WHICH INTEGRATION POLICIES FOR MIGRANTS?

Which Integration Policies for Migrants?

Interaction between the EU and its Member States

Yves Pascouau &
Tineke Strik
(Eds)

Which Integration Policies for Migrants? Interaction between the EU and its Member States
Yves Pascouau & Tineke Strik (Eds)

ISBN: 978-90-5850-848-5

Wolf Legal Publishers (WLP)
P.O. Box 31051
6503 CB Nijmegen
The Netherlands
www.wolfpublishers.nl

Orders for this book can be sent to
sales@wolfpublishers.nl
More information on www.wolfpublishers.nl

Layout: Hannie van de Put

Contents

FOREWORD

Kees Groenendijk, Yves Pascouau & Tineke Strik

Background

The integration of third country nationals in the EU Member States results from a complex process with many different factors promoting or hindering its success. Integration policy therefore covers a wide range of topics – access to employment, education, health care, housing and citizenship – and involves an important number of actors at national, regional and local level. Due to this extreme heterogeneity, integration policy has always been considered as a national, not an EU policy. However, the defining of integration of third country nationals as a common goal of the European Union has catalysed the interaction and mutual influences between the Member States on their integration policies. Several tools and bodies have been established at EU level in order to enhance the coordination of national integration policies. The cooperation in this field prompts the EU and its Member States to formulate a common definition of integration and to rethink integration policies from a new perspective in terms of content, factors and actors.

This 'Europeanisation' of integration policy has consequences both for the national and EU level of decision making. On the one hand, while formulating their integration policy, Member States have to take into account the EU legislation as well as the EU as an actor. On the other hand, since the entry into force of the Amsterdam treaty and the adoption of the Tampere conclusions the EU needs to answer crucial questions relating to the integration of third country nationals who are legally residing in the EU Member States in order to develop an effective common policy in the field of immigration and asylum. After all, the Tampere conclusions envisaged 'fair treatment of third country nationals who reside legally on the territory of its Member States. A more vigorous integration policy should aim at granting them rights and obligations comparable to those of EU citizens'. According to the leaders of the Member States, this integration aim also implied that 'the legal status of third country nationals should be approximated to that of Member States nationals' and that long term residents should be 'granted in that state a set of uniform rights which are as near as possible to those enjoyed by EU citizens'.[1]

These EU principles are reflected in the development of the European policy in the field of immigration and asylum. Some EU Directives directly or indirectly refer to integration issues. This is the case for instance where the provisions enable third country nationals to have access to the labour market or grant them the right to live with their family members. In line with the Tampere conclusions, the preamble (n° 4) of the Directive on the right to family reunification (2003/86/EC) recalls that family reunification facilitates integration of third country nationals in the Member State, which also serves to promote economic and social cohesion, a fundamental Community objective. A similar reference is

1 Conclusion n°. 18 and 21, Tampere European Council, 15-16 October 1999, Presidency Conclusions, SN 200/99, Brussels.

made regarding the importance of the integration of long term residents in the preamble of the Directive concerning the status of third-country nationals who are long-term residents (2003/109/EC). According to the Court of Justice, the meaning and scope of the provisions of this Directive must therefore be sought taking into account the objective pursued by the Directive, namely the integration of third-country nationals who have resided legally and continuously in the Member States (C-571/10, *Kamberaj* and C-508/10, *Commission/ Netherlands*).

At the same time, both Directives offer Member States the possibility to impose certain integration requirements on applicants for this long-term residents status or family reunification. These two different approaches incite to a coherent interpretation of this recent EU legislation in the perspective of the common integration aim.

Integration Requirements introduced in EU Law: State of Play

During the fourty years since the first Regulation on free movement of workers was adopted in 1961 integration policy in the EEC and EU has mainly been an implicit policy. The rights granted to workers from other Member States and their family members did aim at supporting their integration in the country of residence without this being explicitly called an EEC or EU integration policy. The development of the explicit integration policy focusing primarily on migrants from third countries, developed after the Treaty of Amsterdam entered into force in 1999 is a good example how the different levels of policy making within the EU interact and how the locus, the actors and the direction of policy making changes over time.

In the *first* phase (2002-2003) three Member States (Austria, Germany and the Netherlands) introduced the idea of (mandatory) integration policies during the negotiations on the first two directives on legal migration: the Family Reunification Directive (2003/86/EC) and the Long-term Residents Directive (2003/109/EC). Notwithstanding the opposition of most Member States, those three states succeeded in introducing some provisions and preambles on integration measures or conditions in both directives, with the aim to legitimize and facilitate the introduction of obligatory integration exams in their national law.

In the *second* phase (2003-2011) several Member States copied national integration instruments introduced in other Member States, against the background or with the support of the specific provisions in the two directives. The idea of the integration test abroad for family migrants in the Netherlands may well originate from the obligatory German language test introduced in 1997 for non-German family members of *Spätaussiedler*, descendants of ethnic German returning from Russia or Kazakhstan, who acquired German nationality shortly after entry in Germany. Around the change of the century Christian-Democratic politicians in Germany and the Netherland for the first time mentioned a possible language requirement for family reunification. The Dutch integration test abroad introduced in 2006 was first copied in Denmark in an Act of 2007 that, eventually, never entered into force. In Germany the language test abroad for family migrants was introduced in national law in 2007. In the parliamentary debate in Germany repeated references were made to the Dutch and the French model. In France, however, the Dutch model was discussed in parliament but explicitly rejected in 2007. Austria adopted the German model in its legislation in 2011.

In the *third* phase (2006 till today) EU institutions start reminding Member States of the limits on their national sovereignty resulting from the adopted or binding Union law in this area. Moreover, EU institutions mobilise support of national courts in enforcing the new Union law. First the European Commission in its 2006 report on the application of Directive 2003/86/EC in Member States points to the restrictions resulting from that directive and from the general principles of Unions law on the freedom of Member States to introduce integration measures abroad. In 2011 the Commission repeats and specifies this position in its written statement to the Court of Justice in the *Imran* case (C-155/11PPU) and in its Green Paper on the right to family reunification. The Court of Justice in its first judgments on the two directives on legal migration (*Chakroun*, *Kamberaj* and *Commission/Netherlands*) confirms the rights granted to third-country nationals by those directives and the restrictions, thus set on the discretion of Member States.

This case law and the CJEU judgments interpreting the EEC-Turkey association rules trigger national courts in Austria, Germany and the Netherlands[2] to critically review the compatibility with the mandatory integration tests introduced in the national law. In August 2011 the highest social security court in the Netherlands held that mandatory integration courses and exams after admission are incompatible with the standstill and non-discrimination clauses in the Association EEC-Turkey. As a result Turkish nationals are exempted from the integration conditions before and after admission in the Netherlands. A few months earlier, in its written statement in the Imran case, a reference by a Dutch District Court, the Commission held the Dutch integration test abroad to be incompatible with Directive 2003/86/EC. That statement made the *Bundesverwaltungsgericht*, the highest German administrative court, change its position on the compatibility of the German language test abroad with the Family Reunification Directive. In March 2010 that German court held that the relevant German law was compatible with that directive. In October 2011 the same court decided that, considering the position of the Commission in *Imran*, the question of the compatibility of the language test abroad with Directive 2003/86 should be referred to the CJEU. Since the German government granted a visa for family reunification to the spouse in the final stage of that case before the national court, no reference could be made in that case anymore. In May 2012 the Austrian Ministry of Interior issued a circular exempting Turkish family members joining Turkish or Austrian sponsors in Austria from the mandatory integration tests before and after entry as a consequence of judgements of the Austrian *Verwaltungsgerichtshof*, implementing recent case law of the EU Court of Justice.

EU law provisions on integration measures adopted by the Member States in the Council of Ministers first legitimized the introduction of mandatory integration instruments having exclusionary rather than inclusive effects. Later, those Union law provisions and the multiple contacts of national civil servants and politicians in EU fora facilitated exchange and copying of national policy instruments in some Member States. But EU law also acted as an argument against copying in other Member States (France). Finally, the activities of the Commission and the Court of Justice illustrated the limits set on Member States' discretion in this field. These EU institutions triggered enforcement of Union law by national

2 Centrale Raad van Beroep 16 August 2011, *LJN*:BR4959; *Jurisprudentie Vreemdelingenrecht* 2011/416 (Netherlands), Bundesverwaltungsgericht 28 October 2011 case 1C9.10, www.bwervg.de (Germany) and Verwaltungsgerichtshof 15 December 2011, Zl. 2007/18/0430 and VwGH 19 January 2012, Zl. 2011/22/0313 (Austria).

courts in precisely the three Member States (Austria, Germany and the Netherlands) that took the initiative to insert that new perspective on integration policy in EU law. In two of those Member States national authorities have recognized that the EU sets limits on their new integration policy. The Commission and the Court supported the continuity of an EU policy on integration of immigrants, irrespective of their nationality, based on equal treatment, access to employment and education, a secure residence status and the right to family reunification, as agreed by the European Council in Tampere.

Which Integration Policies for Migrants? Interaction between the EU and Its Member States

The growing presence of the EU in the field of migrant's integration raises a series of questions related to the impact of the emerging EU integration policy on Member States' policies. The following questions have led to studies and discussions in this area: To what extent do EU integration policy and national integration policies mutually influence each other? What are the common trends among national and European policies? What are the effects of integration policies on the integration of migrants? To what extent are integration policies linked to migration policies and the legal status of migrants?

In this context, the centre *Migration Asile Multiculturalisme* (Université Libre de Bruxelles), the *Odysseus Network* (chaired by Prof. Philippe de Bruycker, Université Libre de Bruxelles) and the *Centre for Migration Law* (Radboud Universiteit Nijmegen) co-organised a Conference entitled *Which Integration Policies for Migrants? Interaction between the EU and its member States*.

The conference took place in Brussels the 28th and 29th October 2010 and aimed at discussing with relevant academics and stakeholders the impact of the emerging EU policy on Member States policies, and the results of two large academic studies on this topic. The first one, realised by Y. Pascouau in the framework of a contract financed by the Communauté Française de Belgique, is entitled *Integration Requirements in Migrant's Pathways: the Increasing Role of Language and Civic Knowledge*. The second one, realised by Tineke Strik, Anita Böcker, Maaike Luiten and Ricky van Oers with the financial support of the European Integration Fund, is entitled *Integration and Naturalisation tests: the new way to European Citizenship. A Comparative study in nine Member States on the national policies concerning integration and naturalisation tests and their effects on integration*. This study is known as the INTEC project.

In line with these objectives, the conference was divided into three complementary sessions, addressing each one particular side of the issue. The first session, which was held under the aegis of the Odysseus network, focused on the *European Integration Policy*. It aimed at overturning the commonly acknowledged idea that the EU has no competence in the field of integration. Existing rules, bodies and tools prove on the contrary that an important step towards the coordination of national policies has already been taken and that it should give grounds for the development of an EU integration policy with appropriate methods.

The second session addressed the issue of mandatory integration schemes applicable in the EU Member States. This session was held under the auspices of the centre *Migration Asile Multiculturalisme* from the Université Libre de Bruxelles. The centre has conducted under the coordination of Prof. Andrea Rea and with the financial support of the *Communauté française de Belgique*, a transdisciplinary research project entitled *Outsiders in Europe. The For-*

eigner and the 'Other' in the Process of Changing Rules and Identities. The legal side of the project entitled *Integration Requirements in Migrant's Pathways: the Increasing Role of Language and Civic Knowledge* aims at assessing in which of the 23 states covered language and/or civic knowledge requirements were established and at what stage of the migrant's pathway, i.e. in the country of origin, in the host Member State and in the citizenship procedure. The conference was the opportunity to disclose the main results of the research and to give ground to in-depth scrutiny and discussions on trends and impact as well as lawfulness of integration requirements developed in the Member States.

The third and final session was hosted by the Centre for Migration Law of the Radboud Universiteit Nijmegen. The Centre realised the INTEC Project, which sought to assess the effects of language and integration test in nine Member States. Its preliminary results were presented during the conference and followed by discussions on selected national schemes. The INTEC project has conducted a first evaluation of the recent paradigmatic change in policy concepts concerning integration in nine Member States. The main research questions focused on the reasons for the introduction of the obligatory integration requirements, the way in which they had been developed and put into practice and the actual effects of the requirements on immigrants.

This publication includes most of the contributions to this conference, by authors who are involved in migration and integration issues in various ways and in various Member States. They address the above mentioned questions, sometimes discussing it on the national level, sometimes on EU level. It has resulted in a book offering a comprehensive overview of facts, analyses and ideas, which inspires to rethink integration policies. The first chapter includes the contributions discussing various issues relating to the integration policy at EU level. The second chapter specifically focuses on the mandatory integration rules established at EU level. The contributions in chapter three assess the mandatory integration rules established and applied at the national level of certain Member States. Chapter four includes the comparative study of the INTEC project, providing insight into the contribution of language and integration tests to the integration of the persons concerned and the possible intended and unintended effects of the introduction of those tests.

The book was edited by Yves Pascouau and Tineke Strik. The lay-out was produced by Hannie van de Put.

Prof. Kees Groenendijk
Professor of Sociology of Law
Radboud University

Dr. Yves Pascouau
Senior Policy Analyst
European Policy Centre

Dr. Tineke Strik
Assistant Professor of
Migration Law
Radboud University

About the Authors

Diego Acosta Arcarazo is a Lecturer in European Law at the University of Sheffield and holds a PhD in European Migration Law from Kings College London. He has published widely in the area of immigration law and policy including his book *The Long-Term Residence Status as a Subsidiary Form of EU Citizenship* (Martinus Nijhoff 2011).

Anita Böcker is associate professor Sociology of Law at the Law Faculty of Radboud University Nijmegen. Her main research interests are: law and the multi-cultural society; regulation of migration; and the legal and social position of migrants. She has been involved in various international comparative research projects and is one of the Dutch country experts in the SEN Network of socio-economic experts in the anti-discrimination field.

Emmanuelle Bribosia (born in 1971) is Professor of European Law, Anti-discrimination Law and Human Rights Law at the Institute for European Studies (IEE) and at the Law School of ULB (Université Libre de Bruxelles). Since 2007, she has been the Director of the legal department of the IEE. She has a Degree in Law (ULB, 1994) and a PhD on the protection of human rights in EU Law (ULB, 2000). Since 2010, she has been a member of the Transatlantic Study Group on Comparative Anti-discrimination Law. From 2006 she has worked as expert for the European Network of Legal Experts in the Non-discrimination Field where she is the expert for Belgium. For several years, her research has primarily been directed towards Human rights Law and more particularly towards the development of Equality and non-discrimination Law as a tool to manage diversity in Europe and beyond.

Eva Ersbøll is a lawyer and formerly a legal assistant to the Danish Parliamentary Ombudsman. Her Ph.D. is on Danish Nationality in an International and Historical Perspective. She has published on a number of other topics, including Union citizenship, nationality law in Europe, immigration and integration, equality and non-discrimination, the rights of the child and the rights of elderly persons suffering from dementia.

Marie-Claire Foblets, Lic. Iur., Lic. Phil., Ph.D. Anthrop. (Belgium) is Max Planck Director of the newly created Department of Law and Anthropology at the Institute for Social Anthropology in Halle a/d Saale (Germany) and professor of Law at the University of Leuven (Louvain) in Belgium. She has conducted extensive research and published widely on issues of migration law, including the elaboration of European migration law after the Treaty of Amsterdam, citizenship/nationality laws, compulsory integration measures, and anti-racism and non-discrimination policies. In the field of legal anthropology, her research focuses on cultural diversity and legal practice, with a particular interest in minority laws and traditions in contemporary Europe, and their accommodation under State law.

Kees Groenendijk is Emeritus Professor of Sociology of Law at the Radboud University Nijmegen, Netherlands, and Chairman of the Standing Committee of Experts on international immigration, refugee and criminal law (Meijers Committee). From 1995 to 2010 he was Chairman of the Centre for Migration Law at the Radboud University. He has published on national and European law on migration, nationality, discrimination and integration, and on the social and legal status of migrants in Europe.

Mariona Illamola Dausà is Doctor in Law, Director of the European Documentation Center and professor of International Law, specializing in European Union Law, at the University of Girona (Spain). Member of research group ERJAIDI-UE. Author of several publications on immigration policy in the EU.

John Handoll practises law in Dublin. He has a long-standing interest in immigration and integration law and policy and has lectured and published widely in this area. He is a member of the Odysseus network of immigration lawyers.

Kristine Kruma is currently doctoral student at the University of Lund. Her research is on EU citizenship, migration, integration of third country nationals and national citizenship regulation. She is also a judge of the Constitutional Court of Latvia and guest lecturer at the Riga Graduate School of Law. She has been visiting scholar at the Max Planck Institute of International and Comparative Law in Heidelberg and the Centre for Migration in Nijmegen. She is a member of the editorial board of the Baltic Yearbook of International Law and member of Odysseus Network of experts in migration and asylum law. She is ad hoc judge of the European Court of Human Rights for Latvia, Arbitrator at the OSCE Court of Reconciliation and Arbitration and Chairperson of Council of Independent Experts on International and EU law under auspices of the Ministry for Foreign Affairs.

Maaike Luiten has worked as a junior researcher in the field of Migration law at the Law Faculty of Radboud University Nijmegen in 2010. She has been involved in research projects concerning long-term residents and the EEC-Turkey Association and was co-author for the INTEC-project. At the moment she is a lawyer at the Dutch Council of State.

Siobhán Mullally is Professor of Law at University College Cork, where she teaches international human rights law, migration and refugee law and public international law. She is currently a Government of Ireland Senior Research Fellow directing a comparative project on migrant domestic workers. Her publications have appeared in *Human Rights Quarterly*; *Modern Law Review*; *Oxford Journal of Legal Studies*; *International and Comparative Law Quarterly*; *Asian Yearbook of International Law* and *European Human Rights Law Review*. She is the founding Editor in Chief of the Irish *Yearbook of International Law* (Oxford: Hart) and author of *Gender, Migration and Human Rights: Reclaiming Universalism* (Oxford: Hart 2006).

Ricky van Oers is a PhD researcher at the Centre for Migration Law of the Radboud University of Nijmegen. Her research concerns the reasons for introduction and effects of language and integration tests as a condition for naturalisation in the Netherlands, Germany and the UK. Van Oers participated in several international comparative research projects, including the NATAC and EUCITAC projects, which analysed citizenship laws and policies in the EU Member States. She also conducted and coordinated research projects on the implementation in the EU 27 of European Directives on family reunification and long-term resident third-country nationals. For a list of publications, see www.ru.nl/rechten/oers.

Yves Pascouau is Senior Policy Analyst at the European Policy Centre, and is responsible for the European Migration and Diversity Programme. He has researched and published widely on European and national immigration, asylum and integration policies. His current work is mainly dedicated to EU development in the field of immigration, asylum and integration. Prior to joining the European Policy Centre, he worked as researcher in France and at the Université Libre de Bruxelles. He holds a PhD in Law from Pau University in France.

Bernhard Perchinig is a Senior Research Officer at the International Centre for Migration Policy Development (ICMPD) in Vienna and a Faculty Member of the Department of Commercial Law and European Studies at the Danube University Krems and teaches migration and migration policy as a part-time lecturer at the University of Salzburg and the University of Vienna He holds a doctorate in Political Sciences from the University of Vienna (Dr. Phil., 1986). Further to his research and teaching activities he has consulted several international organizations, national and state governments and companies. Since 2006, he chairs the Working Group on Cultural Diversity of the Austrian Commission of UNESCO.

Bernard Ryan is Professor of Migration Law at the University of Kent. His most recent publications have concerned extraterritorial immigration control, integration tests in British migration law and legal aspects of labour migration. He is the co-chair of the Migration and Law Network, which promotes the field of migration law in British universities.

Tineke Strik is assistant professor of Migration Law at the Centre for Migration Law of the Radboud University in Nijmegen, the Netherlands. Her main research field concerns European migration law and its effects on the national legislations of the Member States. She has coordinated the INTEC project, a comparative research on the policies and effects of language and integration tests in nine Member States of the EU. She is currently taking part in the INTI project, a comparative research on the family reunification rules (and its effects) in six Member States. Since 2007 she is also a member of the Dutch Senate for the Green Party and deputy member of the Parliamentary Assembly of the Council of Europe, participating in the Migration Committee.

Nicos Trimikliniotis is an interdisciplinary scholar working in the fields of sociology and law. He is Associate Professor of Law and Sociology and Director of the Centre of the Study of Migration, Inter-ethnic and Labour Relations at the University of Nicosia. He is, since 2008, senior research consultant at PRIO Cyprus Centre. He is the national expert for Cyprus of the European networks of experts on Free Movement of Workers (2008-) and Labour Law (2010-). He is the Cypriot national expert on Independent Network of Labour Migration and Integration Experts (LMIE-INET) for the International Organization for Migration (2009-). He has served as a research associate (national expert) with European University Institute on Citizenship (EUDO, 2009-2010) and on Tolerance, Pluralism and Social Cohesion (ACCEPT, 2011). He also has an association with the University of Cape Town, South Africa. His latest work include: *Contested Integration, Migration and Societal Transformation: European Dilemmas and Challenges* (University of Nicosia Press, 2012); *Re-thinking the Free Movement of Workers: The European Challenges Ahead* (book co-edited with Paul Minderhoud), University of Nijmegen, 2009; *Racism, Migration and Trade Unions in a post-tourist society: Towards a New Paradigm for Cyprus* (in Greek, forthcoming).

Zeynep Yanasmayan is a PhD candidate at the Faculty of Social Sciences in the KU Leuven. She holds an MscEcon degree on Security and Citizenship from the University of Wales, Aberystwyth and an MA degree on European studies from Free University of Brussels (ULB). Her major research interests revolve around integration and citizenship policies, Turkish minorities in Europe, highly skilled migration and diaspora politics. She is currently the Project Manager of the RELIGARE project, European research project on religious diversity and secular models that comprises 13 universities and research centres from across the European Union and Turkey.

Part 1. The EU Integration Policy

Integration of Immigrants in the EU: the Old or the New Way?

Kees Groenendijk

Introduction

The Long Experience with Immigrant Integration in the EC

Long before the European Commission published its first communication on integration policy and long before the European Integration Fund and the Network of National Contact Points were established, the Community had a policy with regard to the integration of immigrants. It was an implicit integration policy, but it was present already in the first community legislation on the free movement of workers, EEC Regulation No. 15, adopted in 1961.[1] The guiding idea behind that policy was that integration of the workers in the host Member State would be stimulated by equal treatment, access to the labor market and education, a secure residence status and the right to family reunification. Family reunification was not defined as a problem but as an instrument supporting the integration of the migrant. The explicit confirmation of family reunification as a right under the Family Reunification Directive by the Court of Justice in its judgment in *Chakroun* is an expression of this traditional approach.[2] This typical Community integration policy developed over decades with steady support from the Court of Justice. It culminated in the citizenship of the Union in 1992. That status symbolized the acceptance of immigrants from other Member States as almost co-citizens. The rules adopted on the basis of the EEC-Turkey Association Agreement are another product of this approach.[3] Over the last decades, the Court in its case-law on the Association EEC-Turkey, constantly reminded Member States and national courts that the association rules are an expression of this integration policy.[4]

In 1999 the European Council in Tampere concluded that this traditional approach should be applied to the integration of third-country nationals as well. '[A]more vigorous integration policy should aim at granting them [lawfully resident third-country nationals] rights and obligations comparable to those of citizens of the European Union'.[5] This was a

1 Article 11-Article 15 of EEC Regulation No. 15 of 12 June 1961, OJ 26 June 1961.

2 ECJ 4 March 2010, C-578/08, *Chakroun*, par. 43 and ECJ 27 June 2006, C-540/03 *Parliament v. Council*, ECR p. I-5769, par. 60.

3 E. Guild, *Immigration Law in the European Community*, chapter 5 (Interpretation of the Turkey Agreement: National Discretion and Community Law Coherence) diss. Nijmegen, Leiden: Martinus Nijhoff 2001.

4 ECJ 17 April 1997, C-351/95, *Kadiman*, par 35. ECJ 16 March 2000, C-329/97, par. 43 and CJEU 29 March 2012, C-7/10 and C-9/10, *Kahveci & Inan*, par. 31-33. In the last judgment the Court in paras 35 and 38 implicitly agreed with the AG Sharpston that the acquisition of the nationality of the host Member State is not the end of the integration process but rather reinforces the integration in the society of that State.

5 Presidency Conclusions on the Tampere European Council of 15 and 16 October 1999, Press Document SN 200/99 par. 4 and par. A(II)(4).

clear confirmation that the traditional integration policy approach, that had been successful for the integration of EU migrants, should be applied in a similar way to third-country nationals. This statement of principles was significantly absent in the policy statement adopted by the European Council in The Hague in 2004[6] and in the European Pact on Immigration and Asylum adopted in October 2008 by the Council at insistence of the French President Sarkozy.[7] But it returned in the conclusion of the European Council in Stockholm in 2009. Under the heading 'Proactive policies for migrants and their rights' the Council stated:

> 'The Union must ensure fair treatment of third country nationals who reside legally on the territory of its Member States. A more vigorous integration policy should aim at granting them rights and obligations comparable to those of citizens of the Union. This should remain an objective of a common immigration policy and should be implemented as soon as possible, and no later than 2014.'[8]

After 11 September 2001 a different approach to integration policy developed in certain Member States. In that approach integration was less seen as a process that may take years or even generations, but more as a stage to be accomplished before the immigrant could be granted admission, a stable residence right or full equal treatment. A secure residence right was seen as the crown on an accomplished integration. Integration policy became part of the control, selection and exclusion of immigrants. It became part of immigration policy. In some Member States this new approach is supplementing the old approach. In other Member States the new approach is competing with the old one or even replacing the old approach.[9]

This development raises three questions.

1) Why would the traditional EU law approach not work for the integration of migrants from outside the EU?
2) To what extent are both approaches reflected in the new EU migration and asylum directives?
3) What are the effects of the new policy approach to integration? Have the new measures assisted integration or been counterproductive?

---

6 Council document 14292/1/04. It was also absent in the Common Basic Principles for Immigrant Integration Policy adopted by the JHA Council in November 2004 under the Dutch EU presidency, see council document 14615/04. On the development of the EU integration policy after 2001 see S. Carrera, *In Search of the Perfect Citizen? The Intersection between Integration, Immigration and Nationality in the EU*, Leiden/Boston: Martinus Nijhoff 2009, and M.C. Foblets, 'The Fragmented Development of EU Immigration and Integration Policy', in: Jan Wouters, Luc Verhey, Philipp Kiiver e.o (eds), *European Constitutionalism beyond Lisbon*, Antwerpen: Intersentia 2009, p. 81-109.

7 Council document 13440/08.

8 OJ 2010 C 115/1 at p. 30, par. 6.1.4.

9 K. Groenendijk, 'Legal concepts of integration in EU migration law', *European Journal of Migration and Law* (6) 2004, p. 111-126; E. Guild, K. Groenendijk & S. Carrera (eds), *Illiberal Liberal States, Citizenship and Integration in the EU*, Burlington: Ashgate 2009; R. van Oers, E. Ersbøll & D. Kostakopoulou (eds), *A Re-definition of Belonging? Language and Integration Tests in Europe*, Leiden/Boston: Martinus Nijhoff 2010.

Some of those questions will probably return in other contributions in this book. I will deal primarily with the second question and make a few remarks about the third one.

EEC Workers as the Prototypical Foreigners

Those who answer that the traditional EU approach cannot work today for third-country nationals because they come from far away countries and adhere to different cultures or religions, tend to forget that in the 1950s and 1960s Italian and Spanish workers were the typical foreigners, coming from what were perceived as clearly different cultures in five of the six original EEC Member States. '*Spaghetti Fresser*' in Germany and the Netherlands was one of the nicknames for Italian workers. Their arrival and presence was not unproblematic at all. In the Netherlands in 1961 there were large scale riots between Italian and Spanish workers and young Dutch natives in three cities in the eastern part of the country. The fights started because the immigrants 'were taking away our girls'. The police, unable to communicate with the foreign workers for lack of a common language on both sides, hit primarily the migrant workers. The riots lasted for several days until a priest who had studied in Rome and the consuls of the two countries intervened. Hundreds of Italian and Spanish workers returned to their country in reaction to their treatment. The main worry in the Dutch Council of Ministers at that time was that the incidents would reduce the possibilities for the Netherlands to recruit the badly needed new workers. The commission established to study the riots advised offering Dutch language courses to the migrant workers.[10] But this advice was disregarded by politicians for more than thirty years.

Fifteen years later, in 1976, together with a colleague, I suggested to Dutch MPs from all five main political parties to amend the Aliens Employment Act, following the Swedish example, to oblige employers who recruited workers from abroad to pay for a 200 hours Dutch language course during working time. None of the MPs was interested. Only the arguments varied between the parties: 'They will return to their own country,' or 'The large companies have interpreters to solve any problem,' or 'They are not interested in our language?' A group of over 100 Turkish workers employed by the Ford factory in Amsterdam shortly after their arrival in 1972 were told by the manager that they would be dismissed when found to be learning or speaking the Dutch language. 'You can communicate with me through the interpreter and you are not supposed to speak with your Dutch colleagues.'[11]

Integration of immigrants is not a new phenomenon. Most EU Member States have a long history of successful integration of immigrants. The main problem is the 'democratic impatience'. Politicians expect integration to take place within a decade, whilst the process of integration often last for one or two generations. If the high expectations are not realized within the unrealistic short time, discussion gets dominated by the idea of 'failed integration' or 'immigrants that are unfit or unable to assimilate'.

---

10 K. Groenendijk, 'Verboden voor Tukkers, Reacties op rellen tussen Italianen, Spanjaarden en Twentenaren in 1961', in F. Bovenkerk, F. Buijs & H. Tromp (red.), *Wetenschap en Partijdigheid, Opstellen voor André J.F. Köbben*, Assen: Van Gorcum 1990, p. 55-95.

11 K. Groenendijk & A. Hahn, *Met recht geslaagd, Nederlandse juristen van Marokkaanse en Turkse herkomst*, The Hague: Sdu 2006, p. 57/58.

Some Problems with the Notion of Integration

Before I deal with the other two questions, I would like to point to some pitfalls of the concept 'integration'. *Firstly*, the word suggests that the new country is a homogeneous whole into which the immigrant can integrate by becoming part of that whole. The use of the word integration suggests that it is clear what the outcome of the integration should be. This underestimates the diversity within the host state and it gives rise to interesting debates on the content of integration tests.[12]

Secondly, in the public debate in some Member States it is suggested that integration is more than participation in the labor market, in schools and in the neighborhood, that integration includes the acceptance of ideas and values. Immigrants should behave, think, and preferably 'become like us'. This idea in my view is hardly compatible with a pluralistic vision of democracy.

Thirdly, the focus in the integration policy debate tends to be on immigrants, what they should do and how they should adapt their behavior and, preferably, their ways of thinking as well. The focus is far less on the behavior of the host society. It is difficult to integrate into a society that is not welcoming or into a labor market with open racial discrimination. It takes two to tango.

Fourthly, in the public debate in our countries the extent to which immigrants, whether they like it or not, are forced to integrate, is often underestimated. In my view the most striking example is the reduction of the average number of children female immigrants give birth to: within a generation it is almost equal to that of the native population. And we should not forget that immigrants also adapt surprisingly rapidly to our bad habits: the occurrence of obesity, breast cancer and other serious illnesses, related to the European way of life, is rapidly rising among immigrants.[13] Many immigrants integrate too much and too quickly and follow our bad habits.

2. Old and New Approaches to Integration Reflected in the New EU Migration and Asylum Directives

The text of three important directives on legal migration, the Family reunification directive,[14] the Long-term residents' directive[15] and the Blue card directive,[16] contain all the

12 E. Guild, K. Groenendijk & S. Carrera, 'Understanding the Contest of Community: Illiberal practices in the EU?', in E. Guild, K. Groenendijk en S. Carrera (eds), *Illiberal Liberal States, Citizenship and Integration in the EU*, Burlington: Ashgate 2009, p. 1-25.

13 D. Thränhardt, 'Integration in der pluralistischen Gesellschaft', in: K. Zimmermann (ed.), *Wechselwirkungen von Migration und Integration im europäischen Mehrebenensystem*, Baden-Baden: Nomos 2010, referring a.o. to L. Hao & J.J.H. Kim, 'Immigration and the American Obesity Epidemic', *International Migration Review* 2009, p. 237-262; see also O. Visser & F.E. van Leeuwen, 'Cancer risk in first generation migrants in North-Holland/Flevoland, The Netherlands, 1995-2004', *European Journal of Cancer* 2007, p. 901-908.

14 Council Directive 2003/86/EC of 22 September 2003 on the right to family reunification, OJ 2003 L 251/12.

15 Council Directive 2003/109/EC of 25 November 2003 concerning the status of third-country nationals who are long-term residents, OJ 2004 L 16/44.

elements of the traditional EU law approach: equal treatment, access to employment and education, secure residence and the right to family reunification. This approach is also clearly confirmed in the preambles of those directives. It is also the thrust of chapter VII (Article 20 to Article 34) of the Qualification directive.[17] However, in the Family reunification directive and the Long-term residents' directive a few but essential clauses were introduced during the negotiations in the text and the preambles, reflecting the new approach. This results in a certain tension, since the word integration has a different meaning in the directives depending on the context.[18] Both in the family reunification directive and the Long-term residents' directive the provisions on integration, depending on their interpretation, potentially could, and in some MS do already, function as a major obstacle to admission, to the rights granted in the directives and to acquiring a secure residence status for large groups of third-country nationals. In the Netherlands the number of applications for the long-term resident permit dropped with 50% after the requirement to have passed the integration exam entered into force in January 2010.[19] In Denmark, that is not bound by the Directive, a similar effect was observed: the number of permanent residence permits issued dropped significantly after the introduction of a more strict language requirement in May 2010.[20]

Specific Clauses on Integration in Recent EU Directives

Clauses on immigrant integration can be found in five directives, the directives on family reunification, on long-term residents, on refugee status, on students and on highly qualified workers, and also in the Commission's proposal for a directive on intra-corporate transferees.[21] The Union legislator in those instruments used four different terms: integration measures, integration conditions, integration criteria and integration programmes.

The term *integration measure* is used in Article 7(2) of the Family reunification directive and in Article 15(3) of the Long-term residents' directive.

The term *integration criteria* is used in the final sentence of Article 4(1) Family reunification directive with regard to the admission of children aged over 12 years. That provision was the subject of the first judgment of the Court on that directive.[22] That exceptional

16 Council Directive 2009/50/EC of 25 May 2009 on the conditions of entry and residence of third-country nationals for the purposes of highly qualified employment, OJ 2009 L 155/17.

17 Council Directive 2004/83/EC of 29 April 2004 on minimum standards for the qualification and status of third country nationals or stateless persons as refugees or persons who otherwise need international protection and the content of the protection granted, OJ 2004 L 304/12.

18 See Groenendijk 2004, fn. 9 supra.

19 The number of application dropped from 28,150 in 2008 and 23,450 in 2009 to 12,260 in 2010 and 9,910 in the first nine months of 2011, Tweede Kamer 33086, no. 6, p. 38.

20 The Copenhagen Post of 2 December 2010 reported that 'September saw 166 rejections and 162 authorisations for permanent residency applications received before the stricter rules came into force. Applications under the new points system the same month resulted in 70 rejections and only one permit.'

21 COM(2010) 378 final of 13 July 2010.

22 ECJ 27 June 2006, C-540/03 *Parliament v. Council*, ECR p. I-5769.

provision may be applied only in Germany,[23] due to the standstill clause that was inserted in the provision because the large majority of Member States strongly opposed this exception proposed by Germany for internal political purposes. In 23 Member States this provision in fact functions as a prohibition on the introduction of integration requirements for minor children.

The term *integration condition* is used in Article 5(2) and Article 15(3) of the Long-term residents' directive. This term is also used in the English and the Italian language versions of the final sentence of Article 4(1) Family reunification discussed above. This may be an indication that integration criteria and integration conditions are identical terms. The use of words 'integration conditions and measures' in Article 15(3) of the Blue card directive in a provision explicitly referring to Article 4(1) and Article 7(2) of the Family reunification directive supports this suggestion. If 'integration criteria' were an overarching term covering both integration conditions and integration measures, there would have been no need to use the two terms in the Blue card directive.[24]

Finally, the term *integration programmes* is used exclusively in Article 33 of the Qualification Directive in all language version I can read.[25]

Integration Programmes, Measures or Conditions?

What can we say about the content of those four terms? Firstly, that they are Union law concepts which have their own independent meaning in European Union law and cannot be defined by reference to concepts of national law. Member States may make national rules on integration, but they are not free to give those terms a purely national content.[26] Article 79(4) TFEU excludes any harmonization of national rules on integration through EU law. But EU law limits the possibilities to use national integration rules as an instrument of immigration control. The terms set certain limits to what can be provided in national rules on integration.

Secondly, from the negotiation documents on the Family reunification directive and the Long-term residents' directive it is clear that the three Member States that repeatedly tried to replace 'integration measures' with 'integration conditions' were unsuccessful. Apparently, the large majority of the Member States believed that the two terms were not identical and that integration conditions would put a greater burden on migrants than integration

23 See also on this issue, H. Labayle & Y. Pascouau, *Directive 2003/86/CE on the Right to Family Reunification-Synthesis Report*, Brussels 2007, 182 p. Report realised in the framework of the Odysseus Network for the European Commission. The report is available on the Website of DG Home.

24 In the Danish language version of that directive 'kriterier' is used where the other language versions use 'condition'.

25 G. Brinkmann, 'The Transposition of the Family Reunification Directive in Germany', in: A.Böcker a.o. (eds.), *Migratierecht en rechtssociologie, gebundeld in Kees' studies, Migration Law and Sociology of Law, Collected Essays in honour of Kees Groenendijk*, Nijmegen: Wolf Legal Publishers 2008, p. 35-42. Article 33 of Directive 2004/83 has been re-casted as Article 34 of Directive 2011/95/EU.

26 ECJ 4 March 2010, C-578/08 (*Chakroun*) par. 45 and ECJ 18 January 1984, 327/82 (*Ekro*), ECR 1984, p. 107, par. 11.

measures.[27] The Commission confirmed the difference between those two terms in its 2011 report on the application of Directive 2003/109/EC in Member States.[28]

Thirdly, for the sake of reducing complexity and on the basis of the comparison of language versions, mentioned before, I suggest that integration conditions and integration criteria are identical terms.

Language Training as the Key Concept

If one would accept these three conclusions, this still does not tell us what is the exact content of the concepts 'integration measure' and 'integration condition'. Here I think the provisions on language training in two directives may be helpful.

Article 15(3) Long-term residents' directive provides that a long-term resident who has fulfilled integration conditions in the first Member State may be '*required to attend language courses*' in a second Member State. The Students' directive in Article 11(d) stipulates that a volunteer may be required '*to receive a basic introduction to the language, history and political and social structures of that Member State*'. An unremunerated trainee may be required to '*receive (...) basic language training so as to acquire the knowledge needed for the purposes of the placement*'.[29] A third-country national student, however, may be required '*to provide evidence (...) of sufficient knowledge of the language of the course to be followed by him/her*'.[30] The requirement for students is clearly higher than for the other two categories. There is a good justification for the requirement to have 'sufficient knowledge of the language' for students. Without such knowledge following courses would not make much sense. For students and migrant workers a language requirement is far easier to justify than for family migrants.[31]

Our analysis reveals three different requirements in the recent EU migration law: the *obligation to prove sufficient knowledge of the language*, the *obligation to attend a language course* and the *requirement to receive basic language training and knowledge of society*. If we add the *right of access to integration programmes* granted by the QD to refugees and beneficiaries of subsidiary protection, we have a fourth variation. This last variation also applies to EU migrants in countries that offer language or integration courses to their own nationals. The equal treatment provisions in Directive 2004/38 and the provision on social advantages in Article 7(2) of Regulation 1612/68 oblige Member States to offer the same access to those courses to EU migrants who want to learn the language of their host Member State. EU migrants have a right to access integration programmes offered by Member States to their own nationals.

A requirement in EU law to comply with integration *measures* (as opposed to integration *conditions*) does not exclude introducing obligations on immigrants, such as the obliga-

27 See Groenendijk 2004, fn. 9 supra and S.R.M.C. Guèvremont, *Vers un traitement équitable des étrangers extracommunautaires en séjour régulier, Examen des directives sur le regroupement familial et sur les residents de longue durée*, diss., Leiden: Meijers Instituut 2008.

28 COM(2011) 585, p. 7.

29 Article 10(c) of Council Directive 2004/114/EC of 13 December 2004 on the conditions of admission of third-country nationals for the purposes of studies, pupil exchange, unremunerated training or voluntary service, OJ 2004 L 375/12.

30 Article 7(1)(c) of Council Directive 2004/114/EC of 13 December 2004 on the conditions of admission of third-country nationals for the purposes of studies, pupil exchange, unremunerated training or voluntary service, OJ 2004 L 375/12.

31 K. Groenendijk, 'Pre-departure Integration Strategies in the European Union: Integration or Immigration Policy?', *European Journal of Migration and Law* 2011, p. 1-30.

tion to attend a language course or receive basic training in language or knowledge of the society. But the concept 'integration measures' does not cover the obligation to prove sufficient knowledge of the language by passing an exam at the same level for all applicants irrespective of their educational level or their personal situation. That is clearly an integration *condition*.

The German versus the French Approach

At this point it is of interest to see the different approaches to the provision on integration measures in Article 7(2) of the Family reunification directive in Germany and France. In Germany, since 2007, third-country spouses have to produce a certificate that they passed a German language exam abroad as a condition for family reunification. Only nationals of seven rich countries, most of them with a predominantly white population, are exempted. The UN Committee on the Elimination of Racial Discrimination held in March 2010 that a similar exception in Dutch law should be amended because it is incompatible with the UN Convention against racial discrimination.[32] There are facilities for learning German sponsored by the Goethe Institute at 480 places in over 100 countries in the world.[33] There are no such facilities for learning Dutch or Danish around the world.[34] In March 2010 the *Bundesverwaltungsgericht*, the highest administrative court in Germany, in a long judgment held that the exemption of certain nationalities did not amount to discrimination. After four pages of interpretation of Article 7(2) Family reunification directive the German court concluded that the requirement to pass a language exam abroad is an integration measure. This question was not referred to the Court of Justice and the German court did not say a word about the *Chakroun* judgment published three weeks earlier.[35] But in October 2011 the same court held that it would have referred the question of the compatibility of the language requirement to the Court of Justice if it would have known the Commission's statement in the *Imran* case.[36] Interestingly, in the *Imran* case the Dutch government granted the visa for family reunification to the Afghan spouse a few days after it had read the Commission's position in that case and a visa was granted to the spouse in the German case shortly before the Bundesverwaltungsgericht would have made its decision. Apparently, both governments wanted to avoid the possibility of an adverse ruling by the Court of Justice.[37]

---

32 CERD/C/NLD/CO/17-18 of 5 March 2010, par. 5.

33 Report of the German Ministry of Foreign Affairs of 10 September 2010, Deutsche Bundestag, Drucksache 17/3090, p. 7.

34 When Denmark finally introduced the integration requirement for admission of third-country national family migrants in November 2010, the spouses and partners were granted three month visas to take the exam in Denmark.

35 Bundesverwaltungsgericht 30 March 2010, *Neue Verwaltungszeitschrift* 2010, p. 964 and *Informationsbrief Ausländerrecht* 2010, p. 331 at par. 23-28. For a (critical) discussion of this judgment and the relevant German legislation, see Reinhard Marx, 'Sprachnachweis und Ehegattennachzug', *Zeitschrift für Ausländerrecht und Ausländerpolitik* 2011, no. 1. The German Court could not have been aware of the opinion of CERD on the Dutch test abroad (see fn 32 supra), since that opinion was published a few days before its judgment was pronounced.

36 Bundesverwaltungsgericht 28 October 2011, case 1C9.10, par. 3, www.bverwg.de.

37 See the order of the CJEU of 10 June 2011, C-155/11PPU that ended the referral by the Dutch in the *Imran* case.

In France there was considerable political pressure to follow the German and Dutch examples. But the French government considered the risk too high that the *Conseil constitutionnel* would hold that an obligation to pass an integration exam abroad violates the constitution and would be incompatible with Article 7(2) FRD.[38] Hence, under the French law, if a spouse in the opinion of the French consul speaks too little French, (s)he will be offered a language course lasting between 40 hours and two months. If the immigrant attends the course he will get the visa and may be required to participate in further language training in France. This is a good example of an integration *measure* in the EU law classification presented above.

3. Effects of Ten Years of National Integration Law in the Netherlands

As a first answer to my third question ('What are the effects of the new policy approach to integration?') I want to mention a few important effect of the new integration legislation in the Netherlands. Others contributors to this book will go into more detail with regard to other Member States. The Netherlands was one of the first EU Member States that started with integration courses offered to migrants from third-countries. In the 1990's those course were first offered to new immigrants and later on also to immigrants who had settled in the country long ago.[39] Since the first Integration of Newcomers Act in 1998 hundreds of thousands immigrants have participated in language and integration courses; the positive effect can hardly be overestimated.

The introduction of formal language and integration test has resulted in a privatization of the selection process and a considerable increase in the required level of knowledge. With each political debate on new legislation a higher level was set, sanctions on not passing the test were made more severe and the percentage of participant who passed was reduced. Frustration and failure to meet the ever higher tests or the official policy aims were built into the legislation.[40]

Formal integration test were introduced with the argument that a uniform test would enhance equal treatment of immigrants. In practice those tests created new forms of inequality: immigrants with less education, older immigrants and immigrants from certain

38 S. Bonjour, 'Between Integration Provision and Selection Mechanism: Party Politic, Judicial Constraint, and the Making of French and Dutch Policies of Civic Integration Abroad', *European Journal of Migration and Law* 2010, p. 299-318 and Y. Pascouau, 'Integration Measures in France: An Evolving Process between Integration and Migration Issues', in R. van Oers, E. Ersbøll & D. Kostakopoulou (eds), *A Re-definition of Belonging? Language and Integration Tests in Europe*, Leiden: Martinus Nijhoff 2010, p. 153-183.

39 I. Michalowski, 'Integration Programmes for Newcomers – A Dutch Model for Europe?', in: A. Böcker a.o. (eds.), *Migration and the Regulation of Social Integration*, IMIS Beiträge No. 24, Universität Osnabrück, Osnabrück: IMIS 2004; H. Vermeulen & R. Penninx (eds), *Immigrant Integration. The Dutch Case*, Amsterdam: Het Spinhuis 2000; I. Michalowski, *Integration als Staatsprogramm, Deutschland, Frankreich, die Niederlande im Vergleich*, diss Münster, Berlin: LIT Verlag 2007.

40 For more details see K. Groenendijk, 'From assisting to requiring integration: Selective citizenship policies in the Netherlands', in: OECD, *Naturalisation: a passport for better integration of immigrants?*, OECD Publishing 2011.

countries of origin had far more problems passing those tests than higher educated, younger immigrants and those from 'Western' countries of origin.[41]

In the Netherlands less than half of the participants in integration courses reached the intended level or passed the exam. The other half did not pass. According to the official evaluation of the 2007 Integration Act in 2007-2009 in total 33,000 immigrants took the exam and 79% passed. At the beginning of 2010 it was estimated that approximately 100,000 immigrants who had started a language course had not yet taken the exam.[42] Possibly, a large part of the participants will never be able to pass.

4. EU law as a Shield against Populist Policies in Member States

Finally, I would like to say a few words about the October 2010 coalition agreement of two traditional parties (VVD and CDA) with the populist party of Geert Wilders.[43] The coalition agreements illustrate what happens if the new approach to integration policies is taken to the extreme. The agreements also illustrate the new role of EU (migration) law as a shield against populist policies in Member States.

The agreements mention as one of the 17 measures aimed at reducing family migration, that the level of the *integration test abroad* will be raised and the content of the test will be broadened.[44] As of 1 April 2011 the level of the test has been raised again by adjusting the computer program. Moreover, the ability to read will be tested by the computer on the basis of the speed and the tone level of the applicant, not unlike a lie detector. From the official evaluation of the test abroad, published last year, it appears that, at the start of the integration course in the Netherlands, the Dutch language knowledge of immigrants who passed the test is only marginally higher than the knowledge of course participants who did not take the test abroad.[45] The contribution of the preparation for the test, if possible at all, to the integration of the immigrants is hard to measure. But the main visible effect of the test is the (temporary) reduction of the number of visa applications for family reunification. The Dutch government always maintained that this reduction was not an aim, only a side effect. The new government made it clear that reduction of family migration, not integration is the primary aim of the test abroad. The coalition agreements are at least honest on this point. But the Commission in its 2008 report[46] and the Court in *Chakroun* made it clear that the requirements of Article 7 Family reunification directive may not be used with the aim of reducing family migration.

Twelve of the seventeen measures in the coalition agreement aiming at reducing family migration cannot be introduced before the Family Reunification directive is amended. In its

41 R. van Oers, 'Citizenship tests in the Netherlands, Germany and the UK', in: R. van Oers, E. Ersbøll & D. Kostakopoulou, *A Redifinition of Belonging? Language and Integration Tests in Europe*, Immigration and Asylum Law and Policy in Europe Series, Vol. 20 (Leiden: Martinus Nijhoff 2010), p. 51-105.

42 Significant, *Evaluatierapport inburgering in Nederland*, Barneveld 2010, p. 28 and 201; see also *Tweede Kamer* 31143, no. 84.

43 *Tweede Kamer* 32417, no. 14; K. Groenendijk & T. Spijkerboer, 'Regulering van migratie en integratie à la Wilders: mag het, kan het en helpt het?', *Nederlands Juristenblad* 2010, p. 2347-2352.

44 *Tweede Kamer* 32417, no. 14, p. 18/19.

45 A. Odé, 'De Wet inburgering buitenland: zelfselectie belangrijker dan selectie', *Migrantenrecht* 2009, p. 288-292.

46 COM(2008) 610 of 8 October 2008.

advice on the proposed new legislation on the integration test abroad the Dutch Council of State questioned[47] the compatibility of the proposal with recent case law of the Court of Justice in the *Chakroun* case and the judgments in *Sahin* and *Commission/Netherlands* on the Association Agreement with Turkey.[48] The government answered that the case law of the Court might develop and that future judgment might shed new light on this issue. I seriously doubt whether Dutch courts, the Commission and the Court of Justice will consider this a convincing answer.[49]

With regard to *integration in the Netherlands* the coalition agreement announces three major changes: (1) the government will no longer pay for the courses, (2) temporary residence permits of those who do not pass the integration exam in time will not be renewed, implying 'voluntary' return or forced expulsion, and (3) the Netherlands will initiate renegotiation of the Association Agreement with Turkey in order to allow imposing on Turkish nationals the obligation to pass the integration exam and all the sanctions in case they do not pass the test in time:[50] administrative fine, reduction of social benefits, no permanent residence permit and mandatory expulsion.

In November 2011 the government in line with its coalition agreement with Geert Wilders introduced a bill that will end payment for language and integration course, reduce the period in which new immigrants are obliged to pass the integration exam, raise the recurrent administrative to be paid if the exam has not been passed and introduce expulsion as an extra sanction. Immigrant may apply for a € 5,000 to € 10,000 loan from the government to pay the course costs.[51] I seriously doubt whether the requirement to pass this exam in order to obtain the EU long-term resident status, when the full costs of acquiring the required level of knowledge will have to be borne by the immigrants, is compatible with Articled 5(2) of Directive 2003/109, the preservation of the *effet utile* of the Directive and the Union law proportionality principle.[52]

In 2007 the Dutch government also decided to stop payment for the courses. This resulted in a 65% reduction in the number of immigrants starting an integration course. Very few immigrants were able or willing to pay the market price, approximately 5,000 euro, for the course. Within a year the new center-left government resumed payment. Why would the effect be different this time? The new sanction, refusal to renew residence permits and expulsion, threatens to turn lawful residents into unlawful residents. In real life,

47 Raad van State opinion of 15 July 2010, *Staatscourant* 2010, no. 13998; see also the relevant Royal Decree in *Staatsblad* 2010, no. 679 and a letter of the Ministers of Interior and of Immigration and Asylum of 14 January 2011, *Tweede Kamer* 32175, no. 15.

48 ECJ 17 September 2009, C-242/06 (*Sahin*) and ECJ 29 April 2010, C-92/07 (*Commission/Netherlands*).

49 The Dutch highest court in social security matters in 2011 held that the standstill clauses in the Association EEC-Turkey does not allow for the imposition of an obligation to attend languages courses and pass an integration exams, as Dutch nationals are exempted from such obligations, Centrale Raad van Beroep 16 August 2011, *LJN*: BR4959 and *Jurisprudentie Vreemdelingenrecht* 2011/416. According to the Dutch Aliens Act, consequently, Turkish national are exempted from the integration test abroad as well.

50 Coalition agreement, *Tweede Kamer* 32417, no. 14, p. 22 and letter of the Minister for Immigration and Asylum of 22 December 2010 to the Second Chamber, *Tweede Kamer* 30573, no. 61.

51 *Tweede Kamer* 33086, nos. 1-3

52 See the Commission's position on the limitations of what can be required under 'integrations conditions' in COM(2011)585, p. 3.

EU migration law (the Family reunification directive, the Qualification directive and the Association Agreement with Turkey) and the EU law principle of proportionality will prohibit expulsion in most cases.[53] But the new 'integration' policy will create insecurity about their residence for a large part of the 100,000 third-country nationals who have enrolled in an integration course during the last years but never took the exam or will never be able to pass the exam. I find it difficult to believe that politicians seriously think that this insecurity will assist the integration of those immigrants and their families. The coalition agreement, negotiated with Geert Wilders, demonstrates that the new approach to integration policy in fact is primarily about immigration control and its main effects are counterproductive with respect to integration. The new policy also demonstrates the important protective role the new EU migration law and the old EU institutions may play in this field in the years ahead.

53 Possibly, the clause about 'fair treatment' of third-country nationals at the beginning of Article 79 TFEU will provide protection against this type of integration policies.

INTEGRATION POLICY IN THE EUROPEAN UNION: THE QUESTION OF COMPETENCE

John Handoll[*]

Introduction

The term 'competence' here refers to the power conferred on public authorities to determine policy and, more particularly, to take measures in a given area.

The area in issue here is that of the integration of third-country nationals legally resident in the European Union (the 'EU').

The 'question of competence' addressed here is whether and to what extent the EU, or the individual Member State, or indeed each of them, enjoys competence in this area. This is considered in relation to a period of time starting with the coming into force of the Amsterdam Treaty in May 1999 and ending, after the coming into force of the Lisbon Treaty, with the present.

It is important to understand from the outset that this area is not occupied by a *single* EU integration policy to the exclusion (or subordination) of individual Member State policies. A rather complex picture involving two elements has instead to be drawn.

The first element is that there are 27 individual Member State integration *policies* which are *supported* (and *incentivised*) by common measures. Before the Lisbon Treaty entered into effect, this support was of a hybrid nature, consisting of EU and inter-governmental measures. Since then, there has been an explicit EU Treaty basis for support measures, though certain 'inter-governmental' features seem to have persisted.

The second element is that, outside this framework of support of national policies, the EU itself has, especially since the entry into force of the Amsterdam Treaty, been able to take measures in the integration area and, in doing so, to pre-empt Member State competence as regards those elements covered by those measures. This activity is rather fragmented and is not sufficient for the EU to be said to have its own 'integration policy', though it undoubtedly has a 'policy on integration'.

The coexistence of these two elements means that the question of competence cannot only be seen in the context of the EU Treaty rules which address the conferral of competences on the Union and determine the scope of the competences thereby conferred. It is also necessary to consider how Member States have been able to work together in relation to an area of *retained* national competence without prejudicing their position in relation to such competence. This issue remains relevant even where supporting powers have been expressly conferred on the EU.

This paper first sets out the Union Treaties' rules on competence, both generally (*Section 2*) and for immigration/integration policies in particular (*Section 3*). Developments in relation to integration policy in the EU are then outlined (*Section 4*).

---

* This article has been finished in December 2011.

A number of specific issues having a bearing on the question of competence are then discussed.

A number of these issues relate to the framework for common measures *supporting* national integration policies (*Section 5*). The focus is on the approach taken by Union Institutions (in particular, the European Council, the Council of Ministers and the European Commission) to the division of competences between the Union and the Member States. After considering the extent to which Member States have retained responsibility for integration policy, the questions of the *need* for supporting measures and the need that such measures should accommodate national differences are then addressed. It is then shortly considered how cooperation has been designed in order to respect Member State powers and at the same time to promote the effectiveness of national policies.

The scope of and exercise of EU powers in relation to integration policy – including powers to take measures supporting national integration policies - are then considered (*Section 6*).

Finally, and by way of conclusion, the impact of the Lisbon Treaty on the question of competence will be discussed (*Section 7*).

We are concerned here with the position of third-country nationals generally. The position of third-country national family members of Union citizens under free movement rules and the Union citizenship provisions is not addressed. Nor is the position of nationals of specific third countries covered by bilateral or international agreements with the EU and its Member States.

This paper draws from a variety of official materials relating to integration policy, including the Treaties, legislative measures, Council conclusions and other documents stemming from the institutions involved. No reference has been made to individual Member State integration policies. Given the time and space constraints, no reference has been made to the rapidly growing academic literature, and other material, in the field.

1. Competence in the Treaties

General

With the entry into force of the Lisbon Treaty on 1 December 2009, the European Union is founded on a recast Treaty on European Union (TEU) and a new Treaty on the Functioning of the European Union (TFEU), together referred to as the 'Treaties'.[1] The Charter of Fundamental Rights of the European Union (the Charter), adopted in 2000 and adapted in 2007,[2] is to have the same legal value as the Treaties.

Each of these three instruments has much to say about competence. Indeed, it is expressly stated in the TFEU that that Treaty 'determines the areas of, delimitation and arrangements for exercising Union competence'.[3]

---

1 See the texts of the Treaties in OJ C83, 30.3.2010, p. 1.

2 *Ibid.*, p. 389.

3 Article 1(1) TFEU.

This Section addresses the general Treaty framework on competence. The following Section addresses the Treaty provisions on competence in the immigration/integration field.

The Position before Lisbon

The focus on this section is on the current position under the Treaties. However, since much of the discussion here relates to a period before the Treaties came into force, a brief outline of the way in which competence was addressed in the past may be helpful.

The introduction by the 1992 Maastricht Treaty on European Union of rules on Community competence in the EC Treaty reflected Member State concerns about 'creeping' competence, seen to be facilitated by the jurisprudence of the Court of Justice. The introduction of these rules can be seen as part of a 'constitutional settlement' reassuring Member States that the Community could not trespass into sensitive areas of Member State power which had not been assigned to the Community.

Article 3b of the newly-named EC Treaty (it had previously been the EEC Treaty) provided that the Community should 'act within the limits of the powers conferred upon it by this Treaty and of the objectives assigned to it therein'.

The exercise of powers by the Community was constrained by the principles of subsidiarity and proportionality. Save for areas where it had exclusive competence, the Community could act, in accordance with the principle of subsidiarity, 'only if and in so far as the objectives of the proposed action cannot be sufficiently achieved by the Member States and can therefore, by reason of the scale or effects of the proposed action, be better achieved by the Community'. Under the principle of proportionality, 'any action by the Community shall not go beyond what is necessary to achieve the objectives of this Treaty'. A Protocol annexed to the EC Treaty addressed the application of the principles of subsidiarity and proportionality

These provisions remained in place until the entry into force of the Lisbon Treaty in December 2009. It will be seen that the current Treaty provisions on competence are rather more detailed than the old. However, the key principle of the limited attribution of Community/EU powers has prevailed throughout.

The Limits of Union Competences

The TEU states that the *limits* of Union competences are governed by the principle of conferral.[4] Under this principle, the Union shall act only within the limits of the competences conferred upon it by the Member States in the Treaties to attain the objective set out in the Treaties.[5]

Competences not conferred upon the Union in the Treaties are expressly stated to *remain* with the Member States.[6]

4 Article 5(1) TEU.

5 Article 5(2) TEU.

6 Articles 4(1) and 5(2) TEU. The statement is 'underlined' in paragraph 1 of the Declaration (No. 18) in relation to the delimitation of competences annexed to the Final Act of the Intergovernmental Conference which adopted the Treaty of Lisbon.

It is recognised that the representatives of the governments of the Member States, meeting in an Intergovernmental Conference, may decide to amend the Treaties, including either to increase or to reduce the competences conferred on the Union in these Treaties.[7]

The Limits of Union Competence and the Charter

The TEU makes it clear that the Charter 'shall not extend in way the competences of the Union as defined in the Treaties'.[8] The 'official' Explanation[9] of Article 51 of the Charter confirms that the Charter may not have the effect of extending the competences and tasks conferred by the Treaties on the Union.[10] Article 51(1) of the Charter provides that its provisions are 'addressed to the institutions, bodies, offices and agencies of the Union with due regard to the principle of subsidiarity and to the Member States only when they are implementing Union law:[11] these entities 'shall therefore respect the rights, observe the principles and promote the application thereof in accordance with their respective powers *and respecting the limits of the powers of the Union as conferred on it in the Treaties*'.[12]

Article 51(2) in turn provides that the Charter 'does not extend the field of application of Union law beyond the powers of the Union or establish any new power or task for the Union, or modify powers or tasks as defined in the Treaties'. The Charter may not therefore have the effect of extending the field of application of Union law beyond the powers of the Union as established in the Treaties.[13] As far as Union powers are concerned, this sets out the 'logical consequences' of the principle of subsidiarity and 'the fact that the Union only has those powers which have been conferred on it': 'fundamental rights as guaranteed in the Union do not have any effect other than in the context of the powers determined by the Treaties'.[14] As far as *Member State* powers are concerned, the Explanation states that 'it goes without saying' that the reference to the Charter in Article 6 TEU 'cannot be understood as extending by itself the range of Member State action considered to be 'implementation of Union law'' (within the meaning of Article 51(1) and referenced case-law of the Court of Justice[15]).

The Use of Union Competences

The *use* of Union competences is governed by the principles of subsidiarity and proportionality.[16]

---

7 See paragraph 3 of the Declaration (No. 18) in relation to the delimitation of competences.

8 Article 6(1) TEU.

9 OJ C303, 14.12.2007, p 32. It is stated that the Explanations do not as such having the status of law and that they are a 'valuable tool of interpretation intended to clarify the provisions of the Charter'.

10 See the Explanation on Article 51 (n. 9), linking Article 51(2) and the second sentence of Article 51(1) to reach this conclusion.

11 See the Explanation on Article 51 (n. 9), referring to the case-law of the ECJ: Case 5/88 *Wachauf* [1989] ECR 2609, Case C-260/89 *ERT* [1991] ECR I-2925, Case C-309/96 *Annibaldi* [1997] ECR I-7493 and Case C-292/97 *Karlsson* [2000] ECR I-2737.

12 Emphasis supplied.

13 Explanation on Article 51 (n. 9), referring to Case C-249/96 *Grant* [1998] ECR I-621, paragraph 45.

14 *Ibid*.

15 See the cases cited in n. 11.

16 Article 5(1) TEU.

Under the principle of subsidiarity, save in areas falling within its exclusive competence, the Union 'shall act only if and insofar as the objectives of the proposed action cannot be sufficiently achieved by the Member States, either at central level or at regional or local level, but can rather, by reason of the scale or effects of the proposed action, be better achieved at Union level'.[17] Under the principle of proportionality, 'the content and form of Union action shall not exceed what is necessary to achieve the objectives of the Treaties'.[18]

The Union institutions are to apply each principle as laid down in the Protocol on the application of the principles of subsidiarity and proportionality.[19] It is stated that National Parliaments ensure compliance with the principle of subsidiarity in accordance with the procedure set out in that Protocol.[20]

The Categories of Union Competences

Three *categories* of Union competences are prescribed in the TFEU. The *scope of* and *arrangements for* exercising the Union's competences are to be determined by the provisions of the TFEU relating to each area.[21]

First, *exclusive Union competence* which means that only the Union may legislate and confer legally binding acts: the Member States may thus act only if so empowered by the Union or for the implementation of Union acts.[22]

Second, *Union competence shared with the Member States*. The Union and the Member States may legislate and adopt legally binding acts.[23] The Member States shall exercise their competence to the extent that the Union has not exercised its competence, or to the extent that the Union has decided to cease exercising its competence.[24] When the Union has taken action in a certain area, the scope of exercise of this competence covers only those elements governed by the Union act in question and therefore does not cover the whole area.[25] As will be seen, shared competence applies to specified areas in the field of the common immigration policy in the area of freedom, security and justice, but *not* to integration policy in terms.

Third, the Union has competence to carry out *actions to support, coordinate or supplement the actions of the Member States* without thereby superseding Member State competence in these areas.[26] Legally binding Union acts in these areas are not to entail harmonisation of Member States' laws or regulations.[27] As seen in the next section, the Union enjoys supportive competence in the area of integration policy: measures incentivising and supporting

17 Article 5(3) TFEU.
18 Article 5(4) TFEU.
19 Article 5(3) and (4) TFEU.
20 Article 5(4) TFEU.
21 Article 2(6) TFEU.
22 Article 2(1) TFEU.
23 Article 2(2), first sentence, TFEU, and paragraph 2, first sentence of the Declaration (No. 18) in relation to the delimitation of competences (the paragraph contains further provisions on the Union deciding to cease exercising its competence in a specific area).
24 Article 2(3), first and second sentences, TFEU.
25 Protocol (No. 25) on the exercise of shared competence, annexed to the TEU and the TFEU.
26 Article 2(5), first sentence, TFEU.
27 Article 2(5), second sentence, TFEU.

Member State action are to exclude any harmonisation of Member States' laws and regulations.

2. Union Competence in the Immigration/Integration Field

Before the Amsterdam Treaty

From the inception of the European Economic Community (EEC) in 1958, the division of powers in the immigration/integration area between the Community and the EEC Member States was not clear. The EEC Treaty did not contain any provisions expressly referring to immigration/integration policy and it was generally recognised this was an area which *in principle* fell within the reserved domain of Member State power.

This did not, however, preclude Community action under the EEC Treaty provisions on, for example, free movement, social policy or international relations even though this might make inroads into the national immigration policy domain. Such an incursion was endorsed by the Court of Justice in the 1987 *Migration Policy Case*,[28] where the Court held – in the face of arguments by Germany and several other Member States – that promotion of the integration into the workforce of third-country migrant workers fell within the scope of the social policy provisions of Article 118 of the EEC Treaty insofar as it was closely linked to employment, but not in relation to the cultural integration of immigrant communities where there was no link with employment and working conditions.

Over time, the Member States recognised the need for some collective action in the immigration/integration area. Such action was seen in terms of inter-governmental cooperation, a mechanism which allowed the Member States to cooperate outside the framework of EEC (and later EC) law in a manner that they thought consistent with their ideas on retained 'sovereign' powers. Such cooperation was not subject to supervision by the Court of Justice and constitutional doctrines such as the principle of the supremacy of Community law did not thus apply *within* the cooperation framework, although the Court of Justice could rule on the frontiers between intergovernmental and Community action.

This cooperation, which intensified after the 1986 Single European Act set out the basis for the Internal Market, initially took place outside a formal Treaty framework. However, with the entry into force of the Maastricht Treaty in November 1993, provisions on immigration policy – including measures on conditions of residence for third-country nationals - were contained in the third-pillar provisions on Cooperation in the Fields of Justice and Home Affairs.[29]

28 Joined Cases 281, 283, 284, 285 and 287/85 *Federal Republic of Germany and others v Commission* [1987] ECR 3203.

29 See, for an example of a relevant measure taken on this basis, the non-binding Council Resolution of 4 March 1996 on the status of third-country nationals residing on a long-term basis in the Member States (OJ C80, 18.3.1996, p. 2).

After the Amsterdam Treaty

With the Treaty of Amsterdam,[30] certain elements of immigration policy came within the competence of the European Community. The activities of the Community henceforth included measures concerning the entry and movement of persons as provided for in Title IV of the EC Treaty.[31] That Title, headed 'Visas, Asylum, Immigration and other Policies related to Free Movement of Persons' provided for the progressive establishment of an area of freedom, security and justice and stated that the Council should adopt 'measures in the fields of asylum, immigration and safeguarding the rights of nationals of third countries', in accordance with Article 63 of the EC Treaty. Article 63 provided, so far as is material here:

> The Council, acting in accordance with the procedure referred to in Article 67, shall, within a period of five years after the entry into force of the Treaty of Amsterdam, adopt:
>
> ...
>
> 3. measures on immigration policy within the following areas:
>   (a) conditions of entry and residence, and standards on procedures for the issue by Member States of long-term visas and residence permits, including those for the purpose of family reunion;
>   (b) illegal immigration and illegal residence, including repatriation of illegal residents;
> 4. measures defining the rights and conditions under which nationals of third countries who are legally resident in a Member State may reside in other Member States
>
> Measures adopted by the Council pursuant to points 3 and 4 shall not prevent any Member State from maintaining or introducing in the areas concerned national provisions which are compatible with this Treaty and with international agreements,
>
> Measures to be adopted pursuant to points ... 3(a) and 4 shall not be subject to the five-year period referred to above.

Integration policy is not expressly referred to in these provisions. However, within the framework set by the October 1999 Tampere European Council and continued by the 2004 Hague Programme, Article 63(3)(a) has been used as the Treaty basis for a number of Directives which contain integration measures applying to particular classes of third-country nationals. It has also, more ambitiously, been used as the Treaty basis for the 2007 Council Decision on the European Fund for the Integration of third-country nationals.[32]

Measures promoting integration could be taken under other provisions of the Treaties, even though these provisions did not refer to 'integration' in terms. These included, in the EC Treaty, measures to combat discrimination[33] (Article 13 EC) and measures supporting

30 See, for the texts of the Treaty of Amsterdam, and the consolidated versions of the TEU and the EC Treaty, OJ C340, 10.11.1997, pp. 1, 145 and 173.

31 Article 3(1)(d) of the EC Treaty.

32 See, further, Section 6, below.

33 Article 13 of the EC Treaty.

or complementing Member State action in policy areas such as social policy,[34] employment,[35] education[36] and health.[37]

The Position after Lisbon

Shared competence applies in the area of freedom, security and justice.[38] This area includes the common immigration policy aimed at ensuring, amongst other matters, the fair treatment of third country nationals residing legally in Member States.[39] The European Parliament and the Council are to adopt measures in relation to, amongst other matters, 'the conditions of entry and residence'[40] and 'the definition of the rights of third-country nationals residing legally in a Member State, including the conditions governing freedom of movement and of residence in other Member States'.[41] As will be seen,[42] this permits the EU to take measures in relation to the integration of third-country nationals going beyond measures supporting national integration policies.

The Union enjoys *supportive competence* in the area of integration of third-country nationals, with Article 79(4) TFEU providing:

> The European Parliament and the Council, acting in accordance with the ordinary legislative procedure, may establish measures to provide incentives and support for the action of Member States with a view to promoting the integration of third-country nationals residing legally in their territories, excluding any harmonisation of the laws and regulations of the Member States.

It should be noted that many of the provisions of the EC Treaty have been essentially retained in the TFEU, although there has been some recasting and amendment. The EU can therefore continue to take measures promoting integration under the non-discrimination provisions,[43] as well as in various policy areas such as social policy,[44] employment,[45] education policy[46] and health,[47] where the role of the EU is to support and complement Member State action.[48]

34 Article 137 of the EC Treaty.
35 Article 127 of the EC Treaty.
36 Articles 149 and 150 of the EC Treaty.
37 Article 152 of the EC Treaty.
38 Article 3(2)(j) TFEU.
39 Article 79(1) TFEU.
40 Article 79(1)(a) TFEU.
41 Article 79(2)(b) TFEU.
42 See Section 6, below.
43 Article 19 TFEU.
44 Article 153 TFEU.
45 Article 147 TFEU.
46 Article 165 and 166 TFEU.
47 Article 168 TFEU.
48 See, further, Section 6, below.

4. Integration Policy in the European Union: An Outline of Developments

General

It is intended here to outline the main developments in relation to integration policy in the EU since the entry into force of the Amsterdam Treaty. These developments should be broadly seen in the context of three successive Programmes: the October 1999 Tampere Programme (1999 to 2004); the 2004 Hague Programme (2005 to 2009); and the 2009 Stockholm Programme (2010 to 2014).

The term 'integration policy in the EU' is used advisedly. It is not the same as 'EU integration policy' and does not prejudge the issue of competence. Over time, the European Council/Council has coined particular terms to cover European action in the areas of integration policy. The term 'European framework on integration' was first used by the European Council in the November 2004 Hague Programme. In the Stockholm Programme, the European Council introduced a different concept – that of 'European cooperation in integration'. The outline below covers actions/developments under the EC Treaty and other actions/developments supporting national integration policies.

The Tampere Programme (1999-end 2004)

Political direction to the development of the area of freedom, security and justice – including the question of the integration of third-country nationals lawfully resident in the Union – was given by the Tampere European Council in October 1999.[49] A common approach had to be developed 'to ensure the integration into our societies of those third-country nationals who are lawfully resident in the Union'. Such integration was seen in terms of 'fair treatment of third-country nationals', with 'a more vigorous integration policy' focussing on rights and obligations of lawfully-resident third-country nationals comparable to those of EU citizens, the enhancement of non-discrimination in economic, social and cultural life, and the fight against racism and xenophobia. After stating that the 'legal status of third-country nationals should be approximated to that of Member State nationals, the European Council addressed the position of long-term residents, calling for the grant of 'a set of uniform rights which are as near as possible to those enjoyed by EU citizens' and endorsing the objective that such long-term residents be offered the opportunity to obtain the nationality of the Member State of residence.

There were some important legislative developments in the course of the Tampere Programme. In the area of non-discrimination, the Racial Equality Directive[50] and the Employment Equality Directive[51] were adopted in 2000. The Family Reunification Directive[52]

49 Tampere European Council, 15-16 October 1999, Presidency Conclusions, paras. 18-21 (Doc. 200/1/99).

50 Council Directive 2000/43/EC of 29 June 2000 implementing the principle of equal treatment between persons irrespective of racial or ethnic origin (OJ L180, 19.7.2000, p. 22).

51 Council Directive 2000/78/EC of 27 November 2000 establishing a general framework for equal treatment in employment and occupation (OJ L303, 2.12. 2000, p. 16).

52 Council Directive 2003/86/EC of 22 September 2003 on the right to family reunification (OJ L251, 3.10.2003, p. 12).

was adopted in September 2003 and the Long-Term Residents Directive[53] was in turn adopted in November 2003: each of these expressly referred to integration concerns.[54] The Victims of Trafficking Directive,[55] containing important provisions on the treatment of vulnerable persons falling within this category, was adopted in April 2004.

The Charter of Fundamental Rights of the EU[56] was proclaimed by the European Parliament, the Council and the Commission in December 2000. With the exception of certain Union citizens' rights, its provisions apply to third-country nationals, as human beings,[57] as residents in a Member State[58] and, in a couple of cases, as third-country nationals.[59]

There was also an institutional debate on the role of the EU in integration policy. Integration policy was addressed as a part of *immigration* policy by the European Commission in its November 2000 Communication on a Community Immigration Policy[60] and its July 2001 Communication on an Open Method of Coordination for the Community Immigration Policy.[61] The initial response, by the June 2002 Seville European Council,[62] stayed close to the rights-based approach taken in Tampere. However, in October 2002, the JHA Council adopted Conclusions on the integration of third-country nationals,[63] which pointed to the importance of integration in EC immigration and asylum policy and paid some attention to the content of *national* integration policies. The Council stated the importance of information exchanges, anticipated the gradual drafting of best practices, and encouraged the establishment of national contact points in the Member States.

The question of integration – both in terms of EU and Member State policies - was addressed in some detail in the Commission's Communication on Immigration, Integration and Employment, adopted in June 2003.[64] The Commission called for a 'holistic approach'

53 Council Directive 2003/109/EC of 25 November 2003 concerning the status of third-country nationals who are long-term residents (OJ L16, 23.1.2004, p. 44).

54 See, further, Section 6, below.

55 Council Directive 2004/81/EC of 29 April 2004 on the residence permit issued to third-country nationals who are victims of trafficking in human beings or who have been the subject of an action to facilitate illegal immigration, who cooperate with the competent authorities (OJ L261, 6.8.2004, p. 19).

56 Charter of Fundamental Rights of the European Union (OJ C346, 18.12.2000, p. 1) (and see, post Lisbon Treaty, OJ C303, 14.12.2007, p. 1).

57 The Title I provisions on dignity (Articles 1 to 5) thus apply to everyone.

58 Certain Union citizens' rights – such as the right to petition the European Parliament (Article 44) – apply not only to Union citizens but also to 'any natural or legal person residing or having its registered office in a Member State'.

59 See Article 13(3) (entitlement of nationals of third countries authorised to work in the territories of the Member States to working conditions equivalent to those of Union citizens) and Article 45(2) (grant of freedom of movement and residence to third-country nationals legally resident in the territory of a Member State).

60 Commission Communication on a Community Immigration Policy (COM(2000) 757 final (22 November 2000)), pp. 19-20.

61 Commission Communication on an Open Method of Coordination for the Community Immigration Policy (COM(2001) 387 final (11 July 2001)), pp. 5 and 11-12.

62 Seville European Council, 21-22 June 2002, Presidency Conclusions, paras. 26-39 (SN 200/1/02 REV 1).

63 JHA Council Conclusions of 15 October 2002 on the Integration of Third-Country Nationals (Council Doc. 12894/02).

64 Commission Communication on Immigration, Integration and Employment (COM(2003) 336 final (3 June 2003)).

and set out its ideas on a more coherent European framework for integration, including the consolidation of the EC legal framework, reinforcing policy coordination, the introduction of 'civic citizenship', action in the fields of employment, social inclusion and economic and social cohesion, combating discrimination, cooperation in the field of education and EU financial support. The Communication also contained a synthesis report on national integration policies.

A response of sorts was made by the General Affairs Council in June 2003 Conclusions on the development of a policy at EU level on the integration of third country nationals legally residing in the territory of the EU,[65] shortly followed by virtually identical conclusions on this subject by the Thessaloniki European Council.[66] These largely developed the thinking set out in the October 2002 Council Conclusions, addressing the development of integration policies 'within a coherent European Union framework, taking into account the legal, political economic, social and cultural diversity of Member States'. To 'intensify' the development of such a framework, the definition of common basic principles was to be envisaged. The conclusions also stressed the importance of developing cooperation and exchange of information within the framework of the National Contact Points on Integration 'with a view in particular to strengthening coordination of relevant policies at national and European Union level'.

In July 2004, the Commission published its First Annual Report on Migration and Integration,[67] which addressed trends in national policies on integration and included an overview on such policies.

Shortly before, in June 2004, the Commission issued an assessment of the Tampere Programme.[68] It stated that integration policy would 'have to be promoted and continued' and that the Union had to 'put in place adequate measures in order to support the action of Member States'.

The Hague Programme

The integration of third-country nationals was one of the themes addressed in the multiannual (2005-2009) Hague Programme adopted by the European Council in November 2004.[69]

The European Council first set out the basis for action:

> Stability and cohesion within our societies benefit from the successful integration of legally resident third-country nationals and their descendants. To achieve this objective, it is essential to develop effective policies, and to prevent the isolation of certain

65 Council Conclusions of 16 June 2003 on the development of a policy at European Union level on the integration of third-country nationals legally residing in the territory of the European Union (Council Doc. 10622/03).

66 Thessaloniki European Council, 19-20 June 2003, Presidency Conclusions, paras. 9 and 28-35.

67 Commission, *First Annual Report on Migration and Integration* (COM(2004) 508 final (16 July 2004)).

68 Commission, *Area of Freedom, Security and Justice: Assessment of the Tampere programme and future orientations* (COM(2004) 401 final (2 June 2004).

69 Brussels European Council, 4-5 November 2004, Presidency Conclusions, paras 14-16, and Annex I, point 1.5 (Council Doc. 14292/1/04 REV 1) (The Hague Programme).

groups. A comprehensive approach involving stakeholders at the local, regional, national, and EU level is therefore essential.

Whilst recognising the progress that had already been made in respect of fair treatment of legally resident third-country nationals, the European Council called for 'the creation of equal opportunities to participate fully in society' and added that 'obstacles to integration need to be actively eliminated'.

In underlining the need for the greater coordination of national integration policies and EU initiatives, the European Council called for the establishment of the common basic principles underlying a coherent European framework on integration. A framework, based on these common basic principles, would 'form the foundation for future initiatives in the EU, relying on clear goals and means of evaluation'. Member States, the Council and the Commission were invited 'to promote the structural exchange of experience and information', with the support of a widely-accessible website.

In the same month, there was an informal meeting of the Ministers responsible for integration in Groningen[70] which paved the way for the November 2004 Council Conclusions on Immigrant Integration Policy in the European Union and the attached Common Basic Principles.[71] These Principles are set out in the table below.

An Annex to the Conclusions provided explanations intended to give direction to each of the Common Basic Principles. The Council stated that the description was indicative, was by no means exhaustive and would be further developed in the future.

These Common Basic Principles had six stated aims: (i) to assist and guide Member States in their integration policies; (ii) to allow Member States to explore how authorities – EU, national, regional and local – could interact and how other actors could be engaged; (iii) to complement and be in synergy with existing legislative frameworks, including international human rights instruments, EC instruments, EU objectives on gender equality and non-discrimination and other EU policies; (iv) to help structuring the regular dialogue between governments and all other relevant institutions and stakeholders at Union level; (v) 'to serve as a basis for and assist the Union to explore how existing EU-instruments relating to integration can be developed further'; and (vi). 'to assist the Council to reflect upon and, over time, agree on EU-level mechanisms and policies needed to support national and local-level integration policy efforts, particularly through EU-wide learning and knowledge-sharing'.

November 2004 also saw the publication of the first edition of the Handbook on Integration for policy-makers and practitioners,[72] addressing the themes of introduction courses for newly-arrived immigrants and refugees, civic participation and indicators.

In December 2004, the Council adopted the Students Directive.[73] This was followed, in October 2005, by the Researchers Directive.[74]

---

70 There is no public record of this meeting.

71 Council Conclusions of 19 November 2004 on Immigrant Integration Policy in the European Union (Council Doc. 14615/04).

72 European Commission, Directorate-General Justice, Freedom and Security, *Handbook on Integration* (1st Edition) (November 2004).

73 Council Directive 2004/114/EC of 13 December 2004 on the conditions of admission of third-country nationals for the purposes of studies, pupil exchange, unremunerated training or voluntary service (OJ L375, 23.12.2004, p. 12).

The Common Basic Principles

1. Integration is a dynamic, two-way process of mutual accommodation by all immigrants and residents of Member States.
2. Integration implies respect for the basic values of the European Union.
3. Employment is a key part of the integration process and is central to the participation of immigrants, to the contributions immigrants make to the host society, and to making such contributions visible.
4. Basic knowledge of the host society's language, history and institutions is indispensable to integration; enabling immigrants to acquire this basic knowledge is essential to successful integration.
5. Efforts in education are critical to preparing immigrants, and particularly their descendants, to be more successful and active participants in society.
6. Access for immigrants to institutions, as well as to public and private goods and services, on a basis equal to national citizens and in a non-discriminatory way, is a critical foundation for better integration.
7. Frequent interaction between immigrants and Member State citizens is a fundamental mechanism for integration. Shared forums, inter-cultural dialogue, education about immigrants and immigrant cultures, and stimulating living conditions in urban environments enhance the interactions between immigrants and Member States citizens.
8. The practice of diverse cultures and religions is guaranteed under the Charter of Fundamental Rights and must be safeguarded, unless practices conflict with other inviolable European rights or with national law.
9. The participation of immigrants in the democratic process and in the formulation of integration policies and measures, especially at the local level, supports their integration.
10. Mainstreaming integration policies and measures in all relevant policy portfolios and levels of government and public services is an important consideration in public-policy formation and implementation.
11. Developing clear goals, indicators and evaluation mechanisms are necessary to adjust policy, evaluate progress on integration and to make the exchange of information more effective.

The Council and Commission Action Plan implementing the Hague Programme was published in August 2005.[75] It was stated that the Plan would be 'implemented in strict compliance with the legal bases laid down in the Treaties and the principles of solidarity, subsidiarity and proportionality'. In relation to the integration of third-country nationals, a Commission communication on a European framework for integration would be adopted in 2005. In relation to the promotion of the structural exchange of experience and information on

74 Council Directive 2005/71/EC of 12 October 2005 on a specific procedure for admitting third-country nationals for the purposes of scientific research (OJ L289, 3.11.2005, p. 15).

75 Council and Commission Action Plan implementing the Hague Programme on strengthening freedom, security and justice in the European Union (OJ C198, 12.8.2005, p. 1).

integration, there would be management of INTI preparatory actions,[76] annual reports on immigration and integration, continuing editions of the Handbook on Integration, and the development of a website.

In September 2005, the Commission adopted a communication on 'A Common Agenda for Integration',[77] providing a 'Framework for the Integration of Third-Country Nationals in the European Union', and containing 'cornerstone' proposals for 'concrete measures to put the Common Basic Principles into practice, together with a series of supportive EU mechanisms'. In December that year, the Council of the European Union and the Representatives of the Governments of the Member States adopted Conclusions on the Common Agenda for Integration[78] which acknowledged the importance of defining a framework at European level for the integration of legally residing third-country nationals in all aspects of society and, in particular, concrete measures for implementing the Common Basic Principles. The Commission was invited to continue to support the activities of the Network of National Contact Points on Integration. There should also be regular (preferably annual) holding of Ministerial discussions and/or Conferences to 'consider pertinent and thematic issues on the integration of third-country nationals in the EU and assess the need for further action'.

The Commission issued its Second Annual Report on Migration and Integration[79] in June 2006 setting out trends in national integration policies and providing a summary report on integration policies and recent trends in the 25 EU Member States.

In July 2006, the European Parliament made an important contribution to the debate in a Resolution on Strategies and Means for the Integration of Immigrants in the EU.[80] Pointing to the seriousness of the integration challenge, the consequences of policy failure and the positive economic results of rising to the challenge, the Resolution contained no less than 33 points addressing a broad range of integration issues.

The December 2006 Brussels European Council[81] identified the steps that needed to be taken in 2007 in relation to a comprehensive European Migration Policy. This included the promotion of integration and intercultural dialogue, fighting against discrimination at Member State and EU levels, strengthening integration policies, and agreeing on common goals and strategies.

The European Council anticipated the importance of the informal Ministerial Conference in Potsdam held in May 2007,[82] where the Integration Ministers tackled the increasingly important question of intercultural dialogue and helped to prepare the June 2007

76 INTI was a European Union (EU) funding programme for preparatory actions promoting the integration in the EU member states of third-country nationals.

77 Commission, *A Common Agenda for Integration. Framework for the Integration of Third-Country Nationals in the European Union* (COM(2005) 389 final (1 September 2005)).

78 Council Conclusions of 1-2 December 2005 on a Common Agenda for Integration (Council Doc. 14390/05).

79 Commission, *Second Annual Report on Migration and Integration* (SEC(2006) 892 (30 June 2006)).

80 European Parliament, *Resolution on Strategies and Means for the Integration of Immigrants in the European Union* (2006/2056(INI) (7 July 2006)). See, also, the Lambrinidis Report (Doc. A6-0190/2006 (17 May 2006).

81 Brussels European Council, 14-15 December 2006, Presidency Conclusions, para. 24(e) (Doc. 6879/06).

82 There is no public record of this meeting.

Conclusions of the Council and the Representatives of the Governments of the Member States on the strengthening of integration policies in the EU.[83]

These Conclusions stressed the need for a global and coherent approach to integration policies and recognised the 'complementary linkage' between immigration and integration. They also emphasised the need to continue to strengthen the integration policies of Member States. They welcomed the initiatives taken to facilitate the exchange of experience and the opportunity provided by the Potsdam meeting 'to review at a political level the scope for further action directed to strengthening the European framework for integration and the integration policies of the Member States, by promoting unity in diversity'. They also welcomed the Commission's publication in May 2007 of the second edition of the Handbook on Integration (which addressed 'mainstreaming' immigrant integration, urban housing, economic integration and integration governance).[84]

Emphasis was given to the importance of the Common Basic Principles as the basis of the European approach to integration and to the need for the Principles to continue to guide the activities of the National Contact Points. The role of the National Contact Points network needed to be strengthened and the Commission was invited to continue to support its activities.

The June 2007 Brussels European Council[85] welcomed the efforts made 'to improve the continued and deepened cooperation at EU level and between Member States in the area of integration and intercultural dialogue'. It particularly welcomed the Council Conclusions on the 'strengthening of integration policies in the EU by promoting unity in diversity' and emphasised the importance of further initiatives to facilitate the exchange of experience on Member States' integration policies.

June 2007 also saw the adoption of the Council Decision establishing the European Fund for Integration,[86] based on Article 63(3)(a) EC. The Fund – totalling some €825 million – is in place for 2007-2013. The establishment of the Fund should be seen in the context of the need stated in the 2004 Hague Programme for the greater coordination of national integration policies, the adoption and implementation of the 2004 Common Basic Principles, and the adverse implications for other Member States and the Union where an individual Member State fails to develop and implement integration policies.[87]

The Commission's Third Annual Report on Migration and Integration[88] was published in September 2007, again addressing trends in national integration policies and containing a summary report on integration policies in 25 of the 27 Member States.[89]

83 Council Conclusions of 12-13 June 2007 on strengthening of integration policies in the European Union: 'Unity in Diversity' (Council Doc. 10267/07).

84 European Commission, Directorate-General Justice, Freedom and Security, *Handbook on Integration* (2nd Edition) (May 2007).

85 Brussels European Council, 21-22 June 2007, Presidency Conclusions, para. 20 (Council Doc. 11177/1/07 REV 1).

86 Council Decision 2007/435/EC of 25 June 2007 establishing the European Fund for the Integration of third-country nationals for the period 2007-2013 as part of the General programme 'Solidarity and Management of Migration Flows' (OJ L168, 28.6.2007, p. 18).

87 See Recitals 4 to 8 of the Preamble to the Decision.

88 Commission, *Third Annual Report on Migration and Integration* (COM(2007) 512 final (11 September 2007).

89 Cyprus and Malta did not reply to the NCPI questionnaire.

In its December 2007 Communication '*Towards a Common Immigration Policy*',[90] the Commission stated that integration policies had to lie at the very core of immigration policies. In relation to legal immigration, the Commission stated that any policy of immigration 'must now go hand in hand with a *policy of integration*, and integration policy has been the subject of a pragmatic approach sustained by *strong political demand*'. Funding from the Integration Fund and other existing instruments would allow work to continue.

In relation to the need for a common policy on integration, the Commission set out in some detail its views on integration challenges and made it clear that 'the potential for significant gains from immigration can only be realised if integration is successful'. The Commission called for a 'renewed commitment' to develop a common immigration policy. This did 'not require any change in the existing competences of the EU, it is a political and practical matter of working together to achieve an outcome which no Member State can achieve alone'. It would include defining 'a plan leading to a common understanding of the kind of immigration Europe needs and the accompanying measures needed to ensure proper integration'.

Shortly after the Commission's Communication, the JHA Ministers and Employment Ministers met, 'in the margins of the Council', for a policy debate on migration, employment and the Lisbon Strategy.[91] In light of the debate, the Presidency concluded, amongst other matters, that 'measures to promote integration are important, including in the areas of skills and education and employment and social policies, as are the efforts of migrants themselves to integrate'.

The Conclusions of the December 2007 Brussels European Council[92] on the question of integration were short. The European Council stated that integration was 'a pivotal element' of the comprehensive European migration policy and called for better coordination between migration and integration policies. In the context of the forthcoming 2008 Year of Intercultural Dialogue, it called on the Commission and the Member States 'to stress the opportunities, benefits and challenges of migration in a pluralistic Europe'.

In its June 2008 Communication on '*A Common Integration Policy for Europe: Principles, Actions and Tools*',[93] the Commission restated the importance of the link between immigration and integration: 'the positive potential of immigration can only be realised if integration into host societies is successful'. The Commission proposed ten common principles underlying the further development of the common immigration policy, grouped under three heading – 'prosperity', 'security' and 'solidarity'. A number of these principles addressed the question of integration.

The June 2008 Brussels European Council[94] welcomed the presentation of the Commission Communication, but signalled that the incoming French Presidency would propose a pact of immigration and asylum. The draft European Pact on Immigration and Asylum was

---

90 Commission, *Towards a Common Immigration Policy* (COM(2007) 780 final (5 December 2007).

91 JHA Council, 6-7 December 2007, 'Migration, Employment and the Lisbon Strategy', Press Release, pp. 8-9 (Council Doc. 15966/07 (Presse 275)).

92 Brussels European Council, 14 December 2007, Presidency Conclusions, para. 25 (Council Doc. 16616/07).

93 Commission, *A Common Immigration Policy for Europe: Principles, Actions and Tools* (COM (2008) 359 final) (17 June 2008).

94 Brussels European Council, 19-20 June 2008, Presidency Conclusions, paras. 8, 78. (Doc. 11018/1/08 REV1).

debated in the informal JHA Council meeting in Cannes in July 2008 and was again addressed by the JHA Council meeting later that month.[95] Agreement was reached in the JHA Council in September 2008[96] and the Pact was adopted by the October 2008 Brussels European Council.[97]

The Pact made it clear that the organisation of immigration had to 'take account of Europe's reception capacity in terms of its labour market, housing, and health, education and social services, and protect migrants against possible exploitation by criminal networks. In the context of the creation of a common area of free movement, it was 'imperative that each Member State take account of its partners' interests when designing and implementing its immigration, integration and asylum policies'.

The European Council made five basic commitments. The first, of clear relevance here, was to 'organise legal immigration to take account of the priorities, needs and reception capacities determined by each Member State, and to encourage integration'. In the context of and managed and concerted immigration policy to be implemented by Member States, the European Council 'stresses the importance of adopting a policy that enables fair treatment of migrants and their harmonious integration into the societies of their host countries'.

Member States were invited, in line with the Common Basic Principles, 'to establish ambitious policies, in a manner and with resources that they deem appropriate, to promote the harmonious integration in their host countries of immigrants who are likely to settle permanently'. These policies should be based on a balance between migrants' rights and duties. They were to include specific measures to promote language-learning and access to employment, and to stress respect for the identities of the Member States and the EU. The Member States were called upon to take into account, by means of appropriate measures, 'the need to combat any forms of discrimination to which migrants may be exposed'.

The European Council also agreed 'to promote information exchange on best practice implemented, in line with the common principles approved by the Council in 2004, in terms of reception and integration, and on EU measures to support national integration policies'.

The aim of the November 2008 Vichy Ministerial Conference was 'to improve the convergence of the concepts and practices of Member States of the European Union in the continuation of the work already started at European level, in particular at the first two ministerial conferences and within the framework of the network of National Contact Points on Integration'. Unlike the earlier Conferences, the Vichy Conference did not just lay the ground 'behind closed doors' for later JHA Council Conclusions, but rather approved its own Declaration, which was reproduced in the November 2008 Conclusions of the Council and the Representatives of the Governments of the Member States on integration policies in the EU.[98]

95 JHA Council, 24-25 July 2008, Press Release (Doc. 11653/08 (Presse 205)).

96 JHA Council, 25 September 2008, Press Release (Doc. 12923/08 (Presse 250)).

97 Brussels European Council, 15-16 October 2008, Presidency Conclusions, paras. 19-20. (Doc. 11018/1/08 REV1) and Doc. 13440/08.

98 JHA Council, 27-28 November 2008, Press Release (Doc. 16325/08 (Presse 344)) and, for the Conclusions, Doc. 15251/08. See, also, Commission, *Strengthening actions and tools to meet integration challenges: Report to the 2008 Ministerial Conference on Integration* (Staff Working Document) (SEC(2008) 2626?).

This Declaration, and the later Conclusions, addressed a number of themes: the promotion of the fundamental values of the EU; the integration process; access to employment and the promotion of diversity in employment; the integration of women and the education of children; intercultural dialogue; and principles of integration policy governance. The Member States agreed 'to give particular attention' to these themes, among other important integration issues, when defining and implementing their national integration policies, in accordance with national specificities and rules'.

In April 2009, the Commission launched two new instruments. First, it established the European Integration Forum, designed to give a voice for representatives of civil society on integration issues. Second, it established the European Website on Integration.[99]

Two important measures were adopted in 2008/2009. In November 2008, the Council adopted a Framework Decision on combating certain forms and expressions of racism and xenophobia by means of criminal law.[100] In May 2009, it adopted the 'Blue Card' Directive, on the conditions of entry and residence (including rules on treatment) of third-country nationals for the purposes of highly qualified employment.[101]

The Stockholm Programme (2010-2014)

The Stockholm Programme,[102] for the period 2010 to 2014, was adopted by the European Council in December 2009.[103] The Programme, which defines the strategic guidelines for legislative and operational planning within the area of freedom, security and justice in accordance with Article 68 TFEU, addresses integration in two separate points.

Point 6.1.4 addresses the issue of proactive policies for migrants and their rights, and repeats the Tampere objective that the European Union must ensure fair treatment of third country nationals who reside legally on the territory of its Member States, and that a more vigorous integration policy should aim at granting them rights and obligations comparable to those of EU citizens. This objective is to be implemented as soon as possible and no later than 2014.

The Commission has therefore been invited to submit proposals for: (a) the consolidation of all legislation in the immigration field, including amendments to simplify and/or where necessary extend the existing provisions and improve their implementation and coherence; and (b) the evaluation and, where necessary, review of the Family Reunification Directive, taking into account the importance of integration measures.

Point 6.1.4 addresses European cooperation in integration. After stating that the successful integration of legally resident third-country nationals remains the key to maximising the benefits of immigration, the European Council addresses the purpose, and the core element, of European cooperation in integration:

---

99 www.integration.eu.

100 Council Framework Decision 2008/913/JHA of 28 November 2008 on combating certain forms and expressions of racism and xenophobia by means of criminal law (OJ L328, 6.12.2008, p. 55).

101 Council Directive 2009/50/EC of 25 May 2009 on the conditions of entry and residence of third-country nationals for the purposes of highly qualified employment (OJ L155, 18.6.2009, p. 17).

102 The Stockholm Programme – An Open and Secure Europe Serving and Protecting the Citizen, (Council Doc. 17024/09).

103 Brussels European Council, 10-11 December 2009, Presidency Conclusions, paras. 25-33 (Council Doc. EUCO 6/09).

> European cooperation can contribute to more effective integration policies in Member States by providing incentives and support for the action of Member States. The objective of granting comparable rights, responsibilities and opportunities for all is at the core of European cooperation in integration, taking into account the necessity of balancing rights and duties.

The European Council identified a number of areas where support of Member States is needed. In the first place, national integration policies are to be supported through 'the further development of structures and tools for knowledge exchange and coordination with other relevant policy areas, such as employment, education and social inclusion'.

The Commission is invited to support Member States' efforts in a number of specific areas:

- through the development of a coordination mechanism involving the Commission and the Member States using a common reference framework, which should improve structures and tools for European knowledge exchange,
- to incorporate integration issues in a comprehensive way in all relevant policy areas,
- towards the identification of joint practices and European modules to support the integration process, including essential elements such as introductory course and language classes, a strong commitment by the host community and the active participation of immigrants in all aspects of collective life,
- towards the development of core indicators in a limited number of relevant policy areas (e.g., employment, education and social inclusion) for monitoring the results of integration policies, in order to increase the comparability of national experiences and reinforce the European learning process,
- for improved consultation with and involvement of civil society, taking into account integration needs in various policy areas and making use of the European Integration Forum and the European website on Integration,
- to enhance democratic values and social cohesion in relation to immigration and integration of immigrants and to promote intercultural dialogue and contacts at all levels.

The European Council invited the Commission to present an Action Plan in the first six months of 2010 to be adopted by the Council. The Commission adopted a Communication on the Action Plan in April 2010.[104]

In 'putting solidarity and responsibility at the heart of our response', the Commission stated that the 'robust defence of migrants' fundamental rights out of respect for our values of human dignity and solidarity will enable them to contribute fully to the European economy and society'. In addressing the question of migrants and their rights, the Commission declared that the EU had to 'strive for a uniform level of rights and obligations for legal immigrants comparable with that of European citizens', and made it clear that such rights were essential to maximise the legal benefits of legal immigration for the benefit of all stakeholders and would strengthen the Union's competitiveness. In relation to integration, there was no mention of 'European cooperation', but simply a statement that the 'integra-

104 Commission, *Delivering an Area of Freedom, Security and Justice for Europe's Citizens: Action Plan Implementing the Stockholm Programme* (COM(2010) 171 final (20 April 2010).

tion of migrants will be further pursued, safeguarding their rights while also underlining their own responsibilities to integrate into the societies in which they live'.

In listing the actions in relation to 'proactive policies for migrants and their rights', the Commission would issue a Green Paper on family reunification (2010), propose a modification of the Family Reunification Directive (2012) and prepare an Immigration code, consolidating legislation in the area of legal immigration (2013). In relation to 'integration', the Commission would launch the third edition of the Handbook (2010), report to the 2010 Ministerial Conference on Integration and prepare a Communication on an EU agenda for integration, including the development of a coordination mechanism (2011).

The 3rd Edition of the *Handbook on Integration* appeared in April 2010.[105] This addressed the question of European exchange of information and good practice and covered a number of themes: mass media and integration; awareness-raising and migrant empowerment; dialogue platforms; the acquisition of nationality and the practice of active citizenship; and immigrant youth, education and the labour market.

The Fourth European Ministerial Conference on Integration was held in Zaragoza in April 2010.[106] The Conference Declaration was reproduced in the June 2010 Conclusions of the Council and the Representatives of the Governments of the Member States on Integration as a Driver for Development and Social Cohesion.[107]

This was the first Ministerial Conference after the entry into force of the Lisbon Treaty and the Ministers recalled that, 'although European cooperation in the field of integration has developed dynamically over the last years, a new stage of cooperation started with the introduction of a specific legal basis for integration in the Treaty of Lisbon which allows Member States to make further progress in this area'.

The Ministers agreed to focus on and to explore the key aspects of integration as a driver for development and social cohesion by incorporating integration issues in a comprehensive way in all relevant policy fields. Particular attention was to be given to employment and education, diversity management and the evaluation of integration policies.

The June 2010 JHA Council also adopted Conclusions on the follow-up to the European Pact on Immigration and Asylum.[108] In relation to integration, the Council stated that efforts in relation to migration policy 'should be complemented by an ambitious integration agenda' building on the Vichy and Zaragoza Declarations. This agenda was to include a coordination mechanism as proposed in the Stockholm Programme and the facilitation of 'mainstreaming of integration priorities in all relevant areas'. It stated that 'expanding the use of indicators and developing European modules to support the integration process should also be important elements of this agenda'. These Conclusions were endorsed by the June 2010 Brussels European Council.[109]

105 European Commission, Directorate-General Justice, Freedom and Security, *Handbook on Integration* (3rd Edition) (April 2010).

106 Ministers for Integration. *Declaration*, European Ministerial Conference on Integration, Zaragoza, 15-16 April 2010 (Council Doc. 8771/10). See, also, Commission, *The consolidation of the EU framework on integration: Report to the 2008 Ministerial Conference on Integration* (Staff Working Document) (SEC(2010) 357 final).

107 JHA Council, 3-4 June 2010, Press release (Council Doc. 10630/1/10 REV 1). For the Conclusions, see Council Doc. 9248/10).

108 Council Doc. 10302/10.

109 Brussels European Council, 17 June 2010, Presidency Conclusions, para. 23 (Council Doc. EUCO 13/10).

5. Supporting National Integration Policies

General

In its December 2007 Communication '*Towards a Common Immigration Policy*',[110] the Commission stated that 'integration policy has been the subject of a pragmatic approach sustained by strong political demand, symbolically reflected in the adoption of common basic principles'.

The statement should be treasured – such imaginative language is rare enough in Commission Communications. At the very real risk of undermining a carefully crafted structure, a number of points appear to emerge. First, reference to a 'pragmatic approach' suggests that debates on competence and other such technical niceties have been left aside. Second, the idea of 'strong political demand' suggests that politicians have driven the process. Third, the adoption of the 2004 Common Basic Principles 'reflects' this pragmatic and politically-driven approach: the term 'symbolically reflected' underlines the importance of the Common Basic Principles and their potential for development.

We are here concerned with the nature of the framework for cooperation by the Member States with respect to *their* integration policies in the period before the entry into force of the Lisbon Treaty. This raises a number of specific issues. First, how Member State powers in the area of integration policy have been characterised. Second, why, given that Member States have 'primarily responsibility' for integration policies, it is necessary for Member States to cooperate in this area. Third, how differences between Member States' integration policies are to be accommodated. Fourth, how cooperation has been designed in order to respect Member State powers and at the same time ensure effective policies.

Characterising Member State Powers

There has been little debate on the issue of national competence in the area of integration policy. Rather, there has been a widespread recognition that integration policy is primarily a matter for the Member States and that common action in the area (whatever its precise legal basis) should strengthen and support national *policies*. The question of competence has thus been left largely unaddressed – simply because it has been accepted that the Member States *are* competent. Instead attention has focused on the way in which Member States can act together in the context of such retained powers.

At the same time, as will be seen, the EC Treaty was used as the legal basis for specific *Community/EU* measures in relation to elements of integration policy. Much of this has been due to the Member States themselves who were prepared, in exercising their law-making powers, to accept a broad interpretation of the key immigration policy provision, Article 63(3)(a) of the EC Treaty, and to use other available EC Treaty bases.

No explicit claims of Member State competence were made by the October 1999 Tampere European Council,[111] though its conclusions on the issue of 'fair treatment of third-country nationals' appear to have envisaged action under the EC Treaty and, to a lesser extent, action by the Member States exercising retained powers (which was, for

110 See n. 90, at p. 4.

111 See n. 48.

example, the case with the European Council's endorsement of the objective that long-term residents be given the opportunity to obtain the nationality of the Member State of residence).

In the 2000 Commission Communication on a Community Immigration Policy,[112] the Commission recognised that integration was primarily the role of the Member States, but stated that this national governmental responsibility was to be shared with 'civil society', notably at local level where integration measures were to be implemented. The 2001 Commission Communication on an open method of coordination for the Community immigration policy[113] set out the Commission understanding of the powers of the Member States in the field of integration policy:[114] it was explicitly recognised that the 'development of appropriate integration strategies is the responsibility of Member States with authorities and other actors at the local, and municipal level having a very important role to play'.

The October 2002 JHA Council Conclusions on the integration of third-country nationals[115] did not specifically refer to either of the Commission Communications and the question of the use of the open coordination method was not addressed. The issue of competence was not addressed in terms. However, it should be noted that reference was made to 'national integration policies' and ideas of cooperation between Member States with regard to such *policies* were advanced, and have since taken root.

In June 2003, the General Affairs Council and, subsequently, the Thessaloniki European Council issued conclusions on the development of a policy at EU level on the integration of third country nationals legally residing in the territory of the EU,[116] in which they made it clear that while primary responsibility for the elaboration and implementation of integration policies 'remains with the Member States, such policies should be developed within a coherent European Union framework, taking into account the legal political, economic, social and cultural diversity of Member States'.

The November 2004 JHA Council Conclusions[117] pointed out that 'integration takes place simultaneously at the individual, family and general community and State levels, and occurs in all facets of life': as a consequence 'successful integration policy must engage the local, regional, and national institutions, with which immigrants interact, in both the public and private realms'. In something of a non-sequitur, the conclusions continued:

> 'The development and implementation of integration policy is *therefore* the primary responsibility of individual Member States rather than that of the Union as a whole'.

In setting out a Common Agenda for Integration[118] in September 2005, the Commission outlined the policy context – pointing to 'a certain amount of convergence in terms of policy and objectives for integration across the EU', the development of a common approach to integration particularly with the Common Principles, the need further to strengthen integration policies at national and EU levels – but stated that 'primary respon-

112 See n. 59, at p. 20.
113 See n. 60, at p. 5, 11.
114 The question of competence in relation to other aspects of immigration policy is not discussed here.
115 See n. 62.
116 See, respectively n. 64, at p. 4, and n. 65, at point 31.
117 See n. 70, at Recital 3.
118 See n. 76, at p. 15.

sibility for the development and implementation of integration policy and measures *nevertheless* remains at the level of the Member State'.[119] In the December 2005 JHA Council conclusions on the Common Agenda,[120] the Council and the Representatives of the Governments of the Member States repeated the Thessaloniki approach and underlined 'the need to strengthen the integration policies of the Member States'.

Why are Supporting Measures Needed?

Given the recognition that the primary responsibility for integration policy lies with the Member States, it may be asked why there is a need for action in the form of supporting measures.

The importance of the link between integration and immigration policy has been repeatedly stated. As the common EU migration policy has evolved, so has the need for effective national integration policies. The November 2000 Commission Communication on a Community immigration policy[121] saw immigration and integration policies as intrinsically linked, and the July 2001 Commission Communication on the open method of coordination[122] argued that the success of the Community immigration policy would 'depend on the extent to which migrants become integrated in their host country'. The October 2002 Council Conclusions[123] saw integration as 'an important element' in the establishment of a European asylum and immigration policy. The November 2004 JHA Council Conclusions[124] saw the successful integration of legally-residing immigrants and their descendants as 'a critical aspect of managing migration' and stated that 'at the same time immigration policy can contribute to the success of integration policy'.

The June 2007 Council Resolution on the strengthening of integration policies in the EU[125] recognised 'the complementary linkage between immigration and integration'. In its December 2007 Communication *Towards a Common Immigration Policy*,[126] the Commission stated that 'any policy on immigration must now go hand in hand with a policy of integration'. The December 2007 Brussels European Council[127] stated that integration was 'a pivotal element' of the comprehensive European migration policy, and called for better coordination between migration and integration policies. The importance of the link was reiterated by the Commission in its June 2008 Communication *A Common Immigration Policy for Europe: Principles, Actions and Tools,*[128] stating that 'the positive potential of immigration can only be realised if integration into host societies is successful'. The link was implicit, but not explicitly stated, in the October 2008 European Pact on Immigration and Asylum.[129] The Stockholm Programme[130] has picked up the argument, stating that the 'success-

119 Emphasis supplied.
120 See n. 77, at Recital 2.
121 See n. 59, at p. 5.
122 See n. 60, at p. 11.
123 See n. 62, at point 5.
124 See n. 70, at Recital 2.
125 See n. 82, at p. 1.
126 See n. 89, at p. 4.
127 See n. 91, at p. 25.
128 See n. 92, at p. 3.
129 See n. 96.
130 See n. 101, p. 64.

ful integration of legally resident third-country nationals remains the key to maximising the benefits of immigration'.

The Hague Programme[131] saw action on the integration of third-country nationals in terms of the benefit successful integration would give to 'stability and cohesion within our societies'. This was reflected in the list of reasons given by the JHA Council in its November 2004 Conclusions[132] why Member State policies had to be successful. The failure of an individual Member State to develop and implement a successful integration policy could have adverse implications for the other Member States and the European Union. This could include impacts on the economy and labour market participation, undermining respect for human rights and Europe's commitment to fulfilling international obligations to refugees and others needing international protection, and breeding alienation and tensions within society. It was 'clearly in the common interest of all Member States of the Union that each individual Member States pursues effective integration strategies'.

In its 2006 Resolution on strategies and means for the integration of immigrants in the EU,[133] the European Parliament pointed to the adverse consequences for the EU of a failure by a single Member State to implement successful integration policies. There could, for example, be under-employment of immigrants, weakening the EU economy and preventing achievement of the Lisbon agenda. Unwelcome workers could be 'driven into the underground economy or into the arms of the EU's economic competitors'. The absence of effective policies could lead to 'negative perceptions of immigrants and to defensive immigration policies'. The European Parliament also pointed to 'fear among citizens subverting respect for human dignity, freedom, democracy, equality, the rule of law and respect for human rights' and to 'perceptions and prejudices about immigrants who have not integrated undermining the Union's successful enlargement'. *Success* in integration would, on the other hand: 'strengthen the Union's economy in the face of global competition'; attract workers, entrepreneurs, scientists and students; result in safer cities and stronger communities; diminish xenophobic tendencies and fortify respect for fundamental rights; and enhance Europe's position in the world.

The October 2008 European Pact on Immigration and Asylum[134] referred to the new challenges brought to the Member States by the creation of a common area of free movement:

> 'One Member State's actions may affect the interests of the others. Access to the territory of one Member State may be followed by access to the others. It is consequently imperative that each Member State take account of its partners' interests when designing and implementing its immigration, integration and asylum policies'.

Accommodating National Differences

Differences in national integration policies not only inform the nature of and content of cooperation, but also underline the need for cooperation in itself.

131 See n. 68, p. 19.
132 See n. 70, at point 4.
133 See n. 79, at Recital E.
134 See n. 96, at p. 3.

The June 2003 Council/European Council Conclusions[135] recognised that national policies should be 'developed within a coherent European Union framework, taking into account the legal, political, economic, social and cultural diversity among Member States'. Though this element is usually left unsaid, it is clear that the idea of *supporting* measures is appropriate where there are divergent national policies. As the 2004 JHA Council Conclusions made clear, 'the precise integration measures a society chooses to implement should be determined by individual Member States'.[136] Thus, it was made clear that the Common Basic Principles aimed at assisting 'Member States in formulating integration policies by offering them a simple non-binding but thoughtful guide against which they can judge and assess their own efforts'.

A somewhat different idea – that cooperation is needed in spite of, or because of, national differences – is also expressed in the 2004 JHA Council Conclusions.[137] It was recognised that that integration policies 'will differ significantly from Member State to Member State' and had to be 'geared to the individual needs of the receiving society, reflecting each individual Member State's history and legal framework'. Such policies might 'also target diverse audiences, the mix which varies between the Member States'. In this context, developing a set of EU common principles was 'essential, *not only given the diversity of experiences and circumstances*, but also given the shared interest that Member States have in agreeing upon shared goals on integration'.[138]

The idea of further strengthening integration policies in the EU 'by promoting unity in diversity' was conceived by the EU Integration Ministers in their informal meeting in Potsdam in May 2007 and reflected in the June 2007 JHA Council Conclusions on strengthening of integration policies in the European Union.[139] Employment of the term 'unity in diversity' seems to have been to be key to the taking of 'further action directed to strengthening the European framework for integration and the integration policies of the Member States'. This term was not discussed, but it seems that 'unity' was *of* the Member States, whilst 'diversity' is *between* them. This was reminiscent of the motto 'united it its diversity' that the European Convention ascribed to 'Europe' in 2003 in the Preamble to the failed Draft Treaty establishing a Constitution for Europe.[140] Although the 'unity in diversity' term may have been useful in obtaining progress in Potsdam, it did not feature in the 2008 Pact[141] or in the thinking of the Council or European Council since then.

The November 2008 Vichy Declaration (and the subsequent Council Conclusions)[142] stressed the challenge of integration faced by all of the Member States, even though, paraphrasing the 2004 Conclusions 'the relevant policies aimed at legally-residing third-country nationals may differ significantly from one Member State to another, depending on their histories and administrative organisations, and concern distinct groups the composition of which may vary from one country to another'. The Member States agreed to give particular

135 See, respectively, n. 64, at p. 4, and n. 65, at point 31.
136 See n. 70, at point 5.
137 See n. 70, at points 6-7.
138 Emphasis supplied.
139 See n. 82, at point 4.
140 OJ C169, 18.7.2003, p. 8.
141 See n. 96.
142 See n. 97, at p. 4.

attention to the themes addressed by the Conference 'when defining and implementing their national integration policies in accordance with national rules'.

Designing Cooperation

A brief chronological survey of developments from Tampere to the present has been provided in Section 4 above. It is proposed here briefly to consider how cooperation has been designed in order to respect Member State powers and at the same time ensure the effectiveness of national integration policies.

Progress may not have been as swift as the Commission (and the European Parliament) would have liked, but there has been a gradual widening and deepening of European cooperation in integration, in terms both of subject-matter and instrumentalities.

The Commission has, of course, provided significant informed input into this process. It has sought, in a series of Communications, to influence policy and to drive the process forward. The desire to drive the process forward, to secure the effectiveness of national integration policies as well as to ensure that national and EU policies work in tandem, was seen in the 2001 Commission Communication on an open method of coordination for the Community immigration policy.[143] The Commission considered that the open coordination method would be the most appropriate way of supporting the Community's policy since, within the Amsterdam Treaty framework, Member States remained responsible for implementing integration policy. The Commission advanced a 'method' under which national policies would be 'harnessed' in order to support Community policy and, over a period, to *develop* that policy. The Communication can be read as implying some future extension of Community powers in the field. Indeed, the Commission stated that the 'use of an open method of coordination, specifically adapted to the immigration field, and as a complement to the legislative framework, will provide the necessary policy mix to achieve a gradual approach to the development of an policy, based, in the first stage at least, on the identification and development of common objectives to which it is agreed that a European response is necessary'.

The Commission early on accepted that its 2001 proposals would not be taken up by the Council. In its 2003 Communication on Immigration, Integration and Employment it proposed instead 'to develop cooperation and exchange of information within the framework of the newly established Group of national contact points on integration with a view, in particular, to strengthening coordination of relevant policies at national level'.[144] The National Contact Points have been key to developments ever since. The 'network works to operationalize and enhance the implementation of technical cooperation, define common objectives, set targets or benchmarks, and strengthen coordination between national and EU policies'.[145] The use of the National Contact Points on Integration has enabled Member States to make more progress than might have been possible with more transparent, centralised structures.

The agenda has been set by the Member States, in the Tampere, Hague and Stockholm Programmes,[146] in Presidency initiatives such as the European Pact on Immigration and

143 See n. 60.

144 See n. 63, at p. 29.

145 See n. 104, at p. 17.

146 See the outline in Section 4, above.

Asylum,[147] in the deliberations of Ministerial Conferences, and in the Conclusions of the Council and the Representatives of the Member States.

The Common Basic Principles have proved to be a key driver in this process, providing a framework for the support of national integration policies and for the development of EU measures. In the context of supporting national policies, the first aim of the Common Basic Principles was stated to be 'to assist Member States in formulating integration policies by offering them a simple non-binding but thoughtful guide of basic principles against which they can judge and assess their own efforts': they could also 'use these basic principles to set priorities and further develop their own measurable goals'.

The Common Basic Principles cover a wide variety of areas and have been built upon and developed over time. The November 2008 Vichy Ministerial Conference addressed a number of key themes/areas, and these were taken up in subsequent Conclusions of the JHA Council and Representatives of the Governments of the Member States.[148] The Member States agreed to give 'particular attention to these themes, among other important integration issues, when defining their national integration policies, in accordance with national specificities and rules'. A similar approach has been taken in relation to the Zaragoza Declaration.[149] Such wording, which appears to give some latitude to the Member States, should be seen in the context of the fact that such Conclusions are, in themselves, not binding.

It is undeniable that the Commission has been able to provide a consistent 'European' voice that could not really be provided by the Member States. This is all the more important since there are EU elements in integration policy and consistency between national and EU measures has to be achieved. However, although it has sought to give direction and many of its ideas have been taken up, the Member States are 'in the driving seat' and some important Commission ideas (in relation, for example, to the use of the Open Coordination Method and 'Civic Citizenship') have not been endorsed. The adoption of the European Pact on Immigration and Asylum[150] – proposed by the French Presidency in the face of different Commission proposals – was undeniably a rebuff for the Commission, which had argued, in its June 2008 Communication on a *Common Immigration Policy for Europe*,[151] for 'coordinated and coherent action by the EU and its Member States' and the 'use of a common methodology for the EU and its Member States to ensure transparency, mutual trust and coherence'.

The Commission has nevertheless made important 'technical' contributions to the process of cooperation with regard to national integration policies. It has worked with the National Contact Points and has drawn national practices together in the three annual Reports on Migration and Integration (2004, 2006 and 2007).[152] It has also been involved with the National Contact Points in the production of the three editions of the Handbook on Integration,[153] collectively setting out 'lessons learned' and 'good practices' across all of the

147 See n. 96.
148 See n. 97.
149 See n. 105.
150 See n. 96.
151 See n. 92, at p. 15-16.
152 See nn. 66, 78 and 87.
153 See nn. 71, 83 and 104.

areas covered by the Common Basic Principles. Last, and by no means least, it hosts the European Website on Integration.[154]

The focus of the above discussion has been on cooperation with regard to national integration policies. Though this is not addressed here, one must not lose sight of the need to ensure that national policies work together with European Union measures in integration policy, including the Immigration Directives discussed in the next Section.

6. EU Powers in Integration Policy

General

Until the entry in force of the Lisbon Treaty, and a new provision – Article 79(4) TFEU – providing a specific legal basis for measures in relation to integration of legally-resident third-country nationals, the area of 'integration' was not addressed in terms in the Treaties.

This did not, however, mean that measures in relation to integration could not be based on Treaty provisions. Even if there was no catch-all provision covering 'integration policy', individual elements of integration policy could be covered by Treaty principles and other policies. This is not surprising since the successful integration of third-country nationals legally residing in a Member States is dependent on action in a wide range of areas, such as the fight against discrimination and social, educational, health and employment policies. Indeed, the 'holistic' approach introduced by the Commission in its June 2003 Communication on Immigration, Integration and Employment[155] and the 'mainstreaming' approach endorsed in the Common Basic Principles[156] mandate the inclusion of integration concerns in a variety of policy areas. Moreover, the success of the EU's immigration policy has been seen as conditional on successful integration, and this has resulted in the migration Directives containing provisions on the treatment of the third-country nationals covered by these Directives, sometimes expressly on integration grounds.

The Common Basic Principles were designed not only to support Member State integration policies, but also to inform EU policies and measures. One of the stated aims was 'to be complementary and in full synergy with existing legislative frameworks, including the international instruments on Human Rights, Community instruments containing integration provisions, EU objectives on gender equality and non-discrimination and other EU policies'. Another was 'to serve as a basis for and assist the EU to explore how existing EU-instruments related to integration can be developed further'. The final aim linked EU action to Member State policies: 'to assist the Council to reflect upon and over time, agree on EU-level mechanisms and policies needed to support national and local-level integration policy efforts, particularly through EU-wide learning and knowledge-sharing.

The reference to action at 'EU-level' glossed over, rather than clarified, the areas of EU/EC competence. This opacity was maintained in the 2005 Common Agenda for Integration,[157] and the Council response.[158] The Common Basic Principles were the key drivers

154 See n. 98.
155 See n. 63.
156 See Common Basic Principle 10, and other Common Basic Principles addressing specific policy areas.
157 See n. 76.
158 See n. 77.

for a framework encompassing cooperation between Member States in relation to their *own* integration policies, supported by mechanisms both within and outside the express scope of the Treaties, *and* action under the Treaties collectively constituting a piecemeal *European Union* policy on integration.

The use of the term 'piecemeal' has no derogatory connotation. Although EU integration policy does not have the breadth of a fully-developed national integration policy, integration concerns are addressed in a number of EU policy areas such as social policy, health policy, employment policy and education policy. The EC Treaty provisions on social policy, for example, made it clear that the Community was to support and complement the activities of Member States on working conditions, including 'the conditions of employment for third-country nationals legally residing in Community territory'.[159] The EC Treaty provisions in relation to these areas – and the 'mainstreaming' of integration concerns in them - are not considered in detail here. However, it should be noted that Community competence in these areas was generally limited to supporting or complementing measures, and that the provisions reflected much the same competence concerns as applied to integration policy. For example, in addition to stating that EC action in relation to social policy was to support and complement national activities, Council action in relation to the conditions of employment for third-country nationals was subject to a unanimity voting requirement.[160]

The Immigration Directives

Integration policy has been treated as an essential element in *immigration* policy and a number of measures under the immigration policy provisions of the EC Treaty have addressed integration questions.

As seen above the Treaty of Amsterdam brought immigration policy as defined into the EC Treaty (albeit with certain intergovernmental legacies which need not be discussed here). Article 63 EC required the Council to adopt measures on immigration policy within a number of areas, including, under Article 63(3)(a) 'conditions of entry and residence'. The meaning of 'conditions of ... residence' is not clear. However, a broad interpretation was mandated by the Tampere European Council, which called for integration of lawfully-resident third-country nationals by ensuring their 'fair treatment' and according them rights and obligations comparable to those applying for EU citizens. This has been followed through in legislation based on Article 63(3)(a) EC. What might be described as 'integration concerns' have been reflected, explicitly or implicitly, in specific provisions on treatment in a number of specific migration Directives.

The various migration Directives adopted between 2003 and 2009 are each based, at least partly, on Article 63(3)(a) EC and each of them contains provisions on the *treatment* – as opposed to *residence* narrowly understood – of persons covered by the Directive.[161] The

159 Article 137 EC.

160 Article 137(3) EC.

161 Council Directive 2003/86/EC of 22 September 2003 on the right to family reunification (OJ L251, 3.10.2003, p. 12) (the Family Reunification Directive); Council Directive 2003/109/EC of 25 November 2003 concerning the status of third-country nationals who are long-term residents (OJ L16, 23.1.2004, p. 44) (the Long-Term Residents Directive); Council Directive 2004/81/EC of 29 April 2004 on the residence permit issued to third-country nationals who are victims of trafficking in human beings or who have been the subject of an action to facilitate illegal immigration, who cooperate →

specific rules on treatment reflect the characteristics of the status of the persons concerned and the reasons for granting them rights of entry and residence. It is, perhaps, stating the obvious that those with rights of long-term stable residence and 'valued' highly-skilled workers enjoy a broader range of socio-economic rights than more temporary residents such as students and researchers, or those with a precarious status, such as victims of trafficking.

In two of these Directives, the importance of 'integration' is expressly stated in the preamble. In the 2003 Family Reunification Directive,[162] it is stated that family reunification 'helps to create socio-cultural stability facilitating the integration of third-country nationals in the Member State, which also serves to promote economic and social cohesion, a fundamental Community objective stated in the Treaty'.[163] Similarly, in the 2003 Long-Term Residents Directive,[164] it is stated that the 'integration of third-country nationals who are long-term residents in the Member States is a key element in promoting economic and social cohesion, a fundamental objective of the Community stated in the Treaty'.[165] An explicit link is made between 'integration' and the equality of treatment to be enjoyed by long-term residents:

> 'In order to constitute a genuine instrument for the integration of long-term residents into society in which they live, long-term residents should enjoy equality of treatment with citizens of the Member State in a wide range of economic and social matters, under the relevant conditions defined by this Directive.'[166]

The reference to 'economic and social cohesion' seems to be intended to support the broader interpretation of Article 63(3)(a) of the EC Treaty as the legal basis for measures on the integration (and not merely 'residence') of third-country nationals covered by the Directives.

The European Fund for Integration

More tellingly perhaps, Article 63(3)(a) was used, perhaps *faute de mieux*, as the basis for the 2007 Council Decision establishing the European Fund for Integration,[167] disposing of € 825 million for the period 2007-2013, though it was made clear that this was a supporting measure.

---

with the competent authorities (OJ L261, 6.8.2004, p. 19) (the Victims of Trafficking Directive); Council Directive 2004/114/EC of 13 December 2004 on the conditions of admission of third-country nationals for the purposes of studies, pupil exchange, unremunerated training or voluntary service (OJ L375, 23.12.2004, p. 12) (the Students Directive); Council Directive 2005/71/EC of 12 October 2005 on a specific procedure for admitting third-country nationals for the purposes of scientific research (OJ L289, 3.11.2005, p. 15) (the Researchers Directive); Council Directive 2009/50/EC of 25 May 2009 on the conditions of entry and residence of third-country nationals for the purposes of highly qualified employment (OJ L155, 18.6.2009, p. 17) (the Blue Card Directive).

162 See n.160.

163 Recital 4 of the Preamble to the Family Reunification Directive.

164 See n. 160.

165 Recital 4 of the Preamble to the Long-Term Residents Directive.

166 Recital 12 of the Preamble to the Long-Term Residents Directive.

167 See n. 161.

The establishment of the Fund should be seen in the context of the need stated in the 2004 Hague Programme for the greater coordination of national integration policies, the adoption and implementation of the 2004 Common Basic Principles, and the adverse implications for other Member States and the Union where an individual Member State fails to develop and implement integration policies.[168]

The *general* objective of the Fund is 'to support the efforts made by the Member States in enabling third-country nationals of different economic, social, cultural, religious, linguistic and ethnic backgrounds to fulfil the conditions of residence and to facilitate their integration into the European societies', primarily focusing on actions relating to the integration of newly-arrived third-country nationals.[169] In order to further this objective, the Fund is to 'contribute to the development and implementation of national integration strategies for third-country nationals in all aspects of society'.

A number of specific objectives of the Fund are also set out:

'(a) facilitation of the development and implementation of admission procedures relevant to and supportive of the integration process of third-country nationals;
(b) development and implementation of the integration process of newly-arrived third country nationals in Member States;
(c) increasing of the capacity of Member States to develop, implement, monitor and evaluate policies and measures for the integration of third-country nationals;
(d) exchange of information, best practices and cooperation in and between Member States in developing, implementing, monitoring and evaluating policies and measures for the integration of third-country nationals.'[170]

The Decision is thus to be seen as establishing a funding mechanism for the support of *national* integration policies. The use of Article 63(3)(a) of the EC Treaty in this context was, to say the least, a creative one. Even assuming it could be used for 'integration' elements in the migration Directives, which in principle were Community measures within the area of 'conditions of entry and residence', the same could not naturally be said for measures 'to promote the integration of third-country nationals in the host societies of Member States within the framework of the Common Basic Principles'.[171] That Article 63(3)(a) was so used – almost in spite of its wording – reflected the imperative need for *Community* funding. Any arguments that Article 63(3)(a) was not an appropriate legal basis for the Decision could be countered by the fact that the Council, acting by unanimity, decided that that Article was to be used as the legal basis for the measure. Whatever interpretative objections could be raised could be met by the praxis of the legislator.

At the same time as deciding that Article 63(3)(a) *could* be used as the basis for the Decision, the legislator could and did decide on the appropriate limits of Community action. The Council was thus at pains to make it clear that measure *supported* Member States' integration policies.

168 See Recitals 4 to 8 of the Preamble to the Decision.
169 Article 2(1) of the Decision.
170 Article 3 of the Decision.
171 Recital 28 of the Preamble to the Decision.

It nevertheless remains the case that, on its wording, Article 63(3)(a) was not an apt basis for Community measures supporting national integration policies where these could not be naturally linked to 'conditions of admission and residence'. In fact, developments since the Treaty of Amsterdam meant that the EC Treaty provisions on immigration were not fit for purpose. This difficulty of 'catch up' was resolved only by the introduction of Article 79(4) TFEU by the Lisbon Treaty.

Non-Discrimination

The principle of non-discrimination has, in particular since the 1999 Tampere Summit, been seen as a key instrument of integration.

Article 12 EC (now Article 18 TFEU), prohibiting discrimination on grounds of nationality within the scope of application of the Treaties, was of limited use as regarded third-country nationals, since 'nationality' has been taken to apply to that of the Member States. However, Article 13 EC (now Article 18(1) TFEU) empowered the Council to take 'appropriate action to combat discrimination based on sex, racial or ethnic origin, religion or belief, disability, age or sexual orientation'. The Council adopted two directives in 2000, one on equal treatment between persons irrespective of racial or ethnic origin[172] and the other on equal treatment in employment and occupation.[173] It is made clear that the prohibition of discrimination should apply to nationals of third countries,[174] but it is expressly provided in each Directive that it 'does not cover differences of treatment based on nationality and is without prejudice to provisions and conditions relating to the entry into and residence of third-country nationals and stateless persons in the territory of Member States, and to any treatment which arises from the legal status of the third-country nationals and stateless persons concerned'.[175] This includes 'access to employment and to occupation',[176] which is particularly significant in the Directive concerning equal treatment *in employment and occupation*! It should, however, be made clear that these provisos should not materially impact on the position of legally-resident third-country nationals who should generally benefit from the national measures implementing the Directives.

The principle of non-discrimination is also an important tool in the migration Directives.[177] Rules on the equality of treatment – which vary depending on the nature of the differing statuses accorded to third-country nationals covered by these Directives – make it clear that there should be equality with nationals of the host Member State in a range of social and economic areas.

---

172 See n. 49.

173 See n. 50.

174 Recital 13 of the Preamble to Directive 2000/43 and Recital 12 of the Preamble to Directive 2000/78.

175 Article 3 of Directive 2000/43 and Article 3 of Directive 2000/78. The same approach is taken in the proposed Council Directive on implementing the principle of equal treatment between persons irrespective of religion or belief, disability, age or sexual orientation (COM (2008) 426 final).

176 Recital 13 of the Preamble to Directive 2000/43 and Recital 12 of the Preamble to Directive 2000/78.

177 See n. 160.

7. The Impact of the Lisbon Treaty

The Lisbon Treaty, which entered in force in December 2009, resulted in a recast Treaty on European Union and a new Treaty on the Functioning of the European Union (TFEU). In the present context, The TFEU addresses the development of a common immigration policy, with its aims including 'the fair treatment of third-country nationals residing legally in Member States', and with the European Parliament and Council empowered to adopt measures on 'the conditions of entry and residence' of third-country nationals as well as on 'the definition of the rights of third-country nationals residing legally in a Member State'.

There is also, in Article 79(4) TFEU, a new specific Treaty basis for the establishment by the European Parliament and the Council of 'measures to provide incentives and support for the action of Member States with a view to promoting the integration of third-country nationals residing legally in their territories, excluding any harmonisation of the laws and regulations of the Member States'.

It should be noted that the new provision is virtually identical to a provision contained in the Draft Treaty establishing a Constitution for Europe,[178] adopted by the European Convention in June 2003, before many of the major developments outlined in this paper. It is a little like the 'fly in the amber' and it has to be questioned whether such a short provision, which was effectively drafted several years before the Lisbon Treaty, is in the light of these later developments fit for purpose.

However, we are stuck with what we have! To a degree, the 'new' provisions have introduced nothing that is fundamentally new, but have only validated the pre-existing position: in other words, the Treaty provisions have caught up with what has been already accepted at political level. Indeed, the idea of 'fair treatment' of legally-resident third-country nationals has been the *leitmotif* of Union action since the Tampere European Council. Measures have been taken at 'EU-level' to incentivise and support national integration policies. However, even this 'validation' is both useful and necessary, given the inadequate legal basis provided by Article 63(3)(a) of the EC Treaty for instruments such as the 2007 Decision establishing the European Fund for Integration.

However, there is more. In its report to the Zaragoza Conference,[179] the Commission pointed to the new '*explicit legal basis* to pro-actively develop European cooperation in the field of integration of legally staying third-country nationals'. It pointed out that the European Parliament will be on an equal footing with the Council and added that 'EU action will become more comprehensive and will allow the further development of integration policy through measures which provide incentives and support for the action of Member States'.

The April 2010 Zaragoza Declaration/June 2010 JHA Conclusions[180] themselves pointed out that 'although European cooperation in the field of integration has developed dynamically over the last years, a new stage of cooperation started with the introduction of a specific legal basis for integration in the Treaty of Lisbon which allows Member States to make further progress in this area'.

How much of this promise will be fulfilled?

---

178 See n. 137, Article III-168(4).

179 See n. 105.

180 See nn. 105 and 106.

European cooperation in integration was, before the entry into force of the Lisbon Treaty, addressed by a hybrid framework of action under the EU Treaty and intergovernmental cooperation (with the latter exemplified by the involvement of 'Representatives of the Governments of the Member States' in establishing non-binding measures and the activities of the National Contact Points on Integration). Even within this hybrid framework, the Commission (and the Parliament) sought a more structured framework for 'coordinated and coherent action by the EU and its Member States'[181] than the Member States were prepared to accept. There was nothing novel about such coordination frameworks. Precedents could readily be found in the Treaty provisions for other policy areas, such as employment policy and social policy.

The Stockholm Programme,[182] which commenced shortly after the Lisbon Treaty came into force, has provided a new momentum, calling, for example, for the development of a coordination of a coordination mechanism using a common reference framework to improve structures and tools for European knowledge exchange (a rather more limited instrument than the Open Coordination Method proposed by the Commission in 2001[183]), the identification of joint practices and European modules to support the integration process, and the development of core indicators in a limited number of policy areas. The JHA Council has endorsed 'an ambitious integration agenda' including these elements[184] and this may start bearing fruit once the Commission has issued its eagerly-awaited Communication on an EU agenda for integration later in 2011.

The types and legal nature of the measures that will be taken remain unclear, and the general wording of Article 79(4) TFEU does not give us any real clues. Article 79(4) enables, rather than requires, the Parliament and Council to act. The provision is to be read in the light of Article 289 TFEU, which provides that the 'ordinary legislative procedure shall consist in the joint adoption by the European Parliament and the Council of a regulation, directive or decision on a proposal from the Commission'. It is not clear what concrete 'measures' will be taken in the near to medium term. Much will depend on the approach taken by the Commission in proposing measures and in the preparedness of the Parliament and especially the Council to adopt such measures. It seems unlikely that much recourse will be had, at least initially, to regulations or directives, and it must always be remembered that 'the harmonisation of the laws and regulations of the Member States is excluded'. Decisions may, of course, be taken in relation to funding, and it should be noted that the European Fund for Integration will need to be extended or replaced at the end of 2013.

Otherwise, it is probable that we will continue to see use made of Ministerial Declarations and Council Conclusions and of other non-binding measures. That 'intergovernmental' elements of the pre-Lisbon framework may not have yet outlived their usefulness is seen in the fact that the June 2010 JHA Council Conclusions on Integration as a Driver for Development and Social Cohesion were adopted by the Council and the Representatives of the Governments of the Member States. The Commission itself has stated that the role of the National Contact Points 'as a place for the exchange of experience and shaping of future policy initiatives should be enhanced'. It could be argued that Article 79(4) TFEU is limited

181 See the discussion on 'designing cooperation' in Section 5, above.

182 See n. 101, at p. 64-65.

183 See n. 60.

184 See n. 107.

to the *possibility* of taking legally-binding measures and that this is an area where *plus ça change, plus c'est la même chose*.

Article 79(4) TFEU does makes a difference. It is undeniable that the legal basis for action which incentivises and supports Member State action in the integration area has, as a result of the Lisbon Treaty, migrated to the EU. There has been a clear competence shift to the extent that action under intergovernmental cooperation outside the framework of the EU Treaty *can* now be taken as measures under the TFEU. However, at the same time, what is being supported and incentivised – that is, 'the action of Member States with a view to promoting the integration of third-country nationals residing legally within their territories' – remains within the domain reserved to the Member States. Indeed, in relation to competence, the reference in Article 79(4) to 'the action *of* Member States'[185] suggests that there is an area of sacrosanct national power which cannot be invaded by Union action, even of only a supportive or incentivising nature.

Certain elements of national integration policy remain highly sensitive. In many Member States, for example, there is an intense debate on the approaches to be taken to integration, with heads of government and 'ordinary' citizens reflecting, in different ways, on the validity of concepts such as 'multiculturalism'[186] and on how acceptance of difference is to be reconciled with adherence to fundamental values.

National identities and essential State functions – in particular national security – have to be respected.[187] At the same time, the need to work together to secure the effectiveness of national integration policies is recognised by all of the Member States. The key challenge is to secure, to reinvigorate the motto, 'unity in diversity'. In this context, integration policy in the EU has been advanced by a mix of the 'Community method' and the 'intergovernmental method'. This has been described, broadly, as the 'new "Union method"'.[188] In the area of integration, the retention of some elements of the 'intergovernmental' method, coupled with the possibilities of action under the TFEU, may continue to be necessary if progress is to continue.

185 Emphasis supplied.

186 See, for example, the statement by German Federal Chancellor Angela Merkel in October 2010 that the multicultural approach 'has failed, utterly failed'.

187 Article 4(2) TFEU.

188 The phrase was coined by German Federal Chancellor Angela Merkel in her November 2010 speech opening the 61st academic year of the College of Europe in Bruges.

Les Politiques d'Intégration de l'Union Européenne et des États Membres à l'Épreuve du Principe de Non-discrimination

*Emmanuelle Bribosia**

Introduction

1. Dès les origines de la construction européenne, les liens étroits entre traitement non-discriminatoire des étrangers et intégration dans la société d'accueil ont été mis en évidence. Ainsi, dans le préambule du règlement 1612/68 relatif à la libre circulation des travailleurs, il était souligné que 'le droit de libre circulation exige, pour qu'il puisse s'exercer dans des conditions objectives de liberté et de dignité, que soit assurée, en fait et en droit, l'égalité de traitement pour tout ce qui se rapporte à l'exercice même d'une activité salariée et à l'accès au logement, et aussi que soient éliminés les obstacles qui s'opposent à la mobilité des travailleurs notamment en ce qui concerne le droit pour le travailleur de se faire rejoindre par sa famille, et les conditions d'intégration de cette famille dans le milieu du pays d'accueil'.[1] L'égalité de traitement ainsi que le droit au regroupement familial sont considérés, dans cette logique, comme des conditions préalables à une intégration dans le pays d'accueil. Certes, ce raisonnement était construit au bénéfice des ressortissants de la Communauté européenne mais, comme le rappelait K. Groenendijk, les Italiens étaient perçus à l'époque comme issus d'une culture différente leur valant parfois le surnom de '*Spaghetti Fresser*' aux Pays Bas notamment.[2]

2. Quoiqu'il en soit, une trentaine d'années plus tard, ce lien étroit entre politique d'intégration et traitement non-discriminatoire va être réaffirmé au bénéfice, cette fois, des ressortissants de pays tiers dans les conclusions du Sommet européen de Tampere, en 1999. Il y est souligné qu' '[u]ne politique plus énergique en matière d'intégration devrait avoir pour ambition d'offrir [aux ressortissants de pays tiers qui résident légalement sur le territoire des États Membres] des droits et obligations comparables à ceux des citoyens de l'Union européenne. Cette politique devrait également favoriser la non-discrimination dans la vie économique, sociale et culturelle et mettre en place des mesures de lutte contre le racisme et la xénophobie'.[3] Au cours de la dernière décennie, la référence à l'importance d'un traitement non-discriminatoire des ressortissants de pays tiers n'a pas disparu des documents officiels européens traitant de l'intégration. Elle est toutefois passée à l'arrière plan et s'est vue supplantée par une insistance soutenue sur les devoirs et les responsabilités du migrant dans ce processus 'à double sens d'interaction réciproque' qu'est l'intégration

---

* Institut d'Etudes européennes-Université Libre de Bruxelles. Le manuscrit a été terminé de rédigé en mars 2011.

1 Règlement 1612/68 du Conseil, du 15 octobre 1968, relatif à la libre circulation des travailleurs à l'intérieur de la Communauté JO L 257 du 19.10.1968, p. 2-12.

2 K. Groenendijk, 'Integration of Immigrant in the EU: the Old or the New Way ?', contribution à cet ouvrage.

3 Conclusions du Conseil européen de Tampere, 15 et 16 octobre 1999, § 18.

dans sa conception nouvelle.[4] En effet, les auteurs s'accordent à décrire un renversement de paradigme à l'œuvre depuis le tournant du millénaire en matière de politiques d'intégration. Traditionnellement considérées comme un processus ou un objectif à atteindre à la réalisation desquels l'octroi de droits sur un pied d'égalité avec les nationaux ainsi que l'octroi d'un statut stable de résidence devaient contribuer, ces politiques connaissent, depuis une dizaine d'années, une mutation importante aboutissant à instaurer la capacité ou la volonté de s'intégrer voire l'intégration elle-même en condition préalable à l'octroi d'un statut stable et au bénéfice de l'égalité de traitement, voire même à l'accès au territoire.[5]

3. Or cette évolution est susceptible d'avoir un impact sur la question de l'applicabilité du principe de non-discrimination fondé sur la nationalité aux politiques d'intégration, selon qu'on les considère comme un volet de la politique migratoire ou de la politique sociale ou d'emploi des États Membres et/ou de l'Union. En effet, en droit international et européen des droits de l'homme, une application moins rigoureuse de l'interdiction des discriminations fondées sur la nationalité, dans le contexte migratoire, a longtemps prévalu, en raison du pouvoir souverain des États de contrôler l'entrée des ressortissants de pays tiers sur leur territoire;[6] qui contraste avec la reconnaissance du caractère suspect des différences de traitement fondées sur la nationalité frappant des étrangers déjà admis sur le territoire.[7] Des remises en cause de cette apparence de légitimité dont jouissait la

4 Voir Programme de Stockholm, décembre 2009, § 6.1.5. et conclusions du Conseil 'Justice et Affaires intérieures' du 19 novembre 2004, 'Principes de base communs d'intégration des immigrants', principes 1, 2 et 6. Il est remarquable à cet égard que le traitement équitable et sur un pied d'égalité des immigrants ne figure qu'en sixième place dans les principes énoncés, loin derrière les deux premiers reconnaissant respectivement que 'l'intégration est un processus dynamique a double sens d'acceptation mutuelle de la part de tous les immigrants et résidents des États Membres' et que 'l'intégration implique le respect des valeurs fondamentales de l'Union européenne'.

5 S. Carrera, *In search of the Perfect Citizen. The Intersection between Integration, Immigration and Nationality*, Leiden-Boston, Martinus Nijhoff Publishers 2009; S. Carrera, 'Towards an EU Framework on the Integration of Immigrants', in S. Carrera (ed.), *The Nexus between Immigration, Integration and Citizenship in the EU*, Challenge Collective Conference, April 2006, p. 2; Leonard F.M. Besselink, 'Unequal Citizenship: Integration Measures and Equality', in S. Carrera (ed.), *The Nexus between Immigration, Integration and Citizenship in the EU*, *op. cit.*, p. 18; Ph. De Bruycker, 'Chronique de jurisprudence consacrée à l'espace de liberté, de sécurité et de justice. Jurisprudence de la Cour de justice au sujet des politiques relatives aux contrôles aux frontières, à l'asile et à l'immigration', *Cahiers de droit européen*, 2010, p. 142; Y. Pascouau, 'Integration Measures in France: An Evolving Process between Integration and Migration Issues', in R. van Oers, E. Ersbøll & D. Kostakopoulou (eds), *A Redefinition of Belonging?*, Leiden-Boston Brill, 2010, p. 153-183, spéc. p. 156.

6 Cour EDH, *Gül c. Suisse*, 19 février 1996, *Recueil des arrêts et décisions*, 1996-I, § 38 et Cour EDH, *Ahmut c. Pays-Bas*, 28 novembre 1996, *Recueil*, 1996-VI, § 67; S. Saroléa, *Droits de l'homme et migrations. De la protection du migrant aux droits de la personne migrante*, Bruxelles: Bruylant, 2006, p. 569 ff.; K. Groenendijk, 'Citizens and third country nationals: differential treatment or discrimination?', in J.-Y. Carlier & E. Guild (eds), *The Future of Free Movement of Persons in the EU*, Bruxelles: Bruylant, 2006, p. 88 ff.; J.-F. Flauss, 'L'étranger entre souveraineté nationale et droits de l'homme', in J.Y. Carlier (ed.), *L'étranger face au droit. XXèmes journées d'études juridiques J. Dabin*, Bruxelles: Bruylant 2010, p. 45-74.

7 Voir références *infra*, § 9.

nationalité comme critère de différenciation en matière migratoire se font jour mais encore timidement à certains égards.[8]

4. Un premier temps de l'étude sera consacré à préciser les contours de l'interdiction de discrimination fondée sur la nationalité, mais aussi sur des critères connexes tels que la race ou l'origine ethnique, en droit de l'Union européenne (I). Dans un deuxième temps, certains éléments des politiques d'intégration de l'UE ou des États Membres seront mis à l'épreuve de ce principe de non-discrimination (II).

I. Les Contours de l'Interdiction de Discrimination fondée sur la Nationalité, la Race ou l'Origine Ethnique en Droit de l'UE

5. Il est admis de longue date dans l'Union européenne que, tant les institutions de l'UE que les États Membres lorsqu'ils agissent dans le champ d'application du droit de l'Union, doivent respecter les droits fondamentaux en tant que principes généraux du droit.[9] Le domaine de l'intégration des ressortissants de pays tiers, qu'il ressorte d'une compétence émergente de l'UE ou de celle des États Membres,[10] ressort globalement de cet encadrement par les droits de l'homme garantis dans l'UE. En témoignent notamment les arrêts rendus par la Cour de justice où elle examine la conformité, au regard des droits fondamentaux, de la directive 2003/86 relative au regroupement familial des ressortissants de pays tiers[11] ainsi que l'arrêt *Chakroun* à l'occasion duquel c'est la législation des Pays-Bas qui est menacée de censure en raison de sa non-conformité à la même directive, interprétée à la lumière des droits fondamentaux.[12] Dans ce dernier cas, pour que les droits fondamentaux reconnus dans l'ordre juridique de l'UE s'appliquent à l'action des États Membres, il sera préalablement nécessaire d'établir un lien de rattachement avec le champ d'application du droit de l'UE.[13]

---

8 O. De Schutter, *L'interdiction de discrimination dans le droit européen des droits de l'homme. Sa pertinence pour les directives communautaires relatives à l'égalité de traitement sur la base de la race et dans l'emploi*, Bruxelles: Commission européenne, direction générale de l'emploi et des affaires sociales et de l'égalité des chances 2005, p. 15.

9 Article 6 § 3 TUE. Les contours du champ d'application du droit de l'UE font néanmoins l'objet de discussions doctrinales. Voir, récemment 'Editorial Comments: The Scope of application of the general principles of Union law: An ever expanding Union?', *C.M.L.Rev.*, 2010, p. 1589-1596 et les références citées en note de bas de page 30.

10 Voir, J. Handoll, 'Integration Policy in the European Union: The Question of Competence', contribution à cet ouvrage.

11 CJCE, arrêt du 27 juin 2006, *Parlement européen c. Conseil*, C-540/03, §§ 22-23 et 104-105.

12 CJUE, arrêt du 4 mars 2010, *Chakroun*, C-578/08, §§ 43-44.

13 CJCE, arrêt du 13 juillet 1989, *Wachauf*, 5/88, *Rec.*, p. 2609 ff.; CJCE, arrêt du 18 juin 1991, *Elliniki Radiophonia Tilleorassi (ERT)*, C-260/89, *Rec.*, p. I-2925 ff.; Conclusions de l'avocate générale Sharpston présentées le 30 septembre 2010, C-34/09, §§ 151-177. Voir aussi, en doctrine, K. Lenaerts & J.A. Gutierrez-Fons, 'The Constitutional Allocation of Powers and General Principles of Law', *Common Market Law Review*, 47, 2010, p. 1629-1669. Attention, dans l'hypothèse où l'action des États Membres ne s'inscrit pas dans le champ d'application du droit de l'UE, cela ne signifie pas qu'elle ne doive pas respecter les droits fondamentaux mais seulement que les garanties et modes de contrôle propres au droit de l'UE ne trouveront pas à s'appliquer. Il faut, dans ce cas, se tourner vers les garanties constitutionnelles de ces droits ou vers la CEDH ou encore vers le droit international des →

6. L'interdiction des discriminations fondées sur la nationalité constitue l'un des principes cardinaux de la construction européenne, depuis ses origines. Même si son statut de droit fondamental a été reconnu par son intégration à l'article 21 § 2 de la charte des droits fondamentaux, elle est encore traditionnellement interprétée comme ne s'appliquant de manière certaine qu'aux différences de traitement entre citoyens européens. De ce point de vue, la question de l'existence et des contours d'un principe général de droit de l'UE interdisant les discriminations fondées sur la nationalité, y compris lorsqu'est en jeu la nationalité d'un État tiers apparaît primordiale (I.1). Plus récemment, depuis l'an 2000, l'Union européenne s'est dotée d'instruments interdisant les discriminations fondées sur la race et l'origine ethnique ou sur la religion notamment et la charte des droits fondamentaux a inscrit une interdiction générale de ce type de discrimination à son article 21 § 1er. Or, sachant que les frontières entre ces différents critères de discriminations sont bien souvent poreuses,[14] il s'impose d'examiner également les potentialités de ces instruments aux fins d'encadrer les politiques d'intégration potentiellement discriminatoires sur la base de ces autres critères, quand la nationalité est utilisée pour camoufler des discriminations fondées sur la race, l'origine ethnique ou plus rarement de la religion (I.2).

I.1 L'Existence d'un Principe Général de Droit de l'UE interdisant les Discriminations fondées sur la Nationalité

7. En droit primaire de l'Union européenne, une interdiction des discriminations fondées sur la nationalité est inscrite dans les traités depuis le traité de Rome de 1957. L'article 18 TFUE (ancien art. 12 CE) stipule que 'dans le domaine d'application du présent traité, et sans préjudice des dispositions particulières qu'il prévoit, est interdite toute discrimination exercée en raison de la nationalité [...]'. Cette disposition générale, ainsi que d'autres consacrant une telle interdiction dans des contextes plus spécifiques en lien avec la libre circulation des personnes, ont traditionnellement été interprétées comme ne s'appliquant qu'aux discriminations affectant les citoyens européens par rapport aux nationaux d'un autre État Membre. Bien qu'une telle interprétation restrictive ait fait l'objet de remises en cause doctrinales,[15] elle a encore été confirmée, en 2009, à l'occasion de l'arrêt *Vatsouras* où la Cour a réaffirmé que

droits de l'homme. (Voir les conclusions présentées par l'avocate générale Kokott, le 25 novembre 2010, dans l'affaire *Shirley McCarthy*, C-434/09, § 60).

14 Voir notamment les conclusions de l'avocat général Bot, dans l'affaire *Mesopotamia Broadcast*, C-244/10 et C-245/10, présentées le 5 mai 201, point 70. 'En ce qui concerne, ensuite, le sens des mots "race" et "nationalité", visés à l'article 22 bis de la directive, nous ne croyons pas non plus qu'ils puissent être compris de la manière restrictive envisagée par la juridiction de renvoi, selon laquelle ils ne viseraient pas des différences de natures ethnique ou culturelle telles que celles pouvant exister entre les Kurdes et les Turcs.' Voir aussi O. De Schutter, *Links between Migration and Discrimination*, European Network of Legal Experts in the non-Discrimination field, Brussels: European Commission 2009, p. 11-24; S. Benedi Lahuerta, 'Race Equality and Third Country Nationals, or How to fight Discrimination with a Discriminatory Law ?', *European Law Journal*, 2009, p. 738-756.

15 K. Groenendijk, 'Citizens and Third Country Nationals: Differential Treatment or Discrimination?', in J.-Y. Carlier & E. Guild (eds), *The Future of Free Movement of Persons in the EU*, Bruxelles: Bruylant 2006, p. 79 ff.; R. Cholewinsky, *Borders and Discrimination in the European Union*, ILPA/MPG 2002, p. 40-41; Chloé Hublet, 'The Scope of Article 12 of the European Communities vis-à-vis Third-Countries Nationals: Evolution at Last?', *European Law Journal*, 2009, p. 757-774.

'[L'art. 12 CE, devenu article 18 TFUE] concerne les situations relevant du champ d'application du droit communautaire dans lesquelles un ressortissant d'un État Membre subit un traitement discriminatoire par rapport aux nationaux d'un autre État Membre sur le seul fondement de sa nationalité et n'a pas vocation à s'appliquer dans le cas d'une éventuelle différence de traitement entre les ressortissants des États Membres et ceux des États tiers'.[16]

Plusieurs types de distinctions fondées sur la nationalité restent, en vertu de cette interprétation, hors du champ de cette interdiction de discrimination, à savoir les différences de traitement entre citoyens européens et ressortissants de pays tiers mais peut-être aussi celles entre différentes catégories de ressortissants de pays tiers. Il est vrai que la consécration de l'interdiction des discriminations fondées sur la nationalité, en tant que droit fondamental, par son inscription à l'article 21 § 2 de la charte des droits fondamentaux de l'Union européenne, devrait être de nature à entraîner une remise en cause de cette interprétation restrictive, notamment par le lien qu'il convient d'établir avec l'article 14 de la CEDH.[17] Toutefois, cette évolution risque peut-être de se heurter au fait que les rédacteurs de la Charte ont repris textuellement le contenu de l'article 18 TFUE (ancien article 12 CE) pour en faire une disposition séparée de la clause anti-discriminatoire générale contenue à l'article 21, § 1er de la Charte et qu'en vertu de l'article 52 § 2 de la charte, il est prévu que les droits de la charte 'qui font l'objet de dispositions dans les traités s'exercent selon les conditions et limites fixées par ceux-ci'.

Même si une évolution n'est pas exclue et que les arguments doctrinaux plaidant en faveur d'une interprétation moins restrictive de cette interdiction, ne manquent pas de pertinence,[18] la mise en évidence d'un principe général de droit UE interdisant les discriminations fondées sur la nationalité, trouvant sa source dans le droit international et européen des droits de l'homme, présente l'avantage d'éviter de devoir entrer dans la controverse. L'entrée en vigueur du Traité de Lisbonne et la valeur contraignante conférée à la charte ne mettent pas fin à la possibilité d'une référence aux principes généraux du droit comme en atteste l'article 6 § 3 du Traité sur l'Union européenne. Afin de déterminer si un droit fondamental doit être consacré en tant que principe général de droit, la Cour se tourne généralement vers la Convention européenne des droits de l'homme qui revêt une signification particulière ainsi que vers les instruments internationaux auxquels les États Membres ont coopéré ou adhéré.[19]

16 CJCE, arrêt du 4 juin 2009, *Vatsouras*, C-22/08 et C-23/08, § 52. Voir à ce sujet, D. Damjanovic, 'Joined Cases C-22/08 & C-23/08, *Vatsouras*, Judgment of the Court (Third Chamber) of 4 June 2009', *Common Market Law Review*, 47, 2010, p. 847-861.

17 Telle qu'interprétée par la Cour européenne des droits de l'homme, cette disposition interdit les discriminations fondées sur la nationalité, sans être nullement limitées aux différences affectant les citoyens de l'UE entre eux (voir Infra, § 9).

18 Voir K. Groenendijk, 'Citizens and Third Country Nationals: Differential Treatment or Discrimination?', *op. cit.*, p. 85 et les références citées. Voir aussi C. Hublet, 'The Scope of Article 12 of the European Communities vis-à-vis Third-Countries Nationals: Evolution at Last?', *op. cit.*, p. 763-770.

19 CJCE, arrêt du 14 mai 1974, *J. Nold*, 4/73, *Rec.*, pp. 491 et s. ; CJCE, arrêt du 15 mai 1986, *Marguerite Johnston*, 222/84, *Rec.*, p. 1651 ff.

8. Il ressort des jurisprudences concordantes de la Cour européenne des droits de l'homme et du Comité des droits de l'homme que l'interdiction des discriminations fondées sur la nationalité a connu un essor en droit international des droits de l'homme depuis les années quatre-vingt-dix.[20] Ainsi comme le souligne J.F. Flauss,

> '[b]ien qu'encore loin d'avoir atteint son rythme de croisière, la résorption des droits ou avantages préférentiels bénéficiant aux nationaux par rapport aux étrangers constitue incontestablement l'une des grandes évolutions structurelles en droit international'.[21]

9. Dans la Convention européenne des droits de l'homme (article 14 CEDH), seule l'origine nationale est mentionnée expressément dans la liste non limitative des critères de discrimination prohibés et non la nationalité en tant que telle. Cela n'a toutefois guère empêché la Cour européenne des droits de l'homme, à partir des années quatre-vingt-dix, d'ériger la nationalité en motif suspect requérant des considérations très fortes pour justifier des différences de traitement exclusivement fondées sur la nationalité.[22] Ont ainsi été condamnées par la Cour EDH des discriminations fondées sur la nationalité dans l'octroi d'allocations de substitution aux allocations de chômage[23] ou d'allocations 'famille nombreuse',[24] ou encore d'allocations pour adulte handicapé,[25] des discriminations dans le calcul d'une pension de retraite[26] ou dans les conditions d'affiliation à un régime de sécurité sociale pour exploitants agricoles.[27] En toute logique, la reconnaissance par la Cour du caractère suspect de la nationalité en tant que critère de différenciation devrait déboucher sur un contrôle plus exigeant et réduire la marge d'appréciation dont jouissent les États Membres pour déterminer 'si et dans quelle mesure des différences entre des situations à d'autres égards analogues justifient des distinctions de traitement'.[28] Comme le souligne Jean-Yves Carlier, il semble que, dans cette jurisprudence de la Cour EDH, 'un

---

20 Comme le souligne O. De Schutter, depuis les années 1990, il semble que la nationalité ait perdu 'l'apparence de légitimité qu'elle pouvait sembler revêtir jadis', 'Links between Migration and Discrimination', *op. cit.*, p. 15.

21 J.-F. Flauss, 'L'étranger entre souveraineté nationale et droits de l'homme', *op. cit.*, p. 63.

22 Voir notamment F. Tulkens, 'L'évolution du principe de non-discrimination à la lumière de la jurisprudence de la Cour européenne des droits de l'homme', in J.Y. Carlier (ed.), *L'étranger face au droit. XXèmes journées d'études juridiques J. Dabin*, *op. cit.*, p. 193-210.

23 Cour EDH, *Gaygusuz c. Autriche*, 16 septembre 1996, § 42 (violation art. 1er Protocole 1er combiné avec l'article 14 CEDH).

24 Cour EDH, *Saidoun c. Grèce* et *Fawsie c. Grèce*, 28 octobre 2010 (violation art. 8 CEDH combiné à l'art. 14 CEDH).

25 Cour EDH, *Koua Poirrez c. France*, 30 septembre 2003 (différence de traitement entre ressortissants français et de certains pays ayant signé une convention de réciprocité, d'une part, et autres étrangers de l'autre pour l'obtention d'une allocation pour adulte handicapé – violation article 1er Prot. 1er combiné à l'art. 14 CEDH).

26 Cour EDH, *Andrejeva c. Lettonie*, 18 février 2009 (refus de prise en compte des années de travail hors de Lettonie pour le calcul de la pension d'une travailleuse au motif qu'elle n'a pas la nationalité lettone mais qu'elle a le statut de non-citoyenne résidente permanente – violation art. 1 Prot. 1 combiné à l'art. 14 CEDH).

27 Cour EDH *Luczac c. Pologne*, 27 novembre 2007 (violation art. 1er Prot. 1er combiné avec l'art. 14 CEDH).

28 Cour EDH, *Gaygusuz c. Autriche*, *op. cit.*, § 42.

renversement de perspective s'opère. A la proportionnalité, succède la 'disproportionnalité': la discrimination est a priori disproportionnée sauf preuve contraire'. L'auteur en déduit deux conséquences méthodologiques: sur le fond, l'existence d'une présomption selon laquelle la nationalité est a priori un critère discriminatoire et, sur la forme, une charge renversée de la preuve en présence de différences de traitement fondées sur ce critère.[29] Il n'en reste pas moins que la Cour de Strasbourg continue, dans certains domaines comme la matière économique et sociale ou, en particulier, la définition des régimes de sécurité sociale, à reconnaître une ample marge nationale d'appréciation aux États, sans que l'articulation entre cette marge d'appréciation et l'exigence de considérations très fortes afin de justifier une différence de traitement fondée sur la nationalité n'apparaisse toujours clairement.[30]

Par ailleurs, dans le contexte de la CEDH, et dans la mesure où le Protocole n° 12 n'a été ratifié que par un nombre restreint d'États,[31] l'interdiction de discrimination ne vaut que 'dans la jouissance des droits et libertés consacrés dans la Convention'. Cela signifie que pour trouver à s'appliquer, l'article 14 de la CEDH doit être combiné avec une autre disposition de la CEDH ou de ses Protocoles et qu'il faut préalablement établir que la situation ou norme discriminatoire tombe sous l'empire d'une de ces dispositions.[32] La Cour est assez souple dans l'interprétation de cette dernière condition et a notamment interprété l'art. 1er du Protocole 1er d'une manière de plus en plus large afin d'y englober les prestations de sécurité sociale notamment, qu'elles soient ou non contributives.

10. Mais si l'on se tourne vers le Pacte international des droits civils et politiques (PIDCP), l'on trouve une clause indépendante d'interdiction des discriminations fondées sur une liste ouverte de motifs (article 26 PIDCP) et la nationalité a été considérée comme incluse dans la notion de 'toute autre situation'.[33] Le Comité des droits de l'homme a précisé la portée des droits du Pacte et de l'interdiction des discriminations dans son Observation générale n° 15 (1986) portant sur la situation des étrangers au regard du Pacte.[34]

---

29 J.Y. Carlier, 'Droits de l'homme et nationalité', *Annales de droit de Louvain*, vol. 36, 2003, p. 243-257, spéc. p. 255-256.

30 Cour EDH *Luczac c. Pologne*, *op. cit.*, § 59 ; Cour EDH, *Andrejeva c. Lettonie*, *op. cit.*, §§ 81-89.

31 Seuls 18 États l'ont ratifié au 1er février 2011, dont uniquement Chypre, l'Espagne, la Finlande, le Luxembourg, les Pays-Bas, la Roumanie et la Slovénie comme membres de l'UE.

32 Cour EDH, *Andrejeva c. Lettonie*, *op. cit.*, §§ 74-80.

33 A ce sujet, voir W. Vandenhole, *Non-Discrimination and Equality in the View of the UN Human Rights Treaty Bodies*, Antwerpen-Oxford: Intersentia 2005, p. 128-129; voir aussi O. De Schutter, 'L'interdiction de discrimination sur la base de la nationalité dans le Pacte international relatif aux droits civils et politiques', in *L'étranger face au droit*, *op. cit.*, p. 151-192. La nationalité n'est pas expressément inscrite dans les motifs de discrimination prohibés mais s'agissant d'une liste ouverte, le Comité des droits de l'homme y a inclus la nationalité, pour compléter l'origine nationale qui elle est expressément incluse. Comité des droits de l'homme, *Ibrahima Gueye et diverses autres personnes c. France*, Communication n°196/1985, CCPR/C/35/D/ 196/1985, constatations du 3 avril 1989, § 9.4.

34 'La règle générale est que chacun des droits énoncés dans le Pacte doit être garanti sans discrimination entre les citoyens et les étrangers. Les étrangers bénéficient de l'obligation générale de non-discrimination à l'égard des droits garantis par le Pacte, ainsi que prévu à l'article 2. Cette garantie s'applique de la même manière aux étrangers et aux citoyens. [...] Les étrangers ont droit à une égale protection de la loi. Il n'y a pas de discrimination entre étrangers et citoyens dans l'application de ces droits.' (Observation générale n° 15, Situation des étrangers au regard du Pacte (27ème session, →

Dans sa jurisprudence, il a jugé discriminatoires des différences de traitement fondées sur la nationalité notamment relativement à la restitution de biens confisqués,[35] dans le mode de calcul d'une pension pour les militaires de carrière[36] et dans la possibilité de siéger au sein d'un conseil d'entreprise.[37]

Dans cette dernière espèce, *Karakurt contre Autriche*, il est intéressant de relever que le Comité s'est prononcé sur le caractère discriminatoire d'une différence de traitement entre deux catégories d'étrangers, à savoir les ressortissants d'un État Membre de l'Espace économique européen, d'une part, et les ressortissants de pays tiers, de l'autre.[38] Or, selon le gouvernement autrichien, cette différence de traitement avait sa source dans les engagements internationaux pris par l'Autriche dans le cadre du traité de Rome et de l'Accord sur l'Espace économique européen (EEE) sur une base de réciprocité et avait pour but légitime 'd'éliminer les différences de traitement entre les travailleurs au sein des États Membres de la CE/EEE'.[39] Une telle justification n'a toutefois pas résisté au contrôle exercé, en l'espèce, par le Comité des droits de l'homme. Alors même qu'il avait déjà constaté dans une précédente affaire, *Van Oord c. Pays-Bas*,[40] 'qu'un accord international instituant un traitement préférentiel en faveur des ressortissants des États contractants pouvait constituer un critère raisonnable et objectif de différenciation', il souligne qu'on ne pourrait en déduire 'une règle générale selon laquelle un tel accord constituerait en soi un critère suffisant au regard de l'article 26 du Pacte' et qu'il faut, au contraire statuer en fonction des faits de

---

1986). Compilation des commentaires généraux et recommandations générales adoptées par les organes des traités, UN doc. HRI/GEN/1/Rev.1 (1994))

35 Comité DH, *Simunek c. République tchèque*, communication no 516/1992, constatations adoptées le 19 juillet 1995; Comité DH, *Adam c. République tchèque*, communication no 586/ 1994, constatations adoptées le 23 juillet 1996; Comité DH, *Blazek* c. *République tchèque*, communication no 857/1999, constatations adoptées le 12 juillet 2001; et Comité DH, *Des Fours Walderode c. République tchèque*, communication no 747/1997, constatations adoptées le 30 octobre 2001.

36 Comité DH, Ibrahima *Gueye et autres c. France*, *op. cit.*, § 9.5 - discrimination découlant d'une loi française prévoyant un mode de calcul d'une pension différent pour les militaires de carrière ayant servi dans l'armée française avant l'indépendance du Sénégal selon qu'ils ont la nationalité française ou sénégalaise). Dans cette affaire, le Comité a exercé un contrôle approfondi des justifications invoquées par le gouvernement français à l'appui de cette différence de traitement fondée sur la nationalité. Il a ainsi considéré qu'il y avait discrimination fondée sur la nationalité car la base retenue pour l'octroi de la pension était les services identiques qu'avaient rendus à la France les militaires. Or un changement ultérieur de nationalité ne constitue pas un motif suffisant pour justifier une différence de traitement. Les différences de situation économique, financière et sociale entre la France et le Sénégal ne peuvent pas non plus être invoquées comme justification légitime. Par ailleurs, de simples difficultés administratives ou la possibilité de certains abus en matière de droit à pension ne sauraient être invoquées pour justifier une différence de traitement (§ 9.5.).

37 Comité DH, *Karakurt c. Autriche* (communication n° 965/2000, constatation du 4 avril 2002 – caractère discriminatoire d'une loi autrichienne réservant aux Autrichiens et aux nationaux des États Membres de l'Espace économique européen la possibilité de siéger au sein d'un conseil d'entreprise).

38 L'on relèvera qu'en raison d'une réserve formulée par l'Autriche relativement à l'inapplicabilité de l'article 26 du Pacte aux différences de traitement entre ressortissants autrichiens et ressortissants étrangers, le Comité n'examine que la partie de la plainte concernant la distinction entre les étrangers ressortissants de pays de l'EEE et les autres étrangers (§ 7.5.).

39 Comité DH, *Karakurt c. Autriche*, *op. cit.*, point 5.5.

40 Comité DH, communication n° 658/1995, *Jacob &Jantina Hendrika van Oord c. Pays-Bas*, Constatation du 23 juillet 1997.

chaque espèce.[41] Et le Comité de conclure qu'eu égard à la fonction dont est investi un membre de comité d'entreprise – promouvoir les intérêts du personnel et veiller au respect des conditions de travail – 'instituer en matière d'éligibilité [...] une distinction visant certains étrangers fondée sur leur seule nationalité n'est pas raisonnable'.[42]

11. Cette jurisprudence mérite d'être rapprochée d'une jurisprudence plus ancienne de la Cour européenne des droits de l'homme (*Moustaquim c. Belgique* et *Chorfi c. Belgique*) à l'occasion de laquelle elle a considéré, au contraire, que la création d'un ordre juridique spécifique, doté de surcroît d'une citoyenneté propre, était en tant que telle, sans vérifier la proportionnalité de la mesure, de nature à justifier objectivement et raisonnablement des différences de traitement entre citoyens UE, d'une part, et ressortissants de pays tiers, de l'autre, relativement aux conditions d'expulsion du territoire.[43] Cette jurisprudence de la Cour européenne des droits de l'homme a fait l'objet de nombreuses critiques doctrinales[44] car, par sa motivation tautologique, elle semblait justifier *a priori* toute différence de traitement entre citoyens européens et ressortissants de pays tiers, sur la seule base de l'existence d'un ordre juridique spécifique et d'une citoyenneté propre à l'UE. Elle est apparue, par ailleurs, difficilement conciliable avec la jurisprudence ultérieure de la même Cour insistant sur le caractère suspect de la nationalité en tant que critère de différentiation ainsi qu'avec celle du Comité des droits de l'homme dans l'affaire *Karakurt c. Autriche* mentionnée ci-dessus.[45]

12. Il importe néanmoins de souligner que les affaires *Moustaquim* et *Chorfi* s'inscrivent toutes deux dans le contexte migratoire puisqu'il y est question de différences de traitement en matière de conditions d'expulsion. Or, la méfiance à l'égard des différences de traitement fondées sur la nationalité s'est avérée traditionnellement moins prononcée lorsque les étrangers concernés se trouvaient en situation de migration, le contexte migratoire jouant souvent comme un filtre aboutissant à un contrôle moins rigoureux des différences de traitement fondées sur la nationalité voire à leur justification automatique.[46] Cela s'inscrit dans la lignée de la réaffirmation constante par la Cour EDH de la souveraineté des États en matière de contrôle de l'entrée des non-nationaux sur leur territoire. Cette souveraineté n'est toutefois pas absolue et doit s'entendre en tenant compte des engagements internationaux des États en matière de droits fondamentaux.[47]

---

41 Comité DH, *Karakurt c. Autriche, op. cit.*, § 8.4.

42 *Ibidem*.

43 Cour EDH, arrêt du 18 février 1991, *Moustaquim c. Belgique,* Série A, n° 193, § 49 ; Cour EDH, arrêt du 7 août 1996, *Chorfi c. Belgique* , *R.D.E.*, 1996, n° 92, p. 36 et s, § 38.

44 Voir notamment à ce sujet: S. Van Drooghenbroeck, 'L'égalité entre étrangers dans la jurisprudence de la Cour européenne des droits de l'homme. Réponses péremptoires. Questions périmées?', *R.D.E.*, 1997, p. 3 ff.; E. Bribosia, 'Les discriminations fondées sur la nationalité dans l'Union européenne à la lumière de la protection des droits fondamentaux', in E. Bribosia, E. Dardenne, P. Magnette & A. Weyembergh (eds), *Union européenne et nationalité. Le principe de non-discrimination et ses limites*, Bruxelles, Bruylant, 1999, p. 215-224; S. Saroléa, *Droits de l'homme et migrations. De la protection du migrant aux droits de la personne migrante*, Bruxelles, Bruylant, 2006, p. 569 ff.

45 Voir *supra*, § 10.

46 S. Saroléa, *Droits de l'homme et migrations. De la protection du migrant aux droits de la personne migrante*, *op. cit.*, 2006, p. 569 ff.

47 'D'après un principe de droit international bien établi, les États ont le droit, sans préjudice des engagements découlant pour eux des traités, de contrôler l'entrée des non-nationaux sur leur sol' (Cour EDH, *Gül c. Suisse, op. cit.*, § 38 et Cour EDH, *Ahmut c. Pays-Bas, op. cit.*, § 67).

C'est ce qui ressort également de l'Observation générale n° 15 formulée par le Comité des droits de l'homme des Nations Unies en vertu de laquelle '[l]e Pacte ne reconnaît pas aux étrangers le droit d'entrer sur le territoire d'un État partie ou d'y séjourner. En principe, il appartient à l'État de décider qui il admet sur son territoire. Toutefois, dans certaines situations, un étranger peut bénéficier de la protection du Pacte même en ce qui concerne l'entrée ou le séjour: tel est le cas si des considérations relatives à la non-discrimination, à l'interdiction des traitements inhumains et au respect de la vie familiale entrent en jeu' (point 5).

13. La posture adoptée par le Comité des droits de l'homme dans l'affaire *Karakurt* nous paraît devoir être privilégiée par rapport à celle de la Cour EDH dans les affaires *Moustaquim* et *Chorfi*. Ainsi, l'existence d'un ordre juridique spécifique ayant instauré une citoyenneté propre ne justifie pas, par elle-même, toute différence de traitement entre citoyens de l'UE et ressortissants de pays tiers. Comme le souligne O. De Schutter, encore faut-il, pour que le principe de proportionnalité soit respecté,[48] que les avantages qui sont accordés aux citoyens de l'UE (et non aux ressortissants de pays tiers) présentent un lien suffisamment étroit avec la notion de citoyenneté, entendue au sens strict, comme recouvrant principalement des droits politiques tels que le droit de vote et d'éligibilité à certaines élections[49] et éventuellement le droit de ne pas être éloigné du territoire.[50]

14. Au vu de sa reconnaissance dans les deux instruments internationaux de protection des droits fondamentaux examinés, tels qu'interprétés par leurs organes de contrôle,[51] l'interdiction des discriminations fondées sur la nationalité – englobant tant les différences de traitement entre nationaux et étrangers que celles entre différentes catégories d'étrangers – doit être considérée comme un principe général du droit de l'UE qui doit s'appliquer tant à l'action des institutions de l'UE qu'à celle des États Membres dans le champ d'application du droit de l'UE (article 6 § 3 TUE). Même si le critère de nationalité

48 O. De Schutter, 'La souveraineté de l'État et les droits de la personne immigrée', *R.D.E.*, 1995, p. 261-270; O. De Schutter, 'La proportionnalité de l'éloignement d'étrangers pour motifs d'ordre public', *R.D.E.*, 1997, p. 177-189; J-Y. Carlier, 'Vers l'interdiction d'expulsion des étrangers intégrés?', *R.T.D.H.*, 1993, p. 449-466.

49 A titre exceptionnel, les instruments de protection des droits de la personne limitent le bénéfice de certains droits aux seuls citoyens (voir notamment l'article 25 PIDCP: 'Tout citoyen a le droit et la possibilité, sans aucune des discriminations visées à l'article 2 et sans restrictions déraisonnables:
- de prendre part à la direction des affaires publiques, soit directement, soit par l'intermédiaire des représentants librement choisis;
- de voter et d'être élu, au cours d'élections périodiques, honnêtes, au suffrage universel et égal et au scrutin secret, assurant l'expression libre de la volonté des électeurs;
- d'accéder dans des conditions générales d'égalité, aux fonctions publiques de son pays.').
Voir aussi les limitations autorisées à certains droits fondamentaux dans le chef des étrangers par l'article 16 de la CEDH. Voir pour une interprétation évolutive de cette disposition au bénéfice des citoyens européens: Cour EDH, *Piermont c. France*, 27 avril 1995, § 94.

50 O. De Schutter, *Links between Migration and Discrimination*, *op. cit.*, p. 45-47.

51 Il importe également de souligner que l'interdiction de discriminations fondées sur la nationalité fait également l'objet d'un nombre important de consécrations dans les droits constitutionnels des États Membres de l'UE et mérite de ce fait d'être intégré dans les principes généraux du droit de l'UE, en tant que résultant des 'traditions constitutionnelles communes aux États Membres' (O. De Schutter, *Links between Migration and Discrimination*, *op. cit.*, p. 55-60).

attire de plus en plus la suspicion en droit international des droits de l'homme,[52] cela n'implique pas automatiquement que toute différence de traitement entre national et étrangers ou entre citoyens UE et ressortissants de pays tiers soit discriminatoire ; mais bien que ces différences de traitement doivent être soumises au test de proportionnalité et ne seront admises que si elles poursuivent un objectif légitime et sont nécessaires, justifiées et proportionnées au regard de celui-ci. Des inconnues subsistent encore quant au niveau de contrôle à appliquer. A cet égard, il ne ressort pas clairement des jurisprudences examinées si un contrôle plus rigoureux impliquant un renversement de la charge de la preuve s'impose dans tous les cas où une différence de traitement fondée exclusivement sur la nationalité est constatée ou si, dans le domaine migratoire et dans celui de la citoyenneté au sens strict, un contrôle moins rigoureux trouve encore à s'appliquer.[53]

I.2 L'Interdiction des Discriminations fondée sur la Race ou l'Origine Ethnique

15. Au vu notamment de la plus grande marge d'appréciation autorisée aux États dans le domaine migratoire, il pourrait s'avérer que l'établissement de mesures voire de conditions d'intégration soient considérées comme justifiées au regard de l'interdiction de discrimination fondée sur la nationalité si elles poursuivent un objectif légitime et sont considérées proportionnées à celui-ci. Dans un tel cas, il peut être utile d'approfondir l'analyse en vérifiant si ces mesures ou conditions différenciées en fonction de la nationalité ne sont pas indirectement discriminatoires en vertu d'un autre motif, et notamment sur base de la race ou de l'origine ethnique.[54]

16. L'interdiction des discriminations fondées sur la race ou l'origine ethnique a fait l'objet d'une consécration plus tardive en droit communautaire que celle fondée sur la nationalité qui est consubstantielle à la mise sur pied d'un marché commun.[55] C'est principalement à partir des années 1990 que cette thématique va faire son entrée, par divers biais, dans le droit de l'UE.[56] Ainsi, à partir du sommet de Dublin de 1990, la condamna-

52 J.F. Flauss, 'L'étranger entre souveraineté nationale et droits de l'homme', *op. cit.*, p. 63; J.Y. Carlier & S. Saroléa (eds), *Droit des étrangers et nationalité*, Bruxelles: De Boeck et Larcier 2005.

53 Voir notamment pour une proposition en ce sens: Sara Benedi Lahuerta, 'Race Equality and Third Country Nationals, or How to fight Discrimination with a Discriminatory Law', *European Law Journal*, 2009, p. 738-756, spéc. p. 748.

54 Un raisonnement similaire pourrait également aboutir à s'interroger sur le caractère indirectement discriminatoire de ces mesures ou conditions en fonction d'autres critères tels que le sexe, la religion ou l'âge notamment. Les développements qui suivent se concentreront néanmoins sur la question de la discrimination indirectement fondée sur la race ou l'origine ethnique qui présente les liens les plus étroits avec les différences de traitement fondées sur la nationalité (O. De Schutter, *Links between Migration and Discrimination*, *op. cit.*, p. 20-23).

55 E. Bribosia, 'La lutte contre la discrimination dans l'Union européenne: une mosaïque de sources dessinant une approche différenciée', in S. Van Drooghenbroeck, S. Sottiaux & Ch. Bayart, *Les lois fédérales du 10 mai 2007 luttant contre la discrimination*, éd. La Charte 2008, p. 31-62; M. Bell, *Anti-discrimination Law and the European Union*, Oxford: Oxford University Press 2002; S. Prechal, 'Equality of Treatment, Non-Discrimination and Social Policy: Achievements in Three Themes', in A. McDonnell (ed.), *A Review of Forty Years of Community Law. Legal Developments in the European Communities and the European Union*, The Hague: Kluwer Law International 2005, p. 255-273.

56 J. Ringelheim, 'L'Europe en quête d'égalité : Genèse de la première directive prohibant la discrimination raciale et ethnique', in *Actes du Colloque Diversité et Discrimination raciale (Paris, 22-23 juin 2007)*, collection Thèmes et Commentaires, Paris: Dalloz 2007, p. 99-119.

tion du racisme et de la xénophobie apparaît de manière récurrente au fil des déclarations adoptées lors des réunions du Conseil européen.[57] Fruit notamment d'une intense campagne de mobilisation de la société civile et d'un contexte politique où le spectre de l'extrême droite refaisait surface, une base juridique permettant de combattre les discriminations fondées notamment sur la race et l'origine ethnique fut introduite dans le traité d'Amsterdam (article 13 CE devenu article 19 TFUE). C'est sur ce fondement qu'en 2000, l'Union s'est dotée d'un instrument spécifiquement destiné à lutter contre les discriminations fondées sur la race et l'origine ethnique, la directive 2000/43/CE relative à la mise en œuvre du principe de l'égalité de traitement entre les personnes sans distinction de race ou d'origine ethnique.[58]

17. Cette directive qui s'applique dans un domaine d'application étendu - emploi au sens large, protection sociale, y compris sécurité sociale et soins de santé, avantages sociaux, éducation, accès aux biens et services, fourniture de biens et de services à disposition du public, y compris logement – est-elle susceptible d'être mobilisée afin d'invalider une politique d'intégration qui s'appliquerait de manière différenciée en fonction de la nationalité, ménageant par exemple des exemptions au bénéfice des ressortissants de certains pays tiers? Le considérant 13 de la directive précise que l'interdiction de discrimination qu'elle contient s'applique également aux ressortissants de pays tiers. Il faut toutefois prendre en compte l'exception introduite à l'article 3 § 2 de la directive qui stipule qu'elle 'ne vise pas les différences de traitement fondées sur la nationalité et s'entend sans préjudice des dispositions et conditions relatives à l'admission et au séjour des ressortissants de pays tiers et des personnes apatrides sur le territoire des États Membres et de tout traitement lié au statut juridique des ressortissants de pays tiers et personnes apatrides concernés'. La formulation de cette exception n'est pas sans ambiguïté et son interprétation est controversée.[59] C'est en particulier la limitation relative à '*tout traitement lié au statut juridique des ressortissants de pays tiers*' qui est difficile à interpréter. Comme le souligne S. Benedi Lahuerta, elle pourrait englober l'accès à l'emploi si l'on se réfère au considérant 13 du préambule de la directive. Toutefois cela s'accorderait difficilement avec l'objectif poursuivi par la directive 2000/43/CE. Une interprétation étroite de cette exception devrait s'imposer comme renvoyant à l'immigration et au contrôle aux frontières mais pas au statut une fois sur le territoire de l'État Membre. Par ailleurs, cette exception ne devrait en tous cas pas aboutir à exclure du champ de la directive des discriminations fondées sur la

57 Voy. Déclaration sur l'antisémitisme, le racisme et la xénophobie (*Conseil européen de Dublin des 25 et 26 juin 1990)*; Déclaration sur le racisme et la xénophobie (*Conseil européen de Maastricht des 9 et 10 décembre 1991)*; Conclusions du Conseil européen de Copenhague des 21 et 22 juin 1993; Conclusions du Conseil européen de Corfou des 24 et 25 juin 1994; Conclusions du Conseil européen d'Essen des 9 et 10 décembre 1994; Conclusions du Conseil européen de Cannes des 25 et 26 juin 1995; Conclusions du Conseil européen de Madrid des 15 et 16 décembre 1995; Conclusions du Conseil européen de Florence des 21 et 22 juin 1996; Conclusions du Conseil européen de Dublin des 13 et 14 décembre 1996.

58 *J.O.* n° L 180 du 19 juillet 2000, p. 22. Depuis l'entrée en vigueur du traité de Lisbonne, il s'agit également d'un objectif assigné à la mise sur pied de l'espace de liberté de sécurité et de justice (art. 67 § 3 TFUE L'Union œuvre pour assurer un niveau élevé de sécurité par des mesures de prévention de la criminalité, du racisme et de la xénophobie, ainsi que de lutte contre ceux-ci).

59 Sara Benedi Lahuerta, 'Race Equality and Third Country Natinals, or How to fight Discrimination with a Discriminatory Law', *European Law Journal*, 2009, p. 738-756. Voir aussi O. De Schutter, *Links between Migration and Discrimination*, *op. cit.*, p. 26.

race ou l'origine ethnique, au seul motif qu'elles sont formellement présentées comme des différences de traitement fondées sur la nationalité (discriminations déguisées).[60]

18. Enfin, l'exception doit, en toute hypothèse, être interprétée conformément aux droits fondamentaux[61] et, en particulier, en tenant compte de la Convention sur l'élimination des discriminations raciales telle qu'interprétée par son Comité.[62] Il est certes vrai que le texte de cette Convention lui-même prévoit qu'elle 'ne s'applique pas aux distinctions, exclusions, restrictions ou préférences établies par un État partie à la Convention selon qu'il s'agit de ses ressortissants ou de non-ressortissants.' (Article 1er § 2) et précise, en outre qu' '[a]ucune disposition de la présente Convention ne peut être interprétée comme affectant de quelque manière que ce soit les dispositions législatives des États parties à la Convention concernant la nationalité, la citoyenneté ou la naturalisation, à condition que ces dispositions ne soient pas discriminatoires à l'égard d'une nationalité particulière' (Article 1er § 3). Toutefois, premièrement, cela n'exclut pas du champ de la Convention des différences de traitement entre différentes catégories d'étrangers qui constitueraient indirectement des discriminations raciales.[63] Deuxièmement, le domaine des politiques migratoires ou des politiques d'intégration n'est pas en tant que tel exclu du champ d'application de la Convention, en vertu de l'article 1er paragraphe 3. Enfin, dans son observation générale n° 30, le Comité sur l'élimination des discriminations raciales a circonscrit étroitement ces exceptions en précisant que 'les différences de traitement fondées sur la citoyenneté ou le statut migratoire constituent une discrimination si les critères pour une telle discrimination, interprétés à la lumière des objectifs et buts de la Convention, ne sont pas appliqués afin de poursuivre un objectif légitime et ne sont pas proportionnés à la réalisation de cet objectif'.[64] Le Comité recommande également aux États 'de s'assurer que les garanties législatives contre la discrimination raciale s'appliquent aux non-citoyens indépendamment de leur statut migratoire (§ 7) et que 'les politiques migratoires n'aient pas pour effet de discriminer sur base de la race, la couleur, l'ascendance ou l'origine nationale ou ethnique' (§ 9).[65]

60 Equality law 'must not accept as a field of exceptionalism beyond its reach discrimination which has as an essential element differential treatment on grounds of race or religion merely because it has been formally categorised as nationality discrimination' (E. Guild, *The Legal Elements of European Identity. EU Citizenship and Migration Law*, Kluwer 2004, p. 250).

61 Au cas où l'exception était jugée contraire aux principes généraux du droit, elle pourrait être invalidée ou devrait, à tout le moins, faire l'objet d'une interprétation conforme à ces principes. Voir pour un raisonnement similaire, les conclusions de l'avocate générale Kokott présentées le 30 septembre 2010, dans l'affaire *Test-Achats*, C-236/09.

62 K. Groenendijk, 'Citizens and third country nationals: differential treatment or discrimination?', *op.cit.*, p. 88; Sara Benedi Lahuerta, 'Race Equality and Third Country Nationals, or How to fight Discrimination with a Discriminatory Law', *op. cit.*, p. 752-754.

63 Voir opinion de Baroness Hale dans le jugement de la *House of Lords* du 9 décembre 2004 *R. v. Immigration Office at Prague Airport and another (Respondents) ex parte European Roma Rights Centre and others (Appellants)* [2004] UKHL 55, para. 101: 'Article 1(2) CERD ... certainly does not mean that State Parties can discriminate between non-citizens on racial grounds'.

64 Observations générales du Comité sur l'élimination des discriminations raciales n° 30 'Discrimination against non-citizens' (1er octobre 2004). Notre traduction. 'Under the Convention, differential treatment based on citizenship or immigration status will constitute discrimination if the criteria for such differentiation, judged in the light of the objectives and purposes of the Convention, are not applied pursuant to a legitimate aim, and are not proportional to the achievement of this aim' (para. 4).

65 Notre traduction.

La pratique du Comité vient corroborer une interprétation stricte des exceptions et large des discriminations prohibées. Ainsi, à l'occasion d'une affaire contre le Danemark concernant le refus d'octroi d'un prêt par une banque danoise sur la seule base de l'absence de nationalité danoise, le Comité va se déclarer compétent pour vérifier si une telle différence de traitement – pourtant entre citoyens et non-citoyens – n'est pas constitutive d'une discrimination au regard de la Convention. Le Comité rejette la justification avancée par le gouvernement danois résidant dans la nécessité d'avoir des garanties de remboursement suffisantes, au motif que

> 'nationality is not the most appropriate requisite when investigating a person's will or capacity to reimburse a loan. The applicant's permanent residence or the place where his employment, property or family ties are to be found may be more relevant in this context. [...] Accordingly, the Committee finds that, on the basis of article 2, paragraph (d), of the Convention, it is appropriate to initiate a proper investigation into the real reasons behind the bank's loan policy vis-à-vis foreign residents, in order to ascertain whether or not criteria involving racial discrimination, within the meaning of article 1 of the Convention, are being applied.'[66]

19. A tout le moins lorsque la nationalité est utilisée comme un 'proxy' (déguisement ou substitut) de la race ou de l'origine ethnique et nonobstant l'article 3 § 2 de la directive, des différences de traitement fondées sur la nationalité doivent pouvoir être confrontées à l'interdiction des discriminations indirectement fondées sur la race ou l'origine ethnique qui découle de la directive 2000/43 dans le champ d'application matériel qu'elle couvre (emploi au sens large, biens et services, éducations, logement, etc.). En dehors de ce champ d'application matériel, il reste possible d'invoquer le principe général de droit d'interdiction des discriminations fondées sur la race ou l'origine ethnique tel qu'il découle des instruments européens et internationaux de protection des droits de la personne.[67]

II. Les Politiques d'Intégration à l'Épreuve de l'Interdiction de Discrimination

20. L'absence de compétence spécifique de l'UE dans le domaine de l'intégration des ressortissants de pays tiers, avant le Traité de Lisbonne, constituait un trompe-l'œil car plusieurs des instruments adoptés dans le cadre de la politique migratoire ou d'asile de l'UE[68] présentent des liens étroits avec l'intégration des ressortissants de pays tiers, voire

66 Committee on the Elimination of Racial Discrimination, *Ziad Ben Ahmed Habassi v. Denmark*, Communication No. 10/1997, U.N. Doc. CERD/C/54/D/10/1997 paras 9.3 – 9.4 (1997), § 9.3.

67 Pour une démonstration de l'existence d'un principe général d'interdiction des discriminations fondées notamment sur la race et l'origine ethnique dans l'ordre juridique de l'UE, au départ notamment des arrêts *Mangold* et *Kücükdeveci*, voir E. Bribosia & T. Bombois, 'Interdiction de la discrimination en raison de l'âge: Du principe, de ses exceptions et de quelques hésitations. Réflexions autour des arrêts Wolf, Petersen et Kücükdeveci de la Cour de justice de l'Union européenne', *RTDE*, 2011/1, p. 41-84.

68 Voir notamment la Directive 2003/86/CE du Conseil du 22 septembre 2003 relative au droit au regroupement familial (*JO*, L 251 du 3.10.2003, p. 12–18) et la directive 2003/109/ CE du Conseil →

autorisent expressément les États Membres à prévoir des mesures/conditions ou programmes d'intégration dans leur législation de transposition faisant, par là-même, entrer ces mesures ou conditions dans le champ d'application du droit de l'UE.[69] Depuis l'entrée en vigueur du Traité de Lisbonne, l'Union européenne dispose d'une compétence spécifique lui permettant d''établir des mesures pour encourager et appuyer l'action des États Membres en vue de favoriser l'intégration des ressortissants de pays tiers en séjour régulier sur leur territoire, à l'exclusion de toute harmonisation des dispositions législatives et réglementaires des États Membres' (article 79 § 4 TFUE). Les politiques d'intégration, en ce compris l'adoption de mesures et/ou conditions d'intégration, restent essentiellement de la compétence des États Membres,[70] mais entrent pour la plupart dans le champ d'application du droit de l'UE.

Le principe général de droit de l'UE interdisant les discriminations fondées sur la nationalité peut être mobilisé à deux niveaux de la politique d'intégration des ressortissants de pays tiers: pour encadrer d'abord l'action des institutions de l'Union et ensuite celle des États Membres lorsqu'elle se situe dans le champ d'application du droit de l'Union. Afin d'illustrer les potentialités d'un tel encadrement, nous analyserons, au regard de l'interdiction des discriminations fondées sur la nationalité, d'abord la directive 2003/109 du 25 novembre 2003 relative au statut des ressortissants de pays tiers résidents de longue durée[71] (II.1.) pour ensuite nous pencher sur les mesures ou conditions d'intégration adoptées par certains États Membres dans le cadre de leur politique de regroupement familial (II.2.)

II.1 La Directive 2003/109 du 25 novembre 2003 relative au Statut des Ressortissants de Pays Tiers Résidents de Longue Durée

21. Il est de jurisprudence constante que la validité d'une directive peut être évaluée à l'aune des droits fondamentaux garantis en tant que principes généraux du droit. Cela a été réaffirmé de manière très nette à l'occasion de l'arrêt *Parlement c. Conseil*, en 2006 où la conformité de la directive 2003/86 relative au regroupement familial des ressortissants de pays tiers était mise en cause au regard de plusieurs droits fondamentaux[72]. Dans cette

---

du 25 novembre 2003 relative au statut des ressortissants de pays tiers résidents de longue durée (*JO*, L 16 du 23.1.2004, p. 44–53).

69 Pour une typologie des clauses en matière d'intégration qui figurent dans des directives en matière d'immigration ou d'asile, voir la contribution de K. Groenendijk 'Integration of Immigrant in the EU: the Old or the New Way ?', contribution à cet ouvrage.

70 Voir J. Handoll 'Integration Policy in the European Union: The Question of Competence', contribution à cet ouvrage.

71 Pour une analyse de la directive 2003/86/CE relative au regroupement familial au regard du principe de non-discrimination, voir E. Bribosia, 'La directive 2003/86 relative au regroupement familial au regard du principe de non-discrimination', *Revue du droit des étrangers*, 2003, p. 517-524. Nous y dénoncions comme constitutives de discriminations fondées sur la nationalité, plusieurs différences de traitement fondées sur la nationalité entre citoyens européens ayant exercé leur liberté de circulation, d'une part, et ressortissants de pays tiers, de l'autre.

72 CJCE, arrêt du 27 juin 2006, *Parlement c. Conseil*, *op. cit.* A ce sujet, voir l'étude de D. Martin, 'La Cour de justice et le droit au regroupement familial: trop ou trop peu! Cour de justice des Communautés européennes (GC) Parlement c. Conseil (C-540/03), 27 juin 2006', *R.T.D.H.*, 2008, pp. 595-609. Voir aussi B. Renauld, T. Bombois & P. Martens, 'Existe-t-il un droit fondamental au regrou- →

affaire, alors que le Conseil contestait la recevabilité du recours au motif que la directive laisserait une certaine marge d'appréciation aux États Membres leur permettant de respecter les droits fondamentaux, la Cour s'est déclarée compétente jugeant que l'existence d'une telle marge d'appréciation 'ne saurait avoir pour effet de soustraire ces dispositions au contrôle de légalité de la Cour' (§ 22). Elle a ajouté qu' 'une disposition d'un acte communautaire pourrait, en tant que telle, ne pas respecter les droits fondamentaux si elle imposait aux États Membres ou autorisait explicitement ou implicitement ceux-ci à adopter ou à maintenir des lois nationales ne respectant pas lesdits droits' (§ 23).[73]

22. A ce jour, aucune mise en cause devant la Cour de justice de la conformité à l'interdiction des discriminations fondées sur la nationalité de la directive 2003/ 109 sur les ressortissants de pays tiers résidents de longue durée n'a par contre été effectuée que ce soit par un recours en annulation ou indirectement par un renvoi préjudiciel en appréciation de validité. A la suite d'une partie de la doctrine,[74] nous examinerons cette question.[75]

23. Cette directive dont l'initiative remonte à mars 2001 s'inscrit dans le prolongement direct de l'engagement pris au Conseil européen de Tampere de rapprocher le statut des ressortissants de pays tiers résidents depuis un certain temps sur le territoire d'un État Membre de celui des citoyens européens et de conférer aux premiers 'un ensemble de droits uniformes aussi proches que possible de ceux dont jouissent les citoyens de l'UE'.[76] Le lien entre l'égalité de traitement et l'intégration y est, par ailleurs, expressément reconnu au considérant (12) du préambule qui stipule qu' 'afin de constituer un véritable instrument d'intégration dans la société dans laquelle le résident de longue durée s'est établi, [il] devrait jouir de l'égalité de traitement avec les citoyens de l'État Membre dans un large éventail de domaines économiques et sociaux, selon les conditions pertinentes définies par la présente directive'.

24. Une première interrogation au regard de l'interdiction de discrimination fondée sur la nationalité réside dans la fixation de conditions et limites à l'égalité de traitement. En effet, la directive garantit au résident de longue durée l'égalité de traitement avec les nationaux en ce qui concerne un large éventail de domaines (article 11: accès à l'emploi et conditions d'emploi et de travail, éducation et formation professionnelle, reconnaissance des diplômes, sécurité sociale, aide sociale et protection sociale, avantages fiscaux, accès et

---

pement familial à Strasbourg, à Luxembourg et à Bruxelles?', in *Liège, Strasbourg, Bruxelles: parcours des droits de l'homme. Liber amicorum Michel Melchior*, Anthémis, pp. 793-827.

73 C'est précisément ce qui a amené la Cour de justice à invalider l'article 5 § 2 de la directive 2004/113 en affirmant qu' '[u]ne telle disposition, qui permet aux États Membres concernés de maintenir sans limitation dans le temps une dérogation à la règle des primes et des prestations unisexes, est contraire à la réalisation de l'objectif d'égalité de traitement entre les femmes et les hommes que poursuit la directive 2004/113 et incompatible avec les articles 21 et 23 de la charte' (CJUE, arrêt du 1er mars 2011, Test-Achats, aff. C-236/09, § 32).

74 K. Groenendijk, 'Citizens and third country nationals: differential treatment or discrimination?', *op. cit.*, p. 88 ff.; M. Bell, 'Civic citizenship and migrant integration', *European Public Law*, 2007, p. 311-333; L. Hallskov, 'The Long-Term Residents Directive: A Fullfilment of the Tampere Objective of Near-Equality?', *European Journal of Migration and Law,* 2005, p. 181-201.

75 Il est à noter que nous ne tenons pas compte dans le cadre de cette analyse d'éventuels statuts privilégiés dont jouissent certains ressortissants de pays tiers tels que les ressortissants turcs qui bénéficient d'un droit élargi à l'égalité de traitement en vertu de l'accord d'association tel qu'interprété par la Cour de justice (ajouter une référence cf. K. Groenendijk, 'Citizens and third country nationals: differential treatment or discrimination?', *op. cit.*, p. 88-94).

76 Conclusions du Conseil européen de Tampere, 15 et 16 octobre 1999.

fourniture de biens et services en ce compris le logement, liberté d'association, d'affiliation et d'engagement dans une organisation de travailleurs ou d'employeurs ou toute organisation professionnelle, le libre accès à l'ensemble du territoire), s'inscrivant dans la même lignée que ce qui avait été réalisé précédemment au bénéfice des ressortissants de l'UE.[77] Toutefois, la logique n'est pas poussée jusqu'au bout puisque des restrictions sont autorisées (art. 11, §§ 1 a), 3 et 4), dont la conformité aux droits fondamentaux mérite d'être testée. Ainsi, tout d'abord, la directive préserve la possibilité pour les États Membres d'exclure les ressortissants de pays tiers de l'accès aux activités qui seraient liées, même à titre occasionnel, à l'exercice de l'autorité publique (article 11 § 1er a)).[78] Une telle exclusion des emplois dans l'administration publique du champ d'application de l'égalité de traitement n'est pas inconnue du droit communautaire (article 45 § 4 TFUE), en incluant les activités qui impliquent une participation même occasionnelle à l'autorité publique, elle va toutefois au-delà de ce que la Cour de justice a toléré pour les citoyens européens.[79] Cette exclusion plus large des ressortissants de pays tiers de l'accès aux emplois publics résiste difficilement à un examen de proportionnalité. La préservation d'un statut distinct et privilégié au bénéfice du citoyen européen pourrait certes être avancée comme objectif légitime dans le cadre de la construction européenne.[80] L'on ne voit toutefois pas bien en quoi exclure les ressortissants de pays tiers résidents de longue durée de ces emplois publics n'impliquant qu'une participation occasionnelle à l'autorité publique pourrait être considéré comme nécessaire à la réalisation de cet objectif. Qui plus est, si l'on prend en compte l'objectif de la directive de favoriser l'intégration des ressortissants de pays tiers, une telle exclusion s'avère même contreproductive. En effet, comme le rappelle M. Bell, d'une part, l'accès aux emplois publics revêt une importance particulière pour l'intégration en ce qu'elle démontre l'engagement de l'État envers l'inclusion des migrants et, d'autre part, les services publics constituent une interface cruciale pour les contacts entre les migrants et l'État.[81]

25. Ensuite, certaines limitations du champ matériel de l'égalité de traitement peuvent apparaître contestables au regard de l'interdiction des discriminations fondées sur la nationalité. C'est le cas, en particulier de la possibilité de limiter l'égalité de traitement en matière d'aide sociale et de protection sociale aux prestations essentielles – à savoir 'au moins, le revenu minimal de subsistance, l'aide en cas de maladie ou de grossesse, l'aide parentale et les soins de longue durée' (considérant 13) (article 11, § 3, c). Cette possibilité de restriction laissée aux États Membres nous semble se heurter à la jurisprudence de la Cour européenne des droits de l'homme relative à l'interdiction de discrimination fondée sur la nationalité contenue à l'article 14 CEDH. Comme cela a été exposé ci-dessus, la

---

77 M. Bell, 'Civic citizenship and migrant integration', *op. cit.*, p. 321.

78 Dans la même veine, l'article 11 § 3 permet aux États Membres de maintenir des 'restrictions à l'accès à l'emploi [...] lorsque, conformément à sa législation nationale ou au droit communautaire en vigueur, ces activités sont réservées à ses ressortissants nationaux, aux citoyens de l'UE ou de l'EEE' (§ 3 a)).

79 M. Bell, 'Civic citizenship and migrant integration', *European Public Law*, 2007, pp. 321-323.

80 L'on rappellera à cet égard que la Cour européenne des droits de l'homme avait, dans les affaires *Moustaquim* et *Chorfi* mentionnées plus haut, justifié une différence de traitement entre citoyens européens et ressortissants de pays tiers en matière d'expulsion en se fondant sur l'existence d'un ordre juridique spécifique, doté d'une citoyenneté propre (voir ci-dessus, point 11).

81 M. Bell, 'Civic citizenship and migrant integration', *op. cit.*, p. 322.

Cour EDH considère la nationalité comme un critère suspect ne pouvant justifier des différences de traitement que s'il existe des 'considérations très fortes'. Or à l'instar de ce que la Cour a jugé dans les affaires *Gaygusuz c. Autriche*[82] à propos d'une allocation d'urgence remplaçant le droit au chômage et *Koua Poirrez c. France*[83] pour une allocation destinée aux adultes handicapés, l'on ne voit pas quelles considérations très fortes pourraient justifier la limitation de l'égalité de traitement des ressortissants de pays tiers résidents de longue durée en matière d'aide et de protection sociales aux seules prestations essentielles.

26. Plus largement, au-delà de le formulation de l'égalité de traitement à l'article 11 de la directive 2003/109, l'on peut tenter de mettre en évidence certaines différences de traitement qui persistent entre citoyens européens et ressortissants de pays tiers résidents de longue durée. Dans son étude de 2006, K. Groenendijk[84] procédait à une comparaison entre le statut du citoyen européen qui réside ou travaille dans un autre État Membre et le ressortissant de pays tiers résidant depuis minimum 5 ans dans un État Membre, tels qu'ils résultent notamment respectivement des directives 2004/38 et 2003/109. Sur les cinq domaines identifiés comme des éléments clé de la citoyenneté, il en épingle trois dans lesquels il est clair que les ressortissants de pays tiers résidents de longue durée bénéficient d'un traitement moins favorable que les citoyens UE et un quatrième où cela dépendra de l'interprétation donnée par la Cour de justice.[85] Outre les différences de traitement déjà mentionnées ci-dessus concernant l'accès aux emplois publics et les restrictions admissibles dans le bénéfice de la protection et de l'aide sociale, les ressortissants de pays tiers n'ont pas le droit de vote et d'éligibilité aux élections municipales. Même si une évolution n'est pas à exclure au vu de l'importance que peut revêtir la participation à la vie politique locale pour l'intégration des ressortissants de pays tiers, ces droits politiques font assurément partie du noyau des droits de citoyenneté, ce qui peut a priori justifier la subsistance d'une différence de traitement fondée sur la nationalité.[86] Concernant l'expulsion pour motifs d'ordre public ou de sécurité publique, les différences de libellé entre les dispositions des deux directives (articles 27 et 28 de la directive 2004/38 et article 12 de la directive 2003/109) ne permettent pas de déterminer avec précision les différences qui seront tolérées *in fine* par la Cour de justice quant aux modalités d'expulsion de ces deux catégories d'étrangers.[87] A cet égard, la jurisprudence *Chakroun* en matière de regroupement familial est prometteuse

82 Voir ci-dessus, point 9.

83 Voir ci-dessus, point 9.

84 K. Groenendijk, 'Citizens and third country nationals: differential treatment or discrimination?', *op. cit.*, p. 88 ff.

85 Il est à noter qu'une analyse plus précise nécessiterait de distinguer en tenant également compte de certaines règles spécifiques concernant les ressortissants de certains pays tiers avec lesquels l'Union a conclu un accord de coopération ou d'association pouvant contenir des règles relatives à la non-discrimination et à la libre circulation. Voir notamment la comparaison effectuée par K. Groenendijk entre les citoyens européens, les ressortissants de pays tiers résidents de longue durée et les ressortissants turcs ('Citizens and third country nationals: differential treatment or discrimination?', *op. cit.*, p. 92).

86 O. De Schutter, *Links between Migration and Discrimination*, *op. cit.*, p. 47.

87 L'on se référera néanmoins utilement à l'arrêt rendu par la Cour de justice de l'UE dans l'affaire *Tsakouridis*, le 23 novembre 2010 (aff. C-145/09, §§ 40-54) où elle précise l'interprétation à donner aux 'raisons impérieuses de sécurité publique' ainsi que ce qui les différencient des 'motifs graves d'ordre public ou de sécurité publique' permettant de justifier une mesure d'expulsion d'un citoyen de l'UE en vertu de l'article 28 de la directive 2004/38.

notamment en ce que la Cour se réfère, par analogie, à sa jurisprudence en matière de citoyenneté européenne, pour interpréter largement les droits des ressortissants de pays tiers reconnus par la directive 2003/86 et réduire la marge nationale de transposition[88] (§ 64). Si les différences potentielles de traitement en matière d'éloignement du territoire qui résultent du libellé des deux directives ne semblent pas devoir être jugée discriminatoires en tant que telles, l'utilisation qui en sera faite par les États Membres pourra faire l'objet d'un contrôle au regard des droits fondamentaux, de l'interdiction des discriminations fondées sur la nationalité et, en particulier du principe de proportionnalité.[89]

27. A l'analyse, certaines des exceptions ou limites au champ d'application de l'égalité de traitement inscrites dans la directive 2003/109 pourraient s'avérer contraires au principe général de non-discrimination fondée sur la nationalité. L'arrêt rendu par la Cour de justice, dans l'affaire *Test-Achats*, le 1er mars 2011, atteste de la disponibilité de la Cour de justice à tirer toutes les conséquences des contrariétés entre, d'une part, les exceptions ménagées dans une directive et, de l'autre, l'objectif qu'elle poursuit et/ou les droits fondamentaux garantis en tant que principes généraux du droit ou consacrés dans la Charte des droits fondamentaux de l'UE. Dans cette affaire, la Cour a, en effet, estimé qu'une exception à l'interdiction des discriminations entres les hommes et les femmes contenue dans la directive 2004/113 (article 5 § 2) n'était pas conforme à l'objectif d'égalité de traitement entre les femmes et les hommes poursuivi par la directive et était incompatible avec les articles 21 et 23 de la Charte des droits fondamentaux de l'UE. Elle a jugé, par conséquent, que la disposition de la directive contenant cette exception était invalide pour l'avenir.[90] Il revient par conséquent aux juridictions nationales d'interroger la Cour à titre préjudiciel sur la validité de ces exceptions et régimes dérogatoires de la directive 2003/109. Quoiqu'il en soit, le respect de l'interdiction des discriminations fondée sur la nationalité constitue déjà une limite à la marge de manœuvre dont disposent les États Membres lorsqu'ils usent de certaines exceptions ou dérogations à l'occasion de la transposition de la directive. C'est particulièrement le cas relativement aux conditions d'intégration auxquelles les États Membres peuvent exiger que les ressortissants de pays tiers satisfassent pour obtenir le statut de résident de longue durée, en vertu de l'article 5 § 2 de la directive.[91]

II.2 Les Mesures et/ou Conditions d'Intégration adoptées par les États Membres

28. Comme cela a déjà abondamment été décrit dans la littérature,[92] les mesures et/ou conditions d'intégration adoptées par les États Membres s'échelonnent schématiquement à

88 Voir ci-dessus, point 5.

89 K. Groenendijk, 'Citizens and third country nationals: differential treatment or discrimination?', *op. cit.*, p. 91 et la référence citée en note de bas de page 32. Voir aussi J. Bast, 'Of General Principles and Trojan Horses – Procedural Due Process in Immigration Proceedings under EU Law', *German Law Journal*, 2010, p. 1006-1024.

90 CJUE, arrêt du 1er mars 2011, *Test-Achats*, aff. C-236/09, §§ 31-33.

91 A ce sujet, voir la contribution de Diego Acosta à cet ouvrage, '"En attendant Godot" or the EU limits to Integration Conditions'.

92 Voir les contributions à ct ouvrage de Y. Pascouau 'Mandatory Integration Schemes in the EU Member States: Overview and Trends' et D. Acosta, '"En attendant Godot" or the EU limits to Integration Conditions', en particulier les références citées aux notes de bas de page 3 à 9.

quatre stades du parcours du migrant: préalablement au regroupement familial avant tout accès au territoire, au moment de l'accès au territoire, au moment de l'octroi d'un statut de résident de longue durée et, enfin, au moment de l'octroi de la nationalité.[93] Si l'on souhaite évaluer ces mesures ou conditions à l'aune du principe général de droit de l'UE d'interdiction des discriminations fondées sur la nationalité mis en évidence ci-dessus, il faut préalablement, pour chacun des stades épinglés, établir le lien avec le champ d'application du droit de l'Union, condition préalable à l'applicabilité aux États Membres des principes généraux du droit de l'UE (1°). Ensuite, à titre d'illustration, nous nous concentrerons sur les mesures d'intégration imposées au migrant, candidat au regroupement familial, dans son pays d'origine, avant même son accès au territoire, afin de les analyser à l'aune de l'interdiction des discriminations (2°).[94]

1°) Le Rattachement au Champ d'Application du Droit de l'UE

29. Les deux premiers stades (avant l'accès au territoire et au moment de celui-ci en vue du regroupement familial) auxquels peuvent se greffer des mesures ou conditions d'intégration sont rattachés au champ du droit de l'UE par l'intermédiaire de la directive 2003/86 relative au regroupement familial des ressortissants de pays tiers en vertu de laquelle les États Membres peuvent exiger des ressortissants de pays tiers candidats au regroupement familial qu'ils se conforment à des mesures d'intégration (notamment article 7 § 2[95]). Les mesures ou conditions d'intégration adoptées par les États Membres relativement au regroupement familial avant l'accès au territoire ou une fois les membres de la famille installés, sont rattachés au champ d'application du droit de l'Union car elles s'inscrivent dans le domaine d'application de la directive et son encadrées par celle-ci. Le troisième stade, qui recouvre les mesures ou conditions d'intégration imposées aux ressortissants de pays tiers au moment de l'octroi d'un statut de résident de longue durée, entre dans le champ du droit de l'Union par un même procédé puisqu'il est couvert par la directive 2003/109/CE du 25 novembre 2003 relative au statut des ressortissants de pays tiers résidents de longue durée (article 5 § 2).[96]

30. Le rattachement au champ du droit de l'Union des mesures ou conditions d'intégration prévues en vue de l'octroi de la nationalité (quatrième stade) est en revanche

93 Voir notamment R. van Oers, E. Ersbøll & D. Kostakopoulou, 'Mapping the Redefinition of Belonging in Europe', in R. van Oers, E. Ersbøll & D. Kostakopoulou (eds), *A Redefinition of Belonging? Language and Integration Tests in Europe*, Leiden-Boston: Brill Publishes 2010, p. 307-332, spéc. 307-312.

94 Pour une analyse des conditions d'intégration fixées en vue de l'octroi du statut de résidant de longue durée, adoptées par les États Membres sur la base de l'article 5 § 2 de la directive 2003/109, au regard des principes généraux du droit et notamment du principe de proportionnalité et de la non-discrimination, voir la contribution de D. Acosta Azcarazo à cet ouvrage '"En attendant Godot" or the EU limits to Integration Conditions'.

95 L'article 4 § 1er contient une dérogation permettant de prévoir des critères ou conditions d'intégration pour les enfants mineurs de plus de 12 ans candidats au regroupement familial. Toutefois, en raison de l'exigence de *standstill* contenue dans cette disposition, en principe, seule l'Allemagne est concernée par celle-ci (K. Groenendijk, 'Integration of Immigrant in the EU: the Old or the New Way ?', contribution à cet ouvrage)

96 Voir à cet égard D. Acosta, '"En attendant Godot" or the EU limits to Integration Conditions', contribution à cet ouvrage.

plus délicat. A priori, un tel rattachement apparaît difficilement défendable vu que les conditions d'octroi et de retrait de la nationalité ressortent de la compétence souveraine des États. C'est d'ailleurs ce qui découle tant de la jurisprudence constante de la Cour de justice selon laquelle la définition des conditions d'acquisition et de perte de la nationalité relève, conformément au droit international, de la compétence de chaque État Membre[97] que de la déclaration relative à la nationalité d'un État Membre (annexée au traité sur l'Union européenne).[98] Toutefois, il est également de jurisprudence constante que 'le fait qu'une matière ressortit à la compétence des États Membres n'empêche pas que, dans des situations relevant du droit de l'Union, les règles nationales concernées doivent respecter ce dernier [...]'.[99] Or, récemment, à l'occasion de son arrêt *Rottmann*, la Cour de justice a affirmé que relèvent du droit de l'UE 'les conditions dans lesquelles un citoyen de l'Union peut, du fait de la perte de sa nationalité, perdre cette qualité de citoyen de l'Union et, dès lors, être privé des droits qui y sont attachés'.[100] S'il ne faut pas négliger les spécificités du cas d'espèce (cas d'apatridie résultant du retrait de nationalité), il ne nous semble pas exclu, au vu des termes larges utilisés par la Cour, qu'elle puisse considérer, dans certains cas, que les conditions mises à l'acquisition de la nationalité d'un État Membre (et pas seulement à la perte de celle-ci) ressortent du droit de l'UE par la connexion qu'elles présentent avec la citoyenneté européenne et, à ce titre, doivent respecter l'interdiction de discrimination découlant du principe général de droit de l'UE mis en évidence ci-dessus.[101] Enfin, comme le relève à juste titre O. De Schutter, il n'est pas exclu non plus que la directive 2000/43

---

97 CJCE, arrêt du 7 juillet 1992, *Micheletti e.a.*, aff. C-369/90, Rec. p. I-4239, § 10; CJCE, arrêt du 11 novembre 1999, *Mesbah*, C-179/98, *Rec.* p. I-7955, § 29, ainsi que CJCE, arrêt du 19 octobre 2004, *Zhu et Chen*, C-200/02, *Rec.* p. I-9925, § 37).

98 La déclaration n° 2 relative à la nationalité d'un État Membre, jointe par les États Membres à l'acte final du traité sur l'Union européenne (*JO* 1992, C 191, p. 98), est libellée comme suit: 'La Conférence déclare que, chaque fois que le traité instituant la Communauté européenne fait référence aux ressortissants des États Membres, la question de savoir si une personne a la nationalité de tel ou tel État Membre est réglée uniquement par référence au droit national de l'État concerné. [...]'. Voir aussi J.Y. Carlier, 'Droits de l'homme et nationalité', *Annales de Droit de Louvain*, 2003, p. 243-257, spéc. p. 245.

99 CJUE, arrêt du 2 mars 2010, C-135/08, *Rottman*, § 41 [voir, en ce sens, arrêts du 24 novembre 1998, *Bickel et Franz*, C-274/96, *Rec.* p.I-7637, § 17 (s'agissant d'une réglementation nationale en matière pénale et de procédure pénale); du 2 octobre 2003, *Garcia Avello*, C-148/02, *Rec.* p. I-11613, § 25 (s'agissant de règles nationales régissant le nom d'une personne); du 12 juillet 2005, *Schempp*, C-403/03, *Rec.* p. I-6421, § 19 (s'agissant de règles nationales relatives à la fiscalité directe), ainsi que du 12 septembre 2006, *Espagne/Royaume-Uni*, C-145/04, *Rec.* p. I-7917, § 78 (s'agissant de règles nationales déterminant les titulaires du droit de vote et d'éligibilité aux élections au Parlement européen).

100 CJUE, arrêt du 2 mars 2010, C-135/08, *Rottman*, § 46 (à propos de la 'situation d'un citoyen de l'Union qui, tel le requérant au principal, est confronté à une décision de retrait de la naturalisation adoptée par les autorités d'un État Membre le plaçant, après qu'il a perdu la nationalité d'un autre État Membre qu'il possédait à l'origine, dans une situation susceptible d'entraîner la perte du statut conféré par l'article 17 CE et des droits y attachés [qui] relève, par sa nature et ses conséquences, du droit de l'Union', § 42.

101 L'arrêt *Ruiz Zambrano* nous paraît appuyer une telle conclusion en ce que la Cour y affirme que 'l'article 20 TFUE s'oppose à des mesures nationales ayant pour effet de priver les citoyens de l'Union de la jouissance effective de l'essentiel des droits conférés par leur statut de citoyen de l'Union (voir en ce sens, arrêt *Rottmann*, précité, § 42' (CJUE, arrêt du 8 mars 2011, *Ruiz Zambrano*, aff. C-34/09, § 42).

soit applicable en cas de conditions d'accès à la nationalité qui s'avèreraient contraires à l'interdiction des discriminations indirectes fondées sur la race ou l'origine ethnique, dans la mesure où cet accès à la nationalité va lui-même gouverner ou faciliter l'accès à l'emploi, à l'éducation ou au logement qui sont couverts par la directive.[102]

2°) Les tests néerlandais et français d'intégration dans le pays d'origine à l'épreuve de l'interdiction des discriminations fondées sur la nationalité, la race et l'origine ethnique

31. L'option de prévoir des mesures d'intégration laissée aux États Membres par la directive 2003/86 (article 7, § 2) a déjà fait couler beaucoup d'encre.[103] La Cour de justice elle-même, à l'occasion de l'arrêt *Parlement contre Conseil* (2006), a précisé qu'il ne s'agissait pas d'un blanc-seing donné aux États Membres et que '[l]'absence de définition de la notion d'intégration ne saurait être interprétée comme une autorisation conférée aux États Membres d'utiliser cette notion d'une manière contraire aux principes généraux du droit communautaire et, plus particulièrement, aux droits fondamentaux [...]'.[104] Dans le contexte du regroupement familial, 5 États Membres ont introduit, à ce jour, des mesures d'intégration dans le pays d'origine, conditionnant parfois l'accès même au territoire de l'État d'accueil (Allemagne, Danemark, France, Pays-Bas, Royaume-Uni).[105] Afin de procéder à l'analyse de leur conformité aux principes généraux du droit de l'Union[106] et, en particulier, à l'interdiction des discriminations fondées sur la nationalité et/ou sur la race ou l'origine ethnique, nous avons sélectionné le cas des Pays-Bas et celui de la France. Les Pays-Bas sont à ce jour ceux qui ont introduit les conditions d'intégration les plus contraignantes[107] tandis que la France a finalement opté pour des mesures non assorties de sanctions.[108]

102 O. De Schutter, *Links between Migration and Discrimination*, *op. cit.*, p. 23. La Cour de justice semble toutefois avoir rejeté une interprétation aussi large concernant une réglementation nationale relative à la transcription des noms de famille et des prénoms dans les actes d'état civil dont elle a considéré qu'elle n'entrait pas dans le champ d'application matériel de la directive 2000/43 (CJUE, arrêt du 12 mai 2011, *Malgožata Runevič-Vardyn*, C-391/09, §§ 41-48.

103 Voir notamment: E. Guild, K. Groenendijk & S. Carrera (eds), *Illiberal Liberal States. Immigration, Citizenship and Integration in the* EU, Farnham: Ashgate 2009; T. Strik, A. Böcker, M. Luiten & R. Van Oers, *Integration and Naturalisation tests: the new way to European Citizenship. A comparative study in Nine Member States on the national policies concerning integration and naturalisation tests and their effects on integration*, contribution à cet ouvrage; K. Groenendijk, 'Legal Concept of Integration in EU Migration Law', *European Journal of Migration and Law*, 2004, p. 111-126.

104 CJCE, arrêt du 27 juin 2006, *Parlement c. Conseil*, *op. cit.*, § 70.

105 T. Strik, A. Böcker, M. Luiten & R. Van Oers, *Integration and Naturalisation tests: the new way to European Citizenship.*, *op. cit.*, p. 13 ff.

106 Une telle mise en cause de la validité des mesures ou conditions d'intégrations nationales devant la Cour de justice peut intervenir par la voie d'un recours en manquement introduit par la Commission européenne ou par un renvoi préjudiciel adressé à la Cour de justice par une juridiction nationale portant sur l'interprétation de la directive 2003/86 et indirectement sur la conformité du droit national à la directive et aux principes généraux du droit.

107 *Wet inburgering Buitenland*, WIB, 2005, *Staatsblad* 2006, no. 94. Pour une présentation détaillée des tests d'intégration mis sur pied aux Pays-Bas, voir T. Strik, A. Böcker, M. Luiten & R. Van Oers, *Integration and Naturalisation tests: the new way to European Citizenship, op. cit.*, p. 9-11.

108 L. 411-8 (Art. 1*er de la loi n° 2007-1631 du 20 novembre 2007)* : 'Pour lui permettre de préparer son intégration républicaine dans la société française, le ressortissant étranger âgé de plus de seize ans et de moins de soixante-cinq ans pour lequel le regroupement familial est sollicité bénéficie, dans son →

32. Sans pouvoir, de manière parfaitement rigoureuse, passer chacune des différences de traitement fondées sur la nationalité liées à ces mesures d'intégration adoptées par les Pays-Bas et par la France au crible de l'interdiction de discrimination fondée sur la nationalité, il s'agit, dans le cadre de cette étude, de livrer les balises du raisonnement qui permettrait d'interroger plus systématiquement leur conformité à cette interdiction.

33. Dans cette optique, la première étape réside dans l'identification des différences de traitement directement fondées sur la nationalité ou indirectement fondées sur la race ou l'origine ethnique, qui résultent de ces tests d'intégration imposés dans le cadre du regroupement familial. Tout d'abord, tant aux Pays-Bas qu'en France les regroupants visés sont tant les ressortissants de pays tiers que les nationaux. Deux différences de traitement fondées sur la nationalité en découlent: premièrement, celle entre les ressortissants de pays tiers, d'une part, et les citoyens européens, de l'autre (a) et deuxièmement, celle entre les nationaux, d'une part, et les citoyens européens de l'autre (b). Ensuite, si l'on se tourne vers les membres de la famille, l'on a, dans les deux pays, une différence de traitement entre les citoyens européens, d'une part, et certains ressortissants de pays tiers de l'autre (c). En outre, dans le cas des Pays-Bas, il résulte de l'exemption dont bénéficient les ressortissants de pays tiers 'dits occidentaux' (les ressortissants de l'EEE ainsi que les ressortissants des États-Unis, Japon, Canada, Nouvelle-Zélande, Australie, Suisse, Corée du Sud et Surinam[109]), une autre différence de traitement, au sein même des ressortissants de pays tiers, selon leur pays d'origine (occidentaux ou non-occidentaux) (d). La question spécifique des ressortissants turcs mérite également une attention particulière au regard des dispositions de l'accord d'association avec la Turquie et de son interprétation par la Cour de justice de l'UE (e). Enfin, des discriminations indirectement fondées sur l'origine ethnique des regroupants pourraient résulter de la mise en œuvre de ces législations (f).[110]

34. La deuxième étape du raisonnement consiste, pour chacune de ces différences de traitement fondées sur la nationalité ou pour celles indirectement fondées sur l'origine ethnique, à examiner si un objectif légitime est poursuivi et si la différence de traitement est proportionnée à cet objectif, à savoir nécessaire, adéquate et proportionnée au sens strict à la réalisation de celui-ci.[111]

---

pays de résidence, d'une évaluation de son degré de connaissance de la langue et des valeurs de la République. Si cette évaluation en établit le besoin, l'autorité administrative organise à l'intention de l'étranger, dans son pays de résidence, une formation dont la durée ne peut excéder deux mois, au terme de laquelle il fait l'objet d'une nouvelle évaluation de sa connaissance de la langue et des valeurs de la République. La délivrance du visa est subordonnée à la production d'une attestation de suivi de cette formation. Cette attestation est délivrée immédiatement à l'issue de la formation. [...]. A propos des mesures d'intégration adoptées en France, voir Y. Pascouau, 'Integration Measures in France: An Evolving Process between Integration and Migration Issues', *op. cit.* Voir aussi la contribution de S. Bonjour, qui met en évidence les motifs politico-juridiques qui expliquent de telles différences entre l'option des Pays-Bas et celle de la France ('Between Integration Provision and Selection Mechanism. Party Politics, Judicial Constraints, and the making of French and Dutch Policies of Civic Integration Abroad', *European Journal of Migration and Law*', 2010, p. 299-318).

109 Ce pays figure dans les pays exemptés pour des motifs historico-linguistiques qui diffèrent des motifs ayant conduit à exempter les ressortissants des autres pays.

110 Pour la facilité de l'exposé, les situations a) et c) recouvrant des différences de traitement entre ressortissants de pays tiers, d'une part, et citoyens de l'UE, de l'autre, tantôt dans le chef du regroupant, tantôt dans celui des membres de la famille, seront étudiées simultanément.

111 S. van Drooghenbroeck, *La proportionnalité dans le droit de la Convention européenne des droits de l'homme. Prendre l'idée simple au sérieux*, Bruxelles: Bruylant 2001, §§ 793 ff.

Membres de la famille – différence de traitement entre les ressortissants de pays tiers selon leur pays d'origine (situation d)

35. La différence de traitement qui affecte les membres de la famille candidats au regroupement familial selon leur pays d'origine (situation d), n'existe qu'aux Pays-Bas et apparaît, à première vue, la plus ostensiblement discriminatoire. Toutefois, nous ne nous y attarderons guère car le caractère discriminatoire de ces exemptions dont bénéficient uniquement les ressortissants de pays dits 'occidentaux' a été préalablement démontré et dénoncé par des organismes de défense des droits fondamentaux ou de lutte contre les discriminations. Ainsi, dans ses observations finales sur les Pays-Bas du 16 mars 2010, le Comité des Nations-Unies pour l'élimination des discriminations raciales a considéré que l'application de la loi néerlandaise sur les tests d'intégration à l'étranger engendrait une discrimination fondée sur la nationalité entre les ressortissants dits 'occidentaux' ou 'non-occidentaux'.[112] Il avait été précédé par le Commissaire aux droits de l'homme du Conseil de l'Europe, Thomas Hammerberg, qui concluait également au caractère discriminatoire de ces mesures dans son rapport sur les Pays-Bas adopté en mars 2009. Le raisonnement le plus détaillé à cet égard est fourni par *Human Rights Watch*, dans un document critique élaboré en mai 2008.[113]

36. Nous nous contenterons ici de reprendre les arguments avancés à l'appui de cette conclusion en les rattachant au test de légitimité de l'objectif poursuivi et de proportionnalité.

La légitimité de l'un des objectifs affirmés à l'appui des tests d'intégration à l'étranger aux Pays-Bas, à savoir, promouvoir une meilleure intégration des migrants au sein de la société néerlandaise, ne semble pas pouvoir être contestée en tant que telle. La Cour de justice de l'UE elle-même n'a-t-elle pas affirmé que '[l]a nécessité de l'intégration peut relever de plusieurs des buts légitimes visés à l'article 8, § 2 de la CEDH' ?[114] Il est nettement plus contestable qu'un test qui ne s'applique qu'à certains membres de la famille, candidats au regroupement, en fonction de leur nationalité, puisse être considéré comme adéquat au regard de cet objectif de favoriser l'intégration de tous les migrants. Le gouvernement des Pays-Bas n'a nullement apporté la preuve qu'il existerait un lien entre le niveau de développement du pays d'origine et la capacité d'intégration du migrant et ne peut prétendre que les ressortissants japonais apprennent plus rapidement le néerlandais que les ressortissants chinois, par exemple.[115] De ce point de vue, la différence de traitement entre ressortissants de pays 'occidentaux' ou 'non-occidentaux' concernant l'exigence d'un test d'intégration préalable au regroupement familial ne paraît pas objectivement justifiée eu égard à l'objectif poursuivi. Qui plus est, l'absence de test préalable à l'admission des mem-

112 CEDR, 'Concluding Observations of the Committee on the Elimination of Racial Discrimination – Netherlands', 16 mars 2010 (Consideration of Reports submitted by states parties under article 9 of the Convention) (CERD/C/NLD/CO/17-18), § 5. A cet égard, l'on relèvera que le Comité pour l'élimination des discriminations raciales inclut explicitement ici dans son champ de contrôle des discriminations fondées sur la nationalité (voir aussi en ce sens CERD, *Ziad Ben Ahmed Habassi v. Denmark*, Communication No. 10/1997, *op. cit.*, § 9.3).

113 *Human Rights Watch*, 'The Netherlands: Discrimination in the Name of Integration. Migrants' Rights under the Integration Abroad Act', mai 2008, p. 26-29.

114 CJCE, arrêt du 27 juin 2006, *Parlement européen c. Conseil*, *op. cit.*, § 66.

115 K. Groenendijk, 'Citizens and third country nationals: differential treatment or discrimination?', *op. cit.*, p. 86.

bres de la famille, ressortissants de pays tiers, des citoyens européens (à l'exception des ressortissants néerlandais) constitue un indice de l'absence de la nécessité de la mesure en vue de favoriser l'intégration.[116] Enfin, les difficultés relatives à la préparation d'un tel test, son coût ainsi que la sanction qui y est liée apparaissent disproportionnés par rapport à l'objectif poursuivi.

Regroupants – Différence de traitement entre nationaux de l'État d'accueil et citoyens de l'UE ayant exercé leur liberté de circulation (situation b)

37. La deuxième situation à examiner recouvre la différence de traitement entre les regroupants selon qu'ils sont des nationaux n'ayant pas exercé leur liberté de circulation ou qu'ils sont des citoyens de l'UE l'ayant exercée (situation b). A priori, la question du caractère éventuellement discriminatoire de cette différence de traitement, au regard du droit de l'UE, est aisément résolue. En effet, il résulte d'une jurisprudence constante que les discriminations dites 'à rebours', à savoir celles qui affectent les nationaux d'un État Membre n'ayant pas fait usage de leur liberté de circulation par rapport aux citoyens de l'UE ayant fait usage de cette liberté n'entrent pas dans le champ d'application du droit de l'UE.[117] De ce point de vue, l'invocation du principe général de droit de l'UE d'interdiction des discriminations fondées sur la nationalité ne serait pas possible puisque la différence de traitement visée se situerait hors du champ d'application du droit de l'UE.

38. Deux remarques nous semblent toutefois devoir être formulées à cet égard. Tout d'abord, comme le souligne l'avocate générale Kokott,

> 'l'on ne peut certainement pas exclure que, à un moment donné, la Cour reconsidère sa jurisprudence et soit amenée, à l'avenir, à déduire de la citoyenneté de l'Union une interdiction de la discrimination des ressortissants nationaux. En effet, le statut de citoyen de l'Union a vocation à 'être le statut fondamental des ressortissants des États Membres permettant à ceux parmi ces derniers qui se trouvent dans la même situation d'obtenir, indépendamment de leur nationalité et sans préjudice des exceptions expressément prévues à cet égard, le même traitement juridique.'[118]

---

116 Le Comité des droits de l'homme a constaté dans une affaire (*Van Oord c. Pays-Bas*, communication n° 658/1995) qu'un accord international instituant un traitement préférentiel en faveur des ressortissants des États contractants pouvait constituer un critère raisonnable et objectif de différenciation sans que l'on puisse pour autant en dégager une règle générale selon laquelle un tel accord constituerait en soi un critère suffisant au regard de l'article 26 du Pacte'. Il n'est dès lors pas suffisant pour les Pays-Bas de se retrancher derrière l'obligation qui découlerait du droit UE de ne pas imposer ces conditions aux membres de la famille des citoyens européens

117 Voir CJCE, arrêt du 25 juillet 2008, *Metock*, aff; C-127/08, Rec. p. I-6241, §§ 77-78 ; voir aussi conclusions de l'avocate générale Kokott, présentées le 25 novembre 2010, dans l'affaire C-434/09, *Shirley McCarthy*, § 40 et les références citées.

118 Conclusions de l'avocate générale Kokott, dans l'affaire *Shirley McCarthy*, *op. cit.*, § 42. Ce faisant l'avocate générale Kokott reprenait, quoique de manière plus modérée, une proposition formulée préalablement par l'avocate générale Sharpston Cette dernière a développé une appréciation particulièrement critique de ce phénomène de discriminations à rebours à l'occasion notamment des conclusions qu'elle a présentées, le 30 septembre 2010, dans l'affaire *Ruiz Zambrano* (aff. C-34/09, §§ 125-138). Elle a doublé cette critique d'une proposition de revirement de jurisprudence adressée à la Cour consistant à fonder, lorsque certaines conditions sont réunies, l'interdiction des discriminations à rebours sur le statut de citoyen européen (article 18 TFUE) (§§ 13-150). Sans embrayer purement et simplement sur la suggestion de son avocate générale, la Cour de justice nous semble avoir fait un →

Ensuite, dans l'attente d'un éventuel revirement de la Cour, il importe de souligner qu'une différence de traitement constitutive de discrimination à rebours peut être examinée par les juridictions nationales au regard de l'interdiction de discrimination garantie en droit national[119] et dans la Convention européenne des droits de l'homme.[120]

Regroupants ou membres de la famille - différences de traitement entre citoyens européens et ressortissants de pays tiers (situations a et c)

39. Le troisième type de différences de traitement à examiner à l'aune du principe général d'interdiction des discriminations recouvre les différences entre citoyens européens et ressortissants de pays tiers, tant dans le chef du regroupant que dans celui des membres de la famille (situations a et c). Comme nous l'avons souligné ci-dessus, en tenant compte notamment de la jurisprudence *Karakurt* du Comité des droits de l'homme, l'existence d'un ordre juridique spécifique ayant instauré une citoyenneté propre ne justifie pas, par elle-

---

pas dans la direction suggérée à l'occasion de son arrêt rendu dans l'affaire *Ruiz Zambrano* (8 mars 2011, aff. C-34/09, §§ 41-42). L'on relèvera toutefois qu'au moment de clôturer cette contribution, la Cour a rendu son arrêt dans l'affaire *McCarthy* en réduisant quelque peu les virtualités de l'arrêt *Ruiz Zambrano*. Elle affirme ainsi que '[i]l s'ensuit que l'article 21 TFUE n'est pas applicable à un citoyen de l'Union qui n'a jamais fait usage de son droit de libre circulation, qui a toujours séjourné dans un État Membre dont il possède la nationalité et qui jouit, par ailleurs, de la nationalité d'un autre État Membre pour autant que la situation de ce citoyen ne comporte pas l'application de mesures d'un État Membre qui auraient pour effet de le priver de la jouissance effective de l'essentiel des droits conférés par le statut de citoyen de l'Union ou d'entraver l'exercice de son droit de circuler et de séjourner librement sur le territoire des États Membres' (§ 56,5 mai 2011, aff. C 434/09 Shirley *McCarthy*). Voir également en ce sens, CJUE, arrêt du 15 novembre 2011, *Dereci*, aff. C-256/11, § 74.

119 A cet égard, la Cour a affirmé que les discriminations à rebours au détriment des nationaux d'un États Membres 'doivent être résolues dans le cadre du système juridique interne dudit État' (CJCE, arrêt du 5 juin 1997, *Uecker e.a.*, aff. C-64/96 e.a., § 23). Voir aussi, à propos de l'attitude de la Cour constitutionnelle belge, B. Renauld, T. Bombois & P. Martens, 'Existe-t-il un droit fondamental au regroupement familial à Strasbourg, à Luxembourg et à Bruxelles?', *op. cit.*, p. 822-827. L'on relèvera à cet égard le recours en annulation introduit par six ONGs, en mars 2012 (n° de rôle 5361), devant la Cour constitutionnelle belge à l'encontre de la loi du 8 juillet 2011 modifiant la loi du 15 décembre 1980 sur l'accès au territoire, le séjour, l'établissement et l'éloignement des étrangers en ce qui concerne les conditions dont est assorti le regroupement familial. A cet égard, les associations requérantes défendent notamment qu'en imposant aux ressortissants belges (regroupants) les mêmes conditions qu'aux ressortissants de pays tiers en matière notamment de revenus et de logement, et donc en imposant des conditions plus strictes aux ressortissants belges qu'aux autres citoyens européens, la nouvelle loi introduit une discrimination entre citoyens de l'UE. Selon ces associations, cette nouvelle législation affectera en particulier les ressortissants belges d'origine turque ou marocaine, ce qui pourrait être constitutive d'une discrimination indirectement fondée sur la race ou l'origine ethnique.

120 C'est sans doute le sens qu'il convient d'attribuer à l'attendu de la Cour, dans l'arrêt *Metock*, où, après avoir rappelé que les discriminations à rebours ne rentrent pas dans le champ d'application du droit communautaire, elle a souligné que tous les États Membres étaient parties à la CEDH qui consacre le droit à la vie privée et familiale en son article 8 (CJCE, arrêt du 25 juillet 2008, *Metock*, *op. cit.*, § 79) . En ce sens, voir B. Renauld, T. Bombois & P. Martens, 'Existe-t-il un droit fondamental au regroupement familial à Strasbourg, à Luxembourg et à Bruxelles?', *op. cit.*, p. 820-821.

même, toute différence de traitement entre citoyens de l'UE et ressortissants de pays tiers. Encore faut-il que cette différence de traitement soit proportionnelle à l'objectif poursuivi.

Si l'on considère d'abord la différence entre regroupants (situation a), le système mis en place tant aux Pays-Bas qu'en France implique, par exemple, qu'au motif de favoriser l'intégration, un ressortissant de pays tiers souhaitant se faire rejoindre par sa femme tunisienne verra son regroupement familial subordonné à la réussite d'un test d'intégration par sa conjointe (Pays-Bas) ou à certaines obligations de suivre des cours de langue préalablement à l'arrivée en France alors qu'un citoyen européen qui veut se faire rejoindre par sa femme de nationalité tunisienne ne se heurtera pas à ces obstacles. Dans un tel cas, il apparaît difficile de soutenir qu'il y aurait une différence d' 'intégrabilité' entre la femme tunisienne d'un citoyen européen et la femme tunisienne d'un ressortissant de pays tiers. Le fait qu'en vertu des règles UE en matière de libre circulation et de séjour, les citoyens européens se voient exemptés de ces mesures d'intégration concernant les membres de leur famille peut légitimement faire douter de la nécessité de telles mesures en vue de l'intégration des ressortissants étrangers. Si ces mesures d'intégration sont véritablement destinées à favoriser l'intégration de celles et ceux à qui elles s'imposent, ne faudrait-il pas, au contraire, en faire bénéficier les membres de la famille d'un citoyen européen?

40. A ce stade du raisonnement, il est nécessaire de distinguer les mesures adoptées par les Pays-Bas de celles de la France. Aux Pays-Bas, aucun cours de langue n'est organisé dans les pays d'origine des migrants et l'accès à des cours privés peut s'avérer prohibitif ; par ailleurs, le passage du test revêt un coût élevé et, de surcroît, l'obtention d'un visa en vue du regroupement familial est conditionnée à la réussite du test.[121] Ces modalités, par leur caractère potentiellement dissuasif et leur impact disproportionné sur certaines catégories de personnes (moins nantis, personnes âgées, analphabètes, etc.),[122] s'avèrent inadéquates et disproportionnées eu égard à l'objectif de favoriser l'intégration et ne nous semblent pas permettre de justifier une différence de traitement entre regroupants, selon qu'ils sont citoyens européens ou ressortissants de pays tiers.

41. L'appréciation est a priori plus nuancée concernant la France où il n'y a pas de sanction en cas d'échec du test à passer dans le pays d'origine et où des cours de langue sont proposés à titre gratuit afin de préparer le test. Ces modalités apparaissent moins contraignantes et pourraient être proportionnées à l'objectif poursuivi. Toutefois, si l'on se penche plus avant sur l'impact de ces mesures sur certains groupes de personnes, elles pourraient également être disproportionnées et rendre discriminatoire la différence de traitement entre regroupants, selon qu'ils sont citoyens de l'UE ou ressortissants de pays tiers. Certains auteurs ont ainsi mis en évidence des effets dissuasifs de l'instauration de ces mesures d'intégration préalables à la délivrance d'un visa notamment vis-à-vis des personnes vivant loin des centres où les formations linguistiques sont dispensées ou des personnes âgées notamment[123]. En outre, alors qu'il y a encore quelques années, l'objectif

121 Pour une présentation détaillée des tests d'intégration mis sur pied par les Pays-Bas, voir 'The Netherlands', *op. cit.*, pp. 9-11

122 Voir *Human rights Watch*, 'The Netherlands: Discrimination in the Name of Integration. Migrants' Rights under the Integration Abroad Act', *op. cit.*, p. 37 ff.

123 Voir notamment C. Cournil & Y. Depigny, 'Contractualisation et externalisation de la politique migratoire: analyse critique de la loi Hortefeux', *Revue de Droit public,* 2008; Y. Pascouau, 'Linking Integration Issues to Migration Ones: An Ongoing Process in French Law', in *Wechselwirkungen von Mi-* →

de favoriser le regroupement familial était considéré en soi comme un moyen de favoriser l'intégration, le recul de près d'un tiers des demandes de regroupement familial en France depuis l'introduction de ces mesures d'intégration à l'étranger semble attester du fait que l'objectif poursuivi serait plutôt le contrôle des migrations 'subies' ou la gestion des flux. Or, la Commission européenne elle-même a souligné, dans son rapport d'évaluation de la directive 2003 /86, que '[c]es mesures [d'intégration] ont pour objectif de faciliter l'intégration des membres de la famille. Leur conformité avec la directive dépend de savoir si elles servent cette finalité et si elles respectent le principe de proportionnalité. Leur conformité peut être discutable en fonction de l'accessibilité à ces cours ou tests, de leur conception et/ou organisation (documents utilisés, prix, lieu, etc.), ou si ces mesures ou leurs effets *servent d'autres buts que l'intégration* (par exemple, prix élevé excluant les familles à faible revenus). [...]'.[124] Les effets de ces mesures pourraient donc les inscrire en contrariété avec les objectifs poursuivis par la directive 2003/86 de favoriser le regroupement familial et l'intégration des membres de la famille.

42. La différence de traitement qui frappe les membres de la famille selon qu'ils sont citoyens européens ou ressortissants de pays tiers (situation c) résiste-t-elle mieux à l'épreuve du principe de non-discrimination ? Si l'on accepte la présomption selon laquelle les citoyens européens seraient plus facilement 'intégrables' que les ressortissants de pays tiers, il semblerait qu'il faille répondre par l'affirmative, dans la mesure où les situations ne seraient pas comparables. Au contraire, si cette présomption n'est pas prise pour acquise, outre la question de la proportionnalité de la différence de traitement examinée ci-dessus (situation a), le fait que les citoyens européens soient dispensés de ces cours de langue et de ces tests ne jette-t-il pas le doute sur la nécessité de la mesure en ce qu'elle vise les ressortissants de pays tiers? Comment justifier, en effet, que ces mesures d'intégration soient présentées comme nécessaire relativement aux ressortissants de pays tiers alors que rien ne serait prévu relativement aux citoyens européens? Paradoxalement, les citoyens européens ne pourraient-ils pas demander à pouvoir bénéficier des cours de langue offerts gratuitement aux ressortissants de pays tiers candidats au regroupement familial, s'ils sont censés favoriser l'intégration? Et, si on pousse le raisonnement dans toutes ses conclusions logiques, n'y aurait-il pas une obligation positive pour la France (ou les autres pays de l'UE) de mettre sur pied, au bénéfice des citoyens européens, de tels cours de langue censés favoriser l'intégration?

Regroupants ou membres de la famille – différence de traitement entre les ressortissants turcs et les citoyens européens (situation e)

43. La quatrième situation à examiner est celle spécifique des différences de traitement entre les ressortissants turcs et les citoyens européens qu'ils soient regroupants ou membres de la famille (situation e). En se fondant sur la jurisprudence récente de la Cour de justice de l'UE,[125] il est plus que probable que certaines mesures d'intégration à l'étranger soient considérées contraires à l'interdiction des discriminations contenue dans l'accord d'association avec la Turquie (article 9) et dans la décision 1/80 (article 10) ainsi qu'à la

---

gration und Integration im Europäischen Mehrebenensystem Rechts- und sozialwissenschaftliche Beiträge, ZERP-Series, Vol. 63: Conference transcript, Bremen 2011.

124 C'est nous qui soulignons. COM(2008)610 final 8 octobre 2008, p. 7-8.

125 CJUE, 29 avril 2010, *Commission c. Pays-Bas*, aff. C-92/07.

clause de *standstill* énoncée à l'article 13 de la décision 1/80.[126] La Cour a, en effet, condamné récemment les Pays-Bas aux motifs qu'

> 'en appliquant aux ressortissants turcs des droits d'un montant disproportionné pour l'obtention de permis de séjour ou la prorogation de ceux-ci par rapport aux droits appliqués aux citoyens de l'Union pour des documents similaires, le Royaume des Pays-Bas a [...] imposé des droits à caractère discriminatoire. Pour autant que ces droits s'appliquent aux travailleurs turcs ou aux membres de leur famille, ces droits introduisent une condition de travail discriminatoire contraire à l'article 10 de la décision n° 1/80. [...].'[127]

Ce raisonnement nous paraît parfaitement transposable aux conditions d'intégration – disproportionnées comme cela a été démontré ci-dessus – imposées par les Pays-Bas aux ressortissants turcs, qu'ils soient regroupants ou membres de la famille, en vue du regroupement familial. C'est d'ailleurs ce qui a été jugé par la Cour d'appel des Pays-Bas (Centrale Raad van Beroep) le 16 août 2011 qui a considéré que le fait de soumettre les ressortissants turcs aux obligations en matière d'intégration était contraire aux articles 9 et 10 de l'accord d'association avec la Turquie.[128]

Regroupants – discriminations indirectement fondées sur la race ou l'origine ethnique (situation f)

44. Au-delà des éventuelles discriminations directes fondées sur la nationalité que ces mesures d'intégration recèleraient, l'ont peut, enfin, s'interroger sur leur caractère indirectement discriminatoire fondé sur la race ou l'origine ethnique des regroupants (situation f). Cette analyse pourrait-elle s'effectuer au regard de la directive 2000/43? L'on a montré dans la première partie de cette étude que les limites du champ d'application fixées par l'article 3, § 2 de la directive 2000/43 doivent s'interpréter restrictivement et en tenant compte des droits fondamentaux. Encore faut-il que le fait de pouvoir se faire rejoindre par un membre de sa famille soit rattachable à l'un des domaines d'application matériel de la directive précisés à l'article 3 § 1er. La notion 'd'avantages sociaux' (article 3, § 1er, f)), qui a fait l'objet d'une interprétation extensive dans la jurisprudence de la Cour, apparaît la plus prometteuse à cet égard. La Cour y a en effet inclus le droit pour un travailleur migrant d'obtenir que son partenaire non marié, non-ressortissant de l'État Membre d'accueil, soit autorisé à y séjourner avec lui.[129] Cette jurisprudence, développée dans le domaine de la circulation des travailleurs ressortissants de l'UE, nous semble pouvoir être

---

126 *Ibidem*, § 49. Il s'ensuit que l'article 13 de la décision n° 1/80 s'oppose à l'introduction dans la réglementation néerlandaise, à compter de la date d'entrée en vigueur aux Pays-Bas de la décision n° 1/80, de toutes nouvelles restrictions à l'exercice de la libre circulation des travailleurs, y compris celles portant sur les conditions de fond et/ou de procédure en matière de première admission sur le territoire de cet État Membre des ressortissants turcs se proposant d'y faire usage de cette liberté. Voir aussi pour une application de cette clause de *standstill* en matière de liberté d'établissement (article 41, paragraphe 1, du protocole additionnel), l'arrêt rendu le 15 novembre 2011, par la CJUE dans l'affaire *Dereci*, aff. C-256/11, §§ 80-101.

127 *Ibidem*, § 75.

128 LJN: BR5210, Centrale Raad van Beroep, 10/4841 WIA. Cette décision est disponible en ligne sur le site web : http://www.rechtspraak.nl/Pages/default.aspx.

129 CJCE, arrêt du 17 avril 1986, *État néerlandais contre Ann Florence Reed*, aff. 59/85, *Rec.*, p. 1283 ff.

utilisée et transposée à la directive 2000/43 permettant d'englober le regroupement familial dans la notion d'avantages sociaux à propos desquels une discrimination fondée sur la race ou l'origine ethnique est interdite.

45. Reste à examiner si le test d'intégration auquel est subordonné l'octroi du visa en vue du regroupement familial engendre une discrimination indirecte fondée sur l'origine ethnique, au sens de l'article 2 § 2 b) de la directive. Conformément à la définition de la directive, le système de tests d'intégration prévu aux Pays-Bas ou en France - apparemment neutre eu égard à l'origine ethnique des regroupants - est néanmoins susceptible d'entraîner un désavantage particulier pour les personnes de certaines origines (marocaine, algérienne ou turque). Ces tests ne résisteront à l'interdiction des discriminations indirectes que s'ils sont objectivement justifiés par un objectif légitime et que les moyens de réaliser cet objectif sont appropriés et nécessaires. Sans remettre en cause l'objectif explicite de favoriser l'intégration des migrants, il importe de vérifier si les mesures y sont proportionnées. Or, pour les Pays-Bas, *Human Rights Watch* a démontré de manière convaincante qu'au sein des citoyens néerlandais regroupants, ces tests d'intégration imposés à l'étranger aux membres de leur famille auraient un impact disproportionné sur les personnes d'origine turque ou marocaine. D'abord, l'imposition de ces tests représente pour ces citoyens d'origine turque ou marocaine un fardeau financier important alors qu'il y a un taux de chômage élevé au sein de cette population et des revenus en moyenne plus bas.[130] Ensuite, des chiffres prouvent que l'introduction de ce test a engendré en pratique une baisse significative des demandes de regroupement familial et, en particulier, celles concernant des ressortissants de Turquie ou du Maroc. Or, il semble attesté également que les ressortissants de ces origines soient plus enclins à se marier avec des ressortissants de leur communauté d'origine. Ces éléments devraient permettre de conclure à une discrimination indirecte car ces tests à l'étranger - apparemment neutres au regard de l'origine ethnique des regroupants en ce qu'ils visent tous les citoyens néerlandais - affectent en pratique les ressortissants d'origine turque et marocaine de manière disproportionnée eu égard à l'objectif d'intégration poursuivi.[131]

46. Même si cela dépasse le cadre de cette étude, l'on relèvera enfin qu'une analyse plus large relative au caractère potentiellement indirectement discriminatoire de ces tests au regard de la religion, de l'âge, du sexe ou de l'origine sociale des personnes visées (regroupants ou membres de la famille) mériterait d'être effectuée, notamment au vu de certaines conclusions résultant de l'analyse d'impact de ces mesures.[132]

Si l'on veut prendre au sérieux les engagements politiques de l'Union européenne qui, depuis le Sommet européen de Tampere, souligne l'importance de favoriser l'intégration des ressortissants de pays tiers, l'interdiction des discriminations fondées sur la nationalité devrait redevenir un préalable à une intégration réussie plutôt qu'une 'récompense', une fois l'intégration réalisée et prouvée.

130 *Human Rights Watch*, 'The Netherlands: Discrimination in the Name of Integration. Migrants' Rights under the Integration Abroad Act', *op. cit.*, p. 29 ff.

131 Pour un raisonnement en ce sens, voir aussi: K. de Vries, *Nationality and Racial discrimination under the Act on Integration Abroad*, Paper presented during the Seminar 'Migration Law and Human Rights', Bergen aan Zee, 21-22 janvier 2010.

132 Voir Rapport INTEC: 'Integration and Naturalisation Tests, the New Way to Citizenship', *op. cit.*

Dans cette optique, face à la montée en puissance des mesures, conditions ou programmes d'intégration obligatoires, adoptés par les États Membres de l'Union, comme autant d'obstacles parsemant le 'parcours du combattant' du ressortissant de pays tiers souhaitant s'intégrer dans la société d'accueil, le principe général de droit de l'UE d'interdiction des discriminations fondées sur la nationalité, voire sur la race ou l'origine ethnique, peut s'avérer un outil utile. Il ressort en effet clairement du droit international des droits de l'homme, qui lie l'Union européenne, que les différences de traitement fondées sur la nationalité quelles qu'elles soient (entre nationaux et étrangers, entre citoyens UE et ressortissants de pays tiers ou entre ressortissants de pays tiers entre eux) ne sont admissibles qu'à condition de poursuivre un objectif légitime et d'être nécessaires, justifiées et proportionnées à l'aune de cet objectif. Si des inconnues subsistent quant au niveau de contrôle à appliquer, notamment dans le domaine migratoire, il n'en demeure pas moins que le caractère suspect des différences de traitement exclusivement fondées sur la nationalité s'affirme de plus en plus.

Ce principe général de droit de l'UE d'interdiction des discriminations vient directement encadrer les instruments et politiques mis en place par l'UE en matière d'intégration. A cet égard, l'on a montré que certaines des exceptions ou limites au champ d'application de l'égalité de traitement, inscrites dans la directive 2003/109 relative au statut des ressortissants de pays tiers résidents de longue durée, pourraient s'avérer contraire à cette interdiction de discrimination. Il incombe aux juridictions nationales d'interroger la Cour de justice, par voie préjudicielle, afin qu'elle puisse, le cas échéant, se prononcer sur l'invalidité de ces exceptions.

Pour ce qui est des mesures ou conditions d'intégration adoptées par certains États Membres, dans le cadre du regroupement familial, une analyse systématique des différences de traitement fondées sur la nationalité, la race ou l'origine ethnique résultant des politiques mises en place notamment en France et aux Pays-Bas a mis en lumière de nombreuses discriminations qui sont déjà, pour certaines, dénoncées devant les juridictions nationales et pourraient l'être, le cas échéant, également devant la Cour de justice par voie préjudicielle.

Il va de soi que le recours au principe général de droit à l'interdiction des discriminations fondées sur la nationalité ne constitue pas la panacée ou le remède miracle face aux questions extrêmement complexes que soulève l'intégration des étrangers. Il n'en est pas moins utile afin d'interroger les politiques de l'UE et des États Membres en la matière, de les confronter aux exigences en matière de droits fondamentaux et de les contraindre à afficher plus clairement leurs objectifs et à garantir plus de cohérence par rapport à ceux-ci.

LES PRINCIPES DE BASE COMMUNS: LE CADRE DE LA POLITIQUE D'INTÉGRATION DE L'UNION EUROPÉENNE

*Mariona Illamola Dausà**

Les Principes de Base Communs (PBC) de la politique d'intégration des immigrants dans l'Union européenne ont toujours été cités comme la base, le cadre de la politique ou de la stratégie européenne d'intégration. Leur finalité est de faciliter le dialogue entre les gouvernements, les institutions participantes et l'Union, en tenant compte du fait que chaque pays va définir la politique d'intégration qu'il souhaite. On peut dire que les PBC doivent déterminer la feuille de route de la politique d'intégration de l'UE. L'objectif du présent article est de montrer pourquoi ils sont considérés comme fondamentaux. Pour y arriver, nous allons parler de leur origine et de leur contenu. Ensuite, nous verrons leurs implications et comment certains documents et actions de l'UE y font référence ou en tiennent compte et jusqu'à quel point ces PBC les influencent. Cette influence est en effet importante car malgré leur caractère non contraignant, les PBC développent une méthode spécifique de coordination des politiques nationales. Finalement, nous allons prendre l'exemple de l'Espagne pour montrer comment un État membre peut prendre en considération les PBC dans sa propre législation.

1. L'origine des Principes de Base Communs

Le débat tenu au niveau de l'UE sur les exigences en matière d'intégration reflète l'importance politique que les États membres accordent à une intégration réussie des ressortissants de pays tiers. L'un des grands thèmes de discussion à cet égard concerne la nature des programmes d'intégration, le type de mesures d'intégration à prévoir et le caractère obligatoire ou pas de ces mesures. Comme le montrent ces discussions, les problèmes auxquels les États membres doivent faire face et la manière dont ils s'efforcent d'y répondre présentent un grand nombre de similitudes. Dans ce contexte et suite aux conclusions de Tampere en matière d'intégration, la Commission a présenté en 2003 la *Communication sur l'immigration, l'intégration et l'emploi,*[1] laquelle signale que la contribution de l'immigration au développement économique peut se faire uniquement si les immigrants sont parfaitement intégrés. Cette communication présente différents aspects qu'il convient de préciser. Le premier considère l'intégration comme un processus à double sens, qui se base sur les

* Je remercie Yves Pascouau pour ses commentaires au cours de l'élaboration du présent travail et Florence Detry pour la révision linguistique réalisée. Cet article se fait avec le support du projet I+D 'La integración de los inmigrantes' DER 2008-00126/JURI, et du groupe de recherche *ERJAIDI-UE,* 2009 SGR 236. Une version en espagnol a été publiée dans la *Revista de Derecho Comunitario Europeo*, enero-abril 2011.

1 COM 2003/336, Communication de la Commission du 3 juin 2003 au Conseil, au Parlement européen, au Comité économique et social européen et au Comité des régions sur l'immigration, l'intégration et l'emploi.

droits et les obligations réciproques de l'immigrant et de la société d'accueil. Le deuxième concerne le caractère holistique de l'intégration pour les immigrants établis et ceux à venir, puisqu'il ne faut pas tenir compte uniquement des aspects économiques et sociaux, mais aussi des questions liés à la diversité culturelle et religieuse, à la citoyenneté, à la participation et aux droits politiques. Le troisième concerne la relation entre intégration, immigration et politiques d'emploi. De même, la Commission propose de développer la coopération et l'échange d'informations dans le cadre du Groupe des Points de Contacts Nationaux sur l'Intégration, et ce en vue de renforcer la coordination des politiques nationales. Ce processus de coopération devra se développer en parfaite complémentarité et synergie avec les autres politiques de l'UE, en particulier les politiques de cohésion et d'inclusion sociales, la politique de lutte contre la discrimination et la stratégie européenne pour l'emploi. Le Parlement européen a accueilli de façon positive cette Communication et a signalé que c'est la première fois qu'un examen sur les trois questions vitales et interconnectées (gestion de l'immigration, nécessité de collaboration avec les pays d'origine et amélioration de l'intégration) a été présenté.

Dans les conclusions du Conseil européen de Thessalonique, daté du mois de juin 2003, les Chefs d'État et de Gouvernement des États membres ont considéré que:

> Si les États membres demeurent responsables au premier chef de l'élaboration et de la mise en application de telles politiques [les politiques d'intégration], celles-ci devraient être élaborées dans un cadre cohérent au niveau de l'Union européenne, en tenant compte de la diversité juridique, politique, économique, sociale et culturelle des États membres. Afin de stimuler la mise au point d'un tel cadre, il conviendrait d'envisager la définition de principes de base communs.'

Plus tard, lors de sa réunion du mois de novembre 2004, le Conseil européen a adopté le Programme de La Haye qui devait avancer et faire face aux nouveaux défis apparus après le Programme de Tampere. Le Programme aborde tous les aspects des politiques relatives à l'espace de liberté, sécurité et justice, y compris l'intégration. A cet égard, l'Union considère que la responsabilité première dans l'élaboration et la mise en œuvre de la politique d'intégration appartient dès lors à chaque État membre plutôt qu'à l'Union dans son ensemble, parce que cette matière concerne en fait tous les aspects de la vie. Ces politiques différeront alors sensiblement d'un État membre à l'autre en fonction des besoins spécifiques de la société d'accueil, étant donné que l'immigration varie d'un pays à l'autre. En même temps, il est évident que tous les États membres de l'Union ont intérêt à ce que chacun d'eux applique des stratégies d'intégration qui soient efficaces, puisque ce qui bénéficie à l'un a des répercussions positives pour les autres.

C'est pourquoi, le Conseil européen a conclu qu'il fallait élaborer une série de principes de base communs sur l'intégration au niveau de l'UE, lesquels devraient mettre en rapport toutes les politiques nationales dans cette matière et servir comme base commune pour un cadre européen cohérent d'intégration. Il a considéré qu'il fallait mettre au point une politique globale et pluridimensionnelle sur l'intégration des ressortissants des pays tiers en séjour régulier.

Dans leurs conclusions, les Chefs d'État et de Gouvernement ont invité la Commission à présenter un rapport annuel sur l'intégration, tout en soulignant l'importance de l'échange d'informations grâce aux Points de Contacts Nationaux sur l'Intégration (PCNI) qui permettent de renforcer la coordination des politiques au niveau national et européen.

Ce réseau de Points de Contacts Nationaux a pour objectif de créer un forum visant à favoriser l'échange d'informations entre les États membres de l'Union afin de trouver les solutions les plus efficaces pour l'intégration des immigrants. Il s'agit, en même temps, d'une plate-forme permettant à chaque État d'être informé sur les structures, les politiques, les projets et les recherches menés en matière d'intégration par tous les autres États, et visant donc aussi à faciliter le partage d'informations et une certaine coordination dans ce domaine.

En adoptant le Programme de La Haye, l'Union a montré son engagement politique dans la coopération en matière d'intégration, ce qui ouvre la porte au développement d'une politique au niveau de l'Union.[2] Il faut tenir compte du fait que l'article 63 TCE prévoyait uniquement la compétence de la Communauté dans le développement d'une politique d'immigration et d'asile, mais passait sous silence la question de l'intégration.[3] Cette situation a changé avec l'entrée en vigueur du traité de Lisbonne. L'article 79 du traité indique que l'Union peut adopter des mesures en matière d'intégration. Seulement, le traité précise que l'Union ne peut adopter des mesures ayant pour effet d'harmoniser les législations nationales. En d'autres termes, les mesures ne peuvent être contraignantes, ce qui explique comme nous le verrons au pont 5 du présent article le choix des instruments utilisés au niveau de l'Union pour traiter les aspects relatifs à l'intégration des ressortissants de pays tiers.

En réponse au mandat du Conseil européen, le Conseil JAI de novembre 2004 a défini les Principes de Base Communs et a souligné que l'intégration est une responsabilité primordiale des États membres plutôt que de l'Union conjointement. En ce sens, le Conseil a souligné que le développement des PBC est essentiel pour avoir des accords sur objectifs communs et aussi parce qu'il y a différents situations nationales. Le Conseil de l'Union a considéré qu'un

> 'aspect déterminant de la gestion des migrations est l'intégration réussie des immigrants en séjour régulier et de leurs descendants. Or, la politique d'immigration peut contribuer au succès de la politique d'intégration. Il est essentiel pour les États membres de maintenir et de développer des sociétés dans lesquelles les nouveaux arrivants se sentent accueillis, qui se caractérisent par un esprit de compréhension et d'acceptation mutuelles et dans lesquelles tous les résidents – nouveaux comme anciens – ont des perspectives claires.'[4]

2. Le Contenu des Principes de Base Communs

Le Programme de La Haye précise que toute initiative future de l'Union s'inscrira dans un cadre fondé sur les PBC, ainsi que sur des objectifs et des outils d'évaluation clairs. Les ministres, au cours de la réunion du Conseil JAI de novembre 2004, ont adopté les onze

---

2 Pour une vision globale de l'origine et du développement de la politique d'intégration de l'UE, voir H. Urth, 'Building a Momentum for the Integration of Third-country Nationals in the European Union', *European Journal of Migration and Law*, 2005, no. 7, p. 163-180.

3 Pour une vision plus approfondie voir P. Lópex Pich, 'La política de Integración de la Unión Europea', *Revista Migraciones*, vol. 22, décembre 2007, p. 221-256.

4 2618ème Session du Conseil 'Justice et affaires intérieures', Bruxelles, le 19 novembre 2004.

Principes de Base Communs. Les explications qui les accompagnent prétendent proposer des orientations indicatives, non exhaustives, devant être étoffées dans l'avenir.

Le contenu des onze PBC est le suivant:

1. *L'intégration est un processus dynamique à double sens d'acceptation mutuelle de la part de tous les immigrants et résidents des États membres*. Il faut que toutes les personnes soient impliquées, tant les immigrants que la société d'accueil, et aient conscience de leurs droits et responsabilités mutuels. Ce principe met en avant le caractère volontariste des politiques d'intégration et génère des droits et des devoirs pour le migrant, ainsi que la nécessité d'un véritable effort de la part de la société d'accueil.
2. *L'intégration implique le respect des valeurs fondamentales de l'Union européenne*. Les valeurs de l'Union sont communes à tous les États membres. Les États membres ont la responsabilité de veiller activement à ce que tous les résidents, comprennent et respectent tout l'éventail des valeurs, des droits, des responsabilités et des privilèges mis en place par les lois de l'UE et des États membres. Toute vue ou opinion qui n'est pas compatible avec ces valeurs fondamentales est susceptible d'entraver la bonne intégration des immigrants dans la société d'accueil et de nuire à la société dans son ensemble.
3. *L'emploi est une composante-clé du processus d'intégration et il est essentiel pour assurer la participation des immigrants, pour favoriser la contribution qu'ils apportent à la société d'accueil et pour rendre cette contribution visible*. Il est nécessaire d'établir des mesures visant à favoriser la reconnaissance des qualifications et la formation, à faciliter l'accès à l'emploi et à lutter contre les discriminations fondées sur l'origine ethnique. Ces actions maintiennent une relation directe avec la Stratégie de Lisbonne et le Processus européen d'inclusion sociale.[5]
4. *Une connaissance de base de la langue, de l'histoire et des institutions de la société d'accueil est un élément indispensable de l'intégration*. Il est essentiel de donner aux immigrants la possibilité d'acquérir cette connaissance par la mise en œuvre de différents programmes permettant de bien réussir l'intégration. Le développement de programmes de formation de base dans plusieurs Etats membres témoigne de l'importance croissante accordée à cet aspect. En même temps, et dans la mesure où l'intégration est un processus à double sens d'acceptation mutuelle il devrait y avoir un respect total de la langue et de la culture des immigrants et de leur descendance.
5. *Il est crucial de consentir des efforts dans le domaine de l'enseignement afin de permettre aux immigrants, notamment à leurs descendants, de mieux réussir et de participer plus activement à la société*. L'enseignement facilite l'éducation, la formation, et l'aptitude à l'emploi. Il favorise également la transmission de connaissances relatives au rôle et au fonctionnement des institutions et des règles de la société, ainsi que la transmission des normes et des valeurs fondamentales qui assurent l'organisation de cette dernière. A ce titre, la lutte contre la sous-performance et le décrochage scolaires, et toutes les formes de délinquance juvénile est prioritaire.
6. *La possibilité pour les immigrants d'avoir accès aux institutions, ainsi qu'aux biens et services publics et privés, sur un pied d'égalité avec les citoyens nationaux et d'une manière non discriminatoire, est un fondement essentiel d'une meilleure intégration*. Le droit de l'UE interdit toute

5 La Stratégie de Lisbonne considère qu'un aspect important pour développer l'économie et le marché de travail sont les actions liées à l'inclusion des collectifs en risque d'exclusion sociale parmi lesquels il y a les immigrants. Ces mesures de support aux immigrants montrent l'importante influence du travail dans l'intégration.

discrimination sur base de l'origine raciale ou ethnique dans les domaines de l'emploi, de l'enseignement, de la sécurité sociale, des soins de santé, de l'accès aux biens et aux services et du logement. Un traitement sans discrimination peut permettre une participation pleine des immigrants dans la société d'accueil. Il faut par ailleurs éviter toute forme de marginalisation. L'existence de dispositions claires et bénéfices pour les personnes qui les respectent facilite unes politiques d'intégration de qualité.

7. *Les échanges fréquents entre immigrants et citoyens des États membres sont un mécanisme fondamental de l'intégration*. Les relations entre les personnes se déroulent principalement au niveau local. L'amélioration des conditions de vie en milieu urbain favorise les échanges qui peuvent aussi être renforcés par la présence de forums, d'activités et d'espaces communs, etc.
8. *La pratique de cultures et de religions différentes est garantie par la Charte des droits fondamentaux et doit être sauvegardée, à moins qu'elle soit contraire à d'autres droits européens inaliénables ou à la loi nationale*. Le respect des nouvelles religions et cultures introduites par les immigrants peut faciliter leur transition vers la société d'accueil et au même temps l'enrichir. Mais les États doivent garantir que les différentes pratiques culturelles et religieuses n'empêchent l'exercice d'autres droits tels que la participation dans la société d'accueil. Le dialogue interculturel et interreligieux sont des exemples pour bien réussir.
9. *La participation des immigrants au processus démocratique et à la formulation des politiques et mesures d'intégration, en particulier au niveau local, favorise leur intégration*. Les immigrants doivent être d'avantage impliqués dans tous les aspects de la vie démocratique. Donner la parole aux immigrants lors de la formulation des politiques qui les concernent directement peut susciter une compréhension mutuelle et favoriser leur sentiment d'appartenance. Dans la mesure du possible, les immigrants pourraient être associés par le biais des élections, du droit de vote, de l'adhésion à des partis politiques, de la participation civique dans des organismes consultatifs ou de la participation sociale.
10. *L'inclusion des politiques et des mesures en matière d'intégration dans tous les domaines politiques, à tous les niveaux de pouvoir et dans les services publics pertinents est un élément important pour la formation et la mise en œuvre des politiques publiques*. L'intégration doit être abordée non seulement d'une façon transversale au sein de toutes les politiques, mais aussi par l'adoption de politiques spécifiques la concernant. La coopération, la coordination et la communication entre tous les acteurs s'avèrent également nécessaires. Au même temps il faut éviter qu'une demande élevée des services publics à cause de l'immigration puisse comporter une baisse de leur qualité.
11. *La définition d'objectifs, d'indicateurs et de mécanismes d'évaluation clairs est indispensable si l'on veut adapter la politique, évaluer les progrès accomplis en matière d'intégration et rendre plus efficaces les échanges d'informations*. Il est important d'évaluer les résultats des actions engagées afin d'analyser les progrès réalisés et de tirer les enseignements des expériences vécues. De cette façon, on pourra éviter de répéter les erreurs commises dans le passé en modifiant les politiques nationales en conséquence et en manifestant de l'intérêt pour les efforts réalisés par les uns et les autres.

On voit que la stratégie d'intégration de l'Union européenne en général et les PBC, en particulier, répondent à une conception holistique qui ne tient pas seulement compte des aspects économiques et sociaux de l'intégration, mais également des aspects relatifs à la diversité culturelle et religieuse, à la citoyenneté, aux droits politiques ainsi qu'à la participation à la vie publique. La réussite de politiques et pratiques en matière d'intégration empêchant l'isolement de certains groupes est un facteur renforçant le respect des valeurs européennes et nationales communs. Pour atteindre ces objectifs, la participation et la collaboration de tous les niveaux de l'administration sont nécessaires.

3. Les Implications des Principes de Base Communs

Les PBC doivent permettre aux États d'évaluer les actions de leurs administrations nationales et également de vérifier si les différents organismes qui ne participent pas à l'intégration pourraient contribuer positivement à cet objectif. Chaque État détermine les mesures concrètes qu'il veut appliquer en fonction des nécessités nationales, tout en bénéficiant à l'intérêt commun de l'Union.[6]

Il s'agit aussi de principes généraux qui peuvent s'avérer utiles tant aux États membres habitués à faire face à une immigration quantitativement importante, États ayant donc un modèle ou un projet politique bien défini, qu'à ceux qui sont devenus plus récemment des pays d'immigration et qui doivent, par conséquent, définir une politique d'intégration.

En premier lieu, les PBC visent à aider les États dans la formulation de leurs politiques d'intégration, en leur procurant des orientations non contraignantes et simples. Ces orientations peuvent servir de base à l'Union pour chercher la manière de développer au mieux ses instruments en matière d'intégration. En deuxième lieu, ces PBC doivent permettre aux États de trouver plus facilement la façon dont les autorités de l'Union ainsi que les autorités nationales, régionales et locales peuvent participer dans le développement et la mise en œuvre des politiques d'intégration. Enfin, et en troisième lieu, les PCB doivent aider le Conseil à développer, sur le plan des politiques européennes, une réflexion portant sur les efforts réalisés au niveau national et local.[7]

En principe, il s'agit de fournir des orientations générales et communes à tous, mais en tenant en compte du fait que la situation dans chaque pays est différente. Le Conseil a dit clairement lors de sa séance de novembre 2004 que *'Les mesures d'intégration concrètes qu'une société choisit de mettre en œuvre doivent être déterminées par chaque État membre.'* On trouve, par exemple, une application pratique de cette idée dans la directive relative au statut de résident de longue durée,[8] qui prévoit la possibilité pour chaque État de demander l'accomplissement de mesures ou de conditions d'intégration pour que ce statut juridique soit reconnu.[9]

6 G. Oude Engberink 'Les ciutats i la integració dels immigrants', in: *II Seminari Immigració i Europa. Cinc anys després de Tampere,* Barcelona: Fundació CIDOB 2005, pp. 107-119.

7 S. Carrera & A. Wiesbrock, *Civic Integration of Third-Country Nationals. Nationalism versus Europeanisation in the Common EU Immigration Policy*, CEPS Liberty and Security in Europe, October 2009.

8 Directive 2003/109/CE du Conseil du 25 novembre 2003 relative au statut des ressortissants de pays tiers résidents de longue durée, JO L 16 du 23.1.2004.

9 S. Carrera, *A Comparison of Integration Programmes in the EU. Trends and Weaknesses*, Challenge Papers no. 1, March 2006; M. Illamola Dausã, 'Medidas o condiciones de integración, España versus Holanda. ¿Un ejemplo a seguir?', in A. Piqueras, N. Jiménez & G. Soto (éds), *Mediterrània Migrant II. I Jornades MEDIMIGRA*, Castelló de la Plana: Universitat Jaume I Servei de Publicacions 2007, p. 339-360; M. Illamola Dausã, 'La Directiva 2003/109 relativa al estatuto jurídico de los residentes de larga duración y su transposición al ordenamiento español', ín F. Aldecoa Luzárraga, J.M. Sobrino Heredia, L.N. González Alonso, A. Pastor Palomar, J. Forner, M. Herranz Ballesteros & C. Pérez Bernárdez →

Le Programme de Stockholm,[10] programme qui suive celui de La Haye et qui fixe les orientations pour les années 2009-2014, soutient que l'espace de liberté, de sécurité et de justice doit être un espace unique de protection des droits fondamentaux. Le respect de la personne, de la dignité humaine et des droits énoncés dans la Charte constitue une valeur essentielle. Cette affirmation n'est pas directement une revendication de l'assimilationnisme, mais pose des limites aux diverses conceptions ou pratiques que l'on pourrait considérer contraires à certaines libertés. Le modèle assimilationniste se base sur la complète assimilation ou intégration de l'étranger aux valeurs nationales traditionnelles dominantes. Au contraire, le modèle multiculturaliste est favorable à la conservation de l'identité collective, à la façon de vivre de chaque groupe et aussi à la propre organisation juridico-privé. Ce modèle prévoit aussi le respect d'unes minimes normes de coexistence qui assurent l'ordre public. Un troisième modèle, le modèle exclusionniste, est caractérisé par une législation restrictive et rigide qui impose de remplir certaines conditions pour avoir accès à certains droits.

Si l'Union européenne, dans sa conception même, se base bien sur le modèle multiculturel, modèle impliquant le respect des diversités culturelles de ses États membres, elle pourrait peut-être le suivre également pour sa politique d'intégration et l'appliquer aux ressortissants des pays tiers. Mais selon les propos de Carrera, *What is the dividing line between an efficient integration policy and the respect of cultural, ethnic and religious diversity?*[11]

De toute façon, aucun pays ne suit un modèle unique et les attitudes des gouvernements et des sociétés changent en fonction des circonstances. Cela s'est passé après les années 90 suite aux conflits dans différentes villes comprenant un très grand nombre d'immigrants. Le résultat a été l'introduction dans différents États membres d'une solution permettant de garantir un minimum de coexistence sur la base de la connaissance de la langue et des institutions du pays de résidence. En ce sens, les PBC justifient l'existence de programmes nationaux d'orientation civique. C'est spécialement le cas du PBC 4 qui défend la connaissance de la langue, de l'histoire et des institutions de la société d'accueil. Mais en même temps, comme il a déjà était signalé, ce PBC 4 proclame qu'un élément majeur de la politique d'intégration devrait également reposer sur le respect total de la langue et de la culture des immigrants et de leur descendance. Suivant cette idée, l'Espagne avait proposé d'inclure une référence expresse pour appuyer le maintien des langues et cultures d'origine, mais cela n'a pas été très bien accueilli par les autres États membres[12]. Bien que cette idée semble sans doute lier l'Espagne au modèle multiculturel, basé sur le respect et la protection des diversités culturelles, on ne voit pas actuellement dans les pratiques du pays cette conception reflétée. Et c'est le cas également du PBC 2, puisqu'il oblige tout résident de l'Union à adhérer et à s'adapter aux valeurs essentielles de l'UE et aux lois de ses États membres, tout en demandant aux États d'assurer que les résidents

---

(coords.), *50º Aniversario de la firma de los Tratados de Roma. Perspectivas desde la Asociación Española de Profesores de Derecho Internacional y Relaciones Internacionales,* Madrid: Marcial Pons 2008, p. 1579-1593.

10 Le programme de Stockholm — Une Europe ouverte et sûre qui sert et protège les citoyens, *JO C 115* du 4 mai 2010.

11 S. Carrera, *'Integration' as a Process of Inclusion for Migrants? The Case of Long-Term Residents in the EU*, CEPS Working Document, no. 219, March 2005.

12 P. Lópex Pich, 'La política de Integración de la Unión Europea', *op. cit.*

comprennent, respectent et profitent, dans des conditions d'égalité, des valeurs, des droits, des responsabilités et des privilèges de l'Union et des États.[13]

Le Comité Économique et Social considère que les PBC

> 'offrent une analyse cohérente du concept européen d'intégration des ressortissants de pays tiers sur la base de l'objectif "d'intégration civique" qui, comme l'énonce le Comité se définit par «la mise sur un pied d'égalité des immigrants avec le reste de la population, en termes de droits et de devoirs, ainsi que d'accès aux biens, aux services et aux canaux de participation citoyenne, dans des conditions d'égalité des chances et de traitement'.[14]

Il soutient également que la création du Forum européen sur l'intégration[15] facilitera l'élaboration de politiques nationales inspirées par les PBC, favorisera la rénovation de la politique de l'UE en matière d'intégration des immigrants, et aidera à donner une certaine cohérence aux politiques et instruments de l'Union.

4. Les Principes de Base Communs dans les Documents et Actions de l'UE

La Commission a mentionné l'intégration comme une des dix priorités du Plan d'action du Programme de La Haye. Cette priorité doit favoriser et permettre profiter de l'impact positif de l'immigration dans notre société et dans notre économie. La Commission a précisé qu'il était nécessaire d'établir un cadre européen pour l'intégration qui respecte les valeurs de l'Union et la non-discrimination en se basant sur les Principes de Base Communs.[16] Ces derniers représentent donc un premier pas décisif vers l'établissement progressif d'un cadre européen en matière d'intégration. Ils constituent en fait une feuille de route à suivre dans la réflexion relative au type d'intégration qui doit être réalisé au niveau européen. Dans ce sens le Conseil, dans ses conclusions et avant d'expliquer les PBC, souligne bien, comme a déjà été indiqué, la prédominance de la compétence nationale dans le développement et la mise en application de la politique d'intégration. Toutefois, le Conseil considère essentiel le développement des PBC sans en donner une justification convaincante. Les explications faites sont indicatives et pas exhaustives, elles uniquement veulent donner des orientations pour arriver au PBC. Il reconnaît tout de même qu'il est de l'intérêt commun de tous les États membres que chacun d'eux puisse disposer d'une stratégie efficace d'inté-

13 Cette idée se trouvait dans les Conclusions du Conseil Européen de Tampere du 15-16 octobre 1999, avec la prévision de la possibilité d'acquisition de la nationalité de l'État d'accueil.

14 Avis du Comité économique et social européen sur le thème 'Éléments pour la structure, l'organisation et le fonctionnement d'une plate-forme destinée à une plus grande participation de la société civile à la promotion de politiques d'intégration de ressortissants de pays tiers au niveau de l'UE', JOUE du 3 février 2009, C 27 (2.4).

15 Le Forum européen sur l'intégration, crée en 2009, donne aux représentants de la société civile l'occasion d'exprimer leurs points de vue sur les questions d'intégration des migrants et de débattre les enjeux actuels et des priorités futures avec les représentants des institutions européennes.

16 COM (2005) 184, Communication de la Commission au Conseil et au Parlement européen - Le programme de La Haye: Dix priorités pour les cinq prochaines années. Un partenariat pour le renouveau européen dans le domaine de la liberté, de la sécurité et de la justice.

gration.[17] Pour ces raisons, dès l'adoption des PBC, on peut en trouver des références dans les différents documents et actions de l'Union.

4.1 *Le Programme Commun pour l'Intégration*

Le Programme Commun pour l'Intégration de 2005 constitue le cadre relatif à l'intégration des ressortissants de pays tiers dans l'Union européenne.[18] Il a pour objectif principal le renforcement de l'application des Principes de Base Communs. Les piliers de ce cadre revêtent la forme, d'une part, de propositions de mesures concrètes visant à mettre en pratique chacun des Principes de Base Communs, et, d'autre part, d'une série de mécanismes de soutien de l'UE. En tenant compte de la situation et des actions existantes, le programme élaboré par la Commission formule de nouvelles suggestions d'actions au niveau national et de l'UE, toutes devant être cohérentes entre elles.

Les États membres ont pour tâche de fixer des priorités et de choisir les actions ainsi que la manière dont elles seront réalisées conformément à leurs situations et traditions nationales. Le texte signale en fait différentes actions possibles, mais plutôt sous forme de guide pour la conception de programmes et de politiques.

Les actions proposées au niveau européen vont élargir et développer des activités dont l'efficacité et l'utilité ont déjà pu être démontrées. Ces actions doivent être considérées comme des composantes importantes des politiques d'intégration nationales et de l'UE. Aussi, le vocabulaire utilisé pour définir les actions proposées est le suivant: renforcer, élaborer, améliorer, promouvoir, coopérer, mettre l'accent, impliquer, informer, envisager, aider, soutenir, organiser, proposer, développer, tenir compte...

Étant donné que le domaine n'est pas régi par des règles juridiquement contraignantes, la Commission souligne l'utilité des échanges d'informations et de bonnes pratiques entre les différents acteurs qui travaillent pour l'intégration. Cette interaction a permis de mettre en lumière un certain nombre d'objectifs et de politiques qui sont similaires dans toute l'Union et qui sont bien reflétés par les PBC. Mais les PBC montrent également que, malgré les efforts réalisés tant par les États membres que par l'Union, les politiques d'intégration doivent encore être renforcées.

De même, la Commission insiste sur la transversalité de la politique d'intégration qui doit être prise en compte dans toutes les politiques. Il s'agit d'un élément essentiel souligné par le PBC 10. Ainsi, la Commission propose certains objectifs pour les actions nationales, tels que le renforcement de la coordination pour la mise en œuvre de la stratégie d'intégration nationale dans les différents niveaux de l'administration ou le soutien de la coopération, de la coordination et de la communication entre parties intéressées. Elle détermine également les objectifs que les actions adoptées par l'Union devront avoir: il s'agit de la consolidation du réseau des Points de Contacts Nationaux sur l'Intégration créés en mars 2003, du développement de la coopération entre institutions et services responsables des questions d'intégration et enfin de l'incorporation des objectifs d'intégration dans les pro-

17 S. Carrera Núñez, *In Search of the Perfect Citizen? The Intersection between Integration, Immigration and Nationality in the EU*, Nijmegen: Wolf Legal Publishers 2008, proof copy, p. 49.

18 COM/2005/0389, Communication de la Commission au Conseil, au Parlement européen, au Comité économique et social européen et au Comité des régions, du 1er septembre 2005, - Programme commun pour l'intégration - Cadre relatif à l'intégration des ressortissants de pays tiers dans l'Union européenne.

grammes généraux pertinents au niveau européen. Les PCNI facilitent le contact entre les représentants des ministres nationaux chargés d'intégration. Ils ont par ailleurs une très grande influence sur le développement du cadre et sur la définition des stratégies. Ces PCNI ont en effet pris part non seulement à l'élaboration des Rapports Annuels sur l'Immigration et l'Intégration de la Commission et à la rénovation de leur conception et méthodologie. Ils ont également pris part à l'élaboration des Manuels sur l'Intégration. Ils possèdent un certain niveau d'indépendance par rapport aux représentants des États formant les groupes de travail du Conseil. Il s'agit d'un forum prenant place à un niveau intermédiaire des institutions européennes et des États membres.

Selon la pratique du PBC 10, le texte suggère aux États différentes idées pour l'établissement de leurs objectifs: renforcer la capacité de collecte, d'analyse et de diffusion des statistiques, ou encore évaluer les procédures d'admission et les programmes d'accueil. Le texte précise également les objectifs concernant les actions de l'Union: se doter d'outils statistiques et d'indicateurs communs; favoriser l'échange d'informations sur les outils nationaux d'évaluation et, le cas échéant, élaborer des critères européens d'apprentissage comparé; encourager une meilleure connaissance des processus d'intégration, y compris l'analyse de l'impact des composantes obligatoires des politiques d'intégration nationales; élargir, grâce à la recherche, la base de connaissances sur les politiques d'intégration et développer le réseau européen des migrations. Ces aspects ont été repris lors de la Conférence Ministérielle en Intégration qui a eu lieu à Saragosse au mois d'avril 2010.

Ce Programme Commun pour l'Intégration a reçu le soutien du Conseil, et la Commission elle-même reprend ses politiques et ses actions dans différents documents, comme par exemple le Plan de politique en matière de migration légale.[19]

De même, ce Programme Commun pour l'Intégration considère qu'il doit y avoir une approche cohérente de l'UE devant impliquer une coopération et un échange d'informations sur l'intégration. Allant dans ce sens, nous pouvons citer les Manuels d'intégration *(Handbook on Integration)*, ainsi que les actions préparatoires INTI et le Fonds pour l'intégration.

4.2 Les Manuels sur l'Intégration

Les Manuels sur l'intégration, à l'intention des décideurs politiques et des praticiens, ont été préparés en étroite collaboration avec les Points de Contacts Nationaux sur l'Intégration. Ils se basent sur différents séminaires techniques organisés par les États et dans lesquels différentes pratiques nationales sont présentées et discutées. Pour assurer un certain niveau d'uniformité, les séminaires sont organisés au moyen d'une structure commune et la Commission prend contact avec un expert indépendant pour l'aider à identifier les principes généraux et les recommandations, et pour l'aider à compiler les meilleures pratiques afin de les inclure dans le Manuel.

Les Manuels ont un rôle de guide dans les échanges d'informations et de meilleures pratiques, et permettent le développement et la promotion des initiatives politiques. Les trois éditions sont le résultat d'une étroite collaboration entre la Commission européenne,

19 COM/2005/0669 final, du 21 décembre 2005, Communication de la Commission - Programme d'action relatif à l'immigration légale.

les Points de Contacts Nationaux sur l'Intégration et le Migration Policy Group en tant que consultant indépendant.

La première édition de cet ouvrage, publiée en novembre 2004,[20] porte sur les programmes d'accueil destinés aux immigrants et aux personnes reconnues comme des réfugiés nouvellement arrivés, sur la participation civique et sur les indicateurs relatifs à l'intégration.

La seconde édition, qui a été publiée au mois de mai 2007,[21] est axée sur d'autres grands enjeux relevés dans les Principes de Base Communs comme le logement et les problèmes urbains, l'accès aux services sanitaires et sociaux, l'intégration dans le marché du travail, la prise en compte de l'égalité des chances et les structures d'intégration. Elle présente par ailleurs des analyses dûment fondées sur lesdits principes.

La troisième édition, publiée en avril 2010,[22] est une compilation de bonnes pratiques concernant les media, les plates-formes de dialogue, l'acquisition de la nationalité et de la citoyenneté active, la jeunesse, l'éducation, le marché du travail et le pouvoir des immigrants.

Les Manuels comprennent des conclusions au lieu de recommandations, ce qui leur confère un caractère juridiquement non contraignant proche des techniques de *soft law*. Leur contenu a été systématisé et mis en relation avec chacun des PBC au moyen d'un document élaboré par le Migration Policy Group. Ce document s'avère être très utile pour les agents qui sont directement impliqués dans la gestion de l'intégration à tous les niveaux.[23] Il a pour objectif de démontrer comment l'échange d'expériences et de bonnes pratiques se trouvant dans les trois Manuels peut servir de guide pour la mise en œuvre des PBC. Dans cette optique, il comprend pour chaque PBC un résumé de son explication officielle et la liste de ses conclusions les plus importantes. Dans le cas où une conclusion concernerait différents PBC, il la reprend dans la liste du PBC le plus significatif. Les conclusions montrent de quelle façon les différentes initiatives nationales peuvent favoriser et renforcer l'intégration des ressortissants des pays tiers.

4.3 Les Rapports Annuels sur l'Immigration et l'Intégration

Les rapports annuels sur l'immigration et l'intégration se fondent sur les réponses données par les États à un questionnaire préparé par la Commission, et analysent les mesures prises au niveau national et de l'Union en matière d'admission et d'intégration des ressortissants de pays tiers. Ils fournissent un aperçu de l'évolution des politiques et contribuent à l'évaluation et au renforcement des mesures d'intégration.

20 http://www.migpolgroup.com/publications_detail.php?id=6 (consulté le 15/10/2010).

21 http://www.migpolgroup.com/publications_detail.php?id=7 (consulté le 15/10/2010).

22 http://www.migpolgroup.com/publications_detail.php?id=268 (consulté le 15/10/2010).

23 *From principles to practice. The Common Basic Principles on Integration and the Handbook Conclusions,* Updated by Thomas Huddleston, MPG, April 2010. The original version of this issue paper was written by Jan Niessen and Mary-Anne Kate and published in June 2007. http://www.migpolgroup.com/publications_detail.php?id=13 (consulté le 15/10/2010).

Le premier Rapport Annuel sur l'Immigration et l'Intégration présenté au mois de juillet 2004[24] analyse les changements de l'immigration et explique les actions prises quant à l'admission et à l'intégration des immigrants au niveau européen et national.

Le deuxième Rapport Annuel sur l'Immigration et l'Intégration[25] signale que la plupart des pays ont adopté des programmes d'introduction, mais ont comme problème commun celui du financement. En ce qui concerne le financement, il serait intéressant que les États puissent considérer les dépenses liées aux politiques d'intégration comme de véritables investissements à long terme, qui leur procureront dans le futur des bénéfices économiques et sociaux. Le réseau des PCNI a proposé de concentrer les politiques d'intégration nationales autour des mêmes champs thématiques que ceux traités dans le second Manuel d'Intégration.[26] Cela a représenté une façon plus structurée de rapprocher les échanges d'informations, les bonnes pratiques ainsi que les politiques nationales, tant de la procédure plus coordonnée des PCNI que des manuels de bonnes pratiques et des rapports annuels.

Le troisième Rapport[27] considère que la plupart des concepts des politiques d'intégration des États membres ont été codifiés par les PBC et se retrouvent, avec quelques différences, dans les stratégies d'intégration. Dans ce rapport, la Commission a conclu que les États membres, en ce qui concerne le PBC 1, ont adopté diverses mesures, mais qu'il s'agit en fait d'un engagement de longue haleine qui demanderait des efforts supplémentaires. La promotion des valeurs de l'Union, présente dans le PBC 2, est considérée comme un élément important des nouvelles politiques et est surtout réalisée dans les programmes d'éducation civique. L'application du PBC 3, qui prévoit l'intégration des immigrants dans le marché du travail, reste un des défis majeurs; elle s'effectue avec des mesures destinées à renforcer la prévention du chômage grâce à l'éducation et à la formation, grâce à des systèmes plus efficaces de reconnaissance des qualifications, grâce à la lutte contre la discrimination sur le lieu de travail et à la promotion de l'emploi des femmes issues de l'immigration. Quant au PBC 4, la plupart des États membres considèrent qu'une connaissance de base de la langue de la société d'accueil est un élément essentiel pour l'intégration. C'est la raison pour laquelle, ils soutiennent le développement de cours de langue dans les programmes d'accueil. Pour encourager la formation et l'éducation liées au PBC 5, il existe des initiatives destinées à faciliter l'intégration scolaire. En ce qui concerne les PBC 6 et PBC 7, il s'agit de promouvoir la coopération entre les acteurs publics et la participation des entreprises à des débats sur l'intégration. Des mesures visant à encourager les échanges entre les immigrants et la société d'accueil commencent également à voir le jour. Le renforcement du dialogue interconfessionnel du PBC 8 apparaît comme offrant des réponses ponctuelles à situations spécifiques de l'actualité. La participation des immigrants au processus démocratique, tel que le propose le PBC 9, est de plus en plus perçue comme un aspect

24 COM/2004/508, Communication de la Commission du 16 juillet 2004 au Conseil, au Parlement européen, au Comité économique et social européen et au Comité des régions - Premier rapport annuel sur la migration et l'intégration.

25 Second Annual Report on Migration and Integration, Commission Staff Working Document, SEC (2006) 892.

26 Le second Manuel d'Intégration est axée sur le logement et les problèmes urbains, l'accès aux services sanitaires et sociaux, l'intégration dans le marché du travail, la prise en compte de l'égalité des chances et les structures d'intégration.

27 COM/2007/0512, Communication de la Commission du 11 septembre 2007 au Conseil, au Parlement européen, Comité économique et social européen et au Comité des régions - Troisième Rapport annuel sur la migration et l'intégration.

essentiel pour une intégration réussie. Le fait que l'intégration soit un aspect transversal a été renforcé en accord avec le PBC 10.

Ce troisième Rapport prévoit que la Commission réfléchisse à une refonte du rapport annuel sur la migration et l'intégration, afin d'en faire un instrument actualisé pour l'analyse comparative de l'évolution des politiques d'intégration.

Suivant cette orientation, en 2009 la Commission européenne a adopté la méthode de suivi pour le contrôle de la mise en œuvre du Pacte européen sur l'Immigration et l'Asile.[28] En le suivent, elle doit présenter, au niveau de l'UE et des États membres, un rapport annuel composé de deux parties D'une part, il comprend un bref rapport de synthèse à caractère politique qui met en évidence les principaux développements intervenus durant la période concernée, les évolutions les plus significatives qui sont envisagées et, finalement, toute recommandation formulée par la Commission. D'autre part, il comprend un rapport plus ample et plus détaillé, indiquant les principales actions menées et évolutions envisagées. Il s'agit de la méthode de suivi qui doit permettre au Conseil européen, lors de son débat annuel, de suivre, tant pour l'Union européenne que pour les États membres, la mise en œuvre des politiques d'immigration et d'asile. La Commission considère le lien entre l'immigration et l'intégration comme une question prioritaire pour l'Union.[29]

Pour faciliter la comparaison des informations, la Commission a adopté une structure commune à laquelle doivent s'adapter les contributions des États membres. Le premier point est destiné à l'immigration légale et à l'intégration. La Commission invite notamment les États membres à mettre en place, selon les procédures et avec les moyens qui leur paraîtront adaptés, des politiques ambitieuses pour favoriser l'intégration harmonieuse dans le pays d'accueil des migrants ayant l'intention de s'y installer durablement. Ces politiques doivent alors être mises en place conformément aux PBC. La Commission demande des informations non seulement sur les actions globales prises dans ce sens, mais aussi, plus concrètement, sur les différents aspects qui font partie des divers PCB, tels que: l'équilibre des droits des migrants et de leurs devoirs, la promotion de l'apprentissage de la langue et de l'accès à l'emploi, le respect des identités des États membres et de l'UE ainsi que de leurs valeurs fondamentales, et la lutte contre les discriminations. Finalement, elle demande à être informée au sujet des actions réalisées pour promouvoir les échanges d'informations concernant les bonnes pratiques mises en œuvre, et au sujet des mesures communautaires de soutien aux politiques nationales d'intégration, conformément aux PBC.

4.4 Déclarations Ministérielles

Le Programme de La Haye d'une partie souligne la nécessité d'une plus grande coordination des politiques d'intégration nationales et des initiatives de l'Union, et de l'autre précise que toute initiative de l'Union doit s'inscrire dans un cadre fondé sur les PBC. Dans cette perspective a été organisée la première réunion informelle des ministres en charge de l'intégration a Groningue le 9, 10 et 11 novembre 2004.

28 COM/2009/0266, Communication de la Commission du 10 juin 2009, au Conseil et au Parlement européen - Méthode de suivi pour le contrôle de la mise en œuvre du Pacte européen sur l'immigration et l'asile.

29 COM/2006/0735, Communication de la Commission du 30 novembre 2006 au Conseil et au Parlement européen - L'approche globale de la question des migrations un an après: vers une politique globale européenne en matière de migrations.

Pour donner un prolongement au débat politique lancé lors de la première conférence ministérielle, et après l'adoption des PBC, une nouvelle étape a été franchie avec la Conférence Ministérielle de Postdam le mois de mai de 2007. Cette conférence a contribué à engager une réflexion sur le dialogue interculturel et à promouvoir le renforcement des politiques d'intégration par la promotion de l'unité dans la diversité.

Étant donné l'application des politiques et des actions relatives aux PBC, ainsi que leur valorisation, les ministres ont souligné, lors de leur réunion à Vichy en novembre 2008,[30] la nécessité de promouvoir les PBC et de les approfondir, essentiellement dans aspects suivants: la promotion des valeurs fondamentales de l'Union, PBC 2; le parcours de l'intégration, PBC 4 et 6; l'accès à l'emploi et la promotion de la diversité dans l'emploi, PBC 3; l'intégration des femmes et l'éducation des enfants, PBC 5; le dialogue interculturel, PBC 7; et les principes de gouvernance des politiques d'intégration, PBC 10 et 11. Il s'agit de domaines d'action qui sont liés à la plupart des PBC, même si dans la déclaration, au moment de la définition de ces priorités ils ne sont pas mentionnés. Le dialogue interconfessionnel et la participation des immigrants dans la vie démocratique restent, quant à eux, en dehors de la déclaration. Les engagements acquis vont se faire dans le respect des spécificités et compétences de chaque pays.

Nous retrouvons la même tendance dans la déclaration finale approuvé par les représentants des gouvernements lors de la Conférence Ministérielle en matière d'Intégration tenue à Saragosse au mois d'avril 2010, dans laquelle les ministres *'conviennent de s'intéresser tout particulièrement aux aspects essentiels de l'intégration, moteur du développement et de la cohésion sociale, en intégrant de manière globale les questions d'intégration dans tous les domaines d'action concernés et en accordant une attention particulière aux questions évoquées'*.[31] Lesdites questions sont l'emploi et l'enseignement, PCB 3 et 5; la participation des citoyens et des immigrants en favorisant le dialogue interculturel, PCB 6, 7 et 9; et l'évaluation des politiques d'intégration, PCB 11. À ces principes, qui sont par la suite définis en actions plus concrètes, il faut ajouter la coordination institutionnelle, PCB 10. Dans son intervention lors de la Conférence, la Commissaire Malmström a affirmé que l'Union doit continuer à baser son travail sur les PBC parce qu'ils couvrent tous les aspects importants de l'intégration et privilégient l'interaction entre les migrants et les citoyens européens.

4.5 *Les Critères Européens d'Évaluation*

La mise en commun au niveau européen des informations concernant les instruments nationaux d'évaluation et l'élaboration des critères européens (indicateurs, critères d'évaluation des performances) est intéressante. Elle permet en effet de favoriser les comparaisons, cependant, dans cet échange d'informations, on doit tenir compte des différents stades dans lesquels se trouvent les États membres en ce qui concerne l'élaboration de leurs propres politiques et stratégies d'intégration et comparer les situations qui se trouvent dans le même niveau de développement.[32]

30 Conférence ministérielle européenne sur l'intégration, Vichy, les 3 et 4 novembre 2008.

31 Conseil de l'Union Européenne du 20 avril 2010, doc 877/10. Conférence Ministérielle Européenne sur l'Intégration, Saragosse, 15 et 16 avril 2010.

32 *Setting up a system of benchmarking to measure the success of integration policies in Europe*, European Parliament, Directorate general Internal policies of the Union, Civil Liberties, Justice and Home Affairs, janvier 2007, IP/C/LIBE/ST/2005-93, pp. 138-149.

Lors de la Conférence Ministérielle de Vichy de 2008 la Commission a signalé que les Modules Européens d'Intégration des Migrants (MEIM) pourraient servir à la construction pour la compréhension des stratégies d'intégration. La Conférence demandait alors aux États membres le développement d'informations et de matériels communs sur les valeurs européennes telles qu'elles sont définies par chaque État, en permettant également d'y inclure leurs propres valeurs.

La initiative multilatérale qui a donné lieu à la Recommandation *'Principles for Monitoring and Evaluation of Integration Policies'* signée à Berlin au mois de juin 2009 par l'Allemagne, la République Tchèque, la France, la Suède et l'Espagne comprend des recommandations pour le processus d'identification du noyau principal des indicateurs, considérés comme une base essentielle pour suivre les politiques d'intégration de chaque État membre de l'Union européenne et pour servir de complément à l'évaluation de leurs résultats.

Dans le même sens de cette Recommandation lors de la Conférence Ministérielle de Saragosse d'avril 2010, il a été proposé d'élaborer un projet visant à évaluer les politiques d'intégration au moyen d'indicateurs qui tiennent compte des contextes nationaux, de l'origine des migrants et des différentes politiques d'intégration et d'immigration des États membres. Les indicateurs vont se baser en principe sur les statistiques officielles et sur des données quantitatives, puis sur des données subjectives et qualitatives qui sont le résultat d'études. Il y a un nombre limité de domaines importants pour l'intégration qui sont identifiés comme prioritaires et qui sont clés pour les PBC (emploi, éducation, inclusion sociale et participation civique).

Finalement, suivant les indications du PBC 11, les critères européens pour évaluer les résultats des actions et tirer des enseignements ont été développés au moyen de modules et d'indicateurs.[33] D'un côté les modules vont faciliter un processus d'apprentissage commun, systématiser les pratiques existantes et profiter des standards européens qui font partie des PBC et du cadre européen. Ils peuvent être utilisés pour désigner les stratégies d'intégration entre les États membres à tous les niveaux.

De l'autre côté, les indicateurs vont faciliter l'évaluation des stratégies et mesures d'intégration. Le déjà cité premier Manuel d'Intégration considère que les indicateurs peuvent être utilisés comme des instruments pour quantifier et qualifier les processus d'intégration, pour résumer les politiques d'intégration compliquées, pour suivre les développements et mesurer les progrès, pour établir des objectifs, pour identifier les impacts des lois, des politiques et des pratiques, pour identifier les acteurs de l'intégration et pour contrôler si leurs obligations s'y sont bien retrouvées, pour prévenir de futures distractions, pour préparer des actions préventives, pour chercher le consensus social lorsque les ressources diminuent et, finalement, pour exposer des aspects qui ont été passés sous silence. Les indicateurs font référence à un nombre limité d'éléments quantitatifs qui signalent les développements importants dans les champs vitaux des politiques d'intégration. Les indicateurs européens seront un complément aux indicateurs nationaux et renforceront les fondements des évaluations au niveau national. Les indicateurs doivent donc être catégorisés en fonction de leur utilisation.[34]

---

33 SEC (2010) 357, Commission staff working document of 19 March 2010, The consolidation of the EU framework on integration. Report to the 2010 Ministerial Conference on Integration.

34 J. Niessen, *Developing and using European integration indicators*, *Strategic thinking on equality and mobility*, Brussels: MPG 2009.

4.6 Le Programme de Stockholm

Le Programme de Stockholm est ambitieux en ce qui concerne l'intégration. Il invite la Commission à aider les États membres en développant un mécanisme de coordination basé sur un cadre de référence qui doit améliorer les structures et les instruments par l'échange de connaissances au niveau européen. Il considère également comme un aspect important la consultation et la participation de la société civile. En relation à l'intégration, il répète l'idée que la *'coopération européenne peut contribuer à améliorer l'efficacité des politiques d'intégration des États membres, en stimulant et en appuyant l'action des États membres'*. Même si les PBC n'y sont pas explicitement mentionnés, on peut les comprendre d'après la rédaction du texte, puisque l'on y trouve la définition d'intégration et les domaines prioritaires d'action auxquels le Conseil européen donne priorité et qui alimentent le contenu des PBC. De plus, le Conseil européen invite la Commission à soutenir l'action des États membres *'par l'élaboration d'un mécanisme de coordination associant la Commission et les États membres et utilisant un cadre de référence commun, qui devrait améliorer les structures et les outils servant à l'échange de connaissances au niveau européen'*. On peut penser qu'il pourrait s'agir de l'application d'une méthode ouverte de coordination.

Le Plan d'action mettant en œuvre le Programme de Stockholm[35] considère que l'Union doit poursuivre ses efforts d'intégration des migrants, en protégeant leurs droits, mais aussi en mettant l'accent sur leur propre responsabilité quant à leur intégration dans les sociétés d'accueil. Une action prévue par le Plan pour 2011 consiste dans l'élaboration, de la part de la Commission, d'une communication portant sur l'agenda de l'UE l'intégration, communication devant inclure le développement d'un mécanisme de coordination. Cette Communication serait la 2ème version du Programme Commun pour l'Intégration de 2005. La relation entre le marché du travail et l'intégration des migrants étant croissante, le Programme de Stockholm et la Stratégie de Lisbonne ont le potentiel d'améliorer et de renforcer les politiques liées aux aspects socio-économiques, culturels et d'intégration civique.

5. Dans Quelle Mesure les Principes de Base Communs sont-ils Obligatoires?

Dans la rédaction du premier objectif des PBC, on affirme littéralement que ceux-ci visent à *'aider les États membres à formuler des politiques d'intégration en mettant à leur disposition un guide simple, non contraignant, mais dont tous les éléments auront été mûrement pesés, contenant des principes de base à l'aune desquels ils pourront juger et évaluer leur propre action'*. Les autres objectifs vont dans le même sens et par conséquent le vocabulaire utilisé s'appuie sur les termes suivants: '*servir de base, aider, compléter, renforcer, contribuer, constituer une référence et une aide*'.

Les PBC tentent de donner la première définition du concept d'intégration dans l'UE. Ils intègrent sous forme de liste harmonisée un certain nombre d'aspects partagés, ayant été cités dans les réponses européennes reçues sur le sujet; il s'agit en général d'une synthèse du point de vue européen, bien que l'on y trouve également d'autres principes ayant une

35 COM/2010/0171, Communication de la Commission du 20 avril 2010, au Parlement européen, au Conseil, au Comité économique et social européen et au Comité des régions - Mettre en place un espace de liberté, de sécurité et de justice au service des citoyens européens - Plan d'action mettant en œuvre le programme de Stockholm.

origine différente par rapport au point de vue classique de l'Union[36]. L'idée des PBC est que les États membres aient la possibilité d'utiliser ces principes de base pour définir leurs priorités et fixer de façon plus précise leurs propres objectifs mesurables, et pour déterminer si ces principes peuvent leur être utiles pour la formulation de leur politique d'intégration. Les PBC établissent les paramètres et identifient les instruments nécessaires pour arriver à une intégration qui soit réussie. Ces PBC fournissent à l'Union une politique *soft* portant sur l'intégration des nationaux des pays tiers; sa nature facultative a été renforcée par la Communication de la Commission datée de 2005 et intitulée *Programme Commun pour l'Intégration.*[37] Celle-ci précise qu'il s'agit d'un ensemble d'actions à caractère indicatif qui laisse aux États l'option de choisir leurs priorités et de s'adapter à leurs propres réalités nationales.

5.1 L'Absence de Compétence Législative de l'Union en Intégration

Le cadre de l'Union, et notamment l'article 79.4 TFUE, ne prévoit pas une harmonisation législative de la politique d'intégration des États membres. Ce nouveau paragraphe introduit par le Traité de Lisbonne permet l'utilisation de la procédure législative ordinaire pour adopter des mesures visant à encourager et appuyer toute action des États destinée à favoriser l'intégration. Cette possibilité, rendra peut-être inutiles les conférences ministérielles informelles. En effet, si le Traité prévoit une procédure législative pour développer les actions en matière d'intégration et donne aux institutions une compétence concrète, on ne voit pas pourquoi le Conseil de l'Union, même informellement, devrait se réunir en dehors de cette procédure pour faire avancer la politique d'intégration.

Nous nous trouvons face à un nouveau stade de coopération, face à un nouvel agenda européen qui permettrait à l'Union de soutenir la politique d'intégration que les États membres doivent mettre en œuvre, et ce par l'adoption de différents moyens tels que les indicateurs, les modules, le développement des PBC et d'autres mécanismes à venir. Le paragraphe 4 de l'article 79 TFUE reflète un esprit différent des autres puisqu'il parle de l'adoption de mesures de soutien, tandis que les autres paragraphes font référence à la compétence de l'Union pour développer une politique d'immigration. Ils prévoient que les institutions européennes adoptent des mesures concrètes relatives aux conditions d'entrée et de résidence, à la définition du statut juridique des résidents des pays tiers, ou vers la prévention de l'immigration illégale. D'une façon indirecte ces dispositions législatives pourront être utilisés comme base pour appuyer les mesures d'intégration que chaque pays veut appliquer en suivant son modèle national; en fait, cela se fait avec, par exemple, les directives de regroupement familial ou de résidents de longue durée.

Les Principes de Base Communs peuvent, en premier lieu, servir de fondement pour définir l'interaction entre les différents niveaux de l'administration (UE et national) en ce qui concerne l'élaboration et la mise en œuvre des politiques d'intégration. Ils permettent de structurer un dialogue régulier entre ces niveaux, tout en y impliquant d'autres acteurs de l'intégration (par exemple, les partenaires sociaux, les ONG, les organisations de femmes et de migrants, les entreprises et d'autres institutions privées). En second lieu, ils

36 S. Carrera Núñez, *In Search of the Perfect Citizen? The Intersection between Integration, Immigration and Nationality in the EU*, *op. cit.*, p. 51-52.

37 COM 2005/389, *op. cit.*

peuvent aider à compléter et à renforcer les cadres législatifs existants. Ils veulent aussi être une référence, d'une part, dans l'étude des moyens visant à améliorer les instruments qui, en matière d'intégration, existent déjà au niveau de l'UE; et d'autre part, dans la définition des mécanismes et des politiques nécessaires pour soutenir la mise en œuvre des politiques d'intégration à l'échelon national et local, en particulier au moyen de l'apprentissage et de l'échange de connaissances à l'échelle de l'UE.

L'Union européenne considère qu'un exposé intégral et coordonné de la politique d'intégration dans les différents niveaux de l'administration est nécessaire et essentiel. En ce sens, selon Bertozzi, le développement et la mise en application de la politique d'intégration constituent une responsabilité primaire de chaque État plutôt que de l'Union dans sa globalité. L'Europe doit être la force dirigeant la construction de l'intégration et doit se préparer pour le changement relatif à la composition de la population, en appliquant le principe de subsidiarité.[38]

En raison de cette absence de compétence législative, l'Union n'a donc que deux solutions pour agir, d'une part, l'utilisation du *soft law,* dont les PBC constituent un élément déterminant et puissant et, d'autre part, l'utilisation de la méthode ouverte de coordination.

5.2 La Méthode Ouverte de Coordination

La Commission européenne a mis sur pied différents mécanismes alternatifs pour favoriser la coordination des politiques des États membres et permettre l'échange d'informations et l'évaluation des mesures. Comme le disent Guild, Carrera et Faure, ces mécanismes de coopération transnationale fondés sur certains principes se différencient des méthodes de prise de décisions traditionnelles, du droit européen et du cadre institutionnel du droit de l'Union, et constituent des méthodes ouvertes de coordination étant aussi bien formelles qu'informelles.[39] Une méthode comme la Méthode Ouverte de Coordination (MOC) prétend encourager la discussion sur l'intégration et promouvoir la convergence progressive des politiques et des pratiques nationales, ainsi que le développement d'objectifs et de standards communs.

L'idée d'appliquer cette méthode à la politique migratoire a été lancée dans deux Communications de la Commission de 2000 et 2001.[40] Malgré le soutien d'autres institutions européennes, les États membres n'étaient pas préparés à suivre la proposition de la Commission et le Conseil l'a donc rejeté.

Dans sa résolution relative à la Communication de 2003 sur l'immigration, l'intégration et l'emploi, le Parlement européen a considéré que la MOC était positive pour promouvoir l'échange d'informations, d'idées et d'expériences.[41] Le Parlement européen a

---

38 S. Bertozzi, *Integration: An Ever-Closer Challenge*, Thinking ahead for Europe, CEPS Working Document, nº 258, February 2007.

39 E. Guild, S. Carrera & A. Faure Atger, *Challenges and prospects for the EU's Area of Freedom, Security and Justice: Recommendations to the European Commission for the Stockholm Programme*, CEPS Working Document n. 313, April 2009, p. 3.

40 COM 2000/757, Communication de la Commission du 22 novembre 2000, au Conseil et au Parlement européen - Politique communautaire en matière d'immigration. COM 2001/ 387, Communication de la Commission du 12 juillet 2001 au Conseil et au Parlement européen sur une méthode ouverte de coordination de la politique communautaire en matière d'immigration.

41 Resolución del Parlamento Europeo sobre la Comunicación de la Comisión sobre inmigración, integración y empleo, P5_TA(2004)0028.

appelé les États membres à élaborer des critères minimums pour la création d'une politique d'intégration en les invitant à coordonner leurs politiques nationales grâce à la méthode ouverte de coordination fondée sur les PBC. En faisant ce type de suggestion dans sa Résolution de juin 2005,[42] le Parlement européen a également donné aux États certaines idées d'actions spécifiques à mettre en œuvre. Toutefois, il s'agit de la répétition de suggestions déjà émises par le Conseil dans son explication des PBC.

Les PBC s'accordent bien avec une structure de MOC modérée et flexible, permettant de renforcer la coopération entre les États membres. Dans cette optique, le rôle des Points de Contacts Nationaux sur l'Intégration s'avère très important pour recueillir des informations sur les bonnes pratiques, identifier les politiques prioritaires, identifier des solutions effectives, évaluer et diriger le progrès. Pour rendre cela effectif, il faut que les États donnent la priorité au travail des PCNI et que la Commission elle-même puisse assurer une bonne structure et un bon support.

Bien que Niessen considère que la politique d'intégration ne se développe pas à travers la MOC, il admet tout de même que sa mise en œuvre demande une infrastructure d'instruments similaires. Ceux-ci incluraient la Charte de droits fondamentaux et les PBC qui servent de guide, un cadre législatif sur certains aspects (admission, résidence...) et, finalement, des plates-formes de coopération entre acteurs gouvernementaux et non gouvernementaux pour faciliter l'échange d'informations et de bonnes pratiques[43].

Cette méthode ouverte de coordination prétend compléter la législation européenne en matière d'immigration et vise aussi à influencer les politiques et les programmes nationaux. L'application d'une politique nationale doit être d'accord avec les PBC pour être valorisée favorablement par le Fonds européen d'intégration. Les Manuels d'Intégration et les Rapports annuels, en coopération avec les Points de Contacts Nationaux sur l'Intégration et avec des experts indépendants facilitent l'échange d'informations et de bonnes pratiques et proposent certaines recommandations. Mais le pouvoir de la Commission se limite surtout à assurer la coordination des États dans la mise en œuvre des PBC, en proposant spécialement certains types d'actions pour mettre en œuvre les PBC au niveau national. Comme déjà signalé, les documents que la Commission utilise se présentent sous différentes formes: des communications, des rapports annuels, des documents internes de travail, des manuels, un agenda, etc., et leur nature et effets ne sont pas très clairement définis. Dépourvus de force juridique contraignante, on peut en fait les définir comme des instruments de *soft law*. L'idée est que les États puissent tirer profit des échanges de bonnes pratiques, même s'il n'y a pas de mécanisme pour garantir qu'ils suivront bien les PBC. Cette *soft law* permet la coordination et aussi le respect des différences nationales, mais pourrait uniquement cette coordination porter atteinte à une bonne base commune?

En réponse à cette question, la réflexion menée par Guild, Carrera et Faure[44] est fort intéressante. Cette MOC peut faire en sorte que la Commission privilégie le consensus et fasse des concessions relatives aux standards communs européens. La MOC a favorisé le fait que certaines politiques nationales d'intégration soient devenues communes dans le cadre de la coopération. C'est le cas par exemple pour les programmes d'intégration civique

42 Résolution du Parlement européen du 9 juin 2005, sur les liens entre immigration légale et illégale et l'intégration des migrants (2004/2137(INI)), P6_TA(2005)0235.

43 J. Niessen, *Developing and using European integration indicators*, *op. cit.*

44 E. Guild, S. Carrera & A. Faure Atger, *Challenges and prospects for the EU's Area of Freedom, Security and Justice*, *op. cit.*, p. 7 and 16.

établis dans le cadre du regroupement familial par plusieurs États membres. L'échange d'informations sur les pratiques suivies par les États membres est certes positif, mais, même si juridiquement est possible, il ne devrait être utilisé pour transférer au niveau européen les politiques nationales plus restrictives. L'établissement de conditions d'intégration pour avoir accès à certains droits ne peut faire l'impasse sur le respect des droits fondamentaux. Les programmes d'intégration civique, les cours et les tests de connaissance de la langue ou de l'histoire du pays d'accueil font partie des PBC qui tentent de donner un cadre pour l'intégration des ressortissants des pays tiers.

La Méthode Ouverte de Coordination favorise l'échange de pratiques, devant être comprises comme *bonnes* pratiques, mais on peut se poser les questions suivantes: qu'est-ce que l'on peut considérer comme une bonne pratique?, Quelle différence y a-t-il entre une bonne et une mauvaise pratique?, Qui possède le pouvoir pour déterminer leur caractère? Une réponse peut consister à considérer comme bonne pratique celle qui donne de bons résultats en matière d'intégration. Mais se pose alors une autre question, dans quel sens favorise-t-elle alors l'intégration? Dans un sens plutôt assimilationniste ou multiculturaliste? Selon nous, la réponse dépendra du modèle de société et, par conséquent, d'intégration que chaque pays, ou que l'Union, désirent établir. Les PBC peuvent être plus 'inclusionnistes' ou plus 'exclusionnistes' en fonction de la valeur que chaque pays octroie à ses pratiques.

6. Les États Membres font-ils Référence aux Principes de Base Communs? L'Espagne comme Exemple

La façon dont les États membres font connaître les PBC, en font la publicité ou montrent leur importance est différente selon les pays.[45] Nous allons nous centrer sur le cas espagnol et ce pour différentes raisons. D'une part, il s'agit d'un nouvel État d'immigration. Un pays qui commence donc à développer une politique d'intégration. D'autre part, le volume de résidents de pays tiers y a augmenté considérablement en peu de temps et entraîne ce faisant des changements dans la société d'accueil.

L'Espagne a été traditionnellement un pays d'émigration et est devenue, il y a quelques années, un pays d'immigration – à la différence d'autres pays de l'Union. Cette situation et cette évolution historique expliquent le développement de sa politique d'immigration et d'intégration.[46] La première loi traitant des aspects relatifs à l'immigration a été celle de

45 Dans le Troisième Rapport Annuel sur l'Immigration et l'Intégration (COM 2007/512 *op. cit*), nous trouvons des références aux différentes pratiques utilisées: 'The CBPs and the Common Agenda are well known by those directly involved in integration policies at national level. Measures aiming at disseminating them further to a wider group of policy-makers and to civil society are undertaken. In Bulgaria and in the Slovak Republic they are discussed and presented to the broader public. They are increasingly mentioned in official declarations and political statements. Some Member States, such as Austria, the Czech Republic, Denmark and Spain, refer to the CBPs on a regular basis when dealing with immigration and integration issues. In the Czech Republic and Greece, the CBPs enriched the debate leading to the adoption of new legislation. They are also explicitly incorporated in some Member States' programmes. (...). In Ireland, the CBPs continue to inform the policy making process and all projects submitted for funding from a recently announced Immigrant Integration Fund are required to reflect the CBPs'.

46 Pour une étude plus détaillée sur le développement de la politique d'intégration en Espagne, voir M. Brusquetas Callejo, B. Garcés Mascareñas, R. Morén Alegret, R. Penninx & E. Ruiz Vieytez, *Immigra-* →

1985,[47] juste avant l'entrée du pays dans les Communautés européennes. Mais si à cette époque les flux migratoires d'entrée en Espagne étaient très faibles, la situation a aujourd'hui changé. La population provenant de pays tiers a augmenté considérablement et se concentre dans certaines Communautés Autonomes (CCAA - régions -), telles que la Catalogne, Madrid, l'Andalousie, Murcie, Valence, les Iles Baléares et les Iles Canaries.[48]

Dans les années 90, les autorités commencent à élaborer une politique d'intégration des immigrants et à concevoir une stratégie au moyen de certaines actions. Un Plan pour l'intégration sociale des immigrants (*Plan para la integración social de los inmigrantes*) a été mis en œuvre. De même, ont été créés le Forum pour l'Intégration Sociale des Immigrants (*Foro para la Integración Social de los Inmigrantes* – organe consultatif du gouvernement) et l'Observatoire Permanent de l'Immigration (*Observatorio Permanente de la Inmigración* – instrument pour suivre l'immigration et l'intégration et faire certaines suggestions de politiques).

La Loi de 1985 a été remplacée en janvier 2000 par la Loi 4/2000.[49] Cette loi a aussi été modifiée au mois de décembre en raison des résultats des élections nationales.[50] En 2003, la Loi 4/2000 a aussi fait l'objet de deux nouvelles réformes.[51] Chacune de ces trois réformes (celle de 2000 et celles de 2003) visait à renforcer la politique d'immigration et de contrôle des flux migratoires, mais aucune ne concernait l'intégration des migrants. Parallèlement à ces procédures législatives, il y a eu l'approbation du Programme Global de Régulation et Coordination de l'Immigration en Espagne (*Programa Global de Regulación y Coordinación de la Inmigración en España - GRECO)* 2000-2004. Ce programme conçu par le Ministère de l'Intérieur introduit la conception de l'apport positif que l'immigration offre à la société d'accueil. Finalement, la pression sociale a placé l'intégration sur l'agenda politique. C'est suite à la participation de spécialistes indépendants, aux considérations résul-

---

tion and Intégration Policymaking in Spain, IMISCOE Working Paper, no. 21, April 2008; S. Carrera Nuñez, *In Search of the Perfect Citizen?. The Intersection between Integration, Immigration and Nationality in the EU*, *op. cit.*, pp. 152-183; R. Ferrero Turrión & G. Pinyol Jiménez, 'Immigration and the Construction of Public Philosophy(ies) of Integration in Spain', in E. Guild, K. Groenendijk & S. Carrera (eds), *Illiberal Liberal States. Immigration, Citizenship and Integration in the EU*, Ashgate 2009, pp. 337-356.

47 Ley Orgánica 7/1985, de 1 de Julio, sobre derechos y libertades de los extranjeros en España (en vigueur jusqu'au 1er février 2000).

48 En 1999, il y avait en Espagne 801.329 résidents étrangers, parmi lesquels 489.126 n'étaient pas citoyens de l'Union Européenne; selon les chiffres du 30 septembre 2010, le nombre de citoyens européens atteint les 2.358.798 et celui des ressortissants de pays tiers atteint les 2.395.704. http://extranjeros.mtin.es/es/InformacionEstadistica/ (consulté le 30 décembre 2010).

49 Ley Orgánica 4/2000 sobre derechos y libertades de los extranjeros en España y su integración social, BOE de12 de enero.

50 Ley Orgánica 8/2000, de 22 de diciembre, de reforma de la Ley Orgánica 4/2000, de 11 de enero, sobre derechos y libertades de extranjeros en España y su Integración Social, *BOE*, de 23 de diciembre.

51 Ley Orgánica 11/2003, de 29 de septiembre de medidas concretas en materia de seguridad ciudadana, violencia doméstica e integración social de los extranjeros, et Ley Orgánica 14/2003, de 20 de noviembre, de Reforma de la Ley orgánica 4/2000, de 11 de enero, sobre derechos y libertades de los extranjeros en España y su integración social, modificada por la Ley Orgánica 8/2000, de 22 de diciembre; de la Ley 7/1985, de 2 de abril, Reguladora de las Bases del Régimen Local; de la Ley 30/1992, de 26 de noviembre, de Régimen Jurídico de las Administraciones Públicas y del Procedimiento Administrativo Común, y de la Ley 3/1991, de 10 de enero, de Competencia Desleal.

tant de différents séminaires d'experts et à la consultation auprès des Communautés Autonomes et des municipalités que le Plan Stratégique de Citoyenneté et d'Intégration (*Plan Estratégico de Ciudadanía e Integración – PECI*) 2007-2010, actuellement en vigueur, a été adopté. Ce Plan définit les principes et les axes fixés par le gouvernement central, dans le but d'être utile à toutes les personnes en général. Il entend en effet renforcer la cohésion sociale en encourageant des politiques publiques basées sur l'égalité des droits et des devoirs, sur l'égalité des chances, sur le développement d'un sentiment d'appartenance à la société espagnole et sur le respect de la diversité.

Dans la présentation du Plan, il est expressément indiqué que les PBC, qui se trouvent annexés dans le document, peuvent être un excellent référent pour définir l'intégration. De même, en ce qui concerne les domaines d'intervention devant être pris en compte pour réussir en matière d'intégration, il y a des références aux textes ou aux instruments européens pour l'intégration, comme les communications de la Commission ou certains PBC bien concrets. En même temps, le Plan consacre le chapitre 4 aux politiques d'intégration au niveau de l'Union européenne et réitéré expressément l'idée que les compétences de l'Union en matière d'intégration consistent uniquement à encourager et à appuyer les mesures adoptées par les États, et que ce sont ces derniers qui conservent la compétence législative exclusive. L'action de l'Union est une stratégie indirecte d'orientation de l'action des États. Les PBC ont justement ce rôle d'orientation. Ils reflètent l'importance croissante des questions relatives à l'intégration dans l'UE et constituent le point de départ pour articuler les actions européennes. Ils représentent le consensus européen minimums en ce qui concerne l'orientation des politiques d'intégration européennes. Cet Plan est complété par l'instrument économique, le Fonds de Support à l'Accueil et l'Intégration des Immigrants et Renforcement Éducatif (*Fondo de Apoyo a la Acogida y la Integración de Inmigrantes y Refuerzo Educativo - FAAIIRE*), par lequel l'Etat offre un apport que les CCAA doivent compléter, mais ce sont elles qui décident dans quelles politiques et actions elles vont investir le financement.

La nouvelle réforme de la Loi espagnole sur l'immigration, qui est entrée en vigueur en décembre 2009,[52] montre une prise de conscience de certains aspects comme le changement dans la composition de la société, le fait qu'il s'agisse de personnes qui ont l'intention de rester dans le pays et le fait qu'il faille éviter l'apparition croissante de conduites xénophobes. En relation à l'intégration,[53] la réforme fait référence au Conseil européen de Tampere en indiquant que la politique d'intégration doit donner aux ressortissants des pays tiers qui sont résidents légaux, des droits et des obligations comparables à ceux des citoyens de l'Union, tout en favorisant l'absence de discrimination. De même, elle se réfère au Pacte européen sur l'immigration et l'asile. Dans l'exposé de motifs, la Loi prévoit le renforce-

52 Ley Orgánica 2/2009, de 11 de diciembre, de reforma de la Ley Orgánica 4/2000, sobre derechos y libertades de los extranjeros en España y su integración social, BOE 299, de 12 de diciembre de 2009, pp. 104986-105031. Une version consolidée de toutes les réformes (Ley Orgánica 4/2000, de 11 de enero sobre derechos y libertades de los extranjeros en España y su integración social, en su redacción dada por las leyes orgánicas 8/2000, de 22 de diciembre, 11/2003, de 29 de septiembre, 14/2003, de 20 de noviembre, y 2/2009, de 11 de diciembre), on la trouve à http://extranjeros.mtin.es/es/NormativaJurisprudencia/Ley_Organica_4_2000.pdf (consultation réalisée le 30 décembre 2010).

53 Pour une étude plus détaillée, voir E. AJA, 'La integración social de los inmigrantes', in D. Boza Martínez, J. Donaire Villa & D. Moya Malapeira (cords.), *Comentarios a la Reforma de la Ley de Extranjería (LO 2/2009)*, Valencia: Tirant lo Blanch 2011.

ment de l'intégration comme un des axes centraux de la politique d'immigration, en tenant compte de l'acquis de l'Union. Le nouvel article *2 bis* fait de l'intégration un principe général qui touche la totalité de la législation parce qu'il établit que l'intégration sociale des immigrants doit se faire par des politiques transversales adressées à toute la citoyenneté. Le nouvel article *2 ter* ordonne les principes et les agissements concernant l'intégration. Bien qu'ils ne soient pas expressément mentionnés, on peut voir dans la rédaction de cet article de la Loi certaines références aux PBC. En ce sens, l'article prévoit que l'intégration doit se faire de façon transversale; dans un respect de coexistence des différentes identités et cultures; en promouvant la participation économique, sociale, culturelle et politique des immigrants; en facilitant par des actions de formation la connaissance et le respect des valeurs de la Constitution espagnole et des valeurs de l'Union; et en developpant des mesures concrètes pour favoriser l'incorporation au système éducatif et l'accès au marché du travail. Ces actions doivent se faire au moyen de l'application de la Loi, des différents plans d'intégration des Communautés Autonomes (CCAA) et des municipalités, qui devront se coordonner, et des programmes biannuels qu' adopteront conjointement le gouvernement et les CCAA à travers la Conférence Sectorielle d'Immigration (*Conferencia Sectorial de Inmigración*). La Loi ne suit ni le modèle multiculturaliste ni le modèle assimilationniste. En revanche, elle reflète bien l'incidence que peut avoir l'apprentissage volontaire de la langue comme un élément stimulateur. Ce seront alors les CCAA et les municipalités qui devront fournir les cours et les services.

Le système particulier des Communautés Autonomes espagnoles implique que le gouvernement central dispose de la compétence exclusive en matière de politique d'immigration mais que ce sont les CCAA qui sont responsables des politiques d'intégration (éducation, santé, logement, assistance sociale...). Elles disposent de compétences attribuées par les statuts d'autonomie et qui peuvent différer d'une Communauté à l'autre. Comme affirme Martínez de Lizarrondo, parce qu'il n'y a pas un plan d'intégration national cohérent, les CCAA et certaines municipalités ont mis en œuvre des plans d'intégration.[54] Depuis 2001, le Conseil Supérieur de Politique d'Immigration (*Consejo Superior de Política de Inmigración)* coordonne les politiques du gouvernement central et des gouvernements autonomes, mais fixe surtout certaines limites.

Le 28 avril 2010, le Parlement de Catalogne a approuvé la Loi d'accueil des immigrants.[55] C'est la première en Espagne[56] et elle matérialise le Pacte National pour l'Immigration[57] (un pacte pour vivre toutes et tous ensembles) qui a été signé en décembre 2008

---

54 A. Martinez de Lizarrondo Artola, 'La integración de inmigrantes en España: el modelo Patchwork', *Revista Migraciones*, no. 26, diciembre 2009, pp. 115-146. Pour une étude plus approfondie de la matière, voir M. Brusquetas Callejo, B. Garcés Mascareñas, R. Morén Alegret, R. Penninx & E. Ruiz Vieytez, 'Immigration and Intégration Policymaking in Spain', *op. cit.*; S. Carrera Núñez, *In Search of the Perfect Citizen? The Intersection between Integration, Immigration and Nationality in the EU*, *op. cit.*, pp. 183-189.

55 Llei 10/2010 del 7 de maig, d'acollida de les persones immigrades i de les retornades a Catalunya, *DOGC núm. 5629* du 14 mai du 2010.

56 Bien que la Loi 15/2008 d'Intégration des Personnes Immigrantes à la Communauté Valencienne ait été publiée avant celle catalane, elle a été influencée, au cours de son élaboration, par l'avant-projet de cette dernière.

57 http://www20.gencat.cat/docs/dasc/03Ambits%20tematics/05Immigracio/03Politiquesplansactuacio/02pactenacionalimmigracio/02continguts/Pdfs/Document_final_PNI_frances.pdf (consulté le 15 octobre 2010).

par la plupart des partis politiques parlementaires, par les agents socio-économiques et par les organisations du secteur. Dans l'exposé des motifs de la Loi, il est fait référence au cadre européen d'intégration à savoir, le Conseil européen de Thessalonique, les Manuels de bonnes pratiques et les PBC. Concrètement, la Loi catalane cite expressément le PBC 4 pour justifier ses programmes de premier accueil destinés à une formation de base sur la langue, l'histoire et les institutions. Un certificat officiel de la Generalitat de Catalogne ou de la municipalité accredittera la réalisation des cours.

Ce document (le certificat) pourra avoir des effets juridiques dans les procédures de l'Administration espagnole (renouvellement de l'autorisation provisoire de résidence, regroupement familial, nationalisation...). C'est-à-dire, même s'il s'agit d'un document non contraignant qu'attribuent les CCAA et qui peut être délégué aux municipalités, l'Administration centrale au moment où elle doit exercer sa compétence en matière d'immigration appréciera l'effort d'intégration du ressortissant du pays tiers en prenant en considération le certificat. Ce certificat n'est pas une condition pour le renouvellement des titres de séjour et autres documents mais il peut aider à compenser le déficit d'une condition requise. Cette innovation introduite par la Loi et son développement[58] va dans la direction d'une mise en relation entre l'intégration et l'immigration, mais ne constituent pas pour l'instant une condition.

7. Réflexions Finales

Les PCB sont intégrés dans toutes les actions de l'Union européenne qui traitent des aspects relatifs à l'intégration des ressortissants des pays tiers. Ils sont pris en compte dans les Manuels d'Intégration, dans les indicateurs ou dans les modules. De même, les États membres y font référence. Cette prise en considération montre la valeur qu'ils possèdent malgré leur caractère non contraignant et de quelle façon ils constituent le guide qui suivent l'Union européenne et les États membres dans le développement et la mise en œuvre des politiques d'intégration.

Les PBC présentent deux caractéristiques importantes. En premier lieu, il s'agit d'une conception holistique qui tient compte non seulement des aspects économiques et sociaux de l'intégration, mais également des aspects relatifs à la diversité culturelle et religieuse, à la citoyenneté, aux droits politiques et à la participation dans la vie publique. En deuxième lieu, il s'agit de la subsidiarité qui implique la nécessaire participation et collaboration de tous les niveaux de l'administration. De même, il faut tenir compte du fait que l'administration n'est pas l'unique acteur dans le domaine de l'intégration, puisqu'il y a bien une multiplicité d'acteurs qui y jouent différents rôles, comme par exemple les associations culturelles, sociales ou sportives, les ONG's, les syndicats ou l'école.

Les PBC doivent faciliter le dialogue entre les gouvernements, les institutions participantes et l'Union. Chaque État détermine les mesures concrètes qu'il veut appliquer en fonction des nécessités nationales, tout en veillant à l'intérêt commun de l'Union qui doit pouvoir en bénéficier.[59]

58 Real Decreto 557/2011, de 20 de abril, por el que se aprueba el Reglamento de la Ley Orgánica 4/2000, sobre derechos y libertades de los extranjeros en España y su integración social, tras la reforma por Ley Orgánica 2/2009, *BOE 103 de 30 de abril de 2011*.

59 G. Oude Engberink, 'Les ciutats i la integració dels immigrants', *op. cit.*

L'Union européenne n'avait pas de compétences explicites en matière d'intégration avant l'entrée en vigueur du Traité de Lisbonne. Le paragraphe 4 de l'article 79 TFUE prévoit que, par la procédure législative ordinaire, des mesures pourront être adoptées afin d'encourager et de soutenir l'action des États en matière d'intégration, à l'exclusion de l'harmonisation des dispositions nationales. Ce nouveau paragraphe confirme l'existence d'un nouvel agenda dans l'Union en matière d'intégration et constitue la base juridique pour le développer. Toutefois, la disposition du traité prévoit qu'il faudra continuer à employer des instruments de nature non contraignante. A ce titre, l'utilisation d'une méthode ouverte de coordination permet de préserver les particularités ou spécificités de chaque État membre.

Pour ces raisons, selon nous, l'Union ne peut faire plus que les actions qu'elle mène à travers les PBC. Ceux-ci sont en fait une sorte de *soft law,* puisque n'étant pas juridiquement contraignants ils sont pris en considération par l'Union dans le développement qu'elle fait de la politique s'intégration et par les États membres dans ses législations et actions nationales. Nous trouvons par exemple le cas de l'Espagne avec références directes et indirectes aux PBC.

Malgré leur caractère non contraignant *per se,* les PBC sont une référence. Les États et l'Union ont assumé le rôle qu'ils ont dans ce sens ou, du moins, les considèrent comme un guide très utile. De fait, les États et l'Union sont en train de développer leurs stratégies et politiques d'intégration en suivant les orientations des PBC. Étant donné la diversité de situations dans les États membres, ce guide ne s'avère-t-il pas peut-être comme la meilleure option?

THE INSTRUMENTALISATION OF EU INTEGRATION POLICY: REFLECTING ON THE DIGNIFIED, EFFICIENT AND UNDECLARED POLICY ASPECTS

Nicos Trimikliniotis[*]

1. Introduction

This contribution will critically evaluate the instruments of EU integration policy (formal, informal and substantial) by examining their contradictions at conceptual and implementation levels. The very notion of 'integration' is contextualised and critically reviewed in practice, both at the level of 'high policy-making' in Brussels, as well as the way it is being understood and implemented in Member States. The notion of integration must be interpreted as an evolving, highly fluid and contested concept, which reflects the balance of forces between different forces both EU and member-state. Also, it needs to be contextualised across the variable geometry and unevenly integrated Member States. The paper firstly places the integration debates in the context of the debates around the so-called crisis of multiculturalism and anti-immigrant and anti-immigration politics. As such, the *instrumentalisation* of migrant integration policy is questioned.

2. Integration – History, Prehistory and Debates

Prehistory of the Current Debates

Integration is a loaded concept and has a highly contested history in the EU of the 21st century. It has a 'prehistory' that dates back to the 1950s and 60s, very much shaped in the postcolonial era after World War II. Two types of prehistories can be identified, each one punctuating in its' own particular way the history of *migrant integration* in the European Union, which really 'takes off' as a pan-EU concept around the millennium.

The first lineage of prehistory is driven by the very logic of European integration as a unifying socio-economic, political and cultural mode. Theoretical approaches vary: neo-functionalist, federalist, liberal intergovernmentalist and more radical theories contest the terrain of integration as a social/political process.[1] This requires contextualisation of the ideals of integration of migrants within the framework and history of the drive towards an 'ever more integrated Europe'; the extent to which we are dealing with a 'faltering project' in need of 'graduated integration' (Habermas 2009) or a question of redefining the demos before we can constitute a European demos (Balibar 2004) are open matters for debate.

---

* I would like to thank Yves Pascouau for his comments on the first draft of this paper.

1 The debates over European Integration continue, see Habermas 2009; Balibar 2004; Wiener & Diez 2003; O'Neill 1996.

The second prehistory derives from the *particular histories of migrant integration processes of EU Member States and beyond*; this aspect is ingrained as the continuation of a post-colonial story in the West/North since the end of Second World War. The history state-led processes of incorporation of migrants stretches 150 years back – particularly in the USA but was really theorised in the 1930s-1950s as assimilation, i.e. the 'melting pot' approach. One strand of the pre-EU migrant integration story stretches across the Atlantic in the USA and Canada, but carries what has often thought of as an 'Anglo-Saxon tradition' from English-speaking world of the UK to Australia. The American functionalist sociologist Talcott Parsons and Chicago School led the way with the AGIL functionalist logic – Adaptation, *Goal-attainment*, Integration, and Latency (see Kostakopoulou 2010). The other strand, the so-called 'continental' story, is so diverse that it cannot be said to have a common framework: the 'Low countries' traditions differ considerably between the now defunct system of 'Dutch toleration and Belgian more republican model; the Scandinavian 'models' have a mixed, to the German and central European ones to the French Republican models and the southern and eastern European approaches. It is rightly questioned whether we can really maintain such distinctions, or indeed whether we can truly speak of 'models' as the very country approaches have been subject to such radical change over time, depending on the content, the Government policy and attitudes, the political-ideological contexts in their contradictory terrain at each particular historic conjuncture that it makes little sense to talk of 'models' as such (Bertossi 2010). They merely become stereotypes, more like caricatures of policy-making structures failing to offer any real insight into the mechanics, power dynamics, the framing and ideological contestations, the evolution, transformations and actual policy practice. State responses to the presence of migrants have varied, but the success of policy-making in achieving the desired goals is questionable (Castles 2004a; 2004b); even today's 'migration state' is hardly responding to the necessity for properly *including* migrants in society (Hollifield 2004).

There is however a marked shift in the conceptualisation and argumentation of integration which occurred somewhere around the turn of the 20th century. As Kostakopoulou points out (2010: 936) 'the civic integration paradigm started superseding multiculturalism towards the turn of the 20th century'. This on the one hand reflects the growing 'conservative reactions against the increasing heterogeneity of communities and the politics of diversity as well as to the security politics prevailing after 9/11'. On the other hand, critics of multiculturalism 'mainly but not exclusively, on the right of the political spectrum, argued that multiculturalism is premised on essentialist conceptions of culture and fosters the creation of bounded enclaves within society' (Kostakopoulou 2010: 936). Having acknowledged this, it also the case that the distinction between 'multiculturalism' and 'integration' is becoming increasingly ambiguous, as migration, integration and multiculturalism become more and more intertwined and blurred in the rhetoric of 'migration crisis'. European debates are increasingly articulated in terms 'crisis of multiculturalism' and 'crisis of migration and integration': the issue of migration/incorporation of migrants in society is increasingly becoming a major cultural/identity polarisation frontier in European politics, even reshaping allegiances and the Left/Right default lines in many instances. The problem is that, as Stuart Hall insists 'the multicultural question' i.e. different groups living together assimilation or degradation is 'the underlying question of globalisation':[2] the question of

2 Quoted by Yuval-Davis et al. (2006: 6).

'integration' is precisely a question of accommodating and living together *despite* differences. However, to make the question meaningful in scrutinising policy or researching the field more widely, it must be turned on its' head. This is the only way to make any study possible as it is next to impossible to extract a generic 'formula' from the various conditions of coexistence in history across Europe and the globe. As rightly reformulated by Anthias (2006) the question becomes as follows: 'under what conditions do people with different languages, cultures and ways of life fail to live in harmony?'.

Dissensus or fundamental disagreement (Rancière 2010) over migration and policy on the incorporation of migrants is often obfuscated as a 'crisis of multiculturalism'; this is in reality a crisis of identity and citizenship in Europe. In the USA, there is a similar discourse on crisis of identity looming. Huntington's last book, with the catchy title, *Who Are We? The Challenges to America's National Identity,* has a similar approach: threatened by the Latino immigration and Huntington speaks of the need to re-affirm the Anglo-Protestant heritage of the country, as essential for the unity of the American nation. The debates over the 'integration of migrants' in the EU, and within each Member State are indicative of the crisis. We have a 'multiculturalism backlash' but this is largely media and political-elite driven, rather than a genuinely popular mood shift against multiculturalism: The so-called 'slow death of multiculturalism' is certainly exaggerated (Vertovec & Wessendrof 2010). Nevertheless, there has been a serious shift in public discourse and the questions relating to migrants (integration, irregular migration, border control and to some degree racism, discrimination and xenophobia) have assumed a prominent role in European politics. The question of migration/integration is an increasingly important political issue across Europe; hence the link with the multicultural question: what sort of society do we have and what do 'we' want? The key question here is defining who 'We' are.

Bertossi (2010: 247) drawing on a comparison of the debates in various EU countries shows that the crisis of integration is currently being disguised as 'crisis of multiculturalism':

> The new politics of integration in Europe is a moment of re-politicisation of ethnicity, race and immigration, which leads to a reframing of traditional discourses on integration-cum-national identity [...]
> The theme 'integration crisis' is a strategic and discursive idiom of European politics today and results in the ultrapoliticisation of immigration, race and ethnicity.

National case studies misguidedly often branded as 'alternative' models of integration (e.g. the so-called 'French republicanism', 'Dutch multiculturalism' and 'British race relations policies' etc) are currently facing concurrent crises precisely because they have undergone the same sort of socio-economic processes and have faced similar shifts in policy/political terms in what he calls 'ultrapoliticisation' (see Silj 2010). These include shifting the emphasis to cultural emphasis where Islam is depicted as 'the main policy problem', emphasis on coercive integration solutions (e.g. culturally value-based citizenship tests). Moreover, we find the expansion of 'mandatory integration regimes' across the EU (Pascouau, 2010), whilst various studies on comparative integration policies show how there is a European trend towards 'coercive integration' targeting working class migrants and with a focus on Muslim, particularly Muslim women, primarily inspired by political demand rather than any successful impact assessment studies.[3] Muslim migration and incorporation into Europe is depicted as a threat to European society, with authors quoting Enoch Powel's infamous rivers of blood speech as if it were 'prophetic' (see Caldwell 2009). Hence, we find more 'politically correct' anti-Muslim and anti-immigrant arguments adopting critical perspectives on the 'failure of multiculturalism' or 'failure of integration' assuming credibility, even academic validity. As Malik (2009) comments on Caldwell's book,

> *Reflections on the Revolution in Europe* is the latest in a succession of books by authors such as Mark Steyn, Oriana Fallaci, Bruce Bawer and Melanie Phillips warning of how immigration, and in particular Muslim immigration, is threatening the very foundations of European civilisation. The melodramatic title of Caldwell's book is a nod to Edmund Burke and reflects his belief that the impact on European of post-war immigration has been as dramatic as the fall of the *ancien regime* in 1789.
>
> What is different about Caldwell is the high praise garnered by his book not simply from right-wing critics of immigration but from many liberals too – there were laudatory reviews in both the *Guardian* and the *Observer*. Caldwell, as Prospect editor David Goodhart puts it in the *Observer*, 'is a bracing, clear-eyed analyst of European pieties.'

As the welfare state is being dismantled, the emphasis shifts from universal goods using socio-economic instruments to means-tested targeting the economically deprived, excluded, marginalised, and in general a shift from any economic functions to symbolic-cultural politics.

The EU migrant integration story to be told is riddled with contradictions from the days of the pre-history of the concept at national level. When it comes to actually implementing the 'common' policy, it inevitably encounters the existing national story, which will be in practice mediated and 'negotiated' on the basis of the instruments, policies and practices developed at EU and national level. This is why the instruments can be crucial in shaping the outcome(s). To talk of the instruments of integration policy, we need to refer to the declared goals, the policy effects, the intended and unintended consequences of various actors, as well as the uses and abuses of the policy. Beyond the rhetoric and the symbolic talk, there are uses and abuses, well-documented about restricting certain types of migrants or groups.

A History of the Current Debates: A Positive Concept Turning Punitive?

From the outset of the current debates on migrant integration in the EU, there were inherent tensions in attempting to legally define the term integration (Groenendijk 2004): his starting point is that 'granting legal status to migrants will enhance integration in society', thus he rightly considers that it is necessary to perceive integration as a two-way process. However, this requires 'making room' in the receiving country to migrants to fit in, to

3 Conference papers presented based on three national examples from the INTEC project at the conference *Which Integration for Migrants? Interaction between the EU and its Member States* (details above) are indicative of this. The papers are: 'Germany: Integration requirement for admission' (Anne Walter, University of Osnabrück, GE), 'Austria: integration requirement for permanent residence' (Bernhard Perchinig, Austrian Academy of Sciences) and 'Netherlands: integration requirement for naturalisation' (Ricky van Oers, Centre for Migration Law Nijmegen, Netherlands).

accommodate and adapt. Groenendijk (2004: 113) distinguishes three alternatives senses of integration which generate three different results in society: (a) a strong residence status and equal treatments for integration; (b) long term residence or naturalisation should be 'remuneration for completed integration'; or (c) 'lack of integration or assumed unfitness to integrate are grounds for refusal of admission'. He is particularly critical of the third perspective as a contradiction in terms, as 'integration from abroad' is an absurdity. It was apparent from those days that there had been tensions resulting from 'the cultural and ideological diversity within the EU' were driving the integration policy astray, as Member States to choose between the first and the third choice. Unless the tensions were resolved Groenendijk (2004: 126) reasoned, then the policy is doomed to fail. By the end of first decade of the new millennium, Kostakopoulou (2010a: 932) would point out:

> Despite the deployment of the notion of a contract, integration is, in reality, a one way process aimed at procuring conformity, discipline and migration control. Civic integration rests on an artificial homogenisation and displays the same elements of paternalism and ethnocentricity that characterised past initiatives.

Some countries are practicing the third choice (c) with the Netherlands, Germany and France leading the way: it is not a question of 'failed integration' but of 'successful restrictive immigration policies' using integration as apologetics as one scholar aptly put it.[4] The UK under the conservatives are turning even more restrictive than 'new Labour' before them and the trend towards making it harder for migrants to access stable settlement and citizenship is well on its way across the EU. The practice of using coercive or mandatory systems of integration seems to be spreading across the EU (Pascouau 2010).

Integration is already a 'legal' concept which is producing legal results (see Groenendijk 2004; Pascouau 2010) in as much is a sociological and political concept. Ali Rattansi (2004) insistence that the British version of integration disguised in the Blair days as 'social cohesion' is essentially a revamped and repackaged version of assimilation, what he has branded as 'new assimilationism'; a critique developed to cover the ways in which there has been a terminological shift away from multiculturalism towards 'civic integration' and 'social cohesion' (Kostakopoulou 2010; Ratcliffe and Newman 2011). With the ascendance of the Conservatives to power in the UK, integration is acquiring even more assilimination-ist. David Cameron's call for a 'more active, muscular liberalism' is indicative of the slippery slope of integration talk as nationalism and Muslim-bashing: he condemned Britain's long-standing policy of multiculturalism as 'a failure' and called for better integration of young Muslims to 'combat home-grown extremism'.[5]

No matter what, the policy of migrant integration has been set in motion and is producing results, legal, political and sociological. In that sense, they are instruments still in the making. In many ways the conceptual framework of the instruments is rather rudimental; in

4 Juergen Bast made this comment, Juergen Bast (2010) 'Integration measures or conditions?', at the conference *Which Integration for Migrants? Interaction between the EU and its' Member States* (details above). The German policy was presented at the same conference by Anne Walter, 'Germany: Integration requirement for admission'.

5 See http://www.smh.com.au/world/multicultural-policies-need-replacing-says-cameron-20110205-1ahxo.html#ixzz1rqKvPWKx.

others they are actually quite well developed. The term integration is central to the EU, but means different things to different actors in terms of the philosophy, the goals, scope and actual operation. There are ideological differences between the various actors and these are dividing the EU structures and the Member States policy-makers, governments and political actors. The Council and the EU Parliament seem to split in three different interpretations of integration, even if the differences appear only to be superficial, underlying them are different philosophies of integration:

1. Those who see integration as a social process, which will include migrants and society.
2. Those who subordinate the 'social' to the 'economic', which is essentially the neoliberal route.
3. Thirdly, those who emphasise the 'cultural' aspects, which may have religious or ethnicist or secularist undertones (exclusivists) versus the pluralist ones stressing the 'multiculturalist' and 'ethnic pluralist' goals as a European tradition of tolerance, etc.

Precisely because we are dealing with a fluid and contested package of policies, the integration package contains within it what can be 'salvaged' as 'positive' or 'constructive' elements in pursuing the goals of accommodating and 'making room' for migrants to adapt in European societies (Groenendijk 2004), which essentially means serving the social needs of migrants as well as enhancing the institutional processes so that society as whole 'opens up' and allows for integration to occur. In this understanding, the burden of integration is not a migrant affair but a societal affair, in which the institutions must accommodate. The argument that the 'old integration policy' was on the whole more open and liberal, whilst the 'new integration policy' is restrictive and exclusionary (Groenendijk 2010) is only partially correct: there has such deterioration of the terms of the debate over integration that the 'old integration policy' seems so benign and open, but in reality the integration logic form its' inception contained such exclusionary and illiberal elements (see Kostakopoulou 2010a; 2010b). Other scholars speak of integration as having 'diverse roles' in the EU context with various actors pushing for different agendas and the tension between the security/identity agenda pursued versus the rights-based approach (Mitsilegas 2007). It is becoming increasingly apparent that the integration package as understood and implemented today contains exclusionary, xenophobic, Eurocentric and ethnocentric elements, which are pandering to and reflecting the current anti-immigrant public opinion driven by forces who want to exploit the latest economic crisis.

From the perspective of this paper, the instrumentalisation of the integration has led to the contradictions identified from the outset to be internalised in the various tools and policy instruments. So far no comparative study investigating the use of the specific aspect of EU toolkit on integration (i.e. the instruments of integration policy) has been published, so as to evaluate the extent of use and abuse, the interpretation, operation and impact, particularly on those at the receiving end. However, there is an abundance of evidence from the vast number of studies undertaken and are currently taking place on the broader issue of integration which illustrate the policy of migrant integration contains serious flaws, if the aims are the smooth incorporation of migrants in European societies: integration means different things in different countries and where they converge is on the common goal of restricting migration.

The State of Integration: Policy, Practice and learning from Migrants

Various studies on integration of migrants in Europe locate a number of problems with the way it is understood and conceptualised by policy-makers in the EU institutions and at national/local level and broadly have similar conclusion as to the state were in. Research findings illustrate how flawed the assumptions are about the reality of migrant integration. Assumptions about aspirations, sense of belonging and ways of life of migrants are highly differentiated, in as much are the so-called natives. For instance, the level of 'satisfaction' and notions of 'belonging' varies across different generations: first generation migrants have positive attitudes, whilst native and second generation migrants similarly share a more critical outlook on political institutions (Maxwell 2010). Incorporation of migrants in societies cannot be measured merely as a state-related process but rather against the totality different domains such as state, market, welfare and culture given that is essentially 'the product of the intersection of migrant aspirations and strategies with regulatory frameworks' (Freeman 2004: 945). Integration must be measured as a *societal process*, not a process that affects only migrants. The rise of racism, xenophobia and anti-migrant politics is a serious matter undermining any notion of integration. There are different explanations put forward for the sources current rise of negative attitudes towards immigrant in Europe (Rustenbach 2010). As shown by the MIPEX study (2011), there is considerable difference between different Member States as to the extent they have implemented the integration acquis, both the 'hard law' and the 'soft law' measures.

The research findings of the two projects referred in this volume[6] are also confirmed by the research project *Prospects for Integration of Migrants from 'Third countries' and their Labour Market Situations: Towards Policies and Action funded by the European Commission* (PRIMTS).[7] This project explored the positions of third country migrants in different economic sectors such as construction, farming, or care sector in the post 2000 period in six EU countries (Cyprus, Finland, Germany, Hungary, Italy, Slovenia). It focused on the precarious migrants. The study found the following relevant conclusions.[8]

Firstly, it confirmed that there are variable meanings of the term integration, from more descriptive to more declaratory uses: the very different migration and integration regimes reflect the particularities in history, national/regional and local contexts as well as the balance of forces in pursuing ethnic/racial, gender and migrant rights to equality and belonging. Most migrants interviewed saw little impact of the rhetoric of integration on the

6 The two research projects are research *Integration and naturalisation tests, the new way to European Citizenship – The effects of integration tests assessed in nine Member States* (INTEC) and the *National Policy Frames for the Integration of Newcomers in Europe. The link between integration and migration* (PROSINT). INTEC was presented by Tineke Strik and the PROSINT by Maren Borkert at conference *Which Integration for Migrants? Interaction between the EU and its Member States*, 28-29 October 2010, organised by the Centre 'Migration Asile Multiculturalisme' (Université Libre de Bruxelles), the Odysseus Network (Université Libre de Bruxelles) and the Centre for Migration Law (Radboud Universiteit Nijmegen).

7 Conducted in the period 2008–2010. Funded by European Commission, European Fund for the Integration of Third-Country Nationals 'Community Actions' 2007, Directorate-General Freedom, Security and Justice. See http://primts.mirovni-institut.si/.

8 For a discussion of the conclusions of the study see Pajnik et al. (2010). Also see Mojca Pajnik & Giovanna Campani (2011) and Trimikliniotis (2011) on further discussion drawn from two books related to the project.

realities of their precarious positions. It was found the term 'integration' as such was hardly ever used migrant workers interviewed; in fact 'even when specifically asked about it, the research showed that many migrants are not familiar with the term 'integration' as such' (Pajnik et al. 2010: 31). For those very few, who seemed to know something about EU-related rights and had specific claims to those rights based on an awareness of the contradiction between declarations and their everyday experience. For the vast majority of participants in the research, the broad integration regime is hardly perceived as a two-way processes as declared; rather they perceive the way it is implement and understood in the various polices win the respective states they living in as conditions and measures to exclude, marginalise and subordinate migrants. Lastly, for a third group of precarious migrant workers the term was unknown to them.

Secondly, despite the remarkable institutional development of policy instruments for integration, the implementation of basic elements for access and participation of migration seems inadequate for low skilled and precarious third country workers. In practice, rather than finding deskilling of migrants *via* their full access and participation in the labour market, we find varying degrees of deskilling for the precarious migrants, i.e. the vast majority of migrants.

Thirdly, another important finding is failure to properly target and deal with what are highly gendered processes. Two dimensions of these are the following: firstly, in terms of gender division of labour in sectors highly feminised (e.g. the care sector; the cleaning and the sex industry). Secondly, issues relating to gender discrimination of migrants are to be addressed in the same way as EU nationals. There is a distinct absence of the gender dimension in EU mechanisms of integration, reflecting perhaps the marginal position of third country migrant women in the gender equality and feminist movement.

Despite the goals for labour integration, there is strong evidence of structural forces which perpetuate the precariousness of migrants (and not only). In terms of labour segmentation, patterns of discrimination, geographical concentrations and housing segregation, higher risk of unemployment and deskilling and lack of opportunities to break the cycles. Many migrant workers in precarious position experience the 'new' integration drive as an exclusionary, in terms of culture, ethnicity, class, gender and religion. Instead of benefiting from measures to enhance their participation, access and belonging, many migrants have experienced increasing marginalisation and repression via the mechanisms to restrict migration.

Finally, it was found that integration measures overall fail to touch upon the most precarious of migrants, the undocumented and informal migrants, rendering this group of migrants precarious in perpetuity. The focus of 'legal migrants' may be founded on politically pragmatic reasons; however it leaves the lives of the most vulnerable to the irregular markets and super-exploitation.

3. The Inchoate Content of the Integration 'Toolkit': Formal, Informal and Substantial Instruments

There are multiple instruments of EU integration policy; they are divided between the 'formal' and the 'substantial'. Also, there are informal elements of policy, which are not always declared, but can be identified with relative ease in the actual implementation and interpretation of policy at national or regional level, illumination various uses and abuses of the jargon of integration. Moreover, there are unintended consequences which must be uncovered. The integration *instruments* are a mixed bag which remain to a large extent declaratory in nature, fixing 'targets' indicators and benchmarking, designed to never meet the logic of a binding legal regime. Policies are left to the Member States to adapt, adopt and implement. There is no essential content but it describe various instruments such as the National Contact Points on Integration (NCPI), the European Website on Integration (EWI) and the European Integration Forum (EIF), the Integration Handbook and the Integration Fund. They are very different in nature and effect - the Integration Fund for instance can fund and promote various actions, including the goals the others are meant to achieve such as the exchange of information, experience and ideas. In this sense the various instruments and tools of integration are very much part of what is sometimes called 'soft Europeanisation', i.e. aiming at leading in the longer-term to the same goals but using means of 'soft experiential processes' to encourage, support and legitimize the social and political goals of integration. However, the same instruments are sometimes used as restrictive, even coercive means invoking the acquis to legitimize such policies. For instance the use of good practices, indicators and benchmarks are essentially voluntary systems believed to be effective in exerting indirect political pressure particularly amongst Member States which want to appear as good exemplars of the policy, or on those trailing behind. However, such voluntary or soft law regimes have their limitations and deficiencies; in particular contexts they can backfire: there can be countries leading the 'bad practices', open the way for negative spiral with no sanctions. Besides, the Lisbon treaty does not allow harmonization of these policy areas.

The Suspended Step of Instrumentalisation: Inchoate Benchmarking and Social Indicators

On the positive side one can see the potential for the development of a more effective system of monitoring and implementing integration policies via a system of standard-setting, benchmarking, measuring the process and evolution on the basis of social indicators. However, as is apparent from the declaration of the European Ministerial Conference on Integration at Zaragoza[9] there was no agreement on developing genuine system of binding indicators to properly compare and evaluate integration policies: the matter was relegated to an annex and referred to a potential to be explored in the future. Only a pilot study was agreed upon. The Zaragoza Conference Declaration agreed:

> To call on the Commission to launch a pilot project with a view to the evaluation of integration policies, including examining the indicators proposed in the Annex to this document and analysing the significance of the defined indicators taking into account the national contexts, the background of diverse migrant populations and different migration and integration policies of the Member States, and reporting on the availability and quality of the data from agreed harmonised sources necessary for the calculation of

9 Fourth European Ministerial Conference on Integration as a Driver for Development and Social Cohesion, which took place on 15-16 April 2010 in Zaragoza.

these indicators. It is also important to promote evaluation mechanisms at local and regional level.[10]

The Annex of the Declaration refers 'a limited number of policy areas of relevance for integration have been identified as priority areas to policy areas and indicators at present,' which would play a role in 'building on national experiences and key areas for the common basic principles.' Hence, employment was placed at the core of the integration process (not merely access to the labour market), whilst education was seen as 'essential in helping immigrants to become successful and more active participants in society'. In this sense, other areas such as social inclusion, participation of immigrants in the democratic process and developing a sense of belonging are also included as policy areas to be measured.[11] The indicators presented in the annex were:

- based on existing and comparable data for most Member States;
- limited in number;
- comparable in time;
- productive and cost-effective;
- simple to understand and easy to communicate; and
- focused on outcome.

There are various studies, many funded by the EU, which have attempted to measure such indicators with varying degree of success in bringing more light as to the state we are in at EU and national level. One project, the Migrant Integration Policy Index (MIPEX),[12] has developed a comparative system of indicators from the different policy areas between different countries.[13] Such a ranking system is particularly useful policy tool to compare and contrast how each country is doing in the various policies, as well getting a global picture on the EU as a whole (and beyond). However, the main criticism is the attempt to reduce the complexity of contextual reality into percentage numbers and abstract graphs, often missing some dynamic issues which are irreducible to numbers. Other studies take a more qualitative and contextual approach to comparison. It is crucial here to stress that at least so far Member States do not agree on making such a regime more robust and shaping common indicators because they do not share same policy priorities in terms of policy goals, reflect-

10 Point 15, of the *Declaration of the Fourth European Ministerial Conference on Integration as a Driver for Development and Social Cohesion*, which took place on 15-16 April 2010 in Zaragoza, 9248/10, Brussels, 4 May 2010, p. 12, at http://register.consilium.europa.eu/pdf/en/10/st09/st09248. en10.pdf (accessed on 10.4.2011).

11 The relevant text reads as follows: 'Employment is a vital part of the integration process, and efforts in education are essential in helping immigrants to become successful and more active participants in society. Not only access to the labour market is important but also entry into society more generally, which makes social inclusion an important area. The participation of immigrants in the democratic process as active citizens supports their integration and enhances their sense of belonging.'

12 See http://www.mipex.eu/ (accessed on 10.4.2011). It is funded by the British Council.

13 Quoting from the MIPEX site: 'MIPEX is a fully interactive tool and reference guide to assess, compare and improve integration policy produced by the British Council and the Migration Policy Group. MIPEX measures integration policies in all European Union Member States plus Norway, Switzerland, Canada and the USA up to 31 May 2010. Using 148 policy indicators it creates a rich, multidimensional picture of migrants' opportunities to participate in society by assessing governments' commitment to integration. By measuring policies and their implementation it reveals whether all residents are guaranteed equal rights, responsibilities and opportunities.' See http://www.mipex.eu/ (accessed on 10.4.2011).

ing the different ideological and political backgrounds and motives of the various actors in EU and national policy-making.

The Integration Handbook: A Flip-side Reading of an Integration Tool

Following the Common Agenda for Integration in 2005,[14] the Stockholm Programme pledged to support Member States integration policies, through the development of structures and tools for knowledge exchange and coordination with other relevant policy areas, such as employment, education and social inclusion. This was to be achieved 'through the development of a coordination mechanism using a common reference framework, which should improve structures and tools for European knowledge exchange'. The amount of initiatives, information and guidebooks produced by EU and EU-related bodies is immense. The European Website on Integration is an initiative of the European Commission under the responsibility of the Directorate-General Home Affairs, providing policy makers and practitioners working on integration in Europe with a tool for the exchange of information and good practice.[15] The European Website on Integration hosts the European Integration Forum, which is meant to operate platform for dialogue on migrant integration.[16]

An important EU initiative to development an agreed framework beyond the common Agreed Principles' across the countries was the drafting of the Handbook on Integration, the third edition of which was launched in Zaragosa in April 2010.[17] The *Handbook*, which is aimed at policy-makers and practitioners, is a well-thought out a framework involving 600 experts, from Governments and civil society, as a result of a seven year process of consultation and discussion on integration, giving guidance and concrete examples on integration. The Director General of DG Justice, Freedom and Security of the European Commission, who prefaced the document, considers that Handbook contains a 'vast range of inspiring, concrete examples' and has resulted the creation of 'a connected, well-functioning community of practitioners' (Handbook, p. 6). It can be thus thought to be the current consensus around which integration measures are drawn. It covers areas such as mass media and integration, awareness-raising and migrant empowerment, dialogue platforms, acquisition of nationality and practice of active citizenship, immigrant youth, education and the labour market. It provides the positive ideas and concrete examples on how integration can be propelled forward.

The Handbook can only be understood in the context of its' use in the way it interact with the current political climate which is not conducive to integration as a positive policy. Therefore the Handbook suffers from the same sort of problems the general policy on integration, particularly as regards the underlying assumptions it contains. A useful exercise to uncover the social and political reality is to inverse the positive spin given to various institutions into negative, so that we can properly read into it the state we are in: we gain such an insight if read the flip-side of the Handbook as very much describing 'the dark side' of integration, in parallel to what scholars working on a different subject matters described as 'the

14 Common Agenda for Integration – Framework for the Integration of Third-Country Nationals in the European Union, at http://ec.europa.eu/ewsi/UDRW/images/items/docl_988_ 232042490.pdf (accessed 1.03.2011).

15 See http://ec.europa.eu/ewsi/en/index.cfm (accessed 1.03.2011).

16 See http://ec.europa.eu/ewsi/en/policy/legal.cfm (accessed 1.03.2011).

17 See http://ec.europa.eu/ewsi/en/resources/detail.cfm?ID_ITEMS=12892 (accessed 1.03. 2011).

dark side of democracy' (Mann 2005) and 'the dark side of Europe'. We can read into the various chapters the opposite of what is prescribed as the current reality. Instead of assuming that there is common agenda for integration (Handbook, chapter 1), we may assume that despite rhetoric the agendas is not shared or common but are quite diverse and often contradictory. Overall, the role of media has hardly been positively promoting integration for migrants, as prescribed in chapter 2 of the Handbook; quite the contrary. There is ample evidence of the destructive, hostile, xenophobic and anti-migrant or at least against certain migrants, particularly Muslim and Arab migrants. The measures taken to deal with the violation of codes of practice have failed to contain xenophobic and anti-immigrant media reporting and depiction of migrants. A classic example is the depiction of Muslim women in the media, or the tension caused as a result of infamous Danish Muhammad cartoons, or the public response to the murder of Theo Van Gogh in the Netherlands. As for the level of awareness and empowerment of migrants (Handbook, chapter 3), this is not something that can be answered easily, as there are huge disparities between groups, ages, genders, class, ethnicity and religion between and within member-states. Certainly in the current negative climate towards migrants, the goal migrant empowerment seems quite far ahead for the vast majority of migrants. Many Member States are not positively inclined towards the acquisition of nationality by migrants, neither are countries encouraging active citizenship, goals prescribed in chapter 5 of the Handbook, as the MIPEX indicators shows. There is widespread migrant youth social exclusion and unemployment, whilst various studies show wide-spread educational segregation and exclusion of migrants, the opposite of what is prescribed in chapter 6. Overall, the Handbook may provide some good prescriptions within various policy areas; however, it fails to recognise the real state we are currently in. This result is that 'good practice' fails really to impact on the structural barriers to enhancing participation, access and belonging of migrants. The Handbook would only be effective once the structural barriers have been knocked down, as part of a more robust system that better combines binding indicators, social policy measures and instruments to 'soft law' approaches.

The Soft Law of Hardening Access: Modularising 'Shared European Values'?

There is a conceptual issue that lies at the heart of the current integration debate relating to the assumptions about 'shared European values': such concepts which are referred to in the 'European modules' developed to assist Member States are by their nature rather nebulous. The problem is that 'European values' are claimed by socialists, liberals, conservatives, even by European racists and neo-Nazis. Various xenophobic and racist discourses are utilizing in the full notion that certain kinds of migrants cannot be integrated as they are 'culturally inept' to adapt and accept the 'European values' and 'liberal norms', for instance Muslims in Europe (see Trimikliniotis 2007). The notion of 'civic integration' left to the individual Member State to define and 'test' whether migrants have been 'integrated' is 'not an innocent concept' (Kostakopoulou 2010b): the assumptions behind 'testing' integration are highly problematic. We are therefore back to the question of implementation of such a mixed bag of not so innocent set of instruments. If Stalin's dictum that 'cadres decide everything'[18] is correct, then as anti-immigrant politics is sweeping across Europe there is little hope that a progressive evolution of the tools and instruments for immigrant integration is likely to emerge. Nevertheless, if we are to learn from history, democratic and popular struggles do impact on policy-making.

Moreover, well thought-out policy designs at EU level do have a powerfully positive impact. Such is the experience of the acquis mandatory regime which is measurable and invites sanctions should the Member States fail to properly transpose and implement the directives. This is thought as the mandatory aspect of integration, which has by and large been successful. The robust anti-discrimination acquis of the Race and Employment directives 43/2000 and 78/2000 had a major impact within every EU country and EU as a whole.[19] A number of directives on family reunification, long-term residence, qualifications, researchers, highly qualified workers, minimum standards of sanitation and measures against employers, on trafficking etc have all contributed to the enhancement of integration of migrants. Also regulations have been used to achieve such goals e.g. the social security regulations (e.g. 1408/71). Moreover, the impact of free movement of persons as a fundamental principle of the EU acquis has been a powerful tool opening new terrains mobility and countering discrimination on the basis of nationality.[20]

The integration instruments on the other hand were designed so as to supplement the above mandatory regime with 'softer tools'. The question then becomes how effective are the various instruments in achieving the goals set out. Given the uncertainty as to the goals of integration, declared and undeclared as well as the consequences, intended and unintended, the picture is blurred. Walter Bagehot famous distinction between the 'dignified' and the 'efficient' elements of the English constitution[21] may have some bearing in distinguishing between the 'formal' and the 'substantive' elements of integration instruments. Nonetheless, it is questionable whether any of the so-called substantial instruments can properly be described as 'efficient' in Bagehot's use of the term: they remain essentially 'dignified', in other words symbolic, declaratory and ideological, even though there is potential to become more 'efficient' tools of integration. The 'formal' tools such as the National Contact Points on Integration, the European Website on Integration (and the European Integration Forum) are particularly useful as means of exchanging information and good practice. They have a potential in developing an EU-wide process of longer-term learning, interacting and mutually exchanging ideas and practices. They are not designed to be policy-making or implementing instruments. Rather, they are like other soft-law instruments in that they are influential as persuasive authorities; however a condition precedent for these to be effective they depend on *political will* to achieve commonly agreed goals. To speak of 'proper' incorporation of migrants into a 'host society' we enter highly

18 J.V. Stalin (1935-1976) 'Address Delivered in the Kremlin Palace to the Graduates from the Red Army Academies', May 4, 1935, from J.V. Stalin, *Problems of Leninism*, Peking: Foreign Languages Press 1976, p. 767-774.

19 See the work produced by the network of experts on anti-discrimination field at http://www.migpolgroup.com/projects_detail.php?id=19 (accessed 10.3.2011); also see Felman 2001; Ellis 2005; Solanke 2009.

20 See European Network on Free Movement of Workers within the European Union, at http://www.ru.nl/law/cmr/projects/current_projects/coordination_of_a_eu/ (accessed 1.3. 2011).

21 See W. Bagehot (1867-2009) *The English Constitution*, at http://www.gutenberg.org/files/4351/4351-h/4351-h.htm.

problematic and outdated sociological logic and vocabulary (see Kostakopoulou 20101a; 2010b). Despite this, if we are to make a positive construction of integration as participation, access and belonging, then integration must be stripped off any exclusionary and xenophobic elements. There is here a false in-built assumption that there is such agreement as to the general aim of integration and all that is left to do to achieve this is a kind of 'fine-tuning', which would be left to the national authorities to adapt such instruments to the specificities of the national, regional and local context. However, as illustrated in this paper this is not the case as there are fundamental opposed tensions in the goals. If a Member State wants to halt the process in their country, the integration instruments can become tools for blocking implementation. More serious is the potential using integration instruments to exclude, to marginalise and to restrict migration, turning the copy/paste logic of mimetic learning against 'good practice', into a copy/paste of 'bad practice' in what becomes a 'race to the bottom'. Such a race leads to social dis-integration in the guise of 'integration'. We have experienced this over the last years such practices in different countries across the EU. The French expulsion of the Roma population to Romania contradicting the principles of free movement, the practices of the Netherlands, Germany and France to implement language tests outside their territory as means of integration prior to entry to the EU, the British, Danish and Dutch restrictive approaches family reunification and the spread of the use of 'integration tests' and mandatory regimes to exclude and punish migrants deemed not integrated or 'integreable' are but some instances where in the guise 'migrant integration' there is logic of disintegration, a race to the bottom. The use of citizenship and integration tests is questioning the liberalism of western democracies.[22]

4. Conclusion: Instrumentalizing Integration in an ever more Exclusionary and Racialised Europe

The construction processes of exclusionary citizenship *via* the discourses on 'testing' whether migrants are integrated is a process that tends to 'racialise' liberal democracy across Europe. Moreover, this process reproduces an exclusionary Europeanisation, as well as novel forms racist/populist mutations present in core of European nation-states and increasing in EU institutions (e.g. European Parliament). Racial, anti-immigrant politics and ideologies and politics of racism are not merely a question of political opportunism; nor is it a marginal phenomenon connected to extreme right-wing groups. Rather it is a mainstream process affecting national and European institutions.[23] Anti-immigrant, xenophobic and racist ideologies of a populist type contain specific elements of the kind of 'closure' required to marginalise, exclude and devalue the 'other': it is *via* the process of 'delineation

---

22 For a discussion see C. Joppke, 'How Liberal are citizenship tests?' (2010) at http://eudo-citizenship.eu/citizenship-forum/255?start=10 (accessed 18 April 2011) – papers by Inez Michalowski, Kees Groenendijk, Ricky van Oers, Amanda Klekowski von Koppenfels, Joseph Carens, Dora Kostakopoulou, Liav Orgad, Randall Hansen, Sergio Carrera, Elspeth Guild and Sarah Wallace Goodman. Also see Guild, Groenendijk & Carrera (2009).

23 See N. Trimikliniotis, 'Populism, Democracy and Social Citizenship: Discourses on "Illegal Migration" or beyond the "Fortress" versus "Cosmopolitanism" Debate', in E. Berggren, B. Likic-Brboric, T. Toksöz & N. Trimikliniotis (eds), *Irregular Migration, Informal Labour and Community: A Challenge for Europe*, Maastricht: Shaker 2007, p. 351-371.

of the internal boundary' (Anthias & Yuval-Davis 1992) generates 'the authoritarian propensity of this political logic' (Laclau 2005: 197). The 'discursive construction of the community' takes a definite form with the processes of criminalisation and illegalisation of migrants as the central element of a *'novel' racist populism and populist racism*.

Prior to the latest economic crisis it could be argued there had been an ideological-discursive shift away from 'welfare chauvinism' towards the notion that certain types of migrants are inherently unable to 'adapt to the western norms'. The question whether there is a mutation of racist politics *via* a paradigm shift within the populist reason is still valid. The logic of so-called migrant deviants or 'lesser breads', thought of as unchangeable and unfixable as they can no longer 'be brought into the law' (see Trimikliniotis 2007) has 'sadly become more or less mainstream, a kind of 'common sense'. However, there is no need to 'displace' various paradigms, particularly when dealing with racialisation processes, as they not only 'happily co-exist' as graded or alternative anti-deviant/anti-immigrant argumentation in discursive strategies, but in the current postmodern logic that anything and everything goes, they reinforce the racialisation process. The point however is not to treat the symptom as the cause, even though in the practice social processes assume their own dynamic and thus causal effect once set in motion. However, a more structural reading may be warranted rather than assuming 'populism' is an adequate explanation fitting into anything and everything. After all the *hatred of democracy* is spreading as elitists or oligarchs refer to 'democracy' pejoratively as 'populism' simply because it threatens *their* order (Rancière 2006).

In this context the debates on integration are increasingly being caught in anti-immigration and anti-immigrant politics. We therefore cannot but fundamentally question how integration is constructed and is *instrumentalised* in an ever more racialised Europe, both within the nation-states and in European institutions.

Bibliography

Anthias, F. (2006) 'Belongings in a Globalising and Unequal World: Rethinking Translocations', in N. Yuval-Davis et al. (eds.), *The situated politics of belonging*, Sage Publications, p. 17-31.

Anthias, F. & N. Yuval-Davis (1992) *Racialised Boundaries: Race, Nation, gender, Colour and Class and the Anti-racist Struggle*, London: Routledge.

Bagehot, W. (1867/2009) *The English Constitution*, Posting Date: August 11, 2009, The Project Gutenberg EBook [EBook #4351], http://www.gutenberg.org/files/4351/4351-h/4351-h.htm.

Bertossi, C. (2010) 'Conclusion – Mistaken models of integration? A critical perspective on the crisis in multiculturalism in Europe', in A. Silj (ed.), *European Multiculturalism Revisited*, Zed Books, p. 235-251.

Castles, S. (2004a) 'Factors that make and unmake migration policy', *International Migration Review,* Vol. 37, No. 3, Fall 2004, p. 812-846.

Castles, S. (2004b) 'Why migration policies fail', *Ethnic and Racial Studies,* Vol. 27 No. 2 March 2004 pp. 205–227.

Fredman, E. (ed.) (2001) *Discrimination and Human Rights, The Case of Racism*, Oxford: Oxford University Press.

Freeman, G. (2004) 'Immigrant incorporation in western democracies', *International Migration Review*, Vol. 38, No. 3, Fall 2004, p. 945-969.

Ellis, E. (2005) *EU Anti-discrimination Law*, Oxford: Oxford University Press.

Guild, E., K. Groenendijk & S. Carrera (eds) (2009) *Illiberal Liberal States: Immigration, Citizenship and Integration in the EU*, Hampshire: Ashgate.

Groenendijk, K. (2010) 'Introductory report: the (legal) notion of integration', in *Which Integration for Migrants? Interaction between the EU and its' Member States*, 28-29 October 2010, conference organised by the Centre 'Migration Asile Multiculturalisme' (Université Libre de Bruxelles), the Odysseus Network (Université Libre de Bruxelles) and the Centre for Migration Law (Radboud Universiteit Nijmegen).

Groenendijk, K. (2004) 'Legal concepts of integration in EU Migration Law', *European Journal of Migration and Law*, 6, p. 111-126.

Hollifield, J. (2004) 'The Emerging Migration State', *International Migration Review,* Vol. 37, No. 3, Fall 2004, p. 885-912.

Joppke, C. (2010) 'How Liberal are citizenship tests?' at http://eudo-citizenship.eu/citizenship-forum/255?start=10 (accessed 18 April 2011).

Kostakopoulou, D. (2010a) 'The Anatomy of Civic Integration', *The Modern Law Review*, (2010) 73(6), p. 933-958.

Kostakopoulou, D. (2010b) 'Introduction', in R. van Oers, E. Ersbøll & D. Kostakopoulou, *A Re-definition of Belonging?*, Leiden-Boston: Brill, p. 1–23.

Laclau, E. (2005) *The Populist Reason,* London: Verso Press.

Malik, K. (2008) 'Book review: Reflections on the Revolution in Europe: Immigration, Islam and Europe by Christopher Caldwell', http://newhumanist.org.uk/2093/book-review-reflections-on-the-revolution-in-europe-immigration-islam-and-europe-by-christopher-caldwell (accessed 20.3.2011).

Mann, M. (2005) *The Dark Side of Democracy: Explaining Ethnic Cleansing*, Cambridge: Cambridge University Press.

Maxwell, R. (2010) 'Evaluating Migrant Integration: Political Attitudes Across Generation Europe', *International Migration Review*, Vol. 44, No. 1, spring 2010, p. 25-52.

Mitsilegas, V. (2007) 'Immigration, Diversity and Integration: The Limits of EU Law', in P. Shah (ed.), *Law and Ethnic Plurality*, Leiden-Boston: Brill, p. 31-45.

Pajnik, M., V. Bajt & S. Herič (2010) *Migrants' Labour and Prospects for Integration: Comparative Report of Six EU Member States*, Working Paper 4, Prospects for Integration of Migrants from 'Third countries' and their Labour Market Situations: Towards Policies and Action (PRIMTS), June 2010.

Pajnik, M. & Giovanna Campani (eds) (2011) *Precarious Migrant Labour across Europe*, Politike Symposion Series, Ljubljana: Peace Institute.

Pascouau, Y. (2010) *Introductory report: outcomes of the ARC/MAM research on mandatory integration measures*, paper for conference *Which Integration for Migrants? Interaction between the EU and its Member States*, 28-29 October 2010, organised by the Centre 'Migration Asile Multiculturalisme' (Université Libre de Bruxelles), the Odysseus Network (Université Libre de Bruxelles) and the Centre for Migration Law (Radboud Universiteit Nijmegen).

Rancière, J. (2006) *Hatred of Democracy*, London: Verso Press.

Rancière, J. (2010) *Dissensus: On Politics and Aesthetics*, London & New York: Continuum.

Ratcliffe, P. & I. Newman, (2011) *Promoting Social Cohesion, Implications for policy and frameworks for evaluation*, London: The Policy Press.

Rustenbach, E. (2010) 'Sources of Negative Attitudes towars Immigrants in Europe: A Multi-Level Analysis', *International Migration Review*, Vol. 44, No. 1, spring 2010, p. 53-77.

Silj, A. (ed.) (2010) *European Multiculturalism Revisited*, London: Zed Books.

Solanke, I. (2009) *Making Anti-Racial Discrimination Law, A comparative history of social action and anti-racial discrimination law*, London: Routledge.

Trimikliniotis, N. (2012) 'Introduction: Contested Integration, Migration and Societal Transformation European Dilemmas and Challenges', in N. Trimikliniotis (ed.), *Contested Integration, Migration and Societal Transformation European Dilemmas and Challenges*, Nicosia: University of Nicosia Press.

Trimikliniotis (2007) 'Populism, Democracy and Social Citizenship: Discourses on 'Illegal Migration' or beyond the 'Fortress' versus 'Cosmopolitanism' Debate', in E. Berggren, B. Likic-Brboric, T. Toksöz & N. Trimikliniotis (eds), *Irregular Migration, Informal Labour and Community: A Challenge for Europe*, Maastricht: Shaker, p. 351-371.

Vertovec, S. & Susanne Wessendrof (ed.) (2010) *The Multiculturalism Backlash, European discourses, policies and practices*, London: Routledge.

Yuval-Davis et. al. (2006) 'Introduction', in N. Yuval-Davis, K. Kannabiran & U. Vieten (eds), *The situated politics of belonging*, London: Sage Publications.

Zaslove, A. (2004) 'The Dark Side of European Politics: Unmasking the Radical Right', *Journal of European Integration*, Vol. 26, No. 1.

Part 2. Mandatory Integration Rules in the EU Context

Mandatory Integration Schemes in the EU Member States: Overview and Trends

Yves Pascouau[*]

Over the last decade, issues related to integration have been questioned on a regular basis in the EU Member States. In the aftermath of urban riots in France and the UK, assassination of prominent persons in the Netherlands or even terrorist attacks in Spain and the UK,[1] the debate on 'failed integration policies' has become stronger. In this context, a link between integration policies and immigration policies has been reinforced aiming at using integration difficulties in order to adopt stricter immigration policies. In other words, difficulties to proper integrate migrants has justified the need to diminish migration flows within some EU States.

This phenomenon aiming at linking integration issues with migration ones and more particularly aiming at using integration issues in the framework of migration management has received an echo at EU level. More precisely, and from mid-2000, capacities or willingness of migrants to integrate into the host society became elements taken into consideration for the acquisition of a more secure status, i.e. the issuance or renewal of a residence permit or the granting of long term residence status.

This development is reflecting in the family reunification directive and the long term residents directive. In both cases, benefiting from the rights enshrined in the texts could be conditioned to the fulfilment of integration measures or conditions. Here, States could take advantage of the transposition process to introduce integration-related rules in their domestic legislation.

The phenomenon has also been taken on board in the different places where integration issues are discussed at EU level in order to coordinate national policies.[2] The development of discussions on this topic created the possibility of an enhanced linkage between integration and immigration.

In a context where mandatory integration schemes, i.e. duties third country nationals are requested to fulfil in order to obtain or continue to benefit from a right, are taking place

* This article was written within the framework of an ARC project financed by the Communauté française de Belgique and managed by the research centre 'Migration Asile Multiculturalisme' from the Université Libre de Bruxelles.

1 See R. Garbaye, *'Emeutes vs Intégration. Comparaisons franco-britanniques'*, *Les nouveaux débats*, Paris: Les Presses de Science-Po 2011.

2 Since the EU has no legislative competence in the field of integration – according to article 79.4 TFEU – the EU has developed a large number of tools and bodies aiming at coordinating national integration policies. The tools are: the Common Basic Principles adopted in 2004 by the Justice and Home Affairs Council (Doc. 14615/04); the Commission's Agenda on Integration (COM(2005)389 final, 01.09.2005); the European Integration Fund (Council Decision 2007/435/EC); Integration Handbooks and the Integration Website (http://ec.europa.eu/ewsi/en/index.cfm). Bodies are: Ministerial conferences dealing with integration issues (Groningen (2004), Potsdam (2007), Vichy (2008) and Zaragoza (2010); regular meetings between national contact points on integration; the Integration Forum.

at national and European level, it has been considered timely and appropriate to launch a large scale research – covering 23 States[3] – to identify where such requirements are applicable. In this view, the research takes into account three steps of the migration process.

The first one concerns the case where third country nationals are asked to fulfil integration duties before accessing States' territory. The second step covers integration measures and conditions to be fulfilled in the host State in the first years of residence or for the acquisition of a long term or permanent residence permit. Finally, the third step is linked with access to citizenship as in several States access to citizenship is conditional upon completion by applicants of different types of testing regarding language and/or civic knowledge.

As regard general results from the research, two main elements deserve to be outlined. First, a common trend in using mandatory integration schemes is taking place among EU States. This phenomenon is fuelled by two main forces. The first one is based on restrictive national policies developed in several States such as the Netherlands, France, Germany and the United Kingdom. These States develop integration requirements in their migration-related policies in order, in the large majority of cases, to make migrants' statuses dependant on the completion of integration duties. This has consequently the potential to make migrants' statutes weaker. The second driving force is based on the Europeanization of migration and integration issues. The development of common rules and the exchange of information between EU States give to such mandatory integration schemes a European wide coverage. As a consequence, they are wide spreading over several Member States.

Secondly, the study highlights that Europeanization of these issues is limited to the development of common trends and does not reach the harmonisation stage. Indeed, rules applicable in each of the EU States are most of time very different even though they concern the same situation and pursue identical objectives. While these differences between national rules and schemes are explained by political, economic, historical or sociological constraints, they remain sometimes very important. This raises the question as to whether harmonisation of national rules is possible, legally[4] and politically speaking,[5] in the near future.

The article aims at giving some insights regarding the two elements above mentioned. It will firstly tackle the issue of integration requirements established by EU States in foreigners' country of origin (1). It will then address the issue of integration measures and conditions applicable to third country nationals legally residing in the host Member State. This part deals with rules applicable during the first years of legal residence and for the acquisition of a permanent/long term residence permit (2). Finally, the article covers integration requirements for the acquisition of citizenship (3).

3 Member States covered by the survey are: Austria, Bulgaria, Czech Republic, Denmark, Finland, Germany, Greece, Ireland, Italy, Latvia, Lithuania, Luxembourg, the Netherlands, Poland, Portugal, Slovakia, Slovenia, Spain, Sweden, the United Kingdom and Norway.

4 Notwithstanding the limit set up by article 79.4 TFEU.

5 This covers the question of the willingness and necessity recognised at political level to harmonise national legislations on integration.

1. Integration Measures in the Country of Origin

1.1 States Implementing such Schemes

The implementation of integration measures in the migrant's country of origin is a new phenomenon. Two main factors made the development of such measures possible.

Directive 2003/86/EC on the right to family reunification[6] is the first one. Article 7, paragraph 2, of the Directive states

> 'Member States may require third country nationals to comply with integration measures, in accordance with national law.'

The provision adds

> 'With regard to the refugees and/or family members of refugees (...) the integration measures referred to in the first subparagraph may only be applied once the persons concerned have been granted family reunification.'

This means that, *a contrario*, the directive opens the possibility to establish integration measures in the migrant's country of origin.[7]

The Dutch legislation is the second factor as this Member State initiated this new mechanism of adopting pre-entry measures in the framework of family reunification. Acting as a precursor in 2006, this State has inspired others such as Germany,[8] France[9] and Denmark.[10] At the time of writing this article, Austria and the United Kingdom have also implemented pre-departure language testing. Hence, 6 out of the 27 Member States have introduced integration abroad mechanisms applicable mainly in the framework of family reunification.

---

6 Council Directive 2003/86/EC of 22 September 2003 on the right to family reunification, OJ L 251/12, 3.10.2003.

7 On this issue see Y. Pascouau, 'Mandatory Integration Provisions in EU and Member States Law', in S. Bonjour, A. Rea & D. Jacobs, *The Others in Europe*, Brussels: Editions de l'Université Libre de Bruxelles 2011.

8 I. Michalowski, 'Integration Tests in Gemany: A Communitarian Approach?', in R. van Oers, E. Ersbøll & D. Kostakopoulou, *A Re-Definition of Belonging? Language and Integration Tests in Europe*, Leiden-Boston: Martinus Nijhoff Publishers 2010; A. Wiesbrock, *Legal Migration to the European Union*, Leiden-Boston: Martinus Nijhoff Publishers 2010.

9 On this issue see Y. Pascouau, 'Integration Measures in France: An Evolving Process between Integration and Migration Issues', in R. van Oers, E. Ersbøll & D. Kostakopoulou, *A Re-Definition of Belonging? Language and Integration Tests in Europe*, Leiden-Boston: Martinus Nijhoff Publishers 2010; Y. Pascouau, 'Linking Integration and Migration issues: an Ongoing Process in French Law', in K. Sieveking, *Wechselwirkungen von Migration und Integration im Europäischen Mehrebenensystem*, Rechts- und sozialwissenschaftliche Beiträge, n° 63, Nomos 2011.

10 E. Ersbøll, 'On Trial in Denmark', in R. van Oers, E. Ersbøll & D. Kostakopoulou, *A Re-Definition of Belonging? Language and Integration Tests in Europe*, Leiden-Boston: Martinus Nijhoff Publishers 2010.

1.2 Different Schemes among States

Among the States implementing integration rules abroad,[11] none of the mechanism established is similar. Whereas one Member State has opted for a very strict type of rules, others have implemented a more flexible system. The Dutch and the French examples are classically put forward to demonstrate this opposition between restrictive and flexible systems.[12]

In the Dutch case, applicants for family reunification need to successfully take a language and knowledge of society test in order to receive the required visa. Applicants have to answer over the phone to questions raised by a computer based in the USA. At the end of the test, the computer indicates whether or not the test has been passed. As long as the test is failed, the visa is not issued and the applicant has to take the test again. In this view, the test conditions the right to family reunification.

French rules do not follow the same path. Applicants for family reunification are requested to take a language evaluation in order to assess their level of French language knowledge. Where the evaluation shows that language knowledge is insufficient, applicants are invited to attend language courses which may not last more than two months. At the end of the classes, applicants receive the visa for family reunification. According to these rules, applicants may be invited to be present at language learning lessons but after attendance and in any case, the visa for family reunification is issued.

To sum up, one system conditions the right to family reunification to successful testing, whereas the other one requires the applicant to take part in a process leading in any case to the issuance of the visa.

1.3 Questions regarding the Conformity of these Schemes with EU Law

While these two examples are typical of the differences existing between national rules, they raise another question regarding their compatibility with the Directive on the right to family reunification. In this regard, it is necessary to take two different approaches based on the directive, on the one hand, and on the jurisprudence, on the other.

As regards directive 2003/86/EC, article 7, paragraph 2, allows Member States to adopt integration 'measures'. It entitles States to adopt rules imposing obligations of means but does not allow them to implement obligations of results. In other words, States can request applicants for family reunification to engage into a process leading to the issuance of the necessary visa but States cannot condition the issuance of the visa to positive results to a test.

In this regards, and according to the Commission's interpretation,[13] it is highly questionable whether the Dutch case is compatible with EU Law. A similar assessment may be

11 This sub-section does not take into account the rules applicable in Austria and the United Kingdom.

12 For a broader and extensive description of systems applicable in the concerned Member States see, T. Strik, A. Böcker, M. Luiten & R. van Oers, *Integration and Naturalisation Tests: The New Way to European Citizenship. A comparative study in nine Member States on the national policies concerning integration and naturalisation tests and their effects on integration*, INTEC project financed by the European Integration Fund, Nijmegen: Centre for Migration Law 2010.

13 'The objective of such measures is to facilitate the integration of family members. Their admissibility under the Directive depends on whether they serve this purpose and whether they respect the principle of proportionality', Report from the Commission to the European Parliament and the Council on →

applicable to the German system where the issuance of the visa is conditioned to the issuance of the proof of sufficient language skills. Such proof is attested by a certificate delivered by appointed institutes on the basis of a language test.[14]

On the other hand, the French system complies with EU Law as the applicant is subject to an obligation of means, attendance to language courses, which does not hamper the issuance of the requested visa to join the sponsor. One mechanism is compatible with the directive whereas the other one is not.

However, and since the ECJ *Chakroun* case law,[15] the compatibly of the French system with EU rules is under question. Indeed, the Court of justice has given the family reunification directive an objective which might have large effects on the establishment of integration schemes abroad.

Asked to interpret provisions regarding income conditions for family reunification the Court stated

> '(...) Furthermore, the margin for manoeuvre which the Member States are recognised as having must not be used by them in a manner which would undermine the objective of the Directive, which is to promote family reunification and the effectiveness thereof.'[16]

Consequently, States are entitled to adopt rules defining conditions for family reunification, but such rules must not run contrary to the objective of the directive which is to promote family reunification. Hence, States are not allowed to adopt rules which aim would be to limit family reunification. As a result, if Member States wish to establish integration measures abroad, such mechanism must, on the one hand, pursue integration purposes and, on the other hand, promote family reunification.

However, the interpretation of the reasoning of the Court may not be limited to the purpose of national rules. It must also be addressed and linked with the effects of national rules. Indeed, rules might be officially adopted in order to enhance integration but in fact pursue a hidden objective which is to deter family members to apply for family reunification. For instance, the introduction of language classes in the family reunification procedure may constitute a deterrent factor for applicants and prevent family members from introducing an application for family reunification. Here, integration measures abroad do not participate to the promotion of family reunification.

On this basis, it is sometimes possible to demonstrate that a State has adopted integration measures in order to limit family migration. The French case is interesting in this regard. Examination of official reports and political statements indicate that the establishment of the language evaluation abroad mechanism pursued the diminution of applications for

---

the application of Directive 2003/86/EC on the right to family reunification, COM(2008) 610 final, 08.10.2008, p. 7-8

14 I. Michalowski, 'Integration Tests in Gemany: A Communitarian Approach?,' in R. van Oers, E. Ersbøll & D. Kostakopoulou, *A Re-Definition of Belonging? Language and Integration Tests in Europe*, Leiden-Boston: Martinus Nijhoff Publishers 2010.

15 European Court of Justice, 4 March 2010, *Rhimou Chakroun v Minister van Buitenlandse Zaken*, Case C-578/08.

16 European Court of Justice, 4 March 2010, *Rhimou Chakroun v Minister van Buitenlandse Zaken*, Case C-578/08, Point 43.

family reunification and succeeded in this regard as the number of visa application for family reunification decreased from up to 26 % since its inception.[17] In linking the purpose and effects of the rules, their compatibility with EU law becomes questionable.

To sum up, the possibility for States to adopt pre-entry integration measures within the framework of family reunification is framed by EU rules and jurisprudence. National rules must pursue an integration purpose and not run counter the objective of the directive neither in terms of political objectives nor in terms of practical effects. While the French mechanism deserves closer evaluation, any new national rule will have to take duly into account these legal limits.

While the compatibly of such mechanisms may *per se* be questioned as they have an immediate effect on the number of applications for family reunification, their establishment may not be forbidden *ab initio*. States still have the possibility to introduce integration abroad schemes as long as they pursue an integration purpose and do not have any major and long term effect on the number of visa applications introduced.

The development of integration measures abroad in the framework of family reunification is a recent phenomenon which has not been widely implemented in the EU Member States. However, it could in the future concern a larger number of States. Indeed, the directive on the right to family reunification does not contain any stand-still clause and the question of establishing such measures is or has been discussed in some States, for instance in Spain during general elections in 2008.[18]

The situation is different when looking at mandatory integration schemes applicable in the host Member States which have been largely implemented.

2. Mandatory Integration Schemes within the States

The issue of mandatory integration schemes within the member States refers to the case where third country nationals are asked to fulfil integration measures or conditions while they are already legally present on the territory of a State.

While, Germany was the only Member State in 1999 requiring third country nationals to prove language knowledge for the issuance of a permanent residence permit,[19] 17 out of the 23 States covered by the research currently impose such a requirement for the issuance or the renewal of residence permit. This question involves now a large number of EU States and demonstrates the impact of benchmarking national policies and of the coordination process between States.

Rules applicable in these 17 States vary significantly in terms of content or in terms of objectives. According to the limited format of the present article, and notwithstanding this variety of national schemes, these rules will be approached and classified under two differ-

17 Y. Pascouau, 'Linking Integration and Migration issues: an Ongoing Process in French Law', in K. Sieveking, *Wechselwirkungen von Migration und Integration im Europäischen Mehrebenensystem*, Rechts- und sozialwissenschaftliche Beiträge, n° 63, Baden-Baden: Nomos 2011.

18 R. Ferrero-Turrión & G. Pinyol-Jiménez, 'Immigration and the Construction of Public Philosophy(ies) of Integration in Spain', in E. Guild, K. Groenendijk & S. Carrera (eds.), *Illiberal Liberal States, Immigration, Citizenship and Integration in the EU*, Farnham: Ashgate 2009.

19 K. Groenendijk, E. Guild & R. Barzilay, *The Legal Status of third-country nationals who are long-term residents in a Member State of the European Union*, Luxembourg: European Commission 2001.

ent categories. The first category deals with nationals schemes where integration requirements have to be fulfilled from the beginning of the sojourn and which may have effect on the renewal of the temporary residence permit and/or the issuance of the long term/permanent residence permit (2.1). The second category comprises Member States where integration requirements are imposed by a formalised test only for the issuance of a permanent/long term residence permit (2.2). The third paragraph will finally address some concluding remarks regarding mandatory integration schemes (2.3).

2.1 Mandatory Integration Schemes applicable from the Entry on the Territory

Two sub-categories may be identified in this group of States. Those which ask third country nationals to engage into an integration contract and those where integration requirements are framed by the law.

Engaging into Integration Contracts

The first category concerns six States (Austria, Denmark, France, Italy, Luxembourg and Belgium) that make use of the integration contract.[20] Among them, rules adopted are different and call for distinction.

Two Member States, France and Italy have developed what can be called the 'short style' integration contract. This denomination relates to the length and effects of integration contracts applied in these States. Regarding the duration, these integration contracts normally last one year and can in certain circumstances be extended to a further year. Regarding the effects, they mainly play a role at the moment of the renewal of the residence permit. In this context, completion of obligations enshrined into the contract are taken into account and assessed when third country nationals apply for the renewal of their temporary residence permit generally after the first year of legal residence in the State. However, fulfilment of the contract may also be taken into account at further steps as it is the case in France where the law indicates that fulfilment of the integration contract may also be taken into consideration when examining application for long term residence permit.

In opposition to 'short style' integration contract, Austria and Denmark have opted for 'long style' integration contracts. These contracts last almost three years in Denmark and five years in Austria. In both cases, third country nationals are compelled to participate to mandatory integration classes, mainly language courses, and fulfilment of these obligations are demanded for the issuance of a permanent/long term residence permit. Here, the contract runs for several years and is directly linked with the long term residence procedure. As the introductory phase is longer and comprises several steps (2 modules to be completed within 5 years in Austria and 3 successive yearly courses ended by exams in Denmark) the level of language knowledge required at the end of the process is higher than in the 'short style' contract.

Finally, Luxembourg and Belgium deserve special attention as models implemented in these States are based on integration contract but the regime applicable is different. In Lux-

20 It must from the beginning be underlined that the term contract is misleading. Indeed, in most cases, third country nationals are obliged to sign the contract and to fulfil obligations enshrined in it. If they do not, sanctions may be applicable. In that sense, the idea conveyed by the term contract of a shared commitment between the foreigner and the States does not apply here.

embourg, a Law adopted in 2008 introduced a voluntary integration contract third country nationals may wish to engage in. But, it looks that involvement into the contract has an important impact on the situation of migrants and makes it more mandatory than voluntary. First, people engaged into the integration contract are given priority in programs set into the national integration action plan. Second, completion of the integration contract is one element that might be taken into account when examining an application for a long term residence permit.

In Belgium, the situation is different. An integration contract exists, based on the 'short term style' and comprising language and civic courses, but it is only applicable for people falling within the scope of Flemish rules.[21] For instance, people falling within the ambit of Wallonia's rules will not be obliged to engage into an integration contract.

In the end five States and one region implement mandatory integration contract. This concerns a little number of States among which one, Luxembourg, does even not recognise the mandatory nature of the contract.

Mandatory Integration Schemes established by Law

In another group of States (Germany, Norway, Slovakia and Spain) integration requirements are organised by the Law without having recourse to so-called integration contracts. Here, attendance to mandatory courses, and in specific situation passing a test, is a condition for the renewal of the residence permit and issuance of the permanent residence permit.

In Germany, third country nationals arriving in the country and not possessing skills in German language have to attend language and civic classes for almost 600 hours. At the end of these classes, foreigners have to take a test in order to have their level of language knowledge assessed. This system aims at providing foreigners with language and civic knowledge. It is also used in the administrative procedure regarding issuance of residence permits. The residence permit is renewed where third country nationals show the intention to reach the required level of language and a regular attendance of the courses. Concerning the issuance of a permanent residence permit, applicants have to provide for the appropriate level of language knowledge.

The Norwegian system is close to the German one, except that there is no test at the end of language and civic training. In this country, third country nationals have to attend language and civic courses for 300 hours. Attendance to those courses is mandatory and failure to fulfil obligations leads to the refusal to issue permanent residence permit.

As regard the situation of Slovakia and Spain, it is not very clear whether these countries have established mandatory integration courses. In Slovakia, the law does not formally organize a mandatory system as such. However, it allows a police department to request a third country national to provide for a document confirming completion of a Slovak language course while applying for the long term residence status. It is possible to interpret the rule in a way that the long term residence permit will not be issued if the applicant has not

21 On the Belgian situation see M.C. Foblets & Z. Yanasmayan, 'Language and integration requirements in Belgium: Discordances between the Flemish policy of "inburgering" and the federal legislators' view(s) on integration of newcomers and migrants', in R. van Oers, E. Ersbøll & D. Kostakopoulou, *A Re-Definition of Belonging? Language and Integration Tests in Europe*, Leiden–Boston: Martinus Nijhoff Publishers 2010.

attended to language courses. In Spain, the new alien's law opens the possibility to condition renewal of the residence permit to the participation to formative actions regarding language and civic learning.

2.2 Mandatory Integration Test applicable for the Issuance of a Long Term/ Permanent Residence Permit

A second category of States is composed with those which use a test for the issuance of a permanent/long term residence permit. The difference with the previous categories is that the question relating to integration duties is focused on the issuance of long term/permanent residence permit and this latter is issued if a test is successfully taken. Such scheme is applicable in the Czech Republic, Greece, Lithuania, Latvia, the Netherlands and Portugal.

However, and notwithstanding the common use of such a procedure, rules applicable in these six Member States differ sometimes in a considerable manner. This is the case for instance regarding the scope of the test. While some States require a language test (Czech Republic, Latvia, Portugal), others ask for the accomplishment of both a language and a civic test (Greece, Lithuania, the Netherlands, United Kingdom). The content of the tests may as well differ. Hence, the level of language knowledge required may vary from level A1 to level B1 of the Common European Framework of Reference[22]. Other differences also exist regarding the preparation of the test. In some States attendance the classes is mandatory whereas it is not in others. As regards the cost of mandatory classes, some are free where others are not.

These differences demonstrate that beyond a common willingness to condition the issuance of the long term/permanent residence permit to a test, States implement this objective in a different fashion.

This overview of integration requirements demonstrates the wide variety of rules and solutions implemented in the States. In short, type of schemes, type of knowledge requested, level of language knowledge required, duration of the course, costs of education are for instance points where differences, sometimes huge, exist. The harmonisation of national rules within the emerging European integration policy may be hard to reach.

2.3 Concluding Remarks regarding Mandatory Integration Schemes within the States

Despite the wide diversity between national rules and models, some conclusions deserve to be outlined regarding integration requirements established in the States.

First, the use of 'integration contracts' is not relevant. On the one hand, migrants are obliged to engage into contracts without having the freedom to choose. In this regard, contracts are all but contracts reflecting the free will of partners. On the other hand, a

---

22 Common European Framework of Reference is a document adopted by the Council of Europe. It provides a basis for the mutual recognition of language qualifications.

small number of States is using these contracts while other States require third country nationals to fulfil the same obligations without obliging them to conclude a formal contract.

Second, the extension of the use of mandatory integration schemes from one State in 1999 to currently 17 cannot be delinked from the emergence of an EU migration policy. The impact of the long term residence directive may not be ignored as well as the development of tools and bodies at EU level addressing integration issues in order to promote the coordination of national policies.

Third, the use of mandatory integration schemes, in particular in the field of family reunification, should be further analyse so as to make sure that integration rules are established to enhance social inclusion and not for the sake of migration management.

3. Mandatory Integration Schemes and Access to Nationality

Eighteen Member States, including Estonia[23] and Norway, require applicants for naturalisation to demonstrate integration skills. This represents almost 75% of the Member States covered by the research. Belgium, Ireland, Italy and Sweden did not establish integration requirements. However, this does not prevent some of them to do so in the future. This is the case for instance for Belgium where the issue of reintroducing language requirements in the naturalisation procedure, abandoned in a law adopted in 2000, is under discussion.[24]

All of the 18 States request applicants for citizenship to prove language knowledge (3.1). The number of States implementing civic knowledge requirements, such as institutions and history knowledge, is less important (3.2). In both cases, rules applicable show differences between Member States.

3.1 Language Knowledge Requirements

While all of the 18 States ask applicants to demonstrate knowledge of the host country's language, differences exist between them.

A first type of difference exists between States which organise a formal examination and those which do not. Austria, Denmark, Germany, the Netherlands and Norway fall within the category of States which do not organise formal examination. These States ask applicants for naturalisation to prove they have already passed adequate language exams in their migration route. Such prove may be brought in different ways according to national rules.[25]

On the contrary, most of the States use a formal examination within the naturalisation procedure. However, a series of differences exists in this category. Some States organise a

23 Estonia is not covered by the research but information provided by the EUDO project website has allowed taking this Member State into account.

24 M.C. Foblets & Z. Yanasmayan, 'Language and integration requirements in Belgium: Discordances between the Flemish policy of "inburgering" and the federal legislators' view(s) on integration of newcomers and migrants', in R. van Oers, E. Ersbøll & D. Kostakopoulou, *A Re-Definition of Belonging? Language and Integration Tests in Europe*, Leiden-Boston: Martinus Nijhoff Publishers 2010.

25 For instance, applicants may provide for an official diploma attesting their level of knowledge or the certificate they have taken prior language tests requested in the framework of their migration route in the host State.

simple oral testing/evaluation (Czech Republic, France and Spain). Here, and as a general rule, the level of language knowledge requested is not very high and language requirement is not central in the naturalisation procedure.

In three other States – Bulgaria, Portugal and the United Kingdom – language skills are assessed on the basis of a written test. The latter may be replaced in Portugal and Bulgaria by the production of certificate of language proficiency. In these two States, the level of language required is not very high. In the United Kingdom, language knowledge may be proven either on the basis of a computer based test, at level B1, or upon attendance to citizenship courses. If the applicant for naturalisation has opted for citizenship courses, he/she needs to prove that he/she has reached the next step of language knowledge.[26]

Finally, Estonia, Finland, Latvia, Lithuania, Luxembourg, Slovakia and Slovenia organise oral and written tests mainly managed by specialised organs or commissions. This procedure shows that language knowledge is considered as a significant element in the naturalisation procedure.

While States apply different procedures, they also demand different performances. Hence, the level of language skills goes from elementary level to advanced speaker. It should however be underlined that the level of language knowledge is an objective element that does not reflect the complexity of the issue.

Indeed, the capacity to learn the language and to acquire the required skills depends on the third country national's capacities and on the possibility given to him/her to receive language classes. This goes from States where no language classes are provided (Bulgaria, Lithuania, Latvia and Slovakia) to the situation where applicants may attend classes on a voluntary fashion (Czech Republic, Estonia, Luxembourg, the Netherlands, Portugal, Slovenia and Spain) or a mandatory basis in the framework of prior procedures (Austria, Denmark, France, Germany, Greece and Norway). The United Kingdom is the only State where language classes are organised in the framework of the naturalisation procedure. In order to disclose the complexity of the issue, it should be underlined that differences have also been found regarding the length and the price of the courses.

The question of language testing for the acquisition of citizenship demonstrates that numerous and sometimes important differences exist between States rules. Without entering into too many details, a similar statement may be drawn as for civic knowledge requirements.

3.2 Civic Knowledge Requirements

Fourteen States require applicants for citizenship to prove civic knowledge. Among those States requirements are very diverse. The great majority of member States require applicants for citizenship to demonstrate knowledge of political institutions, history of the host Member States and values of this latter. A little number asks applicants to provide for knowledge of EU Values.

As regard the type of questions asked, they may vary considerably between States. This is particularly the case where it comes to history as some States ask questions that even natives would hardly have an answer to.

26 For instance, where the applicant possesses a language knowledge equivalent to level A1 at the beginning of the course, he/she has to prove he/she has acquired a level A2 at the end of the courses.

Examination of civic knowledge differs also greatly. Some States do not frame the evaluation in a particular format and evaluate knowledge on the basis of an oral evaluation. Others have established written tests which most of time take the form of a multiple choice questions test. These latter might be very different one from the other – in terms of number of questions, duration of the test, number of goods answers needed, etc ... – and lead to huge differences in terms of difficulties.

Integration requirements for the acquisition of nationality are used in a large majority of States but their regimes vary considerably. In this regard, language and civic knowledge could be considered as a formal element of the naturalisation procedure or constitute a real obstacle to the acquisition of nationality.

4. Conclusions

The research conducted under the ARC-MAM project proved that integration requirements are implemented in an important majority of States. While these requirements remain limited regarding integration measures to be fulfilled in the country of origin, they are more largely shared once third country nationals are on the territory of Member States, i.e. for the renewal of a temporary residence permit, the acquisition of a permanent residence permit or the acquisition of citizenship.

The trend to implement integration requirements is not accompanied with a tendency to implement similar rules. Indeed, schemes and requirements vary significantly between the States and it appears sometimes very hard to find common points of convergences.

This proves that the use of integration requirements is at its first stage of development. Indeed, Member States are experiencing these new possibilities before reaching the further step which would aim at coordinating national policies in a consistent manner. This further step would provide a basis for future harmonisation of national rules in the framework of the emergent EU integration policy.

This coordination process should however avoid a dangerous pitfall which would consist in using integration requirements for the sake of limiting or managing migration flows. This development, emerging in some States, takes the form of requiring migrants to prove language or civic knowledge with the argument of avoiding further integration 'problems'. But, failure to fulfil such requirements has an impact on the migrant's rights and status. This is for instance the case where visa or residence permits are not issued or withdrawn because integration requirements are not or not properly fulfilled. In this regard, States make immigration rules more restrictive, rights more difficult to acquire and migrants' status more fragile.

While the boundaries between integration and immigration have always been very thin, each policy follows a specific objective. Immigration policies seek to define who is entitled to enter and reside into the territory and for which purposes. Integration policies seek to promote social inclusion. In using integration requirements for the sake of restricting migration flows, States are awarding integration policy an exclusion rather than an inclusion purpose.

In times of restrictive policies and xenophobic discourses, it is more than important to recall that integration is a long and complex process which calls not only for migrants' efforts to better integrate but also for the involvement of the receiving State and the participation of the receiving society itself.

Migration Law and Civic Integration in Europe: Reflecting on Mandatory Integration Requirements following *Chakroun*

Siobhán Mullally

With the European Union, the language of multicultural accommodation is increasingly being replaced by policy agendas that are more likely to appeal to the values of social cohesion and civic integration.[1] The preoccupation with integration of migrant communities is reflected in the resurgence of interest in 'pathways to citizenship' and integration testing, both at EU level and in Member States.[2] In recent years, this preoccupation has been marked by a willingness to deploy juridical and punitive tools of immigration control to monitor mandatory integration requirements.[3] Newly expanded forms of integration testing seek to assess the migrant's commitment to liberal democratic ideals and language skills.

At the level of the European Union, integration conditions have increasingly been linked to security and migration control. Integration is now firmly embedded in the range of governance tools deployed by the Union to manage third country nationals within, or aspiring to be within, its borders.[4] Despite the gradual expansion of rights for third country nationals and policy commitments to the 'near equality' and fairness required in the treatment of long-term residents, integration testing has expanded beyond the domain of naturalization, seeking to reach a broader range of migrants.[5]

The expansion of integration testing, and the imposition of thicker integration conditions has not yet been fully tested under European or international human rights law. Yet, this expansion clearly engages rights that are protected both at European and international levels – rights to religious freedom, freedom of expression, to cultural identity, to private

---

1 See: E. Guild, C.A. Groenendijk & S. Carrera, *Illiberal liberal states: immigration, citizenship, and integration in the EU*, Farnham: Ashgate 2009); D. Kostakopoulou, 'Matters of Control: Integration Tests, Naturalisation Reform and Probationary Citizenship in the United Kingdom', 36 *Journal of Ethnic and Migration Studies* 829.

2 See, for example: Home Office, UK Border Agency, *The Path to Citizenship: Next Steps in Reforming the Immigration System* (February, 2008). On the compatibility of citizenship testing with liberalism, see: EUDO Forum on Citizenship, (2010) *How Liberal are Citizenship Tests?*, available at: http://eudo-citizenship.eu/cit-forum/viewforum.php?f=2; On the expansion of integration testing in Europe, see: 'Citizenship Tests in a Post-National Era', International Journal of Multicultural Societies, Special Issue: Vol. 10(1), (2008), discussing recent developments in the Netherlands, Denmark, France and the UK. See also the Special Issue of the *Journal of Ethnic and Migration Studies* edited by M. Vink & R. de Groot (2010, forthcoming).

3 C. Dauvergne, 'Globalizing Fragmentation: New Pressures on Women Caught in the Immigration Law – Citizenship Law Dichotomy', in S. Benhabib & J. Resnik, *Migrations and mobilities: citizenship, borders, and gender*, New York: New York University press 2009, p. 333-355, at p. 334.

4 See: S. Carrera, *In search of the perfect citizen? The intersection between integration, immigration, and nationality in the EU*, Leiden-Boston: Martinus Nijhoff Publishers 2009.

5 See: Council Directive concerning the status of third-country nationals who are long-term residents, 2003/109, [2004] OJ L 16/44, 23.1.2004 and; Council Directive 2003/86/EC of 22 September 2003 on the Right to Family Reunification, OJ L 251/12, 3.10.2003.

and family life and to non-discrimination. The proportionality of states' responses to immigration when such rights are engaged becomes more difficult to justify as the interests at stake touch on core norms of human rights law. Until recently, international law has typically had little to say about state practices on immigration and citizenship. Indeed immigration and citizenship laws are sometimes viewed as the last bastion of the citadel of state sovereignty. Over the last 10-15 years, however, we have seen a greater willingness from international and European human rights bodies to question the historical discretion enjoyed by states in immigration matters.[6] The European Court of Justice has, in some instances, been even more robust in its challenge to Member States.[7]

States, however, have pushed back against the expansion of rights to third country nationals, appealing to national security, public order and to requirements of cohesion and integration.[8] Yielding to this 'push back' may limit the potential of human rights law to challenge states' prerogatives in matters of immigration and citizenship and to protect the rights of migrants and third country nationals in Europe. The rise of the civic integration paradigm is at the heart of debates surrounding the limits of sovereignty of Member States in the EU and the cosmopolitan reach of fundamental rights and non discrimination principles.

This chapter examines the case of *Rhimou Chakroun v Minister van Buitenlandse Zaken,*[9] a case arising from a reference for a Preliminary Ruling on the interpretation of Articles 2 and 7 of Council Directive 2003/86/EC on the right to family reunification (the Family Reunification Directive). The reference was made in the course of proceedings between Mrs Chakroun and the Dutch Minister for Foreign Affairs concerning the refusal to issue a provisional residence permit to Mrs Chakroun. The Chapter begins with an introduction to the evolution of mandatory integration requirements in EU Member States. The judgment of the European Court of Justice in *Chakroun* is then examined. The potential for conflict between integration requirements imposed by Member States at domestic level and the principles of EU law is explored in light of the findings of the Court. The Chapter concludes with a discussion on the implications of the judgment for integration abroad requirements in general, and beyond the context of family reunification.

Integration, Reciprocity and Pre-departure Requirements

The coercive powers of Member States regarding integration have been particularly evident in the expanding set of immigration tools that have developed over the last 5-10 years, both

---

6 See for example, CERD General Recommendation XXX, pt. 4. See also: D.S. Weissbrodt, *The human rights of non-citizens*, Oxford-New York: Oxford University Press 2008; P. Spiro, 'A New International Law of Citizenship', 105 *Am. J. Int'l L.* 694 (2011).

7 See generally, on the role of the ECJ and the European Court of Human Rights in migration law disputes: S. Morano-Foadi & S. Andreadakis, 'The Convergence of the European Legal System in the Treatment of Third Country Nationals in Europe: The ECJ and ECtHR Jurisprudence', *European Journal of International Law*, Vol. 22 (4), 2011, p. 1-18.

8 See generally: A. Edwards & C. Ferstman, *Human Security and Non-Citizens: Law, Policy and International Affairs*, Cambridge University Press 2010.

9 *Chakroun v. Minister van Buitenlandse Zaken*, C-578/08, 4 March 2010.

at national and European levels.[10] Integration conditions have been attached to both the EU Family Reunification and the Long Term Residence Directives.[11] How thin or thick such conditions might be has been left to Member States to determine, allowing considerable discretion to governments in defining the pathways to belonging. To what extent the Court of Justice of the European Union (CJEU) will limit this discretion, drawing on EU legislation, remains to be seen as case law continues to evolve in this field. The Stockholm programme has given a renewed impetus to integration as an element of immigration policy.[12] Further support is provided by the conclusion of the Lisbon Treaty, which allows for incentives and support to be given to Member States' integration initiatives by the European Council and the Parliament.[13] Crucially, Member States retain significant discretion over the integration conditions to be introduced.

The renewed focus on integration in some Member States has taken a juridical form, in legislative initiatives introducing contracts for third country nationals, '*contrats d'acceuil et d'integration*' (CAI) in France, for example, with stringently policed contractual requirements concerning integration.[14] These contracts represent an expansion of integration policy beyond the process of naturalization where requirements of assimilation, albeit relatively thin, have been well established. The consequences of a failure to comply with the terms of the contract, betray the illusion of voluntarism or reciprocity suggested by the language of contract; failing to fulfill the integration requirements imposed may lead to an application for a residence permit or renewal, or family reunification being denied. As Böcker and Strik have noted, the introduction of such requirements 'signifies a reversal of the idea that a secure status facilitates the integration process'.[15] This presumption dominated thinking and practice in EU Member States in the 1980s and 1990s. It also underpinned the earlier positions of the European Commission. Support for this position has been

10 See generally: A. Böcker & T. Strik, 'Language and Knowledge Tests for Permanent Residence Rights: Help or Hindrance for Integration?', European Journal of Migration and Law, Volume 13, Number 2, 2011 , p. 157-184.

11 Supra n. 5.

12 Council of the European Union, The Stockholm Programme – An open and secure Europe serving and protecting the citizens, Doc. 17024/09, Brussels, December 2009. See also: E. Collett, *The EU immigration Pact: from Hague to Stockholm, via Paris*, EPC Policy Brief, Brussels 2008, available at: http://www.epc.eu/TEWN/pdf/304970248_EU%20Immigration%20 Pact.pdf.

13 Treaty of Lisbon Amending the Treaty on European Union and the Treaty Establishing the European Community, Article 63b, OJ C 306 17.12.2007.

14 In France, see: Loi n.° 2003-1119 relative à la maîtrise de l'immigration, au séjour des étrangers en France et à la nationalité of 26 November 2003 and Loi relative à l'immigration et à l'intégration, N°2006-911. See also: Loi n°2007-1631 du 20 novembre 2007 relative à la maîtrise de l'immigration, à l'intégration et à l'asile, introducing the Contrat d'acceuil et d'intégration pour la famille (CAIF), Article 7. At EU level, see: Council Directive concerning the status of third-country nationals who are long-term residents, 2003/109, [2004] OJ L 16/44, 23.1.2004 and; Council Directive 2003/86/EC of 22 September 2003 on the Right to Family Reunification, OJ L 251/12, 3.10.2003. For commentary, see: S. Carrera, ch. 6 and M. Beaujeau, 'Le modèle français d'intégration dans tous ses états: Entre réaffirmations républicaines et tentations populistes', 10 *International Journal on Multicultural Societies* 2008, 27. On developments on family reunification at the EU level, see: D. Kostakopoulou, S. Carrera & M. Jesse, 'Doing and Deserving: Competing Frames of Integration in the EU', in E. Guild et al., *supra* n. 1.

15 *Supra* n. 10, p. 157-158.

eroded over the last decade, however. Secure residence status is now something to be earned following demonstrable compliance with integration requirements.[16]

While integration is often viewed as a two-way process, facilitating the process of adapting to a new society, its institutions and ways of life, the introduction of integration abroad requirements, mark a further shift away from the presumed reciprocity of such a process. The introduction of integration abroad requirements occurs against a background of increasing attempts to restrict family reunification. Integration abroad requirements now operate as a 'switch' for the family migration journey in several Member States, including the Netherlands, France, Austria, Denmark, the United Kingdom and Germany. As Kostapolou has recently noted, the 'absence of serious reflection on the conceptual coherence and justifiability of integration abroad' requirements is puzzling'.[17] The introduction of these new requirements is part of a broader move to limit what has come to be described as '*immigration subie*', (literally, suffered immigration) in favour of '*immigration choisi*'. Family reunification, being less predictable, less susceptible to controlling limits, has been categorized by states and Governments as coming within the umbrella of '*immigration subie*', and as something to be curtailed, restricted and possibly denied.

These restrictions highlight the tensions between the recognition of right to private and family life as deserving of protection as a fundamental right, and the desire of Member States to limit and control family reunification, viewed as a threat to policies of migration management. Against Member States attempts at restriction, the ECJ has increasingly flexed its muscles in this area, elevating the normative priority of respect for family life as a principle of EU law, and questioning attempts by states to subordinate rights claims to utilitarian calculations of the common good. The Commission had, until recently, adopted a somewhat ambivalent position on integration abroad requirements, reflecting the failure at policy level to engage in a robust debate on the conceptual and legal coherence of mandatory pre-departure integration conditions. In its 2005 Communication on a Common Agenda for an Integration Framework for the Integration of TCNs in the EU, the possibility of pre-departure measures playing a role in 'comprehensive migration and development strategies' was acknowledged.[18] Since then, the Commission appears to have stepped back from this position. In its submissions in proceedings on the *Imran* case, the Commission expressed its opinion that the imposition of integration conditions as requirements for the exercise of family reunification rights was not compatible with the Family Reunification Directive.[19] The Commission's submissions in the *Chakroun* case (discussed below) also reflect a general concern to constrain the discretion enjoyed by Member States in implementation of the Family Reunification Directive, with potential implications for integration policies adopted at Member State level.

---

16 *Ibid*.

17 D. Kostakopoulou, 'The Anatomy of Civic Integration', 73 *The Modern Law Review* 933.

18 Communication on a Common Agenda for an Integration Framework for the Integration of Third Country Nationals, COM(2005) 389 final, p. 18.

19 See: ECJ, 10 June 2011, *Bibi Mohammad Imran*, C-155/11 PPU. The Commission specifically stated that Article 7(2) of the Directive did not permit the imposition of a civic integration test abroad as a condition limiting the exercise of family reunification rights. A residence permit was granted by the Netherlands in this case, and so proceedings did deemed to be without purpose before the Court. For further discussion on this see: Y. Pascouau (ed.), *Conditions for Family Reunification under Strain*, Brussels: European Policy Centre2011, p. 93.

Chakroun v. Minister van Buitenlandse Zaken, C-578/08

The *Chakroun* judgment signals the potential for further scrutiny by the Court of Justice of immigration laws adopted by Member States, including in the future, questioning of how and whether integration requirements imposed by Member States comply with EU law.[20] The *Chakroun* case concerned a Moroccan national, Ms Rhimou Chakroun, who was seeking to join her husband Mohammed Chakroun, in the Netherlands. On 10 March 2006, Mrs Chakroun applied to the Netherlands Embassy in Rabat (Morocco) for a provisional residence permit in order to live with her husband. Mr Chakroun, also a Moroccan national, had lived in the Netherlands since 1970 and held permanent residence status. The couple had married in 1972, but Ms Chakroun had continued to live in Morocco. Ms Chakroun was refused a permit on the ground that Mr Chakroun's income at the time was below the minimum income threshold required for family formation under the Dutch Aliens Decree. At the time of the application Mr Chakroun was receiving unemployment benefits. Mr Chakroun's unemployment benefit amounted to only EUR 1,322.73 net per month, inclusive of holiday allowance, and was therefore below the applicable income standard for family formation, which was EUR 1,441.44 per month.

The Dutch Law on Aliens 2000 provided that an application for a fixed-period residence permit may be refused if:[21]

> [...] the alien does not have independent, lasting and sufficient means of support, or the person with whom the alien wishes to reside does not have independent, lasting and sufficient means of support.

It was further specified in the Dutch Aliens Decree 2000 that a residence permit would be granted, in the case of family formation, if the 'lasting and independent net income' was equal to at least 120% of the minimum wage, as set out in the Law on the minimum wage and minimum holiday allowance. Before the Council of State, Mrs Chakroun had raised the question whether Article 7 of the Family Reunification Directive had been correctly implemented in domestic legislation, given the requirement that a sponsor, in cases of family formation, to have resources equivalent to 120% of the minimum wage.[22] She also challenged the distinction made in the Dutch Aliens Decree between family formation and family reunification.[23]

The Council of State ultimately referred two questions to the ECJ: First, whether the requirement of 'stable and regular resources' in Article 7(1)(c) of the Directive 2003/86 could exclude someone who would be entitled to claim special assistance, and; second, whether national legislation distinguishing between applicants for family formation and family reunification was in compliance with the Directive, in particular Article 2(d). Domestic law distinguished between cases where a family relationship existed prior to the sponsor's entry to the Netherlands, and those cases where the relationship was formed while the sponsor was already living in the Netherlands. The minimum level of resources

20 *Chakroun v. Minister van Buitenlandse Zaken*, C-578/08, 4 March 2010.

21 Article 16(1) (c) Law on Aliens 2000.

22 *Ibid.*, para. 24.

23 *Ibid.*, para. 29.

required on the part of the sponsor differed in each case, with a higher threshold set for cases of family formation.

In its judgment, the Court noted that the Preamble to the Directive specifically required that measures concerning family reunification should be adopted by Member States, in conformity with the obligation to protect the family and respect family life, enshrined in several international legal instruments.[24] The Directive, the Court pointed out, respects the principles recognised in particular in article 8 of the European Convention on Human Rights (ECHR) and in the Charter of Fundamental Rights. Much of the debate before the Court concerned the interpretation of Article 7(1) of the Directive, which allows Member States to impose conditions that must be satisfied prior to the grant of family reunification. In this case, the provision in Article 7(1)(c), allowing Member States to require that the sponsor demonstrate that he or she had 'stable and regular resources', which were sufficient to maintain themselves and the family members, 'without recourse to the social assistance system of the Member State', was at issue. The Dutch highest Alien Court *Raad van State* had argued that the minimum wage was an essential reference so as to ensure a minimum standard of living for all Dutch nationals and third country nationals residing in the Netherlands.

Mrs Chakroun challenged the distinction drawn by the Dutch Aliens Decree between family reunification and family formation, a distinction based on whether the family relationship arose before or after the sponsor's entry into the Netherlands. No such distinction is drawn in Article 7(1) of the Family Reunification Directive. If the application in this case had been treated as an application for family reunification, Mr Chakroun's resources would have been greater than the required amount, and presumably, the application would not have been refused. In questioning the distinction between family formation and family reunification, Mrs Chakroun cited the report published on 11 March 2009 by the Council of Europe Commissioner for Human Rights on his visit to the Netherlands, in which he expressed surprise at certain provisions in the Netherlands legislation concerning family reunification.[25] She also cited the report drawn up by the *Wetenschappelijk Onderzoek- en Documentatiecentrum* (Scientific Research and Documentation Centre) of the Netherlands Ministry of Justice evaluating the effect on the migration of foreign spouses to the Netherlands of the increase in income required for purposes of family reunification.[26] In Mrs Chakroun's submission, she argued that the negative aspects described in that report demonstrated that the Netherlands rules run counter to the objective of the Directive.[27] The amount required by the Netherlands authorities for evaluation of the sufficiency of resources was the highest of all the Member States of the European Union.[28]

The Commission, in its submissions, also questioned the link between the level of resources and minimum income levels set and the question whether an application concerned a situation of family formation or reunification – a distinction made in Dutch legislation but not found in the Family Reunification Directive, with the exception of its application to refugees (article 9(2)). The Netherlands Government argued that the level of resources required in the case of family reunification, they suggested, corresponded in fact to the

24 *Ibid.*, para. 44.
25 *Ibid.*, para. 55.
26 *Ibid.*, para. 35.
27 *Ibid.*, para. 35.
28 *Ibid.*, para. 37.

amount 'which is normally sufficient to meet the most basic needs in Netherlands society'.[29] Both Mrs Chakroun and the Commission argued that the Dutch authorities had failed to take account of the long duration of the marriage and, as such, had failed to comply with the requirement of Article 17 of the Directive that there must be an individual assessment in each case.

The Advocate General delivered her opinion on 10 December 2009, notably on UN Human Rights day. In her opinion, Advocate General Sharpston expressed the view that a distinction between family reunification and family formation in the conditions imposed by Member States on level of resources available was not permissible.[30] Objective factors were not available to justify this distinction, unlike the permissible differences in treatment with regard to refugees, where she argued, such objective factors could be pointed to. The Advocate General's opinion draws on the principle of non discrimination to support the rejection of the distinctions made in the domestic law of the Netherlands. The systematic rejection of applications where the family may have a potential entitlement to special assistance was also, she said, contrary to Article 17's requirement of an individual assessment in each case.[31]

The Court agreed in general with Advocate Sharpston's findings and went further in its judgment on the extent and scope of the obligations imposed on Member States by the Directive. The Directive, the Court found, imposed 'precise positive obligations' on States, requiring them, in the cases determined by the Directive, to authorise family reunification of certain members of a sponsor's family, without being left a margin of appreciation.[32] The Court drew again on its statements concerning the scope of obligations imposed by the Directive, in its earlier judgment in *Parliament* v *Council*.[33] Authorisation of family reunification, the Court noted, was the general rule, and the 'margin of manoeuvre' left to states in Article 7, must be strictly interpreted. Specifically actions taken by states should not undermine the effectiveness of the Directive or its objective, which was stated as being to 'promote family reunification'.[34] Importantly, the Court noted that measures concerning family reunification should be adopted in conformity with the obligation to protect the family and respect family life, as recognized in many instruments of international law, and in particular in Article 8 ECHR and in the Charter of Fundamental Rights.

Addressing the specific questions raised by the Netherlands national legislation, the Court noted that the restrictions permitted by Article 7(1)(c) arising from requirements concerning the availability of 'stable and regular resources,' must be limited. In this case, the Court agreed with the Commission's contention in the proceedings, that the difference in level of resources required for family reunification or family formation, could not be defended. The higher amount required for family formation could not be defended as reflecting the minimum level of income needed to subsist in the Netherlands. In a statement that may bring into question general measures imposed by Member States, the Court noted that while states may indicate a 'certain sum as a reference amount' in order to assess the

29 *Ibid.*, para. 37.

30 Opinion of Advocate General Sharpston delivered on 10 December 2009, *Rhimou Chakroun v Minister van Buitenlandse Zaken*, Case C-578/08.

31 *Ibid.*, paras. 56-71 of the Opinion.

32 *Supra* n. 20, para. 41.

33 Case C-540/03 [2006] ECR I-5769, para. 60.

34 *Supra* n.20, para. 43.

availability of 'stable and regular resources', they could not impose a minimum income level below which all family reunifications would be refused. A system, such as that imposed by the Netherlands, would be contrary to the requirement to individually assess the situation of each applicant.[35]

On the distinction between family formation and family reunification, the Court found that the rules set out in the Directive applied to all such cases, without distinction, with the exception of Article 9(2), which applied only to refugees. Citing *Metock*[36] the Court found that Member States were not, therefore, permitted to introduce such a distinction in the transposition of the Directive. This finding was, they said, supported by Recital 6, which seeks to 'protect the family and establish or preserve family life' and by the *travaux préparatoires* of the Directive, cited by Mrs Chakroun, from which it was apparent that there was broad agreement that family reunification should cover both family formation and preservation of the family unit.[37] This interpretation, the Court concluded, was consistent with Article 8 of the ECHR and Article 7 of the Charter of Fundamental Rights, which do not draw any distinction based on the circumstances and time at which a family is constituted.[38]

Conclusions: Implications for Integration Agendas?

The Court's finding is significant. While not addressing specifically the compatibility of integration requirements imposed by Member States, with EU law, it does signal how the Court might analyse and potentially challenge such requirements in the future. The judgment of the Court was limited to responding to the particular questions submitted concerning the financial resources requirements imposed in the context of a family reunification application. However, the analysis applied by the Court and its concern to limit the room for manoeuvre left to Member States so as to ensure that the effectiveness of the Directive was not undermined is of wider significance. It reflects the potential for the Court to ensure that the integration laws and policies adopted at Member State level do not undermine the very purpose of EU legislation. The importance of individual assessments and adherence to the requirements of the ECHR and the Charter of Fundamental Rights are also reinforced.

The positive obligations identified by the Court, as being imposed by the Directive, reflect its willingness to scrutinise the measures adopted at Member State level and their *de facto* impact on the rights protected by EU law. As Weisbrock notes, identifying family reunification or family formation as the general rule from which only limited exceptions are permitted, has several consequences for Member States, including the recognition of parallels between the rights of Union citizens and those of third country nationals.[39] In its judgment, the ECJ invoked the *Eind*[40] and *Metock* judgments to support its conclusions, both cases that directly concerned the rights of Union citizens. The analogy drawn by the

35 *Ibid.*, para. 48.

36 *Metock and Others v. Minister for Justice, Equality and Law Reform*, C-127/08, 25 July 2008.

37 *Supra* n. 9, para. 62.

38 *Ibid.*, para. 63.

39 A. Weisbrock, 'The Right to Family Reunification of Third-Country Nationals under EU Law; Decision of 4 March 2010, Case C-578/08, *Rhimou Chakroun v. Minister van Buitenlandse Zaken*', *European Constitutional Law Review* (2010), 6, p. 462-480, at p. 469.

40 Case C-291/05, *Minister voor Vreemdelingenzaken en Integratie v R.N.G. Eind*, 11 December 2007.

Court, with the rights of third-country nationals, reflects a welcome extension of rights protections within the EU, bringing the Union closer to its objectives of fairness and 'near-equality'.[41]

The *Chakroun* judgment represents a change in the Court's approach to the rights of third country nationals. The case specifically concerns family reunification, but potentially the analogies drawn with the rights of Union citizens could be applied in other situations or with regard to other rights claims. As Martin notes, in *Parliament v Council,* the Court did not discus the possible applicability of EU general principles of law or case-law concerning Union citizens.[42] The Court found that the Directive was in compliance with EU law, provided that it conformed to the requirements of article 8 ECHR case-law. It also found that allowing for the possibility of imposing integration conditions in the specific circumstances of a child over the age of 12 years, arriving independently from his or her family, was compatible with Article 8(2) of the ECHR and in line with the case law of the European Court of Human Rights on family unity rights. The integration conditions to be imposed were limited and were required to be provided by law, and to reflect the specific concern that a child over the age of 12 years, might have more limited potential for integration given their linguistic and education skills. The Strasbourg case-law has, at times, granted lesser protection to family life than EU law protection for the family life of Union citizens.[43] The extension in *Chakroun* of the case-law concerning the rights to family life of Union citizens is, therefore, particularly significant. What is also notable about the *Chakroun* and other judgments of the CJEU is the Court's willingness to go beyond the earlier case law of the European Court of Human Rights, which repeatedly distinguished between the rights claims arising under article 8 in family formation and family reunification claims. Rejecting the distinction between family formation and family reunification claims, the ECJ recognised a 'unified norm' to respect for family life, placing it at the heart of the Union's integration project.

Given the Court's findings that any restrictions on family life must be treated as derogations, and must strictly comply with the principles of EU law, other integration measures adopted by Member States may also be opened up to scrutiny by the Court. The Court did not go so far as to challenge integration abroad requirements *per se*, as these were not the subject of the proceedings before it. The conceptual and normative foundations of such requirements have been questioned by many. While the imposition of such requirements remains permissible, following the Court's judgment, the discretion enjoyed by Member States has been clearly limited and the relevance of principles of EU law affirmed. Already, pre-departure integration testing had attracted the censure of the UN Committee on the Elimination of Racial Discrimination, because of its selective application in the Netherlands to particular nationalities only. The stringency of language testing and the potential for stigmatization of particular communities has also attracted the censure of the Committee.

41 S. Carrera & A. Weisbrock, *Whose Citizenship to Empower in the Area of Freedom, Security and Justice?: The Act of Mobility and Litigation in the Enactment of European Citizenship*, Brussels: CEPS May 2010.

42 D. Martin, 'Comment on European Parliament v Council (Case C-540/03 of 27 June 2006)', *European Journal of Migration and Law* 2007/9(1).

43 See, for example, *Carpenter v Secretary of State for the Home Department*, ECJ Case C-60/00 on 11 July 2002; Case C-200/02, *Kunqian Catherine Zhu and Man Lavette Chen v Secretary of State for the Home Department*, October 19 2004; and more recently: Case C-34/09, *Ruiz Zambrano v Office national de l'emploi (ONEm)*, 8 March 2011; *McCarthy v SSHD*, Case C-434/09, 5 May 2011.

Compliance with the general principle of non discrimination may prove problematic for Member States imposing sweeping integration measures in the context of family reunification Compliance with the requirement of proportionality may also prove a hurdle, even where such requirements apply without distinction between different nationalities, given the importance attached by the Court to the right to respect for family life as a fundamental right.

Beyond the limited circle of immigration theorists, integration testing has not, until recently, attracted much commentary or critique, premised as it was on relatively minimal requirements of civic integration and language competence. At a minimum, compliance of such testing with human rights norms would require the absence of any exclusions based on grounds such as 'race', ethnicity, religion, gender. As the content of such testing becomes 'thicker', we see, yet again, that the claim to universality that underpins the assertion of such values may not be well founded. Rather, it masks a particularism of religious, cultural, and nationalistic affiliations. It also marks a shift away from the earlier presumptions of policy-makers that access to a secure residence status would facilitate and support integration, including through naturalization. These presumptions are now reversed. Integration is now presumed to be a prerequisite to accessing the very status that has in the past facilitated this process.

The *Chakroun* judgment is potentially an important step towards checking the expansion of integration requirements in Member States. Although the judgment is limited in its scope to the particular questions placed before the Court, on financial resources tests, it is potentially of wider application. Key to the findings of the Court and to the conclusions of the Advocate General in the *Chakroun* proceedings, was the absence of a case by case assessment, a requirement that Advocate General Sharpston noted, permeates the Directive. The mere possibility of being able to claim certain types of social assistance in exceptional circumstances (themselves assessed on a case by case basis), cannot be a ground for systematically rejecting an application for family reunification.[44] At the very least, the *Ckakroun* judgment points to the importance of individualized assessments, bringing into question the application of blanket exclusionary rules, including potentially those relating to integration requirements. The potential for failures to comply with requirements of proportionality are many, for example, where the standards of literacy or civic knowledge tests are set too high, or the scope for exemptions is too limited.

As yet, it is unclear whether the CJEU would follow a similar line of reasoning in determining the scope of rights enjoyed by third country nationals under other Directives, such as Directive 2003/109/EC on long-term residence status. Long term residence, as such, may not attract the same level as protection as family reunification, given the more limited protections afforded by international and regional human rights instruments to the right to 'be here' and to remain. Recognition of such rights are constantly evolving, however. The Tampere conclusions, in particular, refer to third country long term residents as deserving a nearly equal treatment compared to EU citizens. Nonetheless, the requirements of proportionality and non-discrimination and the general concern to safeguard the effectiveness and objectives of the Directive could lead to similar conclusions and similar restrictions on the discretion enjoyed by Member States. As Carrera and Weisbrock note, the

---

44 Opinion of Advocate General Sharpston (10 December 2009), *Rhimou Chakroun v Minister van Buitenlandse Zaken*, Case C-578/08, *European Court Reports* 2010, p. I-01839, para. 70.

rights of third country nationals have been the subject of active litigation before the Court of Justice and the Court has, through its jurisprudence, expanded the limits of who is to be considered 'a legitimate holder of EU freedoms'.[45]

Integration abroad requirements reveal the lack of reciprocity underpinning the new integration agendas in many EU Member States. Continuing difficulties are likely to arise when attempting to raise principles of EU law and fundamental rights claims in the context of immigration. The risk of push-back from Member State Governments remains, given the politicization of migration and securitization of migration policy. It remains to be seen whether the potential for greater scrutiny and questioning of integration abroad requirements will be realized.

45 *Supra* n. 41, p. 25.

'En Attendant Godot' or the EU Law Limits to Integration Conditions

Diego Acosta Arcarazo

Abstract

While 'waiting for Godot' (the Court of Justice of the European Union) scholars have discussed at length the contours of integration requirements in European immigration Directives. This paper contributes to the discussion by looking at the possible European Law limits to integration conditions under Directive 2003/109. It begins by briefly summarising the academic debates around these conditions as well as the role of Member States, the Commission and National Courts in their interpretation. It continues by assessing the ways in which some Member States have implemented them, as well as the frequent legislative amendments in order to make them harsher. This opens all sorts of questions, not only legal ones. It is remarkable how, despite the rapid legislative amendments, some Member States claim a stability into which the third-country national would have to integrate. In the last Section, the paper turns to the analysis of the validity of certain integration conditions when confronted with general principles of Union law, such as respect for fundamental rights, proportionality, effectiveness or non-discrimination. I will conclude with some thoughts on what acceptable integration conditions might look like, 'en attendant' the final word by Godot.

1. Prelude: The Actors in the Play

Samuel Beckett's play *En attendant Godot*[1] follows a couple of days in the lives of two characters, Vladimir and Estragon, who are waiting for someone whose name is Godot. In the meantime, they discuss different topics while they occupy themselves eating, sleeping, singing or playing games. Likewise, in the last few years, scholars have conversed at length about the integration conditions under Directive 2003/109[2] while waiting for Godot (the Court of Justice of the European Union). Among other things, the negotiations that intro-

1 Samuel Beckett wrote the original version in French. *Waiting for Godot* is Beckett's translation of his own original. I will cite the English version in this paper: S. Beckett, *Waiting for Godot: a Tragicomedy in Two Acts*, London: Faber and Faber 1959.

2 Directive 2003/109/EC of 25 November 2003 of the Council concerning the Status of Third country Nationals who are Long-term Residents, OJ 2004 L 16/44, 23.1.2004. Member States were required to bring into force the necessary legislation to comply with the Directive by 23 January 2006. Five years later all Member States had implemented it into their national legal orders. Spain was the last one to transpose the Directive via the Ley Orgánica 2/2009, de 11 de diciembre, de reforma de la Ley Orgánica 4/2000, de 11 de enero, sobre derechos y libertades de los extranjeros en España y su integración social, BOE 12 diciembre de 2009. This Law has been developed by its implementing Regulations which entered into force on 30 June 2011, Real Decreto 557/2011, de 20 de abril, por el que se aprueba el Reglamento de la Ley Orgánica 4/2000, sobre derechos y libertades de los extranjeros en España y su integración social, tras su reforma por Ley Orgánica 2/2009, BOE 30 abril 2011.

duced these conditions in the Directive,[3] the possible differences between integration conditions and measures,[4] whether they enable or inhibit integration,[5] the accompanying official discourses[6] and the implementation in different Member States[7] have been discussed. In brief, integration conditions have been identified, categorised, compared, measured, analysed, mapped and attempted to be understood. There has been a consensus in considering integration conditions as the main Achilles' heel of the Directive.[8]

The rest of the characters in Beckett's play are also important for our discussion. Pozzo and Lucky, for instance, represent, in my view, the Member States (at least some of them) and the third-country nationals. Pozzo mistreats Lucky, who carries a heavy suitcase, and controls him with a long rope that restricts him. Lucky functions as a kind of entertainer so Pozzo commands him to dance, think or stand up or otherwise show his compliance.[9] Some Member States have acted in a similar way by asking third-country nationals to do different things in order to prove they have been integrated. The rhetoric surrounding integration has sometimes been harsh with a tendency to implement a restrictive immigration policy.[10] Interestingly, in the play Lucky becomes mute while Pozzo becomes blind, which reflects the blindness of some Member States in introducing harsher and more ambivalent integra-

3 S. Guèvremont, *Vers un Traitement Équitable des Étrangers Extracommunautaires en Séjour Régulier. Examen des Directives sur le Regroupement Familial et sur les Résidents de Longue Durée,* Zutphen: Wöhrmann Print Servie 2009, at p. 368-372.

4 K. Groenendijk, 'Legal Concepts of Integration in EU Migration Law', *European Journal of Migration and Law,* Vol. 6, issue 1, 2004, p. 111-126, at p. 124.

5 S. Wallace Goodman, 'Integration Requirements for Integration's Sake? Identifying, Categorising and Comparing Civic Integration Policies', *Journal of Ethnic and Migration Studies*, Vol. 36, issue 5, 2010, p. 753-772.

6 R. van Oers, E. Ersbøll & D. Kostakopoulou, 'Mapping the Redefinition of Belonging in Europe', in R. van Oers, E. Ersbøll & D. Kostakopoulou (eds), *A Redefinition of Belonging? Language and Integration Tests in Europe*, Leiden-Boston: Martinus Nijhoff 2010, p. 307-332.

7 D. Acosta Arcarazo, *The Long-term Residence Status as a Subsidiary Form of EU Citizenship. An Analysis of Directive 2003/109*, Leiden-Boston: Martinus Nijhoff 2011; S. Carrera, *In Search of the Perfect Citizen? The Intersection between Integration, Immigration and Nationality in the EU,* Leiden-Boston: Martinus Nijhoff 2009; A. Wiesbrock, *Legal Migration to the European Union*, Leiden/Boston: Martinus Nijhoff 2010; R. van Oers, E. Ersbøll & D. Kostakopoulou (eds), *A Redefinition of Belonging? Language and Integration Tests in Europe*, Leiden-Boston: Martinus Nijhoff 2010.

8 K. Groenendijk, 'The Long-Term Residents Directive, Denizenship and Integration', in A. Baldaccini, E. Guild & H. Toner (eds), *Whose Freedom, Security and Justice? EU Immigration and Asylum Law and Policy*, Oxford: Hart Publishing 2007, p. 429-450, at p. 442; S. Boelaert-Suominen, 'Non-EU Nationals and Council Directive 2003/109/EC on the Status of Third-country Nationals who are Long-term Residents: Five Paces Forward and possibly Three Paces Back', *Common Market Law Review*, Vol. 42, issue 4, 2005, p. 1011-1052, at p. 1023.

9 'POZZO: (*with magnanimous gesture*). Let's say no more about it. (*He jerks the rope.*) Up pig! (*Pause.*) Every time he drops he falls asleep. (*Jerks the rope.*) Up hog! (*Noise of Lucky getting up and picking up his baggage. Pozzo jerks the rope.*) Back! (*Enter Lucky backwards.*) Stop! (*Lucky stops.*) Turn! (*Lucky turns...*)...' S. Beckett, *op.cit.*, see fn 1 supra, at p. 22.

10 E. Guild, K. Groenendijk & S. Carrera, 'Understanding the Contest of Community: Illiberal Practices in the EU?', in E. Guild, K. Groenendijk & S. Carrera (eds.) *Illiberal Liberal States. Immigration, Citizenship and Integration in the EU,* Farnham: Ashgate 2009, p. 1-25, at p. 8.

tion conditions, as will be seen below, and the contradiction this causes for principles such as legal certainty.[11]

The final characters are two boys who are both timid and elusive. They come on behalf of Godot to deliver identical messages: Godot will not come that day but might come the day after. Thus, they are the only ones to have a direct relationship with Godot. I am obviously referring, in our EU law immigration context, to the Commission and the National Courts who have also proven to be timid and elusive in their willingness to bring a case on integration conditions before the Court of Justice. This might have to do with the fact that both are well aware of how politically loaded the issue of immigration is. Indeed, Member States have considered this area to be an important part of their sovereignty,[12] which has added to the Commission and National Courts' reluctance to bring cases.[13]

The Commission first referred to the limits of integration measures in its 2008 Report on the implementation of the Family Reunification Directive:

> The objective of such measures is to facilitate the integration of family members. Their admissibility under the Directive depends on whether they serve this purpose and whether they respect the principle of proportionality. Their admissibility can be questioned on the basis of the accessibility of such courses or tests, how they are designed and/or organised (test materials, fees, venue, etc.), whether such measures or their impact serve purposes other than integration (e.g. high fees excluding low-income families).[14]

The Commission assured that it would launch infringement proceedings during 2009 for non-compliance with the Directive.[15] However, it has not yet initiated proceedings against any Member State before the Court and has instead launched, following pressures from the Dutch Government, a new debate on the Directive by publishing a green paper in November 2011.[16] In fact, the Commission has been cautious in this regard and has so far initiated

11 S. Carrera & A. Wiesbrock, *Civic Integration of Third-Country Nationals. Nationalism versus Europeanisation in the Common EU Immigration Policy*, Brussels: Centre for European Policy Studies (CEPS) 2009, at p. 32.

12 B. Melis, *Negotiating Europe's Immigration Frontiers*, The Hague: Kluwer Law International 2001, at p. 124.

13 In the play one of the boys is afraid of Pozzo's (Member States) whip. 'ESTRAGON: What kept you so late? *The boy looks at them in turn, not knowing to which he should reply* (...) Do you know what time it is? BOY: (*recoiling*). It's not my fault, sir. ESTRAGON: And whose is it? Mine? BOY: I was afraid, sir. ESTRAGON: Afraid of what? Of us? (...) VLADIMIR: I know what it is, he was afraid of the others. ESTRAGON: How long have you been here? BOY: A good while, sir. VLADIMIR: You were afraid of the whip. BOY: Yes, sir. VLADIMIR: The roars. BOY: Yes, sir. VLADIMIR: The two big men. BOY: Yes, sir...' S. Beckett, *op.cit.*, see fn 2 supra, at p. 49.

14 Commission Report, On the Application of Directive 2003/86/EC on the Right to Family Reunification, COM (2008) 610 final, 8.10.2008, p. 7-8.

15 *Ibid.*, p. 14.

16 European Commission Green Paper on the Right to Family Reunification of Third-Country Nationals living in the European Union (Directive 2003/86/EC), COM (2011) 735 final, Brussels, 15.11.2011. The Commission will not possibly propose any amendments to the Directive after the cold shoulder that other Member States have given to this proposal. These responses by the Member States can be found at: <http://ec.europa.eu/home-affairs/news/consulting_public/consulting_0023_en.htm>.

very few proceedings in the area of immigration.[17] With regard to the Long-term Residence Directive, the Commission brought the Netherlands before the Court of Justice concerning the excessive fees levied against third-country nationals who wished to apply for a long-term residence permit. The Court recently ruled that these fees were contrary to the principle of effectiveness of the Directive as well as to the proportionality principle.[18] In September 2011, the Commission presented its report on the implementation of this same Directive. As in the case of the family reunification one, the Commission deplored its deficient transposition and announced that it would make full use of its powers including launching infringement proceeding when necessary.[19] It is yet to be seen whether that will be the case or not.

In turn, National Courts were also timid in using Article 267 TFEU to refer migration matters to the Court of Justice.[20] The Cyprus Supreme Court may be mentioned as an example of this controversial practice. In a ruling in 2008 on a question on the interpretation of Article 3 of Directive 2003/109,[21] it rejected the possibility of asking the Court of Justice for a preliminary ruling, despite the fact that it was the Court of last instance and that the matter affected thousands of third-country nationals.[22] In fact, I have argued elsewhere that, based on its previous jurisprudence, the Court of Justice would have probably interpreted this matter in the opposite direction.[23]

Another case in which a National Court was reluctant to refer a question for a preliminary ruling took place in Germany.[24] The *Bundesverwaltungsgericht* (the highest administrative court in Germany) originally decided in March 2010 that the German language test abroad was in conformity with Article 7(2) of the Family Reunification Directive without any reference to the *Chakroun* judgment, and instead considered it to be an *acte clair*. A reference for a preliminary ruling by a Dutch lower court on a similar issue reached the Court of Justice in 2011.[25] The case was unfortunately withdrawn after the Dutch government, concerned about the effects that a ruling would have on its Immigration Law, granted

17 See for example Case C-568/10, *European Commission v Republic of Austria,* on the implementation of Directive 2004/114/EC, the Students' Directive, which was however removed from the register following Austria's compliance.

18 Case C-508/10, *European Commission v Kingdom of the Netherlands*, judgment of 26 April 2012, not yet reported, paragraphs 73 and 77.

19 Report from the Commission to the European Parliament and the Council on the application of Directive 2003/109/EC concerning the status of third-country nationals who are long-term residents, COM (2011) 585 final, Brussels, 28.9.2011.

20 This has changed since the entry into force of the Lisbon Treaty on 1 December 2009 which allows all national courts, including lower ones, to refer a question to the CJEU on migration matters. In fact, there were 17 references for a preliminary ruling on migration matters in 2011, 15 out of which came from lower Courts.

21 *Cresencia Cabotaje Motilla v Republic of Cyprus through the Interior Minister and the Chief Immigration Officer,* Supreme Court Case No. 673/2006 (21 January 2008).

22 See on the case N. Trimikliniotis, *Country Report: Cyprus*, EUDO Citizenship Observatory: January 2010, revised April 2010, p. 17-18.

23 See on this D. Acosta Arcarazo, *op.cit.*, see fn 8 supra, at Chapter IV. The Court of Justice will have the opportunity to discuss this matter as a Dutch Court requested a preliminary ruling on the same Article 3 of the Directive. See reference for a preliminary ruling from the Raad van State (Netherlands) lodged on 20 October 2010 – *Staatssecretaris van Justitie v M. Singh* (Case C-502/10).

24 German Federal Administrative Court (BVerwG), judgment of 30 March 2010, case 1 c 8.09.

25 C-155/11, *Imran* (withdrawn)

the applicant, almost two years after she had requested it, a residence permit.[26] Interestingly enough, the Commission clearly stated in its opinion to the Court that is was not possible under the Directive to refuse a residence permit to a family member on the sole ground of failure to comply with the examination on integration abroad.[27] As previously stated, the Commission has however not initiated any infringement proceedings in that regard to date.

Now that the actors have been presented, it is time to see the play, which takes place in two acts. The first one has been developing in the last few years as Member States have introduced integration conditions. The second one has still to be written.

2. Act I: How are Member States Implementing Integration Conditions?

Integration conditions have become an important issue on the immigration political agendas in several Member States. These requirements have been introduced at four stages: First, some Member States[28] have introduced them as a precondition for family reunification. This first category deals with integration abroad.[29] Second, certain Member States have imposed integration conditions as soon as the third-country national enters the EU. Third, others require proof of some kind of integration when the third-country national wishes to obtain a long-term residence permit. This will be analysed below. Finally, in recent years several Member States have introduced or increased the difficulty of integration conditions as a requirement for acquiring citizenship.[30] Only Belgium has moved in the opposite direction.[31]

The table below identifies which countries require integration conditions in order to grant third-country nationals long-term residence. Whereas in 1999 only Germany required sufficient language knowledge to obtain permanent residence,[32] some Member States

26 The case was withdrawn following the granting of the permit, since it is settled case law that advice on general or hypothetical questions cannot be delivered under the preliminary ruling procedure; see for example Case C-225/02 *García Blanco* [2005] ECR I-523, paragraph 28.

27 Even more interesting is the fact that, following the Commission's opinion, the German Federal Administrative Court distanced itself from its previous ruling and argued instead, in a later case, that a preliminary ruling should have been requested. See BVerwG 1 C 9.10, 28 October 2011.

28 These are France, Netherlands and Germany. Denmark and the United Kingdom have also introduced these measures although they are not bound by Directive 2003/86.

29 See for a summary R. van Oers, E. Ersbøll & D. Kostakopoulou (eds), *op.cit.*, see fn 7 *supra*, at p. 307-312.

30 See R. Bauböck, E. Ersbøll, K. Groenendijk & H. Waldrauch, *Acquisition and Loss of Nationality, Volumes 1 and 2. Policies and Trends in 15 European Countries*, Amsterdam: Amsterdam University Press 2006; R. Bauböck, B. Perchinig & W. Sievers (eds.), *Citizenship Policies in the New Europe*, Amsterdam: Amsterdam University Press 2009.

31 Belgium abolished language and integration requirements in its Belgian Act of 1st March 2000 amending its Nationality Code. See on this M.C. Foblets & Z. Yanasmayan, 'Language and Integration Requirements in Belgium: Discordances between the Flemish Policy of 'Inburgering' and the Federal Legislators' View(s) on the Integration of Newcomers and Migrants', in R. van Oers, E. Ersbøll & D. Kostakopoulou (eds), *op.cit.*, fn 8 supra, p. 271-306, at 277-78.

32 K. Groenendijk, E. Guild & R. Barzilay, *Study on the Legal Status of Third-Country Nationals Who Are Long-Term Residents in a Member State of the European Union*, Nijmegen: Centre for Migration Law, Radboud University of Nijmegen 2000, p. 43.

have made use, in the last few years, of Article 5(2) of the Directive[33] to impose new requirements at two stages. The first column enumerates those who have an integration requirement as soon as the third-country national enters the territory, sometimes by imposing the signature of an integration contract. Here we can mention France, Germany and the Netherlands. The cases of Luxembourg, Italy and Austria are not however exactly the same.

Integration Conditions to acquire Long-term Residence

Group One: Integration when arriving in the Member State	Group Two: Integration Condition when applying for a Long-term Residence permit	Group Three: No Integration Condition imposed to obtain Long-term Residence
• Austria • France • Germany • Italy • The Netherlands • Luxembourg (Voluntary)	• Czech Republic • Estonia • Greece • Latvia • Lithuania • Portugal • Romania • Slovakia	• Belgium • Bulgaria • Cyprus • Finland • Hungary • Malta • Poland • Slovenia • Spain • Sweden

In Luxembourg, the 2008 legislation implementing the Directive provides that the minister responsible for immigration issues will take into consideration the degree of integration before granting a long-term residence permit.[34] For that purpose, a 2011 Regulation[35] introduced a voluntary integration contract which has been applied since October 2011. The contract has a maximum duration of two years and includes a language course (in French, German or Luxemburgish) as well as a civic course and an orientation one. The third-country national is not obliged to sign this agreement and hence integration could be proved by other means when requesting a long-term residence permit. Moreover, both EU citizens and third-country nationals may sign the agreement and it is not only addressed to those who have recently arrived but also to those who have resided for some years in the country.

In Italy, according to new legislation from 2009,[36] amending the Immigration Act,[37] a third-country national entering Italy for the first time will have to sign an integration con-

33 Article 5(2) of Directive 2003/109 reads as follows: 'Member States may require third-country nationals to comply with integration conditions, in accordance with national law.' Denmark, Ireland and the United Kingdom are not bound by the Directive and hence are not included in this enumeration.

34 Article 81 of the Loi du 29 août 2008 portant sur la libre circulation des personnes et l'immigration.

35 Règlement grand-ducal du 2 septembre 2011 fixant les conditions d'application et modalités d'exécution relatives au contrat d'accueil et d'intégration.

36 Legge 15 luglio 2009, n. 94, Disposizioni in materia di sicurezza pubblica. (09G0096), Gazzetta Ufficiale n. 170 del 24-7-2009.

tract. This contract entered into force on 10 March 2012, following the adoption of a Decree in 2011.[38] In brief, those newly arrived third-country nationals who are older than 16 years and who have obtained a residence permit of a least a year of duration are obliged to sign the agreement. There are certain third-country nationals (e.g. those affected by a disability that severely impairs their learning of the Italian language and culture) who do not have to sign the agreement. After its signature, the third-country national is assigned 16 credits. Credits may be gained by performing certain activities which vary in nature, from improving or learning Italian to obtaining a PhD. On the other hand, credits may also be lost if the person concerned fails to comply with certain obligations, such as attending a civic training session providing information about life in Italy, or whether they commit any crime or misdemeanour. Under certain circumstances (health problems, work reasons etc.) the agreement may be suspended or extended. Finally, the agreement is assessed after two years. That assessment may lead to three different outcomes. First, the third-country national will be expelled if he has 0 or less credits. Second, those who have between 1 and 29 credits will see their agreement extended for another year. Third, the third-country national who will have obtained 30 or more credits will have the right to remain in Italy.

Austria could be considered as an intermediate example between the first and the second column. On the one hand, some third-country nationals have to comply with an integration agreement,[39] which consists of two modules: a German language course and a literacy course for those who need it. However, on the other hand, the agreement needs to be fulfilled within the first five years of residence by proving knowledge of German at the level of B1 (it was A2 before). Nevertheless, the 2011 amendment to the Austrian Immigration Law introduces the requirement for certain third-country nationals to proof knowledge of German at the level A2 after only two years of residence. In case of failing to fulfil this obligation, the authorities have the discretion to renew the temporary residence permit.[40] This is an evident example of the introduction of harsher integration conditions in over a period of time. I will provide more cases below.

The second column lists those Member States which require the third-country national to show some kind of integration (language or civic knowledge) when applying for the long-term residence permit. The last column enumerates those Member States which do not impose an integration condition.[41] It is interesting to briefly mention the Belgium case in this last group. Since 2003, the Flemish Community has imposed a policy called 'civic integration'. The third-country national who registers for the first time in the Commune has to sign a contract of civic integration and follow a course on the Dutch language as well as two

37 Decreto Legilslativo 25 luglio 1998, n. 286, Testo unico delle disposizioni concernenti la disciplina dell'immigrazione e norme sulla condizione dello straniero. (Supplemento ordinario n. 139 alla Gazzetta Ufficiale n.191 del 18.08.1998).

38 Decreto del Presidente della Repubblica 14 settembre 2011, n. 179. Regolamento concernente la disciplina dell'accordo di integrazione tra lo straniero e lo Stato, a norma dell'articolo 4-bis, comma 2, del testo unico delle disposizioni concernenti la disciplina dell'immigrazione e norme sulla condizione dello straniero, di cui al decreto legislativo 25 luglio 1998, n. 286.

39 2006 Austrian Settlement and Residence Act, Art 14 (3).

40 See on this case the new Austrian Act: Act amending the Aliens Act 2011, *Fremdenrechtsänderungsgesetz 2011* = FrÄG 2011). See for an analysis B. Perchinig's chapter in this book. See also B. Perchinig, *Country Report Austria*, INTEC Project, Centre for Migration Law, Radboud University Nijmegen 2010, p. 11-16 and p. 19-26.

41 See on both groups of Member States: D. Acosta Arcarazo, *op.cit.*, see fn 8 supra, at Chapter VII.

other courses. In cases of non-compliance an administrative fine may be imposed but its completion is not a requirement for the granting of long-term residence.[42]

For the purpose of this work I am interested in pointing out how some Member States[43] have increased the difficulty of integration conditions over the last few years. This relates to the metaphor that was established earlier with Pozzo's blindness. Hence, what Member States considered in, for example, 2005 as an integrated third-country national may have changed in 2010, so as to consider the same person as non-integrated for the purposes of obtaining long-term residence. This increasing difficulty has gone hand in hand in some cases with a reduction in State support to help the persons concerned comply with the requirements.[44] As Besselink points out, integration has turned from being an issue to be tackled with social measures to one being addressed with immigration law enforced with sanctions,[45] including in some cases expulsion.[46] With this widening of integration requirements as well as the strengthening of their effects in cases of non-compliance,[47] it seems as if Member States would like to get rid of some third-country nationals.[48] In brief, the integration programmes are in many cases sanction-oriented, mandatory and test-based.[49] This is paradoxical and opens all sorts of legal and fairness questions. Regarding the latter it is striking to see how, regardless of the continuous legislative changes, some Member States claim a stability into which the third-country national should integrate. Are third-country nationals mute, like Lucky, when confronted with these developments or are there any legal bases to challenge these integration conditions? I will come back to this question in the next Section. Nevertheless, let me first give four examples, in addition to the Austrian one already mentioned above, of this expansion and increasing difficulty of integration conditions, before moving onto the legal issues.

In Germany, for instance, attending an integration course has been a condition for acquiring long-term residence since 2005. In 2008, however, there were elements that became harsher. First, the language test became compulsory while at the same time there was the introduction of civic examinations. Second, in 2008, the number of hours increased

42 See on this M.C. Foblets & Z. Yanasmayan, *op.cit.*, see fn 32 supra, at p. 285-290.

43 Here I do not intend to give an exhaustive enumeration but to highlight a trend of increasingly harsher integration conditions.

44 I. Michalowski, 'Liberal states – privatised integration policies?' in E. Guild, K. Groenendijk & S. Carrera (eds), *Illiberal Liberal States. Immigration, Citizenship and Integration in the EU*, Surrey: Ashgate 2009, p. 259-276, at p. 261.

45 L. Besselink, 'Integration and Immigration – The Vicissitudes of Dutch "Inburgering"', in E. Guild, K. Groenendijk & S. Carrera (eds), *Illiberal Liberal States: Immigration, Citizenship and Integration in the EU*, Surrey: Ashgate 2009, p. 241-258, at p. 241.

46 This has already taken place in Austria where there had been three deportation orders issued up to 2009, although all three have been appealed. See on this: B. P erchinig, *op.cit.*, see fn 40 *supra*, at p. 23.

47 Y. Pascouau, 'Integration Measures in France: An Evolving Process between Integration and Migration Issues', in R. van Oers, E. Ersbøll & D. Kostakopoulou (eds), *op.cit.*, fn 7 *supra*, p. 153-183.

48 In the play Vladimir asks Pozzo whether he would like to get rid of Lucky to which he answers: 'I do. But instead of driving him away as I might have done, I mean instead of simply kicking him out of his backside, in the goodness of my heart I am bringing him to the fair, where I hope to get a good price for him. The truth is you can't drive such creatures away…' S. Beckett, *op.cit.*, see fn 1 *supra*, at p. 31.

49 D. Kostakopoulou, 'Introduction', in R. van Oers, E. Ersbøll & D. Kostakopoulou (eds), *op.cit.*, fn 7 *supra*, p. 1-24, at p. 8.

from 600 to 900 hours, for those who might need more training, for the language course and from 30 to 45 hours for the civic education course.[50]

In Italy, when the Directive was implemented in 2007, a third-country national was considered to be integrated, and hence could be granted a long-term residence permit, after five years of regular residence without having to pass any language or civic knowledge examination.[51] Only two years later, having resided for a five-year period as well as fulfilling other conditions (e.g. not being a threat to public policy or public security or having sufficient resources) was no longer considered to be valid proof of integration. The 2009 legislation mentioned above[52] introduced the obligation for the third-country national to sign an integration contract as well as the need to pass an Italian language test in order to obtain long-term residence.[53] The third-country national has to attain a level of knowledge of Italian equivalent to an A2,[54] which may be proved by passing an examination or by showing a certificate from certain institutions specified in the implementing Decree.[55]

The Netherlands is also relevant. In 1998, when a first law entitled 'Act on the Integration of New Immigrants' was passed,[56] being integrated meant attending a programme of 600 hours comprising courses on Dutch language and society. However, when the 'Civic Integration Act'[57] entered into force in 2007, being integrated was reformulated in order to mean passing an examination instead of only following a course.[58] Interestingly enough, as of 15 March 2008 it became more difficult to pass the spoken Dutch test, as candidates were required to answer more questions correctly.[59] Hence, the meaning of what it means to be integrated has changed since the previous policy was considered to be ineffective.[60]

In France, the route has been similar. In 2003, new legislation[61] extended from three to five the number of years necessary to be granted permanent residence and introduced the

---

50 I. Michalowski, 'Integration Tests in Germany. A communitarian Approach?', in R. van Oers, E. Ersbøll & D. Kostakopoulou (eds), *A Redefinition of Belonging? Language and Integration Tests in Europe*, Leiden: MartinusNijhoff 2010, p. 185-210, at p. 194.

51 Decreto Legislativo 8 gennaio 2007, n.3 Attuazione della direttiva 2003/109/CE relativa allo status di cittadini di Paesi terzi soggiornanti di lungo periodo.

52 See fn 34 *supra*.

53 Decreto 4 giugno 2010 Modalita di svolgimento del test di conoscenza della lingua italiana, previsto dall'articolo 9 del decreto legislativo 25 luglio 1998, n. 286, introdotto dall'articolo 1, comma 22, lettera i) della legge n. 94/2009. (10A07303) (GU n. 134 del 11-6-2010).

54 *Ibid.*, Article 2(1).

55 *Ibid.*, Articles 3 and 4.

56 Wet inburgering nieuwkomers (Act on the Integration of New Immigrants). It entered into force on 30 September 1998 but was later repealed by the new Civic Integration Act.

57 Wet inburgering, Wi (Civic Integration Act).

58 See on this L. Besselink, *op.cit.*, fn 45 *supra*.

59 This integration has been applicable in the Netherlands since 1 January 2010. See Royal Decree of 29 December 2008, *Staatsblad* 605 (see Article I under R of that Decree) in Article 9.2(2) and (3) of Besluit Inburgering (Royal Decree on Integration). The date of entry of the obligation under Article 21(1)(k) Aliens Act was changed from 21 September 2009 to 1 January 2010.

60 L. Besselink, *op.cit.*, fn 45 *supra*, at p. 247.

61 Loi n. 2003-119 du 26 novembre 2003 relative à la maîtrise de l'immigration, au séjour des étrangers en France et à la nationalité, NOR: INTX 0300040L, Journal Officiel de la République française, 27 novembre 2003.

new condition of Republican integration.[62] This law established the voluntary welcome and integration contract (CAI) for those new third-country nationals who would have the prospect of long-term settlement in the country.[63] In 2006 though, a new law transformed this voluntary contract into a mandatory one.[64] Hence, obtaining long-term residence has been made conditional on complying with the Republican condition of integration and the rest of the requirements established in the contract.[65]

This uncertainty in the integration conditions needed to be fulfilled in order to obtain a more secure status is perhaps best represented by Denmark which, although not bound by the Directive, has changed its requirements several times in the last ten years.[66]

Hence, the question, which immediately arises, is how far may Member States stretch their understanding of integration conditions? Where are the limits imposed by European Law? I turn my attention to these issues in the next Section.

3. Act II: Possible EU Law Limits to the Integration Conditions

The previous Section has considered how the concept of what it means to be successfully integrated has changed in recent years with a new emphasis on obligations coupled with sanctions. However, EU law imposes certain limits on the use that Member States can make of the concept of integration when that might affect the enjoyment of rights by third-country nationals under Directive 2003/109. The concept of integration was first addressed in *Parliament v Council*:

> The fact that the concept of integration is not defined cannot be interpreted as authorising the Member States to employ that concept in a manner contrary to general principles of Community law, in particular to fundamental rights.[67]

Hence, while Member States may certainly introduce integration conditions which a third-country national would need to fulfil before being granted long-term residence, those conditions should not run contrary to general principles of Union law, such as fundamental rights. This is consistent with the fact that the court had already understood in previous cases, such as *Beata*,[68] that Member States did not have full discretion when there was a

62 S. Carrera, 'Nationality, Immigration and "the Republican Integration" in France', in E. Guild, K. Groenendijk & S. Carrera (eds), *Illiberal Liberal States: Immigration, Citizenship and Integration in the EU*, Surrey: Ashgate 2009, p. 315-335, at p. 323.

63 *Ibid.*, p. 324.

64 Loi n. 2006-911 du 24 juillet 2006 relative à l'immigration et l'intégration, NOR: INTX 0600037L, Journal Officiel de la République française, 25 juillet 2006.

65 See on the requirements: S. Carrera, *op.cit.*, fn 62 *supra*, at p. 327-329; Y. Pascouau, *op.cit.*, see fn 47 *supra*.

66 See on this E. Ersbøll, 'On Trial in Denmark', in R. van Oers, E. Ersbøll & D. Kostakopoulou (eds), *op.cit.*, fn 7 *supra*, p. 107-152; E. Ersbøll & L.K. Gravesen, *Country Report Denmark*, INTEC Project, Centre for Migration Law, Radboud University Nijmegen 2010.

67 Case C-540/03, *European Parliament v. Council*, 27 June 2006, [2006] ECR I-5769, paragraph 70.

68 Case C-162/00, *Beata Pokrzeptowicz-Meyer*, 29 January 2003, [2002] ECR I-1049.

reference to national laws in EU legislation.[69] Here, the Court even went a step further by rewriting the derogations in the Directive while interpreting it in conformity with general principles of Union law, such as fundamental rights.[70] Paragraph 60 of the ruling *Parliament v Council* reads as follows:

> Article 4(1) of the Directive imposes precise positive obligations, with corresponding clearly defined individual rights, on the Member States since it requires them, in the cases determined by the Directive, to authorise family reunification of certain members of the sponsor's family, without being left a margin of appreciation.

Considering this, it is hard to identify any plausible reason why the Court would not interpret Article 4(1) of Directive 2003/109[71] in the same manner. Hence, *Parliament v Council* provides the point of departure in order to assess the limits of integration conditions. In turn, the case in *Chakroun* allows taking a step further in that assessment.

Chakroun represents a central ruling for, at least, three reasons. First it establishes the limits in the interpretation of the conditions which need to be fulfilled in order to enjoy the right to family reunification, in accordance with general principles of EU law. Second, it provides a clear example of how seriously the Court takes preambles when interpreting immigration Directives. Third, and related to the previous point, it construes concepts such as social assistance in the same way as for EU citizens.

The facts are well known. Mr Chakroun, a Moroccan national regularly residing in the Netherlands since 1970, wished to have his spouse, whom he married in 1972, reunited with him. However, Mrs Chakroun's application was refused on the ground that her husband was not in receipt of sufficient income. Dutch legislation included a distinction between family reunification and family formation. In the latter case, the third-country national had to have a net income equal to 120% of the minimum wage, whereas in the former it was only 100%.[72] That distinction was considered to be unlawful under the Directive.[73] Regardless of that interpretation, what is of interest here is to see the rationale of the Court in arriving at that conclusion in order to see what possible analogies may be drawn with the Long-term Residence Directive, especially the Court's reinforcement of its commitment to take into consideration the respect for the general principles of Union law. Indeed the Court emphasised the principle of effectiveness. The objective of the Directive, the Court of Justice argued, is 'to authorise family reunification of certain members of the sponsor's family, without being left a margin of appreciation'.[74] Consequently:

69 S. Peers, '"New Minorities": What Status for Third-Country Nationals in the EU System?', in G.N. Toggenburg (ed.), *Minority Protection and the Enlarged European Union: The Way Forward*, Local Government and Public Service Reform Initiative and Open Society Institute 2004, p. 151-162, at p. 157.

70 E. Guild, K. Groenendijk & S. Carrera (eds), *op.cit.*, see fn 10 *supra*, at p. 6.

71 In fact, the Court has recently held that: 'Having regard to the objective pursued by Directive 2003/109 and the system which it puts in place, it should be noted that, where the third-country nationals satisfy the conditions and comply with the procedures laid down in that directive, they have the right to obtain long-term resident status as well as the other rights which stem from the grant of that status'. Case C-508/10, *Commission v Netherlands*, *op.cit.*, see fn 18 *supra*, paragraph 68.

72 Article 3.74 of the Decree on Aliens of 2000 (Vreemdelingenbesluit 2000; 'the Vb 2000') as amended by Royal Decree of 29 September 2004 (*Staatsblad* 2004, p. 496).

73 Case C-578/08, *Rhimou Chakroun v Minister van Buitenlandse Zaken,* [2010],paragraphs 61-66.

74 *Ibid.*, paragraph 41.

> Since authorisation of family reunification is the general rule, the faculty provided for in Article 7(1)(c) of the Directive must be interpreted strictly. Furthermore, the margin for manoeuvre which the Member States are recognised as having must not be used by them in a manner which would undermine the objective of the Directive, which is to promote family reunification, and the effectiveness thereof.[75]

Here again, it would be difficult to argue a different interpretation of the Long-term Residence Directive. The objective of the Directive (the general rule) is granting a long-term residence permit to those third-country nationals who have regularly resided for a period of five years in a Member State. Thus, any condition to that general rule has to be interpreted strictly in order not to run contrary to the objective of the Directive and its effectiveness. This analogy has in fact been established by Advocate General Bot in his recent opinion in *Commission v Netherlands*.[76] The Advocate General has indeed argued in this case that excessive fees levied against third-country nationals willing to obtain a long-term residence permit ran contrary to the principle of effectiveness of the Directive,[77] principle which he has also mentioned in his opinion in *Kamberaj* as limiting Member State's capacity of manouvre when implementing the Directive even when there is a reference to national law on the Directive itself.[78] The Court agreed with the Advocate General in both cases.[79] Principles such as effectiveness, or proportionality, might also be affected, for example, when Member States charge excessive prices for the courses that a third-country national has to follow in order to fulfil an integration condition.[80]

What about other principles of Union law? Certainly the principle of proportionality will have to be respected as well. This principle is intrinsically linked to the principle of effectiveness and has been extensively discussed in the academic literature.[81] Some authors have looked at integration conditions in some Member States in order to confront them with the principle of proportionality.[82] The Court of Justice, as well as National Courts, will have to be attentive to several practices such as lengthy courses (Germany), with a too high level content (Germany again requiring B1 language knowledge, or the Netherlands asking for the same knowledge required to pass a citizenship test), failure of which may

---

75 *Ibid.*, paragraph 43.

76 Advocate General Opinion, Case C-508/10, *Commission v Netherlands*, 19 January 2012, paragraph 61.

77 *Ibid.*, paragraph 80.

78 Advocate General Opinion, Case C-571/10, *Kamberaj*, 13 December 2011, paragraphs 83-84.

79 Case C-508/10, *Commission v Netherlands*, *op.cit.*, see fn 18 *supra*, paragraph 73; Case C-571/10, *Kamberaj*, judgment of 26 April 2012, not yet reported, paragraph 78.

80 In fact, the Court has disregarded the Greek argument that 'in order to set the charges levied for the issue of a residence permit to third-country nationals who are long-term residents, account must be taken of the amount of the contribution which corresponds to the cost of the administrative services provided for the verification not only of the right of residence, but also of the integration of the persons concerned, as a necessary condition for the acquisition of long-term resident status'. Case C-508/10, *Commission v Netherlands*, *op.cit.*, see fn 18 *supra*, paragraph 55.

81 N. Emiliou, *The Principle of Proportionality in European Law. A Comparative Study*, The Hague: Kluwer Law International 1996; E. Ellis (ed.), *The Principle of Proportionality in the Laws of Europe*, Oxford: Hart Publishing 1999; G. de Burca, 'The Principle of Proportionality and its Application in EC Law', *Yearbook of European Law*, Vol. 13, 1993, p. 105-150.

82 For example Carrera looks at the French case. See S. CARRERA, *op.cit.*, see fn 7 *supra*, at p. 404.

entail expulsion (Austria) and which do not seem to be in line with the principle of proportionality,[83] principle which the Court has mentioned in *Commission v Netherlands* as limiting the measures taken by national legislation when transposing the Directive.[84]

Finally, respect for fundamental rights is also central. Article 8 of the European Convention on Human Rights, almost identically reproduced in Article 7 of the Charter of Fundamental Rights, on the right to respect for private and family life will also play a role in the interpretation by the Court of Justice.[85] This also needs to be taken into consideration by National Courts in cases where, for example, a third-country national faces expulsion or non-renewal of a residence permit for non-compliance with integration conditions.[86]

The second reason why *Chakroun* is important, is its illustration of how the Court of Justice takes preambles seriously when interpreting Directives in the area of immigration. In *Chakroun* the Court refers to Recitals 2[87] and 6[88] of Directive 2003/86 and uses them to support its decision. The extent to which the Court will be willing to use preambles when interpreting the Long-term Residence Directive is important with regard to, for example, the principle of non-discrimination. Recital 5 of the Directive reads as follows:

> Member States should give effect to the provisions of this Directive without discrimination on the basis of sex, race, colour, ethnic or social origin, genetic characteristics, language, religion or beliefs, political or other opinions, membership of a national minority, fortune, birth, disabilities, age or sexual orientation.

Hence, Member States should apply the Directive, including the conditions for obtaining long-term residence, in a non-discriminatory manner.[89] However, how far may this reference to non-discrimination be interpreted? There is extensive jurisprudence on the issue of non-discrimination and the Court has interpreted it widely.[90] Moreover, Article 21 of the Charter of Fundamental Rights, to which the Directive makes reference in the third Recital of the preamble, establishes a non-exhaustive list of grounds under which discrimination is prohibited. This means that any other discrimination could also be included.

With regard to the acquisition of long-term residence, some Member States' practices would seem to constitute direct discrimination on grounds of social origin. The prohibition

---

83 S. Carrera & A. Wiesbrock, *op.cit.*, see fn 11 *supra*, at p. 33.

84 Case C-508/10, *Commission v Netherlands*, *op.cit.*, see fn 18 *supra*, paragraph 75.

85 See on the interpretation by the European Court of Human Rights of the right to private life: D. Thym, 'Respect for Private and Family Life under Article 8 ECHR in Immigration Cases: a Human Right to Regularize Illegal Stay?', *International and Comparative Law Quarterly*, Vol. 57, issue 1, 2008, p. 87-112. See on the link between the right to private life and long-term residence D. Acosta, *op.cit.*, see fn 7 *supra*, at ch 9. See also Case of *Sisojeva and others v. Latvia*, Application no. 60654/00, 16 June 2005.

86 This is indeed being assessed by national courts in for example Austria. See B. Perchinig, *op.cit.*, see fn 40 *supra*, at p. 16 and B. Perchinig's chapter in this book.

87 Case C-578/08, *Chakroun*, paragraph 44.

88 *Ibid.*, paragraph 62.

89 M. Jesse, 'Missing in Action: Effective Protection for Third-Country Nationals from Discrimination under Community Law' in E. Guild, K. Groenendijk & S. Carrera (eds), *Illiberal Liberal States. Immigration, Citizenship and Integration in the EU*, Surrey: Ashgate 2009, p. 187-204, at p. 196.

90 A. Eriksson, 'Broadening the Scope of European Non-discrimination Law', *Int J Constitutional Law*, Issue 7, vol. 4, p. 731-753, at p. 733.

of discrimination on the basis of social origin, or socio-economic status, has been established in several international legal instruments, including the European Convention on Human Rights.[91] There is, unfortunately, no case by the European Court of Human Rights on the meaning of social origin. Nonetheless, Advocate General Bot has already referred to recital 5 on non-discrimination to argue that this would oppose the imposition of too high fees having a dissuading effect on those third-country nationals without sufficient economic resources.[92] In addition to that, it seems that some practices would not be lawful under the Directive. For example, in France, third-country nationals with a residence permit mentioning competences and skills do not have to fulfil the welcome and integration contract (CAI).[93] And in Austria, third-country nationals who belonged to the category of 'key workers' (this category is no longer existing in Austria as from 1 July 2011) were considered to have fulfilled the integration agreement per se.[94] Hence, this could be considered direct discrimination:[95] one person is treated less favourably than another (some third-country nationals have to comply with integration conditions in order to be granted long-term residence while others do not) in a comparable situation (both third-country nationals have resided for a period of five years in the Member State) on grounds of social origin (one earns a certain amount of money while the other does not).[96]

It could also be argued that certain integration and language tests may be considered as indirectly discriminatory if it is proved that third-country nationals from certain social or education backgrounds encounter greater difficulty in passing them.[97]

The third reason why *Chakroun* is central, is the Court's interpretation of some concepts in the same way it had already interpreted them for European citizens. Recital 2 of Directive 2003/109 reads as follows:

> The European Council, at its special meeting in Tampere on 15 and 16 October 1999, stated that the legal status of third-country nationals should be approximated to that of

91 See for example Article 2 of the International Covenant on Civil and Political Rights, Article 2(2) of the International Covenant on Economic, Social and Cultural Rights or, most importantly, Article 14 of the European Convention on Human Rights and Fundamental Freedoms. See on this S. Kilcommins, E. McClean, M. McDonagh, S. Mullally & D. Whelan, *Extending the Scope of Employment Equality Legislation: Comparative Perspectives on the Prohibited grounds of Discrimination*, Report Commissioned by the Department of Justice, Equality and Law Reform, Dublin 2004.

92 Advocate General Opinion *Commission v Netherlands*, *op.cit.*, see fn 76 *supra*, paragraph 69.

93 S. Carrera & A. Wiesbrock, *op.cit.*, see fn 11 *supra*, at p. 35.

94 Key workers are those who hold key managerial or technical functions and earn more than 2,466 EUR fourteen times a year. B. Perchinig, *op.cit.*, see fn 40 *supra*, at p. 14. This has slightly changed with the 2011 amendment to the Aliens Act. See on this B. Perchinig's chapter in this book.

95 This is the common definition of direct discrimination in the Race Directive, Article 2(1); the Framework Directive, Article 2(2) (a) and the Equal Treatment Directive, Article 2(1) (a).

96 It is important to underline that highly skilled workers under Directive 2009/50 enjoy a number of derogations from the long-term residence Directive which makes it easier for them to obtain this status. However, there is no derogation from the integration requirement which is also applicable to them. See Article 15(3) of Directive 2009/50/EC of 25 May 2009 of the Council on the Conditions of Entry and Residence of Third-country Nationals for the Purposes of Highly Qualified Employment, OJ 2009 L 155/17, 18.6.2009.

97 A. Wiesbrock, 'Discrimination Instead of Integration? Integration Requirements for Immigrants in Denmark and Germany', in E. Guild, K. Groenendijk & S. Carrera (eds), *Illiberal Liberal States. Immigration, Citizenship and Integration in the EU*, Surrey: Ashgate 2009, p. 299-314, at p. 312.

> Member States' nationals and that a person who has resided legally in a Member State for a period of time to be determined and who holds a long-term residence permit should be granted in that Member State a set of uniform rights which are as near as possible to those enjoyed by citizens of the European Union.

Since the Court, as has been seen, takes preambles seriously when interpreting Directives in the area of immigration, it will no doubt be influenced by its own interpretation of similar concepts for European citizens when dealing with those same concepts for third-country nationals under the Directive.[98]

Chakroun reveals this tendency by interpreting a concept such as social assistance in the same way it had already done for European citizens in *Eind*[99] and by also referring to *Metock*.[100] Advocate General Bot follows the same understanding in *Commission v Netherlands* when discussing the fees to be paid in order to obtain a long-term residence permit.[101]

Considering the aforementioned, the Court could certainly take into consideration its jurisprudence on the concept of integration for EU citizens. According to the reading of the Court, integration is always enhanced by facilitating EU citizens the enjoyment of their rights. There are various reasons for upholding a similar interpretation for third-country nationals. First, this conclusion has been re-stated in two recent rulings affecting EU citizens or their family members: *Ibrahim*[102] and *Teixeira*.[103] Second, that same underlying principle is valid for Turkish workers as well, as the Court has made clear in several rulings.[104] Finally, integration understood as a process which is enhanced by granting rights is also the

98 K. Groenendijk, 'Family Reunification as a Right under Community Law', *European Journal of Migration and Law*, Vol. 8, issue 2, 2006, p. 215-230, at p. 221.

99 Case C-578/08, *Chakroun*, paragraph 46. Article 7(2) of Directive 2003/86 does not specify what is meant by social assistance. The Court makes it clear that it 'refers to assistance granted by the public authorities (...) which can be claimed by an individual (...) who does not have stable and regular resources which are sufficient to maintain himself and the members of his family and who, by reason of that fact, *is likely to become a burden on the social assistance system* of the host Member State during his period of residence' (emphasis added). The same rationale applies for EU citizens.

100 Case C-127/08, *Metock and Others, v Minister for Justice, Equality and Law Reform*, 25 July 2008, [2008] ECR I-06241. See on *Metock*: D. Acosta, 'Immigration in the European Union: Family Reunification after the Metock Case', *UCD Law Review*, Vol. 9, 2009, p. 64-88; C. Costello, '*Metock*: Free Movement and 'Normal Family Life' in the Union', *Common Market Law Review*, Vol. 46, issue 2, 2009, pp. 587-622; S. Peers, 'Free Movement, Immigration Control and Constitutional Conflict', *European Constitutional Law Review*, Vol. 5, 2009, p. 173-196; S. Currie, 'Accelerated Justice or a Step too Far? Residence Rights of non-EU Family Members and the Court's Ruling in *Metock*', *European Law Review*, Vol. 34, issue 2, 2009, p. 310-326; J. Handoll, 'The *Metock* Case. Union Citizenship, Family Reunion and the Abuse of Rights', in P. Minderhoud & N. Trimikliniotis (eds), *Rethinking the Free Movement of Workers: The European Challenges Ahead*, Nijmegen: Wolf Legal Publishers 2009, p. 173-187.

101 Advocate General Opinion *Commission v Netherlands*, *op.cit.*, see fn 76 *supra*, paragraph 66.

102 Case C-310/08, *London Borough of Harrow v Nimco Hassan Ibrahim*, 23 February 2010, paragraph 43.

103 Case C-480/08, *Maria Teixeira v London Borough of Lambeth*, 23 February 2010, paragraph 66.

104 Case C-171/01, *Wählergruppe 'Gemeinsam Zajedno/Birlikte Alternative und Grüne GewerkschafterInnen/UG' and Bundesminister für Wirtschaft und Arbeit and Others*, of 8 May 2003, ECR [2003] I-04301, paragraph 79; Case C-465/01, *Commission of the European Communities v Republic of Austria*, 16 September 2004, ECR [2004] I-08291, paragraph 53.

rationale present in Recitals 4[105] and 12[106] of the Directive on long-term residence. Once more, the Advocate General has also followed this understanding in *Kamberaj* in order to argue for an extensive interpretation of Article 11 of the Directive on the rights to be granted to long-term residence permit holders.[107] Unsurprisingly, the Court also agreed on this with the Advocate General.[108]

The Court of Justice of the European Union will probably assess the elements mentioned and establish a case by case analysis of different integration conditions to see if they comply with the Directive or, whether on the contrary, they run contrary to the main objective of granting a long-term residence permit to those third-country nationals who have regularly resided for a period of five years in a Member State.

4. Dénouement

Considering all these limitations imposed by general principles of Union law a question arises: What kind of integration conditions may Member States introduce? It is obvious that Member States are able to require some kind of integration based on Article 5(2) of the Directive. In my view the best way forward would be to offer courses without imposing any test as this would show that migrants are welcome in their new society.[109] However, if a Member State would like to impose any kind of integration conditions, the Commission's reports, mentioned earlier, could be taken as a starting point. The Commission, in its report on the implementation on the family reunification Directive referred to two elements: the facilitation of integration and respect for the principle of proportionality when looking at issues such as test materials, fees or venue. The report on the long-term residence Directive itself goes a step further by explicitly mentioning the principle of effectiveness and by declaring that the level of the knowledge expected from the applicant needs to be compared with the knowledge of the host society itself.[110]

The Portuguese case provides a good example of a prerequisite which is aimed at facilitating integration. In Portugal, in order to obtain long-term residence, a third-country

105 Recital 4 Directive 2003/109 reads as follows: 'The integration of third-country nationals who are long-term residents in the Member States is a key element in promoting economic and social cohesion, a fundamental objective of the Community stated in the Treaty'.

106 Recital 12 Directive 2003/109 reads as follows: 'In order to constitute a genuine instrument for the integration of long-term residents into society in which they live, long-term residents should enjoy equality of treatment with citizens of the Member State in a wide range of economic and social matters, under the relevant conditions defined by this Directive'.

107 Advocate General Opinion *Kamberaj*, *op.cit.*, see fn 78 *supra*, paragraph 94.

108 Case C-571/10, *Kamberaj*, *op.cit.*, see fn 79 *supra*, paragraphs 86 and 90.

109 E. Guild, K. Groenendijk & S. Carrera (eds), *op.cit.*, see fn 10 *supra*, at p. 9.

110 The report is worded as follows: 'When transposing this provision, Member States must be in line with the purpose of the Directive and take due account of the general principles of EU law, such as the principle of preserving its effectiveness ('*effet utile*') and the proportionality principle. In order to perform such an assessment, the nature and level of the knowledge expected from the applicant, also by comparison to the knowledge of the host society, the cost of the exam, the accessibility of the integration training and tests, the comparison between the integration requirements imposed on a prospective LTR and those applied to prospective citizens (which are expected to be higher), are all valuable indicators'. *Op.cit.*, see fn 19 *supra*, p. 3.

national has to prove basic knowledge of the Portuguese language to an A2 level.[111] In case of non-compliance, the third-country national has the possibility to renew his/her temporary permit but will not be able to obtain long-term residence. The language level may be proved by producing various certificates, as clarified within the implementing Regulation.[112] A second implementing Regulation, which creates the Portuguese courses for speakers of other languages, is certainly of interest for our purposes.[113] This Regulation establishes free, non-compulsory courses. There is no sanction imposed in cases of non-attendance since learning Portuguese is understood as a right, extended to migrants in order to prevent discrimination against them, and not as an obligation.[114] Indeed the Regulation makes reference to the understanding of integration as a two-way process in which migrants and natives adapt to each other's habits, customs, values, religions and languages.[115] This fits well with the Portuguese national integration plan in which immigration is understood as a positive demographic, economic and cultural factor and in which the State is understood to be the main ally in the third-country nationals' integration by creating the conditions for their full participation in society.[116] Hence, the rationale is clear: since learning the language will improve the chances of obtaining a better job, of accessing health care or of participating in the social, cultural and political life of the country, the State will provide the necessary tools.

The Portuguese example certainly respects the two elements proposed by the Commission. It tries to facilitate integration by offering non-compulsory free language courses. It lacks nonetheless an important element, which is that of exemptions for those third-country nationals who are unable to fulfil the integration conditions due to their age, health or other impediment. These exemptions are present, though, in other Member States such as Austria, the Netherlands or Germany.

I would however add a final element to integration conditions implemented in a proportionate manner and allowing for exemptions. This element would be something which could be referred to as 'personalised proportionality'.[117] That would mean that whenever there is any testing imposed in order to acquire long-term residence, Member States should have not only exemptions for specific groups of people but also clauses providing for the granting of long-term residence in other cases. This is similar to some authors' proposals

111 Portuguese Immigration Law, Article 126(1)(e), Lei no 23/2007 de 4 de Julho, Aprova o regime jurídico de entrada, permanência, saída e afastamento de estrangeiros do território nacional, Diário da República, 1.a série –N.º 127– 4 de Julho de 2007.

112 Article 74(g) Decreto Regulamentar no 84/2007de 5 de Novembro, Diário da República, 1.ª série – N.º 212 – 5 de Novembro de 2007.

113 Portaria no 1262/2009 de 15 de Outubro, Diário da República, 1.ª série –N.º 200 –15 de Outubro de 2009.

114 *Ibid.*, preamble.

115 *Ibid.*, preamble.

116 Resolução do Conselho de Ministros no 63-A/2007, Diário da República, 1.ª série –N.º 85 –3 de Maio de 2007, preamble to the Annex.

117 I borrow this concept from Malcolm Ross. See M. Ross, 'The Struggle for EU Citizenship: Why Solidarity Matters', in A. Arnull, C. Barnard, M. Dougan & E. Spaventa (eds), *A Constitutional Order of States: Essays in EU Law in Honour of Alan Dashwood*, Oxford: Hart 2011, p. 283-300. Kostakopoulou has put forward a similar idea when discussing integration measures for family members of third-country nationals. See D. Kostakopoulou, *op.cit.*, see fn 49 *supra*, at p. 10.

that Member States should only test third-country nationals' relative competence[118] so as to take into consideration their different backgrounds with regard to, for instance, education or income.[119] Underlying this rationale is the principle previously highlighted that, after five years of regular residence, a third-country national should be able to obtain long-term residence. Hence, if someone has, for example, attended some language courses but has, nonetheless, failed a test, some sort of personalised proportionality should be taken into consideration. This is not new, as the Court has already used a similar approach in cases such as *Mangold* where there was a breach of the principle of proportionality since 'the personal situation of the person concerned' was not properly acknowledged.[120]

To conclude, the Court of Justice of the European Union will certainly have to address these issues in the coming years in order to ensure certainty on a question of utmost importance for thousands of new Europeans.[121] Since the entry into force of the Treaty of Lisbon, all National Courts, and not only last instance ones, may refer a question to the Court of Justice. Practitioners and other organisations working with migrants in the Member States now have the possibility to raise various issues regarding integration conditions before any National Court so that a question is referred to the Court of Justice.

In the meantime we will keep on discussing this area while waiting for Godot.[122]

118 R. van Oers, E. Ersbøll & D. Kostakopoulou (eds), *op.cit.*, see fn 6 *supra*, at p. 327.

119 E. Guild, K. Groenendijk & S. Carrera (eds), *op.cit.*, see fn 10 *supra*, at p. 8.

120 Case C-144/04, *Werner Mangold v Rüdiger Helm*, 22 November 2005, ECR [2005] I-09981, paragraph 65. See on this A. Eriksson, *op.cit.*, see fn 90 *supra*, at p. 734.

121 Some authors have considered long-term residence to have the potential to become a subsidiary form of EU citizenship or to be an EU citizenship in the making. See on the former concept D. ACOSTA, *op.cit.*, see fn 7 *supra*. See on the latter concept S. Carrera & A. Wiesbrock, 'Whose European Citizenship in the Stockholm Programme? The Enactment of Citizenship by Third Country Nationals in the EU', *European Journal of Migration and Law,* vol. 12, issue 3, 2010, p. 337-359, at p. 358.

122 '-VLADIMIR: Where were you? I thought you were gone forever. -ESTRAGON: They're coming! -VLADIMIR: Who? -ESTRAGON: I don't know. -VLADIMIR: How many? -ESTRAGON: I don't know. -VLADIMIR: (*triumphantly*). It's Godot! At last! Gogo! It's Godot! We're saved! Let's go and meet him....' S. Beckett, *op.cit.*, see fn 1 *supra*, at p. 73.

Citizenship Acquisition: Increasing Trend of Testing Civic Integration

Eva Ersbøll

Introduction

This chapter deals with the increasing trend among European states towards introducing language and societal knowledge tests as a condition for acquisition of citizenship. It examines the purpose and the effects of the tests and argues that there is a need for European cooperation on legal standards within this area. The article's first section takes as a starting point the basic definition of citizenship as a bond between a person and a state that is: citizenship as state membership. It examines the significance of a genuine link between the citizen and his or her state as established in international law and domestic practice. To this end, the development of civic integration requirements is analysed. The second section discusses the impact of migration on citizenship acquisition. It is questioned whether it can be maintained that migration has made access to citizenship less discriminatory and whether the new civic integration requirements in principle can be met by all individuals. The third section deals with the overall importance of citizenship in an age of migration. The fourth section chooses a European perspective and concludes by suggesting common European legal standards for civic integration requirements for naturalisation.

1. The Development of Civic Integration Requirements

1.1 Civic Integration Requirements in International Law and Practice

It is well-established that citizenship law traditionally has been a matter determined by each state under its own law. Still, for more than hundred years, states have cooperated on citizenship issues out of mutual interest, and today it is generally accepted that international law imposes certain limits on the broad domestic powers enjoyed by states within this area.[1]

What the legislator normally takes into consideration when legislating on access to citizenship or nationality (the two terms are used synonymously here) is, as stated by the French professor Paul Lagarde, the intensity of the link connecting an individual to the community.[2]

1 See also the advisory opinion of the Permanent Court of International Justice (PCIJ) on the *Nationality Decrees Issued in Tunis and Morocco (French Zone)* on November 8th, 1921, PCIJ Reports (1921), Series B, No. 4, p. 42, 49, and 57: See now the European Convention on Nationality (1997), article 3(2).

2 Stated before the Nationality Commission and quoted in R. Hansen & P. Weil (eds), *Towards a European Nationality: Citizenship, Immigration and Nationality Law in the EU,* Basingstoke: Palgrave 2001, p. 63.

In the famous *Nottebohm*-case (1955) the International Court of Justice (ICJ) established the 'genuine link-theory', calling for 'a bond of allegiance' and a 'genuine link'.[3] In another famous case on citizenship, concerning the naturalisation provisions of Costa Rica (1984), the Inter-American Court of Human Rights focused on the effective link, the affinity to a country's value system and interests and the relationship with a given political society, its culture, its way of life and its values.[4]

In order to comply with the genuine link requirement states often ask applicants for naturalisation to document their knowledge of the states' language and sometime also of their history, culture, constitutional system etc. Making such demands on applicants for naturalisation is, however, not uncontroversial. In the Costa Rica-case, the Inter-American Court of Human Rights expressed the following viewpoint regarding requirements of being able to speak, write and read and pass an examination on the history of the country and its values:

> These conditions can be deemed, prima facie, to fall within the margin of appreciation reserved to the state as far as concerns the enactment and assessment of the requirements designed to ensure the existence of real and effective links upon which to base the acquisition of the new nationality. So viewed, it cannot be said to be unreasonable and unjustified to require proof of the ability to communicate in the language of the country or, although this is less clear, to require the applicant to 'speak, write and read' the language. The same can be said of the requirement of a 'comprehensive examination on the history of the country and its values.' The Court feels compelled to emphasize, however, that in practice, and given the broad discretion with which tests such as those mandated by the draft amendment tend to be administered, there exists the risk that these requirements will become the vehicle for subjective and arbitrary judgments as well as instruments for the effectuation of discriminatory policies which, although not directly apparent on the face of the law, could well be the consequence of its application.

Thus, it has for long been recognized that the effects of integration tests may be difficult to measure on the basis of the words of an Act on citizenship and also that such tests may have discriminatory effects.

1.2 Civic Integration Requirements in Domestic Law and Practice

Unlike what has been the case in United States and Canada for long, formalised naturalisation tests have not traditionally been a part of the European naturalisation procedures. Still, many European countries have demanded that applicants for naturalisation were able to communicate in the domestic language of the naturalising country. Such language requirements were probably a more widespread phenomenon than often presumed in comparative citizenship studies, since frequently the requirements did not have a legislative basis in a

3 *Nottebohm*-case, Judgment of April 6th, 1955, ICJ Reports (1955), p. 4 ff.

4 Advisory Opinion OC-4/84, January 19, 1984, Inter-American Court of Human Rights (Series A) No 4 (1984) *Proposed Amendments to the Naturalization Provisions of the Constitution of Costa Rica, pr. 59 and 60.*

citizenship Act. Instead, the requirements could follow implicitly from a general 'integration clause' or appear only in secondary law. The lack of transparency with regard to language requirements can be illustrated by the example of the Scandinavian countries.

1.2.1 Scandinavian Tradition for Language Requirements

Denmark, Norway and Sweden have cooperated with a view to harmonise their citizenship legislation since the late nineteenth century. During discussions of the naturalisation criteria in the beginning of the 1920s, delegates from Denmark, Norway and Sweden found it 'evident' that the applicant's ability to speak the language of a naturalising country was of the most utmost importance for the decision on naturalisation. All Scandinavian countries assumed that the relevant authorities continuously, as hitherto, would take the applicants' language skills into consideration.[5] In none of countries, however, the language requirement was included in a citizenship Act. Denmark had since the adoption of the Danish constitution in 1849 considered it decisive that applicants for naturalisation 'were able to speak and understand the mother tongue of the Danish people'.[6] Still, the Danish language requirement was not included in the Danish citizenship Act. Among other things this had to do with the special Danish constitutionally based system according to which foreigners can only acquire Danish citizenship by law, conditioned by their fulfilment of naturalisation requirements agreed upon by a majority in Parliament. In Norway and Sweden there was no counterpart to this special system; still, for other reasons, neither the Norwegian nor the Swedish citizenship Act mentioned the language requirement for naturalisation. The particularity of these two countries was that they both had ethnic groups – namely Laps and Finns – who spoke another language than the main language of the countries, and this was expected to necessitate far reaching exemptions that would be difficult to frame. On this background the Scandinavian delegates deemed it proper not to include an explicit language requirement in the citizenship Acts, and adequate only to deal with the requirement in the administrative guidelines.

The same approach was taken in 1950. The Danish situation was still unique, while the Norwegian and Swedish citizenship Acts of 1950 contained naturalisation conditions regarding age, residence period, conduct, self-support, renunciation of a former citizenship and a declaration of loyalty – but no language requirement. Still, it was anticipated in the preparatory work to the 1950-Acts that applicants for naturalisation had to be able to communicate in the language of the naturalising country.[7]

5 Udkast til Nye Statsborgerretslove, udarbejdet af delegerede for Danmark, Norge og Sverige 1921 (1922) (Draft new citizenship Acts prepared by delegates from Denmark, Norway and Sweden), p. 37.

6 E. Ersbøll, *Indfødsret i international og historisk belysning*, Copenhagen: DJØF Publishing 2008, p. 595.

7 See *Betænkning med udkast til nye statsborgerretslove for Danmark, Norge og Sverige*, afgivet af delegerede for de tre lande (Draft new citizenship Acts for Denmark, Norway and Sweden prepared by delegates from the three countries) (1949); in each country citizens from the other Nordic countries were naturalised on lenient conditions; it was, however, considered necessary to subject Finnish citizens to a language requirement since their language belonged to 'the Finnish language family', cf. p. 43.

1.2.2 *Liberalising Trends in the 1960s*

In the second half of the twentieth century, many countries liberalised their citizenship Acts. Among other things, the naturalisation criteria became less restrictive and often, countries – like Denmark and Finland – applied flexible language requirements taking into consideration the particular situation of the applicant (among other things regard was taken to his or her educational background) or – like Norway and Sweden – repealed their former language requirements. In 1968 Denmark adopted its most lenient naturalisation criteria ever and around the same time in the Nordic countries immigrant descendants became, on attaining majority, entitled to citizenship conditional on ten years of residence.

1.2.3 *Language and Societal Knowledge Requirements in the Baltic States*

In the mid-1990s some restrictive trends appeared in Estonia and Latvia where new naturalisation requirements were adopted after intense debate. It was decided that applicants for naturalisation had to pass a language examination including competence in listening comprehension, conversation, reading and writing. Furthermore, applicants had to demonstrate their knowledge of the constitution and the citizenship Act – and in the case of Latvia, they moreover had to know the national anthem and the history of the country.

These demanding requirements were of course to be seen in the light of the Baltic States' 'sovjetization' for 50 years with immigration on a large scale and rapid ethno-demographic changes which caused fears of national extinction. Still, the requirements caused concern in the international community. Among others the Commissioner of Council of the Baltic Sea States (CBSS) raised the question whether it was at all reasonable to condition the acquisition of citizenship on the pass of a legal exam. In relation to the language requirements the commissioner expressed the following viewpoint:

> In so far as language requirements involve reading and writing proficiency, I find it very important that such requirements are limited to a relatively modest level, and especially that the particular situation of the applicant is taken into consideration.[8]

In the new millennium, surprisingly enough, many Western European countries adopted similar changes of their citizenship Acts – on a considerably less dramatic background.

1.2.4 *Mandatory Integration around 2000*

Around 2000, Denmark and the Netherlands introduced integration Acts. These countries were, thus, among the first to respond to an increasing European criticism of 'failed immigrant integration'. An important part of the integration Acts was the introduction of compulsory language courses and lessons in civics, history and culture. For immigrants who belonged to the target groups (refugees and family reunified persons) lack of attendance to the courses could influence their right to social benefits and access to permanent residence.

8 Commissioner of the CBSS on Democratic Institutions and Human Rights, including the Rights of Persons belonging to Minorities, Ole Espersen: *Criteria and procedures for Obtaining Citizenship in the CBSS Member States*, CBSS 1996, p. 71 ff.

At that time language and societal knowledge test requirements for naturalisation were not a European common feature. Quite the reverse: there was a marked North European trend towards liberalisation of the naturalisations requirements. The explanation offered in literature was that large-scale immigration lead to stable populations of permanent residents which in turn would lead to pressure for the liberalisation of citizenship law. The only noticed exception to this North European pattern was Austria – and this divergence was explained by the extreme right's place in the polity and the consequent decision by mainstream political elites to politicise the question of citizenship law.[9]

1.2.5 Restrictive Trends in the New Millennium

There are indications that the introduction of integration Acts with mandatory language courses etc. functioned as a stepping stone for the introduction of language and integration tests as a condition for citizenship. After 2000 and even more after the terrorist attacks on 9/11 2001, more and more European countries were concerned about 'lack of immigrant integration'. In reply to this, a number of countries introduced formalised language and/or societal knowledge tests requirements for naturalisation, often based on their already existing language course-system.

The formalised tests were introduced in an area of increasing immigrant integration efforts, and the purpose of the tests was improved immigrant integration. In addition, however, the tests were introduced because states wanted to bolster social cohesion, national unity and belonging.[10] So far the general perception had been that immigrant integration would take place during a number of years' residence in the host country. And, as reflected in recommendations etc. from international organs like the EU and the Council of Europe, naturalisation was in itself considered a means of (further) integration.[11]

In a number of states, however, the perception of naturalisation as a means of integration underwent a transformation. A majority among the politicians found that it had been too easy to naturalise and argued that access to citizenship should only be possible at the end of a completed integration process. In their opinion future citizens should prove their attachment to the society and be able to participate and engage actively in the democracy.[12]

---

9 R. Hansen & P. Weil (eds), *Towards a European Nationality, Citizenship, Immigration and Nationality Law in the EU*, Basingstoke: Palgrave 2001, p. 19.

10 See D. Kostakopoulou, 'Introduction', in R. van Oers, E. Ersbøll & D. Kostakopoulou, *A Re-definition of Belonging? Language and Integration Tests in Europe*, Leiden-Boston: Nijhoff Publishers 2010, p. 1.

11 See among others, the Second Protocol amending the Convention on the Reduction of Cases of Multiple Nationality and Military Obligations in Cases of Multiple nationality (ETS no. 14)) that states that 'Acquisition of the nationality of the host country is certainly an important, even crucial factor as far as integration in that country is concerned'; and Commission of the European communities; COM (2003) 336 final *Communication from the Commission to the Council, the European parliament, The European Economic and Social Committee and the Committee of the Regions on the immigration, integration and employment,* pr. 4.3. on Civic citizenship and nationality: tools to facilitate integration, stating that 'Naturalisation is a strategy, which can help to promote integration and which member states should consider when granting residence to immigrants and refugees'.

12 See R. van Oers, E. Ersbøll & D. Kostakopoulou: *A Re-definition of Belonging? Language and Integration Tests in Europe*, Leiden-Boston: Nijhoff Publishers 2010, p. 307 ff.

Like the Baltic States in the 1990s, many European states of today want future citizens to share their value system and a widespread perception is now that citizenship – as state membership – must be earned.

1.2.6 Language and Societal Knowledge Tests, Content and Effect

Thus, in the new millennium, attachment and integration is not any longer measured through long-term residence, and the attachment requirements are not any longer strengthened through extended residence requirements (for which the European Convention on Nationality (1997/ECN) has set a maximum of ten years). Instead, attachment and integration are examined through increasingly restricted language and societal knowledge requirements.

In 2010, 26 out of 32 European countries applied language tests as a condition for naturalisation; in 1998, the comparable number was 22. Among the 26 countries that applied language tests in 2010, 19 used formal tests; the comparable number in 1998 was five (and among them was only one Western European country: Portugal). The trend towards civic knowledge tests is weaker. Civic knowledge tests were applied in eight countries in 1999 (and in only one West European country, namely Austria) while the number was 17 in 2010; among the 17 countries, 12 had introduced formal knowledge tests.[13]

In most countries, the necessary language skills can be proved by examination certificates from language schools, elementary schools and/or educational institutions. If such proof cannot be presented or accepted, applicants must prove their skills by taking specific language and societal knowledge tests before an agency, a special commission or the like established as part of the naturalisation system.[14]

Some countries still test the required knowledge through an informal interview, while others, for instance Norway, consider documentation of language training a satisfactory proof,[15] or they apply a combined system, like the UK which allows applicants to prove their skills by either taking the 'Life in the UK test' or progressing from one level in a language and citizenship course to another. Examinations may be oral or written or both oral and written. In some countries the personal circumstances of the applicant are taken into consideration, while in others, requirements at a fixed level apply to all applicants.[16]

By the use the Common European Framework of Reference (CEF) to classify and compare the different countries' requirements, it appears that most countries require that their future citizens have language skills at either level A2 or B1. Only Denmark applies level B2. It seems, however, that once the test system has been introduced, there is a tendency to set

13 R. Bauböck (EUI, Florence) & I. Honohan (UCD, Dublin), *Access to citizenship in Europe: birthright and naturalisation*, EUDO Dissemination Conference 18-19 November 2010, Brussels http://www.eui.eu/Projects/EUDO/Documents/12-06-BauboeckandHonohanpresentations.pdf.

14 See R. van Oers, E. Ersbøll & D. Kostakopoulou: *A Re-definition of Belonging? Language and Integration Tests in Europe*, Leiden-Boston: Nijhoff Publishers 2010.

15 As of 1 September 2013, foreigners who have a right and a duty to take language training etc. according to the Introduction Norwegian Act must complete the training by passing a test in Norwegian and societal knowledge. The Norwegian citizenship Act has been changed accordingly and requires (in section 8) applicants for naturalization to fulfill their duty as provided in the Introduction Act.

16 See T. Strik, A. Böcker, M. Luiten & R. van Oers: *The INTEC Project: Synthesis Report, Integration and Naturalisation Tests: the new way to European Citizenship*, forthcoming 2012. See also http://menneskeret.dk/files/pdf/INTEC/Synthesis%20Intec%20final%20. pdf.

the requirements higher and higher. In Denmark for instance, the required language level was changed from B1 to B2 and later the pass grad was increased.[17] Other countries have increased the required language level from A2 to B1.[18]

The countries' societal knowledge test is often a multiple-choice-test. The tests' questions may regard the countries' democratic order, legal system, history, geography, population, living conditions, language, immigration, literature, art and/or science. It is not unusual that the questions' degree of difficulty is set so high that the native population has trouble passing the test.

Most countries offer preparation courses for the language tests, while there are a number of countries (like Austria, Denmark, Germany, Latvia and the UK) which do not offer state-regulated preparation courses for the societal knowledge test. Often, however, applicants for naturalisation can prepare for the knowledge test by using the Internet. In some countries, all the questions and answers are published; in others, only sample questions are published and/or a text book may be available.[19]

Some countries offer free language courses while others charge a fee. The prize for a language course may amount to 1,500 – 2,500 Euros (Austria is the most expensive state, but here the naturalisation test is free of charge). For the societal knowledge test most countries require a comparably lower fee – ranging from 25 Euros (Germany) to 89 Euros (Denmark). However, in the Netherlands the costs for the three parts of the central exam may be much higher. Furthermore it should be taken into consideration that in some countries applicants must pay the fee more than once if they fail and want to re-take the test. Finally, considering the total expenses by being naturalised one needs to take into account that an additional application fee is normally required.[20]

In some countries, applicants who have followed the country's primary and lower secondary (school) education are exempted from (some) test requirements. Still, the societal knowledge requirement may apply to both immigrants and immigrant descendants (as in Austria, Denmark, Latvia and the UK). Applicants who suffer from mental or physical impediments may obtain exemption from the test requirements; however, a number of countries have rigid exemption rules.[21]

The pass rates for the tests differ from year to year and from country to country. As regards the knowledge of society tests, the pass rates are high in Austria and Germany. Also in Denmark the pass rate used to be high. The Danish test was introduced in May 2007 and until December 2008 around 97-98 per cent passed. Then, however, the pass rate de-

17 The perception that there is an inclination to set an increasingly high language and societal knowledge level may be untenable in so far as the political situation in a country undergoes a change. In Denmark for instance , it is announced in the new Social Democratic led government's platform (October 2011) that in future applicants for naturalization must have past a Danish language test at level B1 (Danish 2) and a citizenship test that attach importance to the political and every day life which meet citizens in present day life.

18 See T. Strik, A. Böcker, M. Luiten & R. van Oers, *The INTEC Project: Synthesis Report, Integration and Naturalisation Tests: the new way to European Citizenship*, Nijmegen, December 2010 (see Part 4 of this book).

19 *Ibid.*

20 *Ibid.*

21 *Ibid.*

creased dramatically after a strengthening of the test requirements and although there is an upward movement, the pass rate has not risen above 70 per cent.[22]

The long and short of it is that in consequence of the introduction of formalised language and societal knowledge tests, the number of naturalisations has declined in many countries, among them the Netherlands and Denmark where a clear decreasing trend is seen after the introduction of the formalised tests requirements.[23]

2. Citizenship Policies in the New Millennium: Overall Liberal or Recurrently Restrictive?

In recent literature on the development of citizenship in the context of immigration it is argued that there has been a wholesale liberalisation of access to citizenship. This is beyond dispute in so far as many European countries have introduced both *ius soli* acquisition and toleration of dual citizenship. However, the further argument put forward by Joppke in his newest impressive analysis in the book *Citizenship and Migration* – that there has been a general lowering of naturalisation requirements – is worth discussing.[24] Joppke rightly draws attention to the countertrend towards new restrictions in naturalisation post-2001, but he argues that this is a nuance within, not a rollback to, the overall liberalisation of access to citizenship. This viewpoint is substantiated by the argument that the latest restrictions are all individual rather than group level requirements and that in principle, they can be met by all individuals irrespective of ascriptive origin traits; thus, it is reasoned, there has not been a return to the racist or nationalist group level exclusion of the past.

Maybe it is not as simple as that. We have seen that often the new language and societal knowledge test requirements have a selective effect, and often specific groups are excluded. Those who are excluded are primarily groups with low education, illiterates in particular, elderly people, traumatised refugees and – though not defined in ethnic or nationalistic terms – groups from certain parts of the world, among others Asia. The recently completed INTEC research project suggests that at least in the Netherlands and the UK, the introduction of the tests has resulted in a selection of future citizens where the country of origin plays an important role.[25] Similarly with Denmark, where language school teachers have pointed out immigrants from countries with a language from another language family than the Indo-European, for instance the East Asian countries. It is experienced that these groups face significantly more problems passing the tests than others –even to an extent that many may be excluded from reaching the required level.[26]

22 *Ibid.* In December 2010 64.2 percent passed, in June 2011 60.2 percent passed, in December 2011 70.4 percent passed. However, in December 2011 only about 2000 applicants took the test, while the number the preceding years was about 3000. Many applicants have taken the test several times.

23 *Ibid.*

24 C. Joppke, *Citizenship and Migration*, Cambridge: Polity Press 2010, p. 31.

25 See Ti. Strik, A. Böcker, M. Luiten & R. van Oers, *The INTEC Project: Synthesis Report, Integration and Naturalisation Tests: the new way to European Citizenship*, Forthcoming 2012. http://menneskeret.dk/files/pdf/INTEC/Synthesis%20Intec%20final%20.pdf.

26 See E. Ersbøll & L.K. Gravesen, 'Country Report Denmark', in T. Strik, A. Böcker, M. Luiten & R. van Oers, *The INTEC Project: Synthesis Report, Integration and Naturalisation Tests: the new way to European Citizenship*, Forthcoming 2012. See http://menneskeret.dk/files/pdf/INTEC/Denmark% 20Intec %20final.pdf.

Moreover, there are drawbacks to the new test requirements in so far as they apply to immigrant descendants. Although, as Joppke rightly underlines, that application of *ius soli* provisions for immigrant descendants have 'largely remained unaffected by the trend towards stricter naturalisation rules',[27] there are exemptions. Denmark, for instance, repealed in 2004 its more than 200 years' entitlement to citizenship for immigrant descendants. Hereafter, immigrant descendants, who are born and/or raised in the country, need to apply for (un-facilitated) naturalisation.[28] In this case, one can hardly argue that state-membership is contractual, based on a reciprocal *do ut des*. Second generation may have a formal citizenship – the citizenship of their parents' country of origin – but they may not have any independent bond to that country. They need a citizenship of their own – the citizenship of 'their country of origin'. Admittedly, Denmark forms an exception when it comes to abolition of former *ius soli* provisions; still, Denmark is not the only country in which immigrant descendants need to fulfil integration test requirements, see above under 1.2.6.[29] It is incontrovertible that there is a trend towards applying *ius soli*. It is also incontrovertible that even a country like Austria has followed the *ius soli*-trend and granted persons born in Austria facilitated naturalisation by legal entitlement; still, this move is seriously called into question by the many conditions for naturalisation that apply to native-born persons as they do to immigrants.[30]

The argument I wish to put forward is that in an assessment and comparison of citizenship policies of the EU member states, the application of integration test requirements for naturalisation must play a central role.

The application of language and knowledge testing and the application of the *ius soli*-principle may be decisive factors for gaining access to citizenship. As components they may outdo both (in)tolerance of dual citizenship and the length of a residence requirement. This is also reflected in the new 'Citizenship Policy Index' (CPI) constructed by Marc Howard in his extremely interesting book on citizenship policies.[31] The earlier CPI was based on a few key elements: whether a country granted *ius soli*, the length of the residence requirement for naturalisation and whether naturalised immigrants could hold dual citizenship,[32] while the new CPI also incorporates the recent development with language and civic integration requirements.

There can be no doubt that some kind of *ius soli*-acquisition (at birth or after birth) is among the most important elements of a country's citizenship policy – since it entitles immigrant descendants to a citizenship (a citizenship of their own, in 'their own country') and since citizenship without the possibility of *ius soli*-acquisition may be unattainable. The

27 C. Joppke, *Citizenship and Migration*, Cambridge: Polity Press 2010, p. 63.

28 According to the Danish government platform 2011-12, immigrant descendants who are born and raised in Denmark and who have passed the school leaving exam of the Danish *Folkeskole* (lower secondary school) will automatically be offered Danish citizenship, unless they have been sentenced for serious crimes, and all young foreigners who are born and raised in Denmark will automatically be offered citizenship at the age of 18, unless they are sentenced for serious crimes.

29 See also Strik et al. about school drop outs and persons with lower intellectual capacities.

30 See Cinar & Waldrauch, 'Austria', in R. Bauböck, E. Ersbøll, K. Groenendijk & H. Waldrauch (eds), *Acquisition and Loss of Nationality, Volume 2: Country Analyses; Policies and Trends in 15 European States*, Amsterdam: Amsterdam University Press 2006, p. 53.

31 M. Morjé Howard, *The Politics of Citizenship in Europe*, Cambridge: Cambridge University Press 2009.

32 See M. Morjé Howard, 'Comparative Citizenship: An Agenda for Cross-National Research', *Perspectives on Politics* 4, no. 3 (2006), p. 443-455.

same does not count for tolerance of dual citizenship and short residence requirements. It is true that renunciation requirements may have a prohibitive effect on some immigrants' inclination to apply for citizenship, but whether to apply or not that is a decision of their own. If they feel a predominant need for the host country's citizenship, the lesser of two evils may be to acquire that citizenship while loosing the citizenship of origin. The case of the residence requirement is the same. Admittedly, if a liberal country with a residence requirement of three years decides to extend the requirement to five or even ten years, it may be a crucial problem for resident immigrants in acute need of the host country's citizenship; still, all other things being equal, what counts in the long term is that the requirement does not have an exclusive effect.

The case of the language and societal knowledge test requirements is different. These requirements, at least if they stand high, may have a permanent exclusive effect on certain immigrant groups such as uneducated immigrants, elderly and/or disabled immigrants and immigrants from certain regions of the world (with a language belonging to another language family than the European languages). If so, these requirements are in reality much more problematic than even the longest residence requirement and the renunciation requirement…

For the applicants, the size of the problem depends on the overall importance of citizenship in an age of migration.

3. The Significance of Citizenship in an EU Member State

In his thorough analysis of *Citizenship and Migration* Joppke has questioned the future of citizenship. With reference to the works of Yasemin Soysal and Peter Spiro he endorses the viewpoint that citizenship is lightening in the West and that the importance of immigrant visa by far surpasses that of formal citizenship. This is of course, as also underlined by Joppke, a matter of perspective. In all probability the vast majority of the world's population, who cannot enter the territory of the Western countries due to their restrictive immigration policy, will consent. However, it is not unlikely that many immigrants residing in the Western countries consider exclusion from acquisition of the citizenship of their host country to be of equal importance. Spiro forms a picture of a legal immigrant elite, who may choose between permanent residence and citizenship after having cleared the hurdle of territorial access. This picture may reflect the realities in some countries and/or for some resident immigrants. Still, for immigrants who live in the EU member states with constant restrictions of the aliens and citizenship policy, the situation may be different. If these immigrants cannot pass integration tests requirements for permanent residence and/or citizenship, they cannot obtain a secure residence status, and if they have established themselves in the host countries with children at school etc., they may be in a precarious situation which can bear comparison with immigrants who in vain apply for a visa.

In some countries – such as the Netherlands and the UK – the language and societal knowledge requirements for permanent residence and naturalisation are the same.[33] Immigrant groups who face difficulties passing them, are not able to choose a secure status, neither permanent residence nor citizenship. In other countries the requirements for perma-

33 See Strik et al.

nent residence and citizenship differ, but still, both statuses may be difficult to acquire. In a country like Denmark, citizenship may be out of reach for certain immigrants. Denmark has the highest language requirement among the European states (level B2 in CEF) and a societal knowledge test that is considered difficult both in wording and content.[34] It is evident that these requirements do not reflect a lightening citizenship. Immigrants are clearly very persistent and tend to do everything possible in order to become naturalised even when they fail tests and have a very hard time fulfilling the criteria. The importance of citizenship from an immigrant perspective is exemplified in the INTEC project, by a statement, among others, from an applicant who, in vain, had tried to pass the citizenship test. Eventually, she had given up, but immediately reconsidering the matter she said that she might try again. Her reasoning was that 'if they change the legislation, then they may throw out people who have only a permanent residence permit'.[35] The statement reflects an uncertainty felt by immigrants without a secure residence status. Admittedly again, Denmark constitutes an exception – also by having an opt-out from the EU Justice and Home Affairs and thus not being bound by the Council Directive 2003/109/EC concerning the status of third-country nationals who are long term residents; still, the same applies to the UK and Ireland.

Another factor that must be taken into consideration is that in some countries children may not be able to apply for citizenship independently. This is the case in countries like Austria and Denmark, where the strengthening of the test requirements has led to a decline in the number of immigrants who are able to fulfil the requirements for naturalisation, and accordingly a decline in the number of immigrant descendants with citizenship transferred from their parents. There is no doubt that for immigrant parents this arouses profound concern.

Taking into consideration that many European states have introduced integration test requirements as a condition for naturalisation and that still more plan to do so, the policy of testing immigrant integration is to be considered a common European feature. So far, there are huge variations between the countries' legislation regarding language and civic knowledge testing, both as to content and standard, fees, preparation possibilities, target groups and exemption possibilities. However, as already mentioned there has been a tendency towards strengthening the requirements once a test system has been introduced. Language levels have been raised, and moreover there has been a trend towards adding knowledge of society test requirements to language test requirements, as seen in Denmark, Germany, the Netherlands and the UK.[36]

Such tendencies in combination with the tendency seen in most European countries towards developing an aliens policy with the purpose of attracting (first and foremost) highly qualified foreigners – that is: foreigners who 'can and will integrate' – may make citizenship even more important for resident immigrants who do not belong to the new 'elite'.

---

34 When the new government adopts new acquisition rules, as announced in the government platform for 2011-12, acquisition will be facilitated. Still, not all applicants will probably be able to pass a language test at level B1.

35 E. Ersbøll & L.K. Gravesen, *Country Report Denmark; The INTEC-project: Integration and Naturalisation Tests: the new way to European Citizenship* (2010), p. 75. See http:// menneskeret.dk/files/pdf/INTEC/Denmark%20Intec%20final.pdf.

36 See Strik et al.

For long term immigrants and their descendants, citizenship matters in order to feel overall integrated into society; citizenship is of importance for democratic representation and citizenship reflects the full membership of a state.

Therefore, for long term residents and their children there seems to be a pressing need for a clarification of the legal meaning of the principle that 'everyone has a right to a nationality'. The principle was included in the Universal Declaration of Human Rights, article 15, and according to the 1997-European Convention on Nationality (ECN) the citizenship legislation of the state parties must be based on said principle. It is arguable that more state cooperation is needed to this end.

4. European Citizenship-cooperation

The European Convention on Nationality was adopted in an area of liberalisation of citizenship law and the convention in itself contributed further hereto. Citizenship tests were hardly at the agenda in 1997 (with the exception of the Baltic States which was considered a specific case). Still a few years later, a Council of Europe report (2003) on the conditions for acquisition and loss of nationality analysed the citizenship legislation of the members states and found a need for further coordination and harmonisation regarding (among other things) language and integration requirements for naturalisation.[37]

The report asked which degree of knowledge of a host country's language etc. it would be reasonable to require. This question and a question on exceptions from the requirements were to be further discussed. The position of the report was that requirements for knowledge regarding the language, culture and history of the country of which the applicant was seeking citizenship should exclusively be used and regarded as an element of integrating non-citizens and not be used as a discriminatory means for a state to select its citizens.[38]

The report discussed what was meant by 'integration'? It was held that no element of a state's integration law should be contrary to an individual's human rights or discriminatory, nor should 'integration' be interpreted as 'assimilation'.[39]

The Expert Committee on Nationality, which adopted the report, does not exist any longer, but at the 4th Council of Europe Conference on Nationality in December 2010 the participants called upon the Council of Europe to take account of the discussions at the conference, and for this purpose to continue and reinforce its work on citizenship as one of its core concerns and, in particular, to consider possible new standards, principles and rules with regard to access to citizenship as a fundamental human right. Furthermore, the Council should in its future work pay attention to the relationship between integration and citizenship.[40]

It is indeed recommendable that the work on access to citizenship by naturalisation is continued. The rapid development of new citizenship policies in the 21st century furnish

37 Report of 14 January 2003 CJ-NA (2002) 1Committee of Experts on Nationality (CJ-NA), *Conditions for the Acquisition and Loss of Nationality*, adopted by the Committee of Experts on Nationality on the basis of a draft prepared by Mr Andrew Walmsley.

38 *Ibid.*, p. 12.

39 *Ibid.*

40 See the Conference's final conclusions: http://www.coe.int/t/dghl/standardsetting/nationality/Final%20Conclusions%20E.pdf.

good grounds for believing that civic integration tests as a condition for naturalisation is going to be a more lasting phenomenon. Therefore, there is a need to discuss best practices, including among others things questions on target groups, exemptions, relevant knowledge, level, preparatory courses, costs etc. with a view to draft new common European legal standards for civic integration requirements for naturalisation. The debate started by Joppke at the EU citizenship Observatory (EUDO) might form an important basis for such discussions.[41]

41 http://eudo-citizenship.eu/citizenship-forum/255-how-liberal-are-citizenship-tests.

How do We get More out of the EU Citizenship?

Kristine Kruma

Introduction

Since its introduction the EU citizenship has developed as an open concept - incrementally and fragmentary. The important player in this context has been the Court of Justice of the European Union (ECJ). Judgments of the Court on the EU citizenship related matters have divided scholars and commentators into different camps ranging from those who see the EU citizenship as flag-mark to federalism, to those who criticize the Court for going far beyond the EU's competence and granting rights which were not agreed in between the Member States. This might be explained by the fact that attribution of citizenship status and rights derived from it are closely linked with the sovereignty of the Member States.

The ECJ has achieved significant progress in advancing the functional aspects of the EU citizenship. It has strengthened free movement and residence rights as well as attempted to ensure that rule of non-discrimination on basis of nationality is observed. However, the Court's practice in relation to acquisition and loss of the status of EU citizen has been much more limited. It did not intervene into Member State discretion to grant nationality, nor allowed other Member States to attach additional conditions for recognising nationality granted.[1] This is why the ruling in *Rottman*[2] has provoked extensive academic debate on limits of the EU's competence and its role in further development of trans-national identity at the EU level. It has also been discussed in the context of limits on autonomy of the Member States in the field of nationality.

This article will discuss the principles introduced or elaborated in *Rottman*. First, the Court had to answer question on what are the limits for the autonomy of Member States in relation to acquisition or loss of nationality. And, second, under what conditions situation of Mr. Rottman cannot be qualified as purely internal situation. Subsequent developments show that *Rottman* principles might be applied to other situations which relate to exercise of EU citizens' rights. For instance, they might be relevant when dealing with functional aspects of the EU citizenship. This has been exemplified in case-law after *Rottman* and will also be noted in this article. Second part of the article is devoted to questions on the consequences of *Rottman* principles for the application of general rules on loss and acquisition of

1 Case C-192/99 *The Queen v. Secretary of State for the Home Department ex parte Kaur* [2001] ECR I-1237 and Case C-369/90 *Mario Vicente Micheletti and others v. Delegación del Gobierno en Cantabria* [1992] ECR I- 4239

2 Case C-135/08, *Janko Rottman v. Freistaat Bayern* [2010] ECR I-1449. The case concerned an Austrian national subject to criminal proceedings in Austria. In 1995 he left Austria which issues arrest warrant against him. He settled in Germany and in 1998 applied for naturalization there without disclosing information about criminal charges. He became German citizen in 1999 and lost his Austrian nationality. The same year Austria informed Germany on arrest warrant which made German authorities to withdraw German nationality because it was acquired by fraud. The decision was upheld by German Courts and Rottman was deprived of German nationality ab initio. As a result he could become stateless and loose his EU citizenship status.

nationality in the EU. The conclusions will focus on future relationship of EU and national citizenship as well as changes in our general perception of the concept of EU citizenship.

1. Principles derived from *Rottman* and their Application

1.1 Obligation to Pay Due Regard to the EU Law

In *Rottman* the Court had to address the scope of autonomy of Member States in nationality issues. The national court by its questions essentially sought to clarify the scope of obligation to take into account EU context when deciding on withdrawal of nationality leading to statelessness.

The Court already in the *Micheletti,*[3] *Mesbah*[4] and *Chen*[5] cases has established limitations on the absolute discretion of Member States in relation to granting and withholding nationality. In *Rottman* it stated:

> [I]t is for each Member State, *having due regard to Community law*, to lay down the conditions for the acquisition and loss of nationality [....] Nevertheless the fact that a matter falls within the competence of the Member State does not alter the fact that, in situations covered by the European Union Law, the national rules concerned must have due regard to the later.[6] [emphasis added]

In the particular case of deprivation of nationality there is a need to strike a balance between the autonomy of Member States and the EU interests. Therefore, the Court noted that there is an obligation for the national courts to have due regard to the principle of proportionality by taking into account consequences of a decision leading to loss of the EU citizenship.[7] These statements, although in line with previous approach of the Court, require to reflect on the scope of autonomy of EU citizenship from national regulation and even international law.

The importance of this question was emphasized by the Advocate General (AG) Maduro. By reference to *Kaur* he noted that as a principle of customary international law it is for each Member State to determine who are its nationals. This is also confirmed by Declaration No. 2 on nationality annexed to the Final Act of the Treaty on the EU which should be accorded at least interpretative force. Since none of the provisions of EU law regulates the procedure and conditions for the acquisition and loss of the nationality of a Member State or of Union citizenship, this question falls within the competence of the Member

3 Case C-369/90 *Mario Vicente Micheletti and others v. Delegación del Gobierno en Cantabria* [1992] ECR I-4239, para 10.

4 Case C-179/98 *Belgian State v. Fatna Mesbah* [1999] ECR I-7955.

5 Case C-200/02 *Kunqian Catherine Zhu, Man Lavette Chen v. Secretary of State for the Home Department* [2004] ECR I-9925.

6 Case C-135/08 *Janko Rottman v. Freistaat Bayern* [2010] ECR I-1449, para 39 and 41. In para 41 the Court referred also to its previous rulings in cases Case C-274/96 *Criminal proceedings against Horst Otto Bickel and Ulrich Franz* [1998] ECR I-7637, Case C-148/02 *Carlos Garcia Avello v. État belge* [2003] ECR I-11613, Case C-403/03 *Egon Schempp v. Finanzamt München V* [2005] ECR I-6421, Case C-145/04 *Kingdom of Spain v. United Kingdom of Great Britain and Northern Ireland* [2006] ECR I-7917.

7 Case C-135/08 *Janko Rottman v. Freistaat Bayern* [2010] ECR I-1449, para 55.

States.[8] For him once a Member State has declared who are to be considered as EU citizens, the Court is limited by those declarations. Otherwise that would produce a paradoxical solution whereby the secondary would determine the primary: maintenance of Union citizenship would serve as a basis for demanding maintenance of the nationality of a Member State.[9] This statement clearly pleases Member States who might feel insecure in case if the ECJ would attempt to go further in limiting their autonomy regarding nationality issues. At the same time Maduro has also noted:

> The fact nevertheless remains that, if the situation comes within the scope of Community law, the exercise by the Member States of their retained powers cannot be discretionary. It is subject to the obligation to comply with the Community rules.[10]

This statement initially might seem confusing because of the lack of EU regulation on nationality. However, AG Maduro explains that these limits on discretion of Member States stems from requirements established in international law. All three systems – national, international and the EU law – are interrelated. Although international law requires avoidance of statelessness it does not prohibit loss of nationality, even if that would lead to statelessness.[11] In this context the argument of the AG Maduro does not stretch beyond the compounds of international law standards, and since case concerns primarily check on loyalty of nationals, no EU rule has been infringed.[12] Regulation of nationality on the level of Member States would remain dominant if it is in line with both international and human rights regulation. In this context the contents of principle 'due regard to Community law' remains limited to the requirements of international law binding upon Member States.

The reference to limits set by international law are appropriate, however, moderate in the EU context. It narrows the role of the EU principle discussed. For instance, AG Maduro himself mentions the principle of sincere co-operation which can be derived from Article 20 TFEU read together with 10 TFEU (ex 10 TEC) but limits the reference to the academic writings regarding an unjustified mass naturalisation of nationals of non-member States.[13] Invocation of these Articles should not detach EU citizenship from nationality but impose on the Member States an obligation to co-ordinate nationality policies, so that not only in cases of mass naturalization but also in cases of statelessness and deprivation of the nationality role of the EU would be more meaningful.

The ECJ approach was more pertinent if compared to AG Maduro Opinion from the point of view of developing EU law. Apart from references to international law it strengthened the EU element in the test to be applied by national courts. The ECJ emphasised that while Member States do have the right to grant or withdraw nationality, they should examine the consequences at the EU level and take 'due regard to Community law'.[14] Therefore, there is no absolute immunity of Member States in nationality issues. If a Member State

8 Opinion of Advocate General Maduro, 30 September 2009, C-135/08, *Janko Rottman v. Freistaat Bayern* [2010] ECR I-1449, para 19.

9 *Ibid.*, para 24

10 *Ibid.*, para 20.

11 *Ibid.*, paras 27-29 and 33.

12 *Ibid.*, para 33.

13 *Ibid.*, para 30.

14 *Supra* note 7, paras 39 and 45.

leaves the person stateless the loss becomes an obstacle to free movement and residence rights in the EU, which are considered to be fundamental according to EU law. This suggests, as stated by Stephen Hall, that there may be circumstances in which a person who has already acquired the status of a Member State national may be protected by the EU law when subjected to withdrawal procedures and that status withdrawal violated the general principles of law protected by the Court.[15] In this context the application of general principle of proportionality would require national court to take into account a number of factors, *inter alia*, risk of statelessness, length of residence in the Member State, level of integration, social ties in respective Member State and alike.

The Court remained mindful of the international law maxim. It quoted international law provisions on withdrawal of nationality acquired by fraud.[16] Indeed, acquisition of nationality by fraudulent activities *ex lege* is a well established principle of international law and is enshrined *inter alia* in Article 7(1)(b) of the ECN. However, international law on nationality and even human rights law are not exhaustive sources in the EU context. Jo Shaw argues that the Court does not focus on a human rights imperative to avoid statelessness but rather on the EU specific rights which a person will lose.[17] Therefore, the Court does not limit itself to international law considerations, but requires national courts to conduct analysis of situation from the EU's perspective. As rightly observed by Dora Kostakopoulou in this context we can talk about a 'relative autonomy' of Member States in the determination of the conditions for the acquisition and loss of nationality.[18]

The Court did not dwell on legal standing of the provisions of Declaration no. 2 to which AG Maduro referred in his opinion. The ECJ attaches more competences to itself to deal with cases on exercise of citizens' rights. This leads to question raised by Gareth T. Davies, that it remains unclear what the declaration is worth. For him it may be no more than a rejection of harmonization of national citizenship, although even judicial intervention in *Rottman* is harmonization of a sort.[19] The position of the Court can be clarified by interpreting the dual position on *Kaur* it expressed when dealing with *Rottmann*. On the one hand the Court refers to the *Kaur* situation and notes that the situation of *Kaur* is different from that of *Rottman*. On the other hand, as noted by René de Groot and Anja Seling, the ECJ also stated that 'the principles stemming from this judgment with regard to the powers of Member States in the sphere of nationality, and also their duty to exercise those powers having due regard to EU law, apply both to the Member State of naturalization and to the

15 S. Hall, 'Determining the Scope *ratione personae* of European Citizenship: Customary International Law Prevails for Now', *Legal Issues of Economic Integration*, Vol. No. 28(3), 2001, p. 355-360, at 360.

16 *Supra* note 7, paras 52 and 53.

17 See J. Shaw, *Kickoff by Jo Shaw*, March 5 2010, available at EUDO citizenship forum, available at http://eudo-citizenship.eu/citizenship-forum/254-has-the-european-court-of-justice-challenged-member-state-sovereignty-in-nationality-law?start=2, accessed on 5 September 2010.

18 D. Kostakopoulou, *European Union Citizenship and Member State Nationality: updating or upgrading the link?*, 6 July 2010, EUDO Citizenship Forum 'Has the European Court of Justice Challenged Member State Sovereignty in Nationality Law?', 1 July 2010, available at http://eudo-citizenship.eu/citizenship-forum/254-has-the-european-court-of-justice-challenged-member-state-sovereignty-in-nationality-law?start=5, accessed 3 September 2010.

19 See comment by Gareth T. Davies, *The entirely conventional supremacy of Union citizenship and rights* (2010 EUDO citizenship forum) <http://eudo-citizenship.eu/citizenship-forum/254-has-the-european-court-of-justice-challenged-member-state-sovereignty-in-nationality-law> accessed 11 February 2011.

Member State of the original nationality'.[20] Therefore, EU competence in cases of access and loss of citizenship cannot be excluded *in toto* in addition to requirements of international law. This might lead to some sort of harmonization as argued by Davies.

Therefore, on the one hand, *Rottman* can be said to be ground-breaking case in the sense that it added proportionality test to be applied when person can be deprived of nationality according to international law and loose EU citizenship. In this regard, it can be argued that *Rottman* is in line with the Court's previous case-law, for instance *Baumbast*[21] and *Grzelczyk*,[22] requiring individualized approach to personal circumstances of EU citizen which is possible if proportionality test is applied in each particular case including loss of nationality. This might go beyond *lege lata* obligations under international and EU law obligations of Member States. On the other hand, the conclusions are not definitive. Gareth T. Davies has correctly observed that the ECJ is merely trying to prevent a lack of co-ordination between States leading to a Union citizen becoming unnecessarily stateless. It does not dictate any result but only invites to consider proportionality argument.[23] Autonomy of Member States has become more limited because the ECJ has introduced additional principles to be taken into account. At the same time Declaration No. 2 is still applicable for initial determination whether person is entitled to EU citizenship. Moreover, the final decision is left with the national courts, which even by having due regard to EU law can leave Mr. Rottman without national and EU citizenship.[24]

All and all an outcome of *Rottman* has a potential to affect the developments of EU citizenship considerably further. EU interests can be identified in relation to a number of grounds and conditions for loss and acquisition of nationality from the point of view of closer co-operation. Although the EU cannot address all of them at once, they might become subject to Court's jurisdiction and affected by application of principle of proportionality not only in cases leading to statelessness. Moreover, this might lead to repercussions on regulation of EU citizenship in other fields which will be illustrated in the next subsection.

1.2 Principle of 'Substance of Rights'

EU law as a rule is triggered only in cross-border situations. However, EU citizenship cases have identified situations which at the outset might seem internal, but still allow the Court to find jurisdiction. The lack of cross-border character has also been the issue raised by the parties in *Rottman*. However, this argument was not accepted neither by the AG Maduro, nor the Court.

AG Maduro agreed that citizenship as such cannot extend the scope *ratione materiae* of the Treaty to internal situations which have no link with EU law. He also admitted that in

20 *Supra* note 7, para 62. See G.R. de Groot & A. Seling, *The consequences of the Rottmann judgment on Member State autonomy – The Court's avant-gardism in nationality matters* (2010, EUDO Citizenship forum) <http://eudo-citizenship.eu/citizenship-forum/254-has-the-european-court-of-justice-challenged-member-state-sovereignty-in-nationality-law> accessed 11 February 2011.

21 Case C-413/99 *Baumbast, R v. Secretary of State for the Home Department* [2002] ECR I-7091.

22 Case C-184/99 *Rudy Grzelczyk v. Centre public d'aide sociale d'Ottignies-Louvain-la-Neuve* [2001] ECR I-6193.

23 *Supra* note 19.

24 *Supra* note 7, para 55.

Rottman case the link between the withdrawal of naturalization and the EU fundamental freedom is less direct, because *Rottman* did not exercise free movement rights but because he was caught with deliberate deception. However, the fact that he acquired German nationality by exercise of residence rights makes the link with EU law sufficient.[25] At least certain, even remote cross-border element might be relevant for the Court to find jurisdiction.[26] The Court built up on the position of AG and stated:

> It is clear that the situation of a citizen of the Union who, like the applicant in the main proceedings, is faced with a decision withdrawing his naturalization, adopted by the authorities of one Member State, and placing him, after he has lost the nationality of another Member State that he originally possessed, in a position capable of causing him to lose the status conferred by Article 17 TEC [20 TFEU] and the rights attaching thereto falls, *by reason of its nature and its consequences*, within the ambit of European Union law.[27] [emphasis added]

The test 'by reason of its nature and consequences' allows the Court to deal with the case irrespective of the fact that Rottman was not exercising his free movement rights in the 'traditional sense'.[28] In *Rottman* the free movement was acknowledged no to be 'traditional', i.e., Mr. Rottman was solely German citizen who had no links with other countries and who had lost citizenship because of his own conduct. In the context of Article 20 TFEU both the AG Maduro and the Court emphasised that for the purposes of the Court's jurisdiction it is important that Mr. Rottman has moved from Austria to Germany, i.e., nationality laws of two Member States had been applied.

Thus, Article 20 TFEU precludes national measures which have the effect of depriving EU citizens of genuine enjoyment of the substance of the rights conferred upon them as EU citizens. What could be derived is that in cases when the 'substance of rights' is affected no cross-border element is required.[29] These situations by their reason and consequences fall within the ambit of the EU law. Therefore, it has been said that the Court goes beyond the *ratione materiae* of EU law and applies it to situations which can be qualified as purely internal. This is seen as a threat to national immigration matters with possible domino effects on other fields.[30] These statements are, however, too bold because principle has limited application in the context of Article 20 TFEU at least for the time being.

---

25 *Supra* note 8, para 13.

26 However, EU law can be invoked in cases where there is a foreign element, that is, a cross-border dimension. AG Maduro says: 'Only a situation which is confined *in all respects* within a single Member State constituted a purely internal situation' [emphasis added]. Supra note 8, paras 9-10. AG referred to ECJ cases C-64-65/96 *Uecker and Jacquet* [1997] ECR I-3171, Case C-148/02 *Garcia Avello* [2003] ECR I-11613 and others.

27 *Supra* note 7, para 42.

28 *Supra* note 5. The Court established jurisdiction, although persons did not exercise free movement rights in the 'traditional sense', i.e., mother travelled from the UK to Ireland to give birth to her daughter which acquired Irish nationality and thus EU citizenship.

29 Kay Hailbronner & Daniel Thym, 'Case C34/09, Gerardo Ruiz Zambrano v. Office national de l'emploi (ONEm), Judgment of hte Court of 8 March 2011' (2011) 48 (4) *CMLR*, p. 1253-1270, at p. 1255-1256.

30 *Ibid.*, 1257.

The test introduced strengthens the EU citizenship which, according to the Court, is *'intended to be the fundamental status'*.[31] It also makes the regulation on rights of citizens closer to one which has for years been adopted in cases of goods. This reflects the *Dassonville* formula providing that EU law can be invoked when regulation can 'directly or indirectly, actually or potentially' affect or make less attractive free movement rights in the EU.[32] In *Rottman*, person could be deprived of EU citizens' rights in their totality. Therefore, 'the substance of rights' derived from EU citizenship would be inevitably affected. The question arises which situations could potentially fall under 'substance of rights' principle. Apart from withdrawal of status Jo Shaw has noted that possibly the Court has opened the door in *Rottman* to a new phase in its case law. She admits that the dominant focus on transnationalism leaves a huge question mark in relation to the so-called 'wholly internal situations'.[33] Gareth T. Davies even states that all national citizenship laws impact upon the capacity of individuals to enjoy Union citizenship.[34] Therefore, all citizenship regulation potentially might fall within the scope of the EU law. This seems to be broad interpretation. It can be argued that the added value of *Rottman* principles could rather come with gradual re-interpretation of other rights attached to EU citizenship.

1.3 Prospects for Application of Rottman Principles

The evolutionary nature of the EU citizenship concept allows develop interpretation of the primary EU law in order to reach the ultimate goal of the EU citizenship as a fundamental status in EU law. As noted by Advocate General Geelhoed in the *Bidar case*:

> [W]ith respect to matters coming within the scope ratione materiae of the Treaty, citizenship itself may provide a basis for bringing certain matters within that scope where the objectives pursued by the national measure correspond with those pursued by the Treaty or secondary legislation.[35]

Although Rotttman case is very specific factually, the principles applied by the Court can be helpful to develop EU citizenship regulation further by applying these principles to multitude of different other situations concerning rights of EU citizens.

In the context of *Rottman* the question arises what would be its implications in cases when *person possesses EU and non-EU citizenship* and risks to loose EU citizenship. For instance, René de Groot and Anja Seling say that the question is still open.[36] For instance, allowing for loss of EU citizenship in cases if dual non-EU/EU national would possibly contravene EU's aim to facilitate free movement within the EU. In case if EU citizenship is destined to be fundamental status the fact of possessing non-EU citizenship could have only

---

31 *Supra* note 7, para 43.

32 Case 8/74, *Dassonville* [1974] ECR – 837.

33 J. Shaw, *Citizenship: Contrasting Dynamics at the Interface of Integration and Constitutionalism*, EUI Working Papers, RCAS 2010/60, available at http://cadmus.eui.eu/bitstream/handle/ 1814/14396/ RSCAS%202010_60.pdf?sequence=1, accessed 10 January 2011, p. 18.

34 *Supra* note 19.

35 Opinion of AG Geelhoed, 11 November 2004, Case C-209/03 *The Queen ex parte Dany Bidar v. London Borough of Ealing, Secretary of State for Education* [2005] ECR I-2119, para 52.

36 *Supra* note 20.

marginal effect. At the same time it would depend on specific rights invoked and links with the country of EU citizenship if compared to the links to non-EU Member State which nationality might or might not be lost.[37] *Rottman* principles do not exclude possibility for the ECJ to develop further and strengthen proportionality principle in cases when person might loose EU citizenship while retain citizenship of non-EU Member State.

The test on 'substance of rights' represents particular importance in cases concerning *children*. This has already been confirmed by the ECJ in the number of cases. The ECJ has reconfirmed its approach on EU citizenship as fundamental status according to Article 20 TFEU in *Zambrano*[38] by relying on previous rulings, including, *inter alia*, *Baumbast*,[39] *Avello*,[40] *Chen*.[41] In the *Zambrano* case the claim was brought by the third country nationals who were parents to children holding EU citizenship. Since parents residence was illegal they risked to be expelled. Thus, the result would have been that by depriving parents of residence rights and entitlement to work their children could be deprived 'of the genuine enjoyment of the substance of the rights conferred by virtue of their status as citizens of the Union'. This would lead to violation of Article 20 TFEU in relation to children.[42] In this case similarly to *Avello* cross-border element, or the fact that there was no 'traditional movement' like in *Chen*, was not decisive because the genuine enjoyment of the substance of the EU citizen's rights was at stake for children. The ECJ approach in these cases could be further strengthened by reference to the rights of the child and the obligation to serve children's best interests included in Article 24 of the Charter.

The limits of application of the concept of 'substance of rights' since *Rottmann* and *Zambrano* has been further clarified in cases such as *McCarthy* and *Dereci* on rights of *family members* to reside in the territory of Member State which is State of nationality of EU citizen.

37 See for instance Case C-138/02 *Brian Francis Collins v. Secretary of State for Work and Pensions* [2004] ECR I-2703. Case C-224/98 *Marie-Nathalie D'Hoop v. Office national de l'emploi* [2002] ECR I-6191, paras 38-39. The case concerned a Belgian national who returned to Belgium after acquiring secondary education in France and applied for tide-over allowance. The authorities refused to grant her the allowance because she had not acquired secondary education in Belgium.

38 Case C-34/09 *Gerardo Ruiz Zambrano v. Office national de l'emploi*, 8 March 2011 [not yet reported]. Ruiz Zambrano has been residing in Belgium without a residence permit after the rejection of his asylum application and worked without authorization for almost seven years. Attempts to regularize his status were rejected. At the same time coercive measures of deportation were not effected. During their stay in Belgium Mr. Zambrano's family got two children who were registered as Belgian nationals. Their children were born in 2003 and 2005 respectively. Thus the parents, based on their children's citizenship, applied for the right to reside and work in Belgium.

39 Case C-413/99 *Baumbast, R v. Secretary of State for the Home Department* [2003] ECR I-7091. The Court acknowledged not only direct effect of Article 21 TFEU but also confirmed the right to reside of parent, third country national, whose child being EU citizen resided in the country other than country of nationality.

40 C-148/02, *Carlos Garcia Avello v. Etat Belge* [2003] ECR I-11613. The Court found a link to the EU law by reference to the fact that children were citizens of one State of nationality while residing in the territory of another State of their nationality. The Court also did not consider as important the fact that they were resident in Belgium since birth although claimed that their names should be spelled by Spanish traditions, since they held Spanish nationality as well. See also Case C- 353/06 *Stefan Grunkin, Dorothee Regina Paul, Leonhad Matthias Gunkin-Paul v. Standesamt Niebüll* [2008] ECR I-7639 on the use of double surnames by dual citizens – children. The risk of loosing EU citizens rights had been rather remote, however, if compared to *Chen* and *Zambrano*.

41 *Supra* note 5.

42 *Supra* note 38, paras 40, 42-43.

The exceptional character of 'wholly internal situation' which would not trigger 'substance of rights' was established by the ECJ ruling in *McCarthy* where it was confronted with the question whether a dual EU national who had never exercised free movement rights can rely on EU law against the State of nationality.[43] The Court concluded that there is no element in the situation of Mrs. McCarthy that the national measure has the effect of depriving her of the genuine enjoyment of the substance of the rights associated with he status as a Union citizen or of impeding the exercise of her right to move and reside freely.[44] Therefore, cases of family reunification would rarely trigger invocation of Article 20 TFEU if there are no obstacles for EU citizen to move and to reside freely in the EU. Similarly in *Dereci* the Court noted that:

> It follows that the criterion relating to the denial of the genuine enjoyment of the substance of the rights conferred by virtue of European Union citizen status refers to situations in which the Union citizen has, in fact, to leave not only the territory of the Member State of which he is a national but also the territory of the Union as a whole.[45]

The Court further noted that the mere fact that it might appear desirable to a EU citizen, for economic reasons or to preserve family, for the members of his family who are third country nationals to be able to reside with him in particular Member State, is not sufficient in itself to support the view that the EU citizen will be forced to leave EU territory if such a right is not granted. The Court guided national court to deal with the case on basis of Article 8 of the ECHR and to check whether there is possibility that EU citizen would be denied of the genuine enjoyment of the substance of the rights conferred.

Although these cases clarify the application of the 'substance of rights' concept and attempt to delimit national and EU competencies, they also strengthen artificial partitions if compared to other cases discussed in this article.[46] For instance, *Dereci* problem could have

---

43 Case C-434/09 *Shirley McCarthy v. Secretary of State for the Home Department*, Judgment of 5 May 2011 [not yet reported]. The case concerned Mrs. McCarthy, a British and Irish national who had always resided in England. Her husband was a Jamaican national who had no right to reside in England. The applicant invoked her EU citizenship and Irish nationality to obtain residence rights for herself and her husband. She applied for Irish nationality only after marriage to get a passport. In this context the case concerns family unification which is intended to be achieved circuitously by invoking EU law because domestic law in the UK does not permit unification. The important factor was that Mrs. McCarthy, unlike the *Metock* (see note 49 below) situation, did not cross the border at any time. It is interesting to note that the ECJ disregarded the question whether the applicant's Irish nationality is real and effective, while the AG said *expressis verbis* that this issue was irrelevant (see AG Kokott, para 33).

44 *Ibid.*, para 49.

45 Case C-256/11 *Dereci, Heimi, Kokollari, Maduike, Stevic v. Bundesministerium für Inneres*, Judgment of 15 November 2011 [not yet reported]. Case concerned a number of families consisting EU citizens and third country nationals. They entered Austria legally or illegally. All of them were refused residence permits and some of them were subject to expulsion. Paras 66-69.

46 Apart from Zambrano, see also Case C-60/00 *Mary Carpenter v. Secreatary of State for the Home Department* [2002] ECR I-6279, whereas ECJ found jurisdiction despite the fact that Mrs. Carpenter never exercised free movement rights and her husband left his country of nationality only periodically. In Case C-127/08 *Blaise Baheten Metock et. al. v. Minister for Justice, Equality and Law Reform* [2008] ECR I-6241 the ECJ allowed reunification of third country nationals who did not exercise free movement rights with EU citizens who had exercised free movement rights.

been solved on basis of the EU law if families would move few miles and cross the border of the respective Member State or even return after short stay abroad.[47]

In order to overcome these problems there have been suggestions made to revisit interpretation of Articles 18 and 21 TFEU regarding both – application to purely internal situations (Article 21 TFEU) and reverse discrimination (Article 18 TFEU). Concerning the applicability of Article 21 AG Sharpston argued that the right to move and the *free-standing right to reside* should be de-coupled.[48] She offered the following test to be applied in relation to protecting family life:

- A citizen of the EU should not be the claimant in the main proceedings to trigger protection. Third country nationals are protected as family members of EU citizens.
- A fundamental right can be invoked even if the family member is not legally resident.
- The test of threat to public policy or public security should be applied.
- The behaviour of the applicant will be taken into account in order to exclude cases of bad faith.[49]

In relation to *reverse discrimination* AG Sharpston has suggested a modest approach when Article 18 TFEU would be triggered. This would require that three cumulative conditions are met:

- a claim is brought by a citizen of the EU who has not availed themselves of the free movement right but whose situation was comparable to that of other citizens;
- the reverse discrimination complained of would have to entail violation of a fundamental right protected under EU law, leaving the rest of the competence to the ECHR;
- Article 18 TFEU would serve as only a subsidiary remedy, confined to situations in which national law did not afford adequate fundamental rights protection. This condition serves to maintain an appropriate balance between Member State autonomy and the 'effet utile' of EU law.[50]

This approach in applying different Treaty Articles would be more suitable and convincing even in cases like *Zambrano* where access to or loss of citizenship was not contested but rather possibility to explore EU citizens' rights in the future. The question remains whether this is matter of taste or law. AG Sharpston seems to favour the view that movement, even potential movement is methodologically better fitted into Articles 18 or 21 TFEU rather than Article 20 TFEU. The tests offered by the AG is a possible solution which might have far reaching effects on application of EU law. The Charter could also strengthen the argument for re-interpretation of the articles mentioned.[51] As argued by Besson and Utzinger

47 See, for instance, Case C-109/01 *Secretary of State for the Home Department v. Hacene Akrich* [2003] ECR I-9607. Third country national, illegally resident in EU Member State married to EU citizen and then moved to another Member State. Upon return he was refused entry but the ECJ ruled that this violates EU citizen's rights to family reunification if she returns to her Member State of nationality and her husband is refused entry.

48 *Supra* note 38, AG Sharpston, Opinion of 20 September 2010, paras 50 and 100. The approach resembles ECJ rulings where it 'de-coupled' the right of family members to 'accompany and join'.

49 *Ibid.*, para 57-60.

50 *Ibid.*, paras 144-148.

51 However, the Charter applies only in the scope of competences conferred by Member States on the EU, which requires the cross-border test to be satisfied and Case C-256/11 *Dereci, Heimi, Kokollari,* →

the problem with reverse discrimination contradicts the understanding of EU citizenship *qua* fundamental status of Member States' nationals. Similarly to AG Sharpston they suggest applying by analogy the rules applicable to free movement of goods. They also state that reverse discrimination leads Member States to violate their own constitutional principles and the constitutional principle of non-discrimination.[52] Indeed, in dealing with 'purely internal situations' and cases of reverse discrimination, the role of national courts becomes highly important. However, this might not be enough to ensure uniform application of the law throughout the EU and effective implementation of principle of 'due regard to EU law'.

Since EU citizenship is being declared 'fundamental status' and the EU is expanding its competencies by each Treaty amendments, there will be growing number of cases which 'by reason of its nature and its consequences' will trigger invocation of EU law. Despite the criticism of the 'substance of rights' principle to overcome the 'cross-border' test without a sound methodological basis and need to invoke human rights provisions instead[53], there is rather a need to expand 'substance of rights' principle and to apply it also in the context of Articles 18 and 21 TFEU.

2. National Implication of EU Citizenship Regulation

2.1 Revising Grounds for Loss of Nationality

It has not been put to doubt that international law allows deprivation of nationality by the States. In *Rottman* the Court and AG quoted the relevant provisions of the international instruments, i.e., Convention on the reduction of statelessness, European Convention on Nationality (ECN) as well as Universal Declaration of Human rights allowing withdrawal of nationality.

The obligation to avoid statelessness has become part of customary international law. Special Rapporteur Kamto of the International Law Commission has suggested:

> Neither loss of nationality nor denationalization should lead to statelessness. In the case of denationalization in particular, there is a general obligation not to denationalize a citizen who does not have any other nationality. Likewise, nationality cannot effectively be lost unless the person concerned has effectively adopted another nationality. In addition, denationalization should not be arbitrary or based on discriminatory grounds.[54]

Maduike, Stevic v. Bundesministerium für Inneres, 15 November 2011 [not yet reported] para 71, as well as critical note by AG Mengozzi, paras 43-44.

52 Samantha Besson & André Utzinger, 'Introduction: Future Challenges of European Citizenship – Facing a Wide-Open Pandora's Box', (2007) 13/5 *ELJ*, p. 573-590, at p. 583-584.

53 *Supra* note 29, p. 1253 and p.1258.

54 Fourth report on the expulsion of aliens, Maurice Kamto, Special Rapporteur, A/CN.4/594, ILC 60th session, 2008, p. 19. As early as in 1896 the Institute of International law proclaimed that '*no one may lose his nationality or renounce it without acquiring another one; and denationalisation may never be imposed as a penalty*'. International Law Association in 1924 stated that '*a national should not be deprived, by administrative or judicial order, of his nationality whether original or acquired*'. 1930 Hague Convention also →

Apart from Convention on Reduction of Statelessness and ECN, there are a number of principles and norms established under human rights law which limit the discretion of States to withhold or deny nationality on arbitrary and discriminatory grounds.

Article 7 ECN provides for exhaustive list of grounds allowing loss of nationality *ex lege* or at the initiative of a State Party.[55] Most of them are part of customary international law in the context of reduction of statelessness. All together seven grounds are enlisted in Article 7(1) with exceptions mentioned in 7(2) and 7(3). In the context of *Rottman* several grounds deserve brief analysis.

Voluntary Acquisition of Another Nationality (Article 7 (1)a)

Voluntary acquisition of another nationality might serve as basis for loss of Member State nationality and possibly – the EU citizenship. The procedure is present in eleven EU Member States. However, in some countries, such as Germany, the Netherlands and Spain – significant exceptions are provided for.[56] In cases if another EU Member States' nationality is acquired, the loss of nationality in itself does not have consequences for the EU citizenship.

At the same time these policies might place EU citizens at complicated situations especially if they have left their families at home. For instance, EU citizen, national of country A moves to work in EU Member State B. After several years he becomes entitled to nationality of State B. His employer encourages him to apply for citizenship because his work is related to travel to non-EU Member States with which State B has better visa regime. By acquiring nationality of State B, he looses nationality of State A, where his family lives and with which he has otherwise close ties. Different other cases can be mentioned in relation to families who separate because of some family members opt to move in the EU. Although it might not be evident at first sight, the practical difficulties on every-day basis exist in case if person looses nationality because of free movement to another EU Member State. For instance, apart from loyalties and sentiments there might be difficulties in settling private and family matters, ownership, entitlements to participate in political life of the country and alike.

---

dealt with issues of statelessness. It included provision preventing loss of nationality without acquiring another nationality as well as provisions aimed at reducing statelessness occurring at birth. There was also a Protocol relating to a Certain Case of Statelessness attached to the Convention.

55 12 EU Member States have ratified the Convention, while 7 others have signed the Convention. See, http://conventions.coe.int/Treaty/Commun/ChercheSig.asp?NT=166& CM=7&DF=&CL=ENG, accessed 29 March 2012. Taking into account the reluctance of the Court to rely on international law instruments before they have been accepted by all or at least majority of Member States, it might take time when the ECJ will be ready to go beyond provisions of the Convention. See for instance the first reference to the ECHR in ECJ, 28 Octber 1975, C-36/75 *Rutili v. Minister for the Interior* [1975] ECR 1219. The reference was made soon after all EU Member States had ratified the Convention.

56 For details see, G.R. de Groot, M. Vink, I. Honohan, *Loss of Citizenship*, EUDO Citizenship Policy Brief No. 3, available at http://eudo-citizenship.eu/docs/policy_brief_loss.pdf, accessed 10 January 2011, and G.R. de Groot, M. Vink, 'EUDO Citizenship Observatory. Loss of Citizenship: Trends and Regulations in Europe', June 2010, revised October 2010, available at http://eudo-citizenship.eu/docs/loss_paper_updated_14102010.pdf, accessed 10 January 2011.

There are no *lege lata* arguments for the EU Member States to change their nationality laws. They can only be encouraged to re-consider strict approach to nationality regulation and allow for multiple nationality cases or at least make access to nationality easier for former nationals. The neutrality of ECN on multiple nationality cases only supports this approach.

Acquisition of Nationality by Fraudulent Conduct (Article 7 (1)b)

Rottman accepts that a Member State has the right to declare nationality non-existent and a person would become stateless if s/he acquired nationality by fraudulent conduct, false information or concealment of any relevant fact attributable to application. This is one of the most important grounds which is the only one leading to statelessness as confirmed by Article 7(3) of the Convention.

The importance of the ECJ ruling adding EU principles in cases of deprivation of citizenship acquired by fraud becomes more evident when looking at national regulation. At present only five EU Member States do not have fraud provision in their national legislation. Moreover, except for France and Luxembourg other Member States allow withdrawal leading to statelessness. While some Member States provide for time limit of withdrawal of nationality, those limits range from 1-2 years to 15 years.[57] This shows proportionality requirement in different light. It can be argued that extensive period allowing withdrawal, for instance 15 years, is disproportionate for decision on deprivation of nationality in the EU context.

According to Explanatory report to the European Convention on nationality, in cases where acquisition of nationality has been result of the improper conduct, States are free either to revoke the nationality (loss) or to consider that the person never acquired their nationality (void *ab initio*).[58] In the EU context this might be important to establish the scope of obligation of Member State whose nationality a person possessed initially to reinstate former nationality. In that context in *Rottman* AG Maduro was possibly right by arguing that since German nationality was declared void *ab initio* the Austrian nationality of Mr. Rottman should be restored if national legislation allows it. Since the withdrawal of German naturalisation had retroactive effect, Mr. Rottmann had never had German nationality, so that the event triggering the loss of Austrian national never took place.[59] The interpretation quoted above by de Groot and Seling thus cannot be excluded, i.e., obligation to pay due regard to EU law applies to both Member State of naturalization and original nationality.[60] The final decision, of course, remains in the competence of national authorities and courts. All and all the need for co-operation in between different Member States becomes more obvious when dealing with cases like *Rottman*.

57 For details see, G.R. de Groot, M. Vink, I. Honohan, *Loss of Citizenship*, EUDO Citizenship Policy Brief No. 3, available at http://eudo-citizenship.eu/docs/policy_brief_loss.pdf, accessed 10 January 2011.

58 Explanatory Report of the European Convention on Nationality, para 63. Available at http://conventions.coe.int/Treaty/EN/Reports/Html/166.htm, accessed on 11 January 2011.

59 *Supra* note 8, para 34.

60 See section 1.1 above and text preceding footnote 20.

Voluntary Service in a Foreign Military Force (Article 7 (1) c)

Four EU Member States provide for automatic loss of citizenship, if a citizen voluntarily enters the military service of a foreign State, or of a hostile state. Five others provide for withdrawal to be determined by the State. While seven Member States consider that other public service for a foreign State is also considered as ground for loss of citizenship.[61] These policies might amount to disproportionate practices of withdrawal of nationality and should be brought to the minimum among the EU Member States. This is especially so by taking into account the ongoing harmonization process of the access to public service in Member States.[62]

While armed forces, the police, the judiciary, the tax authorities and diplomatic corps in general are sectors performing functions of the State, not all posts in these fields imply the exercise of public authority and responsibility. Therefore, it is doubtful whether a person could be deprived of nationality because of service in non-military forces in another EU Member State. In addition, service in foreign military force should also be revisited among the EU Member States since the adoption of Lisbon Treaty and increasing EU's competence in common security and defence policy sectors.[63] The format, however, will be important, i.e., which forces and according to which mandates are involved. According to Explanatory Report of the ECN participation in a multilateral force on behalf of the State of which the person concerned is a national cannot be considered as service in a foreign military force.[64]

Lack of a Genuine Link with National Habitually Residing Abroad (Article 7 (1)e)

Lack of genuine link due to residence abroad could be the most problematic ground for withdrawal of nationality in the context of the EU. For instance, in case if citizen of a Member State A is absent from the territory of Member State A for many years while residing in the Member State B would allow State A to withdraw citizenship due to the lack of genuine link between State and individual. Yet another situation is possible when person who is citizen of Member State A is absent from the territory of this Member State and resides in non-member State C. In these cases deprivation of citizenship of Member State A would lead to loss of EU citizenship.

Permanent residence abroad is a ground for loss of citizenship in ten EU Member States.[65] There are significant differences with respect to procedures, personal scope, statelessness, age, and the possibilities for citizens to prevent loss of citizenship.

In case of those EU Member States which are parties or at least signatories to the ECN problems are less acute because relevant Article can be invoked only if person possesses

61 *Supra* note 56.

62 See for instance, Case C-47, 50, 51, 53, 54, 61/08 *Commission v. Belgium, France, Luxembourg, Austria, Germany and Greece,* AG Cruz Villalón, 14 September 2010, 24 May 2011 [not yet reported]. Freedom of movement of workers and access to employment in the public service of Member States – Commission Action in respect of the application of Article 48(4) of the EEC Treaty, OJ C-72/2 18.03.1988. Communication from the Commission – *Free movement of workers: achieving the full benefits and potential*, COM/2002/0694 final, 11.12.2002.

63 Articles 42-46 TEU.

64 Explanatory Report of the European Convention on Nationality, para 65. Available at http://conventions.coe.int/Treaty/EN/Reports/Html/166.htm, accessed on 11 January 2011.

65 *Supra* note 56.

another nationality. The Explanatory report to Convention also prescribes that 'lack of a genuine link' can be relied on only in cases if habitual residence abroad continues for generations and State has taken all reasonable measures to communicate with person.[66]

In the context of the EU one could rely on AG Maduro who has said that:

> A State rule providing for loss of nationality in the event of a transfer of residence to another Member State would undoubtedly constitute an infringement of the right of movement and residence conferred on citizens of the Union by Article 18 EC [Article 21 TFEU].[67]

Although there are limited possibilities for a person to become stateless, more co-ordination of nationality laws of Member States concerning loss of national citizenship is desirable. At present there are common EU tests of proportionality and legitimate expectations to be applied by national courts when Article 20 TFEU is invoked. In addition, the ECHR might provide for additional arguments for the ECJ by developing its case law on citizenship and residence issues.[68]

2.2 Solidarity and Acquisition of Nationality

The Court has limited its own jurisdiction in cases of acquisition of EU citizen's status. Thus, in *Kaur case* the Court held:

> [a]doption of that declaration did not have the effect of depriving any person who did not satisfy the definition of a national of the United Kingdom of rights to which that person might be entitled under Community law. The consequence was rather that such rights never arose in the first place for such a person.[69]

Although AG Maduro was sceptic on possibility to introduce any EU conditions on acquisition and loss of nationality, leaving it at the reserved domain of Member States, he himself admitted that obligation to pay 'due regard to Community law' should be applicable in cases of the conditions for the acquisition of nationality.[70] He noted that:

> ... [A]lthough it is true that nationality of a Member State is a precondition for access to Union citizenship, it is equally true that the body of rights and obligations associated with the latter *cannot be limited in an unjustified manner* by the former. In other words, it is not that the acquisition and loss of nationality (and, consequently, of Union citizenship) are in themselves governed by Community law, but the *conditions for the acquisition and loss of nationality must be compatible with the Community rules* and respect the rights of the European citizen.'[71] [emphasis added]

---

66 *Supra* note 64, paras 69-71.

67 *Supra* note 8, para 32.

68 See, for instance, *Kurič and others v. Slovenia* [2010] no. 26828/06, *Tănase v. Moldova* [2010] no. 7/08.

69 Case C-192/99 *Kaur* [2001] ECR I-1237, para 25.

70 *Supra* note 8, para 20.

71 *Ibid.*, para 23.

What is meant by unjustified manner and compatibility with the EU rules remains to be clarified. Even international law contains only limited prescriptions on who should or could be granted nationality and on what conditions. Article 15 (1) of the Universal Declaration of Human Rights states that: '*everyone has the right to a nationality*'. However, this does not entitle a person to any particular nationality. States can still require that person satisfies conditions provided in national law. The ECN contains general requirements on acquisition of nationality in Article 6 ECN. It provides for obligations of States Parties to grant nationality to children and foundlings. Article 6(3) ECN sets residence period required for naturalization which shall not exceed ten years. Article 6(4) places an obligation to facilitate acquisition of nationality for seven groups of persons, for instance, spouses of nationals or persons born on the territory of State Party. Fees, integration requirements, including naturalization exams, or freedom of States to differentiate and introduce facilitated procedures for non-resident applicants for naturalization are not addressed by the Convention.

General harmonisation of nationality laws at the EU level regarding nationality does not seem realistic. First, it might warrant EU Member States to tighten their regulation of the *ius soli* principle. This process would be facilitated by attempting to prevent third country nationals residing in the EU from abusing their residence rights. Second, national citizenship is deeply rooted in national history and traditions of each Member State. However, one can talk about common trends and similarities in naturalization procedures or acquisition of citizenship at birth. It is also possible for the EU to expand its competence on the issues by reference to the principle of 'due regard to Community law'.

In order to give meaning to the statement of AG Maduro the argument can be advanced that the EU law should be taken into account by the Member States when introducing conditions for acquisition of nationality. Member States shall also facilitate the achievement of the Union's tasks and refrain from measures which could jeopardise the attainment of the Union's objectives. Two cases can be mentioned as examples: one generously granting nationality to non-resident kinship holders and another limiting access to nationality.

First, when granting their nationality, Member States should pay due regard to the EU law. Article 4 (3) TEU *inter alia* provides that Member States should take measures to ensure fulfilment of the obligations arising out of Treaties. Since the mid- 1990s, scholars have remarked that EU law would be infringed, if national citizenship laws violated the general principles of EU law, including fundamental rights and the solidarity clause, by failing to consult with Brussels about the possible inclusion of third country nationals 8nto their national population.[72] AG Maduro by reference to academic writing and observations of Hellenic Republic states that EU principle of sincere co-operation could be affected if a Member State were to carry out, without consulting the Commission or its partners, an unjustified mass naturalization of nationals of non-member States.[73]

In the Central and Eastern Europe institution of non-resident external citizenship represents a practice that is at once widespread and widely contested.[74] Benefit laws for ethnic kin groups exist in some 'old' EU Member States (Italy and Greece), and privileged access to citizenship for non-resident persons with close cultural affinity are present in

72 *Supra* note 18.

73 *Supra* note 8, para 30.

74 For a detailed description of cases see Szaboloсs Pogonyi, Mária M. Kovács & Zsolt Körtvélyesi, *The Politics of External Kin-State Citizenship in East Central Europe* (EUDO Citizenship Observatory, October 2010) <http://eudo-citizenship.eu/docs/ECEcompreport.pdf> accessed 2 February 2011.

Denmark, France, Germany, Ireland, Greece, Spain and Portugal.[75] Altogether there are 16 European States that have special naturalization provisions for persons who are perceived as ethnically or linguistically related to the majority population.[76] After 1989, external citizenship for kin-minorities has been introduced in a number of states of East Central Europe, among them EU Member States such as Romania, Hungary, Bulgaria. Romania and Bulgaria offer external citizenship to kin-minorities that live in host States that are not members of the European Union.[77] This can be qualified as compromise reached by Council of Europe intervention on principles of protection of kin-ship holders in neighboring States.[78] Hungarian and Romanian cases have attracted special attention. In 2010 the Hungarian Parliament passed an amendment to the Hungarian Citizenship Act that provides for a preferential and accelerated naturalization of Hungarians who are descendents of former citizens. Many people from neighbouring countries are already applying for Hungarian citizenship.[79] It is estimated that about 80 000 Serbians will apply for Hungarian citizenship. In case of Romania, during 2010 citizenship has been granted to 17000 Moldovans and more than half a million Moldovans work in EU countries.

The 2008 Bolzano Recommendations state that granting citizenship to specific non-resident groups in other countries on the basis of ethnic, national, linguistic, cultural or religious ties may conflict with the rules on prohibition of discrimination.[80] The EU might become an effective mechanism to ensure that these principles of international law are observed. The EU interest in having say on mass naturalizations is because Member States are under obligation to recognize naturalization or granting of citizenship by other Member States without attaching additional conditions. This was at stake in *Micheletti* which arose in the context of Spanish and Italian practice to grant access to their nationality on basis of bilateral agreements with Latin American countries.[81] As argued by Stephen Hall extension of nationality *en masse* could, having regard to *Micheletti*, expose the Community's labour

75 *Ibid.*, p. 2-3.

76 Rainer Bauböck & Sara Wallace Goodman, *Naturalization* EUDO Citizenship Policy Brief, No. 2, October 2010 <http://eudo-citizenship.eu/docs/policy-brief-naturalisation_revised. pdf> accessed March 2011.

77 *Ibid.*, p. 1.

78 See Report of the European Commission for Democracy through Law, *On the Preferential Treatment of National Minorities by their Kin-State*, adopted by the Venice Commission at its 48th Plenary Meeting, Venice 19-20 October 2001.

79 For details see http://eudo-citizenship.eu/citizenship-news/418-hungary-new-citizenship-law-, accessed on 10 January 2011.

80 OSCE High Commissioner for National Minorities 'Bolzano Recommendations on National Minorities in Inter-State Relations and Explanatory Note' (2008) <http://www.osce. org/hcnm/33633> accessed 2 February 2011.

81 For details see G.R. de Groot, 'Latin-American European citizens: Some consequences the autonomy of the Member States of the European Union in nationality matters', *Maastricht journal of European and comparative law*, Vol.9 MJ 2 (2002), p. 115-120. This approach has had considerable impact on the number of persons acquiring EU citizenship 'over night'. For instance, in 2001 taking into account extremely bad economic situation in Argentina, large numbers of persons applied for Spanish passports. According to the Spanish Consulate in Buenos Aires alone 25,400 Argentinean citizens received a Spanish passport in 2001, 21,511 passports were granted in 2000.

market, its markets for services and any markets affected by the right of establishment to serious disruption possibly to the point of jeopardising the Treaty's objectives.[82]

However, before advancing EU role too far one should keep in mind obligation of the EU in Article 4(2) TEU which provides that the Union shall respect the equality of Member States before the Treaties as well as their national identities, inherent in their fundamental structures, political and constitutional. Taking into account that extension of naturalization *en masse* in most cases concern descendants of former nationals and those having close cultural affinity, it is doubtful whether the EU is sufficiently equipped to deal with phenomena of extension of body of citizens *en masse*. The obligation to respect the decisions of other Member States could be limited in two cases. First, national citizenship may not be recognised as valid unless it is granted according to the principles or rules of international law. For instance, nationality is granted *en masse* without individualization required by international law or as a result of imposition without inquiry of individual choice. Second, in cases when massive naturalization policy could lead to violation of Article 4(3) TEU. For instance, States affected could invoke the violation of the principle of good neighbourliness existing in international law.

Second, recently several EU Member States introduced strict naturalization requirements thus making national citizenship less accessible.[83] This, however, should not be done in unjustified manner. It has been argued that coherence of the EU citizenship is being based on transnational integration of national citizenships and as such can be efficiently ensured not by changing the conditions of acquisition of EU citizenship. It should rather be based on Member States facilitating access to naturalization for non-EU nationals residing on their territories. Only in this way can the inherently exclusive nature of citizenship be preserved, and extended on grounds of residence from grass roots and bottom up rather than from EU down to the national level.[84] In this context and by reference to Article 6(4) ECN excessive naturalization requirements would arguably run against the provisions of Article 4(3) TEU. The *lege ferenda* policy argument would be increasing adoption of *ius soli* principle. For the time being application of the principle is somewhat limited. Moreover, some of the Member States have opted for restrictions of application of the principle recently.[85]

Although EU competencies are limited it can act in at least two directions on the basis of Charter provisions. On the basis of Article 21 of the Charter and Article 20 TFEU one could bring a claim against discriminatory provisions of naturalization if such were to appear. In turn on the basis of Article 24(2) of the Charter and Article 20 TFEU a claim can

82 Stephen Hall, *Nationality, Migration Rules & Citizenship of the Union*, Martinus Nijhoff Publishers 1995, p. 66.

83 Several EU Member States have tightened their naturalization requirements, by placing extensive social security requirements, raising fees (up to almost 1000 EUR) and introducing complex naturalization exams. See Rainer Bauböck & Sara Wallace Goodman, *Naturalization (EUDO Citizenship Policy Brief*, No. 2, October 2010) <http://eudo-citizenship.eu/docs/policy-brief-naturalisation_revised.pdf> accessed March 2011.

84 Supra note 52, at p. 581.

85 For details see Iseult Honohan, *Ius Soli Citizenship*, EUDO Citizenship Policy Brief No. 1. Available at http://eudo-citizenship.eu/docs/ius-soli-policy-brief.pdf, accessed 1 April 2012, See also Maarten P. Vink & Gerard R. de Groot, *Birthright Citizenship: Trends and Regulations in Europe*, EUDO Citizenship Observatory, November 2010. Available at http://eudo-citizenship.eu/docs/birthright_comparativepaper.pdf, accessed 1 April 2012.

be brought where children born on the territory of a Member State to stateless parents would not be entitled to acquire citizenship.

Therefore situations might arise when, by applying the principle of 'due regard to Community law', the intervention by the EU and the ECJ is possible. This, however, does not suggest that the EU and the ECJ would alter a citizenship structure based on the principles of *ius soli*, *ius sanguinis* or naturalization as such.

3. Interrelationship between EU Citizenship and National Citizenship

Taking into account latest case-law of the ECJ on EU citizenship there is a room for reflection on current mutual relationship between EU citizenship and national citizenships. The Court did not reflect on this issue in great detail but reiterated that the EU citizenship is intended to be fundamental status of the EU. However, AG Maduro shared his vision on EU citizenship and its relationship with national citizenships.

AG Maduro proposes modest but realistic model of the EU citizenship. He noted that the derived character of Union citizenship in relation to nationality of a Member State flows from its being construed as an 'interstate citizenship' which confers on nationals of a Member States rights in the other Member States, in essence the right of movement and residence and the right to equal treatment, and also vis-à-vis the Union itself.[86] He also suggested the EU citizenship is 'a new form of civic and political allegiance on a European scale' which at the same time 'does not imply the existence of a European people'.[87] Therefore, it is doubtful whether the EU citizenship could gain more by undertaking regulation by itself rather than by inviting Member States to co-operate by liberalizing their national citizenship laws and gradually developing common standards by reference to general developments in international law and EU solidarity principle. For AG Maduro national and EU citizenship are inextricably linked but independent. European citizenship is more than a body of rights which, in themselves, could be granted even to those who do not possess it. He admits that in a way EU citizenship is the product of a decoupling from nationality – it is composed of citizens who do not share the same nationality. Member States intended to show that EU citizenship does not put in question national allegiances. AG Maduro confirms:

> That is the miracle of Union citizenship: it strengthens the ties between us and our States (in so far as we are European citizens precisely because we are nationals of our States) and, at the same time, it emancipates us from them (in so far as we are now citizens beyond our States).[88]

Similarly Jo Shaw argues that quality of EU citizenship is above all its transnational, not its post-national character. She rightly admits that question as to what the content of citizenship at the Union level may be, is related to questions about solidarity which remain con-

86 *Supra* note 8, para 16.
87 *Supra* note 8, para 23.
88 *Ibid.*

tested.[89] Jo Shaw who says that citizenship cases so far have not truly detracted from the status and legal boundaries of national citizenship and shift from complementarity to additionality seems unlikely to make a substantial difference to the political trajectory of EU citizenship.[90] Indeed, the procedure of preliminary rulings results in the final decisions to be taken by national courts taking into account national regulation on citizenship and detailed facts of the case. This is also relevant in the case of *Rottman* the results of which will be definitive only after relevant decisions will be made on the national level. Similarly in *Zambrano* the problem arose not because ECJ imposed its nationality regulation but because Belgian law allowed children born in Zambrano family to be registered as EU citizens. Therefore, the respect for national citizenship laws has been preserved and discretion of Member States regarding acquisition and loss of citizenship is still considerable. However, the ECJ might adopt more pro-active position in cases when functional aspects of EU citizen's status are at stake, especially in case of children.

The achievement of the EU and the ECJ is that it has placed additional criteria and principles to be observed by the national courts in cases of both access and loss of nationality as well as functional aspects of EU citizenship. Gareth T. Davies argues that EU law now applies to, at very least, some aspects of national citizenship law. He qualified this as a minor *coup d'état*. He also suggests that the Court has announced that it is now the supreme adjudicator on the acceptable content of national citizenship law.[91] Dora Kostakopoulou states that what can be reasonably inferred from Member States' relative autonomy in this field is that neither do the Member States enjoy untrammelled authority nor is EU citizenship a superior status that cannot be lost. She also argues that by reference to fundamental status of Union citizenship and *effet utile* of EU law that EU law precludes the automatic loss of Union citizenship if a Union citizen is rendered stateless.[92] On basis of *Rottman* Dora Koustakopoulou proposes an argument that it might be a step forward to detachment of EU citizenship from national citizenship.

These arguments are too far reaching. For the time-being the Court has adopted itself to introducing 'due regard to EU law' and 'substance of rights test' when dealing with citizenship cases. In addition the ECJ has invited to apply international law, including human rights law, standards, as well as deal with the cases on the basis of proportionality principle. Going further would require certain acceptance from the EU Member States. In addition, the Court did not refer explicitly what is meant by proportionality in this context. It noted that this is an issue which the Member States and their courts have to decide upon. To adopt the proposal by Dora Kostakoupoulou would require significant change in thinking about EU citizenship which would rather correspond to federalist approach. Moreover, this approach requires considerable practical and administrative arrangements which can be hardly invented on basis of the ruling of the Court. For instance, to give the EU right for independent regulation of nationality even if in limited fields, would raise the issue on central register of EU citizens, not holding nationality of Member States, identity documents, right to protection in non-EU Member States, entitlement to benefits and alike. The question, thus, arises whether this is indeed necessary at this stage of development of the EU law

89 *Supra* note 33, at p. 10 and p. 18.

90 *Supra* note 33, p. 10 and p. 21.

91 *Supra* note 19.

92 *Supra* note 18.

and whether solutions cannot be found within current architecture of EU and national citizenship.

One could agree with Jo Shaw, AG Maduro and Michael Dougan. Dougan argues that the Court's rulings seem to be premised upon the view that Union citizenship is additional to, rather than merely derived from Member State nationality.[93] However, this does not introduce hierarchy in between national and the EU citizenship. It rather suggests plurality of citizenships which are closely interlinked. None of them requires replacement or abandonment. Their inter-linkage, however, might bring results which are difficult to project at present since they are closely related to social behaviour of EU citizens and their family members as well as national responses by adopting amendments in national citizenship laws. These processes include also national courts and their approaches to this inter-linkage.

Another question which remains to be answered is related to contents of the EU citizenship concept. Scholars so far either read too much into its potential by reference to independent regulation of nationality at the EU level, or leaving too much to political choice of the Member States. Possibly true lies somewhere in between. Dora Kostakopoulou has argued that transformative potential of EU citizenship represents conceptual challenge. She rightly concluded that EU and national citizenships are interdependent and should be examined in their interaction and gradual transformation.[94] Indeed, with each case dealt by the ECJ we are learning more about the possible results of interaction. Progress is incremental and final destination unknown. However, what appears from looking at the developments of the EU citizen concept since Maastricht Treaty is that it has become significant tool for building up transnational status for the benefit of individuals, States and the Union. National citizenship should not be abandoned while the EU can advance more powerful principles on basis of market requirements, new political allegiances and identities as well as political space above the national one.

Conclusions

Over the years the Court has been cautious and opted for a 'consolidating', rather than 'constituionalising' approach to EU citizenship. European citizenship was used as a supplementary basis in order to reaffirm existing EU law.[95] The EU citizenship concept has been more of an evolutionary rather than revolutionary character. The evolutionary concept of EU citizenship has been advanced from declaratory to fundamental status and Member States do have an obligation to take into consideration EU law when taking decisions on nationality. Although recent case-law has been called revolutionary, this article sides with the proposition that recent case law is a new stage of evolutionary character of EU citizenship.

---

93 M. Dougan, *Some comments on Rottmann and the 'personal circumstances' assessment in the Union citizenship caselaw*, 14 April 2010, available at http://eudo-citizenship.eu/citizenship-forum/ 254-has-the-european-court-of-justice-challenged-member-state-sovereignty-in-nationality-law, accessed 3 September 2010.

94 D. Kostakoupoulou, 'European Union Citizenship: Writing the Future', *European Law Journal* (2007) 13(5), p. 623-646, at p. 642 and 646.

95 D. Kostakopoulou, 'Ideas, Norms and European Citizenship: Explaining Institutional Change', *Modern Law Review* (2005) 68 (2), p. 233-267, at p. 244.

The case law so far shows that the EU has been influential in relation to different functions of nationality, while its competence in relation to access and loss remains marginal. For the time being national identities take over the EU's capacity to harmonize nationality laws or any attempts to disentangle EU citizenship from national citizenship regulation. At the same time the ECJ by reference to international law, fundamental rights and general principles of EU law, gradually introduces EU common principles in citizenship cases as well as advances the EU citizenship as fundamental status. General developments in international law are helpful, but there are also issues which are EU specific.

It is highly doubtful whether the ECJ would alter citizenship structure based on principles of *ius soli*, ius *sanguinis* or naturalization as such. The same applies to substantive harmonization of national approaches. At the same time there might be situations triggering invocation of principles developed by the ECJ. The same applies to situations leading to the loss of citizenship. In this context it is equally important that national courts would accept in their mindset that EU citizenship should not be viewed as competitor or even threat to national citizenship but rather additional status providing for additional rights and transnational identity to citizens in European context.

To summarize, the *lege lata* of EU citizenship law requires that: (1) each Member State is supposed to observe international law when granting or depriving of citizenship; (2) when doing so it should also pay due regard to EU law, including the principles adopted by the ECJ; and (3) Member States must respect the citizenship laws of other Member States without imposing additional conditions if the previous two conditions have been observed.

The second criterion was at the centre of this article and there are question marks for further development. The ECJ has introduced the tests of 'due regard to Community law' and 'substance of rights', whereas the situation 'by reason of their nature and consequences' might trigger invocation of EU rights. The concepts of 'due regard to EU law' and 'substance of rights' are clearly not finished concepts. The ECJ will step in to protect personal rights of the citizen on the basis of Article 20 TFEU if there is a risk of losing their status or the exercise of citizens' rights will be hampered. The ECJ has been criticized for delivering open-ended judgments which impede legal certainty and do not provide sufficient guidance for national courts.[96] It is doubtful, however, whether this could have been possible in the context of cases reviewed by the Court. In addition, the tests fit well into incremental development of the EU citizenship concept according to Article 20 TFEU in situations of access to and loss of citizenship. The Court's approach, however, is not entirely elaborated when taking into account other Treaty Articles. This is especially so not only in relation to access and loss of citizenship but also in the context of application of the EU law in 'wholly internal situations' regarding both direct (*McCarthy, Dereci*) and in-direct (*Zambrano, Avello*) functionality aspects of EU citizenship. This does not require re-interpretation of Article 20 TFEU, but rather change of focus on interpretation of Articles 18 and 21 TFEU.

Apart from these developments EU citizenship as a concept should be explored to build upon the EU identity which cannot be done by simply offering certain rights in addition to national citizenship in certain cases appearing in the ECJ list. Belongingness is something in addition to passport, rights and obligations. It also has a social dimension based on historically built dimensions of national cultures. Thus, the EU is facing a much more complicated

96 *Supra* note 29, p. 1268.

task in overcoming historical-cultural differences, not to be erased but enriched by the growing value of the EU dimension.

Part 3. Mandatory Integration Rules in Selected member States

On the Path to Assimilation? Integration Rules in Britain's Migration Law

Bernard Ryan[*]

Introduction

This chapter is concerned with the development of integration rules in immigration and nationality law in the United Kingdom over the past decade. The definition of an 'integration rule' it uses is requirements and principles which relate either to an individual's *capacity for interaction* with persons whose ethnic or national origins are different to theirs, or their *actual interaction* with them. In common with several other long-established immigration countries in Europe, the United Kingdom has introduced a series of such integration rules into its migration law in recent years.[1]

The first section will consider the Labour Government's underlying policy concerning integration requirements between 2001 and its loss of office in May 2010. It will contrast the historic approach, within which integration requirements were very limited, with the more interventionist policy which emerged from late 2001 onwards. It will show that, despite its interventionism, Labour's approach on this subject nevertheless remained relatively cautious, in that it policy statements emphasised respect for cultural diversity, while integration rules were typically justified by reference to the goal of greater social and economic participation by minorities.

The paper will go on to summarise the formal requirements which have been put in place within migration law. Section 2 will set out developments in the requirements for naturalisation as a British citizen: in that area, in 2004, the requirement to demonstrate knowledge of an official language was both extended to spouses, and strengthened, and in 2005 a new requirement to show knowledge of life in the United Kingdom was introduced. Section 3 will analyse the extension, in 2007, of the same requirements of knowledge of English and of life in the United Kingdom to applicants for indefinite leave (a form of permanent residence status). Section 4 will then discuss the extension, since 2004, of English language requirements to the main immigration categories: highly-skilled and skilled economic migrants, the partners of British citizens and persons with indefinite leave, and international students.

In interpreting developments since 2001, this chapter draws upon a distinction proposed by Joppke (2010: 1-4), between 'cognitive' measures and those which concern 'values'. The former are rules which relate to an individual's knowledge of a predominant language and/ or of a state's political and social arrangements. The latter, by contrast, seek to promote certain values, either directly through express requirements, or indirectly, by

* This chapter is based upon the United Kingdom report for a European Integration Fund research project entitled 'Integration and Naturalisation Tests: The new way to European Citizenship' (Ryan 2010). Internet references are correct as of 28 February 2011.

1 The term 'migration law' is used here to include both immigration law and the acquisition of nationality by foreign nationals through naturalisation and registration.

rewarding virtuous behaviour. Joppke himself used this distinction to argue that it is only with the latter category of measures that a state crosses the threshold from liberalism to illiberalism. Here, it is assumed that cognitive measures too are illiberal, as they go beyond the substantive requirements for the given migration category (employment, family, residence, etc), without addressing specific threats to a society's welfare or security. Joppke's approach is instead treated as marking the divide between integration policies which are (merely) illiberal, and those which tend to assimilation. We will see in the concluding section of the paper that, towards the end of its period in office, the Labour Government made two sets of proposals – in *The Path to Citizenship* and *Earning the Right to Stay* – which included 'assimilating' elements. The question now is whether the Conservative/Liberal coalition which came to power in May 2010 will adopt are more overtly assimilationist approach as it develops its migration policy.

1. The Turn to Integration in British Migration Law

Formal requirements concerning the integration of migrants were unknown in the field of immigration law until the past decade, as they applied neither to initial admission nor to the acquisition of indefinite leave. There had though long been a language requirement for persons who sought to obtain British nationality on the basis of residence in the United Kingdom. A requirement of 'adequate knowledge of the English language' was introduced with effect from 1 January 1915 for aliens seeking to naturalise as British subjects on the basis of by residence in the United Kingdom.[2] When the British Nationality Act 1948 separated the category of British subject into citizens of the United Kingdom and colonies (CUKCs), and citizens of newly independent Commonwealth states, it retained the language requirement for naturalisation as CUKCs by aliens.[3] Later, the Immigration Act 1971 introduced a requirement of sufficient knowledge of English or Welsh for Commonwealth and Irish citizens wishing to register as CUKCs after a qualifying period of residence.[4] When the British Nationality Act 1981 introduced the category of British citizenship from 1 January 1983, it provided for the naturalisation of persons other than spouses after five years' residence, including one year without immigration restrictions. Under that Act, all persons – including Commonwealth and Irish citizens – who sought to naturalise on the basis of residence had to demonstrate sufficient knowledge of English, Scottish Gaelic or Welsh.[5]

These various language rules were not applied to those acquiring British nationality through marriage during the twentieth century. Under the 1914 Act, British alien wives acquired British subject status automatically upon marriage to a British subject. The 1948 Act ended the automatic acquisition of nationality by wives, but instead permitted the non-CUKC wives of CUKCs to obtain CUKC status through registration. The 1981 Act then provided for the naturalisation of British citizens' husbands *and* wives after a period of residence in the United Kingdom, but still without any language requirement.

2 British Nationality and Status of Aliens Act 1914, section 2.

3 British Nationality Act 1948, section 10 and Schedule 2.

4 British Nationality Act 1948, section 5A, inserted by Immigration Act 1971, Schedule 1.

5 British Nationality Act 1981, Schedule 1, para 1(1)(c).

The language requirement anyway appears to have been of limited effect prior to 2004, as no procedure was specified for assessing compliance with it. When the Bill which became the 1981 Act was under discussion, the Government's summary of the then practice was that the language requirements

> 'have been operated in a fairly easy-going way. They have essentially been based on an ability to speak rather than write the language ... They do not have to go through all the business of acquiring a knowledge of grammar and the literary skills.'[6]

Thereafter, administrative practice appears to have become even more benign. Whereas in 1982, 2.7% of applications (200 in total) were refused on this ground, in 1996, the figure was 0.15% (27 applications).[7] In 1997, the Home Office policy was to

> 'assume the language requirement to be met where there is circumstantial evidence, such as education in British establishments or employment for a British firm, that that is the case. We only make enquiries about the language requirement of (sic) there is some indication that it might not be met.'[8]

Fransman's summary was that

> 'in practice ... an applicant need do nothing more to satisfy this requirement than complete the application form' (1998: 329).

In retrospect, the limited scope of integration requirements throughout the twentieth century can be seen to have been the accumulated product of several factors. One was the United Kingdom's historically under-developed sense of nationhood (on which, see Cohen 1994: Ch 1). Britain's historical unwillingness to use culture or ethnicity as a marker for membership led it to favour of place of birth as the main criterion for the acquisition of nationality, and to extend a unitary British subject status to its colonies and self-governing dominions. When immigration control came to be developed for aliens – for some categories in 1905, and systematically from 1914 – it therefore focused on whether the individual had the means to support themselves and any dependants, and whether they were a threat to the public good. What aliens were not asked to do was to prove their actual or potential attachment to British culture or society. Even the introduction of a language rule for naturalisation in 1914 was unrelated to domestic policy concerns. Instead, it was designed to protect the common status of British subject, at a time when some dominions had introduced language and literacy tests within their immigration control (Dummett and Nicol 1990: 121-122).

In the post-war decades (1950s-1970s), a second factor was that many of those who migrated to the United Kingdom came from territories that were British, or had recently

6 Home Office Minister Timothy Raison, House of Commons Debates, Standing Committee F, 19 March 1981, col 694, quoted in Fransman 1998: 328-329.

7 Home Office Minister David Waddington, written answer, House of Commons Debates, 6 May 1983 col 163w; Immigration Minister Mike O'Brien, written answer, House of Commons Debates, 2 June 1997, col 3w.

8 Home Office letter of 13 June 1997, quoted in Fransman 1998: 329.

been so. That was the background to their legal rights to enter and live in the United Kingdom, as British subjects in the case of the Commonwealth, and as 'non-aliens' in the case of the Irish. When immigration control was extended to Commonwealth and Irish migrants by the Commonwealth Immigrants Act 1962, they would typically have been familiar with the English language and British culture through their formal education. The application to them of language or cultural tests would therefore have had little point as a device for selection, or for the promotion of integration. Such a development would also in all probability have been open to political criticism, given the continued power of the Commonwealth ideal.

A third factor was the gradual acceptance of ethnic diversity by British policy-makers. In the late 1960s and 1970s, the focus of public policy concerning migrants and ethnic minorities was upon equality opportunity in social and economic life, while by the 1980s and 1990s, cultural recognition had increasingly come to the fore (Favell 1998: Ch 4). Insistence on language or cultural requirements for admission, indefinite leave or naturalisation would have conflicted with both of these goals. By denying full status in the United Kingdom, such an initiative would have implied unequal access to social and economic opportunities for migrants. At the same time, to the extent that it disrupted choices concerning marriage and family residence, it would have been thought at odds with acceptance by policy-makers that minorities could be culturally distinct.

From late 2001, however, the previously limited policy approach to integration rules came to be rejected. The background to these developments was the end of the consensus concerning the acceptance of ethnic and cultural diversity, with the addition of 'community cohesion' to the policy objectives concerning the position of ethnic minorities and migrants. The catalyst for change was a series of riots involving young British Muslim men of South Asian origin in Northern English cities and towns in April-July 2001 (listed in Home Office 2001b: 7). Official reports into the three main locations of the disturbances highlighted social segregation as a major background factor (Bradford Vision 2001; Burnley Task Force 2001; Oldham Independent Review 2001). The same conclusion was offered in its December 2001 report by the Community Cohesion Review Team, led by Ted Cantle, which had been set up to make policy proposals in the field of community cohesion. In its formulation, in many urban areas, 'separate educational arrangements, community and voluntary bodies, employment, places of worship, language, social and cultural networks, means [sic] that communities operate on the basis of a series of parallel lives' (Home Office 2001a: 9).

The initial government response was set out in a report entitled *Building Cohesive Communities* (the Denham Report), also published in December 2001. It endorsed the 'parallel lives' analysis, noting that the disturbances had 'occurred in areas which had become fractured on racial, generational, cultural and religious lines and where there was little dialogue, or much contact, between the various groups across those social divides' (Home Office 2001b: 8). Among its conclusions was that there was a need to promote 'a uniting identity' and 'shared values ...to give people a common sense of belonging,' particularly in the light of 'increased community tensions' following the terrorist attacks in the United States in September 2001 (*ibid.*: 19-20). The theme of 'Common values' was in turn the background to the announcement of the government's intention to make proposals to 'promot[e] citizenship for those entering the country and those seeking naturalisation – including recognition of and adherence to fundamental rights and duties, and to English as our shared language' (*ibid.*: 20).

The result was a series of announcements concerning the reform of nationality law in a Home Office White Paper, *Secure Borders, Safe Haven* (Home Office 2002), published in February 2002. Among these was a proposal for 'a simple examination for citizenship applicants', which it justified in the following terms:

> 'This will strengthen the ability of new citizens to participate in society and to engage actively in our democracy. This will help people understand both their rights and their obligations as citizens of the UK, and strengthen the bonds of mutual understanding between people of diverse cultural backgrounds. It will also help to promote individuals' economic and social integration' (*ibid.*: 11).

It is indicative of the thinking of the time that, within this statement, the policy goal was understood not to be community cohesion alone, but *also* the established principles of promoting participation and respect for diversity.

As the integration agenda was rolled-out by Labour Governments after 2001, the policy justification came to focus primarily on social and economic participation by migrants. When the extension of the requirement to show 'knowledge of life in the United Kingdom' to indefinite leave applications was proposed in February 2005, it was presented as follows: 'permanent migrants must be as economically active as possible; put as little burden on the state as possible; and be as socially integrated as possible' (Home Office 2005: 21). When English language requirements were introduced for skilled workers (Tier 2 of the points-based system), the explanation concerned social integration alone: 'it helps to ensure migrants play a full part in British life outside the workforce' (UK Border Agency 2008: para 45). Equally, when an English language requirement was proposed for spouses and other partners, the main arguments offered were that English would 'assist [their] integration into British society at an early stage,' and 'improve employment chances' (Home Office 2007: 6).

These nuances in government discourse on the integration rules would come to be reflected in the use of 'integration and cohesion' as the official shorthand for the new policy objective. A leading example was the 2007 report of the Government's Commission for Integration and Cohesion. This defined the goal of 'an integrated and cohesive community' to include 'those from different backgrounds hav[ing] similar life opportunities' and 'strong and positive relationships between people from different backgrounds in the workplace, in schools and other institutions within neighbourhoods' (Commission for Integration and Cohesion 2007: 10).

The Labour Government's approach to integration from 2001 therefore remained relatively cautious, as both social and economic participation and respect for diversity retained prominence within it. In the next three sections we will see that that caution had its counterpart in the content of the integration rules which were put in place within migration law after 2001. In Joppke's terms, Labour's reforms focused exclusively upon individuals' cognitive capacities, and did not cross the threshold to the favouring of particular values.

2. Naturalisation

Within the British system, it is necessary to distinguish between 'naturalisation' and 'registration' as routes to the acquisition of British citizenship. Naturalisation is only available to adults, and has historically involved the exercise of discretion by the authorities, particularly as to whether the individual is of good character. By contrast, the concept of registration has historically covered minors and/or cases of entitlement. An important change in this area, however, is that since 4 December 2006 it has been possible for applicants for registration who are 10 or over to be refused registration if they are not of good character.[9] As a consequence, the main difference between naturalisation and registration is that the requirements of knowledge of a language and of life in the United Kingdom apply only to the former.

Individuals' reasons for taking out British citizenship will vary with their circumstances (see EdComs 2008: Ch 5). While some persons may wish to naturalise as British citizens for reasons of social and political attachment, the fees – currently £ 780 in the standard case, with a £ 1010 joint fee for spouses or civil partners who naturalise together – are likely to act as a disincentive unless there are practical advantages. For non-EEA citizens, the main practical advantage of British citizenship over indefinite leave probably concern foreign travel and residence. In particular, British citizenship confers rights to enter and to reside in other EU countries, and visa-free travel to certain other countries, while giving access to British diplomatic protection in most circumstances.

British citizenship also gives a more secure form of residence than possession of indefinite leave. The latter status may be cancelled due to prolonged absence, and those with it remain subject to the rules making deportation mandatory where a person has been convicted of a criminal offence classed as 'particularly serious', or which leads to a sentence of imprisonment for one year or more.[10] In contrast, an individual's nationality status is unaffected by absence, and a British citizen may be deprived of their nationality for public order reasons only if they have another nationality, and only if deprivation would be 'conducive to the public good'.[11] Crucially, this last phrase is given a narrower construction than in the law of deportation, and the policy is to withdraw citizenship only 'on the grounds of involvement in terrorism, espionage, serious organised crime, war crimes or unacceptable behaviours'.[12]

Within the British system, there are two possible routes to naturalisation. The first of these is based solely on lawful residence.[13] The main requirements are that the individual has been lawfully resident in the United Kingdom for the previous five years, has not been absent from the United Kingdom for more than 450 days in that period, and has not been absent from the United Kingdom for more than 90 days in the previous 12 months. The applicant must also have been free from immigration time restrictions over the last 12 months of the qualifying period, which in practice means that they have had indefinite leave or the EU status of permanent resident. When the qualifying rules for indefinite leave and EU permanent residence are taken into account, the result is a minimum eligibility period of *six* years' residence for those who start as economic migrants, refugees, or with humanitarian protection, or who qualify under EU law.

9 This is now in the British Nationality Act 1981, section 41A.
10 UK Borders Act 2007, section 32.
11 British Nationality Act 1981, section 40.
12 UK Border Agency, Nationality Instructions, Volume 1, para 55.4.4 (at 28 February 2011).
13 British Nationality Act 1981, section 6(1) and Schedule 1, paras 1 and 2.

The alternative route is based on being the spouse or civil partner of a British citizen on the date of the application.[14] One difference from the residence route is that in this case it is necessary to be free from immigration restrictions on the date of the application, rather than for the previous one year. More importantly, the qualifying period of residence is less: three years' instead of five years' residence in the United Kingdom, with absences of no more than 270 days over that period. In practice, given the two-year qualifying period for spouses and civil partners to obtain indefinite leave to remain, three years is the effective minimum period of residence required before naturalisation in this category.

The *Secure Borders, Safe Haven* White Paper in 2002, and its implementation by the Nationality, Immigration and Asylum Act 2002, led to a tightening of the integration requirements relating to naturalisation. A first step was that, from 28 July 2004, spouses were made subject to the knowledge requirements applicable to other applicants for naturalisation. This was later applied to civil partners, when that status was created on 5 December 2005.

Secondly, the requirement on all applicants who claimed knowledge of the English language was formalised. From 28 July 2004, it was necessary for the individual either to show that they had passed a language course to English of Speakers of other Languages (ESOL) level 3, or else to have a designated person certify that the individual had an educational qualification which required English language proficiency to at least that level. From 1 September 2004, a further option was certification by a designated person, on the basis of an interview, that the individual had 'knowledge of the English language to the level reasonably to be expected of a person of full age and capacity whose native language is English.' Immigration staff and consular officers were designated persons for both purposes, while notaries and solicitors could certify 'native language' competence in English.[15]

Thirdly, a requirement on all applicants for British citizenship by naturalisation to show 'sufficient knowledge about life in the United Kingdom' came into effect on 1 November 2005. Since that time, the English language and 'knowledge of life' requirements have been met together. The most common way in which the requirements are met is by an individual's passing the 'life in the UK' test (see Kiwan 2008). This test is based on an official handbook, called *Life in the UK: A Journey to Citizenship*, which has to date been published in two editions (Stationery Office, 2004 and 2007). The test questions relate to five factual chapters of the handbook, entitled 'A changing society', 'UK today: a profile', 'How the United Kingdom is governed', 'Everyday needs' and 'Employment'. The test consists of 24 multiple-choice questions, and in order to pass, it is necessary that at least 18 of 24 questions be answered correctly.

Alternatively, an individual may meet the two knowledge requirements by taking and passing an ESOL course which includes defined syllabus material on citizenship.[16] These materials were published in September 2005 as *Citizenship Materials for ESOL Teachers*, and

14 British Nationality Act 1981, section 6(2) and Schedule 1, paras 3 and 4. There is at present no special treatment of unmarried partners when it comes to naturalisation. Because a person starting as an unmarried partner may obtain indefinite leave after two years' residence, the effective minimum period of residence for them to acquire naturalisation is five years.

15 UK Border Agency, Nationality Instructions, Ch 18 Annex E, paras 2.4.2 and 2.5.2 (as of 28 February 2011).

16 British Nationality (General) Regulations 2003 (SI 2003 No 548), reg 5A as amended; Immigration Rules, paras 33B and 33C, as amended.

are available both online and in hard copy.[17] (For details of their development, see Taylor, 2007: 29-38). These materials are divided into these twelve sections: (1) What is citizenship? (2) Parliament and the electoral system, (3) The United Kingdom in Europe, the Commonwealth and the United Nations, (4) The United Kingdom, (5) The United Kingdom as a diverse society, (6) Human rights, (7) Working in the United Kingdom, (8) Health, (9) Housing, (10) Education, (11) Community Engagement, (12) Knowing the law.

The Secretary of State has the power to waive either or both of the knowledge requirements where 'because of the applicant's age or physical or mental condition it would be unreasonable to expect [the person] to fulfil' them.[18] Official guidance indicates that this power is used to exempt individuals suffering from a long-term physical or mental condition that prevents them from learning English or from being tested on their knowledge of life in the UK, and those over 65, or who are nearing the age of 65.[19]

For the purposes of a naturalisation application, it does not matter how long before an application a pass was obtained, and the same pass may already have been relied upon for an indefinite leave application. That raises the question – who might encounter these requirements only at the naturalisation stage? Three main possibilities may be identified:

- An application for naturalisation may be made by someone who acquired indefinite leave before 2 April 2007.
- Some categories are exempt at the indefinite leave stage only (see below). It should be noted in particular that those who start in a humanitarian category encounter the knowledge requirements only at the naturalisation stage.
- EEA nationals and their family members who have resided in the United Kingdom on the basis of EU law for five years obtain the EU law status of permanent resident. This status is broadly equivalent to indefinite leave, but cannot be made subject to language and 'knowledge of life' requirements.

A further point concerns Scottish Gaelic and Welsh, which may be relied upon by an applicant for naturalisation. In theory, these languages are to be assessed within the naturalisation procedure in much the same way as was previously done for English – i.e. the completion of the application in that language is to be taken as evidence of competence, and in other cases an interview is likely.[20] In such a case, knowledge of life in the United Kingdom would be assessed through special arrangements. To date, however, it appears that no-one has relied upon either of these languages to meet the 'life in the UK' requirement.[21] This is not especially surprising, as it is highly unlikely that someone who is not already a British citizen would be more familiar with one of these languages than with English.

Finally, it may be noted that, in *Earning the Right to Stay: A New Points Test for Citizenship* in July 2009, the Labour Government proposed that the requirements of knowledge of English and of life in the United Kingdom would in future be different at the long-term residence and naturalisation stages (Home Office 2009: 9). For the acquisition of a new intermediate right of residence (to be called 'probationary citizenship'), something like the current arrangements would apply, including the test's focus on 'practical information

17 These are available at http://www.niace.org.uk/projects/esolcitizenship/.

18 British Nationality Act 1981, Schedule 1, paras 2(e) and 4(d).

19 UK Border Agency, Nationality Instructions, Ch 18 Annex E, para 1.4 (as of 28 February 2011).

20 *Ibid.*, para 1.2.4.

21 Information provided by UK Border Agency, 30 June 2010.

about life in the UK', and the possibility to show progress to a basic level of English with the ESOL route. For naturalisation, however, what was contemplated was a higher standard: the tests would focus on 'more challenging topics such as the historical and political context,' and progress beyond a basic standard would be required within the ESOL route. This proposal was not taken forward before Labour left office, however, and was dropped as part of the Coalition Government's rejection of its predecessor's proposals concerning long-term residence and naturalisation in November 2010.[22]

3. Indefinite Leave

Within the British immigration system, indefinite leave is a form of permanent resident status. It is usually obtained after a qualifying period of residence in the United Kingdom, in which case the status obtained is indefinite leave *to remain*. The main qualifying periods are two years for a partner, five years for an economic migrant, a refugee or a person with humanitarian protection,[23] six years for those with discretionary leave[24] and ten years for those with a period of lawful residence in any category or categories.

In a limited range of circumstances it is possible to obtain the status prior to admission, in which case it is termed indefinite leave *to enter*. Immigration categories within which indefinite leave to enter possible include the following: former members of the armed forces and their family members; the partner of a British citizen or a person with indefinite leave, with whom they have been living outside the United Kingdom for the previous four years; and, the parent, grandparent or other dependent relative of a British citizen or person with indefinite leave.

The advantages of indefinite leave over the extension of limited leave will depend on the particular category. All those who obtain indefinite leave gain a secure residence status, which is retained provided they are not absent from the United Kingdom for more than two years, and do not fall within the rules on deportation of persons whose presence is deemed not 'conducive to the public good'. Persons with indefinite leave also have the possibility to sponsor a limited range of dependent relatives to come the United Kingdom. Indefinite leave gives eligibility to the full range of social benefits (except for persons with refugee leave, humanitarian protection or discretionary leave, who have access to benefits automatically). Skilled migrants (now under Tier 2 of the points-based system) obtain freedom of employment, while those in family categories gain an autonomous status.

The cost of immigration applications is a further consideration. As of 1 October 2010, the basic cost of an application to extend leave in the main categories is as follows: £ 850 plus £ 250 per dependant for the highly-skilled (Tier 1 of the points-based system); £ 500 plus £ 150 per dependant for skilled workers (Tier 2 of the points-based system); and, £ 500 plus £ 150 per dependant for the family members of British citizens and persons with indefinite leave. Typically, an extension of leave will be for up to three years under Tier 1,

22 For the announcement, see 'The Home Secretary's immigration speech', 5 November 2010, available at http://www.homeoffice.gov.uk/media-centre/speeches/immigration-speech.

23 'Humanitarian protection' corresponds to the concept of subsidiary protection in Council Directive 2004/83/EC.

24 'Discretionary leave' status is primarily for cases where removal would be contrary to the European Convention on Human Rights, but humanitarian protection is unavailable.

and for two years under Tier 2 or for family members. These amounts may be compared to the basic cost of an indefinite leave application at the time of writing: £ 900 for the main applicant, and £ 250 per dependant. Those in humanitarian categories (refugees, humanitarian protection and discretionary leave) are in a distinct position in this regard. They are expected to apply for indefinite leave when their qualifying period comes to an end, but there is in no fee for such an application.

In February 2005, it was announced that the requirements to show knowledge of the English language and 'sufficient knowledge about life in the United Kingdom' were to be extended to applicants for indefinite leave (Home Office 2005: para 39). The requirements were brought into force through amendments to the Immigration Rules, which came into force on 2 April 2007. As with naturalisation, applicants for indefinite leave demonstrate both knowledge of English and knowledge of life in the UK by passing the 'Life in the UK' test, or by passing an ESOL course which includes the required citizenship element.[25]

In principle, the language and knowledge of life requirements apply to all applicants for indefinite leave aged between 18 and 64. Minors may apply for indefinite leave where they are living with a parent or parents who themselves obtain indefinite leave. Equally, persons may apply after reaching 65 through the normal operation of the general rules on economic migration, family migration or the humanitarian categories.

The Secretary of State may waive the requirements for persons 'whose physical or mental condition makes it unreasonable for them to have to meet the requirements'.[26] Further information on how this discretion is to be exercised is provided in official instructions to UK Border Agency case workers.[27] These state that discretion 'must' be exercised to benefit someone 'suffering from a long term illness or disability that severely restricts the ability to attend [ESOL] classes, or prepare for the Life in the UK test', 'is deaf, is a person without speech, or has a speech impediment which limits their ability to communicate in the relevant language' or 'has a mental impairment and may be capable of physically meeting the requirement, but is not able to speak or learn the relevant language.' In other cases, it is stated that 'each application must be considered on its own merits'.

A number of current immigration categories provided for in the Immigration Rules are entirely exempt from the requirements.[28] These are: a foreign national discharged from the armed forces, and their spouse, civil partner or unmarried partner; the partner of a British citizen or person with indefinite leave in the United Kingdom, where the relationship ended through death, or the other person's domestic violence; the parent, grandparent or other dependent relative of a British citizen or person with indefinite leave (who will anyway generally be 65 or over); and, a Turkish businessperson under the association agreement with Turkey.

The two knowledge requirements do not apply either to persons with one of the three humanitarian statuses, to whom indefinite leave is granted outside the Immigration Rules. The policy in this area remained uncertain until relatively recently. The reason was that, when the knowledge requirements came into force for indefinite leave on 2 April 2007, the humanitarian statuses were in a phase of transition. On 1 April 2003, the previous status of exceptional leave to remain, from which there was a qualifying period of four years for

25 Immigration Rules, para 33B.

26 Immigration Rules, para 33G.

27 UK Border Agency, Knowledge of Life in the UK, 15 August 2010, p. 10.

28 *Ibid.*, p. 7-8.

indefinite leave to remain, was replaced by the statuses of humanitarian protection and discretionary leave, with qualifying periods to indefinite leave of five and six years, respectively. Then, on 30 August 2005, those recognised as refugees ceased to be granted indefinite leave, and were instead obtained 'refugee leave' for five years. The result of these two new arrangements was that, in the period immediately after 2 April 2007, there were few, if any, applications for indefinite leave from humanitarian categories, and it was left unclear what the policy would be.[29] It was only as the initial periods of the new forms of leave began to expire – from 1 April 2008 for humanitarian protection, from 1 April 2009 for discretionary leave and from 30 August 2010 for refugee leave - that the policy had to be clarified. In practice, it appears that the policy of non-application of the requirements to humanitarian categories was only definitively resolved in 2010.[30]

Finally, an inconsistency within the British immigration system as a result of the introduction of the knowledge requirements may be noted. This concerns partners of four years' standing, who are eligible for indefinite leave *to enter*, but are also subject to the two knowledge requirements, even though it is not generally possible to meet the requirements while outside the United Kingdom. Special provision is made for persons living outside the United Kingdom as the partner of a UK diplomat, a member of staff of the British Council who is usually UK-based, or a member of staff of the Department for International Development who is a British citizen or has indefinite leave in the United Kingdom.[31] In these cases, the requirements may be met through certification by a designated person, who 'will normally be the head of the [diplomatic] post where the applicant's partner is based'.[32] In other cases, it will be necessary for a partner to travel to the United Kingdom in order to fulfil the knowledge requirements. Should they elect to take up residence before so doing, they are initially treated in the same way as partners who do not meet the four-year rule – i.e. they are given limited leave for a period of up to 27 months.[33] Once they have met the knowledge requirements, however, they may apply for indefinite leave to remain without meeting the usual two-year probationary period for partners.[34]

4. Admission

Since 2004, language requirements have gradually been extended to those seeking admission to the United Kingdom in categories that can lead to indefinite leave. The first group of intending migrants to face a language condition were ministers of religion (a category of

29 This can be seen from pre-April 2007 (but undated) Asylum Policy Instruction on 'refugee leave', which stated that the policy on the requirements was 'still being developed'. This document still appeared on the UK Border Agency website as of 28 February 2011.

30 At the time of writing, official guidance states that applicants with exceptional leave to remain, humanitarian protection and discretionary leave are exempt: UK Border Agency, Knowledge of Life in the UK, 15 August 2010, p. 7-8. While refugee leave is not expressly mentioned, it may be thought covered by the concept of an 'application outside the Rules' there. A summary of the requirements on the UKBA website expressly includes refugee leave: see http://www.ukba.homeoffice.gov.uk/settlement/knowledge-language-life/.

31 Immigration Rules, para 33B(c).

32 UK Border Agency, *Knowledge of Life in the UK*, 15 August 2010, p. 42.

33 Immigration Rules, paras 282(c) and 295B(c).

34 Immigration Rules, paras 287(a)(i)(c) and 295G(c).

skilled worker in the British immigration system), who have been required to demonstrate knowledge of English since 23 August 2004. The reason for singling out this group was to ensure their competence as ministers, while reducing the risk of their promoting an anti-British outlook.[35] The standard that was initially set for them was spoken English to International English Language Test System (IELTS) level 4. From 19 April 2007, this was raised to IELTS level 6, and covered both spoken and written English. In line with that earlier standard, when the skilled worker system was replaced by Tier 2 of the points-based system in November 2008 (see below), ministers of religion had to meet Common European Framework of Reference (CEFR) level B2, rather than the level A1 required for others.[36]

The second group to whom language requirements were applied were the highly-skilled. From 7 November 2006, migrants seeking to enter the UK as part of the Highly Skilled Migrant Programme (HSMP) were required to demonstrate knowledge of the English language, through an IELTS score of 6 – later, CEFR level B2. From 30 June 2008, the HSMP became the 'general' category within Tier 1 of the points-based system. Tier 1 also includes an 'entrepreneur' category, to replace the former business migration and innovator categories, which had not been covered by a language requirement. For Tier 1 (General) and Tier 1 (Entrepreneur), the language level is now set at CEFR level C1, which is classed as equivalent to an IELTS score of 6.5. Tier 1 also includes 'innovator' and 'post-study work' categories, which are not subject to a language rule. In the case of post-study work, the logic is that, in order to qualify, the individual will already have obtained a degree in English in the United Kingdom, having studied there for at least one year.[37] It may be added that Tier 1 is in the process of being curtailed in scope by the Coalition Government at the time of writing. From 6 April 2011, Tier 1 (General) is to be limited to the 'exceptionally talented', with a cap of 1000 places a year, while the abolition of the post-study work category has also been proposed.[38]

Thirdly, skilled workers (other than ministers of religion) have had to satisfy a language requirement under Tier 2 of the points-based system since it came into force on 27 November 2008. In their case, the required level of English is defined in policy guidance as follows: 'you must be able to understand and use familiar everyday expressions and very basic phrases, to introduce yourself and others, and to ask and answer questions about very basic personal details'.[39] This standard is said to be 'closest to' CEFR level A1. Intra-corporate transferees are an exception under Tier 2: they are not subject to the English language rule when they initially obtain admission to the United Kingdom, but must meet it if they seek to extend their stay beyond three years.[40] On 23 November 2010, the Coalition Government announced that the standard required of workers in the Tier 2 (General) sub-category would increase to CEFR level B1 with effect from April 2011.[41] This change will not however apply to the other sub-categories within Tier 2, i.e. ministers of religion

35 'Foreign imams face tougher entry requirements', Times, 6 April 2004.

36 UK Border Agency, *Tier 2 of the Points Based System – Policy Guidance*, 1 October 2010, para 104.

37 It is also possible to qualify with a postgraduate certificate or diploma in education, or a Higher National Diploma obtained at a Scottish institution.

38 See UK Border Agency, *Annual limit for Tier 1 and Tier 2 visa applications*, 24 November 2010, and Home Office 2010: 16.

39 UK Border Agency, *Tier 2 Policy Guidance*, 1 October 2010, para 105.

40 Immigration Rules, para 245ZF(m).

41 UK Border Agency, *Annual limit for Tier 1 and Tier 2 visa applications*, 24 November 2010.

(CEFR level B2), sportspersons (CEFR level A1) and intra-company transferees (CEFR level A1, after three years).

Partners are a further category to whom an English language requirement has been applied for integration reasons. This category covers persons seeking admission as the spouse, civil partner, unmarried partner, fiancé(e) or proposed civil partner of a British citizen or a non-EEA national with indefinite leave. The extension of a language rule to this group had a somewhat convoluted history. A detailed proposal was first made by the Labour Government in a consultation document in December 2007 (Home Office 2007). In July 2008, it then announced that implementation would be delayed, because of gaps in the availability of English language tuition in some countries (Home Office 2008c). Instead, what it contemplated at that point was that partners would either demonstrate the requisite English language ability in the same way as skilled workers, or else would enter an agreement to learn English after arrival in the United Kingdom. In August 2009, the then Government changed tack again, and announced that it would introduce a language requirement from Summer 2011 (Home Office 2009: 23). The standard was to be the same as for skilled workers (CEFR level A1), except that spouses and related would have to show basic competence in spoken English alone, and not both spoken and written English. Eventually, after the change of government in May 2010, the Coalition brought the timing forward, an introduced the requirement with effect from 29 November 2010, based on Labour's plans.

A final English language rule within the United Kingdom immigration control system covers international students. At the time of writing, this rule applies to students who do not intend to study for a degree course, or for a foundation course leading to degree course, or to study the English language. Since 3 March 2010, it has been the responsibility of a course provider to ensure that an intending student in this category has already attained CEFR level B1 before offering them a place to study.[42] In December 2010, the Coalition Government went further, and proposed that *all* international students should have to demonstrate English language competence. Students not intending to study the English language would have to show competence to at least CEFR level B2, while intending English language students would have to demonstrate competence to at least CEFR level C1 (Home Office, 2010: 12). When the March 2010 reform was announced, the reason given for it was the immigration control purpose of preventing the use of the student as a route to residence and employment in the United Kingdom.[43] A similar argument was used in support of the December 2010 proposals, that 'raising the language bar [would] act as evidence of a student's fitness to complete the course' (*ibid.*). On that occasion, however, the Coalition Government added that an English language requirement would 'assist [ ] with their integration with other students and wider society on arrival in the UK' (*ibid.*).

Where a language rule has been applied at the admission stage, the approach is to designate the providers whose tests may be relied upon for the purpose. In each case, a list of approved providers is available on the website of the UK Border Agency.

---

42 UK Border Agency, *Tier 4 changes from 3 March 2010 – Information for Education Providers*, 3 March 2010.

43 Home Secretary Alan Johnson, written statement, House of Commons Debates, 10 February 2010; Home Office 2010.

For all of the groups to whom a language rule has been applied or is proposed, there is an exception for individuals who are nationals of 'majority English-speaking countries'.[44] The sixteen countries which qualify are the following: Antigua and Barbuda; Australia; the Bahamas; Barbados; Belize; Canada; Dominica; Grenada; Guyana; Jamaica; New Zealand; St Kitts and Nevis; St Lucia; St Vincent and the Grenadines; Trinidad and Tobago; and, the USA.

Provision is also made for the exemption of those who previously been educated in English. In the case of highly-skilled workers, skilled workers and partners, there is an exemption for those who have obtained a degree taught in English.[45] For this purpose, it is assumed that a degree was taught in English if it was obtained in the United Kingdom, Ireland or one of countries listed above other than Canada, but degree obtained in other countries could also be relied upon. In the case of international students subject to the English language requirement introduced in March 2010, there is an exemption for those who were school students in the United Kingdom in the previous two years.[46] In its December 2010 consultation, the Coalition Government proposed that in future there should also be an exemption for intending students who have obtained a degree taught in English in a majority English-speaking country.[47] This would not however apply to degrees obtained in other countries.

In the case of partners only, the Immigration Rules also set out exemptions from the requirement in three circumstances: (a) the applicant is aged 65 or over, (b) the applicant has a 'physical or mental condition that would prevent him from meeting the requirement' and (c) 'there are exceptional compassionate circumstances that would prevent the applicant from meeting the requirement.' Exemptions (a) and (b) follow the provision made within the rules governing indefinite leave and naturalisation (see sections 2 and 3, above). Those rules do not however make express provision for 'exceptional compassionate circumstances', as is done by exemption (c) here.

Conclusion: On the Path to Assimilation?

In the period starting in 2001, Labour Governments presented the purpose of integration rules in a nuanced manner, continuing to accept the diversity of communities, and giving particular priority to economic and social participation. This discursive caution corresponded to an important limitation to the measures actually introduced. By focusing solely on knowledge of the English language, or of the basic organisation of British society, the policy limited itself to requirements concerning *cognitive abilities* alone. It stopped short of

44 For Tier 1, this was previously stated in UK Border Agency, *Tier 1 (General) of the Points based System – Policy Guidance*, 6 April 2010, para 178. For Tier 2, it is stated in UK Border Agency, *Tier 2 Policy Guidance*, 1 October 2010, para 107. For partners, it is stated in paras 281, 284, 290, 295A and 295D of the Immigration Rules. For students subject to the 3 March 2010 policy change, it is set out in UK Border Agency, *Tier 4 of the Points based System – Policy Guidance*, 23 July 2010, para 92.

45 See UK Border Agency, *Tier 1 Policy Guidance*, 6 April 2010, paras 192-193 (no longer in force); UK Border Agency, *Tier 2 Policy Guidance*, 1 October 2010, paras 113-114; and, paras 281, 284, 290, 295A and 295D of the Immigration Rules.

46 UK Border Agency, *Tier 4 Policy Guidance*, 23 July 2010, para 91.

47 Home Office 2010: 12.

requiring that those who wished to gain admission, or to obtain indefinite leave or naturalisation, should demonstrate particular *values*, whether directly or indirectly.

Towards the end of the period of Labour Government, however, two policy initiatives contained a values-oriented element. The first of these sought to use migration law to encourage 'active citizenship'. In *The Path to Citizenship*, a consultation paper published in February 2008, it was proposed that those who could not prove 'active citizenship' would need an extra two years' residence in order to qualify for the new status of permanent resident (roughly equivalent to indefinite leave), or to naturalise (see Ryan, 2009: 290-292). The justification for this proposal focused on the implications of 'active citizenship' for community cohesion:

> 'We want to do more to encourage all migrants who wish to stay in the UK permanently to integrate fully into society, including bringing probationary citizens in greater contact with the wider community, showing current British citizens that those seeking to join them as British citizens are earning citizenship by being active rather than passive participants in UK life' (Home Office 2008a: 29).

The proposals in *The Path to Citizenship* were taken forward through the Borders, Citizenship and Immigration Act 2009, which opened the possibility to introduce an 'activity condition' into nationality law. (Full implementation would have required parallel changes to the Immigration Rules.) In the meantime, however, many respondents to *The Path to Citizenship* had expressed unease about the operation of the new principle, believing that it would impose unacceptable burdens on voluntary bodies (Home Office 2008b: 17-18). The range of qualifying activities, and the method of their verification, were therefore referred to a 'design group' in the summer of 2008 (*ibid.*: 18).

For our purposes, the significance of the 'active citizenship' proposal was that, for the first time, the Labour Government crossed the 'values' threshold, by planning to confer a benefit upon virtuous foreign nationals (see Joppke 2010: 3-4). That was seen in particular in the highly conventional list of activities which it was suggested might qualify. These included 'volunteering with a recognised organization', 'running or helping to run a playgroup which encourages the different communities to interact', 'fund-raising activities for charities or schools', 'serving on community bodies, for example as a school governor' and 'running or helping run a local sporting team' (*ibid.*: 29-30). It is inherent in voluntary activity that it reflects the value preferences of those who do, and who do not, engage in it. For that reason, the 'active citizenship' proposal would have meant giving indirect preference to those who held particular values.

That initiative was followed by a more direct proposal concerning migrants' values, in *Earning the Right to Stay: A New Points Test for Citizenship*, published in July 2009. In that document, the Labour Government proposed that, within a planned points system for a new intermediate status of probationary citizenship (to be between initial residence and permanent residence), points would be deducted, or penalties imposed, 'for not integrating into the British way of life' (*ibid.*: 17). However, neither the meaning of this phrase, nor how it might be operationalised, was explained in the consultation document. Instead, respondents to the consultation were asked to indicate which 'attributes' should give rise to these sanctions.

In the event, on 5 November 2010, the Coalition Government announced that it would not proceed with Labour's proposals for 'earned citizenship', which included both of these values-oriented measures.[48] Its argument was that the Labour proposals were 'too complicated, bureaucratic and ... ineffective'. We have seen that the Coalition Government which came to power in 2010 has already tightened language requirements at the admission stage, or proposed to do so, in relation to skilled workers, partners and students. It has also announced that its own proposals in relation to long-term residence will be published in Spring 2011.[49] It seems likely that the result will be further changes to integration rules in relation to indefinite leave (or future equivalents) and/or naturalisation.

In the terms used in this chapter, the question now is whether the Coalition will cross the threshold identified by Joppke, by introducing requirements or principles into migration law which relate to values. This appears especially likely after David Cameron's criticism of multiculturalism in a speech in Munich on 5 February 2011.[50] In that speech, he rejected 'passive tolerance', which 'stands neutral between different values'. He argued instead for 'a much more active, muscular liberalism', as 'a genuinely liberal country ... believes in certain values and actively promotes them'. He went on to list certain of the values which he considered important: 'freedom of speech, freedom of worship, democracy, the rule of law, equal rights regardless of race, sex or sexuality'. Crucially for our purposes, he concluded that such a liberal country 'says to its citizens, this is what defines us as a society: to belong here is to believe in these things.' At the rhetorical level, the current Government has therefore identified an association between values and citizenship. We will soon learn whether it intends to translate that association into new values-oriented elements within migration law.

References

Bradford Vision (2001), *Community Pride not Prejudice: Making Diversity Work in Bradford* [The Ouseley Report].

Burnley Task Force (2001), *Burnley Speaks, Who Listens?* [The Clarke Report].

Commission for Integration and Cohesion (2007), *Final Report: Our Shared Future*.

Cohen, Robin (1994), *Frontiers of Identity: The British and the Others*. London: Longman.

Dummett, Ann and Andrew Nicol (1990), *Subjects, Citizens, Aliens and Others: Nationality and Immigration Law*. London: Weidenfeld and Nicolson.

EdComs (2008), *British Citizenship: Experience and perceptions. An EdComs report for the Lord Goldsmith Review secretariat*.

Favell, Adrian (1998), *Philosophies of Integration: Immigration and the Idea of Citizenship in France and Britain*. Basingstoke: Palgrave.

Fransman, Laurie (1998) *British Nationality Law* (2nd edition). London: Butterworths.

48 'The Home Secretary's immigration speech', 5 November 2010, available at http://www. homeoffice.gov.uk/media-centre/speeches/immigration-speech.

49 This was announced by Immigration Minister Damian Green on 1 February 2011: 'Reforming the immigration system', available at http://www.homeoffice.gov.uk/media-centre/speeches/immigration-speech.

50 'PM's speech at Munich Security Conference', 5 February 2011, available at http://www.number10.gov.uk/news/speeches-and-transcripts/2011/02/pms-speech-at-munich-security-conference-60293.

Home Office (2001a), *Community Cohesion: A Report of the Independent Review Team Chaired by Ted Cantle.*

Home Office (2001b), *Building Cohesive Communities: A Report of the Ministerial Group on Public Order and Community Cohesion.*

Home Office (2002), *Secure Borders, Safe Haven. Integration with Diversity in Modern Britain.*

Home Office (2005), *Controlling our Borders: Making Migration work for Britain.*

Home Office (2007), *Marriage Visas: Pre-Entry English Requirement for Spouses.*

Home Office (2008a), *The Path to Citizenship: Next Steps in Reforming the Immigration System.*

Home Office (2008b), *The Path To Citizenship: Next Steps in Reforming the Immigration System: Government Response to Consultation.*

Home Office (2008c), *Marriage Visas: The Way Forward.*

Home Office (2009), *Earning the Right to Stay: A New Points Test for Citizenship.*

Home Office (2010), *The Student Immigration System: A Consultation.*

Joppke, Christian (2010), 'How liberal are citizenship tests?', in Rainer Bauböck & Christian Joppke (eds), *How Liberal are Citizenship Tests?* (EUI Working Paper RSCAS 2010/41).

Kiwan, Dina (2008) 'A Journey to Citizenship in the United Kingdom', 10:1 *International Journal on Multicultural Societies*, p. 60-75.

Oldham Independent Review (2001), *One Oldham, One Future* [The Ritchie Report].

Qualifications and Curriculum Authority (1998), *Education for Citizenship and the Teaching of Democracy in Schools: Final Report of the Advisory Group on Citizenship.*

Ryan, Bernard (2009), 'The Integration Agenda in British Migration Law', in E. Guild, K. Groenendijk & S. Carrera (eds.) *Illiberal liberal states: immigration, citizenship and integration in the EU.* Farnham: Ashgate.

Ryan, Bernard (2010), *Integration Rules in Immigration and Nationality Law: The Case of the United Kingdom* (unpublished paper within research project on 'Integration and Naturalisation tests: The New Way to European Citizenship'), available at http://www.kent.ac.uk/law/research/documents/ryan-UK-final-1.pdf.

Stationery Office (2004), *Life in the United Kingdom: A Journey to Citizenship.*

Stationery Office (2007), *Life in the United Kingdom: A Journey to Citizenship* (2nd edition).

Taylor, Chris (2007), *ESOL and Citizenship: A Teacher's Guide.* Leicester: National Institute of Adult Continuing Education.

UK Border Agency (2008), *Skilled Workers under the Points-based System (Tier 2): Statement of Intent*, May 2008.

The Integration Agreement in Austria – from symbolic policy to restrictive practice

Bernhard Perchinig

1. The Integration Debate in Austria and the History of 'Integration Testing'

The term 'integration' was not used in federal laws on migration before the 1990s, when the Residence Act of 1992 (*Aufenthaltsgesetz* 1992 = *AufG* 1992) introduced the term 'integration support', targeted at immigrants working legally in Austria, their family members and at recognised refugees. In this law, 'integration' was closely associated with equal opportunities for immigrants. According to Article 11 of the Law, 'their full inclusion in Austrian economic, cultural and societal life and wide-ranging equality of opportunities with Austrian citizens in these areas should be achieved'.

Also on the political level, the term 'integration' gained prominence in the early 1990s. In 1992, the City of Vienna set up the 'Viennese Integration Fund' (*Wiener Integrationsfonds*), the first municipal organisations for the inclusion of immigrants in Austria (Koller 1998). The Fund was quick to criticise the existing legislation, in particular the Residence Law with its strict income and housing conditions as a precondition for residence, and defined integration as a policy to achieve equal opportunities for immigrants. Within civil society, organisations active in supporting immigrants and refugees and humanitarian organisations joined forces and founded 'SOS-Mitmensch' as an umbrella organisation. In January 1993 it organised the 'sea of light', which attracted 300,000 persons, the largest political demonstration since 1945 against xenophobia and the politics of the far right Freedom Party (*Freiheitliche Partei Österreichs, FPÖ*). In the following years, the Constitutional Court passed several decisions declaring the core paragraphs of the Residence Law unconstitutional (König & Perchinig 2003:2f.)

In this political atmosphere, the Social Democratic Party, which at that time formed a coalition with the Conservatives and held the position of Minister of the Interior, embraced a reform of the existing migration law. Under the heading 'integration package' the then Minister of the Interior, Caspar Einem (Social Democrats, SPÖ), a prominent member of the party's left, who had drafted a 'Concept for an Alternative Migration Policy' as a leading staff member of the Viennese Chamber of Labour in 1990 (Einem 1990), announced a complete reform of the existing Aliens Law (*Fremdengesetz* = *FRG*) and the Residence Act intending to strengthen the residence rights of immigrants and ease their access into the labour market. These reform moves were connected to the idea of reducing immigration in exchange for improved integration. 'Integration before new immigration' (*'Integration vor Neuzuwanderung')* became the key phrase of the reform, intended, on the one hand, to give in to the pressure of humanitarian organisations to improve the legal status of immigrants and, on the other hand, to react to the demands of the far right and anti-immigrant FPÖ to completely halt immigration.[1]

In October 1995 the Social Democratic-Conservative coalition government failed to reach an agreement on the budget for 1996 and collapsed. After the elections of December 1995 again a Social Democratic-Conservative coalition government was formed, with the post of the Minister of the Interior being given to Karl Schlögl, a prominent member of the right wing of the Social Democrats. The coalition agreement repeated the slogan, 'Integration before new immigration', but largely cut back on the intended improvements for immigrants, insisting instead on stricter immigration control. Nevertheless, the term 'integration' now was firmly anchored in the Austrian immigration debate.[2]

Consequently, the migration law reform, which was passed by parliament in June 1997 and entered into force on 1 January 1998, was called 'integration package'. It comprised a new Aliens Act (*Fremdengesetz 1997* = FrG 1997) and reforms to the Foreigners' Employment Act (*Ausländerbeschäftigungsgesetz* = AuslBG 1997) and the Asylum Act (*Asylgesetz 1997* – AsylG 1997).

The new Aliens Act referred to 'integration' in two different ways. On the one hand, '*integration support*' was now defined as measures for recognised refugees to be organised by the 'Funds for the Integration of Refugees', an institution set up by the Austrian Ministry of the Interior and the UNHCR in the 1960s, which managed housing and training support for recognised refugees, whereas long-term legally resident immigrants were to bene-fit from measures to *facilitate integration*. On the other hand, the Act associated integration with long-term residence and claimed that family members of long-term resident third-country nationals should gain privileged access to a residence permit due to their '*advanced integration*' (FrG 1997, § 18 (6)). Furthermore, the Act installed an 'Integration Advisory Council' to advise the Ministry of the Interior with regard to the facilitation of integration.

The reform of the Aliens Act was followed by a reform of the Nationality Act in June 1998 (*Staatsbürgerschaftsgesetz 1985* = StbG 1985). Reacting to massive criticism from the FPÖ, that access to Austrian nationality was too easy and even people unable to communicate in German were being naturalised, naturalisation was made dependent on an 'adequate knowledge of German'.[3] The law stipulated that the applicant's knowledge of German should be judged in relation to his/her living conditions (§ 10a StbG 1985). In practice, their knowledge of German was evaluated by the respective authorities based on a personal conversation with the applicant. In general, the ability to communicate 'about issues of everyday life' was regarded as sufficient by the authorities.[4]

After the elections of 1999 had lead to a coalition between the Conservatives (*Österreichische Volkspartei, ÖVP*) and the FPÖ, their first government programme reiterated the main concepts of immigration policy already laid down by the precious Social Democratic-Conservative coalition governments, but linked them closely to security issues. In the governmental programmes of both 2000 (*Bundeskanzleramt* 2000) and 2003 (*Bundeskanzleramt* 2003) migration issues are dealt with under the headings, 'internal security and integration' and 'internal affairs, asylum and integration' respectively. The third chapter of the govern-

1 König & Perchinig 2003, p. 3.

2 König & Perchinig 2003, p. 3.

3 Çinar & Waldrauch 2006, p. 42.

4 Waldrauch & Çinar 2003, p. 264.

mental programme for 2000, entitled, 'comprehensive Integration' for the first time announced the introduction of compulsory German language training for immigrants.[5]

Committing immigrants to fulfilling specific integration measures as precondition for permanent residence was first suggested by the former chairman of the parliamentary faction of the FPÖ, Peter Westenthaler, at a press conference in April 2001. Immigrants should be obliged to sign an 'integration contract', including the obligation to attend a language and integration course as a precondition for a permanent residence permit and the rights associated with that status.[6] This idea was again presented to the Council of Ministers by the Minister of the Interior in August 2001, who suggested a compulsory 'integration contract' requiring new immigrants and all immigrants resident in Austria since 1 January 1998 to attend a 100-hour German course within the first four years of residence in Austria as precondition for a permanent residence status. Half of the costs of the course were to be refunded by the government upon successful completion. In the event of non-compliance, sanctions ranging from financial penalties to expulsion were to be implemented.[7]

The draft bill was accepted within the coalition government two months later – not least to silence the late governor of Carinthia, Jörg Haider (FPÖ), who, after the attacks on the World Trade Center on 11 September 2001, had called for tighter immigration requirements.[8] While the Ministry of the Interior repeatedly pointed to the positive effects of comparable courses on the labour market and societal integration in the Netherlands, the Freedom Party defined the 'integration agreement' as a tool to test the immigrants' willingness to integrate.[9]

In the political debate, the Freedom Party presented the introduction of the agreement as a major political success and as a paradigm shift towards a more restrictive migration policy. The then head of the parliamentary faction of the FPÖ, Peter Westenthaler, described the aim of the agreement as the selection of immigrants willing to integrate and as a remedy for immigration into the welfare system:[10]

> 'We are making it clear that abuse of the social system will no longer be possible in the future. I fully support the negotiated solution of the so-called 'sanction ladder' through which we are saying, Yes, sir! We want to know within 3 years if somebody who came to Austria after 1998 is at all willing and able to integrate! (...) After three years we must be able to ask those people who do not want to integrate why they are in this country in the first place. If they cannot answer, then it is clear what shall happen: they will no longer be allowed to stay here! After all, this is not what the Austrian social system is meant for, ladies and gentlemen! (....)With this law, we are making one

5 König & Perchinig 2003, p. 4.

6 Rohsmann 2003, pp. 68-72.

7 Rohsmann 2003, p. 69.

8 Rohsmann 2003, pp. 73 ff.

9 Rohsmann 2003, p. 75.

10 Mourão-Permoser 2010, p. 198. As Mourão-Permoser rightly comments, Austria was simultaneously negotiating the Family Reunification and Long Term Residence Directive in Brussels and was one of the three countries demanding the imposition of integration requirements. Nevertheless, both directives largely improved the access of resident third-country nationals to social rights in Austria. Mourão-Permoser thus concludes that the imposition of the integration agreement should primarily be understood as 'exclusionary symbolism' (Mourão-Permoser 2010, p. 201).

thing clear: Austria is not and will never be an immigration country. We will make sure of that!'[11]

2. The History of the 'Integration Agreement'

In contrast to the martial rhetoric of Mr. Westenthaler's speech, the amendment of the Aliens Law regulating integration testing had a supportive tone. According to the Article 50a of the amended Aliens Law, 'the Integration Agreement serves the integration of permanently settled aliens. It is aimed at the acquisition of a basic knowledge of German in order to facilitate participation in the economic, cultural and societal life in Austria. This capability may be acquired by attending a German integration course.' The law did not give a further definition of how 'participation in the economic, cultural and societal life in Austria' was to be understood.

The draft was widely criticised by the NGO-community active in the field of migrants' inclusion as hindering integration by linking language acquisition with the right to residence. This strong criticism led to a wide variety of exceptions to the obligation. Thus in practice the integration agreement did not play a big role. According to a report in the daily *Die Presse*, by June 2004 only about 10% of the envisaged target group of some 118,000 immigrants had had to attend the courses.[12]

In the debate following the revelation of the high numbers of exemptions, NGOs, academics and language teachers pointed out that 100 hours were by no means sufficient to really acquire a basic knowledge of German. When, in 2005, the government decided to pass a complete reform of Austria's migration law in order to implement the EU *acquis* on long-term residents and family reunification, it also included a reform of the integration agreement. Now the fulfilment of the integration contract within five years of residence had to be proven as precondition to be granted access to the status of a long-term resident as defined in the EU *acquis*. Knowledge of German at the level A2 of the Common European Framework of Reference for Languages was made the cornerstone of the agreement. Fulfilment of the contract could be either proven by an examination at a recognised training and testing centre or the successful attendance and examination of an integration course of 300 hours. A separate provision for a 75-hour literacy course for illiterate immigrants was included.[13] While there was a vigorous public debate on the imposition of the integration agreement in 2003, the reform of 2005 received only scant attention in public.

Furthermore, an important technical change regarding exemptions was implemented. Whereas, in the previous law, certain categories of people were exempt from the duty to take the test, now those who fulfilled certain conditions were regarded as having fulfilled the integration agreement per se. These included all persons belonging to the category of 'key personnel' – those who held key managerial or technical functions and earned 60% or more of the maximum pensionable income,[14] and all persons who successfully completed

11 Österreichisches Parlament 09.07.2002, 52, cited in Mourão-Permoser 2010, p. 198 ff.

12 *Die Presse*, 17 March 2005, p. 3.

13 Perchinig 2009, p. 243.

14 In Austria, social security contributions are deducted from the gross income up to a certain ceiling, the 'maximum pensionable income'. No social security contributions are deducted from the portion of the salary above this limit. As of 2010, the maximum pensionable income is set at EUR 4,110 per →

vocational training in Austria leading to the national vocational training diploma (*Lehrabschlussprüfung*), or who finished compulsory secondary education in Austria with a positive grade in German, or who finished non-compulsory postsecondary education by taking the *Matura* examination, which allows access to university studies. Exemptions were introduced for health reasons and for children under the age of 14 and for those unable to attend the course because of high age.

This technical change had the effect that, among the number of immigrants reported as having fulfilled the integration agreement, between 50% and 60% of the persons reported as having fulfilled the integration agreement had not, in fact, attended any course or passed any test, but had fulfilled the contract simply by belonging to the category 'key personnel' or by completing school or vocational training in Austria.

The Aliens Law was again reformed in 2009. The reform sharply increased the income requirements necessary for access to the status of a long-term resident third-country national, but did not change the regulations regarding the integration test.

Already in 2007 and 2008 the Ministry of the Interior, held by the Conservative Party, had suggested to follow the Dutch and the German example and to introduce the requirement to learn German as precondition for immigration. The pre-text of the debate was unease about a high number of female spouses from Turkey and the Arab world, who were largely seen as victims of a patriarchal family tradition of arranged marriages. This unease reached deeply into the rank and files of the Social Democratic party. At the same time, lawyers pointed to the fact, that due to the standing jurisdiction of the Austrian Constitutional Court it might not easily be possible to deny a residence permit to an immigrant not having fulfilled the integration contract after five years: In cases involving third country nationals residing with their family five years or more in Austria the Court often had decided, that after such a long time of legal residence the right to private and family life enshrined in the European Convention of Human Rights, which has the status of constitutional law in Austria, would outweigh the interest of the state in migration control and thus the right of residence would have to be granted. There was nearly no debate on the appropriateness of the level of competency in German necessary for integration, and no scientific studies on the topic were contracted.

Since 2009, the Minister of the Interior, Maria Fekter (ÖVP), on several occasions announced that a higher level of language competence (B1) would be required in future as condition for permanent residence, since the current level would not be sufficient for societal and labour market integration,[15] and that knowledge of German at the level A1 would be required before immigration. At these occasions, the minister regularly pointed to positive experiences with these measures in the Netherlands and Germany.

Despite criticism from NGOs and the Green Party, the 'National Action Plan on Integration', which passed parliament on 19 January 2010, reiterated these suggestions and announced that level B1 would be set as the level of knowledge of German necessary to fulfil the integration agreement and level A1 as a pre-condition for immigration to Austria

month (14 times a year). Thus, currently, a minimum gross monthly salary (14 times a year) of EUR 2,466 (= EUR 34,524 per year) is necessary to fulfil the income requirements for being granted the status of 'key personnel'. In 2007, the median yearly income of wage-earners in Austria was EUR 22,815 (*Statistik Austria 2009*, table Unselbständige Erwerbstätige – Überblick).

15 E.g. *Die Presse*, 25 March 2009.

in future.[16] In April 2011, a reform of the Aliens Law passed parliament with the votes of the Conservatives and the Socialdemocrats (Act amending the Aliens Act 2011, *Fremdenrechtsänderungsgesetz 2011* = FrÄG 2011). The Act introduced easier migration conditions for highly qualified immigrants based on a point-system ('Red-White-Red Card') counting basically education, professional experience, age, income and language knowledge on the one hand, and aggravated the demands on language knowledge for access to permanent residence on the other. Furthermore, it improved residence security of children of third country nationals born in Austria.

As of July 1, 2011, the fulfilment of the integration agreement requires the proof of the knowledge of German at the level A2 after two years as condition for the renewal of a temporary residence permit, and of the level B1 after five years as condition for a permanent permit. In case of non-fulfilment the authorities may renew a temporary permit between for a period up to three years, but there is no legal claim for a renewal. As the Nationality Law links the language requirements for naturalisation with the requirements demanded for access to a permanent residence, the amendment also raised the requirement of competency in German for naturalisation to the level B1 of the Common Reference Framework. Furthermore, immigrants wishing to enter Austria, who do not fall under the regulations of the point-system ('Red-White-Red-Card') will have to prove the knowledge of German at the A1 level as a condition to be granted entry. Whereas spouses of Austrian citizens will have to fulfil this condition, spouses of citizens of a member state of the European Economic Area as well as spouses of holders of a Blue Card are exempt.

Qualified immigrants under the point system are exempt from the fulfilment of the proof of knowledge of German at the A2 level, but also have to prove knowledge of German at the level B1 after five years in order to be granted a permanent residence permit. Except of top qualified researchers, university-professors or top-managers, their family members have to prove knowledge of German at the A1 level before being granted the right to join them.

As it is rather unlikely that the Constitutional Court will argue in favour of strong residence rights based on Article 8 of the European Charter of Human Rights after only two years of residence, it will in future be much easier for the authorities to expel immigrants not having fulfilled the requirement to proof knowledge of German at the A2 level after two years.

On April 30, 2012, the Ministry of the Interior issued an administrative circular[17] to all relevant authorities detailing the effects of the decision of the ECJ in the case of Dereci at al.[18] and two decisions of the Administrative Court based on *Dereci*[19] on the implementation of integration conditions in Austria.

According to the circular, the standstill-clause of the Ankara Agreement has to be applied to all Turkish nationals reuniting with their family in Austria and intending to partici-

16 BMI 2010, p. 15.

17 GZ: BMI-FW1710/0037-III/4/2012. Administrative circulars are not published and have no proper legal character; they only explain the view of the Ministry on certain topics, but have no legally binding quality at all. In an interview with the daily *Die Presse* of May 1, 2012, Gerhard Muzak, Professor of Public Law at the University of Vienna, demanded, that the Aliens Law had to be amended to implement the decisions of the ECJ and the Administrative Court.

18 ECJ C256/11, 9.9.2011.

19 Administrative Court, 2007/018/0430, 15.12.2011 and 2011/22/0313, 19.1.2012.

pate in the labour market in the future. According to the standstill-clause, for these Turkish citizens the legal regulations in force as of the date of Austria's accession to the EU (January 1, 1995) would apply. Thus neither pre- nor post-entry conditions would apply, the definition of a family member would have to follow the definitions applicable for Union Citizens and they would be exempted from the age limit for family reunification with a spouse of 21. Only if they intend to get access to the status of a long term resident, they will have to prove knowledge of German at the level B1 after five years of residence. Thus pre- and post-entry testing will cease to be applied for a large group of third country immigrants, and particularly the group, which should mainly be targeted by these measures. The consequences of this development for the future of Austria's integration policies cannot be judged yet at the time of writing.

3. The Integration Agreement in Practice (2003-2011)[20]

The fulfilment of the integration agreement (*Integrationsvereinbarung*) is a precondition for any non-EU and non-EEA immigrant intending to stay in Austria for longer than twelve months within the following two years. The integration agreement also has to be fulfilled by non-EEA spouses of Austrian citizens. Asylum-seekers and recognised refugees do not have to attend the integration courses, since according to the understanding of the government integration cannot start before their case is decided and they are granted the refugee-status. If their asylum application is accepted, they earn the right to residence without fulfilling the integration conditions; if the case is rejected, they either have to leave the country and may be deported or are regarded as not deportable, but in this case they will not be granted a permanent residence permit. In both cases, they are not regarded as legally resident and are not obliged to fulfil the integration-agreement, but they also have no access to the federal subsidies for the costs of language courses offered under the agreement.

Since 'key personnel'[21] and their family members had been regarded as fulfilling the integration contract automatically and any person who has completed compulsory schooling or vocational education in Austria is exempt from fulfilment of the integration agreement, in practice only two target groups had to attend courses or take the necessary language examinations under the regulations in force until June 2011: labour migrants outside the category of 'key personnel' and family members. Under these regulations, there was no labour migration to Austria outside the category 'key personnel' and 'seasonal workers', who both were not obliged to fulfil the integration agreement since 2003. Thus, the integration agreement exclusively targeted persons entering Austria for the purposes of family reunification with third-country nationals or Austrian citizens, and who do not hold an EU or EEA passport[22] and who were not reuniting with a person holding the status of key personnel. In practice, the agreement thus targeted family members of Austrian citizens independently of their income and – since the main criterion for the definition of 'key personnel' was income – of low-income immigrants. Exemptions were only made for medical

20 The following chapter explains the practice of the integration agreement as in force until June 30, 2011.

21 The category 'key personnel' ceased to exist as from July 1, 2011.

22 No other countries are exempt.

reasons and on the grounds of advanced age (to be demonstrated by a certificate from a public health officer) or for minors.

The amendment of 2011 also includes highly qualified immigrants – except of the top category of university professors, researchers or top managers – into the duty to proof knowledge of German at the level B1 after five years of residence as condition to access to the status of a long term resident. Holders of the newly introduced title 'Blue Card – EU' are exempt from this regulation.

Although the Residence and Settlement Act (NAG 2005) speaks of the duty to fulfil the two modules of the integration agreement as a precondition for permanent residence, it does not oblige any immigrant to take an 'integration test'. In fact, until June 30, 2011, there were several possibilities for fulfilling this contract without taking a test or attending a course. The two that were closest to the idea of testing are defined as the combination of a) proof of the ability to read and write (Module 1, NAG 2005, § 14 (5) 1.) and b) 'attendance and successful completion of a German integration course (Module 2, NAG 2005, § 14 (5) 2). This module was to be fulfilled by either successfully attending a German integration course and passing the final exam, or by five years of compulsory schooling in Austria and a positive grade in German at the level of the 9th school year; or by proving a positive grade in German from a foreign school where German is taught at least at the level of the 9th school year; or by demonstrating sufficient knowledge of German (Module 2) by possession of the Austrian Language Diploma in German from any certified Austrian Language Training Institute, or from the Goethe Institute and of the WBT *Weiterbildungs-Testsysteme GmbH*.

Thus in practice, no obligation to attend any integration course exists, but an obligation to prove one's knowledge of German by a certificate from a recognised training institution. According to the amendments of 2011, the situation will change insofar, as the first part of the integration agreement, the test of knowledge of German at the level A2, will have to be fulfilled after two years the latest, and the second part, the test of German at the level B1, after five years the latest. Partial refunding of the course costs will only apply to the A2-exam, but only in the case the test is taken at testing centres of the Austrian Integration Fund according to a new test module, the 'German test for Austria' developed by the Goethe Institute and the German *telc GmbH*.[23] Any other test of the level A2 taken at a certified test centre will also count towards the fulfilment of the integration agreement, but will exclude the right of refunding.

It is interesting to note that the FrÄG 2011 reduced the meaning of integration to language acquisition. Article 14.1 of the amended act states: 'The integration agreement serves the integration of legally resident third country nationals. It aims at the acquisition of deepened knowledge of the German language in order to capacitate the third country national to participate at the societal, economic and cultural life in Austria.' In a further article, the integration agreement is defined as existing of two parts, the first serving the acquisition of elementary and the second the acquisition of deepened knowledge of German (Art. 14.2). No reference whatsoever is made to knowledge of society and politics.

23 Letter of the Austrian Fund for Integration of 20 April 2011, available at: http://www. integrationsfonds.at/fileadmin/Integrationsfond/2_betreuung/2.3_integrationsf%C3%B6rderung/Aussendung_an_Kurstraeger_zur_IV_Neu_2011.pdf, visited June 3, 2011.

Until June 30, 2011, the agreement had to be fulfilled within the first five years of residence, as of July 1, 2011, the first part (A2) has to be taken within two years, the second (B1) within five years. There is no regulation whatsoever concerning the date of commencement. There is the possibility to extend the period for two years by the authorities based on considerations of the specific circumstances of a case. There is no limit on how often a candidate may try to fulfil the agreement by taking the tests.

Until June 30, 2011, the following rules for refunding existed: If successfully passed within one year after immigration to Austria, the costs of the first module (literacy) were refunded 100% (up to EUR 350) by the Austrian Fund for Integration (NAG 2005 § 15.1). Persons entering Austria for family reunification were refunded 50% of the costs of the second module (up to EUR 750), if they successfully passed the examination for Module 2 a) within two years of passing the examination for Module 1, or at least within three years of their immigration to Austria, if they cannot prove their literacy, or b) within two years of applying for the residence permit. A successful examination for Module 2 was proof of the fulfilment of Module 1 (NAG § 15.2). As of July 1, 2011, up to half of the costs of reaching the level A2 will be refunded, if the test is taken within 18 months. At the time of writing the article, there was no information available on the height of refunding, but it is planned to reduce the current limit of Euro 750.- by between a quarter and a third.

Non-compliance leads to gradually increasing penalties. Until June 30, 2011, federal subsidies for participants in the courses were gradually lowered after one year and withdrawn if the first part of the agreement was not fulfilled within two years. It the agreement was not fulfilled within five years, it was possible to extend the period in the event of convincing personal reasons. The extension could last for a maximum of two years and was renewable[24] (NAG 2005, § 14.8).

In cases of non-compliance within five years and no extension of the five yearperiod, the authorities were allowed to impose an administrative fine. Furthermore, they had to consult the alien police in order to determine whether, in view of the applicant's right to private and family life, measures to terminate his residence in Austria were justified. In this case, they had to inform the applicant of the plan not to extend his residence permit and to impose measures to terminate his residence in Austria, giving reasons why the termination of residence is applicable after considering the protection of his right to private and family life. The applicant had the right to react within 14 days. If the authorities did not agree with his arguments, the alien police was informed and started the termination of residence (order to leave Austria, then deportation if this is not followed) (NAG 2005, § 25). In this case, the applicant had the right to appeal as in any other case of deportation.

As of July 1, 2011, subsidies will only be paid out if knowledge of German at the level A2 will be proven after 18 months, there are no subsidies for learning German up to the level B1. Administrative fines may be imposed, if after two years knowledge of German at the level A2 is not proven; and the authorities have, as explained above, inform the aliens police in order to determine whether the temporary residence permit has to be renewed or residence has to be terminated.

24 As the reformed integration agreement entered into power on January 1, 2006, no applications for extension have been filed yet and there is no information about the handling of this provision available.

In practice, only three deportation orders were issued until 2009. All three people are still in Austria and have lodged an appeal against the decision.[25] Since the integration agreement is an administrative act in legal terms, in cases of non-compliance administrative penal law applies. As in any other case of a breach of administrative rules, administrative fines are imposed by the district administrative authorities. No data are available on how often fines have been imposed because of non-compliance with the integration agreement. According to a report in the daily *Kleine Zeitung* of 5 October 2010, a Turkish immigrant living in the Tyrol, who had signed the agreement in 2004, was recently fined EUR 77 for non-compliance. The woman, who had unsuccessfully taken the examination four times, had lodged an appeal but lost the case. According to the Head of the Department for Integration of the State Government of the Tyrol, Johannes Gschier, some 40% of those obliged to fulfil the agreement do not comply in time. The article also cites the Head of the Department for Integration and Residence of the State Government of Styria, Ingrid Koiner, who stated that only very few people are not able to demonstrate fulfilment of the integration agreement within five years. Since January 2011, the number of administrative fines for non-compliance is rising.[26]

The reformed integration agreement entered into force on 1 January 2006. Thus the five year period for the fulfilment of the agreement still is in force and not enough experience has been acquired to evaluate the effects of the threat of expulsion. Since the Austrian Constitutional Court has decided in several cases that after five years of residence the right to private and family life precludes deportation, it is very likely that, in cases of expulsion due to non-fulfilment of the integration agreement brought before the Constitutional Court, the court will declare the deportation order void.

In this case, the person concerned will receive a temporary residence permit for a period between one year and three years (in practice for one year), which has to be renewed annually, and will not have access to the rights associated with the status of a long-term resident according to the EU Directive. Since only those who hold long-term resident status have unlimited access to the labour market in Austria, whereas others need an employment permit that is only granted if no Austrian or EEA citizen is available to fill the position, this might lead to a growing number of de facto long-term residents' being excluded from access to the labour market. Furthermore, equal access to many social provisions, in particular social security payments, are dependent on that status. In most cities, access to council housing is dependent on being an EEA citizen or holding the status of a long-term resident, so those not fulfilling the integration agreement might face serious discrimination in the area of housing.

4. The Politics of Course Organisation

Preparation courses are offered by more than 300 certified institutions, ranging from private language schools, such as Berlitz or Inlingua, to well-established vocational training

25 Mourão-Permoser 2010, p. 210.

26 Telephone information of the Department of Integration and Diversity of the City of Vienna, June 9, 2011.

centres run by the social partners and to small NGOs.[27] The duration of the courses ranges from 100 to 600 hours, depending on the target group, with the majority teaching for 300 hours. The costs vary, but usually were in the range of around EUR 350 for module 1 (literacy) and EUR 1,500 to 2,500 for module 2 (German). The City of Vienna refunds an extra EUR 300 if the immigrant has also attended the Start Vienna programme, consisting of individual advice and coaching on language and vocational training courses and afternoon lectures on life in Vienna, given in the mother tongue of the largest immigrant groups. According to information of a large course provider, the costs for a course leading from the level A2 to B1 will also be in the range of Euro 1.500- to Euro 2.500-.

Until June 30, 2011 there were two main roads to fulfil the integration agreement: Taking an examination according to the model of the Austrian Language Diploma or according to the course model of the Austrian Fund for Integration. The Austrian Language Diploma is modelled according to the European Reference Framework for Languages and is internationally recognised as a proof of knowledge of German according to the ERFL, whereas the course model of the Austrian Funds for Integration only recognised nationally and has not been accepted as a proof of German according to the ERFL by the relevant authorities abroad.

The amendments of 2011 will not change the fact, that as well exams taken at certified test centres following the scheme of the European Reference Framework as those following the scheme of the test of the Austrian Fund for Integration will count towards the fulfilment of the integration contract. But as of July 1, 2011, only those taking an exam following the model of the 'German test for Austria' developed by the Austrian Fund for Integration will be eligible for a (partial) refunding of the course costs. In this case, the tests will have to be taken at test centres of the Austrian Fund for Integration, which did not exist yet at the time of finishing the article.

In Vienna, the largest course provider, the Viennese 'Peoples Universities' (*Wiener Volkshochschulen*), which is regarded as an institution critical to the integration policies of the Ministry of the Interior, had decided not to follow the course model of the Austrian Fund for Integration because of its alleged low didactic quality. Several experts interviewed reported massive pressure of the Austrian Funds for Integration, which is closely linked to the Ministry of the Interior, on the language schools to only follow their model. According to the experts, this conflict is due to the different party affiliations of the ministries administering the different models. The Austrian Language Diploma is administered by an expert unit of the Ministry of Education, which is headed by Social Democratic Minister, whereas the Minister of the Interior and the attached State Secretary for Integration come from the Conservative Party.

According to the experts interviewed, the Ministry of the Interior successively has extended its institutional influence in the field of integration and is interested in pushing aside the influence of the Ministry of Education. There would be a conflict between the ministries involving as well different political attachments and a different understanding of the relation between language acquisition and integration. Whereas the Ministry of the Interior, which was governed by a conservative minister, would select experts mainly from the fields

27 A list of certified institutes can be downloaded from http://www.integrationsfonds.at/fileadmin/Integrationsfond/3_integrationsvereinbarung/downloads/liste_der_zertifizierten_kursinstitute.pdf.

of demography, geography and law, who would follow a conservative understanding of integration as assimilation and were critical to multicultural concepts, the 'epistemic community' linked with the Ministry of Education (governed by a minister of the Social Democratic party) would be rooted in social sciences, pedagogy and linguistics and comprise an understanding of integration focusing on equality and antidiscrimination supporting a positive view on cultural diversity. As experts from these field were known as critics of the governmental integration policies developed by the Ministry of the Interior, this ministry would be interested to weaken their institutional base by developing institutional structures in the field of integration attached to them. The 'Austrian Fund for Integration', which in practice was controlled by the Ministry of the Interior, would be the main tool to dominate the political discourse on integration and to build an institutional setting related to the ministry, in particular through gaining dominance in the field of language training and integration support. With the restriction of the (partial) refunding of the course costs to those courses organised by the Austrian Fund for Integration the Ministry of the Interior has effectively pushed back the influence of the Ministry of Education on the organisation of integration courses, a major area of practical integration policies.

5. Statistical Data and the Open Question of Evaluation

Statistical data on the integration tests are not published by the Ministry of the Interior, the state governments or the Austrian Fund for Integration. The only available statistical data stem from the answers of several parliamentary inquiries to the Minister of the Interior by the Green Party[28] and the Social Democrats.[29]

According to the reply from the Ministry of the Interior to the parliamentary enquiry by the Green Party of 17 January 2008 (3352/AB XXIII. GP), only data about the successful completion of the integration requirements are collected. There are no data available on the number of applications or failed tests, nor a breakdown with regard to age, gender, nationality or income.

28 Parliamentary Enquiry by Member of Parliament Weinzinger and friends regarding the integration agreement of 17 January 2008, 3347/J XXIII. GP, answered by the Ministry of the Interior on 14 March 2008 (3352/AB XXIII GP); Parliamentary Enquiry by Member of Parliament Korun and friends regarding the so-called integration agreement of 8 July 2009, 2638/J XXIV. GP, answered by the Ministry of the Interior on 8 September 2009 (2707/AB XXIV GP); Parliamentary Enquiry by Member of Parliament Korun and friends regarding the integration agreement as a reason for expulsion of 23 December 2009, 4186/J XXIV. GP, answered by the Ministry of the Interior on 23 February 2010 (4128/AB XXIII GP).

29 Parliamentary Enquiry by Member of Parliament Dr. Elisabeth Hlavac and comrades regarding newly-settled immigrants of 14 July 2006, 4670/J XXII. GP, answered by the Ministry of the Interior on 13 September 2006 (4589/AB XXII. GP).

Table 1: Fulfilled integration agreements and number of exemptions 2003–2009[30]

Year	*Required Agreements*	*Fulfilled Agreements*	*Exemptions (1)*
2003	9,114	951	N/A
2004	5,540	1,568	N/A
2005	3,758	1,683	46,383 (2)
2006	22,958	5,795	220
2007	16,690	5,485	181
2008	15,147	4,655	183
2009	N/A	5,219	109

(1) Since 2006, only exemptions on medical grounds are mentioned.
(2) The figure is mentioned in the reply by the Minister of the Interior to a parliamentary enquiry from the Green Party and obviously concerns exemptions according to the rules for the integration agreement as of 2003.

A different picture emerges if the type of fulfilment of the contract is analysed. As explained above, since 2006 completing school in Austria or belonging to the category of 'key personnel' is counted as fulfilment of the integration agreement, without the need to attend an integration course or pass a test. The data provided in the replies from the Ministry of the Interior to the parliamentary enquiries by the Green Party give an overview of the types of fulfilment of the integration agreement from 2006 to 2009.

Table 2: Types of fulfilment of the integration agreement[31]

Year	*Completed education in Austria, key personnel, etc.*	*Proof of German skills by a certificate from a certified institute*	*Other (integration course)*	*Total*
2006	3014	110	2671	5795
2007	2564	122	2799	5485
2008	2759	157	1739	4655

As the data show, only between 37% and 51% of all fulfilments of the integration agreement are based on participation in German and integration courses, most are based on the completion of schooling or vocational education in Austria.

Neither the implementation nor the effects of the integration contract have been evaluated yet. Only a small, 10-page study on 'quality monitoring' is available, published by the Austrian Fund for Integration, the institution responsible for the administration of the courses and the integration examinations, on the Fund's web page.[32] The study was based

30 Own calculations based on Parliamentary Enquiry by Member of Parliament Weinzinger and friends regarding the integration agreement of 17 January 2008, 3347/J XXIII. GP, answered by the Ministry of the Interior on 14 March 2008 (3352/AB XXIII GP); Parliamentary Enquiry by Member of Parliament Korun and friends regarding the so-called integration agreement of 8 July 2009, 2638/J XXIV. GP, answered by the Ministry of the Interior on 8 September 2009 (2707/AB XXIV GP).

31 See footnote 24.

32 ÖIF 2009, http://www.integrationsfonds.at/fileadmin/Integrationsfond/3_integrationsvereinbarung/downloads/IV_Qualit%C3%A4tsmonitoring_final.pdf.

on 84 interviews with officials, 81 interviews with representatives of institutions offering courses, 154 students and 263 students who had already successfully finished their course, and a psychological profile analysis of a further 115 respondents. According to the study, most participants had a positive attitude towards the agreement (54% very positive, 25% positive);[33] 95% of the respondents would also attend a course in German if it were not compulsory, and more than 75% wanted to continue with a course at the next level. The vast majority agreed that they had profited from the course in their private and professional life (ÖIF 2009: 7f.) The teachers interviewed stressed their high motivation and mainly suggested ensuring greater homogeneity with regard to educational background and language competence in the mother tongue on the courses, improvements to the teaching material and the possibility of extending the course length if needed (ÖIF 2009: 11).

Several diplomas, M.A. or Ph.D. theses deal with the present integration contract, but only a few publications are available in scientific journals. Of the theses and academic articles dealing with the integration contract, the majority focus on the political debate surrounding the implementation of the contract or on comparisons with other countries that require fulfilment of integration conditions.

The first study, analysing the political debate surrounding the introduction of the integration agreement, was the diploma thesis by Rohsmann (2003). Scheck (2003) gives a critical analysis of the content of the integration contract and points to the lack of clarity about the goal of integration characterising the contract. Schmiederer (2008) analyses the history of the concept of integration as far as the 1970s and focuses on the shift in the concept of integration from social inclusion to a duty-based approach akin to assimilation. The diploma thesis by Mitis (2003), as well as the article by Feik (2003), compare the Austrian integration contract (as of 2003) with integration courses in Denmark, Germany, the Netherlands and Sweden.

While the aforementioned works concentrate on an analysis of policy documents and scientific literature and analyse the contract implemented in 2003, both the M.A, thesis by Vavken (2009) and the Ph.D. thesis by Mourão-Permoser (2010) include the results of empirical research and analyse the reformed integration contract of 2006. Vavken's M.A. thesis discusses the integration contract in the context of modern theories of justice and argues that the compulsory character of the courses can be justified with reference to the obligation of the state to ensure immigrants' ability to take part in society, which might entail the use of obligations in exchange for an enhancement of abilities. Based on standardised interviews with 258 participants in the integration courses, the author argues that the courses were well-accepted by immigrants and supported their personal development and ability to participate in society.

Mourão–Permoser's Ph.D. thesis in political sciences (2010) contrasts the political debate surrounding the integration agreement with its practical implementation, using interviews with experts and officials form the relevant ministries as its main source. According to the author, the pure linguistic focus and the pragmatic nature of implementation stand in sharp contrast to the martial political rhetoric in the political debate, which portrayed the contract as a tool to weed out immigrants not ready to integrate. The massive difference between the political rhetoric and the actual implementation of the tests would give reason

33 ÖIF 2009, p. 5.

to conclude that their implementation might only be a symbolic exercise to communicate a restrictive approach to immigration to the electorate.

6. The Integration Agreement in the View of Immigrants and Experts

6.1 The View of the Immigrants

The fieldwork for the study was done in Vienna and Wiener Neustadt in Lower Austria in spring and summer 2010 and thus refers to the legal regulations applicable at that time. Interviews were conducted with seven teachers of language training centres offering courses for the fulfilment of the integration contract, six local officials, five representatives of migrant NGOs and twenty five immigrants attending the courses.

In general, all immigrants attending the courses were eager to learn German, because they felt that a sound knowledge of German was a precondition for living in Austria and, in particular, for success on the Austrian labour market. Most often, the respondents were convinced that they would be able to obtain a permanent residence permit after fulfilling the agreement.

Only a few respondents criticised the obligatory character of the course. A few respondents stressed that the obligation would help them to concentrate on learning German. One respondent said: 'If there were no obligation, I would concentrate on finding a job immediately and would not spend so much time learning German. So probably I would only find a bad job. So I am concentrating on learning German and hope to find a better job later.' Some similar statements stressed the need to speak German well in order to find a qualified position – those not able to communicate well in German would only find menial jobs in tourism or the catering or cleaning trade. Another respondent saw the obligation as a positive act by Austria vis-à-vis its immigrants, comparing the situation with parents who also have to put pressure on their children to do their homework sometimes. All the respondents stated that they would also have attended German classes if they were not obligatory. In general, the respondents were quite optimistic with regard to their chances of success and stressed the high quality of the courses, their highly motivated teachers and the good preparation for the examination.

The respondents were generally well-informed about the requirements of the test and the testing procedure. In Vienna, nearly all had been informed about the duty to fulfil the integration requirement and the courses they had to take through the 'Start Vienna' programme. In Lower Austria, the respondents criticised the fact that they did not receive any information from the authorities, but only were informed by the teachers at their language training institute.

Between half and two-thirds of the respondents found the costs of the course rather high. Acknowledging the refund from the Ministry of the Interior (and in the case of the Viennese respondents, from the Viennese government), they pointed to the requirement to pay the total costs in advance and obtain a refund later. Some of them mentioned that they had to borrow the money to pay for the course from friends and relatives. In this respect, most interviewees also mentioned the high income requirements, and not the language test, as the biggest hurdle for gaining access to a permanent residence permit.

The majority of the interviewees agreed that level A2 was not high enough for successful participation in Austrian society, particularly not on the labour market. In this respect, many interviewees criticised the lack of vocational language training and mentioned the problems of acquiring knowledge of the German terms and phrases for tools and processes used in their profession. The lack of financial support for courses leading to a higher level of German was also mentioned critically by many interviewees. Many respondents also mentioned that there was not enough time to learn about life in Austria and that they would be eager to learn more about Austria's society and culture.

6.2 The View of the Teachers

In the view of the teachers the major problems were the different learning experiences and capabilities of the participants. The courses are generally not differentiated by the level of education of the course participants, but by the level of knowledge of German. This educational lack of homogeneity has been described as a major challenge and a problem by all teachers interviewed or, as one teacher mentioned, 'the carpenter is sitting next to the university professor'. According to her, this could provoke a mismatch between group dynamics and learning dynamics: after two or three weeks, the differences in learning speed would become obvious and grow, whereas at the same time group cohesion would develop so that people would not want to switch to another course, even if this would be more suitable for their learning capabilities.

All teachers mentioned that, with the exception of the specific youth courses and the 'Mummy learns German' courses offered only in Vienna, students came from all social groups and age groups. One teacher mentioned that her oldest pupil was a woman of 72 who came to Austria for family reunification and was required to fulfil the agreement despite her age. The educational backgrounds ranged from illiterates to university professors.

According to the teachers, a growing number of asylum-seekers were also attending the courses. Although they were not obliged to do, proof of having passed the language examination would be regarded as a sign of readiness for integration in the appeals procedures in the event of a negative asylum decision. This group did not receive any financial support. The second group without support was European Union citizens from the new member states, a growing number of whom also attended the course to learn German. Although, in most cases, they were living under comparable financial circumstances to immigrants from Turkey, they did not receive any support. Most of them complained of discrimination against third-country nationals.

All teachers reported a high degree of motivation to learn German among the participants. Several teachers mentioned the problem that level A2 was too low for integration into the labour market, but no funding was available for students taking further courses, so many immigrants wishing to improve their German could not attend the courses because of the high costs.

Most teachers had a positive, yet critical view of the effects of course attendance on integration. They stressed that learning German and being able to communicate and take part in society would enhance the self-esteem and self-assurance of the immigrants. Particularly, women coming to Austria for an arranged marriage at an age between 18 and 20 would benefit from the chance to meet other women and see life outside of the family. In this case, the obligation to fulfil the agreement was helpful, because otherwise their husbands would not allow them to leave the home. Furthermore, attending the course and meeting other immigrants in a positive learning setting made them reflect on their motives for immigration and their future in Austria and made them psychologically stronger. From a functional point of view, fulfilling the integration agreement was a precondition for labour market integration and participation in the labour market-oriented courses of the Austrian Labour Market Services and thus directly contributed to integration into the labour market. But the level of the courses was by no means sufficient for success on the labour market.

Nevertheless learning German would only be one aspect of integration, many teachers mentioned. Integration would become a catch-phrase with no meaning and lead to false conclusions: for example, someone could be well-integrated into the labour market but only have friends in his community – according to current understanding he would not be integrated, which would include the idea of the state controlling his private life and be based on a nationalist understanding of Austria as a community of German-speakers. There were many non-integrated German-speakers, as well as persons with no migrant background who had problems taking part in society. The current discourses gave the impression that integration only applies to immigrants. Instead, one should ask about integration for the poorly-educated and the life opportunities they have. The term 'integration' was nothing more than a synonym for membership of the middle classes.

In general, the teachers were fairly critical of the 'one size fits all' approach taken by the integration agreement. Reaching the required A2 level was no problem at all within the 300 hours for academics or for those with a sound educational background and used to learning, but it did pose significant problems for those with a low educational level and little learning experience or low self-esteem. 'Students coming straight from school could easily reach level B1 in 300 hours, whereas an illiterate person might need 600 hours or more to reach A2', a teacher commented. Furthermore, the level A2 was too low for success on the labour market, but as there was no support for reaching a higher level, many immigrants interested to further improve their German would not be able to attend further courses.

In general, it would take between 6 and 12 months to take the examination. Depending on the educational background of the participants, between 85% and 95% of students passed the examination at the first attempt. Those who failed most often passed at their second or third attempt. A few of these then disappeared and those who really could not pass the examination were advised to obtain an exemption certificate from a public health officer.

Most teachers were very critical of the intention of the Ministry to raise the required level of language competence to B1, because the step between A2 and B1 would not be the same as between A1 and A2. Since only another 300 hours were foreseen, it was very likely that the vast majority of students would be able to pass the test successfully. In general, the courses needed more individualisation and a closer association with the living conditions of the students.

6.3 *The View of the Local Officials*

In Vienna, the magistrate has developed a guidance and counselling programme called 'Start Vienna' that is offered to all newly-arrived immigrants. Immigrants attending the counselling session and the information programmes offered in their mother tongue receive a voucher worth up to EUR 300 to be used to pay for the integration courses. According to the interview with the leading civil servant in charge of the programme, around 95% of the newly-arrived immigrants take part in the programme.

The 'Start Vienna' programme consists of a counselling meeting, when immigrants are advised on what language courses to take and informed about the possibilities for vocational training and guidance in their mother tongues or a common language. If necessary, interpreters are present. Counsellors are placed in the department responsible for issuing residence permits so, in practice, a 'one-stop-shop' situation is created.

Clients can return to 'second-level support' if they have further questions. Furthermore, three meetings are held on Saturday evenings, informing immigrants in their mother tongues or a common language about the residence law, the education, health and social systems, the labour market and 'do's and don'ts' of everyday life. Furthermore, a telephone hotline was also set up, offering counselling in eight languages. A webpage (www.start-wien.at) gives further information in fifteen languages and offers an internet-based search for appropriate courses.

Clients receive a 'Viennese education passport' including the vouchers for EUR 300, in which all courses attended and examinations taken are registered. This passport is accepted by the labour market authorities as proof of attendance of the courses, so that the clients do not need to bring all their certificates. In 2009, 2,887 'Viennese education passports' had been issued and therefore 79% of all immigrants who had been issued a first-time residence permit by the City authorities had attended the 'Start Vienna' programme. Furthermore, 5,484 persons had attended the 233 weekend information sessions offered by the magistrate.[34]

In Lower Austria, no comparable counselling structure exists. The immigrants are informed of their duty to fulfil the integration examination by a leaflet written in German, which has to be signed, and are given the addresses of language schools. Thus the teachers in the schools have to do the counselling, which was a major cause for complaint among them.

Although the officials working for the 'Start Vienna' programme were critical about the obligatory character and preferred an incentive system, they also mentioned that this obligation was extremely helpful in making women attending the course. Many men, particularly from Turkey, Asia or the Arab world, who had had an arranged marriage and brought their spouse to Austria, tried to circumvent the agreement and asked whether it was not possible to teach their wives themselves. In these cases, it proved very helpful to point out the obligatory nature of the courses and the potential loss of the residence permit in cases of non-compliance. Then the men agreed to their spouses' attending a course. Additional, women-only courses were available, where these women were sent. Attending the course genuinely strengthened them and gave them the opportunity to get to know other people and interact outside the family. The main positive effect in this case was not so much learning German, but socialising with other women and developing a life outside the family.

According to the officials interviewed, the contract put great pressure on many immigrants because they were not used to learning. One particular problem was the lack of funding for further German classes after reaching level A2. In their counselling sessions, they tried to inform their clients about training possibilities funded by the Labour Market Authorities and to help them gain access to these measures, since otherwise their learning efforts tended to grind to a halt.

34 Start Wien – Überblick 2009, photocopy provided by the MA 17, Magistrate of the City of Vienna.

Most officials stressed the positive effects of the courses. By attending the courses and learning the language, the self-esteem of the immigrants and in particular of immigrant women, was boosted and they were prevented from regression and depression, which was often a reaction to an immigration situation. Nevertheless one should overlook negative aspects, like the threat of losing the residence permit, which only served to generate stress and indicated that immigrants did not belong to society. The language courses should be transferred to a system of incentives and information on the rights of immigrants, of women and children, and protection from discrimination should be included.

6.4 The View of Immigrant Organisations and Advice Centres

Whereas the advice centre representatives and the representative of the women's' organisation mentioned regular enquiries about the integration agreement, the immigrant organisations interviewed did not provide counselling in this field. According to the advice centre representatives, they received about 30 calls per week concerning the integration requirement. Many of these calls did not come from Austria, but from abroad, e.g. from Serbia, and the callers wanted information about which conditions had to be fulfilled for family reunification. The Austrian clients most often needed information regarding the complex calculation of the income required to obtain access to a permanent residence permit.

The high income requirements for receiving a permanent residence permit constituted a huge problem. A growing number of people who had attended the course and passed the examination still were not granted a permanent permit, only a one-year permit, because they did not fulfil the income criteria. In general, people regarded attendance on the course as an obligation, not as coercion. Only a few questioned why they had to fulfil the agreement, most saw it as legitimate that the state should require them to learn German.

All representatives of immigrant organisations and advice centres saw the integration agreement as a barrier to permanent residence. In particular, they criticised the costs and the flexibility of the courses, clearly differentiating between Vienna, where offers of advice by the City and the flexibility of the course providers were regarded positively, and other states, e.g. neighbouring Lower Austria, where no counselling or support structure existed. A further criticism concerned the length of the courses, which were seen as not long enough for poorly-educated people and as not allowing enough time to learn about Austria's history and society. The knowledge acquired was not sufficient for success on the labour market, but there was not enough support for acquiring a better knowledge of German.

The requirements requested and their effects were discussed critically by the respondents. As one respondent stated, 'It is not what you say, but how you say it': no sensible person would argue against learning the lingua franca of the state in which one is living and everyone was aware of the importance of learning German. But the way integration is discussed in public conveys the message that the immigrants do not want to learn German and thus have to be forced to do so. Instead of, say, improving immigrants' chances on the labour market, the measures have instead aggravated and emotionalised the political discourse. No-one discusses the fact that society has to make integration possible by providing opportunities for social mobility, accepting immigration as a reality and welcoming immigrants' (Interview with Immigrant Advice Centre Vienna).

All interviewees agreed that there was a need for better differentiation of the courses depending on the educational background and needs of the students. At the moment, all courses follow the same programme because the law did not allow for differentiation, so it is difficult to adjust to personal learning speeds and learning methods.

7. Conclusions

Whereas the political debate on the integration agreement focused on its function of differentiation between immigrants ready to integrate and those rejecting integration and on preventing immigration into the welfare system, in practice language acquisition is the only target of the integration agreement, which does not include any element beyond language learning.

Given the way the agreement is implemented, several questions concerning its effects do arise: at first, it is interesting to note that no consideration was given to the integration of European Union nationals or long term resident asylum seekers. If, as stated by the law, knowledge of German was a precondition for participation in the societal, economic and cultural life of Austria, there is no valid reason why this should not also apply to Union citizens unfamiliar with the German language. Union citizenship bestows a privileged legal status, but nothing automatic as regards societal integration. If learning German is deemed an essential precondition for the societal integration of third-country nationals, there is no good reason why Union citizens should be able to integrate without this knowledge, except for the unspoken provision that integration was not a target for Union citizens residing in another Member State.

On the other hand, asylum seekers, who quite often stay in Austria for more than five years until their case is decided, also do not have any access to language training or other integration measures. The argument for their exclusion is, that integration only is foreseen for those aspiring the status of a long term resident immigrant, which by definition is not accessible for asylum seekers. Only recognised refugees are offered to attend integration courses, but are not obliged to do so; rejected asylum seekers do not have access to any integration support, even if they have to be granted a right of residence due to humanitarian reasons or non-refoulement clauses. Both exemptions reflect a rather legalistic understanding of integration neglecting the vast body of integration research results in the social sciences.

Secondly, the provision of Art 14 NAG, stating that belonging to the group of key personnel and their family members automatically includes fulfilment of the integration contract, also raises some doubts concerning the fact that a certain income might automatically lead to participation in society, even with no knowledge of German. This idea is particularly questionable, since the income threshold is set at a certain percentage of the maximum pensionable income. Earning one euro less will not grant access to the status of key personnel and thus the person concerned will have to fulfil the integration contract as a precondition for participation, whereas a monthly income one euro higher should automatically entail seamless and guaranteed participation in society. In practice, this legal regulation produces the effect that the number of fulfilled integration contracts communicated to the press and the public is much higher than the number of persons who actually and successfully attend a German language course.

As of July 1, 2011, the situation will change insofar as all labour immigrants entering Austria will fall under the regulations of the newly established points system ('Red-White-Red-Card'). All persons falling into this scheme will be deemed to automatically having proven a knowledge of German at the level A2 - but will have to proof knowledge of German at the level B1 after five years to be granted permanent residence.

Regarding the implementation of the courses, we note the development of a dual approach leading to two different types of course curricula and examinations. This dual approach is most obviously due to a power struggle between the Ministry of the Interior and the Ministry of Education. It is astonishing that, given the pressure to apply efficient budgeting, the existing framework of the Austrian chapter of the ELFR was not used to implement the integration contract, but instead the Ministry of the Interior or, rather, its outpost, the Austrian Fund for Integration, developed its own curriculum and its own testing material.

The 'one-size-fits-all' approach selected obviously does not produce the best results for students. Whereas younger and well-educated pupils were able to reach level B1 in the 300 course hours, this does now allow time for literacy and students with a low level of education might be attracted to learn only for the examination.

According to most interviews, attending the German courses empowers the immigrants and helps them to take part in everyday life. The immigrants attending the courses were eager to learn the language and were highly motivated. In this respect, one of the targets, the ability to participate in societal life, has been upheld by the courses. Nearly all the interviewees agreed that the level of knowledge of German was far too low to participate successfully in the labour market, so that the target of better participation in economic life obviously has not been reached. In this respect, the lack of financial support for further improving one's knowledge of German has to be questioned critically. As the amendments of 2011 will reduce refunding to reaching the level A2, but demand reaching the level B1 after five years, language acquisition will again stronger be linked with the income situation of the person concerned and thus further social divisions among the immigrant population.

Nearly all respondents answered that they did not learn very much about society and politics in Austria – which in public is regarded as the content of the integration courses. In practice, Austria's integration agreement is better described as a language acquisition agreement. In this way, the meaning of integration is reduced to attending a German course and taking a language examination.

Finally, it has to be noted that only a small number of those who were legally obliged to fulfil the integration agreement by 2011 have already done so. The authorities do not know about their whereabouts – some may have left Austria, others might not have been aware of the consequences. Stunningly, no public debate is evident concerning the consequences – loss of the residence permit and possibly expulsion – that might become evident in 2011. A certain number of court cases dealing with the compatibility of the threat of expulsion with Art. 8 of the European Human Rights Convention should be anticipated for 2011. Furthermore, access to the status and rights of a long term resident third country nationals will be hampered in the case of non-fulfilment of the integration agreement.

According to the government, naturalisation should be the culmination of integration. With regard to this idea, we would expect to find an elaborate curriculum leading from the integration contract to naturalisation. In reality, virtually no connection exists between these elements. The integration contract comes at the beginning of the settlement process and naturalisation can only be achieved after ten years of residence. After fulfilling the integration contract, no formal or informal contacts take place between the state authorities and the immigrants regarding naturalisation. Interestingly, the integration contract and naturalisation require the same level of competency in German and set the same income requirements, which stands in sharp contrast to the idea of an integration process culminating in naturalisation. The naturalisation tests themselves do not reflect the actual participation of immigrants in society or their potential contribution to the future of Austria, but follow the line of a didactically old-fashioned *Staatsbürgerkunde* (civic knowledge), which is far removed from modern concepts of civic inclusion and citizenship education.

Overall, the structure of the sequence from the integration contract to naturalisation lacks clarity and consistency. Symbolic messages to the public seem to have been more important than a sound and scientific path towards naturalisation. Furthermore, the lack of evaluation, in particular with regard to the long-term effects of the courses and the lack of public discourse on the effects of the courses are unbelievable.

It is not possible to answer the question about the effects of the courses on migrant integration because no studies on this topic exist. The opinion of the interviewees was divided: while some of them argued that attending the courses and learning the language generally enhanced the self-esteem and self-assurance of immigrants and forced them to plan their future life more carefully, others were critical that language learning alone would not improve their position on the labour market or eliminate structural discrimination.

References

A) Sources

Amt der Wiener Landesregierung (2002) *Entwurf eines Bundesgesetzes, mit dem das Fremdengesetz 1997 (FrG-Novelle 2002) und das Asylgesetz 1997 (AsylG-Novelle 2002) und das Ausländerbeschäftigungsgesetz geändert werden; Begutachtung; Stellungnahme*; MD-VfR - 410/02, 16 April 2002.

Amt der Wiener Landesregierung (2005a), *Entwurf eines Bundesgesetzes, mit dem das Niederlassungs- und Aufenthaltsgesetz erlassen wird sowie das Fremdengesetz 1997, das Gebührengesetz 1957, das Familienlastenausgleichsgesetz 1967 und das Kinderbetreuungsgeldgesetz geändert werden; Begutachtung; Stellungnahme*; MD-VD - 602-1/05, 19 April 2005.

Amt der Wiener Landesregierung (2005b), *Entwurf eines Bundesgesetzes, mit dem das Staatsbürgerschaftsgesetz 1985 (StbG) und das Tilgungsgesetz 1972 geändert werden; Begutachtung; Stellungnahme*, MD -VD - 1565-1/05 Vienna, 17 October 2005.

BKA (Bundeskanzleramt) (2000), *Regierungsprogramm 2000*, http://www.bka.gv.at/2004/4/7/Regprogr.pdf, download 12 February 2006.

BKA (Bundeskanzleramt (2002), *Entwurf eines Bundesgesetzes, mit dem das Fremdengesetz 1997, das Asylgesetz 1997und das Ausländerbeschäftigungsgesetz geändert werden; Begutachtungsverfahren*, GZ 602.846/001-V/A/5/2002.

BKA (Bundeskanzleramt) (2003), *Regierungsprogramm 2003*, http://www.bka.gv.at/2004/4/7/Regierprogr28.2.03.pdf, download 12 February 2006.

BKA (Bundeskanzleramt) (2008), *Regierungsprogramm 2008-2103, Gemeinsam für Österreich*, http://www.bka.gv.at/DocView.axd?CobId=32965, download 22 December 2008.

BMBWK (Bundesministerium für Bildung, Wissenschaft und Kultur) (2002), *Entwurf eines Bundesgesetzes, mit dem das Fremdengesetz 1997, das Asylgesetz und das Ausländerbeschäftigungsgesetz geändert werden*, Stellungnahme zu Zl. 76.201/617-V/1/b/02 vom 5.3.2002.

BMI (Bundesministerium für Inneres) (2002), *Entwurf eines Bundesgesetzes mit dem das Fremdengesetz 1997, das Asylgesetz 1997 und das Ausländerbeschäfigungsgesetz geändert wird, Begutachtungsverfahren*, BMI 76.201/617-V/1/b02.

BMI (Bundesministerium für Inneres) (2010a), *Nationaler Aktionsplan für Integration*, http://www.integrationsfonds.at/fileadmin/Integrationsfond/NAP/nap_bericht.pdf, download 23 January 2010.

Helping Hands (2005), *Stellungnahme*, 36/SN-259/ME XXII. GP.

Kramer, Helmut (2010), *Stellungnahme zum Skriptum zur Vorbereitung für die Prüfung gemäß §10a des Staatsbürgerschaftsgesetzes 1985. Teil I Demokratische Ordnung*, 3 February 2010, Manuscript.

Krumm, Hand Jürgen (2005), *Stellungnahme im Rahmen des Begutachtungsverfahrens zu dem Bundesgesetz mit dem das Niederlassungs- und Aufenthaltsgesetz erlassen sowie das Fremdengesetz 1997, das Gebührengesetz 1957, das Familienlastenausgleichsgesetz 1967 und das Kinderbetreuungsgeldgesetz geändert wird*, 9/SN-266/ME XXII. GP - Stellungnahme zum Entwurf.

Parlamentsdirektion (2005), 952 der Beilagen XXII. GP – Regierungsvorlage – Materialien.

Statistik Austria (2009), *Allgemeiner Einkommensbericht 2008*, http://www.statistik.at/web_de/statistiken/soziales/personen-einkommen/allgemeiner_einkommensbericht/index.html, last visited 7 July 201.

Stojsits, Terezija (2005), *Abweichende persönliche Stellungnahme gemäß § 42 Abs. 5 GOG der Abgeordneten Mag.a Terezija Stoisits zum Bericht 1055 der Beilagen über die Regierungsvorlage (952 der Beilagen): Bundesgesetz, mit dem das Bundes Verfassungsgesetz geändert wird, ein Asylgesetz 2005, ein Fremdenpolizeigesetz 2005 und ein Niederlassungs- und Aufenthaltsgesetz erlassen sowie das Fremdengesetz 1997, das Bundesbetreuungsgesetz, das Personenstandsgesetz, das Bundesgesetz über den unabhängigen Bundesasylsenat, das Einführungsgesetz zu den Verwaltungsverfahrensgesetzen 1991, das Sicherheitspolizeigesetz, das Gebührengesetz 1957, das Familienlastenausgleichsgesetz 1967, das Kinderbetreuungsgeldgesetz und das Tilgungsgesetz 1972 geändert werden (Fremdenrechtspaket 2005)*, 1055 der Beilagen XXII. GP - Ausschussbericht NR.

B) Literature

Çinar, D. & H. Waldrauch (2006), 'Austria', in: R. Bauböck, E. Ersbøll, K. Groenendijk & H. Waldrauch (eds), *Acquisition and Loss of Nationality. Policies and Trends in 15 European Countries*, Vol.2, Amsterdam (AUP), p. 19-63.

Einem, Caspar (1990), *Alternative Optionen der Zuwanderungspolitik*, unpublished manuscript, Vienna (private archive of the author).

Feik, Rudolf (2003), 'Verpflichtende Integrationskurse in der EU', *MigraLex* 2003/ 1, p. 53-58.

Hauer, M., N. Reisinger & A. Stangl (2008), '"Lernen Sie Geschichte!" Eine kritische Analyse der Vorbereitungsunterlagen zum Staatsbürgerschaftstest aus "Geschichte Österreichs"', *ÖDAF-Mitteilungen*, Heft 2/2008, p. 69-82.

Nationaler Kontaktpunkt Österreich im europäischen Migrationsnetzwerk (IOM) (2005), *Integationspraktiken in Österreich. Eine Landkarte über Integrationspraktiken und -philosophien von Bund, Ländern und Sozialpartner*, Vienna (IOM Österreich).

Koller, Jan (1998), *Kommunale Integrationspolitik. Eine Analyse des Wiener Integrationsfonds im Kontext sozialdemokratischer Interessenspolitik*, Diploma Thesis, University of Vienna.

König, K. & B. Perchinig (2003), 'Austria', in: J. Niessen & Y. Schibel (eds), *EU and US approaches to the management of immigration. Comparative perspectives*, Brussels (Migration Policy Group), p. 13-47.

König, K. & B. Perchinig (2005), 'Austria', in: J. Niessen, Y. Schibel & C. Thompson (eds), *Current Immigration Debates in Europe. A Publication of the European Migration Dialogue*, Brussels (Migration Policy Group), p. 11-52.

König, K. & B. Stadler (2003), 'Normative und rechtliche Rahmenbedingungen. Entwicklungstendenzen im öffentlich-rechtlichen und demokratiepolitischen Bereich', in: H. Fassmann & I. Stacher (eds), *Österreichischer Migrations- und Integrationsbericht. Demographische Entwicklungen – sozioökonomische Strukturen – rechtliche Rahmenbedingungen*, Klagenfurt/Celovec , p. 225-261.

Mitis, I. (2003), *Die österreichische 'Integrationsvereinbarung' im Vergleich mit Integrationskursen in anderen europäischen Staaten*, Diploma Thesis, University of Vienna, Vienna.

Mourão-Permoser, Julia (2010), *Redefining Membership. European Union Policy on the Rights of Third Country Nationals*, Ph.D. Thesis, University of Vienna.

Nationaler Kontaktpunkt Österreich im Europäischen Migrationsnetzwerk (IOM Vienna) (2005*), Integrationspraktiken in Österreich. Eine Landkarte über Integrationspraktiken und -philosophien von Bund, Ländern und Sozialpartner*, Vienna (IOM Vienna).

ÖIF (Österreichischer Integrationsfonds) (2009), *Qualitätsmonitoring zur Umsetzung der Integrationsvereinbarung*, http://www.integrationsfonds.at/fileadmin/Integrationsfond/3_integrationsvereinbarung/downloads/IV_Qualit%C3%A4tsmonitoring_final.pdf, download 11 March 2010.

Perchinig, B. (2006), 'Einwanderungs- und Integrationspolitik', in: Emmerich Talos (ed.), *Fünf Jahre Schwarz-Blau. Eine Bilanz des 'Neu Regierens'*, Münster/Vienna (LIT-Verlag), p. 295-312.

Perchinig, B. (2009), 'Von der Fremdarbeit zur Integration? (Arbeits)migrations- und Integrationspolitik in der Zweiten Republik', in: *Österreich in Geschichte und Literatur (ÖGL)*, 53. Jahrgang 2009, Heft 3, p. 228-247.

Perchinig, B. (2010), 'All you need to know to become an Austrian: Naturalisation Policy and Citizenship Testing in Austria', in: R. van Oers, E. Ersbøll & D. Kostakopoulou (eds.), *A Redefinition of Belonging? Language and Integration Tests for Newcomers and Future Citizens*, Leiden/Boston (Koninklijke Brill NV), p. 25-50.

Rohsmann, K. (2003), *Die 'Integrationsvereinbarung' der Fremdengesetznovelle 2002. Integrationsförderung durch Sprach(kurs)zwang?*, Diploma Thesis, University of Vienna, Vienna.

Scheck, R. (2003), *Sprache und Integration. Eine Untersuchung der Integrationsvereinbarung auf ihre Tauglichkeit zur Integration*, Diploma Thesis, University of Vienna, Vienna.

Schmiderer, St. (2008), *Integration: Schlagwort – Zauberwort – hohles Wort. Eine historische und begriffliche Auseinandersetzung im Kontext der österreichischen Immigrationsgeschichte (1970-2005)*, Diploma Thesis, University of Vienna, Vienna.

Stern, Joachim (2010), *Ius pecunia – Staatsbürgerschaft zwischen ausreichendem Lebensunterhalt, Mindestsicherung und Menschenwürde*, Paper presented at the First Conference of Austrian Migration Researchers, Vienna, 21 September 2010.

Vavken, B. (2009), *Verhilft die Integrationsvereinbarung MigrantInnen in Österreich zu 'Chancengleichheit' und 'Beteiligungsgerechtigkeit'? Eine Analyse der Integrationsvereinbarung 2002 und der NAG 2006 im Kontext genderrelevanter Aspekte aus moralphilosophischer Perspektive*, MA Thesis, University of Vienna, Vienna.

Waldrauch, H. & D. Çinar (2003), 'Staatsbürgerschaftspolitik und Einbürgerungspraxis in Österreich', in: H. Fassmann & I. Stacher (eds), *Österreichischer Migrations- und Integrationsbericht. Demographische Entwicklungen – sozioökonomische Strukturen – rechtliche Rahmenbedingungen*, Klagenfurt/Celovec (Drava), p. 261-284.

Weiss, Alexandra (2006), *Bildungschancen von jugendlichen Migranten in Tirol*, Projektbericht, University of Innsbruck.

Pros and Cons of Compulsory '*Inburgering*': Mapping the Views of Newcomers in Flanders and in Brussels

Zeynep Yanasmayan & Marie-Claire Foblets[*]

I. Introduction

The management of cultural diversity is a widely debated topic in Europe. Governments have attempted to address this issue in a variety of ways and with different policies. In recent years, mandatory integration courses and tests have come to the fore and enjoyed public visibility. They have also become highly interlinked with citizenship policy and have been transformed into requirements for the acquisition of nationality. While the use of these new instruments of integration has increased, little is known about their actual effects. Taking this lack in the literature as its starting point, the INTEC (Integration and Naturalisation Tests, the New Way to European Citizenship) project seeks to first provide an overview of the integration tests of nine European countries and then to compare their effects.

The case of Belgium is unique in that its absence of integration tests makes it an 'outlier' amongst the other countries under scrutiny. In order to understand this divergence, it is useful to provide elucidation about the federal system in Belgium. Belgium is composed of three regions (the Flemish Region, the Brussels-Capital Region and the Walloon Region), and three linguistic communities (the Flemish Community, the French-speaking Community and the German-speaking Community). Competences are intricately distributed between the different levels of governance. Within the current system, the federal government is in charge of legislating with respect to nationality.[1] On the other hand, the Communities are the sole responsible bodies for putting forward integration policies. This structure enables separation of the issues of nationality and integration and an option to be independent from each other. The Belgian Code of Nationality[2] in its present form does not require foreigners to provide proof of integration while naturalising. The Act of March 2000,[3] by removing the condition of proof of 'willingness to integrate' and reducing the length of residence required to three years, has made Belgium a country with one of the most liberal legislations in Europe (De Hart & Van Oers 2006; Loobuyck & Jacobs 2006; Foblets 2006; Foblets & Loones 2006). Recent public debates have seen proposals to reverse this trend and re-introduce the integration condition[4] and we briefly touch upon these developments in our concluding remarks.

---

* The authors are grateful to all their respondents for sharing their opinions. Special thanks to Ekaterina Dzhioeva for her invaluable assistance in conducting the interviews.

1 Art. 8 and 9 of the Belgian Constitution.

2 28 Juin1984, Loi relative à certains aspects de la condition des étrangers et instituant le Code de la Nationalité belge, *Moniteur Belge*, p. 10095.

3 1er Mars 2000, Loi modifiant certaines dispositions relatives à la nationalité belge, *Moniteur Belge*, p. 10829.

4 On these recent debates see: Foblets 2011.

With regard to the integration policy, the Flemish Region is the only governance level endowed with a mandatory measure.[5] Newly arrived immigrants in Flanders are entitled to, and some are obliged, to follow an integration programme that comprises societal, vocational and linguistic courses. Nevertheless, the obligation is so far limited to attendance at these courses and there is no official examination to assess the end result. Moreover, as we have described above, attending or not attending the programme has no impact on the acquisition of nationality, or on any residence status for that matter. In brief, unlike other countries in the INTEC research, in Belgium the link between the nationality legislation and integration courses is entangled.

This situation led us to focus on the mandatory integration courses, endorsed as formal policy by the Flemish authorities since 2003, rather than the nationality legislation. The policy is officially entitled '*inburgering*' in Dutch and we refer to it with its original term for 'integration' does not entirely echo the meaning. *Inburgering* denotes the process of 'becoming a citizen', where one is familiarised with the functioning of a society.

The policy of *inburgering,* and hence the entirety of the integration trajectory, is also at the disposal of migrants who come to settle in Brussels. Even though the Flemish government cannot impose it outside the boundaries of Flanders, the offer is still available on a voluntary basis. We noted this differentiation in practice and reflected it in our research design by selecting two cases, namely Brussels and Antwerp.

The methodology of this report is identical to the other national reports within the framework of the INTEC research. It is based partly on the analysis of public debates and existing literature. However, empirical data gathered through face-to-face interviews constitutes the most important source of information. We conducted 34 interviews in total with stakeholders: four with pre-eminent NGOs[6] that have throughout the years accumulated a deep knowledge of the field; five with social orientation course teachers, five with public officials who are in direct contact with migrants and twenty with migrants who have participated in or are currently participating in the courses.[7] The INTEC coordinators designed the questionnaires for all four types of actors. However, due to Belgium's situation, with the coordinators' approval we revised the questionnaires to a certain extent, and particularly included questions about voluntary measures.

Migrants who wish to, or are obliged to, follow integration courses should apply to the reception centres for *inburgering* in their towns. Therefore, our main point of contact in order to reach our respondents was the reception centres in Brussels (hereafter referred to as Bon) and in Antwerp (hereafter referred to as Atlas). It should also be borne in mind that, except for two migrant respondents who were personal connections, all the interviews were arranged by them. Again, with the exception of these two interviews, they all took place in the reception centres. The interviews in Bon and Atlas took in total approxi-

5 Such a mandatory measure has been discussed in the Walloon Parliament on 14 March 2012 but the proposed decree had failed to pass. See on the website of the parliament the proposed Decree 405 (2010-2011) — N° 2.

6 Coordination et Initiatives pour et avec les Réfugiés et Étrangers (CIRÉ), Foyer, La Voix des Femmes, Young Women's Christian Association – Women's Intercultural Centre (IVCA-YWCA).

7 In Brussels, we had three interviews with the social orientation course teachers, three with individual counsellors and eight with migrants who had participated in the classes. In Antwerp, we had two interviews with the social orientation course teachers, two with individual counsellors and twelve with migrants who had participated or were participating in the classes.

mately one and a half months, starting at the end of April and ending at the beginning of June 2010. NGO interviews were also conducted during this period. The length of the interviews differed from informant to informant: between one and a half to two hours with NGO staff, between one to one and a half hours with individual counsellors, approximately two hours with social orientation teachers and approximately half an hour with migrants, with a few exceptions. This schedule required us to make at least three visits to the venues.

Generally speaking, our respondents were welcoming and happy to find a channel through which to make their voices heard. Even though we followed the guidelines provided in the questionnaires, we left space for personal opinions and experiences. In this sense the interviews could be said to have been semi-structured, particularly in the case of migrants. In our interviews with the migrants, we deliberately sought to ensure diversity in our sample. Therefore, it included people with different nationalities, coming from different educational backgrounds and having followed alternative paths in the integration trajectory. The latter means that whereas some of them only received the initial social orientation course and the first level language course, some others continued further studies and made use of the vocational training offered by the Flemish Employment Service (*De Vlaamse Dienst voor Arbeidsbemiddeling en Beroepsopleiding* hereafter referred to as the VDAB) or the like. We obviously took into account the impact that this difference might play in participants' discourses. For instance, a migrant who had not completed the whole trajectory and who, thus, had not followed specialist courses in the VDAB would be more likely to evaluate the programme as less useful for finding a job. Therefore, their appraisals should be seen in this light. Other demographic details are catalogued as follows: 13 out of 20 migrants were female; they were between 26 and 49 years old with a majority in their mid-twenties and thirties. In terms of nationality distribution, we had a great variety: four Moroccans, three Turkish, one Vietnamese, two Tibetan, one Togolese, one South African, one Congolese, one Peruvian, one Jordanian, one Ukrainian, one Iraqi, one Polish, one Moldovan and one Ivorian.

In this report, by looking at two different cases, Bon and Atlas, we seek to examine two aspects of the *inburgering* policy. First, we attempt to shed light on the practices of implementation through the accounts of our respondents. The second objective is to portray the 'perceived effects' of the courses on the lives of migrants. An underlying investigation that we try to achieve by means of the comparative approach is to observe whether there is a difference between mandatory and voluntary measures. We remain reserved in our conclusions and prefer to employ the term 'perceived effects' as the outcomes of a qualitative research are very contingent on the choice of respondents. Not only did we not have control over this process, we also did not reach the migrants who did not attend the courses[8]. This is obviously pertinent for Brussels where participation is entirely voluntary, as well as for Flanders where some migrants simply pay the fine to avoid attending the classes. Due to this sampling strategy, as a rule, the qualitative research was not expected to produce generable results. Nonetheless, the data collected was more in-depth, intelligible and equally policy-relevant.

8 See recent research conducted by HIVA: http://www.hiva.be/resources/pdf/publicaties/R1332.pdf. Their sample also includes people who preferred not to attend the courses.

II. *Inburgering* Policy in Flanders: An Ambitious Political Project

The policy of *inburgering* was first set up by the Decree of 28 February 2003[9] and amended twice, by the Decree of 14 July 2006[10] and by the Decree of 1 February 2008.[11] Whereas the former amendment was aimed at enlarging the target group of the policy, the latter was steered towards making it compatible with the changes regarding asylum applications that had been made to the Foreigners' Law.[12]

The Decree defines *inburgering* as an interactive process that implies rights and duties both for the newcomers and for the Flemish government. The *inburgering* policy strives to create a society based on the values of shared citizenship and of active participation.[13] The concept of *inburgering* is innovative in that it accentuates the commonalities on basic grounds, such as knowledge of the Dutch language, while respecting diversity and different backgrounds. 'The individuality and cultural identity of each citizen needs to be respected, within a set of prevailing norms and values that are to remain the cornerstones of the democratic society' (Gsir *et al.* 2005: 10). Moreover, the policy is now supplemented with the concept note of 15 July 2011[14] which reforms the area considerably by re-baptising the previously minorities policy[15] as integration policy[16] and merging it with the *inburgering* policy. This concept note is expected to lead to a framework decree on integration and *inburgering* in 2012 (Flemish Parliament 2011: 6).

The implementation of *inburgering* calls for a policy of assistance to the newcomers during the first period of their stay. This is, thus, attained through the offer of citizenship trajectories (*inburgeringstrajecten*). The citizenship trajectories are composed of two complementary parts. The first route is the commonly known trajectory that is mandatory for certain groups of people. The second route is, on the contrary, not compulsory since it goes beyond the acquisition of basic knowledge of society and of the language and is, rather, a quest for improving professional skills. This second trajectory does not specifically target immigrants; it is available to everyone eligible for this route. It consists of one-to-one guidance in relation to the future professional itinerary of the newcomer and of specific training. This second route is only available upon completion of the first route and it seeks to help immigrants to fully participate in Belgian society, especially with regard to access to the

9 28 Februari 2003, Decreet betreffende het Vlaamse inburgeringsbeleid, *Moniteur Belge*, p. 24937.

10 14 Juli 2006, Decreet tot wijziging van het decreet van 8 februari 2003 betreffende het Vlaamse inburgeringsbeleid, *Moniteur Belge*, p. 5999014.

11 1 Februari 2008, Decreet tot wijziging van het decreet van 28 februari 2003 betreffende het Vlaamse inburgeringsbeleid, *Moniteur Belge*, p. 108511.

12 15 Decembre 1980, Loi sur l'accès au territoire, le séjour, l'établissement et l'éloignement des étrangers, *Moniteur Belge*, p. 63341.
Following the changes in the asylum application procedure the target group of the *inburgering* policy began to include asylum seekers who had submitted an application more than four months previously instead of asylum seekers whose applications have been declared admissible.

13 Article 2§1 of the 14 juli 2006, Decreet tot wijziging van het decreet van 8 februari 2003 betreffende het Vlaamse inburgeringsbeleid, *Moniteur Belge*, p. 5999014.

14 Vlaams Parlement 1266 (2011-2012) – Nr. 1.

15 Decreet van 28 april 1998 inzake het Vlaamse beleid ten aanzien van etnisch-culturele minderheden, *Moniteur Belge*, 19 Juni 1998.

16 Decreet [betreffende het Vlaamse integratiebeleid (verv. decr. 30 april 2009, art. 2)] tot wijziging van het decreet van 28 april 1998 inzake het Vlaamse beleid ten aanzien van etnisch-culturele minderheden (1), *Moniteur Belge*, 19 Juni 1998.

labour market.[17] The first part of the *inburgeringstrajecten* is, nevertheless, more in the foreground as it includes a wider range of people, due to its compulsory nature. It includes three different programmes: language courses (Dutch as a second language NT2), social orientation and vocational guidance. Moreover, an individual counselling system during the entire programme completes the scheme.[18]

The target group for the *inburgering* policy was initially designed through two criteria: 1) being recently registered in a Flemish or Brussels municipality for the first time; 2) reaching the age of majority.[19] It was tailored only to newcomers who had arrived in Belgium for non-temporary purposes. With the 2006 amendments, the target group has widened significantly, particularly with the inclusion of the established immigrants of non-EU origin, including Belgian nationals born outside Belgium (known as 'oudkomers'), within the scope of the Decree.[20] Ultimately, the target group of the Decree of 2006 as a whole consists of adult foreigners staying in Belgium for non-temporary purposes and adult Belgian nationals who were born outside Belgium and who have at least one parent born outside Belgium. This obviously leads to a much more diversified list of persons, ranging from asylum-seekers who submitted their asylum applications more than four months previously, to Belgian nationals who are receiving social security assistance.

The target group is divided into three categories: compulsory participants, those who are granted priority and those who are not. Compulsory participants are foreigners who have been registered in Belgium for less than twelve months, religious ministers, asylum-seekers who submitted their asylum applications more than four months previously and 'oudkomers' who are dependent on social assistance (i.e. *Centre public d'Assistance sociale* CPAS or in Dutch *Openbaar Centrum voor Maatschappelijk Welzijn* OCMW[21]). This latter category depends on the organisation.[22] The priority group is mainly composed of persons who will be included in the mandatory group eventually, such as resident immigrants with school-age children or immigrants who are renting or are on a waiting list to rent community housing in the Flemish Region. Priority is also given to family members of EU nationals (not Belgians) and minor migrants who have recently arrived.[23]

---

17 Article 4§2 of the 28 februari 2003, Decreet betreffende het Vlaamse inburgeringsbeleid, *Moniteur Belge*, p. 24937.

18 Article 8 and Article 13§1 of the 28 februari 2003, Decreet betreffende het Vlaamse inburgeringsbeleid, *Moniteur Belge*, p. 24937.

19 Article 3§1 of the 28 februari 2003, Decreet betreffende het Vlaamse inburgeringsbeleid, *Moniteur Belge*, p. 24937.

20 Article 3§1 1 of the 14 juli 2006, Decreet tot wijziging van het decreet van 8 februari 2003 betreffende het Vlaamse inburgeringsbeleid, *Moniteur Belge*, p. 5999014.

21 Literally translated as Public Centre for Social Action, CPAS/OCMW is the institution that offers social assistance both financially and psychologically to the most disadvantaged groups in Belgium (i.e. persons who cannot receive an unemployment benefit). CPAS/OCMW operates in a decentralised way; each municipality has a CPAS/OCMW section where the demands are assessed case-by-case.

22 Article 12 of the 14 juli 2006, Decreet tot wijziging van het decreet van 8 februari 2003 betreffende het Vlaamse inburgeringsbeleid, *Moniteur Belge*, p. 5999014 promulgates that the CPAS/OCMW sends out a list of compulsory migrants each month to the reception centres.

23 Article 3§ 4 of the 14 juli 2006, Decreet tot wijziging van het decreet van 8 februari 2003 betreffende het Vlaamse inburgeringsbeleid, *Moniteur Belge*, p. 5999014.

A number of immigrant categories are exempt from the obligation to follow an integration programme. Since the EU Directive (2004/38)[24] on free movement forbids any impediment being imposed on the residence of EU citizens and EEA nationals and their family members, they are exempt from this obligation. In addition, persons who suffer from a serious illness or a mental or physical disability, those over the age of 65 and those who can prove their integration through certain certificates or diplomas are also exempt.[25] Lastly, labour migrants – with the exception of religious ministers – and their families who are assumed to have come for a limited period of time are categorised as exemptions. Two other groups are partly exempt and, therefore, do not have to follow the entire programme. Immigrants who have already fulfilled integration requirements in another EU Member State in order to obtain long-term resident status (in accordance with Article 5 of Directive 2003/109/EC)[26] are only required to attend Dutch language classes.[27] Secondly, asylum-seekers who have submitted their application at least four months previously have to follow the civic orientation part of the trajectory.[28]

In order to register for an integration programme, both newcomers and 'oudkomers' are expected to apply to the reception centre (*onthaalbureau*) of their province once they have registered in a Flemish municipality. In total, there are eight reception centres: one in each of the five provinces (Antwerp, Limburg, East Flanders, Flemish Brabant and West Flanders) and three in the major cities of Antwerp, Ghent and Brussels. There, newcomers sign a 'contract of civic integration' concerning their individual programme. After an initial assessment at the reception centres, migrants are directed to the responsible bodies for different aspects of the programme. Usually, the programme begins within three months of the newcomer's application to the reception centre and overall the training should not last more than one year.[29]

At the end of the courses, an attestation is granted to the migrants who have attended 80% of them. The obligation in Flanders limits itself to attendance; there is no official examination or test that assesses the skills learned on the trajectory. However, the amended Decree offers the possibility of introducing such a test, which seems to be taken off again after being on hold since 2008. An evaluation instrument is to be developed within the course of 2012. The result of that evaluation combined with an A2 level language ability will allow the migrants to receive a certificate of i*nburgering*. None of these measures are in place yet but the Ministry plans to start issuing such certificates by the end of 2012 (Flemish Parliament 2011: 16).

24 The Directive 2004/38/EC on the right of citizens of the European Union and their family members to move and reside freely within the territory of the EU, *Official Journal of the European Union*, L 158 of 30 April 2004.

25 Article 5 § 2 of the 14 juli 2006, Decreet tot wijziging van het decreet van 8 februari 2003 betreffende het Vlaamse inburgeringsbeleid, *Moniteur Belge,* p. 5999014.

26 The Council Directive 2003/109/EC of 25 November 2003 concerning the status of third-country nationals who are long-term residents, *Official Journal of the European Union*, L 16/44 of 23 January 2004.

27 Article 5 § 6 of the 14 juli 2006, Decreet tot wijziging van het decreet van 8 februari 2003 betreffende het Vlaamse inburgeringsbeleid, *Moniteur Belge,* p. 5999014.

28 Article 5 § 7 of the 1 februari 2008, Decreet tot wijziging van het decreet van 28 februari 2003 betreffende het Vlaamse inburgeringsbeleid, *Moniteur Belge*, p. 108511.

29 Article 12 § 2 of the 14 juli 2006, Decreet tot wijziging van het decreet van 8 februari 2003 betreffende het Vlaamse inburgeringsbeleid, *Moniteur Belge,* p. 5999014.

Instead a test that exempts migrants who already possess the necessary knowledge is designed by the University of Antwerp[30] and has already been put into practice in 2011 as a pilot. The Ministry following an evaluation in June 2011 decided to continue the practice of exemption tests, which aims to give the authorities the means to see whether or not a particular person truly needs the social orientation courses. The pilot test that ran through January to December 2011 was in place in Brussels, Antwerp and Ghent only. Since the test is a multiple-choice test, whose content is not public there is a need to expand the amount of questions and to develop a self-study book for migrants who choose this method. By the end of 2012, the Ministry intends to develop these instruments and inquire the possible link between the exemption test and a final evaluation instrument (Flemish Parliament 2011: 23).

As for the sanctions, failure to comply can result in a fine of between 50 and 5000 euros.[31] A fine can also be imposed if the person refuses to cooperate with his or her integration programme or to sign an integration contract. Moreover, failure to complete the integration programme might give rise to the withdrawal of social benefits for people sent by the CPAS/OCMW.

III. *Inburgering* in Practice

An Inquiry into the Perceptions of the Stakeholders of Inburgering

Following the synopsis of the legal basis of the *inburgering* policy, in the following sections we explore the empirical realities concerning the practices and the perceived effects of the policy. These sections draw entirely on the analysis of the qualitative data. Conforming to the framework of the INTEC project, we acted in accordance with the guidelines of the questionnaires. This implied a certain order for the questions, particularly for the migrant interviews: we began with their main reasons for attending the courses, continued with their personal experiences of the courses also including the problems encountered and ended with their evaluations of the courses' utility. Therefore, our report to a certain extent follows the same structure but we also broach several other matters relating to the practices of *inburgering*. Our focus is, nonetheless, inclined towards the social orientation courses as they are, in our view, much more telling with regard to the understanding of 'integration' in the Flemish context since their purpose is to teach the very basics of Belgian/Flemish society to the newcomers. We complemented our presentation with the accounts of the policy executers where relevant.

The questionnaires give prominence to the knowledge of language and of the majority society and seek to see to what extent migrants judge this information to be important for their lives. Besides replying positively to the few direct questions on these topics, a large number of migrants themselves raised the importance of speaking Dutch. Below we describe the various expressions of this in a more detailed way for each of our cases. We were

30 Information gathered from our interviews with the Flemish Ministry of Integration within the framework of a previous study: Foblets & Yanasmayan 2010.

31 Article 25 § 2 of the 14 juli 2006, Decreet tot wijziging van het decreet van 8 februari 2003 betreffende het Vlaamse inburgeringsbeleid, *Moniteur Belge*, p. 5999014.

generally keen to leave enough room for individual articulations and refrained from suggesting answers. A second dimension that came up naturally were the positive repercussions of the courses for the newcomers not only in terms of the acquisition of knowledge but also as a social space. The courses ensured their gradual familiarisation with the social and cultural environment and as a process entrenched the feeling that they are not alone.

Analytically, we kept Brussels and Antwerp as separate cases even though they did not display strikingly different pictures. This was intended for facilitating our later discussion on the obligation. We devoted distinct sub-sections to making the differentiation clear unless the issue at hand was irrelevant for a case or no worthwhile difference was noticed in the discourses.

Motivations: Readiness to speak Dutch

Brussels

Since participation on the courses is voluntary in Brussels, we were more persistent in discovering the factors that influenced migrants' decision to attend them. Following our questionnaire, we paid particular attention to the significance of the acquisition of linguistic skills and knowledge of the majority society.

To start with the language, it would be safe to claim that there was a prevailing awareness that knowledge of the language was pivotal for genuine settlement in the country of residence. Several reasons were given to explain why speaking the language mattered. Two of them stand out as being of crucial importance to almost everyone. First of all, the newcomers were eager to learn Dutch with a view to becoming active in the labour market. Speaking Dutch in Brussels, which is a bilingual region, has become a valuable asset, even a necessity for employment, in recent years. However this should not be seen as a pragmatic involvement since this attitude also conveys an affirmation of their future life in Belgium. This links us to the second reason that was stated unequivocally: the ability to communicate with others. They recognised Belgium as a Dutch-speaking country and displayed a lively interest in understanding its inhabitants and in being understood. Not everyone explicitly mentioned integration as a goal in itself, however similar concerns were raised. For instance, one participant referred to a climate of exchange that was generated by speaking the language and regarded it as '*a way of showing respect to the country that welcomed him*'. Some also evaluated it to be personally rewarding and asserted that speaking the language increased their self-confidence or made them feel comfortable in the society.

Respondents also alluded to personal feelings when questioned about the importance of acquiring knowledge of the majority society. Independence was a theme that recurred in several interviews. They put forward the empowering role of knowing 'how to do things' in a society as a stimulus for attending the courses. They thus thought from the beginning that this knowledge would assist them to stand on their own feet or, as lucidly formulated by a respondent, would give them the assets to be their *own guide in life*. This desire for independence and self-sufficiency usually went hand in hand with an acknowledgement of long-term settlement in Belgium. Although we discuss the content of the courses in the next section, it is worth mentioning here that familiarisation with the laws of Belgium was an influential factor in their judgement. They were interested in discovering the boundaries of the public sphere and the rules to which they were subject. Equally important was learning about their rights.

Looking at the Decree that establishes the legal basis for the *inburgering* policy[32] allows us to see that the migrants' intentions are well in line with the legislator's expectations. The Decree in its amended form in 2006 emphasises promoting the autonomy of the newcomers. A shift in discourse from making migrants familiar with their new environment to promoting their autonomy is noticeable in the amendments made in 2006.[33] The emphasis is reinforced by the new teaching method that has replaced the lecture system with a seminar-like system where participants are encouraged to seek information themselves and participate with their own presentations. Our expert interviews also support this perspective on the part of the public officials.[34]

Antwerp

In Antwerp, our emphasis was less on their private motivations since the assumption was that they had to follow the courses regardless of their interest. To our surprise, half of our respondents did not mention the obligation amongst their reasons for participating in the integration programme. Instead they focused on the necessity of speaking Dutch in daily life in Antwerp and expressed their willingness to learn it. A French-speaking respondent compared the lack of Dutch knowledge to being blindfolded. This elegant metaphor manifests the weight of learning Dutch in the unilingual region of Flanders. Amongst the other half who mentioned 'being obliged' as a reason for attending the classes, many were happy to have done it and valued highly the information they received. There were, nevertheless, a few people who appeared dissatisfied with the courses and mentioned that they would not have gone to the classes had they not been obliged to do so. We expand on this discontentment in the part where we discuss the perceived effects of the courses in Antwerp.

Participation Rate[35]

Brussels

In a number of cases, the motive behind applying to Bon's services has been an interest in learning Dutch. Migrants come to Bon because they hear about its reputation and also the funding it provides for language courses through their social circles. Social orientation courses have, thus, been a bonus that has assisted them much more than they expected. At this initial stage, a limitation with regard to implementation, which relates to the channels of information can be identified. Bon has to rely on informal channels, such as social networks or personal campaigning by ex-participants during their official campaign period. Word of mouth is reportedly the most effective way of 'recruiting' participants. Bon's

32 Decreet van 8 februari 2003 betreffende het Vlaamse inburgeringsbeleid, *Moniteur Belge*, p. 5999014.

33 Please compare Article 2§1 of 28 februari 2003, Decreet betreffende het Vlaamse inburgeringsbeleid, *Moniteur Belge*, p. 24937, with that of the 14 juli 2006, Decreet tot wijziging van het decreet van 8 februari 2003 betreffende het Vlaamse inburgeringsbeleid, *Moniteur Belge*, p. 5999014.

34 Data obtained through interviews with teachers and personal counsellors in the reception centres.

35 For an analysis of the participation rates in all the reception centres, see a study conducted by HIVA about the efficiency & effectiveness of the *inburgering* policy http://www.hiva.be/resources/pdf/publicaties/R1331.pdf.

annual report for 2011[36] indicates that 36,5 % of the participants hear about the courses from previous participants and 9,6% hear about from friends and family. Approximately 20% are referred from the Houses of Dutch (*Huizen van het Nederlands*).[37] Lastly, specific campaigns account for 14,1% of the intake. The problem with informal channels despite their efficacy and persuasiveness is the absence of control over the content that is being transmitted. Nevertheless, because of its unique situation Brussels is unlikely to distribute information through more institutionalised channels, the exception being the Molenbeek municipality, which hands out Bon's brochure to newly registered persons. This notwithstanding, the system is well-established and has enjoyed increased numbers of participants, particularly after 2007 when the government decided to expand its staff. The number of signed contracts has augmented from 622 in 2006 to 1297 in 2007, 1540 in 2008, 1608 in 2009.[38] It made another jump in 2010 with 2097 contracts signed and kept increasing in 2011 with 2126 contracts.[39]

Antwerp

In Antwerp, the recruitment process is more straightforward by virtue of its compulsory nature.[40] In the last years' figures there has been no major fluctuation in the intake with the exception of 2010: 7,647 in 2006, 7,280 in 2007, 6,044 in 2008, 7,569 in 2009[41] and 11,200 in 2010.[42] Among those who presented themselves in 2009, 4,407 signed a contract. The signed contracts rate surprisingly did not increase as much as the intake did in 2010 and remained in a low 5,214.[43] Whereas 2,584 attestations were granted in 2009,[44] in 2010 there were 2,928 attestations.[45] This reveals that the completion rate of the trajectory has increased in recent years as an evaluation study conducted in 2007 indicated that 41.7 % of those who sign a contract successfully complete it (Lambert *et al.* 2007: 21). There has

36 Browsable from http://www.bonrapportannuel.be/fr/cursisten/http://www.bonvzw.be/files/Docs/Nieuws/bon_annual%20report%202009.pdf (retrieved 29 March 2012).

37 The Houses of Dutch are in charge of evaluating the level of Dutch knowledge of the participants and then assigning them to the education centres. Various institutions offer language classes, such as centres for basic education, for adult education and the university language centres.

38 Data accumulated through Bon's annual reports for the given years. Reports downloadable from http://www.bonvzw.be/en/b074763f-8523-4224-b1f0-eaf9ce78df6d.

39 Browsable from http://www.bonrapportannuel.be/fr/werving-amp-intake/ (retrieved 29 March 2012).

40 Also because the municipalities have a structural mission on informing all newcomers, and because the Flemish reception offices receive data (cevi-lists) through the administration in order to contact newcomers directly with a letter.

41 Data from the Atlas annual report of 2009 given by an Atlas official.

42 Data from the Atlas annual report of 2010 http://www.antwerpen.be/docs/Stad/Bedrijven/ Sociale_zaken/ SZ_Integratie/Jaarverslag_inburgering_2010.pdf (retrieved 29 March 2012).

43 It is hard to tell at this point if the low ratio is due to the limited capacity of placement of the reception centre or not but figures of upcoming years would be helpful in identifying the causes of this.

44 Data from the Atlas annual report of 2009 given by an Atlas official.

45 Data from the Atlas annual report of 2010 downloadable from http://www.antwerpen.be/docs/Stad/Bedrijven/Sociale_zaken/SZ_Integratie/Jaarverslag_inburgering_2010.pdf (retrieved 29 March 2012).

also been an increase in the number of contracts signed over the years: 2,285 in 2006, 3,798 in 2007, 4,201 in 2008.[46]

The full trajectory of integration is composed of three different areas of training (language, social orientation and vocational) as well as personal guidance throughout the whole process. The training is designed in a linear fashion: migrants start with the –normally- six-week social orientation courses and then continue with the language and vocational training respectively. Even though our focus is the social orientation courses, we touch briefly on the others as well.

Social Orientation Courses

Social orientation courses are conducted in a number of languages and migrants can choose to attend the course available in the language in which s/he can communicate comfortably. The list is impressive: French, Dutch, Arabic, English, Russian, Spanish, Persian, Turkish, Polish, Tibetan, etc. The groups are also divided by level of education if there is sufficient number of participants. Accordingly, three different groups can be formed: persons who are illiterate or have completed few years of schooling, persons who are university graduates and, finally, a mixed group in between. Occasionally, the results of the covert test employed by the Houses of Dutch as a means of assessing applicants' aptitude for learning are taken into account in this classification. Offering courses adapted to migrants' education level is an essential aspect for improvement of the efficacy of the policy. We have elsewhere[47] drawn attention to the need for a tailored approach that would allow the highly educated to be exposed to a more sophisticated programme and the less well educated to follow courses for a longer period of time. The teachers we interviewed confirmed the validity of this suggestion. They reported that they applied different teaching methods according to the education level of the participants. They gave the highly educated groups more autonomy by asking them to research a theme and present it in the class. In situations where the small number of participants did not permit separate classes, teachers tried to bridge the gap by assigning different homework. The highly educated category could also benefit from customised timing for classes – i.e. 60 or 40 hours of evening classes and Saturday classes. These practices all accentuate the significance of an interactive approach that aims to enhance the satisfaction of participants. Indeed these needs seem to be recognised by the latest policy note of the Flemish government that underlines the significance of a tailored offer (Flemish Parliament 2011: 22).

The content of the courses is determined based on a report of a commission of experts that has been created by the Flemish government.[48] The Commission was charged with suggesting a list of values and principles deemed to be the constituent pillars of Belgian/Flemish society (Foblets & Yanasmayan 2010: 289). The government then published a course book and related materials. It also prepared a teachers' guide in order to ensure that

46 *Ibid.*

47 See Foblets & Yanasmayan 2010.

48 It is important to mention that even before the process with the commission and climo, a common book was prepared by the reception centres that recognise the necessity of working together with professional material.

similar issues were addressed in the courses.[49] This new teaching method, 'climo', (cooperative learning in a multicultural environment) consists of asking the students the subjects they are interested in from the start and engaging them to participate. In Brussels, a week before the classes begin a meeting is organised by each teacher in order to collate the expectations of the students. In Antwerp, this is usually done during the first course where the students are provided with a suggested list of subjects. A number of themes recur in every session, namely legal residence issues, rights of foreigners, social housing and work-related questions. Additionally, some subjects are covered regardless of the demand for them, such as basic information about Belgium's history, geography and political system. The teachers are of the opinion that the new method, by increasing the flexibility of the thought material, has improved responsiveness towards the needs of the migrants.[50]

Brussels

When we juxtapose this with the concerns highlighted by the participants, an analogous picture emerges. The content of the courses is deemed to be very useful at different stages in their lives but particularly in the beginning. The courses provide them with a starting point by not only teaching a little bit about everything in Belgium but also by showing them ways to improve their knowledge. Evidently, they all valorise this knowledge according to their personal experience in life. Therefore, while some stress the importance of learning about rights vis-à-vis the landlords or the social security system that they were not aware of, others are simply happy to have acquired the tools to keep abreast of current events. Themes that pertain to subsistence such as housing, employment opportunities and health system have spontaneously featured in each interview. Transport also stands out as a helpful topic, particularly for migrants from African countries. A majority of the respondents also mentioned being pleased to learn about Belgian culture, Belgian history and its federal system. It can easily be claimed that they are satisfied with the curriculum as a whole. Only when asked specifically did a handful of people utter their wish to hear more about certain topics, such asylum and regularisation procedures. An exception to this promising picture was a respondent who judged the content of the courses as insufficient for her professional ambitions. It is worth expanding on her personal situation as it bears a general message. She came to Belgium six years ago as an asylum-seeker. After spending almost three years without a legal residence she received regular status, which allowed her to attend the courses in Bon. She was about to complete her 2.1. level Dutch course when we interviewed her but she was experiencing a lot of difficulty attending them since she had also had a baby in the meantime. Her family was dependent on a modest monthly CPAS/OCMW salary. The situation, which made it imperative for her to find a job immediately, discouraged her from following the VDAB courses. She wanted to specialise in care for the elderly but the training for it was too long, given her situation. Even though she appreciated what she had learned, especially about the different employment agencies she thought that the informa-

49 As pointed out by a teacher, some themes within the teachers' guide are not appropriate for Brussels as they apply uniquely in Flanders.

50 This is all the more important for Brussels where participation on the courses is voluntary. In addition to the classes both Bon and Atlas organise excursions to different places depending on the wishes of the participants. However, the greater number of such excursions is presented as a strategy on the part of Bon to attract a larger group of migrants.

tion would only be practical when she found a job. This example clearly illustrates that migrants with precarious economic (and legal) situations tend to attach only an instrumental value to the courses. This leads them to overestimate the outcomes of the courses and to a certain extent be disappointed. With a view to overcome such problems perhaps a more perspicuous communication strategy can be developed. It should be made clear to all stakeholders that the courses are meant to be a first step. The concrete outcomes are highly contingent on the situation within the labour market, as well as the social policies with regard to housing, discrimination and education. This would alleviate the burden on the shoulders of the *inburgering* policy by decreasing the expectation that it would offer a blanket solution to all the problems relating to integration.

Antwerp

It is difficult to offer a holistic picture of the situation in Antwerp as we encountered differing views. For instance, this singular case in Brussels was shared by a few more respondents, who expressed that the courses were of a general nature and that they were not helpful in terms of receiving concrete outcomes, such as finding employment. On the other hand, a large number of respondents were highly interested in the topics discussed in the classes. The coverage was deemed to be sufficient for different purposes. Most respondents emphasised the knowledge they had acquired about practical issues like filling in tax forms or insurance policies. Themes touching upon basic life realities were highly cited, such as transportation, the health system, public offices, etc. Again, many expressed appreciation of the documents[51] they had received during the courses and how useful they had been in daily life. Whereas some would have preferred the courses to be more detailed, others were of the opinion that the programme could have been completed within a shorter period. One respondent drew attention to the importance of the teaching skills of the teachers in rendering the course much more entertaining than set out in the book. Another respondent articulated his wish to have more excursions with a view to ensuring 'on-the-site' learning. Some also disapproved of the new method claiming that it was not easy for everyone to look things up on the Internet. A common complaint related to the speed of the procedure. A number of respondents reported having to wait approximately six months after their arrival before being placed on a course, a period during which they lost valuable time and motivation. In comparison to Brussels, it can be said that our respondents in Antwerp remained more critical of the integration programme. We examine below if this had any impact on the perceived effects of the courses.

Dutch as a Second Language and Vocational Guidance

Dutch language courses are administered through the Houses of Dutch, which assign migrants to education centres dispersed around the city. Within the framework of the integration programme, they have to complete at least one module whose duration can vary between 120 to 240 hours, depending on the education level of the applicant. In Brussels, there seems to be a shortage of schools offering 240-hour courses, which are high in de-

51 During the social orientation courses, a pack of documents including important addresses and phone numbers is distributed to the participants.

mand because of the large amount of people at that particular education level. This complicates the placement of migrants onto these courses and might in future cause delays, given the popularity of the courses. In Antwerp, delays for an adequate placement are already a major problem.

At the end of the language module the programme continues with a vocational course. In the mandatory form of the trajectory in Flanders this is given by the VDAB. The course, called 'Kiezen' - which means to choose in Dutch - teaches the participants about their options in the labour market and, accordingly, which training to follow. The attestation of integration is granted at the end of this course. Afterwards interested participants continue to the second trajectory and attend different occupational training courses that usually last between three months to one year. If the migrant already has a profession that s/he can perform in Belgium s/he can also follow customised language courses, like administrative Dutch, at the VDAB. In Brussels, there is a possibility to choose from different actors offering similar or more specialised services. A meeting is organised with the migrant, his/her individual counsellor, the VDAB and Actiris – the Brussels regional public employment service – at the end of the language module. If the migrant has had no previous knowledge of the Dutch language, his/her level is limited to the first module of 1.1. Yet the minimum level for starting the VDAB courses is 1.2. This situation creates irregularity from the point of view of consecutiveness of the trajectory. The reception centres do not finance further language modules but there are other possibilities for funding at the disposal of underprivileged persons.[52]

Challenges Faced by the Participants

Brussels

Clearly, the integration programme requires a considerable amount of self-involvement from the migrants and is a difficult road particularly for those with little education. Dropouts are mainly from this group for whom the trajectory lasts significantly longer. Since we had only one respondent who dropped out, it would not be correct to speculate in general terms. However his case still highlights the importance of a tailored approach. He was placed in a class that did not have a level distinction, which led him to quit after a few weeks. When he was called for a new opening he had already started working and thus could no longer attend the courses. Another example that hints at a need for a more flexible and tailored approach is the situation of the respondent who had difficulty attending the classes because of her baby. Notwithstanding this, our respondents were all determined to improve their Dutch knowledge mostly with the motivation detailed in the section above. Despite the hardship they faced in learning it, they perceived it as an indispensable item. In order not to lag behind the majority society, they agreed it is a fair price to pay. They were very proud when they see that they speak better Dutch than some people who have been in Belgium for several years.

Another hurdle that they face solely in Brussels with regard to language acquisition is that they rarely practice Dutch in their daily life. This is due to the fact that a majority of

52 The VDAB for instance finances the language courses for the migrants who have the intention of undertaking the training it offers.

the population of Brussels is French-speaking despite its official bilingual status. Having noticed the discouraging role the situation plays, Bon seeks to create alternative solutions, like conversation tables.

Antwerp

In Antwerp, the main challenge faced is the delay in the assignment to the appropriate classes. For instance, one respondent, after waiting months to be placed on a language course, had to drop out and wait for the next semester, as the course was not at beginners' level. The problem of waiting seems to be the case more for the language training than for social orientation. A large number of migrants reported difficulty learning Dutch. They particularly had a problem with pronunciation and conversation. Except for one respondent they were satisfied with the quality of the language courses. Another respondent was not pleased with the method of teaching in the language class. She found it frustrating that the teacher expected students to speak Dutch from the very first course. According to her, this exerted too much pressure on the students and did not leave space for them to figure out their learning skills. It must be also mentioned that this respondent had a personal issue with the language teacher, which might have contributed to her negative image.

The teachers and individual counsellors' impressions more or less coincided with the migrants. They indicated that the difficulties encountered were related to the education level, irrespective of cultural and sexual identity. A more alarming account given by the teachers pertained to their inability to reach certain groups of people who could benefit greatly from the courses. We elaborate on this while discussing the obligation.

Personal Guidance

The courses and training in the integration programme are complemented by a system of personal guidance (*begeleiding*) throughout the trajectory. This service is formally envisaged to last for a year but can take up to two to three years for illiterate people whose trajectory progress is slower. During this period, an individual counsellor is allocated to each participant. The individual counsellors' tasks are various: they ensure that the participant in question is appropriately placed on a course, they assist him/her in his/her endeavours to find suitable training, they organise meetings with different actors. In addition to these supervisory duties vis-à-vis the integration programme, they also provide personal 'coaching' to the migrants. Migrants are encouraged to ask their individual counsellors for help with any sort of problems they encounter. A good case in point is a respondent who mentioned calling her individual counsellor with a view to getting help for her emotional troubles and was referred to a psychologist.

Brussels

In our interviews with the individual counsellors in Brussels, we observed their diligent relationships with the participants. Migrants feel free to utilise their help for a number of issues. Individual counsellors function as a bridge that provides the contact with specialised agencies in problematic areas. For instance, a majority of the concerns focus on a professional career. Migrants are eager to know how to find work and where to look for it. They are then directed towards more specialised services for job hunting. It is the same for legal aid vis-à-vis their residence situations. Nevertheless, they personally deal with the issue of the recognition of diplomas. They also take it upon themselves to deal with daily problems that may arise with regard to housing, social security or schooling for those with children. It is part and parcel of their job to make phone calls to the institutions in charge or even to go in person if necessary. Housing in the Brussels region is particularly identified as troublesome, not least due to the exploitative behaviour of landlords.

Antwerp

In Antwerp, the tasks of individual counsellors are comparable to the ones in Brussels with one major difference. In Antwerp, they are also in charge of registering migrants, preparing their contracts and matching them with appropriate courses, whereas in Brussels a separate intake team is responsible for these administrative tasks. Our understanding is that this leaves relatively less time for individual counselling particularly given the larger number of migrants in Antwerp, due to the programme's mandatory nature. Whereas an individual counsellor deals with approximately 110-120 migrants in Antwerp, this number is about 80 in Brussels.

Financial Aspect of the Integration Programme

As opposed to some other European countries within the framework of the INTEC project, in Belgium the courses are free of charge. Even though the Decree offers the possibility to alter this practice in the future, to our knowledge it has not been executed so far. With a view to predicting what would change if the courses were to be charged, we asked our respondents whether they would be willing to pay. Considering that they were all unemployed when they began the courses, they expressed that they would have been rather reluctant. Therefore, charging fees for the courses may put, especially Bon, in a delicate situation by reducing the participation by migrants. Notwithstanding this, the intention of the policy-makers has never been to ask for a fee from underprivileged persons; if it is ever introduced it will be based on the income of the participants. The opinions of public officials are divergent on the topic, however they are all keen to preserve the good intentions of the courses. Some defend the current implementation believing that the offer of free and well-organised courses carries a welcoming message. A teacher in favour of free courses suggested that it would not be fair to ask the participants to pay insofar as there was no guarantee of finding a job after completing the classes. On the other hand, the argument in favour of introducing fees mainly attached to it a symbolic value as a means of handing over some responsibility to the migrants.

Possibility of a Test?

As we have explained in our introduction, integration policy and nationality legislation are competences that lie in different layers of governance in Belgium.[53] Therefore, in the current situation the attestation of *inburgering* does not have any impact on nationality acquisition. However, two developments are on their way, which make it hard to predict the

53 For further information on this discordance see Foblets & Yanasmayan 2010.

future. First, the Flemish government finally decided to introduce an evaluation for the social orientation courses after having put the idea aside for a while. Second, the government that has been formed after 541 days of political deadlock foresees in its December 2011 agreement[54] an amendment to nationality law,[55] which would restore the integration condition. Even though a direct link between the two does not seem very likely for the moment–also given that the Walloon parliament just refused a mandatory integration scheme-, it is still important to mention both planned changes. Different actors we interviewed hold different views vis-à-vis the practice of a test. We try to sketch these below.

Several migrants interviewed in Brussels and Antwerp were sceptical about the possible benefit a test would bring to the system. The information received was perceived to be practical rather than theoretical and thus needed to be internalised and 'performed' in daily life. Therefore, one could easily repeat the topics of study in a test but never use this knowledge later. The capacity that migrants should be endowed with in the end is rather to put into practice what they have learned. Some were categorically opposed to the practice of a test, judging it to be offensive for grown-ups. They mentioned having to deal already with a variety of problems in life and they were of the opinion that a test would only be an additional source of stress. On the other hand, there were few respondents, particularly in Brussels, who argued that a test would help them consolidate their knowledge. One respondent said she would have preferred having a test not for them to evaluate her but for her to assess the quality of the courses. Those who were in favour of the introduction of a test suggested having a differentiated system, which would not penalise illiterates and older people. Whereas the young and educated people could be expected to pass a test, the older and/or less educated should not be forced to take it. The respondents in Antwerp were more committed to the idea of a test that would enable migrants to be exempted from the courses.[56] In particular, respondents who had been living in Belgium for several years and who had to attend the courses later on in their stay preferred to have an examination as they were of the opinion that they already possessed the necessary knowledge. This remark also contains a hidden criticism with respect to the obligation to attend the courses in Flanders. Another alternative that was proposed was to link success in the test to more 'substantial' outcomes, such as the acquisition of nationality.

The views of public officials were more or less separated along the same lines. Following the logic introduced above, a teacher argued that the *inburgering* test should be extended to each part of the country and should be used as the basis for an eventual citizenship test. In contrast with all the other public officials we interviewed she subscribed to a more control-oriented mentality with regard to migration. She contended that migrants should 'deserve' to stay in the country of residence and the test would provide the only way to have 'good' foreigners. This approach differed sharply from the other respondents who considered the test to be coercive. They were worried that compelling migrants to take a test could endanger the bonds they had developed over time. Hence, presence in the class and collaboration with classmates were deemed to be more essential. They stressed that it would be unfair to expect the migrants to acquire a profound knowledge after a six-week course amidst all the

54 See page 134 of the Accord de Gouvernement accessible from http://premier.fgov.be/fr/accord-de-gouvernement-0.

55 Cf. *supra* note 4.

56 It should be noted that at the time of the interviews, the pilot project of exemption tests was not yet in place.

other worries they had vis-à-vis their lives. They also emphasised the incompatibility of a uniform test with the individualised approach that they maintained during the courses. Accordingly, the expectations a teacher developed vis-à-vis one migrant differed widely from another one and thus could not be tested in the same manner.

Reception Centres as Social Spaces

The last aspect that we explore is the impression that the participants maintain regarding their time in the reception centres. Since observing individual perceptions is an unfamiliar approach in policy studies, this particular aspect of implementation often goes unnoticed. However, after having gathered the testimonies of migrants we are convinced that personal relationships between migrants and public officials constitute an important part of the implementation. Particularly in the case of the *inburgering* policy, the contact with the individual counsellors and teachers constitutes in most instances the migrants' first long-term interaction with the majority society.

Our respondents in both Brussels and Antwerp held a very high opinion of this first encounter. They all reported that they had been treated in a very friendly and kind manner. However this seemed to have been taken to another level in Brussels.[57] The positive relationships they maintain have nourished their feeling of belonging: many mention that they feel at home in Bon. The allegiance to Bon remains very strong for migrants who attended the courses years before. Nearly all our respondents were working for Bon voluntarily either by helping with translations or by attending their campaign day/week.

Both Bon and Atlas indeed truly reflect the dual meaning of the French word *accueil*: they not only receive migrants they also welcome them. This feeling also seems to be reinforced, thanks to the representation of diversity within structure. Especially for newcomers who do not speak any of the national languages of Belgium, it is the only place where they can socialise and communicate with others.

The teachers' accounts confirm this positive influence the receptions centres have on the migrants. An additional interaction they point to is between traditionally conflicting groups within the same social orientation course, such as Russians and Chechens both following classes taught in Russian. Therefore, migrants not only learn how to engage with Belgian society but also with a multicultural society.

IV. What are the Effects? A Critical Appraisal by the Target Group

The aim of the *inburgering* policy, as stated by the Decree, is to achieve a cohesive society based on the values of shared citizenship and active participation. The integration programme thus appears as a means to this end, which would, on the one hand, promote foreigners' autonomy and on the other contribute to their recognition as fully-fledged members by the majority society.[58]

57 We prefer not to link this merely to the voluntary nature of the courses as it might simply be due to the lower number of people involved, which makes the atmosphere cosier.

58 Cf. *supra* note 10.

Brussels

Returning to the point mentioned in the motivations section, we can claim that the message of autonomy was clearly conveyed to the participants. They almost unanimously gave accounts of their newly acquired capacity to act on their own due to the information they had received. One respondent referred to the courses as an eye-opener that enlightened her about her life choices. Moreover, they reported that they had a better understanding of Belgian society and their own rights after the classes. They also showed interest in the recent political crisis in Belgium and stated that they would have been unable to comprehend the political sensitivities had not they known about Belgium's history.

Since *inburgering* as a term implies 'feeling acquainted or feeling at home', we also inquired about substantive dimensions of citizenship, such as belonging. We addressed two specific questions to the participants and came across a variety of answers. The first was whether they felt a member of the society, which is one of the purported aims of the *inburgering* policy. All our respondents in Brussels demonstrated a certain sense of affiliation. Even though the list cannot be considered exhaustive, we have attempted to display the different elements that appeared to foster feelings of membership. One element touches upon the idea of engaging with the community. Participating in cultural events, volunteering in Bon or other civil society organisations and thus being in touch with different strata of the society seemed to generate feelings of belonging. At times, this idea is entangled with the previously described phenomenon of autonomy. Hence, some of the responses were along the lines of '*Yes, I feel very good as I can stand on my own feet*' or '*I feel I have to say something if it is not the way it should be*'. One respondent regarded participation on the courses as a contribution to Belgian society and expressed being proud of having contributed. On the other hand, two out of nine respondents in Brussels explicitly mentioned their discontent with the racism within society. One Moroccan respondent, pointing to the problem of stereotyping, felt the burden of being constantly perceived as someone involved in terrorist or criminal activities. The other remark related to another widely known stereotype about migrants 'stealing the jobs' of the majority society. They both identified these personally experienced behaviours as racist and an impediment to their successful integration.

This last comment makes the connection with the second question we addressed to our respondents, namely whether the courses made them feel more integrated into the majority society. A common point that emerged from all the interviews conducted is the necessity to consider the courses as the first step of a long journey. If the policy-makers wish to obtain a more accurate and realistic picture of the effects of these courses, this should be borne in mind. Otherwise, the policy is deemed to fail, due to unfeasible expectations that it cannot deliver. The courses do provide the basics for daily life in Belgium and offer the migrants the tools to successfully cope with it. They also give them a very elementary level of Dutch that can be improved upon by willingness on the part of the migrants. And, lastly, the VDAB courses or their alternatives in Brussels give them valuable hints about their options in the Belgian labour market. Nonetheless, all these need to be supported by surrounding structures that are of vital importance for the lives of the newcomers and that altogether compose the public sphere, such as housing, the health system, employment, education and the like. These structures are precisely the spaces where the interaction that would lead to integration takes place. The courses can thus smooth access to them but cannot guarantee them. On the other hand, improved levels of integration are also contingent on the migrants' own agency in pursuing further what they have learned in the courses. Therefore, the purpose of the courses should be clearly codified as encouraging migrants to make this further step rather than assuming the journey towards integration will be accomplished at the end. In this sense, the reframing of the sector as integration and *inburgering* and the explicit recognition of this aspect in the latest policy note of the Flemish Ministry should be promoted.

The concept of the courses as a first step was widely accepted by the migrants. One respondent's allegory perfectly exemplifies this:

> 'I see Bon as customs; you have to change your jacket at the entry in order to melt into the society. Some people do not go further than the courses, it is up to each and every one of us to enrich what we have gained.'

Some hinted at the need to access other wider structures referred to above but mainly the labour market. They indicated that they would feel more integrated once they were employed, as this would give them the opportunity to interact with different levels of society. Even though the courses had not had a direct impact on their employment status, they had been introduced to different agencies, which had facilitated the process for job hunting. Volunteering in civil society organisations was perceived as an alternative way of reaching and of being active in these structures and thus increasing integration.

A rather unanticipated outcome is how much these courses have been influential in their self-development as social beings. A number of them have acquired or enhanced their hobbies through their encounters in Bon and some of them have actually turned them into their professions. They have been put in contact with other voluntary groups and encouraged to pursue social activities. The activities in which they are now involved are as diverse as poetry, film-making, music and voluntary translation. This reveals that alongside the concrete material information they have received in these courses, equally important are the deeper and positive psychological consequences.

Antwerp

An observation at first glance is the number of people who report being dissatisfied with the courses. Although our methodology, which is qualitative in nature, does not allow us to establish causal relationships in order to explain this difference with Brussels, our belief is that it cannot be solely attributed to sampling strategies. Even a simplistic account of human psychology would reveal that one tends to like something more when the activity is chosen out of free will. Hence it was not surprising to hear statements like '*I would not have gone if I wasn't obliged to*' in Antwerp.

Notwithstanding this, they uniformly stated that their understanding of Belgian society increased after the courses. Learning about the laws and their rights had endowed them with the capacity to become more intensively involved in the society. One respondent declared that it was the way she perceived Belgians that had changed. Now that she could speak Dutch she felt that she had increased levels of friendly exchanges. She thus concluded that the problem had stemmed from her previous lack of linguistic skills rather than a cultural clash. This is precisely the kind of thinking the *inburgering* policy aims to achieve. An interesting discourse we encountered only in Antwerp was the concern they had with regard to their classmates, particularly the migrants who had been living in Belgium for several years. Some referred to them as an obstacle during the courses. Since they were not interested and eager to learn, they ended up compromising the positive effects for everyone. A parallel discourse was about the importance of the courses for this specific group who were perceived to '*stay in their neighbourhood and have no contact with Belgians*'. In order to see the extent the discourse reaches it is useful to directly quote an example:

> 'Actually these courses have nothing to do with Belgium, it is rather aimed to mobilise the uneducated. There is nothing substantial, I only learn things that I cannot learn from my fiancée. I feel as much part of Belgian society as I used to feel before. I see it more as an eye-opener for the uneducated'.

This creates a very paradoxical situation in the sense that it is either 'motivated newcomers' or 'uneducated' established immigrants who belong to the courses but not both at the same time. This reveals that merging these two groups with different problems was perhaps not initially thought through. We return to this point below.

Faced with the question of whether they felt a member of the society after the course, an overwhelming majority of our respondents replied positively. They affirmed feeling more at ease in the society after becoming acquainted with Belgians. One respondent who had grown up in the Netherlands – who thus spoke the language prior to the classes – mentioned that he had been more reserved before and that the courses had helped him to open up. Another respondent stated that the courses helped him to better understand not only Belgian society but also a variety of people coming from different cultural backgrounds. For some, the positive affiliation was conditional on external factors, such as receiving a legal status or obtaining a job. Some respondents' articulation of belonging took their own established communities in Belgium as a reference point, and not necessarily in a positive way. A Turkish migrant reported feeling closer to Belgian society than to the Turkish community members who had been there for several years. A similar account was given by a Moroccan migrant. This might also have been due to the fact that the persons from these established communities who attended the courses were the ones who had been in a way 'penalised' because of their failure to find employment. Yet for some others, their national culture's habitual traits remained very strong and seemed to constitute a reason for alienation from Belgian society, at least initially. One respondent, for instance, categorically refused to be identified as Belgian:

> 'I cannot be a member of Belgium as I will always remain Turkish/a part of Turkey. I am a Turkish who spends a period of her life in Belgium. I am not, I cannot be.'

Comparatively speaking, we received more affirmative answers to our question about integration in Antwerp than in Brussels. Almost all of our respondents confirmed having improved levels of integration. While one referred to the better language skills acquired, the other referred to the capacity to act on his own without having to ask for help for every single thing in his life. A similar account was given by a respondent who said that she no longer felt like a foreigner as she had been equipped with the necessary information. Another respondent was simply happy to see all the efforts aimed at her better integration and reported feeling more integrated out of gratitude. A few respondents also reported that they felt less discriminated against after having completed the courses. This is an important statement in the sense that migrants begin to understand why Belgians 'do things the way they do it' rather than simply labelling these attitudes as racist. However, one respondent complained that the societal rules were too strict and that there was no room for negotiation. He considered this to be an assimilationist inclination, which prevented him from making efforts towards integration. This proves that it is not easy to break essentialist approaches to culture; therefore time and the support of social policies are much needed.

Before talking about the policy implications of our research we would like to draw attention to a recent report published by HIVA that specifically focused on the impact of following *inburgering* trajectory in Flanders (Pauwels & Lamberts 2010). Different from our research, this study made use of a methodology akin to a semi-experimental design. The data is gathered from interviews with respondents who shared a similar profile on sex, age, country of birth and educational level but who differed in their position vis-à-vis the courses. The respondents included persons who started and completed the courses, persons who started the courses but did not complete them and finally persons who chose not to attend the courses at all.

The main rationale behind citing this study is to see to what extent the accounts of the migrants are compatible with our findings. The report indeed confirms that the migrants who started the courses held a high opinion of them and considered them as an added value. Those who did not participate in the trajectory also managed to gather the information taught in the courses, but they had learnt it more slowly and in a more fragmented way. An important difference between both groups however remains in the access to correct judicial information such as labour contract rights, house renting rights, etc., which are apparently much harder to gather through informal networks.

Another striking element that resulted from this study is that half of the respondents had a limited mastery of the Dutch language regardless of their attendance in language courses. One of the conclusions of this report in this regard is that the language courses could still be improved and differentiated between slow and fast learners (Pauwels & Lamberts 2010).

V. Policy Implications

The public officials we spoke to were optimistic yet modest about the effects of the courses. They shared the view that the courses provide the foundation upon which the migrants can build a future. Familiarity with the basic notions of the society helps them to find their own way and come to grips with their lives. The positive feelings they developed from their interactions in the reception centres stimulate integration. Bon and Atlas thus function as a catalyst. The public officials also underlined the psychological impact of meeting new people from different backgrounds, or of simply going out of the house with a particular purpose in mind. Confirmation of the psychological and socialising role of the courses reveal that examining solely the end result of the courses is not sufficient, the process is as important. This also reinforces our argument about the reception centres as social spaces and also why a test would not then be an appropriate mechanism. In terms of concrete outcomes, they acknowledged that the development is idiosyncratic and that substantial changes require longer periods of time, even generations. Yet they believed that there had been an overall increase in knowledge of the society and awareness of professional opportunities.

When it comes to integration, they embraced this compartmentalised approach, which recognises that it is dependent on improvement in other social spaces. Schools and workplaces are most often identified as the major vehicles through which a migrant can socialise with the majority society. Therefore the policy of *inburgering* alone cannot be held responsible for the successful integration of migrants, it needs to be supported by social policies that take into account the diversity of the population in Belgium. Even though the initiatives towards achieving a more inclusive policy are sustained, *inburgering* policy dominates the public debate. This emphasis has in recent years contributed to the false expectations mentioned above. The problem is not so much at the level of the stakeholders who are actively involved in the implementation of the policy but at the level of general public discourse. We can single out two miscalculated moves on the part of the Flemish government that have contributed to this image. First, the introduction of the policy as an innovation from the start gave the impression that the *inburgering* policy would find an answer to all the enduring problems. Moreover, it did not entirely reflect the truth as the reception of the newcomers had been on the agenda ever since the adoption of the minorities' policy. Reception centres that were operating on a voluntary basis in different parts of Flanders and Brussels were reconstituted and gathered together under one heading after the official foundation of the *inburgering* policy. This step did not only fail to recognise the existing programmes of integration, such as COMPAS or TRACE, but also the existing demand for such programmes. The failure to recognise the previous demand for these voluntary schemes led to a misrepresentation of migrants as unwilling to make an effort to follow integration trajectories on their own. Hence they needed to be obliged to do so. We will return to this point when discussing the mandatory nature of the courses. The second mistake, in our view, was to lump together the category of the established residents, the so-called 'oudkomers', with the newcomers whose motivations and problems differ widely. This situation rendered the courses at best less efficient and at worst counter-productive. Even though the lack of language knowledge can perhaps be identified as a common setback, the root causes should be disentangled. The reasons for low levels of successful participation in the labour market or command of the Dutch language in the successive generations of immigrant groups can be explained by a combination of factors ranging from the deficiencies of the education system, to the low human capital of the parents, from the absence of adequate reception measures at the time to a lack of interest towards the country of residence. Therefore, the problems stretched over time cannot be improved with a unitary measure and trying to deal with them under the same heading puts the reputation of the policy in danger. Forcing established residents who are dependent on CPAS/OCMW to follow the courses is also highly discouraging for the newcomers. A number of migrants in Antwerp reported losing interest in the courses because of the attitude they displayed during the courses, like chatting with each other and their low levels of motivation. Below we quote a very telling example:

> 'I didn't feel comfortable being in one class with long staying immigrants. They had their personal questions that were not interesting for me, I wanted to get more general information. What's more old-comers have their prejudices towards Belgians that they shared during the course. It made me slow in making friends among Belgians.'

Looking at it from the perspective of established residents, it is difficult to tell whether they actually learn anything new or they simply fulfil their duty by listening to things they already know or are not interested in knowing. Unfortunately there were very few people in our sample who had been living in Belgium for many years, which made it academically unsound to draw conclusions. However it would be safe to say that within our group the discourses of the newcomers did not match with those of the established residents. Whereas the newcomers were surprised to see that a large number of the established residents did not have a good knowledge of Belgian society, the few established residents we interviewed were of the opinion that the courses were useless for them. In either case, these two groups are not mutually beneficial to each other and their interests do not revolve around the same issues. An alternative solution, if they remain within the target group, can come through the newly instituted exemption test for those who do not need it and subsequently placing them in different classes from the newcomers.

Obligation

This last remark opens the discussion for the main area of investigation of this research, which has so far been implicitly touched upon. The central premise of this chapter is to examine in depth two reception centres of *inburgering*, Atlas and Bon, with a view to seeing to what extent the obligation to attend the courses had an impact on the results achieved. We first present the views of the migrants we gathered and then the pros and cons of the obligation.

In Brussels we asked the respondents whether they would have felt differently if they had been obliged to attend the classes. A considerable number shared the view that as long as the information received was valuable they did not mind having to attend the courses. Another opinion along these lines revolves around the responsibility of the migrant. Two out of nine respondents asserted that it was the duty of the migrant to become accustomed to the country of residence and attending the courses was only a fair trade-off for the opportunities obtained in Belgium. One respondent smoothed this view by suggesting that there should be explanatory mechanisms that would enable migrants to understand that it was in their interest to attend. While acknowledging a migrant's necessity to 'make changes' in a foreign country, another respondent claimed that learning a language had to be out of free will. She argued that the key to learning was taking pleasure in it and imposing the courses endangered this pleasure. Therefore, according to her, migrants were conscious enough to make the right choices for themselves and could take the necessary steps for their integration without being forced to do so. Lastly, one respondent abstained from commenting and limited herself to stating that she did not know if she would have experienced it the same way if she had been obliged to attend. We can discern in the Brussels' case that migrants were grateful for the availability of the free courses that had introduced them to life in Belgium. It seems that the voluntary nature of the programme has strengthened its bona fide character.

In Antwerp, our questions were slightly different, ranging from their first reactions when they found out they had to attend the courses to their evaluation of the courses as a mandatory measure. To our surprise, a large number of the migrants were aware of their obligation to attend integration courses. They even presented themselves to the reception centre before they received the official call-up paper from the municipality. Because of this prior knowledge they were not surprised by the obligation. Most of them were happy about the offer whereas a few of them mentioned that they were suspicious about the use of it in the beginning. The most unfavourable reaction was from a respondent who mentioned that she did not in principle appreciate anything mandatory. She also reported being a little offended as she had the impression of being treated as uncivilised. Even though she had lost her feelings of resentment, she had not really changed her mind about the utility of the courses. Only two of our respondents mentioned that they would not have gone to the courses had they not been obliged to attend. While one of them had been living in Belgium for five years, the other was a newcomer. The former respondent justified her disinterest by her previous years of residence in Belgium and contended that the courses did not really contribute to her knowledge. The latter was the woman mentioned previously who took offence to the obligation. She thus believed that the courses did not teach anything she could not have learnt on her own. On the other hand, the remaining respondents were glad to have completed the courses and were not disturbed by the obligation. Suffice it so say here that their arguments did not differ from the respondents in Brussels.

The mandatory nature of the integration programme in Flanders has been topical from the moment of its introduction. At the political level, while liberal and conservative parties supported the obligation, socialist politicians argued that an obligation could only be fair when sufficient tuition was available and waiting lists for classes had been eliminated (Loobuyck & Jacobs 2006: 112). On the other hand, several scholars (Timmerman, Geets & Van der Heyden 2006: 306; Loobuyck & Jacobs 2006: 112) claimed that the debate was misplaced and that the focus should be on the emancipatory aspect of the obligation, especially for women living in closed minority communities. Based on the qualitative research we conducted with migrants and policy executers, we have attempted to contribute to this debate.

The main advantage of the obligation is clearly the opportunity to reach a wider group. Since the 'marketing' of the courses is carried out through formal public channels, a better level of awareness can be achieved. A corollary to this argument is the goal of emancipation. The obligation brings to light marginalised – or forced to be marginalised – persons such, as spouses who arrive in Belgium through family reunion. The obligation to attend the *inburgering* classes would not only equip them with the necessary tools to attain a certain autonomy but it would also simply give them an opportunity to be away from the authoritarian rule of the family and the community in which they live. Nevertheless, what usually goes unnoticed is that this emancipatory aspect can be best accomplished to the extent that it can be entrusted to a teacher coming from within the community. The recognition and reputation of the teacher within the community reduces the perception of the courses as a threat to the retention of the culture of origin. Another option would be to implant a more severe sanction mechanism that could cause serious deprivation for the migrants. However, in such a scenario the means would no longer justify the ends; putting migrants into economically vulnerable situations with a view to emancipating them is not practicable. In our opinion, this is precisely the weakness of the obligation. It is a slippery slope in the sense that it can easily lean towards more coercive measures. It depends much more on public officials' good will and how well they communicate it. A very welcoming measure in its essence can be misrepresented with a wrong communication strategy. The accounts of the migrants presented above indeed indicate that the message is sometimes less clearly conveyed to the migrants who were obliged to follow the courses.

VI. Conclusion: Future Perspectives

As a conclusion, we would like to reiterate a few observations that appear crucial in order to better grasp and to a certain extent improve the policy of *inburgering*.

The first point to be made is the conceptualisation of the courses as a first step towards a successful process of integration. Integration is not an ultimate outcome that is mathematically achieved through accurate calculations, but rather a continuous engagement, revitalised and developed daily. Social orientation courses assist migrants to make the right start on this journey by offering them the toolkit to survive and encouraging them to further this initial move. Perceiving the courses as a start-up does not undermine the effects of the policy but instead enhances its chances of succeeding by setting up adequate priorities.

A second item that flows from this concern is the necessity to dissociate the *inburgering* policy from the other societal problems that relate to integration, such as unemployment or low education levels. These difficulties faced by the second generation cannot be sufficiently dealt with by the *inburgering* policy and they need to be supported with social policies. Therefore, the *inburgering* policy should not be expected to offer a blanket solution either to all the challenges or to everyone. As we have seen, lumping together the groups of newcomers with the second generation does not generate a fruitful synergy. Unfortunately our data did not provide sufficient information to make a strong claim about whether or not the content of the courses was indeed useful for the second generation. However, it definitely led us to suggest that if the second generation were to be kept in the target group, a distinct class should be assigned to them and perhaps even with slightly different curricula.

Thirdly, concerning the obligation, our contention is that it should be carefully managed so that it continues serving its purpose of reaching a larger number of migrants rather than deterring would-be migrants. Even though there are no striking differences on the perceived effects of the courses in the two cases, the message of 'welcome' is more unambiguously conveyed in the voluntary form of *inburgering*. A clear and coherent communication strategy should be endorsed in order to ensure all three concerns mentioned here. Indeed the recent strategies of the Flemish government mentioned throughout the text – i.e. an integrated framework approach to integration and *inburgering* or the introduction of exemption tests – can be considered steps in the right direction.

Despite the encouraging picture we paint, it remains to be seen what the current political developments in Belgium will engender. One recent event, for instance, is the proposed measures of integration abroad mentioned for the first time in the last four-yearly policy report of the Ministry of Integration. It refers to an enriched cooperation with the Belgian Consulates with a view to offering *inburgering* courses in the country of origin (Flemish Parliament 2009: 33). It is envisaged as a voluntary and free offer that could initially concentrate on certain countries and groups of migrants, such as those who come through family reunification channels (*Ibid.*). The last yearly policy note details this plan of 'Migrating to Flanders - a starter pack for family migrants', which will initially focus on the countries with the highest numbers immigrants in Flanders, namely Morocco, Turkey and Russia (Flemish Parliament 2011: 15). The dissemination of this package of 'Migrating to Flanders', which will be complementary to social orientation courses, will start in these three countries in 2012. The package contains three items: a DVD and a pamphlet, a language guide and a 'backpack'. Whereas the language guide provides an introduction to Dutch language and emphasizes the importance of Dutch knowledge for life in Flanders, the 'backpack' is a practical guide on the necessary documents in order to access employment or education in the country of residence (*ibid.*). These measures have a particular focus on migrants who come to Belgium for family reunification purposes and indeed are part of a larger project to understand the profile of this type of migration. Even though the *Nieuw-Vlaamse Alliantie* (the NV-A literally translated as the New-Flemish Alliance) stance on the issue which proposed making the family reunification visa dependent on the fulfilment of such measures in the country of origin during its election campaign raised doubts, the policy note of 2011-2012 underlines that the offer is free, voluntary and independent of residence permit (*ibid.*).

Yet another issue that is likely to alter the positive atmosphere relates to the nationality legislation. In early April 2010, a draft bill was adopted that aims to increase the length of residence to five years and to re-introduce an integration condition which would consist of proof of 'willingness to integrate' and linguistic competence in one of the national languages of the Kingdom. These changes or similar ones are likely to be adopted in the coming months as the government agreement of December 2011 foresees a reform of nationality law. Accordingly, the expected reform will introduce language and integration requirements for the applicants of naturalisation. It is also stated that economic activity may also be recognised as an element of integration.[59] Therefore the question remains whether any link can be established between *inburgering* and the fulfilment of the integration condition. It is evident from the recent refusal that Wallonia is not favourable to designing a mandatory integration scheme. It is thus difficult to forecast which way the wind will blow; nonetheless it is worthwhile to at least mention the possibilities.

59 Cf. *supra* note 55 for reference.

Part 4. Effects of Mandatory Integration Rules

The INTEC Project: Synthesis Report

Integration and Naturalisation Tests: The New Way to European Citizenship

A Comparative study in nine Member States on the national policies concerning integration and naturalisation tests and their effects on integration, financed by the European Integration Fund

Tineke Strik, Anita Böcker, Maaike Luiten & Ricky van Oers

December 2010

Centre for Migration Law
Radboud University Nijmegen
The Netherlands

Contents

NATIONAL RAPPORTEURS

Co-benificiaries of the Intec project as funded by the Integration Fund:

Austria	Bernard Perchinig, University of Vienna
Belgium	Zeynep Yanasmayan and Marie-Claire Foblets, Catholic University of Leuven
Germany	Anne Walter and Marina Seveker, Institute for Migration Research and Intercultural Studies (IMIS);
Latvia	Kristina Kruma, Riga Graduate School of Law;
The Netherlands	Tineke Strik, Maaike Luiten and Ricky van Oers, Centre for Migration Law, Radboud University;
United Kingdom	Bernard Ryan, Kent Law School.

Other national rapporteurs

Denmark	Eva Ersbøll and Laura Katrine Gravese, Danish Institute for Human Rights;
France	Yves Pascouau, Université Libre de Bruxelles, Belgium.
Hungary	Judit Tóth, Department of Constitutional Law, University of Szeged.

Chapter 1. Research Purpose and Methodology

Tineke Strik and Anita Böcker

1.1 Purpose of the Study

This report presents a comparative study of the policies, practice and data regarding the integration requirements of nine EU Member States. Passing language or integration tests as a condition for naturalization or various types of legal residence rights are topical issues in several EU Member States. A number of common trends regarding this kind of integration policy towards immigrants from third-countries are visible.

Firstly, several Member States have introduced compulsory integration courses and tests as a condition for admission for family reunification, permanent residence, or naturalisation. Secondly, in certain Member States there appears to be a trend towards formalisation of the language and integration requirements. The informal interview between an applicant and a civil servant as part of the naturalisation procedure has been replaced by a formalized test, which often coincides with a raising of the level of required knowledge of the language and of the host society. Thirdly, there appears to be a readiness among Member States to learn from the experiences of other Member States and to copy measures developed elsewhere in the EU. The exchange of information in the Justice and Home Affairs Council, the adoption of the Common Basic Principles on Integration in 2004 and of the Commission's Common Agenda for Integration in 2005, and the informal meetings of EU Ministers responsible for integration have contributed to the openness to experiences of other Member States. Furthermore, most Member States have recently been confronted with the question whether to introduce integration measures or integration conditions in the process of transposing Directive 2003/86/EC on the right to family reunification and Directive 2003/109/EC on the status of long-term resident third-country nationals. Both directives make reference to the possibility of introducing integration measures or requiring immigrants to fulfil an integration condition in order to be entitled to a certain status provided for in those directives. The introduction of the tests reflects a change in ideas on the relationship between legal status and integration.

Although the imitative behaviour of the Member States with regard to integration requirements is rapidly increasing, little is known of the actual effects of this rather recent legislation. Mostly the national legislator mentions the integration of immigrants in the host society as the main purpose of these requirements. Whether the introduction of these new ways of testing integration has actually contributed to better immigrant integration or whether the tests function as a mechanism for selection and exclusion is unknown. Exclusion results in migrants being denied admission to a certain Member State and not obtaining permanent residence status or naturalisation. It is also unclear to what extent being put through an integration test affects the behaviour of potential applicants or how such a requirement is perceived by them. So far there have been few if any empirical studies of the actual effect and impact of the use of integration and naturalisation tests.

The INTEC project has conducted a first evaluation of the recent paradigmatic change in policy concepts concerning integration in certain Member States. The project aimed to provide detailed and reliable information on the content and the impact of compulsory elements in national integration policies. The main research questions focused on the reasons for the introduction of the obligatory integration requirements, the way in which they had been developed and put into practice and the actual effects of the requirements on immigrants. Furthermore attention was paid to the differences between integration requirements with a voluntary and a compulsory nature, the relationship between the different requirements in a Member State and the relationship between the integration requirements of the different Member States. Within the framework of the INTEC project, research was conducted on the national policy and practice concerning these tests and their effects in nine Member States: Austria, Belgium, Denmark, France, Germany, Hungary, Latvia, the Netherlands, the United Kingdom, Hungary and France.[1] The rapporteurs of the two latter Member States conducted the research at their own expense, which forced them to limit the research to a more moderate scale.[2] On the basis of these national reports, the Centre for Migration Law made a comparative study, which is laid out in this report. As this study analyses the impact of compulsory elements in national integration policies, it provides insight into the contribution of those tests to the integration of the persons concerned and the possible intended and unintended effects of the introduction of the tests.

The central aims of the INTEC project have been to collect, analyse and disseminate accurate, systematic, and up-to-date information on the practices and effects of the integration and naturalisation tests in Member States that have introduced such tests. The outcome of this research enables public authorities, both at the national and local level, politicians, immigrants and their organisations as well as academics, journalists and members of the public to form an informed opinion on the different kinds of language and integration tests introduced in the Member States, their contribution to the integration of immigrants, the possible effects of the introduction of these tests and the arguments pro and contra such tests. In this sense the INTEC project may increase the Member States' capacity to develop, implement, monitor and evaluate policies and measures for the integration of third-country nationals and stimulate transnational exchange of good and bad practices with regard to the integration of these nationals. Furthermore, this project aims to disseminate the results of new policies of Member States, not only between the nine Member States concerned but also to all Member States. In order to ensure the dissemination of the research results, the provisional conclusions of the comparative research was presented at an international conference in October 2010. Furthermore, the rapporteurs in all the Member States involved

1 As Denmark does not take part in the EU Justice and Home Affairs *acquis*, the Integration Fund was not able to finance the research conducted in this Member State. To enable the involvement of the experiences in Denmark, the Danish Institute for Human Rights has conducted half of the research at its own expense. The Dutch Centre for Migration Law has financed the other half of the expenses for the Danish research.

2 The French rapporteur was not able to conduct interviews and the Hungarian rapporteur used a limited number of interviews (but instead, of interviewing immigrants she assessed 100 files regarding applications for permanent residence or citizenship). Both rapporteurs will not organise a national seminar on the outcome of their research.

have actively disseminated the outcome of their studies at a national seminar of stakeholders (immigrants, immigrant organisations, local and national officials).

Data collection for the national report as well as this synthesis report ended in October 2010. On the occasion of the publication *Which Integration Policies for Migrants?*, we have a written an afterword on the relevant policy changes introduced between October 2010 and April 2012 in the involved Member States.

1.2 Methodology

The basis of this comparative study is formed by the national reports on nine Member States. These national reports, which encompass more detailed information, are therefore a substantial part of the INTEC project. The authors of the reports are also responsible for the field research in their Member State.[3] The researchers already had extensive research experience on this topic before the INTEC project started. Most of them had published widely on issues of integration, immigration or nationality law in their home country, participated in comparative studies or had themselves conducted comparative studies on integration programmes covering several Member States. Four of the institutions involved participated in the NATAC[4] comparative study on the nationality law and practice in 15 EU Member States (Bauböck, Ersbøll, Groenendijk & Waldrauch 2006). Most of the rapporteurs had also contributed to a study on the national policies concerning the integration of newcomers and/or future citizens in their countries (Van Oers, Ersbøll & Kostakopoulou 2010). These relevant experiences have contributed to the completeness and quality of the national reports and the synthesis report.

The national rapporteurs started their cooperation in a public kick-off seminar in February 2010, where experts on integration policy, linguists, sociologists and civil servants gave an overview of previous research and formulated recommendations for the INTEC project. In a closed setting, the rapporteurs deliberated on the questionnaires for the field research, the selection of the respondents and the criteria and format for the national reports.

In order to formulate the aims of the integration and naturalisation tests, the rapporteurs analyzed the decision making process regarding the integration and naturalisation tests. They included in this analysis the political debates on the actual Bills and comments from advisory bodies, immigrant organisations, academics and other experts. The analysis offered an overview of the arguments and foundations of the introduction of the tests and the way criticism or possible risks had been taken into account. Furthermore the content of the tests, the practical implementation, the target groups and exemptions were described. Using a number of different sources, the rapporteurs investigated the impact of the tests. They assessed criticism and recommendations of (international) experts in literature and reports that appeared after the entry into force of the relevant acts and analyzed the jurisprudence on the integration requirements. Furthermore evaluations of the tests and other

3 The national reports are separately available on the website of the Centre for Migration Law, http://www.ru.nl/law/cmr/projects/intec/.

4 EU funded research in 2004-2005 on the acquisition of nationality in EU Member States: rules, practices and quantitative developments.

related studies and data on the effects of the tests were assessed, including the political reaction to the outcome of the evaluations. The data and number of studies differ per country but also depend on when the tests were introduced. As the naturalisation tests were introduced first, data and literature on this topic were relatively widely available. In some Member States the availability of evaluations was limited or even absent because of the recent introduction of the tests, which was especially the case with the integration and language tests abroad. This was one of the reasons why the rapporteurs also conducted field research in order to collect information on the effects of the tests. Furthermore, the material collected by the interviews offered clarification of the figures, as they revealed the perception by the migrants and other respondents of the integration requirements.

1.3 Interviews

In eight countries, a total of 329 interviews were conducted. Most of the interviews (about 25 in each country) were with immigrants who had been or were required to fulfil integration requirements. In addition, interviews were conducted with teachers of integration courses (about 5 per country); public officials responsible for the application of the integration requirements or the naturalisation legislation (about 5 per country); and staff or active members of immigrant organisations and other NGOs (also about 5 per country). The Dutch research team conducted additional interviews in Turkey, with candidates of the Dutch integration test abroad (10) and their teachers (3). Table 1.1 gives an overview of the interviews conducted in each of the eight countries.

In most countries, the interviews with immigrants were arranged through different channels, and the researchers strived for diversity among the respondents in terms of, e.g., gender, nationality, age and educational level. However, as it was not possible to use interpreters, the research teams in most countries could only conduct interviews with immigrants who were sufficiently proficient in the language of the country of immigration or, e.g., English. Table 1.2 provides information about the methods used for contacting potential respondents and the characteristics of the immigrants interviewed in each country.

Some of the national research teams used additional data collection methods:

- The Hungarian team analyzed 100 files of naturalisation applications in the Office for Immigration and Nationality Affairs.
- The UK research team made a freedom of information request to the UK Border Agency to obtain statistical material concerning the 'Life in the UK' requirement.
- The Danish research team made a request to the Danish Ministry of Integration to obtain statistical data concerning granted and rejected applications for permanent residence filed by applicants who were admitted to Denmark for asylum or family reunification.

Table 1.1 Number of interviews, by country and category of respondent

	Immigrants	*Teachers or staff members language schools/ education centres*	*Public officials*	*Immigrant organisations and other NGOs*	*Total*
Austria	25	7	6	5	43
Belgium	20	5	5	4	34
Denmark	26	5	5	5	41
France	-	-	-	-	-
Germany	27	7	8	7	49
Hungary	25	5	5	2	37
Latvia	28	9	7	4	48
Netherlands (Turkey)	28 (10)	5 (3)	5	5	43 (13)
United Kingdom	16	-	-	5	21
Total	205	46	41	37	329

Table 1.2 Interviews with immigrants

	Number of interviews	*Arranged through:*	*Respondent characteristics*
Austria	25	language centres and immigrant advice centres in Vienna and Wiener Neustadt	16 women, 9 men; 13 different nationalities; mostly admitted for family reunification; half were aged 25 or younger; half had post-secondary education; most had lived in Austria for about a year
Belgium	12 + 8	reception centres in Antwerp and Brussels	12 living in Antwerp (obliged to attend integration course), 8 in Brussels (no obligation); 13 women, 7 men; between 26 and 49 years old; 14 different nationalities
Denmark	14 + 12	administrative agency, local police, language schools, snowball method	- 12 applicants for naturalisation: 9 women, 3 men; nine different nationalities; half were born or raised in Denmark; half were aged 25 or younger; 10 with a middle or high educational level, 2 with a low educational level; - 14 applicants for permanent residence: 9 women, 5 men; ten different nationalities; most had come to Denmark for family reunification; all but one were aged above 25; 11 with a middle or high educational level, 3 with a low educational level.
Germany	27	adult education centres and test centres	8 had passed the integration test abroad as a condition for admission; 12 had passed the integration test in Germany; 10 had passed the integration test for naturalisation; 12 women, 15 men; 18 different nationalities; between 22 and 50 years old, 3 younger than 18
Hungary	25		5 had passed the naturalisation exam; the others were taking it or were attending a course to prepare for it
Latvia	15 + 13	test centre, NGOs, word-of-mouth	15 naturalised citizens, 13 non-citizens

	Number of interviews	*Arranged through:*	*Respondent characteristics*
Netherlands	25 4	test centres in Amsterdam, Nijmegen and Eindhoven; 1 by municipality, 3 by personal network	25 were taking the integration exam (not always clear whether for naturalisation, permanent residence or obligatory, the test is the same); 1 had just started a course, 1 just had applied for naturalisation, 1 was exempted, one did not apply for a permanent residence permit or naturalisation were ; 15 different nationalities (13 were Turkish); 12 between 20 and 30 years old, 12 between 30 and 40 years old; 20 women, 9 men.
(Turkey)	(10)	(language teachers)	(7 had already passed the integration test abroad in Turkey; 3 were still attending a course to prepare for it) (4 between 20 and 30 years old, 4 between 30 and 40 years old) (6 women, 4 men) (5 had academic or higher vocational education)
United Kingdom	16	word-of-mouth and test centres in London and Kent	all 16 had taken the 'Life in the UK' test; 8 women, 8 men; 11 different nationalities; between 21 and 61 years old

CHAPTER 2. TEST ABROAD

Tineke Strik

More and more Member States tend to require a certain knowledge of their language and/or their society as a condition for admission. In 1990, Germany was the first Member State to apply a language requirement for admission, although it was limited to children between 16 and 18 years who applied for subsequent migration in order to reunite with their parents in Germany. In 2005, the German government started to subject two preferential groups to a language test: the spouses and descendants of the so-called *Aussiedler* (ethnic German applicants) and Jewish immigrants (as well as their spouses and descendants) who were aged 15 or older before entry. After having passed the test, the *Aussiedler* and their family members receive German nationality and the Jewish immigrants receive a permanent residence permit. In 2006, the United Kingdom started to require language skills from highly skilled workers and the Netherlands introduced a language and integration test for applicants for family reunification. This last example has been followed and is going to be followed by more and more Member States.

A language requirement for family reunification is applicable in the Netherlands and Germany. Furthermore, the Netherlands requires a certain knowledge of Dutch society. France also tests immigrants abroad on their language level, but only as a method to determine whether they shall be obliged to attend an integration course, not to decide if they are allowed to enter France. At the time or writing the report, three Member States are about to follow the example of the Netherlands and Germany by adding a language requirement to their admission conditions for applicants for family reunification (see the afterword). A language requirement is expected to be introduced in the United Kingdom and Denmark in November 2010. The Danish integration requirements will include knowledge of Danish society. In Austria the introduction of a language test abroad has been announced from October 2010, but a Bill has not yet been brought forward in Parliament.

The national requirements differ with regard to the organisation and implication, the content and level of the test, the target group and the purpose of the integration test. These differences between the Member States will be described below. As the tests involved in family reunification procedures are central, the description starts with the Dutch system.

2.1 Organisation and Costs

Netherlands

The first Member State to introduce the test abroad was the Netherlands. The Civic Integration Abroad Act (*Wet Inburgering Buitenland*, hereafter 'WIB') entered into force on 15 March 2006. The act sets an additional condition for obtaining a regular temporary residence permit, namely that people must first have a basic knowledge of the Dutch language and Dutch society. This basic knowledge will be tested by the Basic Civic Integration Examination in the country of residence of the applicant. The proof of having passed this examination must be handed over on application for admission. Knowledge of the language and Dutch society is tested through an oral examination conducted over the telephone from Dutch Consulates and Embassies abroad, using voice recognition software which is based in the US. This computer programme also decides whether the candidate has passed the examination.

Passing the examination is a condition for granting an authorisation for temporary stay, which is for certain nationalities a necessary document for entering the Netherlands. This authorisation is known as 'MVV'. The migrant must apply for an MVV within one year after passing the examination. After this period, the result of the examination becomes invalid and a new test must be taken in order to be admitted. If the immigrant fails, he/she will not be granted an MVV, and will thus not be admitted to the Netherlands. There is no legal remedy with regard to the outcome of the examination. The applicant is allowed to do the test as many times as necessary, as long as he/she pays € 350 for each examination. The Dutch government does not provide either courses or learning material. It has however compiled a practice pack which can be purchased for € 70.40 and which includes the film, 'Coming to the Netherlands', questions that may be posed during the knowledge of society test, and some language tests. The costs for an admission procedure for family reunification are on average € 1,440, if the migrant passes the test the first time (€ 70 for preparation material, € 350 for the examination, € 830 fee for the visa, € 188 for the residence permit granted after arrival in the Netherlands). These costs do not include the price for a private course, which vary (if available) between € 450 and € 800. As the educational material is not available in all languages, it is not accessible to all applicants. In one case, an applicant from Eritrea objected that he first had to learn English in order to learn Dutch from the educational material. According to the Dutch administrative Court however, this complication did not make the requirement disproportionate. After all, the judge argued, the couple could have a family life in Eritrea or Sudan, from where the applicant originated. Despite worrying reports by Amnesty International regarding the human rights situation in these countries, the court did not take the asylum related aspects of this proposed alternative by the government into account.

Germany

Since the entry into force of the Directives Implementation Act on 28 August 2007, spouses of a German or a third-country national living in Germany have to prove that they are able to communicate in the German language at a certain minimal level as a condition for their admission. Unlike the Netherlands, the German authorities do not test the immigrants' knowledge themselves. Migrants can prove this with a certificate of having passed a recognized test. These examinations are held all over the world by German members of the Association of Language Testers in Europe (ALTE).[5] If an appropriate language certificate cannot be attained in the country of origin, the Diplomatic Mission has to ascertain the level of knowledge of the German language, for instance by a free 'hearing' based on the '*Start*

5 'Start Deutsch 1' test of the Goethe Institute or the telc GmbH, 'Grundstufe Deutsch 1' test of the Austrian Language Diploma (ÖSD) or 'TestDaF' of the TestDaF Institute e.V.

Deutsch 1' test. The '*Start Deutsch 1*' test can be taken in Germany as well as abroad at the Goethe Institute or the telc GmbH (part of the German adult education centre). The Goethe Institute uses its worldwide infrastructure to offer courses and examinations.[6] Although this test is used as a frame of reference by the embassies, it is not important in which way – independently or on the course – the spouse has achieved the required German language skills (Seveker 2008: 199).[7]

According to the evaluation on the language requirement, the waiting period for attending a course is in most cases not longer than two months. For the average participant the duration of the course is about four months. Some Goethe Institutes have developed special courses for migrants with a low education or without experience with the Latin alphabet or learning a foreign language. On the other hand intensive courses are offered to learn the German language within 5 to 7 weeks (Bundesregierung Deutschland 2010: 12-13). The fact that spouses 'all over the world' are able to attend a German language course constitutes a significant difference from the Dutch act. The German authorities facilitate these courses by safeguarding the offer. The costs for the whole procedure are less than half the amount of the Dutch admission procedure. Candidates who have attended a language course at the Goethe Institute pay a reduced fee or are exempted from the test fee. The costs for the admission procedure of a spouse from Turkey amount to € 660 (€ 490 course fee, € 60 test fee and € 60 visa fee, € 50 for the residence permit granted after arrival in Germany).

If the price of a Dutch language course is taken into account, the 'German costs' are less than a third of the 'Dutch costs'. The test can be taken by the spouse as often as required. Just as in the Netherlands, not being able to prove the language skills implies no entry to the German Federation. Whereas the proof of passing the Dutch test is only valid for one year, the language certificate issued by the Goethe Institute does not lose its validity. Nevertheless the German embassy may test the language skills in a visa procedure if the certificate was issued more than a year previously.

France

Since 2007 spouses who apply for family reunification have to meet the requirements of the integration measures. In order to be granted a visa to enter France and join his/her family, the family member has to undergo an evaluation of his/her knowledge of the language and values of French society in the country of origin. The evaluation is conducted by the French authorities (*Office Français pour l'Immigration et l'Intégration*), or contracting parties. If the assessment shows a sufficient level of knowledge, the visa is issued. The applicant will also be exempted from taking part in language sessions on arrival in France within the framework of the welcoming contract (more on this contract in chapter 3). If the evaluation

6 There are currently 149 Goethe Institutes and ten liaison offices in 91 countries as well as test centres in at least 104 countries. Because of the new requirement the institute's networks as well as the licensees' networks were extended. The test centres in Turkey were also extended from three to eight (soon nine), additionally, eight test centres were established in Morocco.

7 The 'way of language acquisition' is of particular importance for ethnic German applicants. Since 1996, they must prove their German language knowledge that must be acquired in a family and be sufficient for basic communication in German in a hearing organised in the country of origin.

demonstrates insufficient knowledge, the applicant is invited to attend courses in the country of origin. These sessions, which deal with knowledge of the language and Republican values, do not last more than two months (180 hours). After attendance, a new evaluation is carried out. If it is successful, the visa is issued and the applicant is exempted from language lessons after arriving in France. If the knowledge is insufficient, the visa is also issued but the authorities determine the length of the formation sessions to be followed in France within the framework of the welcoming contract. Hence, the visa is issued dependent upon attendance on the course, but independently from the level of knowledge the immigrant has demonstrated. Therefore the significant difference between the Dutch and German rules and those of France is that according to the latter passing the test is not a condition for the exercise of the right to family reunification. The test and formation sessions, in the country of origin and after arrival in France, are free of charge and financed by the *Office Français de l'Immigration et de l'Intégration*.

United Kingdom

Whereas the previous three countries only introduced a test for family reunification, the United Kingdom started the introduction of the test in 2004 for ministers of religion. Since November 2006 highly skilled migrants seeking to enter the UK as part of the Highly Skilled Migrant Programme also have to pass a language test or submit proof of sufficient English education. Since November 2008 all skilled workers have to meet the language criterion. In summer 2010, the new Conservative-Liberal coalition announced that the language requirement will also be applied in applications for family reunification from 29 November 2010 (see for the actual entry into force the afterword). If the spouse has to show his/her qualification because he/she is not able to submit relevant proof, this will have to be with an oral test provider approved by the UK Border Agency.

Denmark

Almost simultaneously with the United Kingdom, the Danish government introduced legislation for the application of integration conditions for third-country national spouses of Danish citizens and third-country nationals residing in Denmark. Since 15 November 2010, an applicant for family reunification must pass an immigration test in order to be granted a residence permit on the grounds of family reunification with a spouse/partner in Denmark.[8] The immigration test is an oral one, consisting of a Danish language test and a societal knowledge test. The Danish Act seems to be a copy of the Dutch Integration Act. Besides the similarity in the content and the level of the test, the Danish system has also imitated the Dutch view on supporting the preparation for the test. Instead of offering courses (abroad or in Denmark), a preparatory package has been developed: the most central part

8 The Act authorises the Minister of Integration to determine when the immigration test is to come into force.

of the package is an educational film, 'Life in Denmark'.[9] The aim of the film is to give the participants a realistic general picture of Denmark and the daily life in Denmark. Thus, the film will communicate both facts and values with a view to adapting the expectations of the immigrants to the reality of living in Denmark. Furthermore the package includes a recorded vocabulary list for the language test, 100 images from the film with information about Denmark and Danish society, two samples from the language test and test instructions. The packet costs DKK 50 plus shipping and administration fees (approximately DKK 150 or € 20).

Although the Danish government was inspired by the Dutch example, the Danish application of the requirement differs from the Dutch application in four respects. The most important difference is with regard to the location of the test: instead of the embassies abroad, the examination will be held in Denmark, after the spouse has received a pre-recognition regarding the fulfilment of the other conditions for admission.[10] Applicants subject to a visa requirement will be granted a visa for three months with a view to taking the test in Denmark. Their stay in Denmark will offer them the opportunity to practice the Danish language with their family.[11] The examination has to be taken within three months after arrival in Denmark; however, it is recommended to take the test within the first two and a half months after arrival in Denmark in order to leave time for the examiners to assess the test results. A second difference from the Dutch system concerns the preparation possibilities. The Danish educational film is accessible in a Danish and English version on the Internet. However, in order to watch the film in any other language (it is recorded in 18 other languages) the applicant must buy the preparation package). Thirdly, the validity of the test result is not limited; in the Netherlands, the test has to be retaken if the immigrant does not comply with the other conditions for admission within 12 months after passing the test.

A fourth difference from the Dutch system concerns the method of testing: although the test will also be arranged by a computer-based test system, the test will be evaluated by external examiners. The fee for taking the test is a bit more than the Dutch amount: approximately € 400. During the three month period the test may be re-taken, but then the fee must also be paid again. If an applicant has not passed the test within the three month time limit, family reunification will be refused and a date of departure fixed.

9 'Livet i Danmark', see http://www.nyidanmark.dk/da dk/Integration/integration_af_nyankomne/indvandringsproven/Et+liv+i+Danmark+–+undervisningsfilm+til+indvandringsprøven.htm.

10 According to the analysis, around 1,500–2,000 applicants per year were expected to take the test and most of them (around 70 %) would already stay in Denmark being issued a tourist visa or another kind of residence permit.

11 On the home page of the Ministry of Integration it is stated that it is the applicant's own responsibility to learn Danish which can be done with the help of the applicant's spouse or partner, by taking courses in the country of residence, by buying language courses in the form of books or CDs, or by taking online language courses.

2.2 Level and Content

The Member States that have introduced and will introduce a language test abroad require level A1 or A1 minus of the Common European Framework of Reference (CEFR) for modern languages. The level A1 is the lowest level of proficiency of the categories of the framework (A1, A2, B1, B2 etc.), which encloses basic language skills. A1 minus, which is one step lower than A1, means that the examination candidate understands announcements and instructions, simple questions and answers which are related to his/her immediate personal life, can give elementary information on his/her identity and personal life and can express himself/herself to a very limited degree (with the assistance of isolated words and standard formulas).

Netherlands

The required basic level is A1 minus, and the requirements are limited to listening and speaking skills. The test consists of repeating sentences, answering short questions on basic information, responding to words by saying a word with an opposite meaning, and retelling a short story. The required knowledge of Dutch society consists of 'elementary practical knowledge' on the Netherlands, (including geography, history, legislation and political science), housing, education, the labour market, the system of health care and civic integration. Furthermore the required knowledge covers the rights and duties of migrants and citizens in the Netherlands and the accepted norms in everyday life and in society. The knowledge is tested on a level no higher than A1 minus.

The Dutch government announced that it will raise the level to A1 and extend the language requirements for reading skills at the beginning of 2011. These changes eventually entered into force on 1 April 2011 (see the afterword).

Germany

Spouses have to prove that they are able to communicate in German at least at level A1 in listening, speaking, reading, and writing. Societal knowledge before entering Germany is not required. The test by the Goethe Institute consists of a written individual examination and an oral examination in a group. Two examiners evaluate the test achievements. The tasks of the language test are action-oriented and involve all four language skills. The written examination contains listening, reading and writing. The oral examination is taken in a group (with a maximum of four): each candidate has to introduce himself/herself, provide information and ask for information, as well as make a request and respond to it. Test candidates have to communicate basic information about their name, age, country, address, active working languages, profession and hobbies. They also have to be able to spell their names and to deal fluently with numbers. Furthermore, the appropriate use in everyday situations in Germany by linguistic means is decisive. This means that candidates must be familiar with text types such as signs, posters, catalogues, e-mails, postcards, and similar forms. They must also possess specific information about the country, culture and everyday life.

France

The level of language knowledge is A1.1, which is below A1. Evaluation of language knowledge is based on written and oral tests. Knowledge of French values is tested by oral questions in a language the applicant declares he/she understands.

UK

In the United Kingdom the required language level depends on the residence permit for which the immigrant applies. Highly qualified workers are required to have a score of six (competent user) or above on the International English Language Testing System (IELTS).[12] Applicants for a residence permit which allows them to seek employment, must show proficiency in English equivalent to C1 on the CEFR scale; skilled workers are required to speak English at level A1 (Ryan 2009: 277-98). The English language has to be demonstrated at level A1 in application procedures for family reunification, in an oral test in their home country.

Denmark

As the Danish examination is based on the Dutch example, the level and content of the test are similar to the current Dutch test.

2.3 Target Groups, Exemptions

There is a significant difference between the groups of migrants to which the requirement applies. Applicants for family reunification from outside the EU constitute the main target group. Some Member States however make a distinction within this category on the basis of nationality.

In all Member States migrants can be exempted from the requirement because a sufficient language level has been demonstrated in another way or because a migrant is not able to do the test, for instance because of medical reasons. There are some national differences, especially with regard to the proof of sufficient knowledge.

Netherlands

This entry condition applies to those persons aged between 18 and 65 who meet three criteria: they have applied for admission to the Netherlands with a view to settling permanently, they need to have authorisation for temporary stay, and they are obliged to participate in a civic integration programme after arrival in the Netherlands.[13] In practice this

12 IELTS uses a nine-point scoring system to measure and report on listening, reading, writing, and speaking skills in English. For more on scores, see IELTS, 'Test format and results,' http://www.ielts.org/institutions/test_format_and_results.aspx.

13 Detailed information on this Act is to be found in chapter 3.

obligation primarily concerns applicants for family formation or family reunification with a citizen of the Netherlands or with a migrant originating from a non-EU country.[14] Furthermore this admission requirement applies to ministers of religion coming to the Netherlands in order to enter the labour market.

There are large groups of migrants who are not affected by the act. These include migrants who are not required to apply for an authorisation for temporary stay, who are citizens from the Member States of the EU and EEA, Surinam, Australia, Canada, US, Switzerland, New Zealand, Iceland, Japan and North Korea. Also applicants with a work permit, the self-employed and highly skilled migrants do not fall within the scope of the act. This is also the case for migrants who were granted a status on the basis of the Long-term Residence Directive (2003/109/EC) in another Member State and who fulfilled an integration condition for this purpose. Finally, family members of a migrant with an asylum-related residence permit do not need to pass the test, unless the marriage was concluded after the sponsor was granted a residence permit (family formation). Migrants who are exempted from the obligation to take the integration test in the Netherlands because of their educational background are also exempted from passing the integration test abroad. These are migrants who have spent eight years or more in the Netherlands during childhood and migrants with a school diploma or certificate of education in the Dutch language.

Migrants can also be exempted if they are unable to pass the test due to a mental or physical disability. The legislator refers to the situation where the applicant is blind or deaf or has difficulty hearing, seeing or speaking and is not in possession of audio-visual aids. Proof of this disability requires a declaration from a doctor or expert who is appointed by the head of the embassy or consulate. This medical assessment takes place at the expense of the applicant. Being functionally illiterate does not constitute a ground for exemption. Although the government introduced an oral test with the argument that illiterate persons should also be able to pass, this group will not be exempted from the reading test, introduced in April 2011.

After a national court had ruled in August 2011 that the EEC/Turkey Association Agreement does not allow the Netherlands to oblige Turkish nationals to participate in a civic integration programme after arrival in the Netherlands, the Minister of Integration announced that Turkish nationals were exempted from the integration requirement for admission.

Germany

In Germany, spouses of German citizens or third-country nationals are obliged to pass the test abroad. In the interests of close economic relations, the citizens of certain countries are exempt. These countries are similar to the countries the Dutch government exempted from the test as well.[15] Furthermore, spouses of the nationals who may enter Germany without a

14 Family reunification means that the marriage was already concluded before the applicant was admitted to the Netherlands; in other cases (including marriages with Dutch nationals) the definition family formation is used.

15 USA, Australia, Israel, Japan, Canada, the republic of Korea, New Zealand as well as Andorra, Monaco, San Marino and Honduras, Brazil and El Salvador.

visa are exempted from passing the test. Hence, just like in the Netherlands, family reunification for these nationals residing in Germany is easier than for the 'own nationals'. This is also the case for highly skilled migrants and other migrants whose residence in Germany is considered to be in the German interest. Furthermore, spouses of migrants who have been granted a residence permit for asylum reasons do not fall within the scope of the act.

Germany has a special regulation in the case of the subsequent migration of children between the ages of 16 and 18 years who wish to reunite with their parent(s) residing in Germany. These children have to prove that it can be expected that they will integrate into German society. For this purpose it is assessed whether the child possesses the language ability at CEFR level C1 or if it appears, on the basis of the child's education and way of life to date, that the child will be able to integrate into the German way of life.[16]

The integration requirement is not applicable to spouses whose need for integration is discernibly minimal. This is the case for instance if they are in possession of an academic degree or a comparable qualification or are employed as managing executives, professional sportsmen, journalists or scientists, researchers or teachers. In practice, possession of an academic title appears not to be sufficient for exemption from the required German language knowledge. Moreover, employees of an international company who are based in Germany for no longer than three years, and their spouses, are also exempt. In practice the requirement is targeted to low educated spouses from certain non-Western third countries, i.e. Turkey, Kosovo, Russia or Thailand. The criteria for exemption on the basis of a physical or mental disability are similar to the Dutch criteria. Illiteracy and pregnancy are not grounds for exemption.

France

The French legislation does not, unlike the Netherlands and Germany, make a distinction between nationalities of countries from outside the EU. It has laid down three types of exemptions from the test. The first exemption relates to the age of the applicant: applicants below 16 and over 65 years old are exempt. The second relates to educational background, which implies that the requirement is not applicable to foreigners who completed at least three years of secondary studies in a French school abroad successfully or who completed at least one year of college (University) in France successfully. The third type of exemption involves migrants who have difficulties doing the test because of the general situation in their country (war or a natural or technical disaster) or because of personal circumstances, for instance professional obligations or physical or financial difficulties.

16 The certificate, issued by a reliable and appropriate organisation after passing the language acquisition test, which may not be dated more than one year previously, serves as proof of language ability. It is assumed that children are more easily able to integrate if they have grown up in a Member State of the EU or EEA or if they come from a German-speaking parental home or have attended a German-speaking school abroad for a substantial period.

United Kingdom

The British legislation exempts two categories from the requirement: workers from 16 countries with a majority English population, and migrants who received a bachelor's degree taught in English or an English higher education degree.

Denmark

With regard to nationality, Denmark follows the French example: apart from citizens of the EU and EEA, the requirement applies to all third-country nationals applying for reunification with a spouse or partner (and ministers of religion) (Ersbøll 2010: 129-130). Thus, foreigners coming from countries such as the US, Australia, Canada, Japan and South Korea are also covered (unlike the policy of the Netherlands and Germany). Spouses of migrants with a residence permit granted for occupational or educational reasons do not fall within the scope of the act. The integration requirement will not apply if the foreigner has previously stayed in Denmark for at least five years and fulfils the Danish language requirement for permanent residence.
Exemption from the test requirement is possible under certain special circumstances, for instance where the sponsor is a refugee who cannot take up residence in his/her country of origin due to the risk of persecution or where the sponsor's personal conditions call for exemption. In all cases where a refusal will constitute a violation of the European Convention on Human Rights (ECHR) dispensation must be granted. In general, the integration condition does not apply to foreigners who cannot fulfil the requirements due to serious illness or disability, including post-traumatic stress disorder.

2.4 Purpose of the Test and Debate

Netherlands

The idea that migrants should start their integration before their departure to the Netherlands, emerged from an evaluation of the integration policy in 2004. The parliamentary commission (the Blok Commission) which had evaluated the integration policies of the previous 30 years, concluded that the integration of many aliens had been successful (Commissie-Blok *Bruggen Bouwen*: 2004). According to the commission, their success was only to a relative extent the result of the pursued integration policy. This commission found that 25 per cent of the participants on integration courses did not accomplish the desired A2 level. For this disappointing result, the commission pointed to the weak organisation of the integration education: the slow development of courses, the lack of quality and tailor-made education and the existence of long waiting lists. Although the evaluation had not revealed a certain unwillingness of migrants to integrate, politicians immediately blamed the integration policy for its permissive character. The demand was heard in parliament and government for a radical change in the integration regime by strengthening the responsibility and obligations of the migrant. The government announced the introduction of two kinds of obligations. First, immigrants would be required to pass a basic examination in their country of origin as a condition for family reunification. Second, all immigrants who wished to stay in the Netherlands on a permanent basis would have to pass an integration examination within 3.5 years after their arrival. Failing the examination would entail financial sanctions and the refusal of a permanent or independent status. With the decision to start with integration before entry, the government obviously wanted to be able to apply the refusal of entry as a sanction for not fulfilling the integration requirement.

The government especially targeted its new policy on non-Western spouses of a Dutch citizen or third-country national residing in the Netherlands. According to the government, their immigration would cause the largest integration problems. It stated that 'the large-scale immigration of the last ten years has seriously disrupted the integration of migrants at group level. We must break out of the process of (family) migration which time and again causes integration to fall behind'. In particular, the integration process was thought to have been 'held back by the fact that a large number of second generation migrants opts for a marital partner from the country of origin'. According to the government, 'an important part of these [family migrants] has characteristics that are adverse to a good integration into Dutch society. Most prominent among these – also in scale – is the group of marriage migrants from Turkey and Morocco' (Bonjour 2010: 306). Almost half of the family migrants would belong to these communities and would find themselves in a bad socio-economic position. The government described family migration as a 'self-repeating phenomenon of serial migration' which seemed to be a 'self-repeating phenomenon of continuous growth of ethnic minority groups in a socio-economic deprived position'.

The government mentioned four purposes of the introduction of the integration test abroad. First, the test would enable family migrants to act more independently after their arrival. Second, it would allow them to make a more deliberate and better informed choice on moving to the Netherlands. Third, it would make the migrant and his/her partner residing in the Netherlands more aware of their responsibility for the integration of the newcomer into Dutch society. The government felt that the 'supply-oriented approach' was no longer appropriate, emphasising that the own responsibility of the migrant would fit better into the new approach to integration that it had in mind. In this view, supporting the migrant in his/her preparation for the test abroad would send the wrong signal. Furthermore, offering no support would allow the migrant more freedom of choice in how to prepare for the examination.

As a fourth and final purpose of the WIB, the government expected the integration requirement would work as a 'selection mechanism': only those with the 'motivation and perseverance' necessary to integrate successfully in the Netherlands would be admitted. The government explained it preferred delay or even cancellation of family migration to the situation in which integration after arrival in the Netherlands would lag behind. It stated that reduction in immigration was 'not a primary goal', but nevertheless welcomed the 'side effect' that WIB was expected to result in a decrease in family migration flows by an estimated 25 per cent (Bonjour 2010: 306).

In its Explanatory Memorandum, the government explained how the new requirement fitted in with the European developments, inter alia referring to the Family Reunification Directive and the Long-term Residents Directive. It did not mention that the Dutch government itself was the strongest promoter of the insertion of an optional clause regarding the integration requirements in those directives.[17] The government also considered the integration test abroad to be in line with the 'Tampere conclusions', in which the European leaders of governments in 1999 announced the strengthening of the residence rights of migrants in order to improve their integration (see Tampere conclusions).

The Bill was highly disputed inside and outside parliament for two main reasons (Van der Winden 2006; Spijkerboer 2007). First, policymakers debated the legality of having a mandatory language test without providing sufficient facilities for immigrants to learn Dutch since the government was relying on the free market in the countries of origin to respond to demand for Dutch language instruction. Two official advisory bodies concluded that the test would violate Article 8 ECHR if a large group of family migrants would *de facto* be prevented from living with their spouse or partner in the Netherlands. Second, the linguists who were asked by Minister for Migration and Integration Verdonk to report on the test and the way it was to be administered (in a telephone conversation with a computer), disputed the validity of the language test,[18] as it was based on software developed in the United States for a completely different purpose (Willems 2009: 123-156). The committee which was established by Minister Verdonk in order to advise her on new integration policy concluded that civic integration could not be properly tested abroad. Verdonk did not follow this advice and disregarded the opinion of the linguists she had consulted. In the end, all major parties, except the Green Left MPs, voted for the act, which entered into force in March 2006 (Groenendijk 2010: 13).

One year after the coming into force of the act, the alien chamber of a district court judged that the government was allowed to make the migrant fully responsible for the preparation of the examination. According to the court, the legislator had taken these possible obstacles into account.

Two years after the Integration Act Abroad had entered into force, the NGO Human Rights Watch urged for the abolition of the civic integration examination abroad. The organisation deemed the act discriminatory, as it only applied to family members from 'non-Western' countries. As the difference in treatment had no relation to the aim of the measure (better integration in the country of destination), and the government had failed to justify the difference, Human Rights Watch (HRW 2008: 4 and 24-29) considered the distinction to be (direct) discrimination on the basis of ethnic origin and nationality and therefore incompatible with Article 14 ECHR and Article 26 of the International Covenant on Civil and Political Rights. Although this criticism was uttered with regard to the Dutch legislation, it is also applicable to the distinction the German legislation makes on the basis of nationality. Furthermore, Human Rights Watch argued that the Dutch legislation amounted to indirect racial discrimination (and therefore to violation of the UN Conven-

17 At that time the government only had the idea of introducing the admission condition that the applicant for family reunification would pre-finance the integration course, in which he/she has to participate after admission.

18 The test is taken at a Dutch embassy or consulate in a telephone conversation with a computer equipped with a voice-recognition programme. Also, the person must answer 70 per cent of 30 questions (from a list of 100 published questions) about life in the Netherlands correctly. The Ministry of Justice has published a learning kit with the list and a film about the Netherlands. The kit costs € 65 (about US$ 80). The fee for the examination is € 350 (US$ 431) and has to be paid each time the examination is taken.

tion on the Elimination of All Forms of Racial Discrimination) because it disproportionally affected residents of Turkish and Moroccan origin in the Netherlands who wanted to live with their spouse and children. From the parliamentary debate it appears that the government was especially targeting these two groups. The then Social Democratic Minister of Integration replied that the measure was in compliance with European and international treaties. She mentioned three justifications for the different treatment. First, the requirement was linked with the existing difference between countries whose citizens did not need to apply for an MVV and other countries. Second, citizens who were exempted because of their nationality were in a cultural, economic and social situation from which it could be expected that they had a good understanding of the Dutch social relations, norms and values. Third, the interest in requiring an integration level from them was lower than the Dutch interest in maintaining good foreign and economic relations with these countries. These interests could be at stake if the government decided to introduce an MVV and an obligation to integrate before admission from citizens who were currently exempt from this requirement on the basis of their nationality. The minister added that the Dutch policy served as an example within the European Union. A few months before this reply by the government, a court judged that the WIB was not discriminatory, because the protection of the economic relations with these countries justified the ground for exemption. In March 2010, the Committee on the Elimination of Racial Discrimination (CERD), in its concluding observations on the application of the UN convention in the Netherlands, endorsed the point of view of Human Rights Watch. The CERD found that the exemption led to discrimination on the basis of nationality, particularly between 'Western' and 'non-Western' state nationals, and recommended that the Netherlands review its legislation (CERD 2010).

Two critical comments emerged from the Council of Europe. In 2008, the European Commission against Racism and Intolerance (ECRI) expressed its concerns about the reduction in applications and the fees for the examination. It recommended monitoring the impact of the test abroad and reviewing the system of exemptions, in order to comply with the prohibition of discrimination on grounds of nationality (ECRI 2008: nos. 50, 57 and 58). In spring 2009, the Commissioner for Human Rights of the Council of Europe, Hammarberg, presented his findings on the Dutch policy regarding human rights. In his view, the Family Reunification Directive did not allow Member States to impose passing an examination as a condition for family reunification. He requested the government to review entry conditions for family migration to ensure that tests, fees and age requirements did not amount to a disproportionate obstacle (Hammarberg 2008: par. 4.2, no. 83 and rec. no. 19). In its reply, the Dutch government agreed with this recommendation and referred to the coming results of the evaluation of the WIB.

When it became clear that approximately 90 per cent of the candidates passed the test, the minister considered the introduction of two strengthening measures: raising the limit to pass in order to decrease the number of successful candidates, and increasing the minimum test level from A1 minus to A1, which would make the examination more difficult. Both measures were strongly supported by the majority of the parliament. The limit to pass has been raised since 15 March 2008, but the minister felt that raising the test level to A1 would only be justified if the government would facilitate the preparation of the test. To this end the Minister announced to assess the possibility of cooperation with the Goethe Institute, which supported candidates worldwide with their preparation for the test on the German language.

Statistics showed a significant decrease in the number of applications for family reunification after the introduction of the integration requirement (the first two years 40 percent, later 25 percent. While responding to the evaluation of the integration requirement abroad, the government mentioned this drop in the number of applications without judging this consequence of the measures positively or negatively. It expressed its concern about the fact that a quarter of the partners still had a poor education and that the lasting impact of the integration test appeared to be limited. According to the government, the latter was due to the low level of the examination. It therefore announced that it would raise the examination level to A1 and include a written examination. The government announced that it would develop 'specific material'. With its decision, the government neglected the advice it had requested from experts on linguistic integration. The experts recommended not introducing written tests without proper education, as it would exclude illiterate persons and migrants who had learnt another alphabet. According to the experts, they would only be able to pass the test if they could participate in language courses. In order not to change the way of testing, the Dutch government finally decided to add only a reading test. The reading skills of the migrant are also tested by the computer. Although writing skills are not tested, the reading test requires a certain level of literacy.

Germany

The language test abroad was introduced as a transposition of one of the non-compulsory conditions of the Family Reunification Directive. The debate showed the clear influence of the politics of other countries: in the legal policy debate about the restrictions on the reunification of spouses, reference was made to the integration requirement introduced in the Netherlands. Although the restrictions on the family reunification of spouses are phrased neutrally in the wording of the law and apply to reunification with German nationals as well as foreign nationals, they are meant to avoid the situation where Turks, in particular, who hold traditional values and who are living here, bring very young wives uninfluenced by Western values from their country of origin to Germany. According to the Explanatory Memorandum, the language requirements are justified by three purposes: the need for promoting or demanding integration, the aim to provide protection from forced marriages and violations of human rights, and thirdly the need for protection of the social welfare state.[19] Protection from forced marriages through the introduction of the language test before entry was crucial in public debates and the media. In public discussions in Germany,

19 The position of German law regarding Germans with a migration background becomes even clearer in the justification of economic discrimination, which was introduced with respect to family reunification with Germans. Concerning the requirements guaranteeing subsistence, a decisive factor is whether it is possible to build family unity in the country of origin of a spouse. The law makes a distinction between German nationals: in future, family reunification cannot only be denied to third-country nationals but also to Germans if the sponsor cannot guarantee a sufficient income. The former privilege for spouses of a German ceases to apply. Pursuant to the Explanatory Memorandum, 'special circumstances' exist for persons of whom matrimonial cohabitation abroad can reasonably be expected. This especially concerns holders of dual citizenship with regard to the country whose nationality they possess in addition to German nationality, or Germans who have lived and worked for a fairly long time in the spouse's country of origin and who speak the language of this country.

forced marriage is often defined as a human rights question (Ratia & Walter 2009). According to the Explanatory Memorandum, in-law families use the lack of German language ability deliberately or indirectly to prevent the victims (mostly women) from having an independent social life. The legislator argued that the obligation to attend the integration course after having entered Germany would not have the same effect as attending a course abroad, because of the time it takes before the course starts and the language is learned. In the meantime, the (female) spouse would be subjected to the will of the family-in-law. Furthermore, educated men and women would be more unattractive, according to the family concept of affected circles, and would be difficult to 'control'.

After the introduction of forced marriage as a specific offence in 2005, the debates on how to prevent forced marriages focused only on migration law. This culminated in the two additional new entry requirements – minimum age as well as basic knowledge of the language prior to entry – for spouses of third-country nationals and Germans. Criticism of the constitutional conformity of the provisions and the lack of research on the effectiveness of this restriction and on less general and far-reaching alternatives did not change the dominant view that the protection from forced marriages and dependence of brides justified the language requirement. Nevertheless, the Bill was only desired and promoted by the Christian Democrats. They succeeded in agreement on the Bill in a political compromise with their Social-democratic coalition partners. The SDP got the consent to regularize a large number of asylum seekers who had lived in Germany for years with an insecure status. In return, it had to agree to the Christian Democrats' plan to introduce a language test abroad (Groenendijk 2010).

In general, the Courts have already accepted the arguments of the legislator. The Federal Administrative Court of Germany has confirmed that the regulation is compatible with the Constitution, the Family Reunification Directive and Article 8 ECHR. The Court decided that the principles of proportionality are applied adequately. The Higher Administrative Court of Berlin-Brandenburg (OVG) argued similarly regarding family reunification with a German citizen. The Federal Constitutional Court of Germany has not yet ruled on the issue of inferior treatment in cases of family reunification with German citizens compared to EU citizens, regarding the conflict as a result of so-called 'reverse discrimination' (Walter 2008). However, the invalid application of language requirements in the family reunification of EU citizens' spouses that had initially been practised was changed as a consequence of the judgment of the European Court of Justice on 25 May 2008 in the *Metock* case (Case C-127/08, cf. *8. Lagebericht* 2010: 475). This confirming jurisprudence contrasts the increasing debates in the legal literature on the compatibility of the new language requirements before entry with superior rules of law.

France

In France, the debate on introducing obligatory pre-departure integration measures started in 2006, when an MP published a report that made reference to the Dutch integration test and similar measures under discussion in Denmark and Germany. The relevant Bill, introduced in parliament in 2007, makes explicit reference to the provision allowing (but not mandating) integration measures in the EU Family Reunification Directive. The decision to implement this option to introduce integration measures abroad, was apparently motivated by the same concerns observed in other countries: the number of third-country nationals admitted for family reunification was considered too high in comparison with the numbers of immigrants admitted for employment or study (Carrera 2009b: 315-316). The then Interior Minister Sarkozy coined two phrases: *passer de l'immigration subie à une immigration choisie* ('from passive immigration to selective immigration' — family migration being in the former category) and *une immigration choisie, une integration réussie*. With the second phrase, the Minister claimed a causal relationship between selective immigration and successful integration (Michalowski 2010). Although the integration test was only implemented in the Netherlands in 2006, the French minister pointed out the already positive impact of such measures on the integration of immigrants. MP Mariani mentioned a second argument for the measure; he pointed to the fact that non-renewal of the residence permit due to failure to comply with the obligations of the welcoming contract was difficult because of Article 8 ECHR. He stated that such difficulties could be overcome by integration in the country of origin. In that situation, if attendance at language courses was not completed, the visa could be refused. Hence, integration abroad was not dedicated to the enhancement of integration of third-country nationals but to better manage migration flows.

Although the question relating to integration measures abroad had not been discussed extensively in the parliament, the Bill had been significantly changed before being adopted in 2007. Whereas the Bill established integration conditions (as the issuance of the visa was subordinated to attendance at sessions in the country of origin), the adopted law introduced integration measures without the initially proposed refusal of entry as a sanction for not fulfilling the integration requirement. The original idea of following the Dutch model and requiring the passing of a language test was dropped on legal grounds. It was considered probable that the Constitutional Council, which upon the request of MPs decides on the constitutionality of a Bill immediately after its adoption, would rule that the requirement violated the French Constitution's provision for a right to family life. Moreover, it was considered doubtful whether this requirement would be compatible with France's obligations under the EU Family Reunification Directive, which only allows for integration *measures* and not for integration *conditions* (Pascouau 2010).

United Kingdom

The possibility of introducing a pre-admission language requirement for third-country nationals seeking to migrate to the United Kingdom as the spouse or unmarried partner of a British citizen or a person with a permanent residence permit ('indefinite leave to remain') was mentioned in a government policy document published in March 2007. A detailed proposal was made in December 2007, setting the required level at A1. The integration of the spouses/partners into the community and their employment prospects were mentioned as the main justifications. In yet another policy document of July 2008, a formal requirement to have basic knowledge of the English language was qualified as 'a medium-term goal' because of gaps in the availability of English language courses in countries of origin. In June 2010, the new Conservative-Liberal Democrat government announced its intention to introduce an English language test for non-European spouses and partners coming to join a UK citizen or a settled immigrant. They will be required to demonstrate basic English (at the A1 level) in an oral test in their home country.

Denmark

In 2006, the Danish minority government made an agreement with the Danish People's Party (DPP), an opposition party with an anti-immigrant programme, to revise the country's existing integration policy. Part of the agreement was the introduction of a pre-departure integration test along the lines of the Dutch examination introduced a few months earlier. After the act on the introduction of the integration test had been adopted in 2007, a working group was set up with a view to making a pre-analysis of the implementation of the test. The working group concluded that it would be very costly to establish a testing system abroad (comprising relatively few applicants from many different countries). Accordingly the government and the DPP, in their agreement on the country's budget for 2008, agreed that the 2007 act would be amended. The act was amended in spring 2010 and the new examinations were introduced on 15 November 2010. Cost-benefit considerations played a decisive role in this remarkable policy change.

According to the government, the examination was aimed at increasing the chances of rapid and successful integration of immigrants who would also be better prepared for integration courses after arrival in Denmark. Furthermore, the immigration test should help in securing that foreigners at the outset took responsibility for their own integration and proved their motivation and wish to become part of Danish society. The Minister of Integration underlined from the very beginning that the purpose of the test was not to limit the number of family reunifications – and not to keep foreigners out of Denmark; the government therefore did not expect a distinctive decrease in the number of applications. During the debate in parliament in 2010 the minister made it quite clear that the test would be adjusted in such a way that all 'can make it out'.[20] She underlined that it was not about 'integration', but might be seen as a 'foretaste', making it possible for applicants to document their interest in being integrated and getting familiar with Danish norms. Based on the test some migrants might change their opinion about staying in Denmark – having discovered 'what it is all about' (learning about Danish sexual morality, etc.). The test was supposed to send a signal to newcomers that integration was also about individuals contributing actively and engaging in their own integration; likewise, the test was aimed at giving applicants some realistic expectations about their life in Denmark and the possibilities, requirements, obligations, etc. they would meet.

The introduction of the immigration test has received relatively little attention in the media. During the debate in parliament, it was stressed that the immigration test had not been invented by the Danish government, it had been, allegedly, successfully implemented in the Netherlands – and, according to information received, without having been blamed for violations of international treaty obligations. With regard to one aspect, the government had probably taken the international criticism on the Dutch policy into account. It promised the DPP to examine whether immigrants from Western countries could be exempted, as in the Dutch legislation. However in the Bill implementing this part of the agreement, no such exemptions were provided.

Before the legislative work, a number of NGOs and other organisations and institutions criticized the test for being exclusive, especially taking into consideration the lack of educa-

20 Oral test and preparatory material that do not imply writing or reading abilities.

tion offers and the high fee which as a whole could make it difficult, if not impossible, for poor and/or uneducated applicants to pass. In order to solve some of the alleged problems it was suggested making it possible for migrants to take the knowledge test in their own language. Also opposition parties (including Social Democrats) supported the idea of introducing an integration test provided that all applicants regardless of their educational and financial background were able to pass it. Members of the party proposed offering the immigrants the possibility of an extended stay in Denmark for their preparation for the test. The Minister of Integration rejected the proposals for more support and fewer obstacles, as she stressed that a central element of the test was to strengthen the individual's responsibility to prepare for his/her life in Denmark. Furthermore she pointed out the financial consequences if all applicants were to be offered Danish language education.

Austria

In January 2010, the Austrian Minister of Interior announced a plan to introduce more restrictive immigration rules, one of them being a language requirement for spouses wanting to join their family members in Austria. The Minister explicitly referred to the Dutch case. Some elements of the requirement seem to be similar to the German system: the test will include an oral and written test and the level will be A1. It differs however with regard to the intended target group, as spouses of Austrian nationals will not fall under the scope of the act (Bundesregierung Österreich 2010: 38-39). While the idea is at the time of writing of this report still in the planning stage, it has met with strong criticism from Green politicians and civil rights groups (see the afterword). The Austrian Red Cross said that mandatory language classes in the country of origin would be expensive and unfeasible. In some countries, applicants would have to travel long distances to the embassies or would face danger doing so (Pop 2009; Groenendijk 2010: 19). On 4 October 2010, the Minister of the Interior, Maria Fekter (ÖVP), announced in an interview in the daily *Kurier*, that in the autumn an amendment to the Aliens Law would be passed demanding knowledge of German at the A1 level as a precondition for immigration.

2.5 Consequences of Not Passing the Test

Except for the test applied by the French government, which only serves as a measurement instrument, not passing the test means that family members are not granted reunification with their partners in the Member State. Unless those partners choose to move to the country of origin of their family member (provided that the immigration rules of that country allows them to do so), they will continue to live separately. How long this separation will take, depends on the ability of the spouse to pass the examination. If the partner has to take re-sits, the family reunification will be delayed. If this inability has a permanent character and he or she is not exempted from the requirement, there are two possibilities to live together: in the country of origin of the spouse outside the EU, or in the Member State on a irregular basis. If the spouse who lives in the Member State is an EU citizen who has exercised the right to freedom of movement, they can reunite in his Member State of residence on the basis of Directive 2004/38/EC.

2.6 Effects of the Tests: Statistical Data[21]

The study on the effects of the integration and language tests abroad is limited to the three Member States where the tests are currently applied. In this paragraph a distinction is made between the impact on the number of applications and the impact on the perception, behaviour and integration of the tests. As the French rapporteur was not able to conduct interviews, the second analysis is limited to the Netherlands and Germany.

In all three countries, the number of applications dropped significantly after the introduction of the test abroad. In the Netherlands, the reduction was approximately 40 per cent in the first two years after the introduction of the test. Although this drop may partly be the delayed effect of other restrictive measures introduced in previous years, several studies indicate that the integration test is the main cause of the decline.[22] Although the number of applications slightly rose again in the years afterwards, the number of applications is still significantly lower than before the introduction of the test. In Germany, there was an average 25 per cent reduction in visas for spouses in the first six months of 2008 compared with the same period in the previous year. According to civil servants of German municipalities, the decrease can be ascribed particularly to the introduction of the language test abroad and to the accession of Romania and Bulgaria. The reduction in the number of spouses entering the Netherlands and Germany is the most significant with regard to the countries of origin from where the largest communities residing in the two Member States originate. In the Netherlands the reduction of applications from Turkish and Moroccan spouses is relatively high; in Germany the number of visas issued in Turkey, Kosovo, Russia and Thailand has declined relatively the most (for instance a decline of 38 per cent for Turkish citizens).

Netherlands

With regard to the Turkish and Moroccan nationals living in the Netherlands, statistics show a decrease in the number of marriages with a spouse living abroad. Whereas in 2001 more than half of the Turkish and Moroccan second or third generation migrants concluded a marriage abroad, in 2007 only 20 per cent of them chose a partner abroad. They mostly still marry a person from the same ethnic community, but more and more with a person already living in the Netherlands. This development seems to be connected to the more restrictive admission criteria, especially the income requirement, the integration test abroad and the age limit (Dagevos & Gijsberts 2009: 19). As these groups of immigrants were explicitly targeted by the act, the government's policy seems to have been successful for this part. This development however does not explain the whole drop in the number of applications. We do not know what the current family situation is of the persons who don't apply anymore. Did they come to the Netherlands irregularly or do they live separately? Until now no research has been conducted on their situation, and policymakers do not pay

---

21 Unless otherwise stated, the figures in this section have been taken from the national INTEC reports.

22 IND, *Monitor Inburgeringsexamen Buitenland*, april 2008, p. 6; IND, *Jaarresultaten 2006*, Den Haag, maart 2007, p. 3; Sociaal Cultureel Planbureau, *Jaarrapport Integratie 2007*; Dagevos & Gijsberts 2009, p. 316; WODC, *Korte termijn evaluatie Wet inburgering buitenland, eindrapportage,* Ministerie van Justitie, januari 2008.

attention to this 'black hole'. Nevertheless the figures show that a number of persons do not manage to pass the examination, no matter how many times the examination is taken. Although the pass rate for candidates taking the examination for the first time remains on average 89 per cent, the pass rate is lower for migrants who have to take the examination twice or more (72 per cent). The pass rate is also lower in the case of elderly migrants and the lower educated.

It is not easy to make a comparison between the data on the Dutch and German statistics because the drop in the Netherlands concerns the number of applications, while the drop in Germany concerns the number of applications granted. In the Netherlands, spouses tend to take the test and apply for admission only if they are quite sure that the visa will be granted. This behaviour might be caused by the high costs involved in taking the test and paying the fees for the application. The number of applications granted increased even after the introduction of new and strengthened requirements. This outcome could be related to the change in population of the applicants the statistics show: nearly 75 per cent of the candidates have had an average or high education, whereas in 2005 around 53 per cent of the applicants for family reunification were illiterate or low educated. Researchers who conducted the evaluation of the integration test abroad called this phenomenon a kind of 'self-selection' (Odé 2009 and Regioplan 2009). This self-selection seems to affect family reunification harder than family formation (which means that the marriage is concluded after the sponsor was granted a residence permit), as figures show that the number of applications for reunification have recovered less than those for formation. This could be explained by the fact that this group of family members probably includes relatively more elderly and lower educated migrants (e.g. family members of victims of war). Hence, although the Integration Act Abroad particularly aimed to affect young spouses, it seems to have hit other groups harder.

Germany

Unlike the situation in the Netherlands, third-country nationals wanting to (re-) unite with their spouse in Germany do not seem to refrain from application because of the language test. However they are rejected more often than in the Netherlands, mostly due to their failure of the test. Respondents at the Goethe Institute signaled a certain number of spouses who register for the test unprepared. In 2008 the pass rate was on average 59 per cent, in 2009 this percentage increased to 64. This increase is presumably related to the attendance of future spouses at language courses in Germany.[23] The language teachers interviewed in this study emphasized an increase in interest in the language course at level A1 in Germany. Regarding the tests taken abroad, a slight difference is visible between the pass rate of candidates who attended a German language course at the Goethe Institute (74 per cent) and the pass rate of candidates who did not do so (61 per cent). In some specific countries such as Turkey, the difference is more significant: in Turkey the pass rate in 2008 was 60 per cent (92 per cent of the course participants succeeded, 57 per cent of the other candidates succeeded), in 2009 the pass rate increased to 68 per cent (92 per cent of the participants

23 In order to be admitted to Germany, they had mentioned a different purpose for their stay in Germany, in the visa procedure, than language acquisition for family reunification.

succeeded, 64 per cent of the other candidates). During the first six months of 2009, one-fifth of the candidates who passed the test had participated in the preparatory course at the Goethe Institute. Although the so-called 'external' candidates might have used other preparation methods (private courses, the Internet, courses in Germany), participating in the course specifically preparing for the test seems to have improved the chances of passing substantially. According to the evaluation by the government, the significant difference in the pass rate of candidates who attended a course at the Goethe Institute and the other candidates, reveals a difference in quality of the courses. The quality of private courses is worse compared to the courses offered by the Goethe Institute, or at least unpredictable and they are not preparing adequately for the test (Auswärtiges Amt 2010). In the evaluation, the differences in the pass rates and the number of resits is related to two factors: the differences in (the quality of) course offerings and the differences in education level of the spouses. The percentage of female candidates passing the test proved to be significantly higher than the percentage of successful male candidates.

The evaluation shows that the largest decline in the numbers of visas issued was in the first six months, when spouses had to prepare to take the test. Although the number of visas issued for reasons of family reunification is still lower than before the introduction of the test, the government concludes on the basis of its evaluation of the act that the number is now on the level that was to be expected if no language condition had been introduced. To substantiate this conclusion, the government refers to the fact that the number of applications for family reunification from Turkey already declined before the introduction of the test. According to the government a structural decrease in the number of visas issued is in line with the development world wide (Bundesregierung Deutschland 2010: 2-3 and 45-47).[24] The German rapporteurs are more cautious in their conclusion: they ascertain an increase in the number of family reunifications in 2009, but they notify that the pattern is irregular, as the numbers per quarter differ. This can be influenced by seasonal factors. A comparison of the same quarters in different years, seems to indicate a recovery to a certain extent of the decline immediately after the introduction of the language condition.[25]

France

In France, the number of visas issued for family reunification in the first six months of 2009 was 27 per cent below the level in the same period for 2008, before the new policy was introduced. The drop is considered to be the result of the strengthening of the rules applicable to family reunification and the introduction of the test. With regard to the latter, this factor is probably much less determining compared to the Netherlands and Germany, while passing the test is not a condition for admission to France. Failing the test only delays the family reunification for two months at most. Nevertheless, in literature on this topic refer-

24 According to the evaluation, the number of visas issued for family reunification from Turkey was 19.426 in 2002, 10.208 in 2006 and 6.905 in 2009. The test has been introduced on 1 October 2007. No specific reasons are given for the decline since 2002. The introduction of the *Zuwanderungsgesetz* on 1 January 2005 only implied slight changes in the right to family reunification.

25 The statistics on the second quarter of 2007-2009 show the number of visas issued: 2007 (no test): 9267, 2008: 7771, 2009: 8053. The third quarter: 2007 (no test): 8603, 2008: 8445, 2009: 9027. The fourth quarter: 2007 (introduction test) 5147, 2008: 8093; 2009: 8289.

ence is made to the difficulties migrants meet if as a result of the test they have to attend a course. If they live far from the education institute, following the course could constitute a financial and organisational burden, despite the fact that the education offered is free (Cournil & Depigny 2008).

2.7 Effects of the Tests: Interview Results

Netherlands

On the basis of our interviews, it can be concluded that most migrants are positive about learning about Dutch society as preparation for their migration to the Netherlands. Some respondents emphasized they would also have prepared on Dutch society without a test. The respondents confirmed that learning the Dutch language abroad does not seem to substantially contribute to their knowledge of the Dutch language. Preparing for the test itself causes a lot of stress and tension, and takes time and money. Four out of ten respondents interviewed in Turkey were offended and angry about the requirement. One of them pointed to the fact that Dutch citizens are not obliged to learn Turkish before being admitted to Turkey. Most of the respondents were of the opinion that learning the language in the Netherlands would be easier and more appropriate than learning it abroad.

All respondents emphasized that preparation for the test would have been impossible or at least much more difficult without having attended a course. Participating in a course also offers the possibility of getting into contact with other future inhabitants of the Netherlands, and getting more realistic expectations of living there. Female candidates especially seem to benefit from this. These respondents were in the fortunate position of being able to attend a course. Immigrants lacking this opportunity also lack these advantages and will face more problems with passing the test.

Preparing for the test constitutes difficulties in some situations, especially because of the lack of support from the Dutch authorities. According to the Moroccan organisation, migrants living in rural areas have problems travelling to the embassy several times (as well as communicating with the embassy from a distance) and finding preparation material. Often a course is not available to them. The Dutch Refugee Council pointed to the extremely harsh situation in (former) war countries. The family members have to travel (twice) through unsafe areas, sometimes to an embassy settled in another country. They also lack educational material and sometimes even the Internet or electricity. Also the respondents in Turkey who were able to follow lessons, pointed to some negative consequences. According to teachers it was difficult for migrants who worked full time to do the course. One respondent had to give up her job in order to be able to follow the lessons. As the admission procedure had been delayed, she had already waited for a long time without an income. More respondents felt negative about the fact that they had to invest a lot (in time and in money) while the outcome of the application procedure was insecure. Also the combination of requirements caused stress, as the outcome of the test was only valid for one year. In one case the partner in the Netherlands had lost his job in the meantime: the migrant would have to take the test again. Some respondents knew migrants whose relationship had broken down as a result of the ongoing problems and frustrations because of the test and the whole application procedure.

The language teachers in Turkey pointed out that most of the participants on their courses were young and relatively highly educated. One teacher in the Netherlands noticed that after the introduction of the WIB, he only received highly educated newcomers. This confirms the observed change in the background of the migrants in the evaluation of the Integration Act (see section 2.6). According to the teachers and migrants in Turkey, illiterate persons, elderly migrants and the low educated suffer the most from the integration requirement. One respondent and one teacher pleaded for an exemption for elderly persons. The Dutch Refugee Council pleaded for an exemption for migrants with psychological problems.

Furthermore more than one-third of the respondents interviewed in the evaluation of the act, expected that specific groups would have less chance of passing the examination. They referred to illiterates and low educated immigrants, some also referred to elderly immigrants. The average age of family migrants who come from a country where the integration requirement applies has dropped slightly since the introduction of the act, while their average level of education has increased. According to the researchers this could imply that the act triggers a degree of self-selection, whereby the elderly and lower educated are being deterred most by the integration requirement. The researchers therefore advised investing in specific information for the elderly, illiterate and low educated, in order to remove their psychological barrier. In their view, the level of the examination is suitable for these groups as well. The advisory committee involved in this evaluation, doubted the compatibility of the integration test abroad with Article 7 (2) of the Family Reunification Directive, as the criteria regarding the proportionality of the measure might not be fulfilled. More in general, the advisory commission advised improving facilitation of the preparation for the examination (Regioplan 2009).

Germany

The conclusion of the Dutch evaluation that the integration test abroad constitutes a form of self- selection was also drawn by a respondent from a German migrant advisory service, who summarised: 'Only men and women who can read and write may marry de facto.' A German language teacher pointed out that the content of the tests causes extra problems for certain groups, as the tasks are related to aspects of daily life in Germany, which are not familiar to all test candidates abroad.

From the immigrants' point of view, listening is the most difficult discipline in the test abroad. The spoken language in the recordings for the test and the speech of officials in the Diplomatic Mission is regarded as rapid. To some extent, migrants explain the high number of retakes by the fact that the test candidates do not pass the listening part of the test or they sit the test without being prepared for it. Not preparing for the test seems to be related to a lack of motivation to comply with the requirements. According to the respondents at the Goethe Institute, teachers abroad have difficulties gaining support among the migrants regarding the purpose of the requirement and motivating them to prepare for the test.

The German authorities and the Goethe Institute experienced cases of avoidance as well as attempts at fraud. To improve identity controls, registration for the test takes place in person and on a different day from the test itself. Sometimes the oral tests and the written tests take place on different days as well. These measures are seen as a burden by those affected because of distances to the examination location and the financial expense. In some countries (the rapporteurs mention Nigeria), problems regarding authenticity of documents and certificates arise because they are not registered in the country.

The visa procedure is repeatedly criticised in that it lacks transparency and constitutes, in addition, a tripwire. The fact that the authorities can repeatedly control the language ability during the visa procedure is perceived by migrants as trickery and an arbitrary measure. In order to combat fraud, migrants were asked at the Embassy in Thailand, for example, what colour their blouse was and they had to write down their name and address, although they had already passed the language test. There were also complaints about spouses who were tested by the Foreigner's Authority a second time after arrival in Germany.

Interviewed Germans who wanted their spouse to join them in Germany, perceived their position as inferior to EU citizens whose spouses were not subject to the language test: 'I did not understand it, why am I suddenly in a minority?' To avoid the language test before entry, a certain number of Germans take up temporary residence in a neighbouring European country in order to enable the subsequent migration of a spouse as an EU citizen.

Migrants and municipal officials in Germany viewed the possibility of learning German through courses abroad as positive because a basic command of the language would help the persons involved to make purchases by themselves, to ask questions independently and to make the newly arrived immigrants more self-confident. The courses also promote social contacts with other spouses. This prevents especially female spouses getting into an isolated position after arrival in Germany. Not only teachers of integration courses, but also migrant advisory services and migrants regard the courses as positive but see the costs and efforts involved in the test as a burden. The respondents of the migrant advisory service did not question the obligation for migrants to learn the German language; however, they have spoken out against the fact that this is bound to the tests in the visa procedure.

The fulfilment of language requirements is associated with strenuous effort, psychological burdens, partner stress and family stress: 'Many people are at breaking point over it, which means that I give these couples advice about family reunification and then transfer them to my colleague in the department of separation and divorce'. From the migrant advisory services' point of view, this regulation reinforces the imbalance of power between women and men and makes a wife emotionally and financially dependent on her husband. 'We often had dramatic cases; a girl in Afghanistan had to go to Kabul, through enemy territory, not only to take the course, but also to apply for a visa. Then she was smuggled across the border. [...].'

The stress that goes along with the language requirement does not seem to correspond with the effect on the migrant of having passed the test on language ability. Most of the teachers of integration courses interviewed as part of this study considered that the output of the language test before entry was low and the costs for those involved were high. Generally, the teachers in Germany do not regard the results of the language test at level A1 as significant because of differences in the language ability at the first level of proficiency. They sometimes experience that migrants who passed the test abroad, are not able to speak a word of German.

Do the Tests Promote Integration?

Netherlands

The purpose of the Dutch test was fourfold. First, acting independently after arrival; second, promoting a more deliberate and better informed choice to migrate to the Netherlands; third, emphasizing the migrants' own responsibility and fourth, selecting the motivated and persevering migrants.

With regard to the language level, the official evaluation did not reveal large differences between migrants who took the examination abroad and migrants who did not do so. The researchers noticed only slightly better listening skills by migrants who took the examination at their time of arrival in the Netherlands in comparison with migrants who did not take an examination abroad. The researchers based this conclusion on a comparison between these two groups of their level of listening during the intake soon after admission to the Netherlands. The researchers suggested that this difference might also relate to the changing background of migrants.

Most of the interviewed migrants in Turkey expected that their preparation would enable them to act more independently in the Netherlands (see a doctor, go shopping). It is noteworthy that this expectation does not correspond with the experience of the three respondents who had already entered the Netherlands after having passed the test. The level appears to be too low and the knowledge too soon forgotten for them to be able to act independently in the Netherlands. Also four out of five teachers in the Netherlands hardly noticed any difference between migrants who did the test abroad and others. One explanatory factor could be the time that passes between the test and the start of a course in the Netherlands. Most of the respondents argued that learning the language in the Netherlands would be much quicker and more effective. According to one teacher, knowledge of Dutch society is regarded as the most useful education. It helps them to prepare for their stay in the Netherlands. Two teachers pointed to the importance of the contact old participants kept with each other in the Netherlands, which prevented them from isolation. This advantage is of course only applicable to immigrants who are able to attend a course. As the organisation of courses is left to the free market, there are private courses only in the main countries of origin.

The purpose of emphasizing the migrant's own responsibility for his/her integration, seems to have the side-effect of making migrants feel frustrated, as they experience a lot of difficulty in meeting the integration requirement without any support from the government. From the interviews we learned that most of them already felt responsible for preparing for their stay in the Netherlands. The difficulties they had to overcome were not experienced as proportionate. The absence of any offer of courses affected this perception.

The purpose of promoting a more deliberate and better informed choice is only partly achieved with regard to migrants who attended a course, if the teacher is aware of the importance of promoting realistic expectations of residence in the Netherlands. Learning the language from a book does not stimulate a more deliberate choice. As the organisation and quality of courses is completely left to the free market, the authorities do not influence this effect.

Although respondents often mentioned motivation as a crucial element for meeting the integration requirements, the interviews confirm the figures that the test abroad creates selection on age and education. This type of selection differs from the purpose of the policy makers to select on motivation and perseverance. Given the reduction in the number of applications and the relatively high educational level of the remaining applicants, one could conclude that the government's planned selection and reduction in the numbers appears to have been effective.

Germany

The purpose of the German language test abroad is to promote integration and to protect against forced marriages. Migrants and migrant advisory services in Germany have repeatedly pointed at the discrepancy between what is demanded and the knowledge that those involved actually possess after the test abroad. 'I do not think it is good because people do not speak German after passing the test.' Nevertheless none of the migrants interviewed emphasized that the language requirements for the subsequent migration of spouses were easy to fulfil.

At the same time, it is not possible to judge whether the test protects those affected from forced marriages. It was quite incomprehensible to all the interviewees how the language test could prevent forced marriages. Migrants, their spouses and migrant advisory services have repeatedly felt that the language test does not prevent forced marriages. The achievement of this latter purpose is also hard to find out, as figures on the scope of the existence of this phenomenon are lacking.

According to the evaluation of the government however, teachers abroad had noticed in some cases that women deliberately failed the examination in order to avoid a forced marriage in Germany. Furthermore, the teachers observed that the attendance of the courses promotes a greater awareness by young candidates of the drastic personal changes involved in their migration to Germany. Learning the elementary aspects of the German language would motivate them to continue language lessons after arrival in Germany (Bundesregierung 2010: 2).

Taking into account the figures on applications and the perception of the respondents, one can conclude that the test has a selective effect and is perceived by migrants and advisory organisations as an offence against family life. At the same time it is highly doubtful whether the language test promotes integration or prevents forced marriages. These administrative procedures and costs on the part of the authorities, as well as the efforts made and expenses incurred by those affected would appear to be disproportionate to a low success rate, taking into account the low language skills the teachers in Germany observe. Integration assistance through language courses is perceived as an advantage, as it prepares spouses for their life in Germany and perhaps motivates them to continue studying the language. The causal connection between the proof of language ability and the claim to family reunification however constitutes the problem.

2.8 Summary and Conclusions

Overview of National Practices and Differences

The Member States can be categorised as the ones that require language skills in reading and writing as well as in listening and speaking (Germany and in future Austria), and the Member States that limit their requirements to listening and speaking skills (Netherlands, Denmark, United Kingdom). The Member States of the first category accompany the written and oral test with an infrastructure of education. This German choice to support migrants in their preparation for the test, expresses its policy (introduced in 2005) of promoting and demanding integration. Although the demanding aspect has gained weight since 2007, the promoting element facilitates migrants to fulfil the language requirements.

The latter category of Member States, which have only introduced an oral test, do not organise an infrastructure of language courses. This clear division will come to an end at the moment the Dutch government introduces the written test in April 2011. No courses in the Dutch language will be offered, despite the opinion of the previous government and of experts that the requirement of written skills without the possibility of attending a course, will result in the exclusion of low educated and elderly migrants from family reunification.

France also offers courses (and obliges migrants to participate), but only to prepare family members for their stay in France. Unlike the other Member States with language requirements, France does not require a certain level of knowledge as a condition for admission. It applies an effort obligation, not a result obligation. According to the French rapporteur, the French government wanted to ensure compliance with Article 7 (2) of the Family Reunification Directive. The European Commission seems to agree with the French interpretation of the limits of the directive. According to the Commission, integration tests can only be admissible if they promote integration of the family members, without undermining the purpose of the directive, namely the protection of family life. Whether or not the requirement is proportionate and to what extent applicants are supported in their preparation, are determining factors for the admissibility of the test (Commission 2008: 7-8).

The systems of the two Member States which will only introduce an oral test, offer better preparation possibilities than the Dutch system. Observance of the British discussion on the decision to apply a language test reveals that the availability of English language courses was a main consideration. Although the British government will not organise courses, it can be taken for granted that access to an English language course worldwide is easier than access to a Dutch or Danish course. Although the Danish government only chose to examine the applicants in Denmark for financial reasons, this decision may possibly enable migrants to attend a language course in Denmark. This will probably be much more effective than learning the language abroad.

Table 2.1: Language or integration requirements for family reunification[*]

Country	*Required to pass a test for admission*	*Level and content*	*Target group*	*Costs*	*Entry into force*
Netherlands	Yes Test abroad No course is offered education material for sale	A1minus from 1 January 2011: A1 Oral, language and society	third-country nationals in need for a visa applying for family reunification (18-65) with third country or own national, except spouses of refugees and highly skilled	€1440 excluding a course	15-03-2006
Germany	Yes Test abroad Course is offered	A1 written and oral, language	Identical to Netherlands, except age (16-65)	€660 Including a course	1 -09-2007
France	No Two other conditions: Signing integration contract and attendance course (if knowledge is insufficient)	A.1.1 (below A1) Oral and written, language and society	third-country nationals applying for family reunification (16-65) with third country or own national	Free	1-01-2008

* The language proficiency levels referred to are those set out in the Council of Europe's 'Common European Framework of Reference: Learning, Teaching, Assessment'. A person with level A1 proficiency is defined as: 'Can understand and use familiar everyday expressions and very basic phrases aimed at the satisfaction of needs of a concrete type. Can introduce him/herself and others and can ask and answer questions about personal details such as where he/she lives, people he/she knows and things he/she has. Can interact in a simple way provided the other person talks slowly and clearly and is prepared to help.'

Country	*Required to pass a test for admission*	*Level and content*	*Target group*	*Costs*	*Entry into force*
Denmark	Yes Test in DK Education material is offered for free	A 1 minus Oral language and society	third-country nationals applying for family reunification (18-65) with third country or own national	€400	15-11-2010
United Kingdom	Yes Test abroad No course is offered	A 1 language oral	Spouses of a third country or own national, except those of a 'majority English-speaking country'	£644	29-11-2010 (expected)
Austria	Yes No course is offered Test abroad	A1 language oral and written	Family members of third-country nationals	unknown	unknown

This means that compared with the other Member States that have followed the Dutch example, immigrants applying for entry to the Netherlands will face the most difficulties in preparing for the examination. This will be even more difficult after the examination requirements are strengthened (April 2011). At that moment the examination will be the most difficult one in all involved Member States, while the preparation possibilities will be the least.

The costs involved with the language or integration test abroad for migrants, show significant differences between the Member States. Taking into account the fees, the Dutch application procedure for family reunification is far more expensive than those of other Member States. France is placed on the opposite end of the spectrum, as it does not charge the expenses for the test and courses to the applicant.

With regard to the target groups, the Netherlands and Germany make a distinction within the category third-country nationals. The nationals from 'Western countries' (including Japan and South Korea) do not fall within the scope of their acts. This distinction is made in order not to harm the economic relations with these countries. The other Member States however have not followed this example. As a result of the free movement rights, citizens of the EU and EEA and their family members are not affected by the language or integration tests. It is worth mentioning that with the exception of Denmark Turkish citizens are affected by the requirements, despite the EC-Turkey Association Agreement. The decision of the EU Court of Justice of 29 April 2010 on the scope and impact of the standstill clauses of this agreement has made application of the test abroad to Turkish citizens highly doubtful. This question however is hardly addressed in the Dutch and German public and political debate in reaction to this judgment. Own nationals of the Member States are not protected by EU law. Whereas all involved Member States apply the requirement also to spouses of their own citizens, Austria has decided not to do so.

Political Arguments

Even though the Member States copied the Dutch ideas, different arguments were used for the justification of the introduction of the test abroad. Where the Dutch government emphasized the improvement of the social position, stressing the migrants' responsibility to integrate and the promotion of a more deliberate choice for the Netherlands, the German government mentioned the promotion of integration and protection of the social welfare state. As the major justification, however, it stressed the importance of the combat of forced marriages. This latter argument by Germany was copied by the Dutch government as justification for the strengthening of the requirements. The Danish government not only copied the Dutch test, but also the arguments for its introduction. The motivation differed with regard to two aspects: the government put more emphasis on making migrants familiar with the Danish norms, which could lead to the decision not to migrate to Denmark. Secondly, the Danish government stressed that it was not aiming for a reduction in the number of migrants. The British government also did not refer to a reduction in immigrants. The British initiative was first justified by an MP as a measure to combat so-called 'ghettoisation', but the proposal for the test itself formed part of proposals concerning forced marriages. In its announcement on the introduction of the test, the Austrian government mentioned the test as a restrictive immigration rule, which implies the purpose of reducing the number of spouses coming from outside the EU.

The Dutch government seems to have changed its arguments in favour of the test abroad over time: at the introduction of the test improving the social position of migrants was the central purpose. After the evaluation however, the government substantiated the strengthening of the requirements with the purpose of raising the level of education of the spouses, with the aim of the protection (of the bride) from the family-in-law and the need to combat forced marriages. At the time of introduction of the test abroad, the initial choice of an oral form and a low level were argued with reference to illiterate and low educated migrants: they should also be able to pass the test. Now that the level is to be raised, this argument seems to have lost its validity. The previous position of the government that the level could only be raised to A1 if an infrastructure for education was provided has also vanished without any debate or argument. This evolution of arguing in favour of the test abroad, feeds the impression that the test is especially applied as an instrument of immigration control.

Whereas Germany and Denmark referred to the Netherlands to legitimise the requirement, France did so in order to prove that the requirement was effective (although the Dutch test had only just been introduced). At its initial proposal, the French government was the first Member State to express the explicit aim of reducing the number of third-country nationals admitted for family reunification and selecting candidates on their chances to integrate successfully. Although these purposes were to a certain extent similar to those of the Netherlands, the government decided not to make passing the test a condition for admission because of incompatibility with the French Constitution and the Family Reunification Directive.

The Dutch legislation did not convince the French civil servants and politicians of the lawfulness of the measure, but it seems to have convinced the German and Danish ones (referring to the rule of law in the Netherlands). The wide international criticism of the Dutch test abroad had not been included in the debates in these Member States, except for the criticism of the distinction between nationalities. Whereas this criticism did not affect the Dutch rules, it may have resulted in the absence of distinction between nationalities in Denmark. With regard to other elements of the criticism, the introduction of the test abroad in Germany, Denmark, and to a certain extent the United Kingdom and Austria, was legitimized by the previous introduction in the Netherlands without having taken the critical international reports on the Dutch practice into account.

Although the Member States which introduced a language or an integration test abroad seemed to have been inspired by the Netherlands, they all made different choices on its implementation. Besides the already mentioned choices regarding the assistance in learning the language, the differences in the target group is noteworthy. The fact that France and Denmark did not follow the Dutch and German example to distinguish certain nationalities, indicates that they did not want to risk a violation of the prohibition on discrimination on the basis of nationality. At the time the act was discussed in Denmark, much international criticism was uttered on the distinction the Netherlands made between nationalities in applying the integration act abroad. Hence, international criticism and jurisprudence directed at the Dutch policy has not led to changes in the Dutch integration requirement, but it has actually influenced the Danish integration requirement. The distinction the United Kingdom makes emerges from the language that is used in the countries of origin. This can be considered as an exemption because of sufficient knowledge of the language.

Impact of the Integration Requirement

In all three Member States the introduction of the test abroad has led to a drop in the number of applications or admissions for family reunification. It is remarkable that this effect also occurred in France, where the outcome of the test can result in a delay of just two months. Perhaps the obligation to attend a course (far from the place of residence) also constitutes an obstacle for applying for family reunification. After the first dramatic drop, the number of visas issued by the Netherlands and Germany increased again. This partial recovery indicates that some of the migrants managed to adjust to the new requirement. Furthermore, preparation for the test takes time, which partly explains the sharp drop immediately after the introduction of the test. In the Netherlands more ethnic Turks and Moroccans marry a person already residing in the Netherlands, partly as a result of the cumulation of more restrictive admission conditions. The figures of the Netherlands show that the remaining spouses from outside the EU are younger and more highly educated than the population of spouses before the introduction of the test. The statistics on applicants for family reunification in the German report do not include figures on educational background and age, but the German respondents also estimated that the language requirement selects on education and age. The selecting effect of the test is probably less significant in Germany than in the Netherlands, as applicants for the German test are supported in their preparation by a course.

The conclusion of respondents in the Netherlands and Germany are quite similar on a number of aspects. First, they share the opinion that the language requirement only results in a slight improvement of the language skills of the spouses. Taking into account the stress, time and money that are involved in passing the test, many respondents think there is no balance between the efforts and the result. Probably this imbalance is partly caused by the fact that learning the language of a country where you have never been is much more difficult than learning the language when you practice it in daily life. All respondents in both Member States acknowledged that learning the language after arrival is much more effective. Another reason is that some of the applicants are not used to learning (a language). The differences in pass rates in Germany also show that passing the test partly depends on the quality of the courses. Introducing a uniform quality mark or certification would perhaps improve the overall quality of the courses. The preparation for the Dutch test is even harder because of the lack of courses or the dependence on private courses without a quality mark. This will constitute an even larger problem after the introduction of the written test. Organizing an infrastructure of education abroad would diminish the risk of exclusion of certain groups. Furthermore it would encourage social contacts after arrival and result in more realistic expectations of life in the Netherlands. Hence, two purposes expressed by the Dutch government of the introduction of the test can be better achieved by personal education abroad.

Another similarity is the problems migrants meet when they live in (post-)war countries like Afghanistan. The absence of an embassy or education institute forces them to travel through unsafe areas several times. Also the absence of electricity or other elementary infrastructures constitute obstacles to the preparation for the test. These were probably the reason for the French government to exempt migrants living in these areas from taking a test and attending a course.

In general, migrants we interviewed were positive about the possibility of preparing for their stay in the Netherlands or Germany. Women seemed to be more motivated to learn and more positive about the requirement than the men. The ones who were able to attend a course (of good quality) gained social contacts, more self-confidence and a more realistic expectation about their future life. According to migrants preparing for the Dutch test, preparing on society was more useful than learning the language abroad. There was a broad consensus for the view that migrants should be required to learn the language of their new home country. A majority of the respondents thought, however, that this requirement should not be imposed before departure. According to most respondents however, the largest problem was the link between acquiring a certain level of knowledge and admission. A substantial proportion of respondents pointed out that the absence of individual considerations while applying this general requirement, sometimes resulted in distressing situations.

In cases where it is difficult for the migrants to take responsibility, one may question whether the effort which is demanded is proportionate in relation to the right to family life and the purposes of the test. Regarding the question whether the purpose of the test is achieved, the research so far makes clear that the effects on language skills are marginal and the effects on integration are unknown for two reasons. First, the tests have been introduced only recently, and getting integrated takes time. Second, research on integration shows that the level of integration depends on several factors. An effect which is already evident is the reduction in the number of applications, especially from lower educated and elderly migrants. The tests serve as a selection based only on education and age, instead of the intended selection based on motivation or the combat of forced marriages. Both Dutch and German governments do not seem to assess accurately whether the tests are effective in relation to their goals, or take other effects for granted. The fact that the Dutch government decided to introduce a written test because (inter alia) 25 per cent of the applicants is (still) low educated implies that the actual effect of the test (higher percentage of highly educated spouses) has now become its purpose. This shift in the argumentation for the application of the test abroad makes it more difficult to assess the effectiveness of the measure.

In the Netherlands and Germany however, the highest national courts have accepted the arguments for the tests and judged that the requirement is in compliance with the Constitution (Germany), Article 8 ECHR (both Member States) and the Family Reunification Directive (both Member States). In both countries this judgment is also made with regard to illiterates. In the Netherlands this was also the case regarding a migrant who failed the test four times, as well as a migrant who was forced to first learn English in order to read the educational material, as this was not available in his mother tongue. Until now, no preliminary reference has been made to the Court of Justice.

CHAPTER 3. INTEGRATION TESTS IN THE COUNTRY

Anita Böcker

More and more EU Member States have defined language or integration requirements that must be met by immigrants admitted for non-temporary stay. The nature of the requirements differs. In some countries, newcomers are required to attend language or integration courses during their first year(s) of residence. In other countries, they are also required to successfully complete these courses by passing an examination. Other countries again require immigrants seeking permanent residence to pass an examination without, however, obliging them to attend a course.

3.1 Description of the Requirements

Currently, immigrants are required to pass an examination in seven of the nine countries in this study. Austria, Denmark, France, Germany, Latvia, the Netherlands and the United Kingdom have made access to permanent residence conditional upon the passing of a language (and knowledge of society) examination for particular categories of immigrants. In Belgium, the Flemish Region requires newly arrived immigrants to attend an integration programme, but this is not a condition for access to permanent residence. In Hungary, immigrants are neither required to pass an examination nor to attend a course as a condition for access to permanent residence. The requirements differ also with regard to, e.g., content and level, target groups and exemptions, costs for the immigrant, and sanctions for non-compliance. The requirements are summarized in table 3.1 and briefly discussed below.

Table 3.1: Integration tests after admission to the country

Country	*Are immigrants required to pass an examination?*	*Are they (also) required to attend an integration programme or course?*	*Is knowledge of the language tested (required level*)?*	*Is knowledge of society tested?*	*Year of entry into force*
Austria	Yes	Formally, no	Yes (A2)	No	2003
Belgium	No	Yes, but only in the Flemish Region	n.a.	n.a.	2003 (programme)

Country	*Are immigrants required to pass an examination?*	*Are they (also) required to attend an integration programme or course?*	*Is knowledge of the language tested (required level*)?*	*Is knowledge of society tested?*	*Year of entry into force*
Denmark	Yes	Yes	Yes (B1)	No (but a new, 'active citizenship' test will be implemented in 2011)	2002 (test; introduction programme: 1999; test at level B1: 2007)
France	Yes, but only if their level of language proficiency is assessed to be below A1.1	Yes	Yes (A1.1)	No	2007
Germany	Yes	Yes	Yes (B1)	Yes	2005
Hungary	No	No	n.a.	n.a.	n.a.
Latvia	Yes	No	Yes (A2)	No	2003
Netherlands	Yes	Municipalities can oblige immigrants to attend a programme	Yes (A2)	Yes	2007 (integration course: 1998)
United Kingdom	Yes	No, but if their level of English is below B1, they may opt for attending a course	Yes (B1 or, if they have opted for attending a course, progress of at least one level)	Yes	2007

* The language proficiency levels referred to are those set out in the Council of Europe's 'Common European Framework of Reference: Learning, Teaching, Assessment'. A person with level A1 proficiency is defined as: 'Can understand and use familiar everyday expressions and very basic phrases aimed at the satisfaction of needs of a concrete type. Can introduce him/herself and others and can ask and answer questions about personal details such as where he/she lives, people he/she knows and things he/she has. Can interact in a simple way provided the other person talks slowly and clearly and is prepared to help.' A person with level A2 is defined as: 'Can understand sentences and frequently used expressions related to areas of most immediate relevance (e.g. very basic personal and family information, shopping, local geography, employment). Can communicate in simple and routine tasks requiring a simple and direct exchange of information on familiar and routine matters. Can describe in simple terms aspects of his/her background, immediate environment and matters in areas of im-

mediate need.' A person with level B1 is defined as: 'Can understand the main points of clear standard input on familiar matters regularly encountered in word, school, leisure, etc. Can deal with most situations likely to arise whilst travelling in an area where the language is spoken. Can produce simple connected text on topics which are familiar or of personal interest. Can describe experiences and events, dreams, hopes and ambitions and briefly give reasons and explanations for opinions and plans.'

Austria

Since 1 January 2003, Austria has required that non-EU/EEA immigrants fulfil an 'integration contract' during their first years of residence in the country. Compliance with this requirement is a condition for the renewal of a residence permit or the issuance of a permanent residence permit. One of the ways to fulfil the integration contract is to successfully complete a German language and integration course at a certified institute. In 2005, the required level of language proficiency was raised from A1 to A2. At the same time, the time period within which the integration contract had to be fulfilled was extended from four to five years. Since 2005, the language and integration courses have consisted of two modules. The first module (75 hours) aims at imparting reading and writing skills to illiterate immigrants; the second module (300 hours) aims at imparting a basic knowledge of German (level A2). About a quarter of those who rely on a language and integration course first attend the literacy module. The course is completed by a written and oral language examination, held by the teachers and graded by the teachers as 'pass' or 'fail'. The integration contract can also be fulfilled without attending a German language and integration course, by passing a language examination at level A2 at a certified language school. The government intended to increase the required level of language proficiency from level A2 to B1, but it seems to have abandoned this idea. At the time of writing of this report the Minister of the Interior had recently announced, however, that the time period within which the integration contract had to be fulfilled will be reduced from five to two years (see the afterword).

Belgium

Since 2003, newly arrived immigrants in Flanders are entitled and some are obliged to follow an integration programme. The obligation is limited to attendance at the courses and there is no official examination to assess the end result. Immigrants who have attended 80 per cent of the courses receive an attestation. Immigrants who belong to the target group are required to sign and fulfil a 'contract of civic integration' in which the content of their integration programme is specified. The first, obligatory, part of the programme consists of a Dutch language course, an introduction to Flemish and Belgian society, and career guidance. The level of language proficiency targeted in the language course is A1. The second part of the integration programme is only available upon completion of the first part and seeks to help immigrants to fully participate in Belgian society. The programme normally does not last more than a year.

Denmark

In 1999, Denmark introduced integration requirements as a condition for the issuance of a permanent residence permit, and these requirements have since been increasingly raised. In 1999, it was required that applicants for a permanent residence permit had to complete an introduction programme. In 2002, they were required to have also passed the language examination at the end of the programme. In 2007, the required level of language proficiency was set at B1. In addition, it was required that the applicants had had employment for at least 2.5 years within the last seven years. The language and employment requirement together were labelled 'the integration examination'. The current requirements, which have been in force since June 2010, include a strengthened employment requirement (2.5 years within the last three years) and furthermore they include an 'active citizenship' requirement (which can be fulfilled by passing a special 'active citizenship' test or through active participation in an organisation for at least twelve months) and a requirement to fulfil 'supplementary conditions relevant to integration' (which can be fulfilled by having had full-time employment for at least four years within the last 4.5 years, having completed certain forms of education, or having passed a Danish language test at level B2). The 'active citizenship' test, which at the time of writing the report was foreseen to be introduced in mid-2011 (see the afterword), will resemble the naturalisation test. However, the level will be somewhat lower and it will consist of only 15 questions, ten of which must be answered correctly. Newcomers are entitled to three years of Danish language tuition. The municipalities have to offer each newcomer an integration programme. Its content should be based on an assessment of the newcomer's skills, background and needs and must be laid down in an individual contract. The programme includes a language course. The language courses are offered at three levels: A2, B1 and B2 (targeting foreigners according to their previous schooling). Each course lasts three years and each course is completed by an examination. By the 2010 amendment of the Aliens Act it was decided that the integration programme also has to include an 'active citizenship course'.

France

Since 1 January 2007, non-EU immigrants who intend to stay in France for more than one year have been required to sign and fulfil a 'welcoming contract'. Depending on their level of language proficiency, they may be required to attend a language course. If the level of language proficiency has not been evaluated in the country of origin (see chapter 2), it will be determined after the immigrant's arrival in France, during the course of the interview where the welcoming contract is signed. The language test consists of a multiple choice exam and an oral and written proficiency test (Carrera 2009a: 338). If the immigrant does not have the required level of language proficiency, he will be required to attend a French language course as part of the welcoming contract. The course lasts a maximum of 400 hours and aims at imparting a basic level of French (A1.1, which is lower than A1). Students who pass the examination at the end of the course receive the *Diplôme Initial de langue française*. The welcoming contract also comprises civic formation (6 hours) and an information session about daily life in France (1-6 hours). All training and information sessions are organized by the *Office Français de l'Immigration et de l'Intégration* (OFII). The welcoming contract has to be fulfilled within a year. It is considered fulfilled when the immigrant has attended the training and information sessions and acquired the *Diplôme Initial de langue française*. Only about one in four or five newcomers are required to attend a language course; a large majority of the 'newcomers' in France have sufficient French language skills to be exempted from this part of the welcoming contract. A Bill that at the time of writing of the report was foreseen to be discussed in the end of 2010 proposes to raise the required level of language proficiency and to strengthen the obligation to fulfil the welcoming contract (see the afterword).

Germany

Already in 1990, Germany started to require a basic knowledge of the German language from applicants for a permanent residence permit. The *Zuwanderungsgesetz*, which entered into force in January 2005, provides that non-EU immigrants in Germany can be required to successfully complete an integration course as a condition for the issuance of a permanent residence permit. The current integration course consists of a basic and an advanced language course (600 or 900 teaching hours) and an orientation course (45 teaching hours). The language course aims at imparting an intermediate level of German (B1). The orientation course aims at imparting a basic knowledge of the legal system, culture and history. Both the language and the orientation course are completed by an examination. The current language examination has been in use since July 2009. It is a tiered examination, testing not only level B1 but also level A2. The test is passed when B1 has been achieved, that is, when three of the four parts (speaking, listening, reading and writing) have been passed with B1. Candidates who achieve level A2 receive a certificate of their language skills, and obtain the opportunity to take the advanced language course again (up to 300 hours) to reach level B1. The examination currently in use at the end of the orientation course was introduced in January 2009. Candidates have to answer at least 13 out of a total of 25 questions correctly to pass this test. The 25 questions are derived from a catalogue of 250 questions based on the three modules of the curriculum of the orientation course.

Hungary

In Hungary, immigrants are neither required to pass a test nor to attend a programme as a condition for access to permanent residence. Adult refugees can be obliged to attend a Hungarian language course and optionally an integration course as a precondition for receiving a welfare benefit, but since 2008 this obligation has no longer been applied.

Latvia

Since 2003, Latvia has required certain categories of applicants for permanent residence to pass a language examination. The same requirement has applied to applicants for the EU long-term resident (LTR) status since July 2006. The required level of language proficiency is A2. The examination is organized by the Centre of State Education Curricula. It consists of a written and an oral part and tests listening, reading, writing and speaking skills. Candidates who do not pass the test have to wait at least three months before they are allowed to take it again. General information about the examination and a sample examination are available on the Internet; there also is a book. The Centre of State Education Curricula offers no courses, but it has certified a number of teachers and published their names and contact details on its website.

Netherlands

In 1998, the Netherlands introduced obligatory integration courses for newly arrived non-EU/EEA immigrants. In January 2007, a new law entered into force which requires not only 'newcomers' but also immigrants who settled in the country before 2007 to pass an integration examination. In January 2010, passing the examination became a requirement for permanent or independent residence status. Newcomers have to pass the integration examination within 3.5 years from the issuance of their first residence permit. The examination consists of a practical examination and a central examination. The practical examination tests the language skills of the candidates in daily life situations. Candidates can pass this examination by submitting a portfolio (containing evidence of 20 situations in which the candidate has had to speak Dutch, e.g., registering a birth), taking part in an assessment (an oral examination during which the candidate has to take part in four role-plays), or by a combination of both. The central examination consists of three parts. The 'spoken Dutch test' is a telephone test in which the candidate has to repeat sentences, answer questions and give brief accounts of stories. The 'digital practical test' and 'knowledge of Dutch society test' are taken using a computer. The digital practical test consists of questions about daily life situations. The knowledge of Dutch society test consists of about 43 questions about work and income; manners, norms and values; housing; health and health care; history and geography; authorities; polity and the constitutional state; and education and upbringing. The level of the examination is A2 (or, for settled immigrants, A1). Immigrants who are already proficient in Dutch can prove this by passing a 'short exemption test'. The level of this test is higher than that of the integration examination, B1 instead of A2. Another route has been created for highly educated immigrants: they can take the 'NT2' (Dutch as a second language) state examination, which has a higher level than the integration examination and gives access to higher vocational education and university.

United Kingdom

Since April 2007, immigrants who apply for indefinite leave to remain (a form of permanent residence permit) are required to demonstrate sufficient language knowledge and sufficient knowledge about life in the United Kingdom (the same requirements as were already in effect for those applying for naturalisation). Depending on their level of English, they can do this by passing the 'Life in the UK' test, or by successfully completing an English for Speakers of Other Languages (ESOL) course which includes defined syllabus material on citizenship at an accredited college. Those who are already proficient in English will take the 'Life in the UK' test, which is pitched at level B1. It is a computerized test consisting of 24 multiple-choice questions about national institutions, society, employment matters and everyday matters such as housing, money, health and education. It is based on an official handbook. The test outcome is communicated automatically to the UK Border Agency. Those whose level of English is lower than level B1 will need to attend combined ESOL and citizenship classes. There is no set format for these courses. The courses are generally provided by further education colleges (run by the government of each of the four component parts of the United Kingdom) or by adult education services (provided by local authorities). Applicants using this route must demonstrate progress of at least one level to obtain the required 'ESOL Skills for Life' qualification. Relatively few immigrants use this route. Since the introduction of the language and 'Life in the UK' requirements, 81 per cent of applicants for indefinite leave have met the requirements by passing the test; 12 per cent have relied upon an ESOL qualification; and 8 per cent have been exempted.

3.2 Preparation for the Examinations

In five of the seven countries where immigrants are required to pass a language or integration examination, there are publicly regulated and/or funded courses that prepare them for this examination. In Denmark, France and Germany, immigrants who belong to the target groups are (or can be) obliged to attend these courses. In Austria, formally there exists no obligation to attend these courses; immigrants who are required to prove their language skills can also do this by passing a language examination at a certified institute. In the Netherlands, the government sought to privatise the integration courses. The idea was to make the immigrants themselves responsible (also financially) for acquiring the required knowledge and skills; the government would only define the requirements. However, it soon became clear that this did not work, and the municipalities were again made responsible. They can require immigrants who belong to the target groups to attend a course. The centre-right government that came into power in October 2010 intends to change the system again.

Two other countries with examinations do not provide public courses to prepare for them. In Latvia, no official courses are provided to prepare for the Latvian language test which applicants for permanent residence must pass. Immigrants have to prepare themselves by studying a book or by taking lessons with a certified teacher. In the United Kingdom, there are no official courses to prepare for the 'Life in the UK test'. Immigrants have to prepare themselves by studying the official 'Life in the UK' handbook. However, immigrants who do not have sufficient language skills are offered another route. They can attend combined language and citizenship classes at an accredited institute and, instead of taking the 'Life in the UK' test, submit a formal letter from the institute in question, setting out their initial and final levels reached.

The Flemish Region of Belgium does not require immigrants to pass an examination, but it does require them to attend official integration courses.

3.3 Costs

As the following table shows, there are large differences in the costs of the examinations and courses for the immigrants. Whereas the language courses in Denmark and Flanders and all training and information sessions in France are free of charge for immigrants who are obliged to attend them (and in Denmark also for other resident immigrants), immigrants in other countries have to pay at least part of the course costs themselves. Immigrants in Germany pay € 650 and immigrants in Austria pay € 750 to € 2,500 for their language and orientation courses.

Table 3.2: Costs of examinations and courses

Austria	Immigrants have to pay fees for the courses they attend to fulfil their integration contract. The literacy module normally costs € 350, the German language module € 750 to € 2,500. If the first module is successfully completed within one year, the costs are reimbursed. If the second module is successfully competed within two years (or three years for those who first completed the literacy module), half of the costs (up to a maximum of € 750) are reimbursed. Persons who only take the language exam pay a fee of € 50 to € 100.
Belgium (Flanders)	The language courses are free of charge for all participants (compulsory as well as voluntary participants).
Denmark	Municipalities are required to offer newly arrived immigrants free language tuition for up to three years. Candidates who want to take a language exam without having attended a course may be required to pay a fee of about € 130. A cost-based fee will be charged for the 'active citizenship test'.
France	All training and information sessions are financed by the Office Français de l'Immigration et de l'Intégration (OFII).
Germany	Immigrants who attend a language and integration course pay € 1 per teaching hour; the total costs are normally € 645. Recipients of welfare or unemployment benefits can apply for an exemption. Immigrants who pass the integration exam within two years can claim half of their contribution back. The test fee (for those who take the exam without having attended a course) differs per federal state; in most states, it is between € 95 and € 125.
Hungary	n.a.
Latvia	The fee for the language test is 10 LVL (about € 14).
Netherlands	Immigrants who are offered a course by their municipality can be required to contribute € 270 to the costs of their course and exams. For others, the costs are much higher. The fees for the three parts of the central exam are € 126 in total. The fee for the practical exam is € 104 (portfolio) or € 250 to € 1,200 (assessment). Those who choose to follow a course will also have to pay a course fee. The costs are partly reimbursed if the integration exam is passed within 3.5 years. It is also possible to get a loan. The fee for the short exemption test is € 81 and the fee for the NT2 state exam € 90.
United Kingdom	The fee for the 'Life in the UK' test is £ 34. The official 'Life in the UK' handbook costs £ 9.99 in hard copy. The costs of the ESOL courses (for immigrants whose level of English is below B1) vary depending on the provider and the kind of course. There are exemptions from fees for, e.g., persons in receipt of social benefits and persons in humanitarian categories, and reduced fees for persons protected by EU free movement law and the partners of settled persons who have been resident in the United Kingdom for one year.

Both in Germany and Austria, immigrants who pass the examination within a given time period can claim part of their contributions back. In the Netherlands, the municipalities may demand that immigrants contribute € 270 to the costs of their integration courses (including examination fees). The costs for immigrants who prepare for the integration examination on their own are much higher. The examination fees also vary widely. Candidates in Denmark normally do not pay a fee.

3.4 Target Groups and Exemptions

Seven countries (plus the Flemish Region in Belgium) require non-EU/EEA immigrants to pass an integration test and/or to complete an integration programme. The target group has been defined differently by each country. However, it always includes newly arrived immigrants who have been admitted for family reunification, and in most countries, a large majority of the target group falls into this category. EU/EEA citizens and their family members are always excluded from the target group. The family members of own nationals, on the other hand, are always included. In the United Kingdom, however, the parent, grandparent or other dependent relative of a British citizen or settled person are exempt from the 'Life in the UK' test.

Immigrants who have been granted asylum do not always belong to the target group; they are not required to pass an integration test or complete an integration programme in Austria, Latvia and the United Kingdom. (In the Flemish Region in Belgium, on the other hand, asylum seekers who have stayed in the country for more than four months have to attend a course on Flemish and Belgian society.)

Many labour migrants in all countries with integration requirements will not have to fulfil these requirements because their stay is (assumed to be) of a temporary nature. The Austrian legislation contains an explicit exception for highly skilled labour migrants ('key personnel'): non-EU/EEA immigrants who intend to stay in Austria for more than 24 months have to sign an integration contract, but 'key personnel' (and their family members) are regarded as already having fulfilled the integration contract. France has a similar exception for holders of a 'skills and talents' visa; they are not required to fulfil the welcoming contract. The Dutch legislation contains an exception in the opposite direction: ministers of religion are the only category of (assumedly) temporary migrants who are required to complete an integration course in the Netherlands. A similar exception exists in the Flemish Region of Belgium, where all labour migrants with the exception of ministers of religion are exempt from the obligation to attend an integration programme. In Denmark, the Integration Act was amended in 2010 to include labour migrants (including EU/EEA citizens) on a voluntary basis. The reason for this amendment was that the number of migrants admitted for employment had more than tripled since 2001. In the United Kingdom, Turkish businesspersons recognized under the association agreement with Turkey are exempt from the 'Life in the UK' test. The other countries do not have exceptions for Turkish citizens. However, two Dutch courts recently ruled that imposing integration requirements on Turkish workers is contrary to the non-discrimination provisions and the standstill clauses of the association agreement with Turkey. At the time of writing of the report, the Dutch government had just lodged appeals against these decisions (see the afterword).

In most countries, immigrants who can prove their integration or knowledge of the language with particular diplomas or certificates are not required to take the examination. In most countries, young immigrants who are still in education are not required to take the examination either. Most countries also have age limits. Several countries have limited the target group to persons aged between 18 and 65; other countries have exemptions for older persons or pensioners and/or for younger persons.

In addition, most countries have exemptions for disabilities or long-term illnesses that severely restrict the ability to speak or learn the language or to prepare for the integration test. The formulation of this exemption in the Danish legislation (handicapped persons may be exempted from fulfilling requirements, which they are not able to fulfil, provided that it is required by 'Denmark's international obligations, including the UN Convention on the Rights of Persons with Disabilities') has aroused much criticism, because it leaves wide margins of discretion to the immigration authorities. In Germany, immigrants who have to look after a handicapped family member can also apply for an exemption.

The United Kingdom also has exemptions for, e.g., victims of domestic violence and foreign nationals discharged from the armed forces. In Denmark, foreigners 'with strong ties to Denmark' are exempted from the new 'active citizenship' and 'supplementary conditions' requirements; this exemption applies to foreigners belonging to the Danish minority in South Schleswig, former Danish citizens, foreigners with Danish parents, and Argentinian citizens with Danish parents or grandparents.

In Germany, the Netherlands and the Flemish Region in Belgium, not only newly arrived immigrants but also immigrants who have lived in the country for a long time (and who may already have a permanent residence permit) can be obliged to pass an examination or to attend a course if their language skills are considered to be insufficient. In Germany, this applies to foreigners who receive unemployment benefits and to foreigners who have 'special integration needs'. The latter category includes parents of minor children living in Germany who are dependent on social assistance. In the Netherlands, it applies to foreigners who do not have a diploma proving that they have sufficient knowledge of the Dutch language; they can be obliged to attend a course and to pass an examination (at level A1) even if they have a job. Moreover, having attended an integration course under the previous legislation (which required newcomers to attend a course targeted at level A2, but which did not require them to pass the examination at the end of the course) is no ground for exemption. In the Flemish Region in Belgium, it applies to foreigners as well as foreign-born Belgians who receive social assistance.

3.5 Consequences of not Passing the Test

Sanctions

In seven countries (plus the Flemish Region in Belgium), non-EU/EEA immigrants are required to pass an integration test and/or to complete an integration programme. The consequences for immigrants who fail to comply differ from country to country and may range from not being eligible for permanent or independent residence status to being threatened with expulsion. Failure to comply may also lead to financial penalties (administrative fines, withdrawal or cutting of social benefits) in half the countries studied.

Table 3.3: Consequences of failure to pass test or to attend course

Country	Consequences for entitlement to permanent residence permit	Consequences for renewal of temporary residence permit	Administrative fine	Consequences for social benefits
Austria	YES	(YES)	YES	NO
Belgium (Flanders)	NO	NO	YES	YES
Denmark	YES	NO	NO	YES
France	(YES)	(YES)	NO	NO
Germany	YES	(YES)	YES	YES
Latvia	YES	NO	NO	NO
Netherlands	YES	NO	YES	YES
United Kingdom	YES	NO	NO	NO

(YES) between brackets means that the consequences are not straightforward.

In Latvia and the United Kingdom, immigrants who are not able to prove that they have sufficient knowledge of the language (and of 'Life in the UK') are not eligible for permanent or long-term residence status and the rights attached to it. They will have to apply for renewal of their temporary residence permit. In these countries, there are no other penalties.

Denmark and the Netherlands have also made access to permanent residence status (and the rights attached to it) conditional on the passing of a language (and knowledge of society) test, but, in addition, these countries have financial penalties for immigrants who fail to comply with the obligation to complete an integration programme. In both countries, these immigrants' social benefits may be cut. In the Netherlands, the failure to complete an integration programme may also be punished by an administrative fine. An evaluation study in the latter country found that half of the municipalities surveyed were reluctant to impose such a fine, because they did not think it would help or because they considered it too heavy a sanction for immigrants with a low income. Other municipalities, however, considered the maximum fine too low (Significant 2010). In its coalition agreement, the centre-right government that came into power in October 2010 announced to make it possible to withdraw the temporary residence permits of immigrants who do not pass the Dutch language and integration test.

In Germany, there is a certain reluctance to emphasise the obligatory nature of the integration programmes and tests (cf. Joppke 2007). The 'right' to participate is stressed. Many newcomers are 'entitled' as well as 'obliged' to enrol on an integration course. Those who pass the test at the end of the course will be granted a permanent residence permit (provided that they fulfil all other requirements for such a permit). However, not having passed the test will not automatically lead to the refusal of a permanent resident permit. It will depend on whether the immigrant in question has attended the course 'properly'. On the other hand, gross and repeated failure to comply with the obligation to attend a course may also, although again not automatically, have consequences for the renewal of the temporary residence permit. As the immigrant's duration of stay in Germany, his/her ties with Germany, and the consequences for his/her family members must be taken into account, this penalty will rarely be imposed. However, failure to comply may also be punished by an administrative fine or the reduction or withdrawal of the immigrant's benefit.

Austria has made access to permanent residence status conditional on the successful completion of an integration contract (or the passing of a language test). The integration contract has to be completed within the first five years of residence, but this period may be extended, on request, for a further two years (and the extension may be renewed). An immigrant's failure to fulfil the integration contract may also have consequences for the renewal of his/her temporary residence permit, but as in Germany, this penalty will rarely be imposed. The failure to fulfil the integration contract may also be punished by an administrative fine.

In France, the immigration authorities can take the fulfilment of the welcoming contract into consideration at the first renewal of the residence permit (a draft law proposes to extend this to any renewal) and in deciding on the application for a permanent residence permit. Non-fulfilment does not automatically lead to non-renewal of the temporary permit or non-issuance of a permanent permit. The issuance of a permanent permit is conditional on 'republican integration' into French society, the evaluation of which leaves wide margins of discretion to the immigration authorities. It is not clear how much weight they attach to the fulfilment of the welcoming contract in deciding on applications for permanent permits. However, a video on the website of the OFII suggests that such a permit will not be issued if the welcoming contract has not been completed. There appear to have been no cases where immigrants were refused a renewal of their temporary permit on this ground.

Unlike the above-mentioned countries, Belgium has not made access to a permanent residence status conditional on the fulfilment of an integration requirement. However, the Flemish Region requires some immigrants to attend an integration programme. The failure to comply with this obligation can lead to financial penalties. It may be punished by an administrative fine or by the withdrawal or reduction of social benefits.

Consequences regarding the Residence Rights

In most Member States, the rights of migrants are strengthened with the obtainment of a permanent residence status. A permanent residence permit offers its holder greater security of residence than a temporary permit. The level of security offered by the permanent status, differs from country to country. In the Member States where the permanent residence permit offers the highest security, the permit can be lost on three grounds only: fraud, long absence from the country, or long prison sentences. Third-country nationals holding a permanent status in these Member States do not have to fear losing their residence rights in the event of, e.g., unemployment, dependence on public assistance, offences against public order, or, if they were admitted to the country on asylum related grounds, in the event of an improvement of the situation in their country of origin. Furthermore, in many Member States there are other rights attached to a permanent status. Like the level of security, these rights vary between the Member States

In Austria, holders of the long-term resident status have unlimited access to the labour market, whereas others need an employment permit that is only granted if no Austrian or EEA citizen is available to fill the position. Furthermore, equal access to many social provisions, in particular social security payments, is dependent on a permanent residence status. Federal or provincial school subsidies are only granted to pupils who have at least one parent with a permanent resident status. In most Austrian cities, access to council housing is also dependent on being an EEA citizen or holding the status of a long-term resident.

In Germany, holders of a permanent residence permit have advantages with regard to family reunification, employment, and finding accommodation.

In the United Kingdom, the advantages of indefinite leave over the extension of limited leave will depend on the particular category. All persons with indefinite leave have the possibility to sponsor a limited range of dependent relatives to come to the United Kingdom. Indefinite leave also gives eligibility to the full range of social benefits (except for persons with refugee leave, humanitarian protection or discretionary leave, who have access to benefits automatically). Migrants in sponsored skilled workers categories obtain freedom of employment, while those in family categories gain an autonomous status. The costs of immigration applications are a further consideration. The costs of applying for extension of the permit regularly are much higher than the costs for an application for indefinite leave.

In addition to formal rights, a permanent resident status may also give its holder access to, e.g., a mortgage or an employment contract. In most countries, banks will not grant mortgages to migrants with temporary residence permits, and many employers will be hesitant to offer them an employment contract.

3.6 Purposes and Debates

In each of the countries where immigrants are required to attend an integration programme and/or to pass a language or integration test, the stated aim is to foster their integration. The background to the introduction of the requirements was, in nearly all cases, an apparent or perceived crisis of integration (Michalowski 2007). Two main concerns are discernible in the debates in most countries. The first is to make permanent immigrants economically self-supporting, to lower their unemployment rates and to reduce the costs they incur to the state in the form of welfare expenses. The second concern, which became more important with the post-2001 wave of terrorist activities and unrest associated with Muslim communities in the United Kingdom, Spain, France, the Netherlands, Denmark, and Germany is to familiarise immigrants with the history and culture of the country of immigration and to inculcate in them the values and principles of liberal democracy. There are other, more latent aims and concerns as well, such as the desire to limit access to permanent residence to 'well integrated' immigrants (which, for that matter, is an increasingly manifest aim in Denmark and the Netherlands) or to assure the native population that the government or the mainstream political parties are managing the crisis efficiently (cf. Joppke 2007).

Denmark

Among the countries studied, the Netherlands and Denmark were the first to introduce compulsory integration programmes for newcomers. The Netherlands did so in 1998, Denmark in 1999. A few years later, Denmark was also the first country to make permanent residence conditional upon the passing of an examination. It did so in 2002, when the liberal-conservative government that came into power in 2001 adopted a new aliens policy. The policy was based on three pillars, one of which was the strengthening of the requirement of being self-supporting. When the integration programme was introduced in 1999, it was compulsory, but the public responsibility to provide opportunities for immigrants to integrate on an equal footing with other citizens was stressed. Since then, there has been a shift to emphasizing the immigrant's responsibility for his/her own integration. This resulted in 2002 in an amendment of the integration legislation to the effect that immigrants had to pass a language examination as a precondition for obtaining permanent residence, and it has since led to far-reaching amendments. In 2010, in the legislative debate about the latest amendment, it was explicitly stated that one of the aims was to make it more difficult for immigrants who are 'not well integrated' to obtain permanent residence.

Austria

In Austria, the idea of an integration examination for immigrants was first put forward in 2001, when an FPÖ politician suggested restricting access to permanent residence to immigrants who could demonstrate sufficient knowledge of German and of Austrian society. Immigrants should be obliged to sign an 'integration contract', including the obligation to attend a language and integration course as a precondition for permanent residence. Referring to the positive experiences with this type of integration measure in the Netherlands, the FPÖ's coalition partner, the (Christian Democrat) ÖVP, supported the suggestion. The coalition government agreed on a draft Bill later the same year. In the political debate, the FPÖ presented the introduction of the integration contract as a major political success and as a paradigm shift towards a more restrictive immigration policy. The head of the parliamentary faction of the FPÖ described the contract as a device for selection and as a remedy for immigration into the welfare system. The SPÖ (Social Democrats) and the Greens sharply criticised the Bill of law as preventing integration. The law itself as adopted in 2002 (*Fremdengesetz* 2002) defined the aim of the integration contract as: 'It is aimed at the acquisition of a basic knowledge of German in order to facilitate participation in the economic, cultural and societal life in Austria.'

Germany

In Germany, the idea of obligatory integration courses for immigrants was first put forward by the Süssmuth Commission (2001). Referring to the experiences with this type of integration measure in the Netherlands and Sweden, the commission proposed introducing similar courses in Germany. Though the 'right to participate' was stressed, the possibility of obliging immigrants to participate was an important instrument from the beginning. It was justified by the importance of the aim to be reached (the promotion of integration) as well as by the argument that women who were isolated at home could be accessed and brought into German society using this instrument. The integration courses were introduced in the *Zuwanderungsgesetz* 2004, which was approved on a cross-party basis. The aim of the courses as stipulated in the law is to acquaint foreigners with the way of life in the Federal Republic of Germany so that they can act independently in all areas of daily life. To the extent that there was debate on the integration courses, it focused mainly on who was to pay (the immigrant or the state, and if the latter, the federal government, the states, or the municipalities) and what type of sanctions (positive or negative) should be used. Eventually compromises were reached on both issues. Although there was reluctance to emphasise the compulsory aspect of the courses, this aspect has become increasingly important. Currently, the government plans to introduce integration contracts based on the French model. These contracts which, just like the integration courses, would apply to new arrivals as well as immigrants who have lived in the country for years should help to make integration efforts 'more binding'.

Netherlands

In 1998, the Netherlands was the first country to introduce a compulsory integration programme for newly arrived immigrants. Following the 9/11 terrorist attacks, the rise of Pim Fortuyn and his subsequent murder shortly before the 2002 elections, a centre-right government came into power. It decided to reform the 1998 legislation, the results of which were disappointing. According to the government, a more compelling and result-oriented integration policy was required to combat the 'failed integration of large groups' of immigrants. The government announced that immigrants seeking permanent residence in the Netherlands would be required to pass an examination. The explanatory memorandum to the Bill which was sent to parliament in September 2005 stated that in order to 'fully participate in Dutch society', immigrants needed to have knowledge of the Dutch language and to know and accept Dutch norms and values. The most important issue in the legislative debate on the Bill was whether naturalized citizens born outside the EU/EEA should be included in the target group. They were included in the initial Bill. The Council of State advised that this was discriminatory. The government revised the Bill so that specific categories of naturalized citizens would be included (recipients of social benefits, parents of underage children, Ministers of Religion). After a second negative advice from the Council of State, the idea to include naturalized citizens was abandoned altogether.

United Kingdom

In the United Kingdom, integration requirements were unknown in the field of immigration law until recent years. This may be explained by several factors. One was that many of those who migrated to the United Kingdom in the post-war decades came from territories that were, or had been, British. Another factor was the gradual acceptance of a form of ethnic pluralism by British policy-makers. In the late 1960s and 1970s, the focus was on ensuring equality of opportunity in social and economic life, while by the 1980s and 1990s, cultural recognition had increasingly come to the fore. Insistence on language or integration requirements would have conflicted with both of these versions of pluralism. Recent years, however, have seen language requirements rolled out at all stages of the immigration and nationality law system, and the introduction of the 'Life in the UK' test for first naturalisation and then indefinite leave. The background to these developments was that the consensus concerning an unqualified version of cultural pluralism had come to an end. The catalyst for change was a series of riots involving young British Muslim men of South Asian origin in Northern English cities and towns in 2001. Official reports highlighted social segregation as a major background factor. The initial government response was set out in a report entitled *Building Cohesive Communities*. One of its conclusions was that there was a need to promote 'a uniting identity' and 'shared values' to give people 'a common sense of belonging'. From 2002, social and economic participation has become more important in the policy discourse. When the extension of the requirement to show 'knowledge of life in the UK' to indefinite leave applications was proposed in February 2005, it was part of a policy concerning social and economic participation: 'permanent migrants must be as economically active as possible; put as little burden on the state as possible; and be as socially integrated as possible'.

Latvia

Unlike the debates about language or integration requirements in 'old' EU Member States, the debate in Latvia has not concentrated on the need to promote the integration of immigrants. The numbers of third-country nationals are insignificant in Latvia. The Latvian debate has concentrated on former-USSR citizens who migrated to or were born in Latvia during Soviet occupation and who after 1991 did not qualify for Latvian citizenship. When the Long-term Residence Directive was transposed into Latvian law in 2006, the debate in the *Saeima* focused mainly on whether these former USSR citizens should be entitled to EU citizenship and what requirements they would have to meet to acquire the LTR status. The leftist parties sharply criticized the Bill which proposed to require former-USSR citizens to apply for the status and to pass a language examination and not singling them out as a special group. Otherwise, there has not been much debate about the introduction of a language examination for applicants for permanent residence as well as for the LTR status. There is a broad consensus that knowledge of the language should be required. The stated aim of the language requirement is that it is a device for integration into Latvian society.

France

As in other countries, the background to the introduction of integration requirements for immigrants seeking permanent residence in France was an apparent failure of immigrant integration. After the 2002 elections (in which the extreme right were very successful), a centre-right government came into power. It announced that all new immigrants would be invited to sign a *contract d'accueil et de l'intégration* (CAI). The Loi Sarkozy of November 2003 made the granting of a ten-year residence card dependent on *l'intégration republicaine*, defined in the law as 'knowledge of the French language and of the principles that constitute the French Republic', but it did not specify how such integration was to be determined. With the entry into force of the Loi Sarkozy II of July 2006, the CAI became compulsory. The explanatory memorandum to the Bill explained that this was to reinforce the route towards 'republican integration' and to enable a better evaluation of an immigrant's integration (Michalowski 2007; Joppke 2007; Carrera & Wiesbrock 2009). The move from voluntary to compulsory courses and to making permanent residence conditional upon the fulfilment of the CAI has not aroused much debate in France. This may be explained by the circumstance that the proposals were part of larger projects, which contained other more sensitive issues.

3.7 Effects of the Requirements: Statistical Data[26]

Numbers of Immigrants Targeted, Attendance Rates and Pass Rates

Statistical data on the number of immigrants who are obliged to attend or pass an integration programme or test, and their attendance and pass rates are not available for all countries studied. It is clear however, that the numbers of immigrants who have to fulfil integration requirements vary widely. In France in 2008, only 21.5 per cent (14,265 persons) of the immigrants who signed a welcoming contract were required to attend a language course. A large majority of the 'newcomers' in France have sufficient French language skills to be exempted from this part of the welcoming contract. In other countries, a much larger proportion of the newcomers are affected by the requirements, either because a large majority are not proficient in the language of the country (Austria, Denmark, Germany, the Netherlands, the Flemish Region in Belgium), or because there are no exemption possibilities for immigrants who are already proficient in the language of the test (United Kingdom). Thus, in Austria in the period January 2006- June 2009, about 81,000 immigrants enrolled on a language and integration course. In Denmark in 2008, 37,833 newcomers followed a Danish language course; about 60 per cent were obliged to do so. In Germany in 2009, 54,062 immigrants were obliged to attend a language and integration course; among them were 33,474 newcomers, 27,746 recipients of unemployment benefits, and 2,842 persons who had lived in Germany for a longer period of time (Integrationsbeauftragte 2010: 239). In the Netherlands in the period January 2007-December 2009, 127,000 immigrants (49,000 of whom were newcomers) received notice from their municipality that they would have to pass the Dutch language and integration examination; 83,000 of them (36,000 newcomers) enrolled on a course. In the United Kingdom in the period April 2007-June 2010, nearly one million immigrants sat the 'Life in the UK' test.

The attendance rates of those who are obliged to attend a course or programme appear to be quite high, at least in countries where data are available. For example, in France in 2008, 87 per cent of the newcomers who were required to do so did attend a language course. In Germany in 2009, the attendance rate of immigrants who were obliged to attend a language and integration course was 80 per cent, and it is estimated that only 8-10 per cent refuse to attend. In the Flemish Region in Belgium, 64 per cent of the immigrants who signed an integration contract in 2007 received an attestation after having attended at least 80 per cent of the classes; the proportion was 68 per cent for those who were obliged to attend as against 56 per cent for those who were entitled but not obliged to (De Cuyper 2010: 53). In the Netherlands, attendance rates have increased since municipalities can oblige immigrants to enrol on a course.

The pass rates for the language and integration tests in use in the different countries appear to vary substantially. For example, in France, 90 per cent of the newcomers who attended a language course in 2008 passed the (level A1.1) test at the end of the course. In the Netherlands, in December 2009, the pass rate stood at 79 per cent for all those who had taken the (level A2) Dutch language and integration examination since its introduction in January 2007 (26,000 out of 33,000 candidates). The pass rate for those who sat the exam-

26 Unless otherwise stated, the figures in this section have been taken from the national INTEC reports.

ination for the first time in 2009 was 74 per cent. In Denmark in 2008, 87 per cent of those who enrolled for the examination passed it. The pass rate was highest at level A2 (99 per cent) and lowest at level B2 (81 per cent). In Latvia, 74 per cent of those who took the (level A2) language examination required for permanent residence in the years 2007-2009 were successful. Among the candidates were also, however, persons who took the examination to be admitted to particular professions. In the United Kingdom, too, 74 per cent of the immigrants who sat the (level B1) 'Life in the UK' test in the period July 2007-June 2010 were successful.[27] In Germany, 46 per cent of those who attended a language and integration course in the period 2005-2008 attained the required level of language proficiency (B1); it has since increased to over 50 per cent. The pass rate for the nationally standardized knowledge of society test, which was introduced in 2009, is much higher (90 per cent).

Pass rates in themselves do not say much as long as it is not known what proportion of the target group has taken the test. In Austria, a wide gap was found between the number of immigrants who enrolled on a language course in the period January 2006-June 2009 (81,000) and the number of those whose fees were refunded after having passed the examination (7,480). Only a small proportion seemed to have been prepared to sit the examination upon completion of the course; most seemed to postpone it. In the Netherlands in the years 2007-2009, 127,000 persons were given notice that they would have to pass the Dutch language and integration examination within the next 3.5 years; those who had fulfilled this requirement by the end of 2009 (24,000 persons) were probably not representative of the entire population, but above average, motivated and able. The pass rate for the Dutch examination is therefore likely to decrease somewhat in the coming years.

Pass rates broken down by nationality are available for the United Kingdom's 'Life in the UK' test.[28] The pass rates vary greatly by nationality. The global pass rate, for all nationalities, for the period November 2005-June 2010, stands at 71 per cent. The total pass rate for the 17 states which are designated as 'majority English-speaking' in the British immigration system is 86 per cent, as against 70 per cent for the rest of the world. There is however significant variation among the English-speaking states. What emerges is differentiation between developed and developing countries. New Zealand, Australia, the USA, Canada, and Ireland have a combined pass rate of 98 per cent. For the other 12 designated states, all in the Caribbean area, the pass rate is only 70 per cent. There is also significant variation among the non-English-speaking states. Whereas the pass rates for Singapore and Japan stand at 95 per cent, various other Asian nationalities have pass rates below 50 per cent. This variation again suggests differentiation by level of development. Another impression from the pass rates by nationality is that there is differentiation by immigration category. Many of the nationalities with relatively low pass rates have had substantial numbers of persons granted humanitarian status in Britain over the past decade or more; examples are Sri Lanka, Angola, Kosovo, Afghanistan, Iraq and Turkey.

27 The data were obtained by the UK research team through a freedom of information request to the UK Border Agency. The data do not distinguish between applicants for indefinite leave and for naturalisation, and the data are by test attempt rather than individual.

28 The data were obtained by the UK research team through a freedom of information request to the UK Border Agency. The data do not distinguish between applicants for indefinite leave and for naturalisation, and the data are by test attempt rather than individual.

Pass rates broken down by sex, age group and country of origin are available for the Netherlands. Three years after the introduction of the language and integration test, the pass rate stood at 76 per cent for women, and 83 per cent for men. Younger candidates are more likely to be successful than older ones. The pass rate stood at 85 per cent for candidates younger than 36, and 60 per cent for candidates older than 55. As in the United Kingdom, the pass rates in the Netherlands also vary considerably by nationality. The pass rate for Turkish candidates is 63 per cent, the pass rate for Polish candidates 93 per cent. It is 90 per cent for candidates from the former Soviet Union, 85 per cent for candidates from former Yugoslavia and Iraq, 80 per cent for candidates from Afghanistan and 74 per cent for Moroccan candidates.

Comparable data are not available for the other countries studied. However, in Denmark, where language courses are offered at three levels (A2, B1, B2), immigrants from non-Western countries are proportionally overrepresented in the lowest-level courses. Many students who are enrolled on a level A2 course will not be able to pass the level B1 examination (the level required for a permanent residence permit).

In Germany, the first results of a longitudinal study show that a younger age, a higher educational level, and not having been born in Turkey, Russia or another former Soviet Republic or South or East Asia have a positive effect on the progress achieved during the course (Rother 2009).

Effects on Permanent Residence and Security of Residence

In most of the countries studied, it is too early to establish the effects of the integration requirements on the number of applications for and grants of permanent residence.

The integration requirements which were introduced in Germany in 2005 apply to newcomers who were admitted to the country from 2005 onwards. As a permanent residence permit can be obtained only after five years of residence in Germany, the first cohort falling under the 2005 legislation will not apply for it until 2010. Thus, it is too early to assess the effects of the requirements on the number of applications for, and grants of permanent residence in Germany.

Immigrants in Austria have to fulfil an 'integration contract'. The current contract was introduced in 2005 and newcomers are required to fulfil it within their first five years of residence in the country. Thus in Austria, too, it is too early to establish an effect on the numbers of granted permanent residence permits. However, an immigrant's failure to fulfil the integration contract may also have consequences for the renewal of his/her temporary residence permit. In the years 2006-2009, about 46,000 residence permits were issued to immigrants in the potential target group. The number of fulfilled integration contracts was much smaller (9,200). A tentative conclusion from these figures is that the coming years (when the five-year period for the first cohorts of immigrants falling under the 2005 legislation expires) may see a large number of legal disputes. These disputes will have to clarify whether and when family migrants who have failed to fulfil the integration requirements within the required time period can be deported.

In the Netherlands, passing an integration examination has been a requirement for permanent residence only since January 2010. The Dutch statistics for the first six months of 2010 do show a decline in the number of applications for permanent residence in comparison to the previous year. This decline is probably at least partly attributable to the integration requirement. However, the fee for these applications was also raised (Ministerie van Justitie 2010: 31). Moreover, the drop in the number of applications for permanent residence could also be due to more immigrants applying for naturalisation right away, without first applying for a permanent resident permit, as the integration examination also gives access to naturalisation. To see this effect in the numbers for naturalisation takes more time.

As from April 2007, all applicants for indefinite leave in the United Kingdom have been required to demonstrate sufficient language and 'Life in the UK' knowledge. The introduction of the requirements has not led to a decline in the number of grants of indefinite leave. However, it cannot be concluded from this that the requirements have not had deterrent effects, because higher levels of immigration from the late 1990s onwards increased the pool of potential applicants for indefinite leave. A further problem is that, even if a reduced propensity to obtain indefinite leave could be shown, it could be due to other causes, including in particular the increased fees for these applications in recent years.

In Denmark, the number of applications for permanent residence permits has declined sharply since 2006 (from an annual average of 12,000 in 2003-2005, to less than 5,500 in 2006-2009). At the same time, the proportion of rejected applications rose (from less than 20 per cent in 2003-2005 to on average 40 per cent in 2006-2009).[29] The drop in the number of applications can be attributed to the seven-year residence requirement which was introduced in 2002 (and which applied to immigrants who applied for a residence permit from 1 March 2002 onwards; immigrants who had applied for or had been issued a residence permit before that date were eligible for a permanent permit after three years of residence). The drop in the proportion of granted applications is probably at least partly attributable to the requirement to pass a language test, which was also introduced in 2002, and sharpened up in 2007. Refugees have been affected most severely by the new requirements. Before 2006, less than 10 per cent of refugees' applications for a permanent permit were refused; in 2008 and 2009, the refusal rate was more than 50 per cent. The refusal rates for family migrants increased from less than 30 per cent before 2006, to 47 per cent in 2006, 39 per cent in 2008 and 36 per cent in 2009. The number of granted permanent residence permits for both refugees and family migrants will probably drop further in the coming years. As of 26 March 2010, all applicants for permanent residence have to fulfil the more restrictive requirements which entered into force on that date. Moreover, children can no longer apply for a permanent residence permit; they have to wait until they are 18 years old, and some will have to wait longer because they will not be able to fulfil all requirements at once.

For Latvia, where applicants for a permanent residence permit have been required to pass a language examination since July 2006, data are available only for the years from 2006 onwards. A tentative conclusion from these data is that the introduction of the requirement has not resulted in a significant decline in the number of permanent permits granted.

---

29 The data were obtained by the Danish research team through a request to the Danish Ministry of Integration. The data pertain to decisions in the years 2003-2009 on applications for permanent residence filed by applicants who were admitted to Denmark for asylum or family reunification. It was not possible to obtain similar data for applicants who were admitted for work or study.

Effects on Integration

In most of the countries studied, the effects of the requirements on the integration process of the target groups have not yet been systematically evaluated. An official evaluation published in the Netherlands in 2010 stated that it was too early to assess the effects of the current integration requirements on the integration process of the target group. In Germany, a longitudinal study (in which 4,000 students in language and integration courses are interviewed at the beginning, at the end, and a year after completing their course) is being conducted but has not yet been completed (Rother 2009).

An effectiveness measurement of Danish municipalities' integration policies found that refugees and family migrants were finding employment or starting education more quickly than previously. The proportion of refugees and family migrants who arrived in 2006 and who got a job or started education after one year had doubled compared to those who arrived in 2000. However, the study did not examine whether the integration requirements (which had been sharpened up since 2002) played a role in the progress. According to the study, the progress was possibly attributable to more efficient municipal policies and the economic situation (Hansen 2009).

The effects of the Flemish integration policy were evaluated in 2010. The evaluation study used different methods, including linked data files and interviews. The results showed that immigrants who had completed an integration course more often had a job than immigrants of the same age, gender, nationality, educational level, etc., who had not started or completed an integration course. The impact on other dimensions of integration was rather limited. Those who had completed an integration course did not have more interethnic contacts than those who had not started or completed a course. Furthermore, half of those who had completed a course did not have more than just a basic level of Flemish three or four years later, when they were interviewed (Pauwels & Lamberts 2010: 119 ff).

3.8 Effects of the Requirements: Interview Results

We interviewed immigrants and other actors in six of the countries that require immigrants to attend an integration course and/or to pass an integration examination after their admission to the country.[30]

Most of the interviews were with immigrants: 25 immigrants were interviewed in Austria; 20 in Belgium; 14 in Denmark;[31] 27 in Germany; 25 in the Netherlands; 16 in the United Kingdom (127 interviews in total). The immigrant respondents in the Netherlands were interviewed in test centres; most of them had just taken the examination which gives access to permanent residence as well as naturalisation. All the respondents in the United Kingdom had taken the 'Life in the UK' test; no interviews were conducted with immi-

30 The Latvian research team also conducted interviews, but these interviews focused exclusively on the naturalisation examination.

31 These 14 respondents were interviewed about their experiences when seeking permanent residence. The Danish research team conducted 12 more interviews with immigrants who had applied for naturalisation.

grants who attended combined ESOL and citizenship classes. All the respondents in Belgium had attended an integration programme; 12 of them had been obliged to do so (in Antwerp); 8 others had voluntarily attended (in Brussels).

In addition to these interviews with immigrants, interviews were conducted with teachers and language school representatives (7 in Austria; 5 in Belgium; 5 in Denmark; 7 in Germany; 5 in the Netherlands); public officials (6 in Austria; 5 in Belgium; 3 in Denmark; 8 in Germany; 5 in the Netherlands); and immigrant organisations and other NGOs (5 in Austria; 4 in Belgium; 5 in Denmark; 7 in Germany; 5 in the Netherlands; 5 in the United Kingdom). More information about the interviews can be found in chapter 1.

Opinions on the Requirements

In general, the immigrants interviewed thought that a language requirement in some form was fair. They felt that knowledge of the language was a precondition for making a life in their country of immigration. However, in Denmark, some respondents found the required level of language proficiency (B1) unreasonably high, and in the Netherlands, many thought that the requirements should apply only to newcomers.

In countries which also have knowledge of society requirements, these were less well received than the language requirements. In the United Kingdom, a minority of the immigrants interviewed thought that the official 'Life in the UK' handbook contained information which it was important to know; there was also criticism that the information was potentially out of date. Some respondents thought that the 'Life in the UK' test was questionable because it set a standard that British-born persons could not meet. Similar criticisms were voiced by respondents in the Netherlands. They felt that they were asked to subscribe to norms and values which were not theirs, or that they had to learn things which no Dutch-born person would know. In Germany, on the other hand, opinions were more mixed. The advanced language learners among the respondents found the orientation course the most interesting part of their integration programme.

In general, the immigrant respondents had positive opinions about the courses offered in Austria, Denmark, Germany, the Netherlands and the Flemish Region in Belgium. Most of them did not seem to mind their compulsory nature. Several respondents in Austria stated that they would not have invested that much effort in learning German if they had not been obliged to do so. On the other hand, about half of the respondents in Denmark stated that they would have learnt Danish anyway –even if it had not been a requirement for permanent residence. In Belgium, the research team's impression was that the respondents in Brussels were somewhat more satisfied with the courses they attended voluntarily than immigrants in Antwerp were with their compulsory courses. In the Netherlands and the Flemish Region in Belgium, not only newcomers but also settled immigrants can be obliged to complete an integration programme. In the Netherlands, the settled immigrants among the respondents objected to this obligation. They thought that it came too late for them. Some of the respondents in Antwerp (who were themselves newcomers) complained that the settled immigrants in their class were not motivated to learn Flemish and were spoiling it for their classmates.

Some of the impressions gained in the interviews with immigrants were confirmed in the interviews with teachers. Particularly in Austria and Denmark, the teachers and language school representatives thought that most of their students attended the courses not (just) because they were obliged to do so or because they wanted to qualify for permanent residence, but because they wanted to learn the language. It should be noted, however, that in both countries (and also in the Netherlands and Germany) a growing number of students attended the courses voluntarily. Some of the teachers in Germany, on the other hand, thought that the attendance rates for their courses would drop if there was no obligation. One of them pointed out that he had many English-speaking students, who managed to get by quite well in Germany speaking English.

Some of the teachers in Austria and nearly all the teachers and language school representatives in Germany and Denmark thought that the required level of language proficiency (A2 in Austria, B1 in Denmark and Germany) was too high for particular groups of immigrants. The Austrian teachers also complained that the 300 hours of the language module of the integration contract were too short to also impart knowledge of society to their students. Most Austrian teachers were very critical of the plans to raise the required level of language competence to B1.

According to the local officials interviewed in Austria, quite a few newcomers saw the language and integration courses as something positive and some were really thankful that the courses were offered. Though some of the officials were critical of the compulsory nature of the courses, they also thought that it was extremely helpful in making women attend the course. The local officials in the Netherlands thought that certain groups of immigrants would not attend an integration course if there was no obligation. This regards women who are disencouraged by their husband to integrate in Dutch society and migrants with a fulltime job and mothers with young children. These two groups are often too busy to prepare voluntarily for the test. Furthermore, settled immigrants often objected to having to attend a course and take an examination. Particularly those who had already attended a course under the previous legislation were indignant that they were not exempted from the new requirements. Immigrants from the United States and Japan and, more in general, immigrants who already had a job often reacted with disbelief when informed that they had to attend a course and pass an integration examination. In Germany, there seemed to be regional differences. Whereas local officials in Munich spoke of a 'run' on the courses in that city, teachers and local officials in Potsdam found it more difficult to attract students. This difference is possibly attributable to regional differences in employment opportunities for immigrants.

Groups Facing Difficulties Fulfilling the Requirements

In the United Kingdom, the results from the interviews with immigrants and NGOs confirmed some of the impressions given by the statistics. The 'Life in the UK' test is relatively straightforward for those with fluent English, but difficult for those with a lower level of English, particularly if they have had little formal education, and no experience with computers. Many in humanitarian categories, some in family categories (especially women) and some older people seem to fare less well.

As stated, teachers and language school representatives in Austria, Germany and Denmark thought that the required level of language proficiency (A2 in Austria, B1 in Denmark and Germany) was too high for particular groups of immigrants. The German teachers thought that students with little formal education could attain level A2 if they did their best, but not level B1. According to the Danish language school respondents, there was a group of immigrants who were stuck in the language school system because they would never be able to pass the B1 level examination. Besides people with little formal education, this group consisted of people who did not have a talent for languages and people whose first language belonged to another language family than the Indo-European. The Austrian teachers pointed out that illiterate students could not attain level A2 within the 300 hours of language training provided in Austria. This group consisted mainly of women from Turkey and Arab countries with little or no formal education and low self-esteem. The 75 hours of literacy training were also insufficient to learn to read and write.

Various respondents in Denmark pointed out that a large group of immigrants who had been working and supporting their families and thought that 'that was what was expected of them' now faced difficulties having to work and take a language course at the same time. Especially people with little education, refugees and women had problems fulfilling both requirements.

Teachers and local officials in the Netherlands also thought that particular groups faced difficulties fulfilling the integration requirements in their country. They were thinking of elderly people, illiterates and others with little formal education and traumatised refugees. Chinese immigrants who had lived in the Netherlands for many years also had difficulties learning Dutch. Immigrants with a job and young mothers found it difficult to combine fulfilling the integration requirements with their normal activities.

Various respondents in Austria, Denmark, the Netherlands and the United Kingdom pointed out difficulties with getting exemptions for disabled or, e.g., traumatized persons. Respondents in Denmark thought that the rules lacked transparency. Respondents in the United Kingdom pointed out the absence of a specific procedure for exemption on grounds of incapacity before an application was made. Respondents in the Netherlands thought that traumatised refugees sometimes had difficulty obtaining the required medical certificate. Respondents in Austria thought that the threshold for exemption on grounds of incapacity was too high.

Effects on Integration

The immigrants interviewed had different opinions about the importance of the integration requirements for their integration. In Austria, the majority of those who had already passed the examination, found the course helpful in their daily life. Two of them reported that it had helped them to get a promotion at their workplace. At the same time, many stated that in order to feel part of Austrian society, it was not sufficient to speak German, there also had to be a tolerant and welcoming climate, which they had not found in Vienna. In Belgium, almost all immigrant interviewees reported an improved level of integration. Some of them referred to the language skills they had acquired; others explained that they were better able to get by without having to ask for help all the time. A few respondents also reported that they felt less discriminated against after having completed the integration programme. The immigrant interviewees in the Netherlands also stated that they were better able to manage in daily life. However, a settled immigrant who had been obliged to attend an integration course after years of residence in the Netherlands stated that she had learnt everything she needed in daily life in practice. In Denmark, half of the respondents stated that they would have learnt Danish anyway. Also half of the respondents stated that they had integrated into Danish society not so much due to the language course but to other factors, such as family, friends and work. Several respondents stressed that they felt excluded by the Danish aliens law; the language course had not changed this. The immigrant interviewees in Germany stressed that they did not feel part of German society because of their knowledge of the language, but because of their having a job and paying taxes in Germany. In the United Kingdom, nearly all respondents were sceptical about the likelihood that the 'Life in the UK' test would lead to integration. One respondent was surprised even by the suggestion that integration was one of the test's objectives. The high degree of scepticism among the interviewees in the United Kingdom is perhaps attributable to the fact that many newcomers in the United Kingdom are already proficient in the language of their country of immigration. This is different in the other countries studied.

Most of the non-immigrant respondents were reluctant to claim that the integration requirements contributed to the integration process of those who have to meet them. In Austria and the Netherlands, many respondents pointed out that level A2 (the required level for permanent residence in both countries) was not sufficient for successful participation in the labour market. The same was said by respondents in Germany about level B1. The respondents did not think that applicants for permanent residence should be required to attain a higher level of language proficiency. However, they thought that it was unrealistic to expect an effect on the immigrants' integration in the labour market.

In all countries with compulsory courses, there were many respondents who claimed that these had emancipatory effects for particular groups, e.g., young mothers and (other) immigrants who belong to rather closed communities, and who would not (be allowed to) attend an integration programme if there was no obligation. Particularly in Germany and Austria, many respondents stressed that the psychological effects of the courses were probably more important than the language progress made by the immigrants who participated in the courses. They spoke of 'boosting the self-esteem' of immigrants (particularly immigrant women) with little formal education, and of 'making them feel at home' in their country of immigration. On the other hand, particularly in Austria, some respondents stressed that in the end, factors such as discrimination and the closed nature of mainstream society were more important for the integration process of immigrants than integration programmes and examinations.

Effects on Permanent Residence and Security of Residence

In most of the countries studied, failing to fulfil the integration requirements may have consequences for the immigrant's access to permanent residence. In a few countries, it may even have consequences for the renewal of the immigrant's temporary residence permit.

In the interviews in the United Kingdom, several examples were mentioned of immigrants who could not apply for indefinite leave to remain because they had not (yet) passed the 'Life in the UK' test.

The interview results in Denmark confirmed that the sharp decline in the proportion of granted applications in Denmark was partly attributable to the requirement to pass a language examination. However, many immigrant interviewees stressed that rather than the examination in itself, the combination with other requirements constituted a problem for them. The (former) requirement of active participation in the language classes was particularly difficult to combine with that of being in full-time employment. Some respondents were nervous and confused about the new requirements which were to be introduced at the time of the interviews. The immigrant respondents in Denmark considered it very important to obtain permanent residence. They said that they would therefore continue to make an effort. One respondent decided to close his shop to get more time to study for the language examination.

The decline in the Dutch numbers of applications for permanent residence since January 2010 can be attributable to the integration requirement, but also to more immigrants applying for naturalisation right away, as the integration examination gives access to naturalisation as well as to permanent residence. The interviews in the Netherlands provided some evidence that this might be the case. Most of the respondents who were preparing for the examination stated that their final aim was to apply for naturalisation. They wanted to be safe or 'get rid of all the crap' connected to not being a Dutch citizen.

In Austria and Germany, local officials and other respondents thought that the income requirements in these countries constituted a bigger hurdle than the language and integration requirement. Immigrants with low educational levels would have difficulties fulfilling both requirements. These impressions were confirmed in the interviews with immigrants in both countries. Several immigrant organisations reported a growing sense of unease in immigrant communities because of the threatening denial of the renewal of the temporary residence permit or the granting of a permanent residence permit. In Vienna alone, more than 3,000 persons who had been admitted to the country in 2006 would not yet have fulfilled their integration contract.

3.9 Summary and Conclusions

The Requirements

Seven of the nine countries in this study (Austria, Denmark, France, Germany, Latvia, the Netherlands and the United Kingdom) have made access to permanent residence conditional upon the passing of a language (and knowledge of society) test for particular categories of non-EU/EEA immigrants. In five of the seven countries there are publicly regulated and/or funded courses to prepare for the test, and in four countries (Denmark, France, Germany and the Netherlands), immigrants who belong to the target group are (or can be) obliged to attend these courses.

The content of the test differs from country to country, but it always includes a language examination. The required level of language proficiency varies from A.1.1 in France to B1 in Denmark, Germany and the United Kingdom. The target group differs also from country to country. However, it always includes newcomers who have been admitted for family reunification, and in most countries, a large majority of the target group falls into this category. EU citizens and their family members are always excluded from the target group (although in Denmark they now are invited to participate, and in several other member States they can participate voluntarily). The family members of own nationals, on the other hand, are always included. In Germany and the Netherlands, not only new arrivals, but also immigrants who have lived in the country for a long time can be obliged to successfully complete a language and integration course if their language skills are considered to be insufficient.

In five countries (Austria, Denmark, Latvia, the Netherlands, the United Kingdom), immigrants in the target group are not eligible for permanent or long-term residence status and the rights attached to it unless they can prove sufficient knowledge of the language (and society) of the country. In Germany and France, too, immigrants seeking permanent residence are in principle required to prove sufficient language knowledge, but the consequences for those who fail to do so are less straightforward than in the other five countries. On the other hand, both in Germany and France as well as in Austria, an immigrant's failure to comply with integration requirements may also have consequences for the renewal of his/her temporary residence permit. However, this penalty will rarely be imposed.

In most countries where integration requirements were introduced, there has been a tendency to strengthen them (by raising the required level of language proficiency or by sharpening the sanctions for non-compliance) and/or to extend the target group.

Purposes and Debates

In each of the countries where non-EU/EEA immigrants are required to pass a test, the stated aim is to foster their integration. The background to the introduction of the requirements was, in nearly all cases, an apparent or perceived crisis of integration. Two main concerns in the debates in most countries were to make permanent immigrants economically self-supporting, and to inculcate in them the values and principles of liberal democracy. However, in many cases there were other, more latent aims and concerns as well, such as the desire to limit access to permanent residence status to 'deserving' immigrants or – in countries where populist anti-immigrant parties achieved electoral successes – to assure the native population that the government or the mainstream political parties were managing the crisis efficiently. These latent goals may also explain why, particularly in Denmark, the Netherlands, Austria and France, there has been a tendency to introduce new or stricter requirements without having evaluated the effectiveness of the previous requirements.

Effects on Integration

In most of the countries studied, the effects of the requirements on the integration process of the target groups have not yet been systematically evaluated. Most existing evaluation studies have been restricted to the implementation of the requirements.
The immigrants interviewed for this study had different opinions about the importance of the integration requirements for their integration. Most of the other respondents (teachers, public officials, NGOs) were reluctant to claim that the integration requirements for permanent residence contributed to the integration process of those who have to meet them. Many of them thought that the required levels of language proficiency for permanent residence were not sufficient for successful participation in the labour market. The respondents did not think that applicants for permanent residence should be required to attain a higher level of language proficiency. However, they thought that it was unrealistic to expect an effect on the immigrants' integration in the labour market. On the other hand, in all countries with compulsory courses, there were many respondents who claimed that these had emancipatory effects for particular groups, e.g., young mothers and (other) immigrants

who belong to rather closed communities, and who would not (be allowed to) attend a course if there was no obligation.

Effects on Permanent Residence and Security of Residence

In most of the countries studied, it is too early to establish the effects of the integration requirements on the numbers of applications for and grants of permanent residence. In Denmark, however, the requirement to pass a language test appears to have caused a decline in the proportion of granted applications for permanent residence. Refugees have been affected most severely. The results of the interviews in Denmark confirmed that the drop in the proportion of granted applications was partly attributable to the requirement to pass a language examination. However, many immigrant interviewees stressed that rather than the examination in itself, the combination with other requirements constituted a problem for them. The (former) requirement of active participation in the language classes was particularly difficult to combine with that of being in full-time employment.

In Latvia, the requirement to pass a language test does not appear to have led to a decline in the number of permanent permits granted. Likewise, in the United Kingdom, the requirement to demonstrate sufficient language and 'Life in the UK' know-ledge has not led to a decline in the number of grants of indefinite leave to remain. However, it cannot be concluded from this that the requirement has not had deterrent effects, because the pool of potential applicants for indefinite leave has increased in the past decade. Interviews in the United Kingdom confirmed that in a number of cases migrants were not able to apply for indefinite leave to remain because they had not (yet) passed the 'Life in the UK' test.

In the other countries studied, it is too early to establish an effect on permanent residence. In Austria and Germany, most respondents thought that the income requirements in these countries constituted a bigger hurdle than the language and integration requirement. However, in both countries, an immigrant's failure to comply with the language and integration requirements may also have consequences for the renewal of his/her temporary residence permit. In the coming years, legal disputes may have to clarify whether and when this penalty can be imposed on family migrants.

With regard to the consequences of not obtaining a permanent residence permit, it can be concluded that, apart from not gaining security of residence, in a number of countries this can lead to less access to the labour market, housing and social benefits. Those practical consequences of being unable to exercise a permanent residence right as well as the more insecure position can hinder integration. In this way integration requirements can have a counterproductive effect on the integration of immigrants who face difficulties fulfilling the requirements.

Groups Facing Difficulties Fulfilling the Requirements

The (future) effects on permanent residence are likely to be more severe for some groups than others. With regard to the 'Life in the UK' test, data on pass rates for different nationalities as well as the results from the interviews indicated that many migrants in humanitarian categories, some in family categories (especially women) and some older people therefore fare less well. In Denmark, data on applications for and grants of permanent residence indicated that refugees have been affected most severely, and this was confirmed in the interviews with language school representatives. In Germany, the first results of the above-mentioned longitudinal study indicated that a higher age, a lower level of education and having been born in Turkey, a former Soviet Republic or South or East Asia had a negative effect on the progress achieved during a German language and integration course. Most of the teachers and language school representatives interviewed in Denmark, Germany and Austria thought that the required level of language proficiency (B1 in Denmark and Germany, A2 in Austria) was too high for immigrants with little formal education. Teachers and local officials in the Netherlands also thought that elderly people, illiterates and others with little formal education and traumatised refugees faced difficulties fulfilling the integration requirements in their country.

The effects of the requirements on permanent residence and security of residence undoubtedly merit specific further examination, both at the overall level, and by certain key characteristics (principally immigration category, gender, age, and nationality).

CHAPTER 4. INTEGRATION TESTS IN THE NATURALISATION PROCEDURE

Maaike Luiten & Ricky van Oers

4.1 Description of the tests

Currently, integration tests are applied as a condition for naturalisation in seven of the nine countries under consideration in this study. In Belgium, immigrants applying for naturalisation are not required to prove integration, since the condition to show 'sufficient willingness to integrate' was abolished with the introduction of changes in Belgian nationality law in 2000 (De Hart & Van Oers 2006: 325). In France applicants for naturalisation are required to have assimilated into the French community, which means that they are required to have sufficient knowledge of the French language and the rights and duties conferred by French nationality. This knowledge is however not tested in a test, but in an interview with a civil servant at the local *préfecture*. Applicants are required to be able to speak and understand French in order to be able to face daily and basic communication. In the interview, the civil servant can take the personal circumstances of the applicant, such as his/her educational background, social condition and age, into account.[32]

In the other countries under consideration, knowledge of the language and/or the society is either tested in an integration test, or proof of such knowledge, for instance by submitting a secondary school diploma, is required. Prior to the introduction of these requirements, language skills and integration were often assumed (UK), or tested in an informal interview (Denmark, Netherlands, some German states). The requirements are shown in table 4.1 and will be briefly described below.

Austria

In Austria, a language requirement for naturalisation has been applied since 1998, when naturalisation was made dependent on an 'adequate knowledge of German', to be tested in an interview about issues of everyday life, in which the living conditions of the applicant could be taken into account. The language requirement was strengthened on 1 March 2006. Since that date, knowledge of the German language at level A2, both orally and in writing, has been required.

32 Despite French language skills, an application for French nationality will be denied if an immigrant is considered to have not sufficiently socially or culturally integrated into French society. This for instance is the case if an immigrant only lives within his/her own community or has a way of life which is incompatible with belonging to the French community. The wearing of an integral veil (*niqab*) has led to the refusal of the application of a Muslim woman in 2008, and more recently in 2010, the naturalisation application of a man who forced his wife to wear a *niqab* was denied (Klekowski Von Koppenfels 2010: 11).

Table 4.1: Integration requirements for naturalisation

Requirement *Country*	*Knowledge of the language*	*Knowledge of society*	*When introduced?*
Austria	Yes, level A2, oral and written language skills.	Yes, tested in knowledge of society test.	Language skills required since 1998, formalisation of language requirement in 2006. Knowledge of society since 2006.
Belgium	No.	No.	N.A.
Denmark	Yes, level B2, oral and written language skills.	Yes, tested in *Infødsretsprøve*.	Formalisation of the language requirement in 2002 (level B1), level B2 since 2006. Knowledge of society since May 2007.
France	Yes, tested in informal interview.	No.	
Germany	Yes, level B1, oral and written language skills.	Yes, tested in Einbürgerungstest.	Language skills since 2000, formalised language test since August 2007, knowledge of society test since September 2008.
Hungary	No, not explicitly tested.	Yes, oral constitutional examination.	October 1993.
Latvia	Yes, level B1, oral and written language skills.	Yes, written or oral knowledge of society test.	July 1994.
Netherlands	Yes, level A2, oral and written.	Yes.	Formalized language and knowledge of society test since 2003. Original 'naturalisation test' replaced by 'integration examination' at same level in 2007.
UK	Yes, level B1, but course at lower levels.	Yes, 'Life in the UK' test.	Formalised language requirement since 2004; in November 2005 language requirement merged with knowledge of society requirement.

Language skills at level A2 are also required in order to obtain a permanent residence permit. Hence those who fulfilled the language requirement at permanent residence stage are not required to fulfil the language requirement when applying for Austrian nationality. Furthermore, a naturalisation test, in which applicants for naturalisation have to prove 'basic knowledge' of the democratic order of the Austrian Republic, the history of Austria and the history of the province of residence, was introduced on 1 March 2006. The test is a multiple-choice test consisting of 18 questions, which are drawn from a set of published sample questions. The curriculum of the test follows the curriculum of the fourth year of compulsory secondary school.

Denmark

Denmark requires its future citizens to have language skills at level B2 of the CEF, which is the highest level of language skills required in the countries examined in this study. Language skills at level B2 have been required since 2006. Prior to 2006 and starting in 2002, language skills at level B1 were required, whereas before 2002, applicants for Danish nationality were merely required to be able to speak and understand the Danish language. In 2008, the pass mark threshold for the Danish language test was increased. A multiple-choice knowledge of society test was introduced in Denmark in May 2007 (*indfødsretsprøve*). The test, which costs about €89 and can be taken twice a year, consists of 40 questions, five of which concern recent events, and the remaining 35 are based on a textbook, which e.g. deals with Danish history from the beginning of the Viking age (750 A.D.), geography, population, language, immigration, democracy, literature, art and science. In November 2008, the number of questions that were needed to be answered correctly in order to pass the test was raised, the time offered to complete the test was shortened and the questions were no longer accessible in advance; thereafter the pass rate in the test dropped (see below). In summer 2010, after the content of the knowledge of society test had been criticized by experts in history, political science and other branches of science and it turned out that for some questions none of the multiple-choice answers were correct, the Minister of Integration announced that she would consider replacing the multiple-choice test with a test consisting of open questions.

Germany

Naturalisation applicants in Germany are required to prove language skills at level B1. This level has applied since 2000, but since initially there were no nationally standardised tests, the language requirement was applied differently in practice. Whereas some *Länder* required oral and written language skills, in other *Länder* only oral language skills sufficed. The requirement was hence formalised, which means that since August 2007, applicants for naturalisation have been required to submit evidence, for instance in the form of a language certificate, that they have command of the German language orally and in writing at level B1. Level B1 equals the level of language which is tested in the final test of the integration courses within the framework of the Residence Act (*Aufenthaltsgesetz*), as is the case in Denmark for level B2 language courses. The certificate immigrants obtain when they pass the final test at the end of the integration course can hence be used to fulfil the language requirement for naturalisation. Furthermore, since 1 September 2008, applicants for naturalisation have been required to show sufficient knowledge of the legal system, the society and the living conditions in the Federal Republic of Germany (Article 10(1)(6) of the German Nationality Act) by passing the so-called *Einbürgerungstes*' (naturalisation test). The naturalisation test consists of 33 multiple-choice questions, of which at least 17 need to be answered correctly. Whereas the content of the naturalisation test is based on the content of the integration courses (Article 10(7) German Nationality Act), passing the orientation test at the end of the integration course of the Residence Act will not suffice for naturalisation.

In the German state of Baden-Württemberg, a number of specific questions are added to the integration test. If there are doubts that the applicant has carried out activities which are not in compliance with the Constitution and an inquiry to the Office for the Protection of the Constitution supports these doubts, then the applicant must dispel these doubts in an interview with the naturalisation authority.

Hungary

In Hungary, applicants for naturalisation are required to pass an examination on constitutional issues. Knowledge of the Hungarian language is not tested as such, but a high level of Hungarian is required to fulfil the other requirements for naturalisation. The constitutional examination is taken orally and in writing, and only those who master Hungarian perfectly will generally pass it. The examination currently consists of 21 topics defined in a textbook, which mentions the knowledge of pupils in the final year of elementary school as the threshold for the knowledge tested. However, according to the Hungarian rapporteur, the textbook is based on the knowledge of a moderately well educated person with good linguistic competence. The topics include Hungary's constitutional structure and state symbols. In 2006, the topics of the examination were extended to literature, art, science and national history, starting from the establishment of the state in the 10th century. This thematic extension of the examination was an internal decision by the Ministry of Interior and the amendment was passed as a technical requirement. The content of the test was criticized after a weekly journal found that 90 per cent of Hungarians interviewed in the streets could not answer the questions.

The Hungarian constitutional examination is managed by local administrative offices (20 in total), which organise the examinations before a board generally consisting of lawyers, administrators and teachers (the examination board). Whereas the format of the examination and its major components are regulated by Government Decree, each county administrative office has its own in-house rules on the management and procedure of the examination including how to assess the oral and written tests (e.g. how many points are required to pass the examination). This means that the level of difficulty of and pass rates in the examination will not only depend on the composition of the examination board, but will also vary between the counties, and potential applicants for naturalisation will temporarily change their domicile to take a test in a county which has a reputation of setting 'easy' examinations, a trend which was recognized by the metropolitan administrative office.

Latvia

When Latvia regained its independence in 1991, after having been occupied by the Soviet Republic for half a century, Latvian became the only official language. The requirements for Latvian citizenship were the topic of a political debate, which was closely related to the large group of former citizens of the USSR living in Latvia. Due to a lack of agreement, Latvian membership in the Council of Europe was postponed until the adoption of a new citizenship law. The High Commissioner on National Minorities of the Organisation for Security and Cooperation in Europe (OSCE) urged the government not to formulate language requirements for citizenship which would constitute an obstacle to naturalisation. The level should not exceed conversational knowledge, the authorities should be lenient in applying the requirements and elderly persons and the disabled should be exempted from the requirement. The law finally adopted nevertheless included the requirement to read and write Latvian and understand official Latvian information. In 1998, pressure emerging from the process of accession to the European Union and low naturalisation rates led to the decision to simplify the requirements for elderly persons and to the reduction in questions regarding history and societal knowledge.

Future citizens are required to have written and oral command of Latvian at level B1. Knowledge of society is also tested. The language examination consists of two parts. The first part tests the applicant's ability to listen and understand, to read, write and communicate on topics of daily life. This part takes 90 minutes. The examination consists of multiple-choice questions. The writing part consists of two tasks: completing a form with personal information and writing an essay. The second part of the examination is a 15-minute interview. A person is allowed three attempts to pass the examination. If these attempts are not successful the naturalisation application has to be made anew.

Applicants who take the knowledge test orally have to demonstrate their knowledge of the national anthem and answer questions. Thirty minutes are granted for preparation and the examination itself takes 15 minutes. Answering the questions in writing takes 45 minutes. In this case, knowledge of the national anthem can be demonstrated orally or in writing. The knowledge examination consists of both multiple-choice and open questions. Ten general questions on the history of Latvia and eight questions on the Constitution are included in the examination.

The Netherlands

The Netherlands requires oral and written Dutch language skills at level A2. Since 1 April 2007 these skills, together with knowledge of the Dutch society, need to be proven in the 'integration examination', the passing of which is also required for immigrants who have an integration obligation under the WI or, since 2010, for those applying for permanent residence.[33] Prior to 1 April 2007, knowledge of the language at level A2 and knowledge of society were tested in the naturalisation test, which in turn replaced the 'integration interview' on 1 April 2003.

33 For a description of the content of the integration examination, see paragraph 3.1 above.

The United Kingdom

In the UK, future citizens are required to have knowledge of the English language and of 'Life in the UK'. Proof of sufficient language skills at level B1 has been required since July 2004. Applicants can also fulfil the language requirement by showing sufficient knowledge of Welsh or Scottish Gaelic. Prior to 2004 language skills were also required, but the language requirement was of limited effect, since there was no procedure specified by which language capacity could be assessed. Home Office policy was to assume that the language requirement was met in case of 'circumstantial evidence' such as education in British establishments or employment in a British firm. Enquiries would only be made in case of indications that the language requirement would not be met. On 1 November 2005, the requirement to have 'Life in the UK' knowledge was introduced. Since that date, both knowledge requirements, i.e. knowledge of the language and knowledge of Life in the UK, can be fulfilled by passing the 'Life in the UK' test at level B1. An alternative route to citizenship is however offered to those with language skills below level B1: they can follow an 'ESOL with citizenship course', in which they need to make progress to the next level of language proficiency. There are hence two 'routes' to citizenship. As in the Netherlands, the same integration requirements apply for permanent residence.[34] Those who fulfilled the knowledge requirements by either passing the Life in the UK test or by submitting a certificate of attendance on an ESOL course for ILR will hence not face new requirements when applying for citizenship.

A proposal that fulfilment of an 'active citizenship' requirement will shorten the period of residence required for citizenship has been made. The fate of the proposal at the time of writing the report was still uncertain (see the afterword).

4.2 Preparation for the Tests and Costs

All of the countries under consideration offer some form of preparation for the language and/or integration test for naturalisation. Whereas this statement may appear self-evident, in the Netherlands no possibilities for preparation existed for the naturalisation test, the predecessor of the integration examination, which applied until 1 April 2007. Furthermore, the content of the naturalisation test was undisclosed and no sample questions were published. Currently, candidates for the integration examination can follow an integration course, in which knowledge of the language and of Dutch society are taught, or practise the different parts in the examination on the Internet. In most cases, taking part in the preparation courses will be funded by the municipalities, if the migrant is obliged to pass the integration test.[35]

Courses are also set up by the administrative offices in Hungary. The costs of these courses vary between € 5-10. Candidates can however also choose to follow courses set up

34 Fulfilment of the knowledge requirements has been required for the status of 'Indefinite Leave to Remain' since 2 April 2007. For more information regarding the content of the 'Life in the UK' test and the ESOL with citizenship courses, see paragraph 3.1 above.

35 See paragraph 3.3 above.

by NGOs or private agencies, or study from a textbook. The text of the book was criticized by an agency providing preparatory courses because of the dry and old-fashioned style of language.

No state-regulated preparation courses for the knowledge of society test are offered in Austria, Denmark, Germany, Latvia and the UK. From the interviews it became apparent that such courses had been set up by volunteers in the UK. In Austria, the largest provider of courses for the integration agreement had set up a course in 2006, but no one had enrolled. Furthermore, the association had never been contacted by immigrants wishing to find a course. Hence, apparently there was no need felt by immigrants to prepare for the test on a course. Latvia organized courses during the nineties, with external assistance. Courses were supposed to be set up in Germany, but in the end this hardly occurred because of limited demand. One-day preparation courses are however offered by the adult education institute (*Volkshochschule*) of Munich and in Hamburg, politics classes for immigrants, offered since the 1970s, are currently used as a means to prepare the topics of the test. These classes are offered in the form of a ten-day seminar for which educational leave can be obtained. Instead of attending a course, people can prepare for the knowledge of society test using the Internet, since all questions and answers are published. Furthermore, booklets have been published. To prepare for the language test at level B1, immigrants can follow an integration course within the framework of the Residence Act. Costs for the course are normally €645, but reduced fees may apply.[36]

In Austria and Denmark, immigrants can also prepare for the language requirement on a language course. In Austria, following module 2 of the integration agreement, which consists of 100 to 600 hours of language teaching, will lead to level A2. Costs for the course vary between € 1,500 to € 2,500.[37] In Denmark, free three-year language courses are offered to foreigners who are covered by the Integration Act. However, only about 53 per cent of the students are enrolled on a language course at level B2 – the level required for naturalisation.

As regards the knowledge of society test, in Austria candidates can prepare for the test by studying the preparation material published by the federal and provincial governments, the published sample questions, or by a training programme which can be bought at the website www.staatsbuergerschaft.com. The training programme costs €12 for the basic version and €18 for the advanced version. In spring 2010 the learning brochure on democratic structures and history of Austria was removed from the website of the Interior Minister following critical questions by the Green Party. In 2008, the brochure had been criticized in a scientific article in the journal for German as a Foreign Language for inter alia containing factual mistakes and didactically questionable explanations. Furthermore, according to the authors of the article, explaining Austrian history at the level of the fourth grade of secondary school using level A2 of language competence was not possible. In February 2010, the brochure was again criticized by a renowned political scientist who stated that the brochure would by no means realise the aim of the Nationality Law to inform about

36 Taking part in the course is free for recipients of social welfare and unemployment benefits, see paragraph 3.3 above for more detailed information.

37 50 per cent of the costs may be refunded if the test is passed within a certain amount of time, see paragraph 3.3.

the democratic structure of Austria at the level of the fourth grade and would rank below an acceptable level of a scientifically sound and didactically meaningful civic education. Whereas the Interior Minister has stated that the brochure would be evaluated, rewritten and republished on the website, this so far has not occurred. Candidates for the knowledge of society test will hence have to consult other sources to prepare for the test.

Danish candidates in the *infødsretsprøve* can prepare by studying a textbook which can either be bought, viewed on the Ministry of Integration website, or downloaded as an MP3 file. Until November 2008, all questions which could come up during the test were published on the Internet, together with the answers. However, this system was criticized (and the pass rate of almost 100 per cent was considered too high), and in November 2008 it was decided to no longer publish the answers on the Internet.[38]

Applicants for naturalisation in Latvia can prepare themselves by studying a book on the Latvian language examination (€ 2.60), a book on basic questions on Latvian history and Constitution (€ 4.80) and a book with recommendations on the methods of preparation for the examination on *Satversme*, the national anthem and history (€ 2). The lack of courses is a major problem in Latvia. Projects on integration do exist, but are short-term. Recently the number of providers for courses increased and courses are offered for € 35. However these types of providers just offer their participants exactly the same material as the Naturalisation Board distributes for free. These free EU-supported programmes are offered to target groups, such as parents of children belonging to minorities and teachers. However, the number of participants is rather low because of limited resources. The Agency recently released an online learning programme at level A1, which is available in both Russian and English.

Finally in the UK, candidates for the Life in the UK test can prepare by studying five of nine chapters from the second edition of the handbook '*Life in the UK: A Journey to Citizenship*' (£ 9.99), published by the Stationery Office, which is the official publisher, but a private company. The Stationery Office also published preparation material, namely a study guide and a practice q&a with 400 sample questions and answers based on the handbook. It should be noted that, whereas the advisory commission on the implementation of the knowledge requirement advised the publication of a handbook for those with a reasonable command of English, they never intended the handbook to become the basis for a standard test on knowledge of Life in the UK. Rather, the commission envisaged that the requirements should be met through some form of education, also for those competent in English. The use of the handbook and the testing of knowledge in the Life in the UK test hence show that the system has departed far from the educational intentions of the advisory group.

38 Furthermore, more questions need to be answered correctly in order to pass the test, and within a shorter period of time, see above.

Table 4.2: Costs

Austria	A training plan for the test costs € 12 (basic version) or € 18 (advanced version). The preparation script and the naturalisation test are free of charge. Depending on the state where the naturalisation takes place, and the title under which the naturalisation is granted, fees range from € 621 to € 1,878 . Costs for the language course vary between € 1,500 to € 2,500.
Belgium	Not applicable.
Denmark	The costs for the citizenship test are € 89. A fee of € 134 has to be made upon application. Renewed applications are free of charge.
France	Not applicable.
Germany	Language test costs € 100 or higher, except Berlin where the costs are € 23. The Einbürgerungstest costs € 25. A fee of € 645 has to be paid for the language course. Furthermore, a fee of € 255 has to be paid for the application.
Hungary	The fee for the language test is € 20.
Latvia	Handbooks with prices varying between € 2 and € 4.80. Courses are offered for € 35 (but they do not add anything to the free courses). Free courses are also offered by the State Language Agency. The fee for naturalisation is € 28. A fee of € 4.30 is set for the poor and unemployed, family members of families including three or more minor children, pensioners, severely and moderately disabled persons and persons attending duly accredited education establishments. Persons exempted from fees are the politically repressed, very severely disabled, orphans and children who are not cared for by parents and persons who are registered for social benefits.
Netherlands	Immigrants who are offered a course by their municipality can be required to contribute € 270 to the costs of their course and exams. For others, the costs are much higher. The fees for the three parts of the central exam are € 126 in total. The fee for the practical exam is € 104 (portfolio) or € 250 to € 1,200 (assessment). Those who choose to follow a course will also have to pay a course fee. The costs are partly reimbursed if the integration exam is passed within 3.5 years. It is also possible to get a loan. The fee for the short exemption test is € 81 and the fee for the NT2 state exam € 90. Prices for a single application are € 567. In case someone jointly applies with his/her partner the fee is € 719. Stateless persons and those who are granted a residence permit on asylum grounds receive a € 50 reduction on each application.

United Kingdom	The fee for the 'Life in the UK' test is £ 34. The official 'Life in the UK' handbook costs £ 9.99 in hard copy. The costs of the ESOL courses (for immigrants whose level of English is below B1) vary depending on the provider and the kind of course. There are exemptions from fees for, e.g., persons in receipt of social benefits and persons in humanitarian categories, and reduced fees for persons protected by EU free movement law and the partners of settled persons who have been resident in the United Kingdom for one year. The fee for a single application is £ 780 and in case someone jointly applies with his/her partner the fee is £ 1,010.

4.3 Exemptions

All immigrants wanting to obtain citizenship via naturalisation are required to fulfil the language and knowledge of society requirements for naturalisation. The consequences of not fulfilling the requirements will be that the nationality for the country under consideration will not be granted, and that the immigrant will retain an inferior legal position, be it either as a legal permanent or temporary resident. Generally speaking, two categories of persons can however be exempt from passing the necessary tests: those whose knowledge of the language and the country is already considered to be sufficient, and those of whom it cannot be expected that they will ever be able to fulfil the requirements due to mental or physical impediments or age.

4.3.1 Exemptions on the Basis of Sufficient Integration

Native speakers

In Austria, native speakers of German are exempt from submitting a language certificate when applying for naturalisation. In the Netherlands, immigrants from Belgium (Flanders) or Surinam can be exempt if they can submit a high school diploma proving that a pass mark was obtained for the subject 'Dutch'.

Applicants following education or having obtained a diploma

Apart from the UK, in all of the countries under consideration, immigrants who have followed education in the country or are still in school, are exempt from showing proof of sufficient language skills and/or passing the knowledge of society test as a condition for naturalisation. They are considered to have sufficient language skills and/or knowledge of society. The UK does not provide an exemption ground for immigrants who are either in school, or who have obtained a diploma. All applicants for naturalisation will have to submit a Life in the UK test certificate (or an ESOL-with-citizenship course certificate) when handing in their applications.

Apart from in the UK, the language and knowledge of society requirements will hence mostly apply to first generation immigrants, who have not gone to school in the country in which they want to naturalise, and to school dropouts. Furthermore, in some countries the proof of having passed a certain examination (if recognized to that end) is considered adequate proof of the necessary language skills or exemption from the language and/or knowledge of society requirements (Austria, Denmark). Therefore, besides first generation migrants, the integration requirements mainly also apply to those second generation immigrants with lower intellectual capacities. Lastly in Hungary, the exemption regulation for immigrants with a diploma mainly seems to have been introduced to the benefit of ethnic Hungarians. Immigrants who have completed their secondary schooling in the 'host' country will generally be second generation immigrants, who in most of the countries under consideration can benefit from facilitated access to citizenship such as option or declaration.

In Austria, having a secondary school diploma will not lead to exemption from either the language requirement or the knowledge of society test. As regards the language requirement, only those who are in school can be exempted from proving sufficient language skills (level A2). Furthermore, exemption is made conditional on obtaining a positive grade in the subject 'German'. Exemption from the knowledge of society test can only be acquired if someone has obtained a positive grading in the subject of 'history and civics' at the level of the fourth year of compulsory secondary school. Those who have come to Austria past the compulsory schooling age and who for instance have obtained a diploma granting access to University or a University degree, will hence not be exempt from either the language requirement or the knowledge of society test.

In Denmark, the entitlement to naturalisation for second generation immigrants, hence those born, raised and gone to school in Denmark, was repealed in 2004. Thus, second generation migrants need to fulfil all naturalisation requirements. Most of them will, however, be able to prove their adequate skills in the Danish language by having passed grade 9 or 10 of Danish public school with a mark of 4 or higher in each Danish discipline (a mark of 2 is sufficient to pass the school leaving examination and a mark of 7 is considered an average). All applicants for naturalisation will have to pass the knowledge of society test. The interviews with police officers in Denmark showed that the majority of applicants for naturalisation, i.e. between 70 and 80 per cent, prove Danish language skills by submitting a diploma from a Danish school. This statement suggests that most applicants for naturalisation are second generation immigrants who attended school in Denmark and who until 2004 had an entitlement to citizenship. This may indicate that many first generation immigrants face difficulties fulfilling the naturalisation criteria, among others the high language requirement.

In Latvia persons who graduated from elementary, secondary or higher education where the instruction language was not Latvian, and who have passed a centralized examination in Latvian, are exempted from the language test if they apply within two years following this examination. Applicants who have been educated in Latvian are not bound by such a time limit. Both groups have to take and pass the knowledge examination.

In the Netherlands, secondary school diplomas or higher will lead to exemption from passing the integration examination. Furthermore, persons who are not following secondary education or who have not (yet) obtained a secondary school diploma are exempt if they have followed education in the Netherlands for a period of eight years during the obligatory schooling age (5-16). This exemption clause has applied since 1 January 2007. Before, school dropouts or those still in high school would not be exempt from passing the test. However, in practice it appears that civil servants apply the list of diplomas leading to exemption very strictly. A recent example is that of a Danish applicant with a PhD in Dutch language and literature who had to take the language test for naturalisation, because this study was not on the list of the civil servant.

Germany, like the Netherlands, exempts immigrants who have obtained a German secondary school diploma or higher or who have attended a German school from proving sufficient language skills. Four years 'successful' attendance in a German speaking school suffices for exemption. Furthermore, those who progress to the tenth class of the intermediate secondary school, comprehensive school or grammar school are exempt from the language requirement. To be exempt from passing the *Einbürgerungstest*, only certificates of 'general' education lead to exemption. An academic degree will hence not necessarily lead to exemption from the knowledge of society requirement. In Baden-Württemberg this ruling has been interpreted as meaning that only those who obtained a university degree in public administration, law and politics are exempt from the naturalisation test.

In Hungary, students studying for a certificate in Hungary are exempt from passing the constitutional examination. Since 2006, persons who attended public elementary school where the subjects were taught in Hungarian, whether in Hungary or in another country, are also exempt. The introduction of this exemption clause means a facilitation of the naturalisation procedure for ethnic Hungarians, the majority of whom will have attended public school with curricula in Hungarian. A visit to the website of the Office for Immigration and Nationality Affairs shows that problems however often occur regarding the burden of proof. A further extension of the exemption regulation to the benefit of ethnic Hungarians is foreseen. Starting on 1 January 2011, immigrants with a Hungarian ascendant or whose origin from Hungary is probable will be exempt from passing the examination if they can prove they have knowledge of Hungarian.

In all of the countries mentioned above, only proof of sufficient integration 'in black and white', i.e. on the basis of a generally rather limited list of diplomas, will lead to exemption from fulfilling the language and knowledge of society requirements. Persons who have integrated in a different way, for instance through working and residing in the country of which they want to become full members, will be required to submit proof of integration by submitting language and knowledge of society test certificates. In the Netherlands, complaints uttered by municipal officials who saw themselves obliged to refer immigrants, who were obviously well integrated, to an integration course or an integration test, led to the preparation of an amendment of the exemption regulation to provide for a possibility to exempt obviously integrated immigrants.

4.3.2 Exemption on the Basis of Age or an Impediment

Age

Persons who have reached a certain age will be exempt from fulfilling the language and knowledge of society requirements in Austria, France, Germany, Hungary and the UK. The exact age someone will need to have attained is not specified in Austria. Persons who want to be exempt from fulfilling the requirements on age grounds will need to submit a certificate from a public health official that they are unable to fulfil the requirements due to their health. In Germany, persons who have reached the age of 60 and who have been living in Germany for a period of 12 years will be exempt from the requirements. In Hungary and the UK, persons aged 65 or over will be exempt.

A general exemption on age grounds is not provided in the Netherlands and in Denmark. In Denmark, until 2002, persons aged over 65 were exempt from showing language skills in the integration interview. With the formalisation of the language requirement, this exemption possibility for older immigrants was repealed. In the Netherlands, those who have reached the age of 65 can opt for Dutch citizenship, which means that they are not required to pass the integration examination. Option is however only possible after a period of residence of 15 years.

In Latvia there is also an exemption for persons below a certain age. Naturalized persons can opt for citizenship for their children under 15 years old. However, in practice a problem of so-called 'forgotten children' has arisen, i.e. where parents acquire citizenship but forget to file an application for registration of their children. When these children reach the age of majority they have to follow the normal procedure for naturalisation.

Mental or physical impediments

In all countries under consideration, exemption from fulfilling the language and knowledge of society requirements may be obtained if someone suffers from a mental or physical impediment. The impediment needs to be proven in a doctor's attestation in which the relationship between the impediment and the inability to fulfil the requirements is made clear.

In Denmark, possibilities for exemption on the basis of a mental or physical impediment are rather limited, following a reduction of these possibilities in 2006. Exemption is only granted under exceptional circumstances in cases where the applicant is suffering from a very serious illness. Immigrants suffering from PTSD (posttraumatic stress disorder) are explicitly excluded from obtaining exemption. Decisions regarding exemption are taken by the Naturalisation Committee behind closed doors and in principle no reason for refusing the application for exemption is given. The immigrant organisations interviewed stated that being granted exemption was almost impossible and some stressed that the rules were rather unclear. Several respondents had never experienced a case where a person had been exempted; one organisation even saw blind people's applications for exemption turned down. A number of the respondents called for more grounds for exemption, especially as regards PTSD.

In the UK also the exemption procedure appears to be applied with rigidity. In the UK, staff members from law centres complained about the absence of a specific procedure for exemption before an application is made. Those who want to be exempt need to file their applications together with the documents on the basis of which exemption might be granted. If exemption is not granted, the applicant will lose the application fee, even if further information or documents might have led to the application succeeding. One law centre once saw the application of a deaf and dumb person refused. Only after issuing a pre-action protocol saying that judicial review would be taken if the decision was not reviewed, was the application granted.

Illiteracy

In most of the countries under consideration, illiteracy is not explicitly mentioned as an exemption ground. Only the Netherlands and the German state of Bavaria appeared to have introduced a special procedure for illiterates. In the German state of Bavaria, a special language test, the so-called *Alpha*-test, is used for illiterates. There is, however, no adapted knowledge of society test for illiterates. Since reading and writing skills are required to complete this test, passing it will prove an insurmountable barrier for illiterates.

In the Netherlands, those who are illiterate or disabled have the possibility of exemption from the naturalisation test. An illiterate candidate who wishes to qualify for exemption has to be illiterate in both Dutch and his or her first language, and has to show that a serious attempt has been made to learn Dutch. Subsequently, illiterate candidates have to undergo a feasibility investigation They will be exempted from the naturalisaton test only if the outcome of this feasibility investigation is that they will not be able to learn Dutch at A2 level within the next five years. Since 1 April 2007, the immigrant is however in this case also required to pass the 'test spoken Dutch'. For the feasibility investigation, € 287 is charged. The fact that illiterate candidates have to undergo an expensive examination, for which they have to travel to Amsterdam, before they can be exempted from the naturalisation test or, since 1 April 2007, the integration examination, may constitute a barrier to naturalisation for this category of immigrants.

4.4 Purpose of the Tests

Different reasons for introduction of the tests/requirements were expressed in the countries under consideration and can be summarized in three categories.

Changing Opinion on the Function of Naturalisation

As we have seen above, prior to the introduction of formal language and knowledge of society tests, basic oral language skills, which were tested in an informal interview, were required for naturalisation in Austria, Denmark, some German states, and the Netherlands. At that time, naturalisation in Denmark and the Netherlands was regarded as a step (Netherlands) or a 'crucial positive element' (Denmark) in the integration process.

In the Netherlands, the the Minorities' Policy departed from the central idea that a good legal position would be beneficial to an immigrant's integration. This view formed the basis for the requirements for naturalization, as codified in the *1985 Rijkswet op het Nederlanderschap* (Dutch Nationality Act). Naturalisation became a right rather than a favour. In order to further open up access to Dutch nationality, the renunciation requirement was abolished in 1992. Christian Democrats in the Parliament in the course of the 1990s however started to express a different opinion on the place of naturalisation in the integration process than the government, of which they also formed part, had done so far: instead of a step in the integration process, naturalisation should be the end of a completed integration process. Furthermore, the rise in the number of naturalisations, which was especially high after the abolition of the renunciation requirement, according to the Christian Democrats showed that naturalisation had become 'too easy'. They therefore started lobbying for the introduction of written language skills and knowledge of society as conditions for naturalisation. Eventually, these requirements were introduced after sufficient support was gained from other political groups. After the introduction of the naturalisation test, the Conservative Liberal Minister for Integration repeatedly referred to naturalisation as 'the crown' on the integration process.

In Denmark, the view that naturalisation is a means rather than an end of integration was rejected by the centre-right Danish People's Party (DPP). In 2002, the DPP entered into an agreement about the naturalisation criteria with the governing parties (Conservatives and Liberals), after which inter alia the language requirement was strengthened. Hence, the governing parties, as the DPP had always done, also rejected the idea of naturalisation as a means of integration. Instead, they contended that 'the acquisition of citizenship presumes that the applicant is already integrated in Danish society'.[39]

Whether naturalisation was explicitly seen as a means for integration by the Austrian government prior to the introduction of the knowledge of society and language skills at level A2 requirements in 2006 is unclear. However, when the Austrian right-wing Freedom Party (FPÖ) entered into a coalition government with the Christian Democratic ÖVP in 1999, it expressed the view that naturalisation should come at the end of the integration process. Previously, criticism regarding the naturalisation procedure expressed by the FPÖ had already led to the introduction of the condition of 'adequate knowledge of the German language' in 1998. Like the Christian Democrats in the Netherlands, the FPÖ argued that acquisition of Austrian nationality was 'too easy'. The introduction of a language requirement apparently did not have the effect intended by the FPÖ, since it started a stronger lobby for stricter naturalisation criteria in 2005. The high number of naturalisations according to them showed an unfavourably liberal attitude to nationality. The new rules regarding naturalisation came into effect on 1 March 2006.[40] Hence, both in the Netherlands and in Austria, the wish to reduce the number of naturalisations explicitly played a role in the debates preceding the reinforcement of the language and integration criteria for naturalisation.

Increased Integration

In many of the countries under consideration, the introduction and strengthening of the language requirements and the introduction of the condition of societal knowledge have been justified using the argument of improved immigrant integration. The way in which this desire was worded, however, varied.

In Austria, for example, naturalisation is seen as a culmination of integration, which can only be reached with a good knowledge of German. In Denmark, language and societal requirements must secure that new Danish citizens have such knowledge of the Danish language, culture, etc. that they can get along in Danish society, follow the developments and debates and thus participate in the Danish society on an equal footing with the rest of the Danish population. Social and economic participation in society was also primarily the focus of policy justification in the UK. Examination for citizenship was perceived to strengthen the ability of new citizens to participate in society and to engage actively in the democracy.

---

39 Letter from the former Minister for Integration dated 7 June 2006.

40 Besides the requirement to prove language skills at level A2 and the introduction of the knowledge of society test, other requirements for naturalisation were also strengthened. The residence requirement was increased and naturalisation is refused to applicants who have received social support payments in the three years preceding the applications.

In Germany, in the eyes of the government, the formalisation of the language requirement was necessary to guarantee the immigrants' participation in the political decision making process. Only the possession of oral language skills, which was considered to be sufficient in some states, was considered insufficient for proper political decision making skills.

In Hungary, the examination of constitutional issues was introduced with the expectation that applicants should have fundamental historical and constitutional knowledge by passing an examination demonstrating their attachment to Hungary. The test was also considered to contribute to the moral relevance of Hungarian citizenship.

In Latvia, naturalisation requirements, especially the language requirement, were considered to be a basis for building a civil society and for defining a shared system of values. During the Soviet occupation many immigrants from the former Soviet republics came to Latvia. After regaining independence, Latvia had to ensure state continuity. This implied that fundamental laws and the Constitution in force before the Soviet occupation had to be revived and only the persons who were citizens at the time of the occupation as well as their descendants were recognised as Latvian citizens. In order to ensure the existence of Latvia, including its own identity, the language requirement was compulsory, while many persons were bilingual (Latvian and Russian) or had no knowledge of Latvian at all. The naturalisation requirements set by the Citizenship Law in 1994 were hence aimed at persons who came to Latvia during the Soviet era.

A More Uniform Interpretation of the Language Requirement for Naturalisation

In Germany and the Netherlands, the wish for a more uniform interpretation and application of the language requirement led to a formalisation of the language test. In the Netherlands, this formalisation at the same time implied a strengthening of the language requirement. In Germany, it meant a strengthening of the requirement in the *Länder* that previously only tested oral language proficiency.

Research conducted in the Netherlands in 1988 had pointed out that the language requirement was applied differently in the municipalities. Whereas the manual for the application of the Dutch Nationality Act stated that only oral language skills were required, ten per cent of the municipalities also required written language skills. The 1992 Bill, which proposed the official abolition of the renunciation requirement, hence also contained a reformulation of the language and integration requirement. A more precise formulation of the language and integration requirement would enhance equality and fairness in its application.

In Germany, next to a different application of the language requirement, the requirement to declare loyalty to Germany's free and democratic basic order also led to different practices in the *Länder*. It was hence decided to add the requirement of knowledge of the legal and social system and the way of life in the Federal territory, generally to be proven in a naturalisation test, as a condition for naturalisation. Since only the state of Baden-Württemberg employed questions within the framework of the declaration of loyalty, the introduction of the naturalisation test implied a strengthening of the overall naturalisation procedure in the other German states.

4.5 Consequences of not Passing the Test

Migrants who are not exempted from the requirement to pass the test, will not be able to naturalise as long as they do not pass the test. This has consequences for their political rights, especially the right to vote or to be voted as a politician. Although in some Member States migrants enjoy voting rights on the municipal level if they fulfill certain conditions (for instance after a legal residence of five years), participation in regional or national elections is reserved for citizens. Furthermore, certain professions can only be practised by citizens, like the profession of judges or certain administrators. Which professions belong to this category, varies from country to country. Another consequence of not obtaining citizenship is that migrants do not enjoy the highest level of security of residence. Although the exact conditions for withdrawal varies from country to country, they are in all Member States more strict regarding citizenship than regarding the permanent residence permit. These three kinds of consequences (political rights, professional rights and security of residence) can influence the degree of integration of migrants.

4.6 Effects of the Tests: Statistical Data[41]

The way statistics are compiled differs considerably between the countries that are part of this research, which leads to the situation that the topics addressed in the national reports are not always the same.

Number of Applications, Naturalisations and Refusals

In Austria, Denmark, Latvia and the Netherlands the number of persons who naturalise is declining. In Germany differences between the federal states exist, since the federal Nationality Act is implemented differently in the states. In France the language and other requirements do not appear to have affected the number of applications. Hence, the number of naturalisations have remained more or less similar over the years. For Hungary there are no statistics on this issue. Because of the difference between the countries, each country will be described individually below.

In Austria there has been a continuous decline in the number of naturalisations since 2004, in particular since 2006. The number of persons was 26,259 in 2006 and 14,041 in 2007 with further declines in the following years. This decline can be explained by several factors. The large group of refugees from former Yugoslavia became smaller because they had reached the ten years of residence required for naturalisation between 1998 and 2004. Another reason can be found in the restriction of naturalisation criteria. According to some of the interview respondents, elderly migrants who speak poor German may be put off the idea of naturalisation because of the test. Most respondents thought, however, that the stricter residence and income requirements are more likely to explain the decline in naturalisations. Furthermore, Directive 2003/109/EC was implemented in Austrian law, which equalized the status of long-term residents to that of Austrian citizens in terms of access to

41 Unless otherwise stated, the figures in this section have been taken from the national INTEC reports.

the labour market, social rights and access to housing. This took away some of the importance to naturalise.

In Denmark the number of naturalisations decreased after 2002 due to implementation of stricter rules in that year. To a large extent the drop in 2003 was caused by the formalisation of the language requirement, which meant that applicants were forced to put their applications on hold until they had passed a language examination at level B1. In 2004 and 2005 the number increased again because more and more immigrants had taken the necessary language examinations. However, with the rise of the required language level from 2006 (from B1 to B2) a new decrease has occurred and this time the decrease appears to have a more permanent character. Furthermore, the number of refusals of applications increased in 2002, 2003 as well as in the period 2007-2009. Refusals have increasingly been given due to a lack of Danish language proficiency. However, at the moment two new important grounds for refusal account for the largest percentage of the number of refusals: the requirement for passing the naturalisation test and the requirement for self-support.

In Germany, there was a decline in naturalisations from 2000 to 2006, while in 2006 the numbers increased slightly. However, in 2007 and 2008 numbers decreased again, followed by a slight increase in 2009. At the same time, the number of foreigners eligible for naturalisation on the basis of their time spent in Germany is high. In 2007, only 2.9 per cent of those eligible on such grounds were naturalised (Integrationsbeauftragte 2010: 443). Mention should be made of the fact that naturalisation rates differ considerably between the German states and cities because of different interpretations of the naturalisation requirements, differences in the length of the procedure and differences in administrative quality. The number of naturalisations increased in seven states, whereas there was a decrease in nine states. The organisation of a campaign to promote naturalisation has proven to have a positive effect on the number of naturalisations in Stuttgart, where the number of applications rose by ten per cent in 2009.

In Latvia, the accession of Latvia to the EU in 2004 and was one of the causes for a considerable rise in the number of naturalisations. However, after 2006 the numbers dropped significantly, probably because since then non-citizens could also apply for the EU Long-term Residence status if they wanted to get a certain level of freedom of movement within the EU. The required level of knowledge for obtaining this status is lower than the test regarding Latvian citizenship.

In the Netherlands a differentiation can be made between the period before the entry into force of the revised Dutch Nationality Act in 2003, introducing the formalized language and integration requirement in the form of the naturalisation test and reinforcing the residence requirement, and the period after this revision.[42] The number of applications for naturalisation was much higher before the coming into force of the revised Dutch Nationality Act. Compared to 2002, the year before the revised Dutch Nationality Act entered into force, the number of applications for naturalisation decreased by two-thirds in 2004. In 2008, the number of applications was still more than half as low as the number of applications filed in 2002. From 1997 to 2001, hence prior to the introduction of the revised

42 Prior to the entry into force of the revised Dutch Nationality Act on 1 April 2003, ordinary residence of five years would suffice for naturalisation. As of 1 April 2003, the residence must have been lawful and uninterrupted.

Dutch Nationality Act, a decreasing trend in the number of applications can also be seen.[43] The decreases in the number of naturalisations in the years prior to the introduction of the revised Dutch Nationality Act, however, were not as sharp as the decrease which can be noticed later. The conclusion can hence be drawn that the revision of the nationality legislation has been the most important cause of the strong decrease in the number of applications for naturalisation. In 2007, the naturalisation test in the Netherlands was replaced by the integration examination. Other requirements for naturalisation remained unaltered. The new decrease in the number of naturalisations in 2007 and 2008 can hence probably be ascribed to the introduction of the integration examination, which has the same level as the naturalisation test, but which is more extensive and expensive. In the years to come, a rise in the number of naturalisations can however be expected, since there has been a rise in the number of persons passing the integration examination (see below).

In the UK, the number of naturalisations has not declined since the formalisation of the language requirement and the introduction of the knowledge of 'Life in the UK' requirement in the years 2004 and 2005. On the contrary: one can even see an increase in naturalisations despite the strengthening of the requirements. In the four calendar years prior to 2004, the average number of naturalisations was 78,564 and in the four full years since 2005, the average number was 117,441. An explanation for this is the fact that higher levels of migration to the UK from the 1990s onwards increased the pool of potential applicants for both an indefinite leave to remain (permanent residence status) and naturalisation. This upward trend makes it difficult to identify any deterrent effect since the language and Life in the UK requirements were introduced. Another problem is that even if a reduced propensity to obtain naturalisation could be shown, this could also be due to other causes, such as the increased fees for the application.[44]

Pass Rates

Pass rates for the knowledge of society tests in Austria and Germany are high. In Austria according to an article in the weekly 'News' of 1 August 2007, the pass rate for the test at first attempt was on average 90 per cent in Austria. Three other reports on the success rate for naturalisation testing show higher pass rates, e.g. 95 per cent in 2010. In Germany from the day the *Einbürgerungstest* entered into force (1 September 2008) to 31 March 2010, 106,831 people took part in the test, with a success rate of 98.5 per cent. Pass rates also used to be high in Denmark, where until December 2008, 97 per cent of all candidates passed the test successfully. After the introduction of a new test in December 2008, the pass rate dropped considerably: more than three-quarters of the candidates failed the test. Since then the pass rate has risen, being 54.5 per cent in December 2009, and there is reason to believe that the pass rate for June 2010 will further increase. It should be borne in mind, however, that as well as the knowledge of society test, applicants for naturalisation in

43 This can probably be ascribed to the re-application of the renunciation requirement in 1997. But the reduction may also partly be due to the effect that a large share of the Moroccan and Turkish immigrants, the two largest immigrant groups in the Netherlands, had been naturalised by that time (Böcker, Groenendijk & De Hart 2005).

44 In 2005 these fees were £ 200, increased to £ 575 in 2007, £ 655 in 2008, £ 720 in 2009 and £ 735 in 2010.

Austria, Denmark and Germany will also have to fulfil the language requirement which especially in Denmark appears to form a high barrier (see analysis of interviews in paragraph 4.6).

In Latvia, the pass rates for the naturalisation examinations have been declining over the years. During 2004 and 2005, when naturalisation reached its peak, the percentage of those who failed the knowledge test was 3.7 per cent and 4.8 per cent respectively, but by 2007 and 2008 those figures had already reached 10.4 per cent and 17.8 per cent. The results for the language examination are similar. During 2004 and 2005, respectively 10 and 16 per cent of all participants in the language examination failed. In the years thereafter, the failure rates increased, reaching a peak in 2009 when almost 40 per cent of all language examination candidates failed. This can be explained by two factors: the decrease in the offer of courses financed by the state and the lower educational level of the current group of applicants.

The Hungarian report mentions an estimated success rate of 70 per cent in the constitutional examination. From interviews it becomes clear that the failure rate is 10 per cent. Furthermore, the second attempt is in most cases successful. The composition of the Examination Board has a strong influence on the pass rate.

In the Netherlands the pass rate for the naturalisation test, in force from 1 April 2003 to 1 April 2007, was 60 per cent of all those who enrolled for the test and eventually took it. The others did not turn up after they were confronted with the obligation to pay for the test (as well as the fee for naturalisation), or they did not turn up for the second part of the test or failed the test. Departing from the number of actual participants, the pass rate for the test is higher, namely 74 per cent. On 1 April 2007, the integration examination replaced the naturalisation test as a condition for naturalisation. Since the integration examination is also a condition for permanent residence, the results in this examination are considered in paragraph 3.3 of this report. With a pass rate between 72 and 74 per cent, the pass rate for the integration examination is more or less similar to the pass rate for the former naturalisation test. The absolute number of persons passing the integration examination is however much higher. Whereas a total of 14,300 persons passed the naturalisation test during the four years it was in force, with 49,500 persons passing the integration examination in the period 2007-June 2010, the number of successful candidates in this test appears to be three times higher. It is hence expected that the number of naturalisations will rise in the future. It however remains to be seen whether this expected rise will have a permanent character, since plans were at the time of writing in the making to put a stop to the financing of integration courses (see the afterword).

Number of Exemptions

Statistical data on the number of immigrants who are exempted from the language and knowledge of society requirements are only available for Denmark and the Netherlands. In Denmark the number of exemptions from the language requirement has decreased, possibly because the practice of the Naturalisation Committee has been restricted in parallel with the restrictions on the requirements for naturalisation.

In the Netherlands in the first one and a half years after the introduction of the naturalisation test, around 85 per cent of all applicants for naturalisation were exempt from passing the test on the basis of a diploma. Around three per cent of all applicants were exempt due to language or medical impediments, which leaves twelve per cent of all applicants who actually took the test (INS 2004: 33). More recent statistics show that in the years 2005 to 2008, 4.5 per cent of all the applicants whose application was granted were exempt on the basis of a medical or language impediment. Furthermore, the percentage of persons who successfully passed the naturalisation test before applying for naturalisation has risen to between 25 and 29 per cent (INS 2007: 71).[45] The majority of all applicants for naturalisation is hence exempt from passing the required test, mostly on the basis of a diploma.

Age

In the countries that had data as regards the age of the naturalised immigrant (Germany and the Netherlands), the age group of persons between 18 and 35 accounts for most of the naturalisations. In Germany naturalized migrants are increasingly becoming younger. The average age of persons who were naturalized in 2007 was 30.5 years and the average age of persons who were naturalized in 2009 was 29.5 years. In Latvia approximately one-third of the naturalized non-citizens consists of persons from 18-30 years and the number of older people opting for naturalisation is decreasing. By representing two-thirds of the candidates who passed the naturalisation test, the group of immigrants aged 18 to 35 are by far the most represented age category that registered for and passed the test in the Netherlands as well. Representing one-third of the total, immigrants aged between 35 and 65 represent the second largest group who registered for and passed the naturalisation test. Immigrants aged 65 years or older are the least represented category among immigrants registering for and passing the test. Furthermore, the pass rate for this age category is significantly lower than the pass rates for the younger age categories. With 62.2 per cent, the pass rate for those candidates aged 18 to 35 is highest. The pass rates appear to reduce with age, since candidates aged 35 to 65 passed the test less often. With 40 per cent, the pass rate for candidates aged 65 years or older is lowest.

Nationality

Applications for naturalisation and/or pass rates for the tests broken down by nationality are available for Hungary, Germany, Latvia, the Netherlands and the UK. In Hungary 90 per cent of naturalized persons are native ethnic Hungarians. A spot check among 101 applications in 2009 showed that 69 per cent of the applications were made by ethnic Hungarians. In Germany most naturalized foreigners are from Turkey (24,647 in 2009). In Latvia the largest share of naturalized citizens are former citizens of the USSR: they have submitted 68 per cent of all naturalisation applications in the 14 years since the introduction of naturalisation. This corresponds to their share among the non-citizens of Latvia (on 1 July 2009 66 per cent of non-citizens were former citizens of the USSR). The following groups are Belarusians (10 per cent applications and share among non-citizens 13 per cent) and Ukrainians (9 per cent of applications, 9.5 per cent among the non-citizens).

45 Since accurate data on the number of persons passing the test before applying for naturalisation were not available, the percentage was based on an estimate using available numbers.

In the Netherlands and the UK, pass rates in the tests broken down by nationality are available. In both countries, the pass rates clearly differ between the countries of origin. In the UK, it appears that pass rates for countries with a high level of development are higher. The pass rates furthermore suggest that there are differences of outcome per immigration category: countries from which many refugees and family migrants originate generally have low pass rates (see above paragraph 3.7).

In the Netherlands the pass rates also vary considerably between the nationalities.[46] As in the UK, the introduction of the test has resulted in a selection of future citizens in which the country of origin plays an important role.

Gender

In Latvia the cumulative figures since naturalisation started in 1996 until the end of 2009 show that 63 per cent of all naturalisation applicants have been women. In 2009 for the first time there were more men applying than women. In the Netherlands the absolute number of men (12,248 - 7,286) registering for and passing the test is also higher than the absolute number of women (11,463 - 7,017). However, the difference is small. Women score better (62 per cent) than men (59 per cent) as regards success rates.

4.7 Effects of the Tests: Interview Results

Opinions on the Requirements

In general, examinations testing language and societal knowledge are supported by the interviewees in all countries. Both immigrants interviewed in Austria who were preparing for the naturalisation test approved the duty to take a test and saw it as a self-evident right of the state to impose such an obligation. A similar feeling of understanding as regards the obligation to meet naturalisation requirements exists in Denmark and Germany, where in most cases naturalisation tests (and orientation courses) are considered a good opportunity to learn about history and current affairs and to gain an understanding of society. Furthermore, the Naturalisation Office and the police in Denmark indicate that migrants who currently apply for naturalisation have a better knowledge of the Danish language than former applicants. However, fewer immigrants apply for naturalisation, which is probably due to the language requirements. In Latvia citizens and non-citizens generally support the examinations. Latvian officials and language teachers are positive about the naturalisation process.

Although a general sense of understanding is present among interviewees, critical comments have been made. The immigrants interviewed in Denmark can be divided into two groups, low educated migrants to respectively higher educated migrants and/or second generation migrants. Half of the applicants for naturalisation interviewed were born and/or raised in Denmark. Some of the respondents of this latter category think it is 'unreasonable' or 'unfair' that they have to comply with naturalisation requirements. The second genera-

46 This was already explained in paragraph 3.7.

tion migrants consider themselves Danish and feel offended that they have to prove this by taking a test. They can, however, prove their language skills by showing a diploma from a Danish public school. It appears that in Denmark the well-educated immigrants form the largest part of naturalized immigrants. In Latvia some non-citizens felt humiliated that they had to take a test. Two NGOs supported this view. However, survey data show that the number of persons who think that the naturalisation process is humiliating has decreased. Most academic graduates in Germany believe that the test is not necessary for them because they are already equipped with an appropriate level of relevant knowledge. Other migrants showed little understanding for the meaning of the naturalisation tests: 'I live and work here. What a German does, I am also doing. Why should I not vote and why must I take the test?'

Opinions on the Content of the Test

While most naturalisation tests were initially concentrated on knowledge of the language, during the last five years the requirements of the test have been extended to knowledge of society and history, constitution and values and norms in Austria, Denmark, Germany and the UK. In the Netherlands and Latvia, societal knowledge has been part of the formalized test from the beginning. In France and Hungary this knowledge is tested in an interview. Nevertheless, in general migrants consider the language requirement as the most difficult part of the test.

In Germany and Latvia the naturalisation test is not perceived to be difficult. In Germany, it was questioned, both by migrant advisory services and migrants, whether the naturalisation test makes an individual into a loyal citizen and an equal member of society. Naturalized respondents in Latvia indicated that the tests consist of simple questions and that the contents are relevant. Conversely, non-citizens think that the examinations should be easier, especially for the elderly. All Latvian officials and NGOs interviewed noted that the most difficult part of the examination was the written part of the language examination. Furthermore, the Office of Citizenship and Migration Affairs received complaints about history questions, such as 'what happened on 17 June 1940?'.

In Denmark persons in all categories interviewed indicated that the naturalisation requirements, especially the level of the language requirement, were too high. According to immigrant organisations the language requirement is the hardest to fulfil and it is criticized, also by language teachers, for excluding less well educated immigrants from becoming Danish citizens. Some organisations point out as a good thing that the conditions are standardized. Some migrants, furthermore, stated that the content of the knowledge of society test is, for example, irrelevant or superficial. With regard to questions on history there are strong doubts whether young native Danish citizens would know the answers. Language teachers in Denmark complained that what was tested, was if 'the applicant has learned the text book by heart'.

In the Netherlands the answers by the migrants show a wide variety of what they think of the test. Their opinion on the usefulness of the test seems to be more uniform. In particular the ability to speak the language is seen as a very important aspect to function in everyday life. Part of the critique by the different interviewees is directed at the content of the knowledge of Dutch society test: are these questions useful and do natives know the answers? Some immigrants considered the questions regarding behavior and values and norms as unnecessary brainwashing. Furthermore, municipalities indicated that compiling the portfolio places a heavy burden on the migrant.

In the UK a common assessment indicates that the handbook contains unnecessary information and potentially outdated information. Test candidates confirm that the test is relatively straightforward for those with fluent English language skills. One respondent said that the test asked things native British citizens did not even know. Some candidates had ideas for reformation of the tests, such as an interview to assess the candidate's Life in the UK knowledge. Also two candidates thought the test was too easy for what it purported to assess.

Although the examination in Hungary only constitutes of a knowledge test on constitutional issues, the questions are so difficult that a high level of Hungarian is required (at least C1 level). Officials therefore only advise immigrants with high language abilities to take the examination. This explains the low failure rate despite the fact that the test is very difficult.

Preparation for the Test

In all countries respondents prepared themselves for the test, for example, by following a course, self-study or experience in practice. In Germany most test candidates prepared for the test on the Internet. Orientation courses contain complex vocabulary and require a higher level of proficiency than A2/B1 levels. Immigrants who possess limited German language skills often pass naturalisation tests by learning the answers by heart.

In Austria, according to teachers, candidates only rarely attend a language course. In most cases naturalisation takes place after at least ten years of residence in the country and it can be expected that persons have acquired enough knowledge of the German language by that time to pass the language test at Level A2. Some candidates are, however advised to attend a course if the official in charge believes that the applicant has insufficient knowledge of the language. Teachers furthermore indicate that there is no demand for language courses and that immigrants prepare their test at home. Two immigrants interviewed were indeed advised to follow a course before taking the test and they were well informed about the possibility of downloading learning material.

In Denmark the language teachers stated that there were not enough possibilities for preparation for the knowledge test. In the Netherlands a number of the candidates for the naturalisation test prepare for the test by following an integration course. This course has been introduced within the framework of the Integration Act. As prior to the entry into force of this act, candidates for the naturalisation test were not supported in their preparation for the test, it can be concluded that the Integration Act (which also includes the integration requirement for a permanent residence permit) facilitates the preparation for naturalisation. The suggestion was made by teachers in the Netherlands that more attention could be paid to ordinary day-to-day worries or cultural affairs. Most migrants were satisfied with the contents of the courses. Some officials of the municipalities however mentioned the fact that a lot of attention was paid to passing the tests (teaching for tests) and that the main goal – learning the Dutch language – might disappear out of sight.

As regards preparation in the UK all test candidates relied on the handbook, several also on questions and answers and many had visited unofficial Internet websites to test their skills.

The major fear of examinees in Hungary is that they will not understand the questions asked at the examination, because they differ from the preparatory material. Fear for the examination appeared to be a major reason for Latvian non-citizens not to apply for Latvian citizenship. A number of them felt too old and had insufficient knowledge of the language. Due to the lack of Latvian courses, this group is not able to overcome its insufficient knowledge.

Motives to Naturalise

According to Austrian NGOs naturalisation is more and more becoming an expression of the decision to stay in Austria forever. This was confirmed by one of the migrants interviewed. Naturalisation would also prevent immigrants from legal discrimination and practical hassles. One immigrant wanted his children to become Austrian citizens and therefore the whole family decided to naturalise. According to NGOs the interest has dropped since the introduction of the long-term residence status, in particular among older migrants, who often feel too old to learn the German language well enough and to pass the test. This group is also less interested in free movement and voting rights. It appears, according to NGOs, that young people also often opt for the EU long-term residence status instead of naturalisation, as this status is easier to obtain and facilitates movement within the EU.

In Germany the reasons given for naturalisation were predominantly of a pragmatic nature: to have the freedom to travel, to have a German passport and avoid stress when dealing with the authorities, to join dependants who had already become German. In some cases, the right to political participation was also mentioned as a motive. The ability to travel was also one of the main motives to naturalise in Latvia. Other main motives, emotional as well as pragmatic, were for example the wish to belong to the country, have voting rights, the fact that the applicant would continue to live in Latvia, the partner was a citizen of Latvia or the fact that citizenship was needed in order to find a job. Some non-citizens did not opt for naturalisation because they wanted to maintain closer ties with Russia. Loss of their status would be an obstacle for travelling to Russia.

Most respondents in the Netherlands were participating in a course and/or the test because they were under the obligation to integrate, but indicated that after the test they wanted to apply for naturalisation. This integration obligation of the Integration Act made the barrier to opting for naturalisation lower. The most important motive particularly for naturalisation was that these migrants wanted to be safe, or, to put it differently, to 'get rid of all the crap' connected with not being Dutch. Interest groups, particularly refugee organisations, also mentioned this consideration, indicating that naturalisation was the ultimate guarantee for refugees of not running the risk of being sent back to their country of origin. Migrants themselves mentioned mainly practical reasons: improvement of their current situation, or as a requirement for further education or a (better) job. They also indicated that the possession ultimately, of a Dutch passport would grant them the most secure position. Also the fact that some of these migrants had partners who already had a Dutch passport stimulated them to get in an equal position. A particular practical motive, as in Germany and Latvia, was the idea that the possession of a Dutch passport would allow the holder to travel far more easily around the world.

Groups facing Difficulties fulfilling the Requirements

According to interviews with the support and services centres in Austria, elderly people who speak poor German may be deterred from naturalisation because of the test in Austria. Also in Latvia older persons face more difficulties with the language examination than others and are often afraid of taking it. However, younger people have more problems with the knowledge examination.

In Hungary having Hungarian language skills is the highest barrier for non-Hungarian speaking (non-ethnic) migrants. Non-Hungarian speakers are screened out through this examination, which means a hindrance in the acquisition of nationality. According to respondents the Latin alphabet and Hungarian pronunciation are difficult for Russian, Serbian, Chinese or other Asian examinees.

In the Netherlands, certain groups find it difficult to meet the requirements: elderly people and low educated migrants, illiterates in particular, Asian migrants and traumatized refugees.

In the UK the test is relatively straightforward for those with a good command of English, but language and Life in the UK requirements have greater impact on certain groups. Many persons in humanitarian categories, some in family categories – especially if they are women – and some older people fare less well. Those groups are now less free to naturalise than they would have been had the naturalisation requirements not applied.

Exemptions

In four countries, the results of the interviews contain some information on the opinions as regards exemptions. One respondent in Denmark finds the possibilities for exemption too poor. A number of immigrant organisations call attention to the need for more grounds for exemption, especially as regards post-traumatic stress disorder. Applications for exemption from the language requirements are often submitted on physical or mental health grounds or on word-blindness. The Danish Naturalisation Office notes that only very serious health problems that prevent the person from fulfilling the requirements constitute a valid ground for exemption. Latvian NGOs and a British legal advisor argued for more exemptions on grounds of ages. British respondents mentioned the absence of a specific procedure for exemption on grounds of incapacity before an application is made. In the Netherlands, a release of the requirement for traumatised migrants can be given on medical grounds. However, not all doctors are familiar with traumata of refugees, which, according to teachers and refugee interest groups, lead to difficulties and stress while preparing for the test.

In the Netherlands, Germany and Austria respondents complained about the limited number of officially recognised diplomas that creates an exemption from this requirement. Dutch municipalities and teachers mention cases in which certain diplomas do not appear on the list when they should. In Germany, the way authorities deal with language requirements is a problem. In one case, the authority in charge refused to recognise a language certificate that had been issued at an earlier date, although the naturalisation applicant spoke fluent German (8. Lagebericht 2010: 445). In the Netherlands and Austria, an academic degree from a university in the country does not count as fulfilment of the language and societal knowledge requirements. In the Netherlands, a Danish assistant professor in Dutch literature had to do a short exemption test in order to prove her language skills. In Austria, a

Mexican citizen had a similar experience, despite his Ph.D. in history from Vienna University with a thesis on the subject of Austrian history in the 20th century, written in German.

Problems and Obstacles Experienced

In Denmark it was pointed out as a problem that the test is held only twice a year, since candidates will have forgotten the knowledge they gained in that time.

In Hungary the requirements for the level of Hungarian as well as the level of knowledge have not been defined. The missing transparency of the examination order and assessment methods has attracted critics. In the Netherlands similar problems occur, as the content of the test is kept secret, although there is some exercise material available. Not knowing what will be asked increases the stress of migrants taking the test. Municipalities and course institutions also mention the lack of feedback to the candidate as regards the mistakes he/she has made as a downside of the learning effect of a candidate.

In the UK the potential difficulties, according to a volunteer who ran study classes, include a lack of education in the country of origin or experience of computers. Immigrants are concerned and scared that the process is complex and they are not used to studying and taking examinations. Another problem indicated by a migrant organisation and a law centre was the lack of time for preparation due to work obligations. A law centre also mentioned the situation where it was difficult to get family support to get a woman out of the house and into a language course.

In the Netherlands, the level of the short exemption test is B1, while the level of the naturalisation test is A2. Despite a national judgment that this higher requirement is not in compliance with the Integration Act, the authorities did not lower the level.

Effects on Integration

In some countries, doubts were expressed on the presumption that a naturalisation test would lead to a better integration in society. For the majority of respondents in Denmark, passing the test on knowledge of society did not lead to a feeling of being integrated into Danish society. In Germany and the Netherlands, immigrants who had no problems meeting the requirements already felt part of society and stated not to be better integrated after meeting the requirements. The test resulted in the feeling, especially of higher educated migrants, that their integration was unappreciated. According to some German officials the tests are not an appropriate method to integrate, because someone could pass the test without understanding or dealing with the content. Furthermore, the certified level B1 is not sufficient for any profession, because the language ability at this level is quite elementary. This is why immigrants who pass the tests can improve their economic situation only to a limited extent. Dutch language teachers also criticized that the actual 'certificate' (A2) had no value whatsoever regarding subsequent training or education; it could not be compared with the so-called basic qualification needed for further education or the job market.

In Latvia immigrants appreciate naturalisation differently from language teachers. Immigrants do not consider naturalisation as a means to facilitate integration. Non-citizens (especially former USSR citizens) do not feel invited to acquire citizenship, mainly because of historical reasons and personal feelings regarding Latvian citizenship. Most of them thought that the test had an adverse effect on integration. Conversely, language teachers say that examinations are necessary for integration into society. Language and knowledge of history are crucial to making daily life easier and for making persons feel better at work and positive about Latvia.

In the UK there was general agreement among candidates that the test did not contribute to their integration. A frequent statement that was made was that the test was only about memorisation, and was therefore not suited to test integration. According to two respondents of advice centres, minority groups seek the company of persons from the same background, e.g. a Somali would socialize with other Somalis, whether they spoke English or not. One volunteer at a migrant organisation however pointed to the positive effect of tests: they would give the person a sense of achievement and would make them feel more confident.

4.8 Summary and Conclusions

The Requirements

Seven of the nine countries under consideration in this study (Austria, Denmark, Germany, Hungary, Latvia, the Netherlands and the UK) apply integration tests as a condition for naturalisation. The knowledge of language and a knowledge of society are tested, or proved in another way, for instance by a relevant diploma. All of the above mentioned countries offer some form of preparation for the language and/or integration test for naturalisation. In four of the seven countries (Austria, Denmark, Germany and the Netherlands) there are publicly regulated and/or funded courses to prepare for the language test. In the Netherlands and Denmark, these courses were not introduced for the preparation of the naturalisation test, but within the framework of the Integration Act. As the test on the basis of this act has the same content as the naturalisation test, the courses serve in practice as a proper preparation for naturalisation. No state-regulated preparation courses for the knowledge of society test are offered in Austria, Denmark, Germany, Latvia and the UK. Hungary is the only country where knowledge of language is not explicitly tested. In France the language requirement is tested in an informal interview and in Belgium no language requirement is applied.

In the six countries where knowledge of language is required the level differs. The level is the highest in Denmark (B2). As regards the knowledge of society test it is difficult to estimate in which country this requirement is the hardest to fulfil.

It appears that once tests are introduced, requirements for naturalisation have only been strengthened. In Austria, for example, where a language requirement for naturalisation has been applied since 1998, the requirement was made uniform and strengthened in March 2006. In the same year also a knowledge of society test was introduced. This trend of adding knowledge of society requirements to the language test in naturalisation procedures can also be seen in Denmark, Germany, the Netherlands and the United Kingdom. The strengthening of the requirements affects the number of applications, naturalisations and refusals. The decrease in these numbers is partly due to restriction of naturalisation criteria, but is also influenced by other factors. In the United Kingdom for example an increase can be observed, despite the strengthening of the requirements. This is presumably related to the increase in the number of immigrants in the last decade.

In the Netherlands and the United Kingdom the same integration requirements apply for naturalisation as for permanent residence. Hence, no new requirements are applicable when a person applies for citizenship. It is thus to be expected that the number of naturalisations in the Netherlands will increase, since there has been a rise in the number of persons passing the integration examination. With regard to 'oldcomers', this effect could be less evident, as for them the required level for the granting of permanent residence is lower. In Austria and Germany fulfilling the language requirement for permanent residence means exemption from this requirement when applying for naturalisation.

Although in general testing language and societal knowledge is supported and understood by most interviewees in all countries, some criticism exists. These critical remarks mostly concern the content of the tests or study material, especially the questions asked in the knowledge of society tests. These were often deemed not to be relevant, or even useless or primitive. Furthermore, in most countries various problems and/or obstacles in the naturalisation procedure exist. For instance, in Denmark it is considered a problem that the knowledge test is only held twice a year and in Hungary the minimum level of required knowledge is unclear. In the Netherlands, the questions of the test are kept secret, which complicates the preparation for the test.

Exemptions

In all countries, except the United Kingdom, immigrants who have followed education in the country or who are attending school, are exempted from proving sufficient language skills and/or passing the knowledge of society test as a condition for naturalisation. Persons who have reached a certain age are exempted from fulfilling the language and knowledge of society requirements in Austria, France, Germany, Hungary, Latvia, the Netherlands and the United Kingdom. In all countries under consideration, exemption from the requirements may be obtained if someone suffers from a mental or physical impediment.

From interviews in Denmark, Latvia, the Netherlands and the UK it appears that respondents think that there are few possibilities for exemption and that exemption is difficult to obtain.

Purposes

In the countries under consideration different reasons for introduction of the requirements and/or tests were expressed. The reasons mainly fell within three categories. Firstly, in some countries the opinion on the place of naturalisation in the integration process changed. In the Netherlands, for example, there is a shift from seeing naturalisation as a step in the integration process to naturalisation as 'the crown' on the integration process. Secondly, a more uniform interpretation of the language requirement for naturalisation was an important factor for formalizing naturalisation tests in Germany and the Netherlands. Finally, in many countries, the introduction and strengthening of the language requirements and the introduction of the condition of societal knowledge have been justified by the argument that the requirements would promote the integration of migrants.

The situation in Latvia can be considered special because of the former Soviet occupation and the need to ensure state continuity. In Latvia, naturalisation requirements, especially the language requirement, were considered to be a basis for building a civil society and for defining a shared system of values.

Effects on Integration

From interviews conducted for this study, it appears that in most countries under consideration it remains questionable whether naturalisation tests lead to better integration in society. Most migrant respondents in Denmark, Germany, Latvia and the UK were of the opinion that the test did not contribute to their integration. Conversely, other respondents pointed to the positive effects of naturalisation testing. Language teachers in Latvia, for example, said that examinations are necessary to integrate in society because knowledge of language and history are crucial in daily life.

In Denmark and the Netherlands most migrants experienced that attending a course and the need to practice, increased their sense of independence. In most countries, having passed the test is not recognised as a proof of certain skills on the labour market.

Groups facing Difficulties fulfilling Requirements

Some groups find it more difficult to meet the naturalisation requirements than others. Especially older people find it difficult to meet the naturalisation requirements in Austria, Latvia, the Netherlands and the UK. This is confirmed by data on the number of naturalisations and pass rates broken down by age. In Hungary the high language skills necessary to pass the test on constitutional knowledge is the highest barrier for the ethnic minorities who do not speak Hungarian. In Latvia, younger people have more problems with the knowledge examination. In the United Kingdom many persons in humanitarian categories, some in family categories – especially if they are women – fare less well.

Based on pass rates broken down by nationality it can be suggested that in the Netherlands and the UK, the introduction of the test resulted in a selection of future citizens in which the country of origin plays an important role. As the other national reports did not produce similar figures, we could not compare these conclusions with other Member States.

CHAPTER 5. SUMMARY AND CONCLUSIONS

Tineke Strik

A comparison of the developments in the nine Member States, clearly shows a growing preference to impose integration conditions at the earliest possible stage and, in this regard, to connect the right to residence with an integration requirement. In this chapter, we will analyse the political perception lying behind this development. In this analysis we included possible relations between the policy developments of the different Member States. As this research has concentrated on the effects of the integration measures and conditions, we will describe in this chapter what the relevant conclusions regarding the different tests have in common. Finally, we will formulate some recommendations for best practice as well as for future research.

5.1 From an Effort Obligation to a Result Obligation: An Overview

In most Member States the first type of integration requirement has been applied in a naturalisation procedure. Until the beginning of this century, this condition was limited to knowledge of the language. In most countries the fulfilment of this requirement was assumed (United Kingdom) or assessed in an informal interview with a civil servant (Netherlands, some German states, Denmark, France). Since 2000 the tendency has grown in different Member States to apply uniform criteria and to assess the language requirement in the form of a formalized test, often combined with an assessment on societal knowledge. Currently, seven of the nine Member States assess the required knowledge by a test.

At the same time politicians have called for the need to prove knowledge of and respect for the national values and norms. In France, the interview was not replaced by a test but the French values and norms have become increasingly important in the assessment. The new requirement for future French citizens to show adherence to them, indicates that the emphasis on assimilation in French integration policy has grown. Considering the growing attention paid to national values and norms in the integration policies of other Member States, this could be a common trend.

Before 2000, naturalisation had been seen as a step in the integration process, which supported migrants to become more integrated. For this reason, a large number of politicians were convinced at that time that granting citizenship to migrants living permanently in their country, was in the national interest. At the beginning of the twentieth century this conviction made way for the shift towards the idea that migrants should deserve citizenship, as it marked the final stage of the integration process. This changing approach to migrants not only affected the requirements for citizenship, but also those for residence rights.

Table 5.1 Overview of the introduction and level of the tests

Country	*Passing test requirement for admission*	*Obligation attendance courses in country*	*Passing test requirement for permanent residence*	*Passing test requirement for naturalisation*
Austria	Yes A1 future (2011)	Formally no	Yes A2 2003	Yes A2 1998 language requirement 2006 test lan-guage/society
Belgium	No	Yes, only in Flemish region 2003	No	No
Denmark	Yes A1 minus 15 Nov 2010	Yes 1999	Yes, test since 2002, level B1 since 2007 ('active citizen-ship' test from 2011)	Yes 2002 B1 2006 B2 2007+society
France	No	Yes	Yes A1.1 2007	No, knowledge is assessed by an interview 2005 2010 +adherence to principles French Republic
Germany	Yes A1 Oct 2007	Yes 2005	Yes B1 2005	Yes B1 2000 language 2007 language test formalised 2008 +society
Hungary	No	No	No	Yes 1993 constitution
Latvia	No	No	Yes A2 2003	Yes B1 1995 Language and socie-ty
Netherlands	Yes A1 minusMarch 2006 (A1 Jan 2011)	Yes 1998-2007 Municipality can oblige participation since 2009	Yes A2 2010 (2007 obliga-tion to pass)	Yes A2 2003 test language/ society 2007 +portfolio
United King-dom	Yes A1 Nov 2010	No, there is possibility below level B1	Yes B1 or progress of at least one level if opted for a course 2007	Yes B1 2004 language test 2005 + society

Since 2000 national governments have started to require a certain language level from applicants for permanent residence. Germany has a longer history in this respect: a simple knowledge of the German language has been required for a settlement permit since 1990. Although language courses were already available in most countries, from the middle to the end of the 1990s the offer of courses became more structured and extensive. The overall view was that authorities had to support migrants in learning the language. There was a consensus for the idea that not only would language skills promote integration, but also that access to work, the right to family reunification, permanent residence and citizenship would foster integration. Relatively soon after the introduction of a more structured education regime, newly arrived migrants became obliged to participate in education programmes. In most countries this requirement to make an effort to integrate was the first step towards an obligatory integration policy. Not attending a course initially led at most to a reduction in social welfare benefits. In Denmark the government started to offer an introductory programme for newly arrived migrants in 1999. If they did not attend the course, their application for permanent residence could be refused. The efforts of a migrant to learn the language, hence became connected to his/ her residence rights.

The next step towards a connection between integration and residence rights, has been the development of an integration test for the acquisition of a permanent residence right (currently, in seven of the nine Member States a test is taken for this purpose). The obligation to attempt to learn the language or learn about society, was now replaced by the obligation to achieve a certain result.

After acceptance of the idea that a migrant must first show a certain level of integration before having the right to permanent residence, politicians thought it would be strange to require less from a migrant who applied for a stronger legal position, citizenship. Although in most Member States the integration requirements were first introduced in the naturalisation procedure, the introduction of integration requirements for permanent residence rights seems to have strengthened the integration requirement for citizenship in Denmark, Austria, Germany and the Netherlands.

Furthermore, the introduction of integration requirements for residence rights seems to have promoted the need for the introduction of integration requirements at an earlier stage, namely in the admission procedure. By this last step, the integration policy has become connected with immigration policy, whereby the migration rules have been adapted for integration purposes. In 2011, knowledge of language (and of society) will be required by five Member States as a condition for family reunification. According to the French rules, admission will be denied only temporarily (at most two months), in order for the migrant to learn the language before arrival in France. The developments and the political debates clearly show that five Member States followed (or are going to follow) the example of the Netherlands, which first introduced this condition for admission.

Also this new policy has emerged from the trend we previously described: before 2000, in most Member States the dominant view was that the right to family reunification promoted integration of immigrants. Compared to a situation in which family members live separately in different countries, living as a family unit was assumed to be more favourable to integration. For this reason the right to family reunification has been laid down in the EU rules for free movement of workers. This stance was also taken by the Member States during the negotiations on the Family Reunification Directive (between 2000 and 2003).[47] Just before and after the adoption of the directive, political support grew for the idea that family reunification could pose a threat instead of a stimulus to integration. Therefore, family members should first prove their prospects for integration before being admitted.

In a policy where a stronger legal status is no longer used as an instrument for the improvement of integration, the responsibility for the integration lies more on the shoulders of the migrant. But between the Member States where migrants first have to prove their integration before their residence rights are strengthened, there is a large difference in the extent to which they still show their responsibility. An important indicator of the responsibility the Member State takes is the extent to which it offers education on language and societal knowledge to migrants. Germany (with its policy of 'promoting and demanding') and France (integration contract) explicitly express the notion of shared responsibility, and Denmark also acts in this way by offering good quality courses for free. In the Netherlands, the notion of shared responsibility between the state and the individual migrant for his/her integration process has lost political support. This attitude has been demonstrated by the reluctance to safeguard language courses abroad and, more recently, by the announcement in the Coalition Agreement of the new right-wing government Rutte to withdraw its (financial and organisational) responsibility for the integration education in the Netherlands.

The political development described above, is applicable to Denmark, the United Kingdom, Germany, Austria, the Netherlands and to a lesser extent to France. What is striking in this regard, is that in some Member States (particularly Denmark and the Netherlands) from the moment it was decided to strengthen the integration requirements (for naturalisation) or introduce them (for permanent residence or admission), the levels were quickly raised soon afterwards. Sometimes the requirements were strengthened again one year after the previous strengthening. As these decisions could not have been based on evaluations of their effects, they apparently emerged from political preferences.

Three Deviating Member States

The reports on Belgium, Latvia and Hungary show a different development, partly due to a different historical background.

The integration policy in Belgium deviates from the other Western Member States, as no language or integration requirements have to be fulfilled in the naturalisation procedure. Only the Flemish government applies an obligation to integrate to migrants living permanently in Flanders, which is limited to the signing of an integration contract and the attendance at courses. Failure to comply with this obligation can lead to a fine, but does not affect the migrants' residence rights. Though the Flemish region tends to emphasise the importance of knowledge of language and society more and more, the overall Belgian policy still supports the notion that a successful integration of migrants primarily depends on social and inclusive policy, taking into account the diversity of the Belgian population.

47 See Preamble of Directive 2003/86/EG, no. 4: 'Family reunification is a necessary way of making family life possible. It helps to create socio-cultural stability facilitating the integration of third-country nationals in the Member State, which also serves to promote economic and social cohesion, a fundamental Community objective stated in the Treaty.'

The developments in Latvia and Hungary deviated from the Western Member States. The naturalisation requirements in Latvia were adopted in 1994 in order to fulfil one of the criteria for entering the Council of Europe, which implied that residents of a Member State should have access to citizenship. Nevertheless the introduction of the naturalization procedure caused a profound political debate. The Latvian development shows that naturalisation in Latvia was, for historical reasons, a sensitive issue. Certain politicians associated citizenship with loyalty, and were hesitant to enable large numbers of former USSR citizens to become Latvian citizens. To this end, the language requirement proved to be an effective instrument. Although the level of this language requirement for the Longterm Resident status is lower (A2) than the level for Latvian citizenship (B1) and does not include a requirement for societal knowledge, the number of applications for citizenship is much higher than the number of applications for the LTR status. One can conclude somewhat ironically that pressure from the Council of Europe and the European Union led to relaxation of the language and societal knowledge criteria in a new Member State, whereas the development in the older Member States show an increasing level of requirements for citizenship. Considering the growing call for proof of adherence to Western values and norms, loyalty has replaced integration as a national interest in the discussions on citizen- ship in the Western Member States.

The introduction of the constitutional and societal knowledge requirements in the Hungarian naturalisation procedure, besides language requirements, was justified by a reference to other national practices in Europe. In this way, the government aimed to preserve and emphasise the constitutional, cultural and historical heritage of Hungary. From January 2011 onwards, ethnic Hungarians living outside Hungary will be able to apply for Hungarian citizenship. Furthermore, applicants in Hungary will be obliged to take an oath or pledge of allegiance before the local mayor of the municipality of the migrant's residence.

5.2 Do Integration and Naturalisation Tests Improve Integration?

As the requirements or the strengthening of them have only been introduced relatively recently, it is too early to draw conclusions on the extent to which they have promoted integration. Several rapporteurs but also many respondents emphasise that successful integration, besides knowledge of language and society, depends on many other factors as well. Furthermore, knowledge of the language of the Member State is not always necessary to become integrated, especially if the migrant lives in an environment where another language, for instance English, is spoken.

A Flemish evaluation showed that migrants who had accomplished their integration course, more often acquired a job than the ones who did not finish the course. Danish research (Hansen 2009, see also paragraph 3.7), which found out that a more efficient municipal integration policy resulted in more employment participation, indicates that the necessary support can take different forms.

The above mentioned Flemish evaluation however also revealed that participation in the course does not always result in a substantial improvement in the language skills or in social contacts with Flemish citizens. This outcome confirms the limitation of integration programmes, to which many respondents pointed. According to Austrian respondents, a receptive society is crucial for their participation and hence, for their integration. These respondents missed a welcoming approach, and therefore felt isolated.

The interviews revealed that there is much support for learning about society before departure to the Member State, but less for learning the language. Learning the language however is perceived as the most valuable part of the courses after arrival. Respondents attending these courses were more sceptical about the societal knowledge they had to learn, for different reasons. Some found the content was not very useful, and others could not believe it would help them to integrate.

The empirical part of the research shows a paradoxical conclusion with regard to the different tests. On the one hand, the language level is perceived as insufficient to improve the migrant's labour market position. The level for admission is insufficient to act independently, the level for permanent residence is insufficient to be successful in the labour market. On the other hand, the level is perceived to be too high in order to include all migrants who are willing to integrate.

This latter perception has already been confirmed by the decline in the number of applications for family reunification (in Germany and the Netherlands), and can be expected to result in an increasing number of denials of applications for a permanent residence permit. The sharp decline in the number of permanent residence permits granted, which we currently see in Denmark, is expected in Austria, the Netherlands and the United Kingdom as well. The current pass rates are influenced by the practice that, until now, only the most motivated and able candidates have taken the test.

In some countries, a side effect of the introduction of the test for permanent residence rights is the introduction of language and integration courses – and vice versa. In general, migrants were positive about their participation in these courses, which strengthens their motivation to continue learning the language. Furthermore, participating offers the opportunity for making social contacts, which prevents them from isolation and promotes their integration as well. Furthermore, these contacts and learning to speak and practice, strengthens the self-confidence of migrants. These effects, from which women seem to benefit the most, occur at the courses in the countries abroad as well as in the Member States after arrival. Although most migrants are motivated to attend the courses, many respondents indicated that the obligatory character had a positive effect on the participation of a certain number of immigrants. It sometimes stimulated migrants more, but it also facilitated the participation of women from closed communities, who would otherwise have been kept at home. Most migrants who did not need such a stimulus, were not bothered by the obligation.

How do the Consequences of Failing the Test Affect Integration?

The consequence for certain groups of being excluded from admission or a stronger legal status, will not serve their integration, or the integration as a general purpose. This is especially the case with regard to family reunification (where the marriage already existed before the migrant in the Member State was granted a residence permit), Failing the test and therefore being denied access (to the Member State or a stronger residence right) results in stress for both spouses, and prevents both of them from having a positive attitude to society. The delay in family reunification and the concentration on trying to fulfil the criteria will also withhold the spouse living in the Member State from integration or participation. If children are involved, the delay in the reunification will also affect their interests and their integration. The circumstances of family members waiting for admission can be unsafe if they live in (former) war countries. Although spouses of recognized refugees are, according to the Family Reunification Directive, exempted from the integration test, spouses who live in a (post) war situation like in Afghanistan or Sudan, face similar problems as family members of recognized refugees.

If migrants retain their temporary residence permit because they cannot meet the requirements for the granting of a permanent residence permit, they will in general have fewer integration possibilities. Migrants with a temporary residence permit, depending on the Member State where they live, may be barred from full access to the labour market or social benefits or from voting in local elections. The most important consequence of not obtaining a permanent residence right is the continuation of insecurity regarding the residence right. If for instance an income requirement is no longer fulfilled, migrants may face withdrawal of their permit or expulsion. This consequence is the most distressing for refugees or migrants who obtained a permit on humanitarian grounds. After all, they can be expelled to a country where they risk persecution or arbitrary violence, which has perhaps caused trauma. Undoubtedly, this uncertainty will affect their prospects for integration. Though the integration conditions are meant to promote integration, the opposite effect can be produced with regard to migrants who are willing to integrate, but who lack the capacity to pass the tests. Furthermore, in some Member States they may lose their temporary residence permit if they do not fulfil the integration requirements (for example Austria, and in future the Netherlands).

Which Groups are Affected the Most?

As mentioned above, refugees (and migrants in a post-war situation) and their family members can suffer relatively the most from being denied admission or a permanent residence right. Figures on pass rates by nationality and the interviews indicate that they actually fail the tests relatively more often. This can be related to the harsh circumstances they live in abroad, or the trauma they suffer after arrival. This could be called an unintended effect, as most governments seemed to have other categories in mind when they introduced the integration tests. Most governments want to select for motivation and prospects for integration or to combat forced marriages. These purposes are more related to family formation than family reunification, and to migrants who are free to choose where to live. This is not the case with refugees and their family members. These objections do by no means indicate that their integration prospects are bad. A survey on the Danish local policy towards refugees and family members indicates that the effectiveness of integration policy also depends on the quality of organization and the extent to which this policy is prioritized (Hansen 2009). The connection of the integration policy with their legal status is however problematic and counterproductive, as a lower security of residence or less social or political rights can affect the degree of integration.

Other most affected groups mentioned by many respondents are elderly people and the low educated. These groups have, besides migrants with a refugee background, the largest problems in meeting the integration criteria at all three stages. They lack experience with learning (a foreign language), or are not even familiar with the Latin alphabet. The duration of the course often appears to be too short for the lower educated and illiterates.

Germany, the Netherlands and Flanders also oblige migrants who are already settled to meet integration requirements (passing the test or, like in Flanders, participating in a course). Elderly migrants, who have already lived in the Member States for a long time, also lack motivation, because, in their view, the attention paid to their integration is too late. Another significant difference seems to be that migrants originating from developing countries and non-Western countries have lower pass rates than migrants from developed and Western countries. This could be related to a lower educational background, the lack of experience with computers or to the larger differences in culture and language between the Member State and their home country.

As a matter of fact, all third country nationals can be affected by these integration requirements for the granting of a legal status, especially because an individual consideration of the circumstances and interests is lacking. This development outdistances the position of third-country nationals from those of EU citizens, to whom integration requirements are not applicable. Although the European Council announced in 1999 that the rights of third-country nationals should become as comparable as possible to those of EU citizens, the developments have turned in the opposite direction. However, this so-called Tampere conclusion aimed to promote the integration of third-country nationals.[48]

Besides third-country nationals, the own nationals of the Member States are affected as well. With the strengthened conditions for family reunification and for a stronger legal status for their spouses, the difference between their position and the position of EU citizens to whom the free movement rules apply, has become larger. This phenomenon of 'reverse discrimination' could affect the support for the European Union. Considering the strengthened conditions, the previous plea by the European Commission for equal treatment of the two groups with regard to family reunification, has become all the more relevant.

5.3 Recommendations

The research findings indicate that migrants benefit from language and integration courses, as it improves their language abilities as well as their social contacts, their independence and self-confidence. In general, migrants are highly motivated to participate in language education. They do not seem to be motivated by the obligation to attend a course, but because they like to learn the language and get in touch with other participants. For some specific groups the obligation to attend the course can have a positive effect on their motivation or actual participation. This particularly concerns women who are not supported by their husbands to integrate and migrants who face difficulties combining the courses with their daily activities, such as a full-time job or raising and taking care of young children.

48 Conclusion no. 18. 'The European Union must ensure fair treatment of third-country nationals who reside legally on the territory of its Member States. A more vigorous integration policy should aim at granting them rights and obligations comparable to those of EU citizens. It should also enhance non-discrimination in economic, social and cultural life and develop measures against racism and xenophobia', Presidency Conclusions, Tampere European Council 15 and 16 October 1999, SN 200/1/99.

However, especially if attendance to integration education is obligatory, more flexibility is needed in order to take the individual circumstances of migrants into account. This is with regard to the organisation of courses, for instance, more evening courses for migrants who are employed and preferably also more flexibility by their employers to grant them time for education. With regard to young parents, child care at the education centre facilitates their attendance. Also more flexibility towards the exemptions from the requirements is advisable. This is in relation to migrants who can clearly demonstrate sufficient knowledge of language or society, as well as migrants who are not able to meet the requirements. Finally, flexibility towards the level of the education offered is necessary. As the knowledge level and the ability to learn differ greatly, sufficient differentiation in the education offer is crucial for the motivation and progress of the participants. Special attention should be paid to possibilities to better attune integration education to regular education or the labour market. Therefore language education, combined with the development of special courses for migrants who lag behind but also for those who want to make more progress, would promote an effective integration policy. This is the case for language education abroad as well as education in the country. The research clearly shows that especially young migrants who have arrived recently in the Member States, benefit from language and integration education. It could be reconsidered whether it is useful to oblige older migrants (mostly the ones who have resided in the Member States for a long time) to attend the courses and pass a test. It would probably be more efficient and adequate to offer elderly migrants education and tailor-made support for their integration, without obliging them to attend courses.

This research, however, did not find any reason to promote the connection of the integration requirements with the granting of a certain legal status (admission, permanent residence or citizenship). This connection is not necessary to motivate migrants, and it inevitably leads to the exclusion of certain groups from a secure legal status. The effects of this exclusion will hamper their integration, rather than promoting it. With regard to the integration requirement for admission, the exclusion also results in affecting family life and violating the right to family reunification, as laid down in the Directive on the Right to Family Reunification. In most Member States, this connection between the level of integration and the granting of certain residence rights has been made relatively soon after the introduction of a language education infrastructure. Although the added value of this connection has not been proven, most respondents emphasised its positive effect on integration of the migrants should not be overestimated. As the negative side effects of this connection are already clear, it is recommended that this policy is reconsidered.

Furthermore, the respondents demonstrated a broad consensus about the limited effect of language and integration policy on the actual integration of migrants. Other factors, such as a receptive society, an effective combat of discrimination and equal opportunities on the labour market, are just as or even more crucial. To be effective, integration policies should pay attention to these elements.

More Research Necessary

In order to monitor closely the effectiveness but also the side effects of the introduction of the tests, it is recommended that research is conducted on the situation of migrants who are not able to meet the integration requirements, and are therefore prevented from admission, permanent residence or citizenship. Until now, little is known about their circumstances and choices. As more Member States intend to introduce the language requirement for admission, and the effects of the integration requirement for the granting of permanent residence rights will become clear in the coming years, this would be the proper moment to initiate such empirical research.

The European Union has a long tradition in integration policy without the use of tests for the granting of a legal status. It could be worthwhile to assess the factors which led to a successful integration of EU citizens who made use of their freedom of movement. Looking at this experience, but also to best practices regarding the integration of third-country nationals, may be more effective than continuing to cumulate and strengthen the integration conditions.

AFTERWORD

The data collection for the INTEC report was finished in October 2010. Since then, many developments have taken place regarding integration tests and integration policy of the involved Member States. Below you find an overview of the main developments. The data for this update were collected in April 2012.

Test Abroad

After the completion of the INTEC report, three Member States have followed the example of the Netherlands and Germany by adding a language requirement to their admission conditions for applicants for family reunification. In November 2010, the United Kingdom introduced a language requirement at level A1 and Denmark introduced a language and integration requirement at level A1 minus. In both Member States this knowledge is tested in an oral examination. In Austria the language test abroad is applicable since July 2011 and consists of a writing, reading, listening and speaking test at level A1. The three Member States did not develop an education system abroad in order to support the preparation for the test; Denmark does offer a preparation kit. Just as in the Netherlands and Germany, these new admission requirements in Denmark and the United Kingdom only apply to third-country family members of their citizens or of their third-country national residents.

Although Denmark initially had not exempted nationals from certain third countries from the requirement, it adapted its legislation later on in order to exempt nationals from the United States, Canada, Australia, Israel, Japan, New Zealand, Switzerland and South Korea. The United Kingdom only exempts nationals from majority English speaking countries. In Denmark, the government abandoned its initial plan to exempt Turkish nationals on the basis of the Association Treaty EC/Turkey. By contrast, in the Netherlands, the minister of integration announced in September 2011 that Turkish nationals were exempted from the integration requirement for admission. This was the consequence of a ruling of 16 August 2011, in which the Central Appeals Tribunal decided that the language and integration requirement for Turkish nationals and their family members is in violation of the EU-Turkey association agreement. Turkish nationals who took the examination abroad on or after 16 August 2011 are eligible for a refund of their examination fee; travel and subsistence expenses may also be reimbursed.

In Austria, applicants for a residence permit as an 'exceptionally qualified person' and family members of holders of such a permit, as well as applicants for the Blue Card and citizens of the European Economic Area and Switzerland, are exempt. On April 30, 2012, the Austrian Ministry of the Interior forwarded an administrative circular to all relevant authorities outlining the effects of the decision of the ECJ in the case of Derici and several decisions of the Austrian Administrative Court on the effects of the Ankara-Agreement on family reunification. According to the circular, the standstill clause has to be applied to all Turkish nationals falling under the Ankara Agreement, who intend to work in Austria in the future, including family members. For this group the legal regulations in force on January 1, 1995 (the date of Austria's accession to the EU) apply. This implies inter alia that family members of Turkish nationals falling under the Ankara Agreement and Turkish family members of Austrian citizens who intend to take up employment in future are exempt from the pre-entry test.

In Denmark, the right-winged government decided to develop a new immigration test at level A2. However, before this new test was developed, the new government (Social Democratic - Social Liberal - Socialist People's Party) installed in October 2011 decided that the new test is not to be introduced. The new coalition announced that priority will be given to integration instead of exclusion. In March 2012 it presented a Bill in which the immigration test for family reunification for spouses is repealed. Instead a new Danish language test at level A1 as a condition for continuous residence will be introduced. Spouses and partners will be granted more time to pass the test in Denmark: instead of within three months (the condition for admission), they will have to pass the test as a condition for continuous stay within six to nine months after admission. In the Netherlands, however, the integration requirement has been strengthened since April 2011, with the rise of the required language level to A1 and the extension with a reading test. Candidates must achieve a higher score in order to pass the test. At the same time the hardship clause for the integration requirement, laid down in the Aliens Decree, was extended because denying admission on the sole ground that the applicant has not passed the test, would be unjust (*onbillijk*). In the Aliens Circular this criterion was defined as a combination of individual circumstances which make it permanently impossible for the applicant to pass the test. In May 2011 the Dutch Ombudsman criticized the government for applying the hardship clause too rigidly: in the past five years the government had only used this clause in five cases. In the same month, the European Commission took the position that denying family reunification for the sole reason that the applicant had not passed the integration examination, is not in compliance with article 7 (2) of the Directive regarding the Right to Family Reunification. The Commission took this position in the *Imran* case, in which a Dutch district court requested the EU Court of Justice for a preliminary ruling. The underlying case of this request concerned an Afghan illiterate mother who took the test at the embassy of Pakistan several times, but failed to pass it. Her husband and her eight children resided in the Netherlands. A week after the Commission had sent its position to the Dutch government, the mother was granted permission to reunite with her family. With this decision, the Dutch government succeeded to avoid a judgment of the EU Court of Justice on the compatibility of the Dutch integration requirement with the Directive on the Right to Family Reunification.

The Flemish region of Belgium, Flanders, which doesn't impose an integration condition on family members who want to reunite with their spouse residing in Flanders, has developed a preparation kit for this target group. This kit, the so-called 'Migrating to Flanders – a starter pack for family migrants', will initially only be disseminated in the countries with the highest numbers immigrants in Flanders, namely Morocco, Turkey and Russia. The dissemination of this package will start in 2012 and will be complementary to an offer of social orientation courses. The package contains three items: a DVD and a pamphlet, a language guide and a 'backpack'. Whereas the language guide provides an introduction to Dutch language and emphasizes the importance of Dutch knowledge for life in Flanders, the 'backpack' is a practical guide on the possibly necessary documents in order to access employment or education in the country of residence. Although the right-winged party *Nieuw-Vlaamse Alliantie* (literally translated as the New-Flemish Alliance) proposed to make the granting of a visa for family reunification dependent on the fulfilment of integration measures in the country of origin, the Flemish Ministry of Integration underlines that the offer is free, voluntary and independent of the obtainment of a residence permit.

Integration Tests in the Country

Since July 2011 migrants residing in Austria have to prove their knowledge of the German language at A2 level after two years of residence as a condition for the renewal of their temporary residence permit. In case of non-fulfilment the authorities may renew a temporary permit for a period up to three years, but there is no legal right to a renewal. It is considered rather unlikely that the Constitutional Court will protect family life based on Article 8 of the European Convention of Human Rights already after two years of residence. Therefore the Austrian government expects it to be much more easy to expel immigrants not having fulfilled the requirement to prove knowledge of German at the A2 level after two years. As a result of the *Derici* case and several judgments of the Austrian Administrative Court, Turkish nationals who fall under the scope of the Ankara Agreement are exempt from this obligation. Qualified immigrants who reside in Austria on the basis of the so-called 'Red-White-Red-Card' as well as those holding a 'Blue Card' and those holding a temporary residence permit for a certain professional group (e.g. artist, journalist, scientist) are also exempt from the fulfilment of the proof of knowledge of German at the A2-level. Since July 2011, the required knowledge level for obtaining a permanent residence permit has been raised from A2 to B1. Those who are exempt from the language requirement after 2 years of residence, still have to meet the integration requirement connected to the obtainment of a permanent residence permit. Partial refunding of the course costs will only take place if the A2 examination is passed within two years after arrival, provided that the test is taken at testing centres of the Austrian Integration Fund according to a new test module, the 'German test for Austria' developed by the Goethe Institute and the German *telc GmbH*. The passing of a test of another certified test centre will count as having fulfilled the integration agreement, but will be excluded from the right of refunding. In Vienna, the largest course provider, the Viennese 'Peoples Universities' (*Wiener Volkshochschulen*), which is regarded as an institution critical to the integration policies of the Ministry of the Interior, had decided not to follow the course model of the Austrian Fund for Integration because of its alleged low didactic quality. Several experts interviewed reported massive pressure of the Austrian Fund for Integration, which is closely linked to the Ministry of the Interior, on the language schools to only follow their model.

In Denmark, the new government installed in October 2011, has presented a Bill on 26 April 2012 in order to relax the requirements for permanent residence rights and naturalisation. Regarding permanent residence rights, the government plans to repeal the point system and the active citizenship test for permanent residence (introduced in 2010). The required knowledge level will be lowered from B1 to A2. A migrant may acquire permanent residence after five years. The migrant has to prove having had full-time employment or education during three years within the last five years. There will still be a requirement on self-support, but certain benefits will not count as a contra-indication for self-support. Refugees may be exempted from the general rules after eight years residence.

In France, the law adopted in June 2011 has emphasized the obligation to respect the welcoming contract. For the decision on the renewal of the temporary residence permit, the administrative authority takes into account the extent to which the migrant complies with the welcoming contract regarding fundamental values of the Republic, and to which he seriously participates in civic and linguistic training. Before, these factors were only taken into account at the first renewal of the residence permit.

In the Netherlands, the language and integration requirement for Turkish nationals has been abolished. This means that having passed the language and integration examination is no longer a condition for obtaining a permanent residence permit and that municipalities may no longer oblige Turkish nationals to participate in language and integration courses or impose penalties on those who do not participate. This decision resulted from a ruling of 16 August 2011, in which the Central Appeals Tribunal (*Centrale Raad van Beroep*) judged that the language and integration requirement for Turkish nationals and their family members negatively affects their legal position in the Netherlands and is not in compliance with EU-Turkey association law.

Integration Tests in the Naturalisation Procedure

The Austrian Nationality Law links the language requirements for naturalisation with the requirements for a permanent residence permit. Therefore the rise of the latter to level B1 as of July 2011 also led to the rise of the required level for naturalisation to B1. In practice, implicitly B1 was required already before, as the naturalisation test requires an understanding of German at the level B1 at least.

In Belgium the coalition agreement of December 2011 announced a reform of nationality law. The expected reform will introduce language and integration requirements for the applicants of naturalisation. According to the agreement, economic activity may also be recognised as an indication of integration.

In Denmark, the new government has announced a change of the requirements for naturalisation, in order not to exclude anyone from citizenship. To this aim, it has decided to lower the required language level for citizenship from B2 to B1, and to change the citizenship test in such a way that importance is attached to aspects of everyday life and political life, met by citizens in a modern society. In addition, dual citizenship will be accepted. Furthermore, the applicant has to be self-supporting during 2,5 years out of the last 5 years. Other requirements for citizenship will remain the same. However, the second generation of immigrant origin will (again) be offered Danish citizenship by the age of 18 years, unless they have committed serious crimes, and if an applicant is able to prove he suffers from a Post Traumatic Stress Syndrom, he will be exempt from criteria which he or she is not able to fulfil.

In France, a decree adopted in October 2011 has set the level of language knowledge required for naturalisation at B1. Moreover, as from January 2012, applicants are required to submit proof of their language knowledge in the form of a diploma or certificate. A decree adopted in January 2012 stipulates that the applicants' level of knowledge of French history, culture and society must be equivalent to the level of knowledge acquired on these subjects at the end of elementary school. This knowledge is assessed by means of a multiple choice test by the civil servant who also conducts the personal interview in order to evaluate the applicant's ‘adhesion’ to the French principles and values. Applicants also have to demonstrate sufficient knowledge of rights and duties conferred by French citizenship as well as 'adhesion' to essential principles and values of the Republic. In January 2012, another decree has established the Charter of rights and duties of French citizens. This Charter has to be signed by every applicant for citizenship.

In Latvia, several initiatives have been undertaken by the local governments to organise language courses, which has led to a slight increase of the number of participants. It is expected that starting from 2013 free language courses will be offered by the Society Integration Fund. The program was terminated in 2009 due to lack of resources. Free trial exams are also offered during information days organised by OCMA. There are also ongoing debates in the Parliament on amendments to the Citizenship Law which can affect naturalization procedures. As the Citizenship Law is one of the most sensitive laws in Latvia, it is difficult to estimate which amendments will be adopted. One of the amendments would imply that citizens will be tested on their loyalty. The Parliamentary debate concentrates on the way loyalty can be tested. Furthermore, the bill provides for an exemption from both the language and knowledge tests for graduates of minority schools as well as registering non-citizen children automatically.

The Dutch centre-right government that came into power in October 2010 has proposed to amend the Dutch Nationality Act (*Rijkswet op het Nederlanderschap*) in order to strengthen the requirements for naturalisation. The language and integration requirement (which is the same as the one for permanent residence) will not change, but several new requirements will be implemented. Applicants for naturalisation will have to fulfil an income requirement and a so-called qualification requirement. The latter requirement means that applicants will have to show that they have completed two years of vocational training or work experience. Furthermore, this Bill proposes a language examination for migrants who want to acquire Dutch citizenship by way of option. The option procedure was initially meant to give certain categories of immigrants, including older immigrants with a long duration of stay in the Netherlands and second generation immigrants, the possibility of acquiring Dutch citizenship by lodging a simple, unilateral declaration. Finally the Bill limits the number of situations in which dual citizenship is allowed. As the Dutch government resigned in April 2012 and new elections will be held in September 2012, the proposal will not be discussed in Parliament before the elections. The fate of this Bill depends on the outcome of the elections.

Overview of the level of the tests in use in April 2012[*]

Country	*Admission*	*Permanent residence*	*Naturalisation*
Austria	A1	B1	B1 + KoS
Belgium	-	-	-
Denmark	A1	B1 + KoS (government intends to lower level from B1 to A2 and to repeal KoS)	B2 + KoS (government intends to lower level from B2 to B1)

Country	*Admission*	*Permanent residence*	*Naturalisation*
France	(A1.1)	(A1.1)	B1 + KoS, but no special language test: naturalisation candidates must submit proof of their language skills in the form of a diploma or certificate
Germany	A1	B1	B1 + KoS
Hungary	-	-	test on knowledge of the constitution, the passing of which requires fluency in Hungarian
Latvia	-	A2	B1 + KoS
Netherlands	A1	A2 + KoS	A2 + KoS
United Kingdom	A1	B1 (or progress of at least one level if opted for a course)	B1 + KoS

* (Level) between brackets means that passing the test is not a straightforward requirement. KoS = knowlegde of society.

BIBLIOGRAPHY

Bauböck, R., E. Ersbøll, K. Groenendijk & H. Waldrauch (2006), *Acquisition and Loss of Nationality, Volume I: Comparative Analyses: Policies and Trends in 15 European Countries*, Amsterdam: University Press.

Böcker, A., K. Groenendijk & B. de Hart (2005), 'De Toegang tot het Nederlanderschap. Effecten van twintig jaar beleidswijzigingen', *Nederlands Juristenblad* 80(3) p. 157-164.

Bonjour, S. (2010), 'Between Integration Provision and Selection Mechanism. Party Politics, Judicial Constraints, and the Making of French and Dutch Policies of Civic Integration Abroad', *European Journal of Migration and Law*, no. 3, p. 299-18.

Bundesregierung Deutschland (2010), *Bericht über die Evaluierung des Nachweises einfacher Deutschkentnisse beim Ehegattennachzug nach dem Aufenthaltsgesetz: Sprachlern- und Sprachtestangebote, Visumverfahren,* Berlin: Auswärtiges Amt, Beauftragte der Bundesregierung für Migration, Flüchtlinge und IntegrationBundesregierung Österreich, *Nationaler Aktionsplan für Integration, Massnahmen*, 19 January 2010, www.integration.at.

Carrera, S. (2009a), *In Search of the Perfect Citizen? The Intersection between Integration, Immigration and Nationality in the EU*, Leiden/Boston: Martinus Nijhoff.

Carrerra, S. (2009b), 'Nationality, Immigration and "the Republican Integration" in France: Normativisation, Expansionism and Externalisation', in E. Guild, K. Groenendijk & S. Carrera, *Illiberal Liberal States: Immigration, citizenship and Integration in the EU,* Burlington, VT: Ashgate, p. 315-336.

Carrera, S. & A. Wiesbrock (2009), *Civic Integration of Third-Country Nationals. Nationalism versus Europeanisation in the Common EU Immigration Policy,* www.ceps.eu.

CERD (2010), *Report on the Netherlands*, Committee on the Elimination of Racial Discrimination, Seventy-sixth session 15 February to 12 March 2010, CERD/C/NLD/CO/1718.

Commission (2008), *Report from the Commission to the European Parliament and the Council on the Application of Directive 2003/86/EC on the Right to Family Reunification*, COM (2008) 610, 8 October 2008.

Cournil, C. & Y. Depigny (2008), 'Contractualisation et externalisation de la politique migratoire: analyse et critique de la loi Hortefeux', *Revue de droit public*, no. 4, p. 1045-1079.

Cuyper , P. de (2010), *Deel 2. Het inburgeringsbeleid in Vlaanderen: de efficiëntie en effectiviteit geëvalueerd*. Leuven: HIVA.

Dagevos, J. & M. Gijsberts (2009), *'Ontwikkelingen in integratie op hoofdlijnen',* in J. Dagevos & M. Gijsberts, *Jaarrapport Integratie 2009,* The Hague: SCP.

ECRI (2008), *Third periodical report on the Netherlands*, Strasbourg, European Commission against Racism and Intolerance.

Ersbøll, E. (2010), 'On trial in Denmark? ', in R. van Oers, E. Ersbøll and D. Kostakopoulou, *A Re-definition of Belonging? Language and Integration Tests in Europe*, Leiden: Martinus Nijhoff Publishers, p. 107-148.

Groenendijk, K. (2010), *Predeparture Integration Strategies in the European Union: Integration or Immigration Policy?*, Washington DC: Migration Policy Institute.

Groenendijk, K., E. Guild & H. Dogan (1998), *Security of Residence of Long-Term Migrants. A Comparative Study of Law and Practice in European Countries*, Strasbourg: Council of Europe.

Hammarberg (2009), *Report by the Commissioner for Human Rights Thomas Hammarberg, on his visit to the Netherlands*, 21-25 September 2008, 11 March 2009.

Hansen, L.M. (2009), *Effectiveness measurement of Danish municipalities integration policies from 1999 to 2007*, Copenhagen: The Ministry for Immigration, Refugee and Integration Affairs.

Hart, B. de & R. van Oers (2006), 'European Trends in Nationality Law', in R. Bauböck, E. Ersbøll, K. Groenendijk & H. Waldrauch (eds.), *Acquisition and Loss of Nationality; Policies and Trends in 15 European Member States. Volume I: Comparative Analyses*, 317-357. Amsterdam: Amsterdam University Press. Also available via http://www.law.ed.ac.uk/citmodes/files/NATACCh7.pdf.

Integrationsbeauftragte (2010), *8. Bericht der Beauftragten der Bundesregierung für Migration, Flüchtlinge und Integration über die Lage der Ausländerinnen und Ausländer in Deutschland*, Berlin: Integrationsbeauftragte.

Joppke, C. (2007), *Do obligatory civic integration courses for immigrants in Western Europe further integration? Focus Migration*, Policy Brief no. 8. www.focus-migration.de/uploads/tx_wilpubdb/PB08_IntegrationCourses_02.pdf.

Klekowski von Koppenfels (2010), 'Citizenship Tests could signal that European States perceive themselves as Immigration Countries', in R. Bauböck & C. Joppke (eds.), *How Liberal are Citizenship Tests*, 11-14. EUI Working paper accessible via http://eudo-citizenship.eu/docs/RSCAS_2010_41.pdf.

Michalowski, I. (2007), *Integration als Staatsprogramm: Deutschland, Frankreich und die Niederlande im Vergleich*. Münster: LIT Verlag.

Michalowski, I. (2010) 'Integration tests in Germany. A communitarian approach?', in R. Van Oers, E. Ersbøll and D. Kostakopoulou, *A Re-definition of Belonging? Language and Integration Tests in Europe*, Leiden: Brill Publishers, p. 185-210.

Ministerie van Justitie (2010), *Rapportage Vreemdelingenketen. Periode januari-juni 2010*. Den Haag: Ministerie van Justitie.

Oers, R. van, E. Ersbøll & D. Kostakopoulou (2010), *A Re-definition of Belonging? Language and Integration Tests in Europe*, Leiden: Martinus Nijhoff Publishers.

Oers, R. van (2006), *De Naturalisatietoets Geslaagd? Een Onderzoek naar de Totstandkoming en Effecten van de Naturalisatietoets*, Nijmegen: Wolf Legal Publishers.

Odé, A. (2009), De Wet Inburgering Buitenland: zelfselectie belangrijker dan selectie, *Migrantenrecht* 2009, no. 7, p. 288-292.

Pascouau, Y. (2010) 'Integration Measures in France: An Evolving Process between Integration and Migration Issues', in: R. van Oers, E. Ersbøll & D. Kostakopoulou, *A Redefiniton of Belonging? Language and Interation Tests in Euope,* Leiden: Brill, 153-83.

Pauwels, F. & M. Lamberts (2010), *Deel 3. De impact van inburgering*, Leuven: HIVA.

Pop, V. (2009), 'Austria eyes language tests for migrants', *EU Observer*, 16 January 2009, http://euobserver.com/9/29165.

Ratia, E. & Walter, A. (2009), *International Exploration on Forced Marriages. A study on legal initiatives, policies and public discussions in Belgium, France, Germany, the United Kingdom and Switzerland*, Nijmegen: Wolf Legal Publishers.

Regioplan (2009), *De Wet Inburgering Buitenland, een onderzoek naar de werking, de resultaten en de eerste effecten*, publication no. 1754, www.regioplan.nl or TK 2008-2009, 32 005, no. 1.

Rother, N. (2009), *Das Integrationspanel. Entwicklung von alltagsrelevanten Sprachfertigkeiten und Sprachkompetenzen der Integrationskursteilnehmer während des Kurses.* www.bamf.de.

Ryan, B. (2009), 'The immigration Agenda in British Migration Law', in E. Guild, K. Groenendijk & S. Carrera, *Illiberal States: Immigration, Citizenship and Integration in the EU,* Burlington, VT: Ashgate, p. 277-298.

Seveker (2008), *Sprachkurse im Kontext von Integration und Aussiedlung. Am Beispiel der Altairegion/Westsibirien*, Saarbrücken: VDM Verlag Dr. Müller.

Significant (2010), *Evaluatierapport Inburgering in Nederland.* www.rijksoverheid.nl.

Spijkerboer, T. (2007), *Zeker weten: Inburgering en de fundamenten van het Nederlandse politieke bestel*, Den Haag: Sdu.

Walter A. (2008), *Reverse Discrimination and Family Reunification*, Nijmegen: Wolf Legal Publishers.

Willems, W. (2009), De politiek aan de knoppen van de machine: spraaktechnologie in het inburgeringsbeleid', in Huub Dijstelbloem & Albert Meijer (eds), *De migratiemachine: de rol van technologie in het migrantenbeleid*, Amsterdam: Van Gennep, p. 123-156.

Winden, J. van der (2006), *Wet inburgering in het buitenland*, Den Haag: Sdu.

Bibliography

De Cuyper, P., *Inburgering in Vlaanderen, de efficiëntie en effectiviteit van het beleid geëvalueerd (deel 2)*, HIVA, Leuven: Kuleuven 2010.

De Hart, B. & R. van Oers, 'European Trends in Nationality Law', in: R. Bauböck *et al.* (eds), *Acquisition and Loss of Nationality, Volume I: Comparative Analysis; Policies and Trends in 15 European Countries*, Amsterdam: Amsterdam University Press 2006.

Flemish Parliament (2009), *Beleidsnota Inburgering & Integratie 2009-2014,* 186 (2009-2010) – Nr. 1, 23 oktober 2009 (2009-2010).

Flemish Parliament (2011), *Beleidsbrief: Inburgering en Integratie, Beleidsprioriteiten 2011-2012*, 1313 (2011-2012) – Nr. 1, 24 oktober 2011 (2011-2012).

Foblets, M.C., 'Les changements de la loi sur la nationalité Belge', in: B. Khader, M. Martiniello, A. Rea & C. Timmerman (eds), *Penser l'immigration et l'intègration autrement*, Brussels: Bruylant 2006.

Foblets, M.C. & S. Loones, 'Belgium', in: R. Bauböck *et al.* (eds), *Acquisition and Loss of Nationality, Volume II: Country Analyses*, Amsterdam: Amsterdam University Press 2006.

Foblets, M-C. & Z. Yanasmayan, 'Language and integration requirements in Belgium: Discordances between the Flemish policy of "inburgering" and the federal legislators' view(s) on integration of newcomers and migrants', in R. Van Oers, E. Ersbøll & D. Kostakopoulou (eds) *A Re-definition of Belonging? Language and Integration Tests in Europe*, Leiden: Brill 2010.

Foblets, M-C, 'De Belgische nationaliteit in eer hersteld? Nieuwe wendingen in de appreciatie van integratie, Europees burgerschap en procedures van nationaliteitsverkrijging', in : M.-C. Foblets, M. Hildbrandt, J. Steenbergen (eds), *Liber Amicorum Réné Foqué*, Gent: Larcier 2011, p. 319-348.

Gsir, S., M. Martiniello, K. Meireman & J. Wets, 'Belgium', in: J. Niessen, Y. Schibel & C. Thompson (eds), *Current Immigration Debates in Europe: A Publication of the European Migration Dialogue*, 2005, downloadable from http://www.migpolgroup.com/multiattachments/2959/DocumentName/EMD_Belgium_2005.pdf.

Loobuyck, P. & D. Jacobs, 'The Flemish immigration society: Political challenges on different levels', in: L. d'Haenens, M. Hooghe, D. Vanheule & H. Gezduci (eds), *New Citizens, New Policies? Developments in Diversity Policy in Canada and Flanders*, Ghent: Academia Press 2006.

Lambert, M., P. De Cuyper, J. Geets, L. Struyven, C. Timmerman, S. van den Eede & J. Wets, *Het Vlaamse Inburgeringsbeleid geëvalueerd*, 2007, downloadable from http://binnenland.vlaanderen.be/inburgering/onderzoek/pdf/Het%20Vlaamse%20Inburgeringsbeleid%20gee valueerd_synthese.pdf.

Pauwels, F. & M. Lamberts, *De impact van inburgering in Vlaanderen (deel 3)*, Leuven: HIVA 2010.

Timmerman, C., J. Geets & K. Van Der Heyden, 'Les Nouveaux Arrivants en Flandre', in: B. Khader, M. Martiniello, A. Rea & C. Timmerman (eds), *Penser l'immigration et l'intègration autrement*, Brussels: Bruylant 2006.